Oracle Press™

Oracle9*i*AS Building J2EE™ Applications

Oracle Press™

Oracle9*i*AS Building J2EE™ Applications

Nirva Morisseau-Leroy

In collaboration with Ekkehard Rohwedder, Luis Amat, Ashish Parikh, and Gerald Momplaisir

McGraw-Hill/Osborne

New York Chicago San Francisco
Lisbon London Madrid Mexico City
Milan New Delhi San Juan
Seoul Singapore Sydney Toronto

The McGraw-Hill Companies

McGraw-Hill/Osborne
2600 Tenth Street
Berkeley, California 94710
U.S.A.

To arrange bulk purchase discounts for sales promotions, premiums, or fund-raisers, please contact **McGraw-Hill**/Osborne at the above address. For information on translations or book distributors outside the U.S.A., please see the International Contact Information page immediately following the index of this book.

Oracle9*i*AS Building J2EE™ Applications

1234567890 FGR FGR 0198765432

ISBN 0-07-222614-5

Publisher
Brandon A. Nordin

Vice President & Associate Publisher
Scott Rogers

Acquisitions Editor
Jeremy Judson

Project Editor
Janet Walden

Acquisitions Coordinator
Athena Honore

Technical Editors
Ekkehard Rohwedder, Mikael Ottosson, Andy Tael

Copy Editor
William McManus

Proofreader
Karen Mead

Indexer
David Heiret

Computer Designers
Tabitha M. Cagan, Kathleen Fay Edwards

Illustrators
Michael Mueller, Lyssa Wald

This book was composed with Corel VENTURA™ Publisher.

I dedicate this book to many mothers: Marie Therese Limousin (my mother); Renee Morisseau-Leroy (my mother-in-law); my sisters, Paula Erie, Louise Erie, Ginette Erie, and Mireille Erie; and my daughter, Tara.

–Nirva Morisseau-Leroy

About the Author

Voted by *Oracle Magazine* "Most Innovative Application Developer of the Year," Nirva Morisseau-Leroy, MSCS, is an Oracle Database Administrator and Java Application Developer at the National Oceanic and Atmospheric Administration – University of Miami Cooperative Institute for Marine and Atmospheric Sciences, and is assigned to the Hurricane Research Division of the Atlantic Oceanographic & Meteorological Laboratory. Morisseau-Leroy has over 16 years of information systems experience as an Oracle DBA, application developer, and MIS director, utilizing Java, JDBC, SQLJ, Enterprise JavaBeans, SQL, and Oracle PL/SQL. Trilingual (French, Spanish, and English), Morisseau-Leroy is the primary author of several Oracle Press books, such as *Oracle9*i *SQLJ Programming, Oracle8*i *Java Component Programming with EJB, CORBA and JSP*, and *Oracle8*i *SQLJ Programming*. Morisseau-Leroy has published several papers in database and Java conferences and is a winner of several awards. She can be reached at nmorisseauleroy@data-i.com.

About the Contributing Authors

Ekkehard Rohwedder (M.Sc. in Computer Science, Carnegie Mellon University) joined Oracle Corporation in 1996. He has been leading the development of the Oracle SQLJ and JPublisher products. He is interested in programming language technologies that make programmers' lives easier and more productive. Ekkehard was a technical editor and a collaborating author for *Oracle9*i*AS Building J2EE Applications* and a technical editor for *Oracle9*i *SQLJ Programming*. He can be reached at ekkehard.rohwedder@oracle.com.

Luis R. Amat, Jr., MSCS, is a Technical Manager in the Software Engineering and Development national practice for Oracle Consulting's Advanced Technology Solutions organization. He is sought after worldwide by Oracle clients for his software architecture and development insight, especially in the area of enterprise Java. He is a founding member, architect, and developer of the Oracle9*i*AS MVC Framework for J2EE (aka Cleveland Framework). He can be reached at luis.amat@oracle.com.

Ashish Parikh is an Architect with the Advanced Technology Solutions Software Engineering and Development Group at Oracle Corporation. He is a named expert in the field of Distributed Computing and Middleware Architectures, has presented abstracts for Java One 2002, and has authored a number of articles on J2EE, J2ME, security, and Web Services. He is also the President of the Bay Area chapter of the Worldwide Institute of Software Architects, through which he evangelizes software architecture paradigms. He can be reached at ashish.parikh@oracle.com.

Gerald P. Momplaisir, MSCS, has numerous years of information technology experience. In the past ten years, he has specialized in Oracle, object-oriented systems, and networking technologies. His love for database systems and object-oriented technologies led him to join Oracle Corporation, where he is now a Senior Principal Consultant. He has co-authored both the *Oracle8*i *SQLJ* and *Oracle9*i *SQLJ*

Programming books from Oracle Press. He has also written articles for the Oracle Technology Network (OTN) web site. He has participated in major J2EE development efforts as lead developer and lead architect. He can be reached at gerald.momplaisir@oracle.com.

About the Technical Editors

Ekkehard Rohwedder (M.Sc. in Computer Science, Carnegie Mellon University) joined Oracle Corporation in 1996. He has been leading the development of the Oracle SQLJ and JPublisher products. He is interested in programming language technologies that make programmers' lives easier and more productive. He can be reached at ekkehard.rohwedder@oracle.com.

Mikael Ottosson is a Technical Director, Business Development, Oracle9*i* Application Server (Oracle Corporation). He has over five years of experience using Java and J2EE and is currently involved in helping Oracle's largest customers and partners successfully implement Java and J2EE-based applications on Oracle9*i* Application Server.

Andy Tael is a Director of Business Development, Oracle9*i* Application Server (Oracle Corporation). He is currently involved in helping Oracle's largest customers and partners successfully implement applications on Oracle9*i* Application Server.

Contents at a Glance

PART I
Overview

PART II
Building J2EE Business Tier Components

PART III
Building J2EE Web and Presentation Tier Components

PART IV
Appendixes

Contents

PART II

Building J2EE Business Tier Components

PART III

Building J2EE Web and Presentation Tier Components

PART IV
Appendixes

Acknowledgments

his book was made possible by the efforts of many people. Many special thanks to my technical editors, Ekkehard Rohwedder, Mikael Ottosson, and Andy Tael. I especially appreciate their support, advice, feedback, and above all their excellent technical suggestions during the development of this project. Special thanks to Dr. Maryse Prezeau for her advice and support, and to my daughter Gina Morisseau-Leroy McDaniel, Web Graphic Design Specialist, who designed the GUI for the J2EE application presented in the book. Many thanks to Lars Ewe, Principal Product Manager (Oracle Corporation). Lars is very experienced in Java, J2EE-based solutions, and application frameworks like TopLink, and helped put together one of the applications presented in Chapter 3 using Oracle9*i* TopLink. I would like to thank Melody Liu, Principal Business Development Manager, and Lisa Goldstein, Senior Product Manager, both from Oracle Corporation, who have assisted me during many months with this project. Thanks to Marc Horowitz for allowing us to use his personal site to manage the flow of our documents. Many special thanks to my contributing authors, Ekkehard Rohwedder, Luis Amat, Ashish Parikh, and Gerald Momplaisir. Thanks to Dr. Mark D. Powell, Atmospheric Scientist, and his H*WIND team at the National Oceanic and Atmospheric Administration's Hurricane Research Division; Dr. Joseph Prospero, CIMAS Director and professor at University of Miami (Miami, Florida); and Jeremy Judson, Athena Honore, Janet Walden, Bill McManus, Karen Mead, and David Heiret of the McGraw-Hill/ Osborne editorial staff.

Foreword

he growth of the Internet and the e-business revolution has lead to a shift of enterprise applications running off desktop computers to running on application servers. Java has emerged as the primary language being used to develop these applications. Java 2 Enterprise Edition (J2EE) provides a comprehensive set of services such as transaction management, reliable messaging, security, naming, and connectivity to allow large-scale enterprise applications to be built quickly and productively. The adoption of the J2EE specification by the developer community and by large software vendors has lead to its evolution today as the most popular programming model for the Internet. However, in addition to developer productivity, enterprise applications also need a software platform that addresses issues such as performance, scalability, high availability, and security. Increasingly, these requirements affect every application developed today, regardless of whether it is aimed at powering a dynamic web site or an enterprise transaction processing system, and regardless of whether it is intended to run on an organization's internal network or on the Internet.

Oracle recognizes that the emergence of Java as a viable platform for large-scale enterprise applications has made J2EE an important part of a developer's toolkit. We have designed Oracle9*i* Application Server (Oracle9*i*AS) to be a 100 percent standards-compliant environment for J2EE applications, with complete support for JavaServer Pages, servlets, and Enterprise JavaBeans. Oracle9*i*AS is lightweight and easy to use and has a number of features that have been specifically designed to make the Java developer very productive. It is also designed to run J2EE applications with unmatched performance, scalability, and reliability. Throw in servlet and EJB clusters; a centralized, web-based management environment; a world-class integrated development environment in Oracle9*i* JDeveloper; a world-class Java-database mapping facility; the substantial tools, utilities, documentation, and knowledge available from Oracle; and developers all over the world, and you have a clear winner when it comes to an enterprise application server—Oracle.

Oracle9iAS Building J2EE Applications, by Nirva Morisseau-Leroy and her contributing authors, Ekkehard Rohwedder, Luis Amat, Ashish Parikh, and Gerald Momplaisir, is the book you need to understand J2EE and to develop high-quality Internet applications using Oracle9*i*AS Containers For J2EE. The chapters are filled with real-life applications that demonstrate how to effectively design, develop, deploy, and manage J2EE applications. It has been meticulously researched and is designed to provide you with information you need to become productive as quickly as possible with Oracle9*i*AS. I was very pleased with the quality and timeliness of the book and the careful organization and structure with which the book leads you all the way from introductory information to the most advanced concepts using carefully designed examples to make the concepts easy to understand. It will serve as an invaluable guide as you learn how to develop unified, scalable, and secure applications using Oracle9*i*AS Containers For J2EE.

Thomas Kurian
Senior Vice President, Oracle9*i*AS
Oracle Corporation

Preface

o you want to run your J2EE applications faster, more securely, and more reliably? Do you want to develop and deploy J2EE applications more easily and more productively? If your answer to these questions is yes, you are reading the right book. By using the Oracle9*i* Application Server (Oracle9*i*AS) to develop and deploy your J2EE applications, you will be more productive and you will sleep better at night knowing that your applications run faster, more securely, and more reliably than on any other application server. Yes, these are bold statements, but we think that after reading this book you will agree. Through real-world examples, we give you a thorough and in-depth understanding of developing J2EE applications on, and deploying them to, Oracle9*i*AS.

So, What Do I Get?

This book targets experienced J2EE developers as well as newcomers to the wonderful world of Java and J2EE. In this book, we cover all of the components you need to know within the J2EE 1.3 specification to be able to develop real-world, robust applications. We give you a review of the basics of each component, show you useful examples in each chapter, and teach you how to configure and deploy the components to Oracle9*i*AS Containers For J2EE (OC4J). This book also gives you all the tips and tricks you need to take full advantage of OC4J's developer-friendly features, such as hot deployment, auto deployment, auto generation of client stubs, auto generation of deployment descriptors, tools to expose standard components as Web Services, tools for deployment and management, and much more. But, development is only half the battle. Reading this book will also give you in-depth knowledge about how to configure OC4J to optimize performance and availability as well as ensure high levels of security for your J2EE application. We show you how to install OC4J, configure data sources, use external JMS providers, configure and use security such as JAAS, plug in a framework, deploy applications, and we offer you other tips and tricks.

We show you everything you need to know to be really productive using Oracle9*i* Application Server.

We have divided this book into three parts:

In Part I, we give you an overview and history of J2EE and all of its components, including roles, packaging, frameworks, and design patterns. We also give you an overview of Oracle9*i* Application Server and in-depth coverage of OC4J services such as JDBC, data sources, JNDI, RMI, and SQLJ.

In Part II, we start developing the business logic for our sample application. We introduce you to Enterprise JavaBeans (EJB), and show you how to use all its different flavors, including message-driven beans, to encapsulate your business logic, handle transactions, and use design patterns and local interfaces.

In Part III, we cover the presentation layer using servlets and JavaServer Pages.

Furthermore, we cover security and show how to enforce security in your application using Java Authentication and Authorization Service (JAAS). You will learn how easy it is to expose different components as Web Services.

Thank you for purchasing this book. I hope you will find it to be a valuable resource when developing and deploying your J2EE applications on Oracle9*i* Application Server.

Mikael Ottosson
Technical Director, Business Development
Oracle9*i* Application Server
Oracle Corporation

Introduction

This book is about developing Java client-side and server-side software components using the J2EE technology. More importantly, this book covers the different deployment scenarios of these components to the Oracle9*i*AS Containers For J2EE (OC4J), release 3 (9.0.3). OC4J is a J2EE-compliant application server; thus, applications residing in OC4J are portable and can live in any J2EE-compliant application server. Specifically, this book focuses on the different technologies that comprise the J2EE technology; the "core" components of OC4J; how to use the J2EE technology in application analysis, design, and implementation; and how to deploy applications to OC4J.

Throughout this book, you will learn how to develop and deploy J2EE components that live in OC4J and manipulate data residing in an Oracle9*i* data server and Oracle8*i* database versions 8.1.7 and 8.1.6. You will use the components that you build in this book as simple business objects, but, more importantly, you will deploy them using component models such as Enterprise JavaBeans (EJB), servlets, and JavaServer Pages (JSP). These component models are part of the J2EE platform and allow companies to deploy the same application into a variety of deployment servers and to distribute the same application to a variety of clients, including Java stand-alone programs, EJB, JSP, servlet, or web browser clients.

Additionally, you will learn how to build applications using Oracle9*i*AS TopLink. Oracle9*i*AS TopLink, one of the latest additions to the Oracle9*i*AS technology stack, is a well-known technology that adds an industry-leading object-relational mapping and data-integration solution to the Oracle9*i*AS stack. It can help you overcome the object-relational impedance mismatch in all kinds of architectures, including JSP/servlet, classical two- or three-tier, and EJB architectures. To learn more about Oracle9*i*AS TopLink, see http://otn.oracle.com/software/products/ias/devuse.html

Part I (Chapters 1, 2, and 3) provides an overview of J2EE, an OC4J user guide, and OC4J services. Chapter 3 covers the different technologies that OC4J supports, such as JDBC, SQLJ, Java Naming and Directory Interface (JNDI), Java Message

Service (JMS), and Oracle9*i*AS TopLink, and explains how to use these technologies when developing your applications.

Part II (Chapters 4, 5, 6, and 7) teaches you the fundamental concepts of the Enterprise JavaBeans (EJB 2.0) architecture. In these chapters, you will build simple and advanced database EJB components, in the forms of entity beans, session beans, and message-driven beans, and deploy them to OC4J. Specifically, in Chapter 7, you will learn how to configure and set up Oracle Advanced Queuing as a JMS provider and develop JMS clients that produce and receive messages using point-to-point (PTP) and publish/subscribe (pub/sub) messaging systems. In the PTP domain, the destination for message delivery is called a *queue,* whereas in the pub/sub domain, the destination for message delivery is called a *topic.* Note that in order for you to run the application that you will develop in Chapter 7, you need OC4J release 9.0.3 or higher and Oracle9*i* database, release 9.3 or higher.

In Part III (Chapters 8, 9, 10, and 11), you will learn about OC4J security, OC4J and Web Services, servlets, and JavaServer Pages. In Chapter 9 (covering Web Services), Chapter 10 (servlets), and Chapter 11 (JSP), you will build client applications that use the business objects and EJB components that you build in Parts I and II.

For quick references on the details that we present in the chapters, we have included four appendixes in Part IV: Appendix A (OC4J XML Configuration Files), Appendix B (OC4J Security), Appendix C (Enterprise JavaBeans API Reference), and Appendix D (OC4J J2EE-Specific DTD Reference).

CAUTION
The applications that you will develop in this book require OC4J, release 9.0.3 or higher.

In this book, you will develop the *Purchase Order Financial System,* a J2EE application that manipulates data relating to purchase orders stored in an Oracle9*i* data server. The Purchase Order Financial System is a real-life application that was designed for the Atlantic Oceanographic and Meteorological Laboratory, Miami, Florida, an Environmental Research Laboratory of the National Oceanic and Atmospheric Administration, part of the U.S. Department of Commerce.

In this introduction, we present the use cases of the application, the *Purchase Order* database schema, and the SQL script to set up and configure Oracle Advanced Queuing as a JMS provider. The elements presented here will facilitate the assimilation of the contents of the book.

The Purchase Order relational database schema, a "pure" relational database, is part of a database design presented in Gerald Momplaisir's 1997 master's thesis, "Design of a Financial Administrative System Using the Semantic Binary Model," for the School of Computer Sciences, Florida International University. This schema is easy to understand but still useful and has been used successfully in a number of programming textbooks. We have used the Purchase Order financial schema, quite intensively, in our previous publications: *Oracle9*i *SQLJ Programming,* by N. Morisseau-Leroy, M. Solomon, and G. Momplaisir (Oracle Press, Osborne/McGraw-Hill, June 2001); *Oracle8*i *Java Component Programming with EJB, CORBA and JSP,* by N. Morisseau-Leroy, M. Solomon, and J. Basu (Oracle Press, Osborne/McGraw-Hill, September 2000); and *Oracle8*i *SQLJ Programming,* by N. Morisseau-Leroy, M. Solomon, and G. Momplaisir (Oracle Press, Osborne/McGraw-Hill, November 1999).

The introduction of the book is divided into several sections:

- Use Cases (provides the use cases on which we based the applications that you will develop)
- Database Schema (presents the Purchase Order database schema, which is used in all chapters in which you learn to develop J2EE applications)
- Set Up and Configure Oracle Advanced Queuing as a JMS Provider
- Providing Feedback to the Authors
- Retrieving Examples Online
- Disclaimer

Use Cases

In this section, we present the use case specifications of the Purchase Order Financial System that you will build in the book. There are five use case specifications:

- **Manage Employee** Allows a budget officer to create, view, update, and delete an employee. You will implement the business logic requirements in Chapter 5.
- **Purchase Order System** Allows an employee of a company to enter a purchase order from a web browser prior to purchasing goods from a company. You will implement the business logic requirements in Chapters 5 and 6.
- **Purchase Order Approval** Allows a budget officer to approve or disapprove employee purchase requests. You will implement the business logic requirements in Chapter 7.

- **Manage Department** Allows a budget officer to create, view, update, and delete a department. You can download the code implementation of this use case from www.data-i.com and www.osborne.com.
- **Manage Project** Allows a budget officer to create, view, update, and delete a project. You can download the code implementation of this use case from www.data-i.com and www.osborne.com.

Manage Employee

The Manage Employee use case allows a budget officer to create, view, update, and delete an employee.

Actor

The actor is the budget officer.

Preconditions

- The database schema must exist.
- At least one department exists (see the section on the Manage Department use case).
- The budget officer has been authenticated and authorized to use the system.

Flow of Events

The use case begins when the budget officer chooses the "Manage" URL location from their web browser.

Main Flow

Create a New Employee:

1. The budget officer selects to create a new employee from the menu.
2. The browser displays an empty employee web form.
3. The budget officer, the title, first name, last name, telephone, e-mail, and the department can be selected from a drop-down list of departments.
4. The budget officer clicks the Create button of the new employee.
5. A confirmation page is displayed to the budget officer, showing the new employee number.

Alternate Flows

View an Employee:

1. The budget officer selects to view an existing employee from the menu.
2. The browser displays a list of employees.
3. The budget officer selects an employee order to view.
4. The system retrieves and displays the selected employee.

Modify an Employee:

1. The budget officer selects to modify an existing employee from the menu.
2. The browser displays a list of employees.
3. The budget officer selects an employee order to modify.
4. The system retrieves and displays the employee.
5. The budget officer updates and makes changes to the employee.
6. The budget officer clicks the Save Changes button of the employee.
7. The system displays a confirmation page.

Delete an Employee:

1. The budget officer selects Delete Employee from a menu.
2. The browser displays a list of employees.
3. The budget officer selects the employee to delete.
4. The system retrieves and displays the employee.
5. The budget officer clicks the Delete Employee button.
6. The system displays a confirmation page.

Unable to Create or Modify Employee:

If a system error occurs when the budget officer tries to modify or enter a new employee, the system displays an error message and returns to where the error occurred. The budget officer has the option to continue or cancel.

Purchase Order System

The Purchase Order System use case allows an employee of a company to enter a purchase order from a web browser prior to purchasing goods from a company.

Actors

The actors are employees who need to enter or manage purchase orders.

Preconditions

- The Purchase Order relational database schema must exist.
- The user has been authenticated and authorized to use the system.

Flow of Events

The use case begins when the employee chooses the "Purchase Order" URL location from their web browser.

Main Flow

Create a New Purchase Order:

1. The employee selects to create a new purchase order from a menu.
2. The browser displays an empty purchase order web form.
3. The employee enters the following purchase order information:
    - Vendor information: name, address, city, state, and ZIP. The employee also has the option to choose the vendor from a drop-down list of vendors previously entered into the system. If the employee selects a vendor from the list, the system populates the form with the vendor information from the selected drop-down list.
    - Each item, on a separate line, that they wish to purchase from the vendor: project number, unit (ea, lb), quantity, and the estimated cost of the item.
4. The employee clicks the Create button of the purchase order.
5. A confirmation page is displayed to the user, showing their new purchase order number.

Alternate Flows

View a Purchase Order:

1. The employee selects to view an existing purchase order from a menu.
2. The browser displays a list of purchase orders that the employee has entered.
3. The employee selects a purchase order to view.
4. The system retrieves and displays the purchase order selected by the employee. The display includes all information that the employee previously entered for the purchase order, including the approval status.

Modify a Purchase Order:

1. The employee selects to modify an existing purchase order from a menu.
2. The browser displays a list of purchase orders that the employee has entered into the system but that have not been approved by the budget officer (see the following section regarding the Purchase Order Approval use case).
3. The employee selects a purchase order to update.
4. The system retrieves and displays the purchase order corresponding to the purchase order entered by the employee.
5. The employee updates and makes changes to the purchase order.
6. The employee clicks the Save Changes button of the purchase order.
7. The system displays a confirmation page.

Delete a Purchase Order:

1. The employee selects Delete Purchase Order from a menu.
2. The browser displays a list of purchase orders that the employee has entered into the system but that have not been approved by the budget officer (see the following section regarding the Purchase Order Approval use case).
3. The employee selects a purchase order to delete.
4. The system retrieves and displays the purchase order corresponding to the purchase order selected by the employee.
5. The employee clicks the Delete Purchase Order button.
6. The system displays a confirmation page.

Unable to Create or Modify Purchase Order:

If a system error occurs when the employee tries to modify or enter a new purchase order, the system displays an error message and returns to where the error occurred. The employee has the option to continue or cancel.

Purchase Order Approval

The Purchase Order Approval use case allows a budget officer to approve or disapprove employee purchase requests.

Actors

- Employees who have entered purchase orders.
- The budget officer who approves purchase orders.

Preconditions

- The Purchase Order relational database schema must exist.
- The budget officer has been authenticated and authorized to use the system.

Flow of Events

The use case begins when the budget officer chooses the "Purchase Order" URL location from their web browser.

Main Flow

Approve Purchase Orders:

1. The budget officer selects Purchase Approval from a menu.
2. The system retrieves a list of purchase orders awaiting approval.
3. The browser displays a purchase order.
4. The budget officer has the option to enter comments in a description field.
5. The budget officer selects Approve or Disapprove.
6. The system generates and sends an e-mail to the employee who entered the purchase order.
7. The browser displays the next purchase order.

8. Steps 3 through 6 are repeated until all purchase orders have gone through the approval process.

Alternate Flow

There is no alternative flow.

Unable to Create or Modify Purchase Order:

If a system error occurs when the budget officer tries to approve a purchase order, the system displays an error message and returns to where the error occurred. The budget officer has the option to continue or cancel.

Manage Department

The Manage Department use case allows a budget officer to create, view, update, and delete a department.

Actor

The actor is the budget officer.

Preconditions

- The Purchase Order relational database schema must exist.
- The budget officer has been authenticated and authorized to use the system.

Flow of Events

The use case begins when the budget officer chooses the "Manage" URL location from their web browser.

Main Flow

Create a New Department:

1. The budget officer selects to create a new department from the menu.
2. The browser displays an empty department web form.
3. The budget officer enters the new department's name and short name.
4. The budget officer clicks the Create button to add a new department.
5. A confirmation page is displayed to the budget officer, showing the new department number.

Alternate Flows

View a Department:

1. The budget officer selects to view an existing department from the menu.
2. The browser displays a list of departments.
3. The budget officer selects a department order to view.
4. The system retrieves and displays the selected department.

Modify a Department:

1. The budget officer selects to modify an existing department from the menu.
2. The browser displays a list of departments.
3. The budget officer selects a department order to modify.
4. The system retrieves and displays the department.
5. The budget officer updates and makes changes to the department.
6. The budget officer clicks the Save Changes button of the department.
7. The system displays a confirmation page.

Delete a Department:

1. The budget officer selects Delete Department from a menu.
2. The browser displays a list of departments.
3. The budget officer selects a department to delete.
4. The system retrieves and displays the department.
5. The budget officer clicks the Delete Department button.
6. The system displays a confirmation page.

Unable to Create or Modify Department:

If a system error occurs when the budget officer tries to modify or enter a new department, the system displays an error message and returns to where the error occurred. The budget officer has the option to continue or cancel.

Manage Project

The Manage Project use case allows a budget officer to create, view, update, and delete a project.

Actor

The actor is the budget officer.

Preconditions

- The Purchase Order database schema must exist.
- The budget officer has been authenticated and authorized to use the system.

Flow of Events

The use case begins when the budget officer chooses the "Manage" URL location from their web browser.

Main Flow

Create a New Project:

1. The budget officer selects to create a new project from the menu.
2. The browser displays an empty project web form.
3. The budget officer enters the name, start date, and initial funding for the project.
4. The budget officer clicks the Create button to add a new project.
5. A confirmation page is displayed to the budget officer, showing the new project number.

Alternate Flows

View a Project:

1. The budget officer selects to view an existing project from the menu.
2. The browser displays a list of projects.
3. The budget officer selects a project order to view.
4. The system retrieves and displays the selected project.

Modify a Project:

1. The budget officer selects to modify an existing project from the menu.
2. The browser displays a list of projects.
3. The budget officer selects a project order to modify.
4. The system retrieves and displays the project.
5. The budget officer updates and makes changes to the project.
6. The budget officer clicks the Save Changes button of the project.
7. The system displays a confirmation page.

Delete a Project:

1. The budget officer selects Delete Project from a menu.
2. The browser displays a list of projects.
3. The budget officer selects a project to delete.
4. The system retrieves and displays the project.
5. The budget officer clicks the Delete Project button.
6. The system displays a confirmation page.

Unable to Create or Modify Project

If a system error occurs when the budget officer tries to modify or enter a new project, the system displays an error message and returns to where the error occurred. The budget officer has the option to continue or cancel.

Database Schema

Throughout the book, you will develop J2EE applications that manipulate a "pure" relational database—that is, a financial schema called the Purchase Order schema. The Purchase Order relational database schema is part of a database design presented in Gerald Momplaisir's 1997 master's thesis, "Design of a Financial Administrative System Using the Semantic Binary Model," for the School of Computer Sciences, Florida International University.

Note that all the J2EE applications that you will develop in this book have been tested and deployed in the Oracle9*i* Application Server, specifically in OC4J, release 3 (9.0.3). The Purchase Order schema has also been tested against the

Oracle8*i* database, releases 8.1.6 and 8.1.7, and the Oracle9*i* database, release 9.0.1, and all of them have been deployed in OC4J.

SQL Scripts to Create the Financial Purchase Order Database Schema

Use the following `createposchema.sql` SQL script to create the Purchase Order database schema in the Oracle9*i* database:

```
-- File Name:  createposchema.sql
DROP TABLE DEPARTMENT CASCADE CONSTRAINTS
/
CREATE TABLE DEPARTMENT(
deptno        NUMBER(5),
shortname     VARCHAR2(6),
longname      VARCHAR2(20))
/
DROP TABLE ACCOUNT CASCADE CONSTRAINTS;
/
CREATE TABLE ACCOUNT (
accountno      NUMBER(5),
projectno      NUMBER(5),
deptno         NUMBER(5)),
PRIMARY KEY ( accountno ))
/
DROP TABLE EMPLOYEE CASCADE CONSTRAINTS
/
CREATE TABLE EMPLOYEE(
employeeno     NUMBER(7),
deptno         NUMBER(5),
type           VARCHAR2(30),
lastname       VARCHAR2(30),
firstname      VARCHAR2(30),
phone          VARCHAR2(10),
email          VARCHAR2(30))
/
DROP TABLE VENDOR CASCADE CONSTRAINTS
/
CREATE TABLE VENDOR (
vendorno     NUMBER(6),
name         VARCHAR2(30),
address      VARCHAR2(20),
city         VARCHAR2(15),
state        VARCHAR2(15),
zip         VARCHAR2(15),
country      VARCHAR2(15))
```

```
/
DROP TABLE PROJECT CASCADE CONSTRAINTS
/
CREATE TABLE PROJECT (
projectno         NUMBER(5),
name      VARCHAR2(20),
start_date        DATE,
amt_of_funds      NUMBER,
PRIMARY KEY( projectno );
/
DROP TABLE PURCHASE_ORDER CASCADE CONSTRAINTS
/
CREATE TABLE PURCHASE_ORDER (
requestno         NUMBER(10),
employeeno        NUMBER(7),
vendorno          NUMBER(6))
/
DROP TABLE LINE_ITEM CASCADE CONSTRAINTS
/
CREATE TABLE LINE_ITEM (
requestno         NUMBER(10),
lineno            NUMBER(5),
projectno         NUMBER(5),
quantity          NUMBER(5),
unit              VARCHAR2(2),
cost              NUMBER(8,2),
actualcost        NUMBER(8,2),
description       VARCHAR2(30))
/
DROP TABLE APPROVAL CASCADE CONSTRAINTS
/
CREATE TABLE APPROVAL (
requestno        NUMBER(10),
budgetofficer    NUMBER(7),
approved         CHAR(1),
reasons          VARCHAR2(30))
/
```

Use the following `poconstraints.sql` SQL script to create additional constraints on the tables of the Purchase Order database schema:

```
-- File Name: poconstraints.sql
alter table DEPARTMENT
  ADD CONSTRAINT deptno_pk PRIMARY KEY(deptno)
  USING INDEX TABLESPACE INDX
/
ALTER TABLE ACCOUNT
```

```
  ADD CONSTRAINT accountno_pk PRIMARY KEY(accountno)
  USING INDEX TABLESPACE INDX
/
ALTER TABLE PROJECT
  ADD CONSTRAINT projectno_pk PRIMARY KEY(projectno)
  USING INDEX TABLESPACE INDX
/
ALTER TABLE ACCOUNT
  ADD CONSTRAINT acc_deptno_fk
  FOREIGN KEY(deptno)
  REFERENCES DEPARTMENT(deptno)
/
ALTER TABLE EMPLOYEE
  ADD CONSTRAINT employeeno_pk PRIMARY KEY(employeeno)
  USING INDEX TABLESPACE INDX
/
ALTER TABLE EMPLOYEE
  ADD CONSTRAINT emp_deptno_fk
  FOREIGN KEY(deptno)
  REFERENCES DEPARTMENT(deptno)
/
 ALTER TABLE vendor_list
  ADD CONSTRAINT vendorno_pk PRIMARY KEY(vendorno)
  USING INDEX TABLESPACE INDX
/
ALTER TABLE Purchase_Order
  ADD CONSTRAINT requestno_pk PRIMARY KEY(requestno)
  USING INDEX TABLESPACE INDX
/
ALTER TABLE LINE_ITEM
  ADD CONSTRAINT lineno_pk
  PRIMARY KEY(requestno,lineno,projectno)
  USING INDEX TABLESPACE INDX
/
ALTER TABLE LINE_ITEM
  ADD CONSTRAINT lineitem_requestno_fk
  FOREIGN KEY(requestno)
  REFERENCES PURCHASE_ORDER(requestno)
/
ALTER TABLE APPROVAL
  ADD constraint requestno_fk FOREIGN KEY(requestno)
  REFERENCES PURCHASE_ORDER(requestno)
 /
```

Use the following `posequences.sql` SQL script to create the relationships on the tables of the Purchase Order database schema:

```
File Name: posequences.sql
CREATE SEQUENCE deptno_SEQ
  START WITH 200
  INCREMENT BY 1
/
CREATE SEQUENCE projectno_SEQ
  START WITH 300
  INCREMENT BY 1
/
CREATE SEQUENCE employeeno_SEQ
  START WITH 100
  INCREMENT BY 1
/
CREATE SEQUENCE accountno_SEQ
  START WITH 1000
  INCREMENT BY 1
/
CREATE SEQUENCE cardno_SEQ
  START WITH 311200
  INCREMENT BY 1
/
CREATE SEQUENCE vendorno_SEQ
  START WITH 400
  INCREMENT BY 1
/
CREATE SEQUENCE requestno_SEQ
  START WITH 500
  INCREMENT BY 1
/
CREATE SEQUENCE lineno_SEQ
  START WITH 1
  INCREMENT BY 1
/
```

Next, we present the SQL script to set up Oracle AQ as a JMS provider.

Set Up and Configure Oracle Advanced Queuing as a JMS Provider

In this section, we present the SQL script to set up and configure Oracle AQ in an Oracle9*i* database. OC4J allows you to plug in message providers and third-party messaging systems, such as Oracle AQ, IBM MQSeries, Sonic Software's SonicMQ, and SwiftMQ (from swiftmq.com). In Chapter 7, you will build the Approval application that satisfies the business logic requirements of the Purchase Order Approval use case specification presented in the "Use Cases" section of this

Introduction. The Approval application uses Oracle AQ as a JMS provider. A JMS provider is a messaging system that implements JMS in addition to the other administrative and control functionality required of a full-featured messaging product. It is the entity that implements JMS for a messaging product.

Oracle AQ supplies queue and topic message implementations. Message queuing functionality allows applications on Oracle databases to communicate asynchronously via messages in AQ queues. Oracle AQ has additional features, such as e-mail notifications and transformation useful for Internet applications. AQ operations can also be performed over the Internet via HTTP(s) and e-mail. To learn more about Oracle AQ, see the *Oracle9*i *Application Developer's Guide – Advanced Queuing, Release 1 (9.0.2)* technical manual and/or http://otn.oracle.com/products/aq/content.html. For detailed information regarding Oracle AQ setup and configuration, see the "Setting Up Oracle Advanced Queuing as a JMS Provider" section of Chapter 7.

Here is the SQL script to set up and configure Oracle AQ as a JMS provider:

```
-- Connect as system/password
connect system/password

-- Using the existing SCOTT database user
-- Just grant that user the AQ_USER_ROLE:
GRANT "AQ_USER_ROLE" TO "SCOTT";
ALTER USER "SCOTT" DEFAULT ROLE  ALL;

-- Creating the AQUSER database user
CREATE USER "AQUSER"  PROFILE "DEFAULT"
    IDENTIFIED BY "x" DEFAULT TABLESPACE "USERS"
    TEMPORARY TABLESPACE "TEMP"
    QUOTA UNLIMITED
    ON USERS
    ACCOUNT UNLOCK;

-- Grant the following Oracle system privileges to AQUSER
GRANT "AQ_USER_ROLE" TO "AQUSER";
GRANT "CONNECT" TO "AQUSER";

-- Setting up the PROCESSTOPIC Topic

-- 1. Create the queue table
BEGIN
  DBMS_AQADM.CREATE_QUEUE_TABLE ( queue_table=> 'AQUSER.PROCESSTOPIC',
   queue_payload_type=> 'SYS.AQ$_JMS_MAP_MESSAGE',
   sort_list=> '', comment=> '',
   multiple_consumers=> TRUE, message_grouping=> DBMS_AQADM.NONE,
   non_repudiation => DBMS_AQADM.NONE,
   storage_clause=> '', compatible=> '8.1',
   primary_instance=> '0', secondary_instance=> '0');
  COMMIT;
```

```
END;

-- 2. Create the actual Topic destination
BEGIN
  DBMS_AQADM.CREATE_QUEUE(queue_name=> 'AQUSER.PROCESSTOPIC',
   queue_table=> 'AQUSER.PROCESSTOPIC',
   queue_type=> DBMS_AQADM.NORMAL_QUEUE,
   max_retries=> '0', retry_delay=> '0',
   retention_time=> '0', comment=> '');
  COMMIT;
END;

-- 3. Start the Topic destination
BEGIN
  DBMS_AQADM.START_QUEUE('AQUSER.PROCESSTOPIC', TRUE, TRUE);
  COMMIT;
END;

-- ################## --
-- Setting up the EMAILQUEUE Queue

-- 1. Create the queue table
BEGIN
  DBMS_AQADM.CREATE_QUEUE_TABLE ( queue_table=> 'AQUSER.EMAILQUEUE',
   queue_payload_type=> 'SYS.AQ$_JMS_TEXT_MESSAGE', sort_list=> '',
   comment=>'', multiple_consumers=> FALSE,
   message_grouping=> DBMS_AQADM.NONE,
   non_repudiation => DBMS_AQADM.NONE, storage_clause=> '',
   compatible=> '8.1', primary_instance=> '0',
   secondary_instance=> '0');
  COMMIT;
END;

-- 2. Create the actual Queue destination
BEGIN
  DBMS_AQADM.CREATE_QUEUE(queue_name=> 'AQUSER.EMAILQUEUE',
   queue_table=> 'AQUSER.EMAILQUEUE',
   queue_type=> DBMS_AQADM.NORMAL_QUEUE,
   max_retries=> '0', retry_delay=> '0',
   retention_time=> '0', comment=> '');
  COMMIT;
END;

-- 3. Start the Queue destination
BEGIN
  DBMS_AQADM.START_QUEUE('AQUSER.EMAILQUEUE', TRUE, TRUE);
  COMMIT;
END;
```

```
-- Connect as AQUSER
connect aquser/x
/
-- Grant privilege to the AQUSER.PROCESSTOPIC Topic
BEGIN
DBMS_AQADM.GRANT_QUEUE_PRIVILEGE (privilege=>'DEQUEUE',
   queue_name=>'AQUSER.PROCESSTOPIC', grantee=>'SCOTT',
   grant_option=>FALSE);
   COMMIT;
END;
BEGIN
DBMS_AQADM.GRANT_QUEUE_PRIVILEGE (privilege=>'ENQUEUE',
     queue_name=>'AQUSER.PROCESSTOPIC', grantee=>'SCOTT',
     grant_option=>FALSE);
COMMIT;
END;
-- Grant privilege to the AQUSER.EMAILQUEUE Queue
BEGIN
DBMS_AQADM.GRANT_QUEUE_PRIVILEGE (privilege=>'DEQUEUE',
    queue_name=>'AQUSER.EMAILQUEUE', grantee=>'SCOTT',
    grant_option=>FALSE);
COMMIT;
END;
BEGIN
DBMS_AQADM.GRANT_QUEUE_PRIVILEGE (privilege=>'ENQUEUE',
   queue_name=>'AQUSER.EMAILQUEUE', grantee=>'SCOTT',
   grant_option=>FALSE);
COMMIT;
END;
```

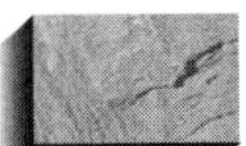

CAUTION
Oracle AQ requires Oracle9i database, release 9.3 or higher. To run the Approval application that you develop in Chapter 7, you also need OC4J release 9.0.3 or higher.

Providing Feedback to the Authors

The authors welcome your comments and suggestions on the quality and usefulness of this book. Your input is important to us. You can send comments to us via electronic mail:

- Nirva Morisseau-Leroy at nmorisseauleroy@data-i.com
- Ekkehard Rohwedder at ekkehard.rohwedder@oracle.com

- Luis Amat at luis.amat@oracle.com
- Ashish Parikh at ashish.parikh@oracle.com
- Gerald Momplaisir at gerald.momplaisir@oracle.com

Retrieving Examples Online

The use case specifications, schema scripts, Oracle AQ setup script, and program source code can be found at the Oracle Technology Network (http://otn.oracle.com), www.data-i.com, and www.osborne.com. Note that Oracle9*i*AS Application Server, Oracle9*i*AS Containers For J2EE, and other Oracle software also can be downloaded from http://otn.oracle.com.

Disclaimer

The programs presented here are not intended for use in any inherently dangerous applications. It shall be the reader's responsibility to take all appropriate fail-safe, backup, redundancy, and other measures to ensure the safe use of such applications.

PART I

Overview

CHAPTER 1

Introduction to J2EE

While most of this book will guide you through J2EE using Oracle9*i*AS Containers For J2EE (OC4J) mostly by example, this chapter presents a more generic introduction to the J2EE 1.3 specification. You will learn about the concepts and technologies available through the J2EE platform and how and when to use J2EE when designing and developing enterprise applications. Specifically, you will cover the following topics:

- J2EE fundamentals, history, and future
- J2EE technologies
- The technical value of using, or not using, J2EE in projects
- J2EE architecture
- J2EE application components and containers
- J2EE services
- Packaging and deployment
- J2EE roles
- J2EE design patterns
- Sample application and methodology

J2EE Fundamentals, History, and Future

Enterprise-wide applications are not as naturally unified or straightforward as other applications. Potentially intricate distribution, security, reliability and performance requirements are a few of the risks to consider. Those complexities and risks are compounded even further when one considers Internet and other web deployments with their potentially immense application user populations. The Java 2 Enterprise Edition (J2EE) specification arose out of a need to mitigate these risks and lower the sometimes-prohibitive costs that come with building a secure, high-performance enterprise application. The following are but a few of the features that mitigate those risks and costs:

- Unified, scalable, and platform-independent language for all application tiers: Java
- Component-based approach to development, design, assembly, and deployment
- Unified security model

- Design-by-contract approach: clean interfaces and expected behavior between tiers delivered through a comprehensive suite of APIs
- Allows for separate development roles and easier integration of both new and legacy components

The J2EE specification is currently in version 1.3, and a public draft of the 1.4 specification is currently available. Each release brings with it a more complete realization of the vision of unified, low-risk, low-cost enterprise applications.

J2EE Technologies

J2EE consists of separate technology areas and design patterns (or blueprints) for building a successful system using those technologies. The technology specifications provided by J2EE are those required by developers to build enterprise systems with Java, those required to connect to existing enterprise information systems, and those for enabling simpler programming and component customization. While we certainly do not want to cover each of the APIs in great detail, a quick review of each of the technologies available through the J2EE 1.3 specification is certainly applicable.

JDBC 2.0 The JDBC API provides an abstraction layer to almost any relational or tabular data source. It provides authentication, connection, SQL, and transactional APIs, among others. Programmers can use the same code for accessing any vendor's data source through the use of a JDBC driver for that data source. Because of the ubiquitous nature of data and data sources in most enterprise applications, you will find that JDBC permeates most of the technologies in the J2EE technology stack, and therefore is mentioned throughout most of this book. Chapter 3, however, contains information on how to use JDBC in Oracle9*i*AS to connect to an Oracle database.

JNDI 1.2 The Java Naming and Directory Interface (JNDI) APIs provide interfaces to directory services such as, but not limited to, lightweight directory access protocol (LDAP), JDBC data sources, EJB Homes, JMS (Java Message Service) Connections, Network Information Service (NIS), and Domain Name System (DNS). Naming services are an integral part of the way J2EE components find services, other components, and legacy systems. Developers can refer to component customization data declaratively (by name) so that customizing software will not require code changes in the system or the components themselves. Chapter 3 provides more details on JNDI and its uses in OC4J.

JTA 1.0 and JTS Transaction management is a J2EE standard service for simplifying distributed systems development. It also ensures data integrity by enforcing strict rules for accessing and manipulating enterprise data, by making sure a transaction either finishes completely or does not go through at all. The Java Transaction API

(JTA) enables a distributed transactional system or application to access a transaction manager, as defined by the Java Transaction Service (JTS), as well as the J2EE server and the application itself abstractly and independently of implementation specifics through Java interfaces. A JTS transaction manager provides transactional demarcation and synchronization services, resource management, and propagation of information for a transactional system.

Servlet 2.3 The Java Servlet API is a container-managed, stateful alternative to Common Gateway Interface (CGI) applications. Servlets are deployed and managed by a dedicated part of the J2EE container that is closely integrated with the container's security subsystem. For a discussion on containers, see "J2EE Components, Containers, and Services" later in this chapter. A servlet's sole purpose is to receive HTTP requests, generate dynamic data, usually HTML, and deliver an HTTP response. The Java Servlet API also introduces the concept of an HTTP session that allows an HTTP client to make stateful calls to the servlet container. Servlets do not release all of their resources for each request, as do typical CGI applications, but rather stay resident and ready for often-concurrent requests from HTTP clients. Hooks into the servlet and the session's life cycles are available through servlet event listeners and, beginning with the 2.3 Java Servlet specification, developers can use filter chains to make successive transformations on the HTTP request or response. See Chapter 10 for a detailed discussion on how to build servlets and deploy them to OC4J.

JSP 1.2 JavaServer Pages provide a way for developers to use a templated view for dynamic HTML content. A JSP is usually an HTML page containing pieces of interspersed embedded Java code (scriptlets) or custom or standard tag libraries. Tag libraries provide for a cleaner separation between the view and controller tiers of an application, although techniques and patterns exist to enable this separation though the use of scriptlets (see "J2EE Architecture" later in this chapter for more details on application tiers). Using tag libraries rather than scriptlets, moreover, frees JSP developers from having to know or understand Java code, by allowing them to place a functional HTML-like tag into a JSP for rendering at run time when the JSP is compiled once into a Java servlet and run. Chapter 11 provides a thorough discussion on JSPs and shows how they might apply to the Purchase Order application referred to throughout the book.

EJB 2.0 Enterprise JavaBeans serve as a J2EE application's business logic layer. Business logic is code that helps tie enterprise systems and data to an application's web or other presentation tiers. EJBs provide access to a potentially stateful, remote, transactional, secure (under J2EE's unified security platform), and scalable business logic tier. EJBs are not, therefore, used for generating user interfaces, nor are they used for handling client requests. Those tasks are typically handled by the presentation-tier components (servlets, JSPs, client applications, and so on). The three types of EJBs (session beans, entity beans, and message-driven beans) and their deployment and options for persistence are examined in detail in Chapters 4, 5, 6, and 7 and are used extensively throughout this book as the Purchase Order system's business logic.

The EJB 2.0 specification brought enhancements in the areas of entity bean persistence and interbean relationships. Developers can now declaratively express interbean relationships in descriptor files without having to understand the underlying storage structures. The 2.0 specification also introduced an EJB query syntax called EJBQL, integration of session beans and JMS through message-driven beans, and the ability to create and use local interfaces as an alternative to remote interfaces. With the introduction of local interfaces, EJB calls can now be streamlined if the caller and the EJB are in the same container.

RMI-IIOP Remote Method Invocation (RMI) is a set of APIs that allows users to create distributed Java applications. Java serialization and Java Remote Method Protocol (JRMP) are used to make remote procedure calls on objects. Objects can also be marshaled and unmarshaled from server to client and back if needed. The J2EE standard supports JRMP to allow objects access to other objects in other address spaces. Clients can employ RMI-IIOP to communicate with EJBs. RMI-IIOP is an implementation of RMI over the OMG IIOP standard that allows EJB interoperability with Common Object Request Broker Architecture (CORBA) objects regardless of programming language. It provides the full functionality of a CORBA object request broker (ORB), so developers can write Java CORBA code without licensing additional software. Component providers can write remote interfaces in Java that can then be translated to an Interface Definition Language (IDL) and implemented in any other language for which there is a CORBA ORB and mapping. CORBA is an Object Management Group (OMG) standard for enabling language-independent object distribution (see www.omg.org).

JMS 1.0 J2EE product providers implement the Java Message Service (JMS) API to support enterprise messaging through systems such as Oracle Advanced Queuing (AQ), IBM MQSeries, SonicMQ, SwiftMQ, and others. JMS provides developers with an asynchronous messaging system that allows decoupled systems to process information when it is most convenient for them. Business-to-business (B2B) and

Enterprise Application Integration (EAI) projects often rely heavily on JMS and its implementations. There are two models under which JMS developers can work: publish-and-subscribe (pub/sub) and point-to-point (PTP). Publish-and-subscribe is used when multiple processes (the subscribers) need to receive the same message from another process (a publisher), and point-to-point is employed when one process needs to send a message directly to another known process. See Chapter 7 for a discussion on message-driven beans, a type of EJB that encapsulates JMS in order to allow J2EE applications to manage processes asynchronously. The chapter also contains an overview of JMS.

JavaMail 1.2 The JavaMail API provides protocol-independent support for an e-mail system. It provides facilities for both reading and sending e-mail and contains several built-in implementations for standard mail protocols: IMAP, POP3, and SMTP. Developers can subclass the abstract classes in the API to provide support for other protocols such as MAPI, NNTP, LotusNotes and other protocol providers. Please refer to Sun's J2EE web site for more details on the J2EE-mandated JavaMail API.

JAF 1.0 The JavaBeans Activation Framework (JAF) integrates MIME (Multipurpose Internet Mail Extension) with Java technologies and the Java platform. It provides support for mapping file types to MIME types and is closely integrated into the JavaMail API for handling data included in e-mail. Most developers will not need to interface directly with the JAF.

JAXP 1.1 Given that all J2EE module descriptors are implemented as XML documents, XML technology is an integral part of the J2EE platform. The Java API for XML Processing (JAXP) supports implementation-independent processing of XML documents through DOM, SAX, and XSLT. There are two main APIs for representing and parsing XML documents. The Document Object Model (DOM) represents a tree-based model, while the Simple API for XML (SAX) is an event-based API that provides callbacks for parsing events (such as starting and ending of elements and documents) that an application's handler implementations can use when parsing XML documents. Extensible Stylesheet Language Transformations (XSLT) is a language used for converting XML documents into other structured document formats (usually XML) based on templates.

The implementation-neutral interfaces promoted through JAXP allow developers to declaratively switch between parser implementations to take advantage of their particular strengths. Depending on the requirements, a system may need a parser that performs faster without much regard to memory usage, while other systems may require a parser with a conservative memory usage policy. Oracle provides a

JAXP-compliant parser with all of its products. The Oracle parser also supports the Oracle XML Development Kit (XDK). Refer to the Oracle Technology Network for information on the XDK.

JAAS 1.0 The Java Authentication and Authorization Service (JAAS) is designed to provide developers with a common, standard, pure-Java framework and API for authentication and assigning and verifying user privileges. JAAS provides Pluggable Authentication Module (PAM) support for authenticating users via any number of authentication providers: LDAP, other JNDI sources, operating system, XML file, and so forth. It also supports single sign-on and an access control policy for user-based, group-based, and role-based authorization. The JAAS specification is new in J2EE 1.3. Prior to the J2EE 1.3 specification, there were no standard mechanisms for J2EE security, and each application server provider had the ability to remain compliant and implement its own security infrastructure as long as it provided the requisite security interfaces to the servlet, EJB, and other Java specifications. Chapter 8 contains an overview of J2EE security, JAAS, and JAZN, Oracle's JAAS implementation.

JCA 1.0 The Java Connector Architecture (JCA) provides a standard, abstract API for connecting EJBs and enterprise applications into Enterprise Information Systems (EIS), the bottom tier of the J2EE technology stack. This layer consists of anything containing computer-available enterprise information: database servers (relational and nonrelational), mainframes, ERP and CRM systems, workflow systems, and countless legacy applications and feeds. The connections are accomplished through resource adapters. These adapters are analogous to JDBC drivers for relational databases.

Sun Microsystems' J2EE web site (http://www.j2ee.com) is filled with freely available API listings and generic documentation. The Oracle Technology Network (http://otn.oracle.com) also contains helpful documentation, including information specific to OC4J and other products.

The Technical Value of Using, or Not Using, J2EE in Projects

Most projects can be developed using J2EE technologies, but not all Java development projects require all the technologies provided by J2EE to be successful. A system's desired functionality can be delivered in any number of ways. For example, a screen for editing data can be achieved using J2EE technologies just as well as using a C++-based client/server application. Functional requirements are not typically the reason that you use J2EE. Instead, the desired capabilities of a system or its nonfunctional requirements will help determine if or how J2EE technologies are a good fit. Target audience, scale, reliability, performance, and flexibility are a few things to consider. Functional requirements, on the other hand, are not usually good indicators of whether or not a project should be developed using J2EE, because requirements can be fulfilled, quite frankly, using almost any technology set. Moreover, it is often necessary to leave an existing system in place to provide a given functionality for an enterprise system. The important thing to remember is that J2EE's component- and interface-based approach to technology and all phases of development allows for easier integration with legacy systems.

Consider two enterprise applications: one is a high-volume, e-commerce web site for selling and auctioning books and other merchandise; the other is a medium-volume, case-tracking system for a medium-sized law firm. The nonfunctional requirements for each are the significant deciding factors when arriving at an appropriate architecture. While it is desirable to strive for and achieve positive results with regard to nonfunctional requirements, it is often quite expensive to do so. Table 1-1 compares possible nonfunctional requirements for the two applications. A full J2EE implementation of the law firm's case-tracking application may be unnecessary when considering nonfunctional requirements alone. That fact, coupled with functional requirements, may point toward a quick yet well-designed, web-centric application, while the e-commerce application would most likely benefit from a carefully designed model-view-controller (MVC)-focused, EJB-centric application. See the following "J2EE Architecture" section for more information on MVC architecture and web- and EJB-centric approaches to J2EE development.

Nonfunctional Requirement	Internet E-Commerce Web Site (Need)	Intranet Law Firm Case-Tracking Application (Need)
Availability	High	Medium
Reliability	High	High
Capacity	High	Low
Extensibility	High	Low
Flexibility	High	Low
Performance	High	Medium
Scalability	High	Medium

TABLE 1-1. *Nonfunctional Requirements Affect Architecture*

J2EE Architecture

A typical J2EE architecture aims to separate applications into separate, manageable, and often interchangeable tiers or layers, given a well-conceived design. When designed and managed properly, these tiers can be developed and even maintained somewhat independently and in parallel, providing for a clear separation of roles and allowing for resources specializing in different technologies. A full discussion on J2EE roles follows later in the "J2EE Roles" section.

Generally speaking, a well-architected J2EE system follows the well-documented MVC (model-view-controller) design pattern created by and for Smalltalk-80 users. This approach, pictured in Figure 1-1, separates the data objects (model) from the way they are presented to the user (view) and the way in which the user controls them (controller). The MVC architecture is still considered to be a strong foundation for applications. Within the last few years, these three-tiered applications, while a step in the right direction, have slightly limited the reuse of components built upon them. There is now an almost industry-wide agreement that a well-designed, scalable application should consist of at least four layers, with the presentation logic separated from the business logic, allowing for reuse of business objects among applications (refer to Figure 1-2). These multitiered systems, however, are still applications of the MVC pattern.

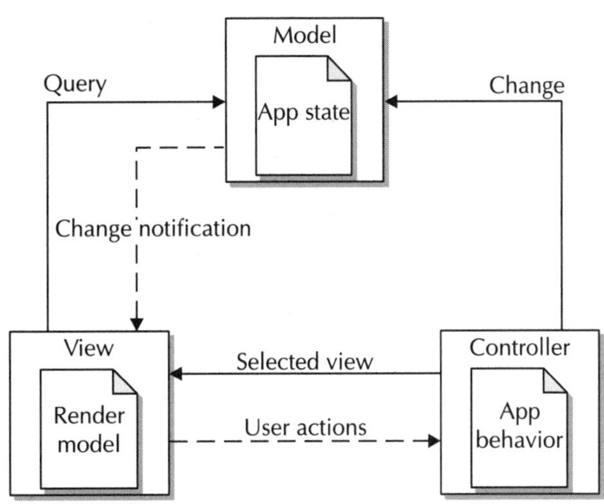

FIGURE 1-1. *Model-view-controller (MVC) architecture*

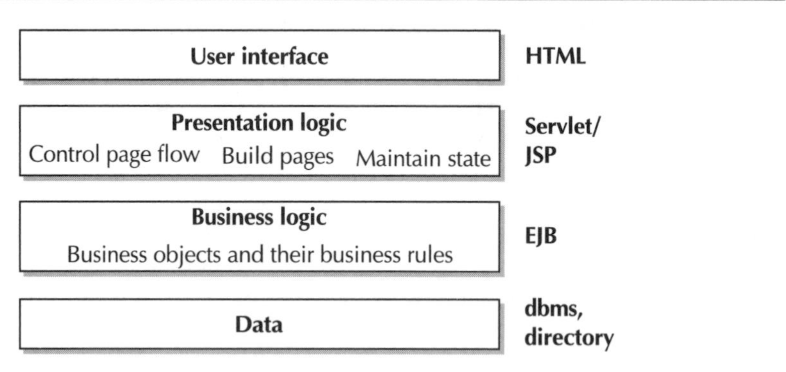

FIGURE 1-2. *MVC architecture in J2EE*

The MVC pattern is the basis from which the other key J2EE patterns (discussed later in the "J2EE Design Patterns" section) are derived. Figure 1-2 represents a multitiered version of the MVC approach that illustrates the mapping of typical J2EE technologies into four basic layers. The J2EE specifications and blueprints have taken the lead in the movement toward multi-tiered systems, and their support is still growing rapidly. The different technologies available through the J2EE platform (discussed previously in the "J2EE Technologies" section) are typically well suited for their roles in one of the four promoted tiers.

There are ways, however, to apply J2EE technologies in a system aside from the complete MVC approach. The Sun J2EE BluePrints describe two major approaches to designing J2EE applications: the web-centric and EJB-centric approaches. The strict EJB-centric approach best approximates an MVC system design by distributing a system's various technologies among the various tiers, specifically concentrating on business logic stored in EJBs. This approach should yield thin presentation layers and robust business logic and enterprise infrastructure layers. The web-centric approach, however, tends to concentrate technologies in the presentation tiers. Unlike the EJB-centric approach, the web-centric approach yields more-complex, thicker presentation tiers and does not usually feature a separate EJB tier for serving up business logic.

While both the EJB- and web-centric approaches typically yield fully functioning systems, they differ in their degrees of maintainability and *scalability* (the measure of a system's ability to handle greater load by applying more hardware to it). As is usually the case, a system's maintainability is inversely proportional to the speed at which it can be initially developed. In other words, the more flexible and maintainable a system is, the longer it takes to get it out the door. Although incorporating patterns and reuse and following established development processes can mitigate this up-front

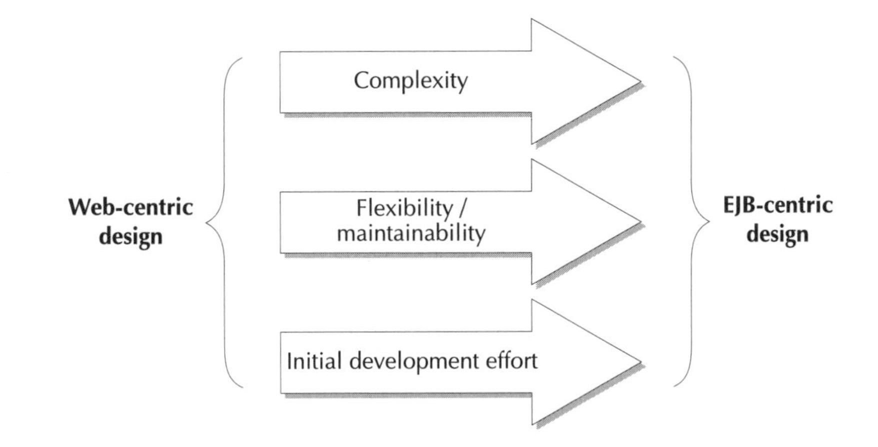

FIGURE 1-3. *Web-centric vs. EJB-centric design*

overhead quite a bit, the problem is still typical of most development organizations. Initial time and cost are not always, however, the only contributing factors to a system's design, especially when considering the flexibility, scaling, and general performance required of typical Internet applications. Designs are rarely "cookie-cutter" or absolute endeavors, so architecting a J2EE system requires you to pay attention to all the factors that come into play along the spectrum from web-centric to EJB-centric (MVC) approaches. Figure 1-3 helps illustrate these factors.

J2EE Components, Containers, and Services

As previously mentioned, J2EE promotes a component-based approach to development, design, assembly, and deployment. A *component* is a unit of software in an application. Components not only serve projects and applications by enabling division of labor, but also provide an easy mapping of application behavior and enable assembly- and deployment-time behavior. J2EE provides built-in run-time environments for its components. These environments, called *containers,* provide specific and standard services for components. Because the services are standard, components can be developed for any J2EE-compliant server, and developers can expect that the same services will be present in any J2EE server regardless of the vendor. There are two main containers in full J2EE servers: a web container (servlet and JSPs) and an EJB container. The container-specific component deployment mechanisms (XML descriptors) for the containers are described in the following section, "Packaging and Deployment."

J2EE web containers provide web component (servlet and JSP) functionality to clients. Web components are responsible, in conjunction with the web container, for handling client requests and delivering appropriate, secure, timely, and correct responses. The web container is also responsible for session management. EJB containers provide transaction and life-cycle management services for EJB components. They also provide services for finding EJB Homes. J2EE's unified security model pervades both the web and EJB containers and, therefore, allows a session to be authenticated and authorized through a Java security principal in either layer. Both containers also facilitate components' access to JDBC data sources.

Packaging and Deployment

J2EE provides a simple and effective way to package the separate components into modules that make up a system into a special Java Archive (JAR) file called an Enterprise Archive (EAR) file. Each of the standard modules that comprise an EAR file (web archives, EJB components, resource archives, and client applications) is also packaged using specially named JAR files per component type. The information describing those archives, and their deployment specifics, are stored in XML files called *descriptors*. The structure for each standard J2EE module and descriptor is described in the following sections.

Enterprise Archive File

The EAR file, a standard JAR file with an .ear extension, contains one or more standard J2EE modules and a J2EE application descriptor typically named `application.xml`. Each J2EE module (including web, ejb and application modules, and client applications) is deployable separately from the EAR file with its own descriptors, but the EAR file helps to gather the components for an application into one repeatably deployable and standard archive. The J2EE modules are each registered with the application descriptor usually in the EAR file's META-INF directory. Figure 1-4 illustrates the modules typically found in an EAR file. J2EE applications are usually contained within a single EAR file, but may, in the case of an application suite, for example, span multiple EAR files.

Web Module (WAR File)

The WAR file, a JAR file with a .war extension, contains all the web-tier components for the J2EE application. These components include the following:

- Compiled servlet .class files and the classes upon which they depend. These .class files can be optionally archived in libraries as JAR files.
- JavaServer Pages (JSP) and the classes upon which they depend.

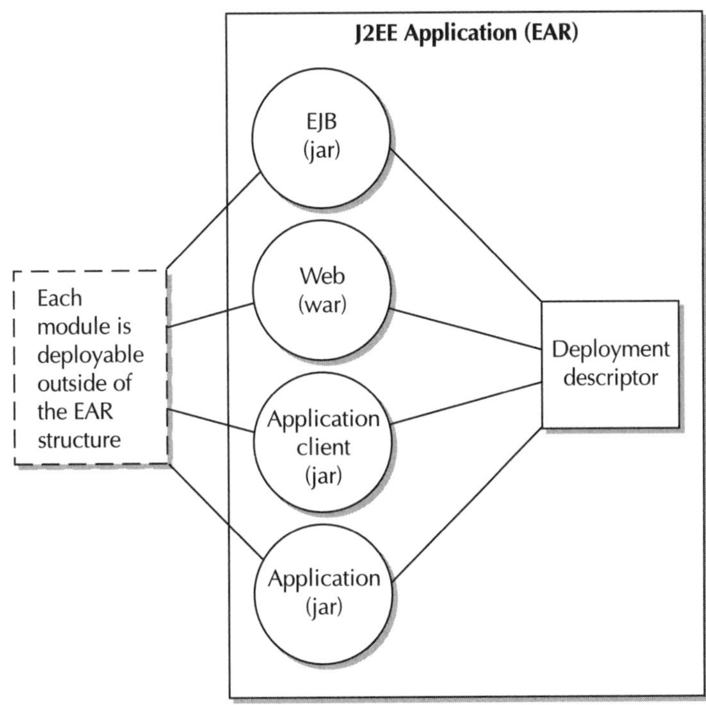

FIGURE 1-4. *J2EE application enterprise archive structure (EAR file)*

- Static web documents such as HTML pages, images, PDFs, and so forth.
- Compiled applet .class files and the classes upon which they depend. Applets are client-side applications that are embedded in HTML and typically run inside a web browser. Their Java archives are served from web servers alongside their host HTML pages.
- A Web module deployment descriptor (`web.xml` file).

The Servlet specification mandates that a WAR file have the structure illustrated in Figure 1-5.

The `web.xml` file describes the web-tier components (servlets and JSPs) contained at the context root. A *context root* is a name that gets mapped to the document root of a web client. For example, if your context root is named my_site, then the URL http://*localhost*:8888/my_site/index.html will retrieve the index.html page from the document root of the server running on port 8888 on your local machine. Like other

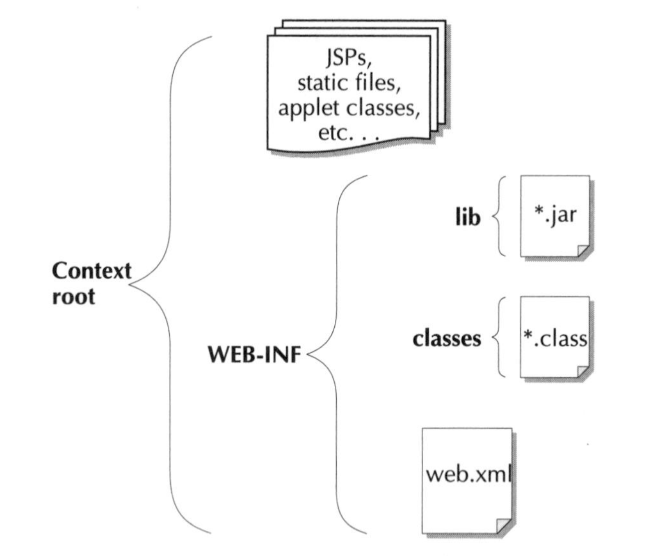

FIGURE 1-5. *Web module archive structure (WAR file)*

descriptors, the `web.xml` file contains security information. It also contains information regarding references to other J2EE components. See Chapters 10 and 11 for more information regarding web-tier components, and see Chapter 8 for an introduction to J2EE security.

EJB Module

Enterprise JavaBeans are packaged as compiled classes in a standard JAR file. An `ejb-jar` file also contains an `ejb-jar.xml` descriptor file under the JAR file's META-INF directory. The EJB descriptor contains information about the EJBs contained in the JAR file. An EJB file developer should also create a client-side `ejb-jar` file including all the classes and files required of a client accessing the EJB module on the server side. See Chapter 5 for a more detailed discussion regarding EJBs, their standard EJB descriptors, and how to access a server-side EJB module.

Client Applications Module

An client applications module is packaged in a standard JAR file with a .jar extension. The JAR file should contain the compiled .class files comprising the client application and a client application deployment descriptor. The client application can use the client-side `ejb-jar` file mentioned in the preceding "EJB Module" section for accessing the application's EJBs.

Resource Adapter Module

A Java Connector is packaged in a resource archive in a standard JAR file with a .rar extension. This RAR file should contain the Java JAR files containing classes and interfaces that implement the resource adapter and the required Connector architecture. The RAR file should also contain utility files, native libraries, and documentation needed to support the resource adaptor. Lastly, the file should also contain the resource adapter deployment descriptor. The Java Connector Architecture is also discussed briefly in the "J2EE Technologies" section earlier in this chapter.

J2EE Roles

The J2EE specification not only provides for separation of developer roles, but also describes the roles of all parties involved in development. The clearly defined roles outside of the immediate development team, J2EE product provider and J2EE tool provider, help to unite the industry around the J2EE standard. The developer-specific roles, in turn, help to unite the development team around the technology and provide guidelines related to their individual responsibilities. While it may seem trivial, these well-defined roles are just another way that J2EE helps to mitigate risk and lower cost for a typical enterprise application. It is important to note that these roles do not have to be filled by separate individuals. Most development scenarios use the same person in various development roles, and some companies, including Oracle Corporation with its OC4J and Oracle 9*i* JDeveloper products, play multiple nondeveloper roles. Each role and each of its subroles is described in the following sections.

J2EE Product Provider

The product provider is the company or entity that provides implementations of the J2EE APIs, containers, and other features described in the J2EE platform. These include, but are not limited to, operating system, application server, web server, and database server vendors. Subsets of some of the product provider roles are defined in the EJB, JSP, and Servlet specifications. The EJB specification defines the enterprise bean provider, EJB container provider, and EJB server provider roles. The JSP specification defines the JSP container provider role, and the Servlet specification defines the servlet container provider, web container provider, and web server provider roles. Oracle, for example, supplies products in all these areas except the operating system and provides implementations of various APIs (JDBC, JAXP, JAAS, and so on) to access the various components. Oracle9*i*AS Containers For J2EE contains the entire application server component including a highly scalable web server and a J2EE-compliant server (OC4J). Oracle9*i*DB is, of course, Oracle's popular database server.

Tool Provider

The tool provider is the company or entity that creates and delivers development tools used by the individuals in the application component provider, application assembler, and application deployer and administrator roles. Oracle 9*i* JDeveloper provides not only functionality for use throughout the full J2EE development life cycle, but also a plug-in API for integrating specific vendor-provided or custom extensions to the tool to make users more productive. Plug-ins are available for code formatting, integration to different frameworks, launching external processes, and other useful things.

Application Component Provider

The application component provider is the company or entity that creates web-tier components, client-side application components, or business-tier components (for example, EJBs) for use in enterprise Java applications. These developers can work in parallel if the appropriate design patterns are employed for the application. Application content providers can assume the role of a client application developer, a web component developer, or an enterprise bean developer. Each of these roles is described in the following sections.

Client Application Developer

A client application developer delivers a JAR file containing the J2EE application client. The client application developer is responsible for:

- Writing, compiling, and unit testing the source code for the client application
- Specifying the deployment descriptor for the client
- Archiving the compiled Java classes, user interface (UI) artifacts, and deployment descriptor files into the JAR file

Web Component Developer

A web component developer delivers a WAR file containing the web component for an enterprise application. The web component developer is responsible for:

- Writing, compiling, and unit testing the servlet source code
- Writing JSP and HTML files; this task is often delegated to UI-specific resources
- Specifying a deployment descriptor (`web.xml`)
- Archiving the compiled Java classes, JSP, HTML, UI artifacts (for example, images), and web deployment descriptor files into the WAR file

Enterprise Bean Developer

An enterprise bean developer delivers an `ejb-jar` file that contains the EJB and its descriptors. The enterprise bean developer is responsible for:

- Writing, compiling, and unit testing source code for the EJB
- Specifying a deployment descriptor (`ejb-jar.xml`)
- Archiving the compiled Java classes and EJB deployment descriptor into the `ejb-jar` file

Application Assembler

The application assembler is the company or entity that receives application component archives from application component providers and assembles them into an EAR file for a given application. The EAR file structure is described earlier in the "Packaging and Deployment" section. The developer is responsible for:

- Archiving EJB, JAR, and WAR files created previously by the application component providers into an EAR file for the application
- Verifying that the application components that go into the EAR file are compliant with the J2EE specification
- Specifying the deployment descriptor (`application.xml`) for the EAR file

Application Deployer and Administrator

The application deployer and administrator is the company or entity that configures and deploys the J2EE application (EAR file) and manages the infrastructure and environment where the application runs. The deployer moves the application components to the J2EE server and generates the product-provider-specific components for the application.

The deployer and administrator is responsible for:

- Verifying that the EAR file contents are compliant with the J2EE specification
- Moving the application (EAR file) to the J2EE-compliant server
- Modifying the deployment descriptor of the J2EE application for the environment under which it will run
- Deploying the application (EAR file) to the J2EE server

Realizing J2EE's promise of componentization, reusability, and maintainability for a project may seem like a huge undertaking given the many roles listed here. Different vendors' implementations of standard J2EE products and their tools support improve a developer's productivity and add value to the seemingly meticulous tasks needed to successfully develop and deploy a J2EE application. Oracle9*i*AS Containers For J2EE, for example, provides the HTML-based Enterprise Manager for centrally managing the distributed nodes of OC4J server. While the Oracle Enterprise Manager simplifies management and administration, Oracle9*i* JDeveloper simplifies J2EE development.

J2EE Design Patterns

Design patterns are nothing more than reusable solutions to recurring problems. They are a convenient way of reusing proven and simple code and concepts between programmers and projects or applications. Because the vision of J2EE is so focused around enterprise applications that exhibit some common problems, it is no wonder that a design pattern catalog grew out of the effort alongside the technologies themselves. While it is possible to describe various design patterns in any J2EE system, Sun's J2EE BluePrints web site describes only a few key patterns in its Patterns Catalog (see http://java.sun.com/blueprints/patterns/j2ee_patterns/catalog.html) because they can be applied to most J2EE applications. These patterns, described next, are all part of the larger model-view-controller pattern (see the previous "J2EE Architecture" section) and are included in the catalog. These patterns are by no means unique to J2EE, or to Java for that matter, but are commonly used to simplify and provide proven architectural solutions for J2EE-centric projects.

Front Controller

The Front Controller pattern provides a single access and control point for each of an application's views. In typical J2EE applications, this central component is located in the web tier and is usually a controlling servlet. Most J2EE application frameworks use this pattern as a central part of their web-tier run-time environments. When a system's views are represented by JSPs, the controlling servlet forwards control to the appropriate JSP. This is in line with the MVC design pattern, as previously illustrated in Figure 1-1.

Session Façade

The Session Façade pattern provides a single, "design-by-contract" oriented interface to the business logic tier of an application. For most applications, this is represented through a set of session EJBs that encapsulate sometimes complex transactions through and between entity EJBs. In other cases, the Session Façade is represented through simple Java interfaces or through other, non-EJB, business logic abstraction components.

In all cases, however, the web-tier or application component clients to the business logic are unaware as to the implementation of the business logic. Instead, they interact with the business logic tier through the Session Façade. This pattern may be coupled with an abstract factory pattern to find and deliver a business logic implementation of the Session Façade determined via a declarative file or any other number of environmental settings. See Chapter 6 to learn how to implement the Session Façade pattern.

Value Object

The Value Object pattern serves to limit multiple transfers of fine-grained data through a one-time transfer of the data in a course-grained object. This pattern commonly helps economize network and computing resources by limiting round trips between application tiers and by limiting the number of procedure calls for an application. Value objects used to transfer data between the web and business logic tiers typically map one-to-one to entity EJBs. If the value object were not used, then passing remote entity beans between tiers and the subsequent getter and setter method calls on those beans could, depending on the location of the tiers, result in wasted network round trips. Instead, a value object, representing and often implementing the same interface as the entity bean, is passed once each time a query is performed and each time the entire bean needs to be persisted. Figure 1-6 shows how serializable value objects are often passed between tiers and referred to at any tier. The originally

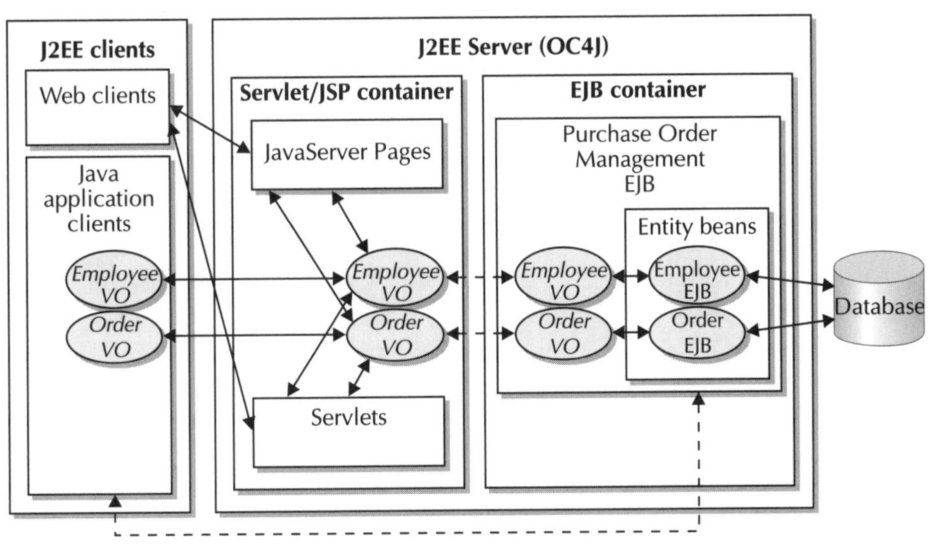

FIGURE 1-6. *Value objects are passed between tiers*

persisted values are retrieved only once in the EJB tier and used to populate the value objects. See Chapter 6 to learn how to implement the Value Object pattern.

Page-By-Page Iterator

The Page-By-Page Iterator pattern retrieves sublists of a large remote list one sublist (page) at a time. Retrieving a large amount of data one chunk at a time is more efficient than trying to access the entire, often cumbersome, list all at once and then using local and middle-tier resources to divide the data into chunks. Furthermore, local or middle-tier resources would be strained due to the number of finder method and getter and setter calls if the data were retrieved using entity beans. Instead, the Page-By-Page Iterator pattern should be used in combination with value objects. The pattern should be used only when retrieving or transmitting the entire data set at once would take too much time, the user will be interested in only a page at a time, the entire data set will not fit in the client's display, or the entire data set will not fit in memory.

Data Access Object

The Data Access Object pattern serves to separate business logic components from the actual logic that does data access by placing data access logic into a separate interface whose implementation may contain code specific to a particular vendor or data source. A bean-managed persistent (BMP) entity EJB named `EmployeeEJB`, for example, might contain code specific for interacting with an Oracle database, but when that persistence code is extracted into an `EmployeeDAO` interface that the `EmployeeEJB` delegates to, then the `EmployeeEJB` code becomes more vendor independent and reusable across different deployments of the application. An `EmployeeDAOOracle` object, in turn, implements the `EmployeeDAO` interface. Figure 1-7 shows how several persisting implementations of an interface may be present for an entity bean while only one is used per deployment.

Fast Lane Reader

The Fast Lane Reader pattern makes an exception to using entity beans or any other entity-based components for read-only data. The performance benefits from using a data access object or straight JDBC far outweigh those of going through the entity bean layer. In fact, there are few benefits to entity beans when the underlying data is read-only. The Fast Lane Reader pattern can also be used in cases where the data is not read-only but the need for efficiency and performance outweighs the need for the data to be up-to-date.

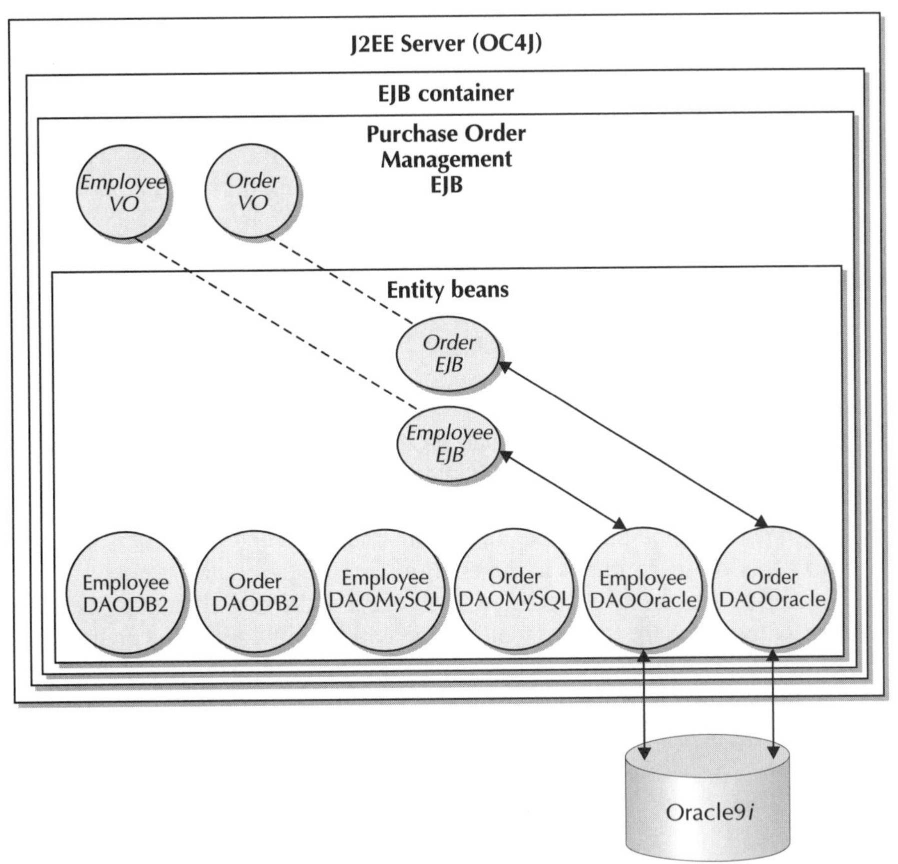

FIGURE 1-7. *Data access objects implement persistence-specific functionality*

Sample Application and Methodology

Throughout the book, you will be building and reading about the design and implementation of a sample Purchase Order application. It is a web-based J2EE application for employees to enter purchases. The expenses are then approved or rejected by management through a similar web interface that the employees see. The application and its use-case-driven design artifacts are presented in the Introduction of the book. While the design of the system was rather quick given its small size and scope, a typical J2EE application, or any application for that matter, should most likely be designed in iterative phases with early mitigation of architectural risks. Unified Process (RUP) and Agile Methods (Extreme Programming, SCRUM, and so forth) are two of the more popular methodologies that support such an approach. A *methodology* is a set of techniques, deliverables, approaches, and stages that a development group can use to deliver and maintain software projects efficiently, repeatedly, and effectively. It is important that you use a common methodology when developing any system, to increase productivity, manage complexity, and avoid costly mistakes. Although the J2EE specification serves to lower risk and cost of enterprise projects, it is still all too easy for projects to fail without the proper approach, guidance, and oversight that a methodology gives you.

This chapter, although relatively broad in scope, serves as merely an introduction to J2EE and its various concepts and principles. Throughout the rest of this book, you will drill down into many of the technologies discussed here. While this chapter's focus was primarily on the J2EE standard, the remaining contents of this book will focus on how to apply those standards in the environment; in particular, the fully J2EE-compliant and certified OC4J container. Each of the following chapters is dedicated to portions of the standard that we believe you will find interesting and useful.

Starting with Chapter 2, you will apply the general J2EE knowledge that you learned in this chapter to a specific product. Chapter 2 introduces you to how the J2EE standard is implemented by a J2EE product provider; specifically by Oracle through OC4J.

CHAPTER 2

Oracle9*i* Application Server Containers For J2EE (OC4J) Overview

n this chapter, you will learn how to install and configure the stand-alone or single-instance version of the Oracle9*i*AS Containers For J2EE (OC4J). More importantly, you will learn the steps necessary to successfully deploy J2EE applications to OC4J.

OC4J is written entirely in Java and executes on the standard Java Development Kit (JDK) virtual machine. The latest release of OC4J, 9.0.3, provides a fully J2EE 1.3 certified environment that includes a JSP translator and runtime (1.2), a Servlet engine (2.3), an Enterprise JavaBeans (EJB) container (EJB 2.0), and the rest of the J2EE services such as Java Naming and Directory Interface (JNDI), JDBC (JDBC Extension 2.0), Java Message Service (JMS) 1.0, Java Authentication and Authorization Service (JAAS) 1.0, Java Transaction API (JTA) 1.0. To learn more about how OC4J supports these J2EE services, see Chapter 3.

The target audience of this book, and thus this chapter, is developers using the stand-alone version of OC4J. The scope of this chapter is not to teach you how to manage the enterprise features of OC4J, such as load balancing, clustering, and failover. For enterprise configuration of OC4J, you should use the Oracle Enterprise Manager (OEM) tool or the Distributed Configuration Management (DCM) command-line utility. To learn more about how to manage OC4J with OEM, you should consult the *Oracle9iAS Containers For J2EE User's Guide* technical manual from Oracle Corporation.

You will also learn how to use the OC4J administrative command-line tool (`admin.jar`) and its options. You will use the `admin.jar` tool to deploy applications to OC4J in stand-alone mode. Additionally, you will see step-by-step examples of how to deploy J2EE applications to OC4J.

Specifically, you will learn about the following topics:

- Installing and starting OC4J
- OC4J startup options
- Using the stand-alone OC4J command-line options
- Deploying J2EE applications to OC4J
- Performing OC4J debugging

Installing and Starting OC4J

It is simple to install OC4J onto your system. Follow these steps to install and start OC4J:

1. You should first have the J2EE 1.3 APIs.
2. Download the stand-alone version of OC4J from Oracle Technology Network (OTN) at http://otn.oracle.com.

3. Unzip the downloaded file.
4. You have successfully installed OC4J. The default HTTP web server port is 8888. If there are conflicts or you want to change the port number, go to the .../`j2EE/home/config` directory. Open the `http-web-site.xml` file and change 8888 to another port.
5. Update the administrative password with the following command from the .../`j2ee/home` directory:

   ```
   java -jar oc4j.jar -install
   ```

   You will be prompted to enter a password after issuing the preceding command. This command will modify the administrative user called "admin." The command will rewrite the .../`j2ee/home/config/principal.xml` file configuration and the `admin` user password will be updated in the file.
6. To start OC4J, enter the following command from the prompt to start:

   ```
   java -jar oc4j.jar
   ```

7. Use the following URL in a web browser to test the installation of OC4J:

   ```
   http://localhost:8888
   ```

OC4J Startup Options

You can provide OC4J with different startup options. These options are used to verify information of the container; provide information to the container; and get information from the container. The following is the syntax for the startup:

```
java -jar oc4j.jar <options>
```

Table 2-1 lists the options.

Option	Description
`-config [file]`	Specifies a configuration file other than the default `server.xml`.
`-validateXML`	Strictly validates all the configuration files. This is useful if you have modified the configuration files and want to verify the syntax. If this is not specified, no validation occurs. *Note: This option requires a connection to the Internet.*

TABLE 2-1. *Options for Application Deployment*

Option	Description
`-out [file]`	Specifies a file to route the standard output to. Messages printed to `System.out` and those from the servlet logging interface are logged in this file. If not specified, all output is written to standard output.
`-err [file]`	Specifies a file to route standard error to. Messages printed to `System.err` and those written to standard error are logged in this file.
`-install`	Installs the server and activates the admin account. Rewrites the configuration files to match the operating system line feed. This should only be used the first time OC4J is installed.
`-userThreads`	Enables context lookup support for user-created threads.
`-quiet`	Suppresses standard output.
`-version`	Prints the version number and exits.
`-help`	Prints the help message.
`-verbosity`	Provides more information from OC4J to the standard output. This value is an integer between 1 and 10. The default level is 3, and 10 is the highest level of debugging.
`-monitorResourceThreads`	Enables backup debugging of thread resources; enable this only if you have problems that seem to relate to threads getting stuck in critical sections of code (release 9.0.3 only).
`-rewriteXML`	Rewrites bad XML files (after prompting) as accurately as possible. *Caution: If you have corrupt XML files, you may lose data when rewriting if they're badly written (release 9.0.3 only).*

TABLE 2-1. *Options for Application Deployment* (continued)

Managing OC4J Through the Command-Line Tool

In this section, you will use the options of the OC4J Administration Management JAR (`admin.jar`) tool. You use the `admin.jar` command-line tool to manage the OC4J server in stand-alone mode and to deploy J2EE applications to the application server. The `admin.jar` tool can only be used with the stand-alone version of OC4J. Additionally, an instance of OC4J must be running in order to use this tool.

The `admin.jar` command-line tool allows you to administer OC4J from a client-admin console using a command line. The syntax is as follows:

```
java -jar admin.jar ormi://<oc4j_host>:<oc4j_ormi_port> <admin_id>
      <admin_password> <options>
```

where:

- `<oc4j_host>` is the name or IP address of a computer running OC4J.
- `<oc4j_ormi_port>` is the RMI port that can be found in the …`/j2ee/home/config/rmi.xml`. The RMI port number is optional if the default port of `23791` is used.
- `<admin_id>` and `<admin_password>` are the administrative username and password that can be found in the …`/j2ee/home/config/principal.xml`.

The `admin.jar` tool options are subdivided into four categories:

- General OC4J administration
- Application deployment
- Web site administration
- Data source administration

General OC4J Administration

In this section, we provide the `admin.jar` options to shut down and restart OC4J. Note that the use of `admin.jar` assumes that an instance of OC4J is running.

Shutting Down OC4J

Use the **`-shutdown`** option of the `admin.jar` tool to shut down OC4J. Here is the syntax:

```
java -jar admin.jar ormi://<oc4j_host>:<oc4j_ormi_port> <admin_id>
  <admin_password> -shutdown [ordinary | force][reason]
```

There are three optional subswitches associated with `-shutdown`:

- **`ordinary`** Allows each thread to terminate normally. This is the default mode.

- **force** Terminates all threads immediately.
- **reason** A string that is logged with the termination.

Here is an example of how to shut down an OC4J instance:

```
java -jar admin.jar ormi://localhost:8888 admin adminPassword
-shutdown force
```

Restarting OC4J

Use the **-restart** option of the `admin.jar` tool to restart OC4J. Here is the syntax:

```
java -jar admin.jar ormi://<oc4j_host>:<oc4j_ormi_port> <admin_id>
  <admin_password> -restart [reason]
```

There is an optional switch, `reason`, that is associated with `-restart`. This switch is a string that is logged with the restart.

Here is an example of how to restart an OC4J instance:

```
java -jar admin.jar ormi://localhost:23791 admin adminPassword
-restart
```

NOTE

You should use the `-restart` option when the OC4J application server has been previously started with `oc4j.jar`.

Options for Application Deployment

This section shows you how to deploy applications on OC4J. You will learn two ways to deploy applications. You will first see how to deploy applications using an "exploded" directory. You will then learn how to deploy applications using the standard J2EE way of deploying applications, with an EAR file.

In this section, we provide the `admin.jar` options to deploy J2EE applications to OC4J. Use the **-deploy** option of the `admin.jar` tool to deploy your application to OC4J:

```
java -jar admin.jar ormi://<oc4j_host>:<oc4j_ormi_port> <admin_id>
    <admin_password> -deploy -file <path/filename>
    -deploymentName <deploy_name> -targetPath <deploy_dir>
```

Here is an example of how to deploy an application to an OC4J instance:

```
java -jar admin.jar ormi://localhost/ admin adminPassword  -deploy
-file \oc4j\Chapter05\chapter05.ear -deploymentName -targetPath
\j2ee\home\application\chapter05
```

Use the **-bindWebApp** option of the `admin.jar` tool to bind a web application:

```
java -jar admin.jar ormi://<oc4j_host>:<oc4j_ormi_port> <admin_id>
    <admin_password> -bindWebApp <app_deploy_name><web_app_name>
                                 <web_site_name><context_root>
```

Here is an example of how to bind the web application to an OC4J instance:

```
java -jar admin.jar ormi://localhost/ admin adminPassword
-bindWebApp chapter05 chapter05 http-web-site /chapter05
```

Table 2-2 summarizes the application deployment options of the `admin.jar` command-line tool.

Next, we present the `admin.jar` options for managing web sites.

Options for Web Site Administration

The administration tool can be used to administer OC4J's built-in HTTP server. However, when you move your application into production, it is recommended that you use Oracle HTTP Server (OHS) to communicate with OC4J. OHS communicates with OC4J through a module called `mod_oc4j`. Refer to the beginning of this chapter for a discussion of the stand-alone OC4J instance versus the full installation of Oracle9*i*AS.

Use the **-site** option of the `admin.jar` tool to administer web sites. This option will modify the corresponding web site configuration's XML files. For example, you can use the following syntax to install a new web site:

```
java -jar admin.jar ormi://<oc4j_host>:<oc4j_ormi_port> <admin_id>
    <admin_password> -site -add -host <hostname> -port <portnumber>
                -display-name <name> -virtual-hosts <virtual_host>
```

Option	Description
`-deploy`	Deploys (or redeploys) an application. Supply application information in the following subswitches: **`-file <path/filename>`** The path and filename of the EAR file to deploy. **`-deploymentName <deploy_name>`** The user-defined application deployment name. **`-targetPath <deploy_dir>`** The path on the server node to deploy archives into. The default is the `applications/` directory. It is best to provide a target path to the directory where the EAR file is copied for deployment. If `-targetPath` is not specified, the EAR file is copied to the `applications/` directory. OC4J maintains a unique name for the EAR file. Thus, when you redeploy the EAR file, OC4J renames the file by prepending an underscore character (_) in front of the name to ensure that another application's EAR file is not overwritten. Each successive deployment will cause another underscore character to be prepended to the EAR file. However, if it is the same application, the `applications/` directory contains a separate EAR file for each deployment. If you provide a target path, this problem does not occur. **`-parent <parent_appname>`** The parent application of this application. When deployed, any method within the child application can invoke any method within the parent application. This is a means to enable methods in one JAR to see EJBs that have been deployed in another JAR. This is useful to deploy all service EJBs in a single JAR file, where its users declare the service application as its parent. The default is the global application. **`-deploymentDirectory <path>`** If not specified, the application is deployed into the `application-deployments/` directory. To change where the application is deployed, provide a path with this option. If you supply the string "[NONE]", the deployment configurations are always read from the EAR file each time the application is deployed. **`-cluster`** Signals that the application should be deployed to all currently live nodes within the cluster.

TABLE 2-2. *Options for Application Deployment*

Option	Description
-bindWebApp <app_deploy_name> <web_app_name> <web_site_name> <context_root>	Binds a web application to the specified site and root. **<app_deploy_name>** The application name, which is the same name used in -deploymentName on the -deploy option. Also note that this is the same name that is saved in the <application name= <app_name> variable in the server.xml file. **<web_app_name>** The name of the WAR file contained within the EAR file—without the .war extension. **<web_site_name>** The name of the <name>-web-site .xml file that denotes the web site that this web application should be bound to. This is the file that will receive the web application definition. **<context_root>** The root context for the Web module. This option creates an entry in the OC4J <name>-web-site .xml configuration file that was denoted in the <web_site _name> option value.
-cluster	Deploys the application to all live nodes within the cluster.
-undeploy <appname>	Removes the deployed J2EE application from the OC4J web server. The <appname> is the name provided on the -deploymentName subswitch. This results in the following: The application is removed from the OC4J runtime and the server.xml file. Bindings for all the application's Web modules are removed from all the web sites to which the Web modules were bound. Application files are removed from both the applications and application-deployments directories. **-keepFiles** Prevents application files from being removed. However, the application is removed from the runtime and the Web modules are unbound.

TABLE 2-2. *Options for Application Deployment* (continued)

As with **-deploy**, there are subswitches associated with **-site**. Table 2-3 summarizes the web site administration options of the admin.jar command-line tool.

Option	Description
-site -add	Installs a new web site. Supply information with the following subswitches: **-host <hostname>** The host where the web site exists. **-port <portnum>** The web site port. **-display-name <name>** The name of the web site. **-virtual-hosts <virtual_hosts>** The virtual hosts of the web site. **-secure <true|false>** The value is `true` if the web site is secure, and otherwise is `false`. **-factory <factory_name>** The name of the `SSLServerSocketFactory` class if you are not using the Java Secure Socket Extension (JSSE). The JSSE defines a provider interface that other security providers can implement. Sun Microsystems provides its own implementation in `com.sun.net.ssl.internal.ssl.Provider`. **-keystore <keystore>** The relative or absolute path to a keystore. **-storepass <password>** The keystore password. **-provider <provider>** The provider used if using JSSE; defaults to `com.sun.net.ssl.internal.ssl.Provider`. **-needs-client-auth <true|false>** If set to `true`, a client that wants to access a J2EE web site needs to identify itself with a digital certificate. If set to `false`, a client does not need to identify itself with a digital certificate. The default is `false`.
-site -remove	Removes an existing web site. Supply the host and port of this web site with the following subswitches: **-host <hostname>** The web site host to be removed. **-port <portnum>** The web site port to be removed.
-site -test	Tests an existing web site. Supply the host and port of the web site to be tested with the following subswitches: **-host <hostname>** The web site host to be tested. **-port <portnum>** The web site port to be tested.
-site -list	Lists all existing web sites.

TABLE 2-3. *Options for Web Site Administration*

Option	Description
-site -update	Updates an existing web site. Supply information with the following subswitches: **-oldHost <hostname>** The old host of the web site. You can change the web site host and port with the "old" and "new" subswitches. **-oldPort <portnum>** The old port of the web site. **-newHost <hostname>** The new host of the web site. **-newPort <portnum>** The new port of the web site. **-display-name <name>** The new display name of the web site. **-virtual-hosts <vhosts>** The new virtual hosts of the web site. **-secure <true|false>** If set to `true`, the web site is secure. If set to `false`, the web site is not secure. The default is `false`. **-factory <classname>** The new name of the `SSLServerSocketFactory` class if you are not using JSSE. **-keystore <path>** The new relative or absolute path to a keystore. **-storepass <password>** The new keystore password. **-provider <provider>** The new provider used if you are not using JSSE. **-needs-client-auth <true|false>** If set to `true`, a client that wants to access a J2EE web site needs to identify itself with a digital certificate. If set to `false`, a client does not need to identify itself with a digital certificate. The default is `false`.

TABLE 2-3. *Options for Web Site Administration* (continued)

Next, you will use the `admin.jar` tool options to manage OC4J data sources.

Options for Application and Data Source Administration

The **`-application [name] [command]`** subcommand of the `admin.jar` tool allows you to manage OC4J applications and data sources. The `-application` command takes in a name of an application before the subswitch command. This `<name>` can be the global application name or any J2EE application:

- The global application name, installed originally as default, specified in the name attribute of the `<global-application>` tag in the `server.xml` file.

- A specific application name defined within an `<application>` tag in the `server.xml` file.

CAUTION
The name of the application should not be enclosed in quotes.

If you want OC4J to manage your data sources, you can configure the `data-source.xml` file by using `admin.jar`. For example, you can use the `-listDataSource` option of the `-application` command to list all the OC4J data sources:

```
java -jar admin.jar ormi://<oc4j_host>:<oc4j_ormi_port> <admin_id>
<admin_password> -application default -listDataSource
```

The following command lists all the data sources of a running OC4J instance:

```
java -jar admin.jar ormi://localhost admin adminpassword
-application default -listDataSource
```

Table 2-4 shows the options for the `-application` command.

Option	Description
`-application <name> -restart`	Restarts the application. This triggers auto-deployment if enabled and a file has been touched.
`-application <name> -addUser <username> <password>`	Adds a user to the security file (`principals.xml`).
`-application <name> -dataSourceInfo`	Retrieves the dynamic usage information about the installed `DataSource` objects.
`-application <name> -listDataSource`	Retrieves the statically configured information about each installed `DataSource` object.
`-application <name> -testDataSource`	Tests an existing `DataSource`. Supply information with the following subswitches: **`-location <location>`** The namespace location for the `DataSource`. For example, `jdbc/DefaultDS`. **`-username <username>`** The username you use to log in, along with a password. **`-password <password>`** The password to log in with.

TABLE 2-4. *Options for Application and Data Source Management*

Option	Description
-application <name> -installDataSource	Installs a new DataSource. Supply information within the following subswitches: **-jar <JARfile>** The JAR file containing the driver that is to be added to the library of the server. **-url <URL>** The JDBC database URL. **-location <JNDIlocation>** The namespace location for the raw source. For example, jdbc/NirvaDS. **-pooledLocation <JNDIlocation>** The namespace location for the pooled source. For example, jdbc/ NirvaDS. **-xaLocation <JNDIlocation>** The namespace location for the XA source. For example, jdbc/xa/DefaultXADS. **-ejbLocation <JNDIlocation>** The namespace location for the container-managed transactional data source. This is the only data source that can perform global JTA transactions. For example, jdbc/DefaultDS. **-username <username>** The username you use to log in. **-password <password>** The password you use to log in. **-connectionDriver <driverClass>** The JDBC database driver class. **-classname <DSclass>** The data source class name, such as com.evermind.sql.DriverManagerDataSource. **-sourceLocation <jndiDS>** The underlying data source of this specialized data source. **-xaSourceLocation <jndiXADS>** The underlying XA data source of this specialized data source.
-application <name> -removeDataSource	Removes an existing DataSource. Supply information with the following subswitch: **-location <JNDIlocation>** The namespace location for the DataSource. For example, jdbc/DefaultDS.

TABLE 2-4. *Options for Application and Data Source Management* (continued)

Option	Description
-application <name> -updateDataSource	Updates an existing DataSource. Supply information with the following subswitches: **-oldLocation <JNDIlocation>** The old namespace location for the DataSource. For example, jdbc/DefaultDS. **-newLocation <JNDIlocation>** The new namespace location for the DataSource. For example, jdbc/DefaultDS. **-jar <JAR>** The JAR file containing the driver to add to the library of the server. **-url <URL>** The JDBC database URL. **-pooledLocation <JNDIlocation>** The namespace location for the pooled source. For example, jdbc/DefaultPooledDS. **-xaLocation <JNDIlocation>** The namespace location for the XA DataSource. For example, jdbc/xa/DefaultXADS. **-ejbLocation <JNDIlocation>** The namespace location for the data source for container-managed transactions. This is the only data source that can perform global JTA transactions. For example, jdbc/DefaultDS. **-username <username>** The username you use to log in. **-password <password>** The password you use to log in. **-connectionDriver <driverClass>** The JDBC database driver class. For example, com.mydb.Driver. **-classname <DSClass>** The data source class name. For example, com.evermind.sql.DriverManagerDataSource. **-sourceLocation <jndiDS>** The underlying data source of this specialized data source. **-xaSourceLocation <jndiXADS>** The underlying XA data source of this specialized data source.

TABLE 2-4. *Options for Application and Data Source Management* (continued)

Deploying J2EE Applications to OC4J

In this section, you will learn how to deploy J2EE applications to OC4J. To illustrate how to deploy an application, you will deploy the applications that you will develop in Chapter 5. This chapter consists of a web application that contains a servlet and several EJB components.

You should use tools such as Oracle9*i* JDeveloper for deploying your applications to OC4J. Oracle9*i* JDeveloper provides you with an easy-to-use graphical tool to accomplish this. You will use different ways of deploying applications in this chapter so that you will get a better understanding of how J2EE applications are deployed on OC4J.

OC4J supports both deployment of Enterprise Archive (EAR) files and deployment of applications using an exploded directory conforming to the J2EE standard. You will deploy applications using both methods.

Chapter 5 will give you an example of a J2EE directory structure. In Chapter 5, the root of the development directory for the applications is **`chapter05`**. The structure of the development directory is as follows:

- **chapter05** Root directory of your J2EE application
    - **META-INF** Directory where your `application.xml` file is located (and possibly your `orion-application.xml` file), which defines the modules you have in your J2EE application.
    - **src** Directory where all the source files are located.
        - **META-INF** Directory where the `ejb-jar.xml` deployment descriptor file and the `orion-ejb-jar.xml` OC4J-specific deployment descriptor file are located.
        - **purchase** Package indicating the starting point of the `Purchase` application.
            - **ejb** Package consisting of the source code of your EJB components.
                - **bmp** Package consisting of the source code of all your bean-managed persistent (BMP) entity beans.
                - **cmp** Package consisting of the source code of all your container-managed persistent (CMP) entity beans.
            - **util** Package consisting of the source code of your utility classes.
            - **vo** Package consisting of the source code of your value object classes.
        - **webapps** Package consisting of the source code of the testing servlet program.
            - **test** Package.
    - **classes** Root directory for your EJBs: the EJB module.

- **META-INF** Directory where the `ejb-jar.xml` deployment descriptor file and the `orion-ejb-jar.xml` OC4J-specific deployment descriptor file are located.
- **purchase** Package indicating the starting point of the Java class files of the `Purchase` application.
  - **ejb** Package consisting of the class files of your EJB components.
    - **bmp** Package consisting of the class files of all your bean-managed persistent (BMP) entity beans.
    - **cmp** Package consisting of the class files of all your container-managed persistent (CMP) entity beans.
  - **util** Package consisting of the class files of your utility classes.
  - **vo** Package consisting of the class files of your value object classes.

- **web** Root directory for your Web module, containing your .jsps, .html pages, and tag libraries.
  - **WEB-INF** Directory where your `web.xml` file is located (and possibly your `orion-web.xml` file).
    - **classes** Starting point for your Web module's classes.
      - **webapps** Package.
        - **test** Package consisting of the class files of your servlets.

Configuring the OC4J data-sources.xml File

If your application will access a database, as the application in Chapter 5 does, you will need to define an OC4J data source. You can do this by modifying the OC4J `data-sources.xml` file. Before deploying your application, you need to register your data source with OC4J. You can do that by using the `admin.jar` tool, discussed earlier in this chapter, or by manually modifying the OC4J `data-sources.xml` file. This file is located in the OC4J's .../`j2ee/home/config` directory.

In this section, you will manually modify the `data-sources.xml` file. The beans that you will create in Chapter 5 will use a data source called `jdbc/nirvaDBDS`. You need to specify that data source in the OC4J `data-sources.xml` file.

In the OC4J's `data-sources.xml` file, Oracle provides a default `DataSource` example that uses Oracle JDBC-driver to create the connections. For your example, modify the file as follows:

```
<!-- Original source from Oracle -->
<data-source
            class="com.evermind.sql.DriverManagerDataSource"
            name="OracleDS"
            location="jdbc/OracleCoreDS"
            xa-location="jdbc/xa/OracleXADS"
            ejb-location="jdbc/OracleDS"
            connection-driver="oracle.jdbc.driver.OracleDriver"
            username="scott"
            password="tiger"
            url="jdbc:oracle:thin:@localhost:1521:oracle"
            inactivity-timeout="30"
      />

<!-- Your datasource -->
<data-source
            class="com.evermind.sql.DriverManagerDataSource"
            name="nirvaDBDS"
            location="jdbc/nirvaDBCoreDS"
            xa-location="jdbc/xa/nirvaDBXADS"
            ejb-location="jdbc/nirvaDBDS"
            connection-driver="oracle.jdbc.driver.OracleDriver"
            username="scott"
            password="tiger"
            url="jdbc:oracle:thin:@yourhost:your-port-no:your-sid"
            inactivity-timeout="30"
       />
```

NOTE
Adding a new data source is one of the few configuration changes that requires a restart of OC4J.

You can deploy applications both by using EAR files and by using an exploded directory conforming to the J2EE standard (as does our `chapter05` directory structure). You will learn how to deploy using both ways. Note that using an EAR file is the standard way to deploy J2EE applications to an application server. However, during development, you may find it useful to deploy your J2EE applications using an exploded directory.

Deploying an Exploded Directory

OC4J also supports deployment of an exploded directory structure. If you have the chapter05 code unzipped in the `/chapter05` directory, you should do the following to deploy the application:

1. Create an `application.xml` file in your `/chapter05/META-INF` directory.
2. Create a `web.xml` file in your `/chapter05/WEB-INF` directory.
3. Edit the OC4J `server.xml` file under the `$OC4J_HOME/config` directory and add the following entry:

   ```
   <application name="chapter5" path="file:///d:/chapter05"
              auto-start="true" />
   ```

   Note that the "file:///" prefix takes care of the forward slash / and backslash \.
4. Edit the `http-web-site.xml` file and add the following entry:

   ```
   <web-app application="chapter5" name="chapter5" root="/chapter5" />
   ```

Note that OC4J supports hot deployment. Thus, you do not have to restart the server.

If you want a clean deployment of an application deployed to OC4J, you should do the following:

1. Stop OC4J.
2. Delete the application directories under `application` and `application-deployments`.
3. Start OC4J again:

   ```
   java -jar oc4j.jar
   ```

OC4J will then do a clean install of the application.

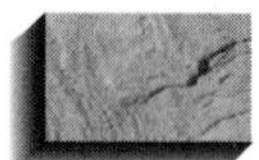

NOTE
You can find an `application.xml` file for the exploded approach under `chapter05/META-INF`, called `application-exploded.xml`.

A J2EE application can contain the following modules:

- **Web applications** Typically, a web application can consist of several components, such as servlets, JSPs, HTML pages, tag libraries, and utility classes. These components are part of the Web application module and are packaged in a WAR file.

- **EJB applications** The EJB application module (`ejb-jar` files) includes Enterprise JavaBeans (EJBs).
- **Client applications** The Client applications module includes client application programs and is contained within a JAR file.

You will next deploy the newly created EAR file application of Chapter 5. In the following section, you will learn step by step how to deploy an EAR file to OC4J.

Archiving Applications

You will next deploy the web application that you will develop in Chapter 5 as an EAR file. To do this, you need to package the application in a J2EE EAR. You will do this by following the steps described in this section. Again, use the compiled classes and files for Chapter 5 to create the EAR file of this section.

Packaging the Application: Creating the EAR File

This application consists of a *Web module,* containing only the `LocalClient Servlet`, and an *EJB module,* containing two CMP beans and one BMP bean.

Let's start by creating the WAR file:

1. Open a command prompt, and position yourself in the web directory (**chapter05/web**).
2. Create a WAR file by typing the following at the command line:

   ```
   jar cvf chapter05-web.war WEB-INF
   ```

3. Copy `chapter05-web.war` to the root directory, `chapter05`.
4. Position yourself in the `classes` directory.
5. Create a JAR file by typing the following command at the command line:

   ```
   jar cvf chapter05-ejb.jar META-INF ejbapps vo util
   ```

6. Copy `chapter05-ejb.jar` to the root directory, `chapter05`.
7. Modify the `application.xml` file in the `chapter05/META-INF` directory. For example:

   ```
   <?xml version="1.0"?>
   <!DOCTYPE application PUBLIC "-//Sun Microsystems,
         Inc.//DTD J2EE Application 1.2//EN"
        "http://java.sun.com/j2ee/dtds/application_1_2.dtd">
   <!-- The application element is the root element of a
         J2EE application deployment descriptor.  -->
   ```

```
<application>
      <display-name>Chapter5</display-name>
      <module>
            <web>
                  <web-uri>chapter05-web.war</web-uri>
                  <context-root>/</context-root>
            </web>
      </module>
      <module>
            <ejb>chapter05-ejb.jar</ejb>
      </module>
</application>
```

8. Position yourself in the root directory, `chapter05`.
9. Archive the `chapter05-web.war`, `chapter05-ejb.jar`, and `META-INF` directory to an EAR file. Type the following to create the EAR file:

```
jar cvf chapter05.ear chapter05-web.war
  chapter05-ejb.jar META-INF
```

You are now done. You should have a `chapter05.ear` file. You are ready to deploy.

If your application will access a database, then you need to define an OC4J data source. You can do this by modifying the OC4J `data-sources.xml` file. Refer to the "Configuring the OC4J data-sources.xml File" section earlier in this chapter to learn how to create OC4J data sources. Next, you will deploy the EAR file of the application.

Deploying an EAR File to OC4J

To deploy an EAR file on OC4J, follow these steps:

1. Copy the `Chapter05.ear` file to your OC4J's `applications` directory. If your OC4J home directory is `/.../j2ee/home`, then you will copy it to the `/.../j2ee/home/applications` directory. The EAR file can be placed anywhere, but in this example, you will use the OC4J `applications` directory.
2. Edit the OC4J `server.xml` file, found under your `$OC4J_HOME\config` directory. Add the following entry:

```
<application name="chapter5" path="../applications/chapter05.ear"
auto-start="true" />
```

3. Edit `http-web-site.xml` to bind your Web module to this J2EE application. Add the following entry:

```
<web-app application="chapter5" name="chapter05-web"
    root="/chapter5" load-on-startup="true" />
```

NOTE
The name must correspond to whatever name you gave the WAR file, and the root will be your virtual path where you can reach your application.

OC4J supports hot deployment; therefore, if OC4J is running, it will immediately pick up and deploy this application. If OC4J is not running, you can start OC4J by following the instructions described earlier in this chapter. You can start OC4J by typing the following:

```
java -jar oc4j.jar
```

You can test the deployment by typing the following URL in a web browser:

```
http://localhost/chapter5
```

Debugging in OC4J

OC4J provides several debug options for developers to track down sources of problems and generate information on activities performed by subsystems of OC4J. These debug options can be set for a particular subsystem while starting up OC4J. Table 2-5 lists the debug options available with OC4J release 2. These debug options have two states, either true or false. By default, these are set to false. (Please note that some of these debug options may become obsolete in future releases of OC4J, or Oracle may introduce completely different mechanisms for debugging in the future.)

You can start OC4J with one or more debug options. The default value for these debug options is false. For example, if you want to generate debug information on HTTP session events, then you have to start OC4J as follows:

```
java -Dhttp.session.debug=true -jar oc4j.jar
```

Debugging Subsystem	Debug Option	Description
HTTP	`http.session.debug`	Provides information about session events
	`http.cluster.debug`	Provides information about HTTP clustering events
	`http.error.debug`	Prints all HTTP errors

TABLE 2-5. *Debug Options*

Debugging Subsystem	Debug Option	Description
JDBC	`datasource.verbose`	Provides information on error generated at the creation of data source and connections using data sources and connections released to the pool
	`jdbc.debug`	Provides very verbose information when JDBC calls are made
EJB	`ejb.clustering.debug`	Turns on EJB clustering debug messages
	`transaction.debug`	Provides debug information on transactions; useful for JTA debugging
JMS	`jms.debug`	Prints JMS debug information

TABLE 2-5. *Debug Options* (continued)

After OC4J is started with a specific debug option, the debug information will be generated and routed to standard output. For example, you will see HTTP session information redirected to your OC4J console as follows:

```
EvermindHttpServletRequest.getCurrentSession(), session=null
Created session with id 'fe0da992ddd74b00ac98d1d859bd0733'
 at Tue Jul 23 20:37:41 PDT 2002, secure-only: false

EvermindHttpSession.beginRequest()

EvermindHttpServletRequest.getCurrentSession(), session=HTTP
Sessionfe0da992ddd74b00ac98d1d859bd0733

EvermindHttpSession.endRequest()
```

If you want to save the debug information, you have to redirect your standard output to a file, as in the following example:

```
java -Dhttp.session.debug=true -jar oc4j.jar -out oc4j.out -err oc4j.err
```

You can also start OC4J with proper level of verbosity by using a number between 1 and 10. For example, you can start OC4J standalone as follows:

```
java -jar oc4j.jar -verbosity 10
```

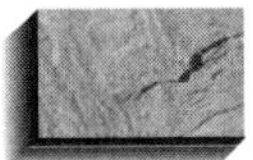

NOTE
Turning on excessive debugging information can potentially slow down your applications and cause problems by filling system files when those are redirected to other files.

This concludes this chapter. You will see further examples of how to deploy J2EE applications in upcoming chapters, starting with Chapter 5.

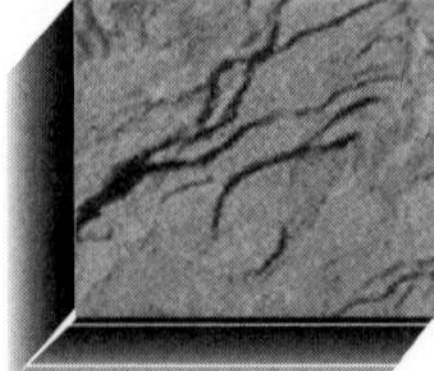

CHAPTER 3

OC4J Services: Overview

In Chapter 2 you learned about the features of Oracle9*i*AS Containers For J2EE (OC4J). In this chapter, you will learn about the different technologies that OC4J supports and how to use these technologies when developing your applications.

Specifically, you will encounter the following topics:

- Java Database Connectivity (JDBC)
- Static and dynamic embedded SQL for Java: SQLJ
- Java Naming and Directory Interface (JNDI)
- Data sources
- Java Remote Method Invocation (RMI)
- Java Authentication and Authorization Service (JAAS), Oracle HTTP Server, and Java Message Service (JMS)
- Java Transaction API (JTA)
- Java Connector Architecture
- Oracle9*i*AS TopLink

Java Database Connectivity

JDBC is a Java API for executing SQL statements. JDBC provides a standard way for Java programs to access relational databases. OC4J provides full support for JDBC release 2.0 and earlier. With Oracle JDBC release 9.2 and later, some JDBC 3.0 features are also supported. OC4J applications can access both Oracle and non-Oracle databases. Oracle Corporation provides JDBC drivers to access Oracle8.0, Oracle8*i*, and Oracle9*i* databases. Also, Oracle has licensed the Merant JDBC drivers to access non-Oracle databases, such as IBM DB/2 UDB, Microsoft SQL Server, Informix, and Sybase databases. These drivers are available for download at http://otn.oracle.com.

JDBC Connections

In this section, you will learn how to use JDBC to connect to an Oracle database. More importantly, you will develop a JDBC application that will teach you step by step how to use JDBC to access Oracle database servers. In the "Oracle9*i*AS TopLink" section, you will learn how Oracle9*i*AS TopLink uses Oracle JDBC drivers to connect to Oracle databases. In the "OC4J and Data Sources" section of this chapter, you will learn how to use OC4J applications to access Oracle database servers.

Oracle provides four JDBC drivers:

- **Oracle Thin driver** A 100-percent Java driver for client-side use without an Oracle installation. Use this driver in OC4J and any Java program (application, applet, servlet, or JSP). Note that clients that are using this driver can reside anywhere on a network.
- **Oracle OCI driver** Requires an Oracle client installation on your computer. Use this driver for client-side programs that reside anywhere on the network where an Oracle client has been installed.
- **Oracle server-side Thin driver and server-side internal driver** Used by Java/SQLJ stored procedures that reside in the Oracle database server.

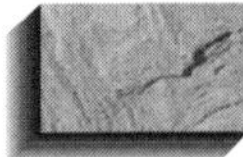

NOTE

Oracle has two versions of the Thin and OCI drivers: One is compatible with JDK 1.2.x and the other is compatible with JDK 1.1.x. The JDK 1.2.x versions support standard JDBC 2.0. The JDK 1.1.x versions support most JDBC 2.0 features, but must do so through Oracle extensions because JDBC 2.0 features are not available in JDK 1.1.x versions. In addition, Oracle JDBC release 9.2 and later also provides `ojdbc14.jar`*, a version for use under JDK 1.4 and later with support for JDBC 3.0.*

The JDBC drivers comply fully with JDBC 2.0, including the following:

- **Data source support** See the "OC4J and Data Sources" section to learn more about OC4J data sources.
- **Java Transaction API (JTA) and XA connection support** The JTA API allows you to demarcate transactions in a manner that is independent of the transaction manager implementation. XA resource is used in distributed transaction processing (DTP) environments.
- **Complete data type support** Support for advanced data types, such as BLOB, CLOB, character streams, abstract data types, collections, and, with Oracle9*i* Database Release 1, support for abstract data types with inheritance.

- **JDBC 2.0 connection pooling** Full support for the JDBC 2.0 connection pooling facilities.
- **Advanced features** Advanced features, such as support for Transparent Application Failover (which allows the midtier to redirect connections to a "failed-over" node when an Oracle database fails), scrollable result sets, batch updates, Unicode support, and several other advanced capabilities.
- **OC4J JDBC drivers** These are certified with Oracle8.0, Oracle8*i*, and Oracle9*i* database servers.

Connecting to Oracle via a Java Application

The following Java application, `ConnectToOracle.java`, demonstrates how to use the Oracle Thin driver to connect to an Oracle database:

```
/*
*     Program Name:   ConnectToOracle.java
*
*     Purpose:        A simple Java application that
*                     demonstrates how to connect
*                     to an Oracle database using
*                     the Oracle Thin JDBC driver.
*/
package app;
// Step 1: Import the java.sql package
import java.sql.*;

public class ConnectToOracle {
  public static void main(String[] args)
          throws SQLException {

    // Step 2: Load the Oracle JDBC driver
    DriverManager.registerDriver(new oracle.jdbc.OracleDriver());

    // Step 3: Connect to the database
    // using the Oracle Thin JDBC driver
    // Use the following connection string to connect:
    // Connection conn = DriverManager.getConnection
    //                  ("jdbc:oracle:thin:@" +
    //                  yourDatabaseServer,
    //                  dbUserName, dbPassword);


    Connection conn = null;
```

```
    try {
          conn = DriverManager.getConnection
                        ("jdbc:oracle:thin:@" +
                           "data-i.com:1521:ORCL",
                            "Scott", "tiger");
          System.out.println("Connected.");
    } // End of try
    catch (SQLException e) {
        throw new SQLException ("Unable to Connect!!!"
                                      +e.getMessage());
    } // End catch
    finally {
        try {
             if (conn != null) conn.close();
        } catch (SQLException ex) {}
    } // End finally

    // Step 4: Please, do close the connection
    conn.close();
  } // End of main()

} // End of ConnectToOracle class
```

Output from the ConnectToOracle Class

If the `ConnectToOracle` class was able to connect to the database, you should get the following output:

```
Connected.
```

NOTE
Use the `ConnectToOracle` class to check your Oracle JDBC installation.

SQLJ

OC4J supports the SQLJ language for directly embedding SQL statements in Java code. SQLJ is a version of embedded SQL that is tightly integrated with the Java programming language. SQLJ consists of a set of syntax and programmatic extensions that define the interactions between SQL and Java. The term SQLJ refers to a series of specifications for ways to embed SQL in Java. Prior to the Oracle9*i* SQLJ release, SQLJ complemented the JDBC dynamic embedded SQL model with a static embedded SQL model. JDBC provides a dynamic SQL interface for Java, whereas with Oracle9*i* SQLJ, dynamic embedded SQL access (similar to JDBC's) is supported in addition to

SQLJ's traditional embedded SQL access. Refer to *Oracle9*i *SQLJ Programming* (McGraw-Hill/Osborne, 2001) to learn more about Oracle 9*i* SQLJ.

In this section, you will learn how to develop a SQLJ application to manipulate data stored in an Oracle database. Specifically, you will create the `EmployeeTool` class, which manipulates the `EMPLOYEE` table. In the "Oracle9*i*AS TopLink" section of this chapter, you will use Oracle9*i*AS TopLink to generate the `purchase.model.Employee` class, an object-relational mapping for the `EMPLOYEE` table. In Chapters 10 and 11, you will create Java clients (servlets and JavaServer Pages) that use the `purchase.model.Employee` class.

The `EMPLOYEE` table is part of the Purchase Order database schema presented in the Introduction of the book. As a reminder, in Listing 3-1, we show the definition of the `EMPLOYEE` table.

Listing 3-1: The `EMPLOYEE` table

```
CREATE TABLE EMPLOYEE(
employeeno     NUMBER(7),
deptno         NUMBER(5),
type           VARCHAR2(30),
lastname       VARCHAR2(30),
firstname      VARCHAR2(30),
phone          VARCHAR2(10),
email          VARCHAR2(20))
/
```

The EmployeeTool Class

The `EmployeeTool` class is a Java application. The nice thing about this class is that the `EmployeeTool` class can be used alone or as a helper class for any Java client such as a Java application, servlet, JavaServer Page, applet, or EJB component. In Chapter 5, you will learn how to build the `EmployeeLocal` EJB component, a bean-managed persistent (BMP) entity bean that uses the `EmployeeTool` SQLJ class.

The `EmployeeTool` class consists of the following:

- **The `EmpIter` SQLJ iterator** A SQLJ iterator is similar to a JDBC result set in that it holds the result returned by a `SELECT` statement. In the `EmployeeTool` class, the SQLJ `EmpIter` iterator is used to hold a collection of `employeenos`. A SQLJ iterator is represented by a Java class. At translation time, the SQLJ translator will translate the SQLJ `EmpIter` iterator declaration into a Java declaration for a Java class `EmpIter`. This `EmpIter` class will contain:

- A `next()` method that retrieves data from the iterator row by row.
- An *accessor* method, `employeeno()`, that returns the values of the `employeeno` column in the row currently being processed.
- A `close()` method that deactivates the iterator instance.

- **The `public Collection getEmployeeIds (Connection conn)` method** This method and the remaining methods in this list use an input parameter of type `java.sql.Connection`. In this method, you use the `EmpIter` SQLJ iterator to retrieve a set of employee IDs that are stored in the `EMPLOYEE` table.
- **The `public EmployeeVO getEmployeeInfo(Connection conn, …)` method** This method queries the database and returns an `EmployeeVO` object consisting of data related to a specific employee. `EmployeeVO` is a value object class, a business object that is passed by value as a serializable Java object to and from the `EmployeeTool` SQLJ class.
- **The `public EmployeePK getEmployeeno(Connection conn, …)` method** This method queries a database and returns an `EmployeePK` object to the caller. `EmployeePK` is a Java class, a primary key class that is used to uniquely identify an EJB entity bean. Refer to Chapters 4 and 5 to learn more about primary key classes and value objects.
- **The `public void insertNewEmployee(Connection conn, …)` method** This method inserts an employee in the database.
- **The `public void removeEmployee(Connection conn, …)` method** This method permanently removes an employee record from the database.
- **The `public void updateEmployee(Connection conn, …)` method** This method updates an employee's data.
- **The `private DefaultContext getDefaultContext(Connection conn)` method** This method converts a `java.sql.Connection` object to a SQLJ `DefaultContext` connection object.

Here is the listing of the `EmployeeTool` class:

```
/*
*      Program Name:     EmployeeTool.sqlj
*      Purpose:          To manipulate the EMPLOYEE table
*
```

```
*/
package purchase.util;
import sqlj.runtime.ref.DefaultContext;
import java.sql.SQLException;
import java.sql.Connection;
import purchase.ejb.bmp.EmployeePK;
import purchase.vo.EmployeeVO;
import java.util.Vector;
import java.util.Collection;

public class EmployeeTool {

  // Declare a SQLJ named iterator to
  // store the query result from the database.

  #sql iterator EmpIter( long employeeNo );

  // Empty constructor
  public EmployeeTool () { }

  public Collection getEmployeeIds (Connection conn)
         throws SQLException   {

    System.out.println("Inside EmployeeTool.getEmployeeIds");
    Vector employeeIds = new Vector();

    // Create an instance of EmpIter
    EmpIter anEmpIter = null;

    // Create an instance of DefaultContext
    DefaultContext ctx = null;

    try {
      // Get a SQLJ connection
      ctx = getDefaultContext(conn);

      // Populate the SQLJ iterator with
      // data from the EMPLOYEE table
      #sql[ctx] anEmpIter =
        { SELECT employeeNo
          FROM EMPLOYEE
        };
      System.out.println("Query EmployeeTool.getEmployeeIds");
      while (anEmpIter.next()) {

        // Create an EmployeePK object
        EmployeePK employeePK
              = new EmployeePK(anEmpIter.employeeNo());
```

```
        // Add the object to the Vector
        employeeIds.add(employeePK);

      }  // End of while

      return employeeIds;

    }  // End try
    catch( SQLException e ) {
     throw new SQLException("EmployeeTool: Unable to get employee ids"
                  + e.getMessage());
    } // End catch
    catch (java.lang.NullPointerException e) {
      e.printStackTrace();
      throw new SQLException("EmployeeTool:Unable"
           +" to get SQLJ Connection "  + e.getMessage());
    } // End of catch block
    finally {
      try {
        if (anEmpIter != null) anEmpIter.close();
      } // End try
      catch (SQLException e1) {}
      try {

        // Close only the SQLJ Connection
        ctx.close(ConnectionContext.KEEP_CONNECTION);

      } // End try
      catch (SQLException e2) {}
    } // End finally

  } // End of getEmployeeIds()

  public EmployeeVO getEmployeeInfo(Connection conn,long anEmployeeNo)
    throws SQLException   {

    System.out.println("Inside getEmployeeInfo()!!");
    DefaultContext ctx = null;
    EmployeeVO employeeVO = null;
    long employeeNo;
    long deptNo;
    String type;
    String lastName;
    String firstName;
    String phone;
    String email;
```

```
    try {
      ctx = getDefaultContext(conn);
      #sql [ctx]  { SELECT employeeNo ,deptNo,
                      type, lastName, firstName, phone, email INTO
                      :employeeNo,:deptNo,:type,:lastName,
                      :firstName,:phone, :email
                  FROM EMPLOYEE
                  WHERE employeeNo = :anEmployeeNo
      };

      employeeVO =
        new EmployeeVO(employeeNo, deptNo, type, lastName,
                       firstName, phone, email);

      System.out.println("Inside getEmployeeInfo()-- Record!!");

      return employeeVO;

    }  // End try
    catch( SQLException e ) {
      throw new SQLException ("EmployeeTool: Unable "
                  + "to get employee info " + e.getMessage());
    } // End catch

    finally {
      try {
           ctx.close(ConnectionContext.KEEP_CONNECTION);
      } // End try
      catch (SQLException e) {}
    } // End finally

  } // End of getEmployeeInfo()

  public EmployeePK getEmployeeno(Connection conn,
                                  EmployeePK employeeNoPK)
    throws SQLException   {

    long anEmployeeNo = employeeNoPK.employeeNo;
    System.out.println("Inside getEmployeeNo()!!" +anEmployeeNo);

    DefaultContext ctx = null;

    try {
      ctx = getDefaultContext(conn);

      // Get an employeeNo
      #sql [ctx] { SELECT employeeNo INTO :anEmployeeNo
             FROM EMPLOYEE
```

```
          WHERE employeeNo =
               :(employeeNoPK.employeeNo)
     };

    System.out.println("Inside getEmployeeNo()-- Record!!");

    return employeeNoPK;
  }  // End try
  catch( SQLException e ) {
    throw new SQLException("EmployeeTool: Unable to get employeeNo "
                           + e.getMessage());
  } // End catch
  finally {
    try {
      ctx.close(ConnectionContext.KEEP_CONNECTION);
    } // End try
    catch (SQLException e) {}
  } // End finally

} // End of getEmployeeno()

public void insertNewEmployee(Connection conn,
                              long employeeNo, long deptNo,
                              String type, String lastName,
                              String firstName, String phone,
                              String email)
  throws SQLException    {

      System.out.println("Inside insertNewEmployee()!!");
      DefaultContext ctx = null;

      try {
           ctx = getDefaultContext(conn);
           // Get an employeeNo
           #sql [ctx] { INSERT INTO EMPLOYEE
                     VALUES(:employeeNo,:deptNo,
                            :type, :lastName,
                            :firstName, :phone,
                            :email)
           };

           System.out.println("I insertNewEmployee()-- Record!!");

      }  // End try
      catch( SQLException e ) {
           throw new SQLException ("EmployeeTool: "
                +"Unable to insert new employee"
                                   +e.getMessage());
```

```
        } // End catch
        finally {
          try {
              ctx.close(ConnectionContext.KEEP_CONNECTION);
          } // End try
          catch (SQLException e) {}
        } // End finally

  } // End of insertNewEmployee()

  public void removeEmployee(Connection conn,
                             EmployeePK employeeNoPK)
    throws SQLException  {

    System.out.println("Inside removeEmployee()!!");
    DefaultContext ctx = null;

    try {
      ctx = getDefaultContext(conn);
      // Get an employeeNo
      #sql [ctx] { DELETE FROM EMPLOYEE
                   WHERE employeeNo = :(employeeNoPK.employeeNo)
      };

      System.out.println("I removeEmployee()-- Record!!");
    }  // End try
    catch( SQLException e ) {
      throw new SQLException ("EmployeeTool: Unable "
          +" to get remove employee " + e.getMessage());
    } // End catch
    finally {
      try {
        ctx.close(ConnectionContext.KEEP_CONNECTION);
      } // End try
      catch (Exception e) {}
    } // End finally

  } // End of removeEmployee()

  public void updateEmployee(Connection conn,
                             long employeeNo, long deptNo,
                             String type, String lastName,
                             String firstName, String phone,
                             String email)
    throws SQLException  {

    System.out.println("Inside UpdateEmployee()!!");
```

```
    DefaultContext ctx = null;

    try {
      ctx = getDefaultContext(conn);
      // Get an employeeNo
      #sql [ctx] { UPDATE EMPLOYEE
                   SET deptNo = :deptNo,
                   type = :type,
                   lastName = :lastName,
                   firstName = :firstName,
                   phone = :phone,
                   email = :email
                   WHERE employeeNo = :employeeNo
      };

      System.out.println("I UpdateEmployee()-- Record!!");
    }  // End try
    catch( SQLException e ) {
     throw new SQLException ("EmployeeTool: Unable to Update employee"
                  + e.getMessage());
    } // End catch
    finally {
      try {
        ctx.close(ConnectionContext.KEEP_CONNECTION);
      } // End try
      catch (Exception e) {}
    } // End finally

  } // End of updateEmployee()

  private DefaultContext getDefaultContext(Connection conn)
    throws SQLException  {

    return new DefaultContext(conn);

  } // End of getDefaultContext

}  // End of EmployeeTool class
```

Java Naming and Directory Interface

In this section, you will learn how to use JNDI in OC4J applications. JNDI is specified as part of J2EE and provides a standard interface for locating users, machines, networks, objects, and services. One of these types of objects is the data source. Data sources provide an alternative mechanism to connect to a database. To learn more about data sources, see the "OC4J and Data Sources" section later in this chapter. The value of using JNDI and data sources to specify database connections instead of performing connections directly in Java code via `java.sql.DriverManager` is that you can decouple the application code from the database configuration against which the application is run. Thus, JNDI provides an important layer of abstraction that allows you full flexibility when deploying your applications.

JNDI is defined to be independent of any specific directory service implementation. JNDI provides naming and directory functionality to Java programs. You use a naming service to store various types of objects and associate or bind names to these objects. A directory service is similar to a naming service. Unlike a naming service, a directory service allows you to store attributes with the directory objects.

The JNDI architecture consists of an API and a service provider interface (SPI). The JNDI API is used by application programs to access naming and directory services; the JNDI SPI is used to attach a provider of naming and directory services. The JNDI class libraries, in the form of `jndi.jar`, are distributed with OC4J.

The JNDI API consists of five packages:

- **`javax.naming`** Contains classes and interfaces for accessing naming services. It defines a `Context` interface for looking up, binding/unbinding, and renaming objects and creating and destroying subcontexts. The `lookup()` method is the most commonly used operation.
- **`javax.naming.directory`** Extends the `javax.naming` package and provides functionality for accessing directory services in addition to naming services. It contains the `DirContext` interface that represents a directory context. The `DirContext` interface extends the `Context` interface and defines methods for examining and updating attributes associated with a directory object.
- **`javax.naming.event`** Contains classes and interfaces for supporting event notification in naming and directory services.
- **`javax.naming.ldap`** Contains classes and interfaces for using features that are specific to the Lightweight Directory Access Protocol version 3 (LDAP v3).
- **`javax.naming.spi`** Provides the means by which developers of different naming/directory service providers can develop their own implementations and make them available to applications via JNDI.

OC4J provides a complete JNDI 1.2 implementation. The JNDI service provider in OC4J is implemented in an XML-based file system. OC4J applications use JNDI to obtain naming contexts that enable the application to locate and retrieve objects such as data sources, local and remote EJB components, JMS services, and many other J2EE objects and services.

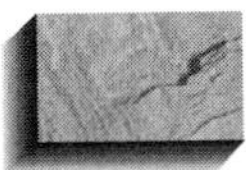

NOTE
This section presents a brief overview of JNDI. To learn more about JNDI, see http://java.sun.com/products/jndi/index.html.

JNDI Lookup Mechanism

You can use JNDI to perform naming operations, including read operations and operations for updating the namespace. In this section, you will learn how to use JNDI to look up a resource. Looking up a resource involves two steps:

1. Create an initial context object. In JNDI, naming and directory operations are performed relative to a context. There are no absolute roots. JNDI defines the `InitialContext` class, which provides a starting point for naming and directory operations. Once you have an initial context, you can use it to look up other contexts and objects. The `InitialContext` class extends `Object` and implements `Context`.

2. Look up the object using the JNDI name. Use an `InitialContext` object to look up a J2EE or another resource. The type of object that is returned by `lookup()` depends both on the underlying naming system and on the data associated with the object itself.

The JNDI Environment

The `InitialContext` class has two constructors:

- **`InitialContext()`** Use this constructor in applications that have been deployed to OC4J; that is, applications that reside in OC4J, such as servlets, JSP programs, and EJB components.
- **`InitialContext(Hashtable env)`** Use this constructor in applications that reside anywhere on a network; that is, applications that need to specify JNDI environment parameters.

The `InitialContext()` constructor creates a `Context` object using the OC4J default context environment. When you start OC4J, it constructs a JNDI context for each application that is deployed in the application server. OC4J provides the *global application,* which is the default application for each application in an OC4J instance. The global application is defined in the OC4J `server.xml` file.

You learned about the `server.xml` file in Chapter 2. Recall that OC4J is made aware of your applications when you register them in the OC4J `server.xml` file. Refer to Chapter 2 to learn how to register your application in the `server.xml` file.

User-written applications inherit properties from the global application. However, user-written applications can override property values defined in the global application, define new values for properties, and define new properties as required.

The `InitialContext(Hashtable env)` constructor takes a Java `Hashtable` object as a parameter that contains properties required by JNDI. The JNDI properties are as follows:

- **`INITIAL_CONTEXT_FACTORY`** This is a value for the `java.naming.factory.initial` property. When you create a new initial context object, you need to specify which initial context factory that the new object will use. Use the `INITIAL_CONTEXT_FACTORY` property to do so. An initial context factory allows you to locate objects in OC4J. See the "Initial Context Factories" section, later in this chapter, to learn about initial context factories.
- **`PROVIDER_URL`** Use this property to specify the URL that the application client uses to look up objects on the server. `RMIInitialContextFactory` also uses the `PROVIDER_URL` property to search for objects in different applications.
- **`SECURITY_PRINCIPAL`** Use this property to specify the name of the users to whom you gave access to OC4J. Client applications must use this property. OC4J requires this property in order to authenticate the client. This property is not required for server-side code.
- **`SECURITY_CREDENTIAL`** Use this property to specify the user password. This property works jointly with the `SECURITY_PRINCIPAL` property. Like the `SECURITY_PRINCIPAL` property, the `SECURITY_CREDENTIAL` property is required from client applications for OC4J to authenticate the client, and is not required for server-side code.

Next, we provide a brief overview on the initial context factories. To learn more about these initial contexts factories, see the *Oracle9iAS Containers For J2EE Enterprise JavaBeans Developer's Guide and Reference* technical manual.

Initial Context Factories

There are three initial context factories that applications can use to look up objects in OC4J:

- **`ApplicationClientInitialContextFactory`** Clients use this factory to construct the initial context object for looking up resources such as OC4J EJBs or data sources. You can specify this property in the application code itself or in a `jndi.properties` file. When clients use the `ApplicationClientInitialContextFactory` property, they can look up local or remote objects using the `java:comp/env` mechanism. Local objects are objects that reside in the same JVM as the client, whereas remote objects reside in different JVMs.

- **`ApplicationInitialContextFactory`** For applications that reside in the Oracle9*i*AS Containers For J2EE, OC4J can establish default properties for JNDI. OC4J uses this factory as the default value for the `java.naming.factory.initial` property. OC4J applications using `ApplicationInitialContextFactory` can locate all resources referenced in the `web.xml`, `orion-web.xml`, or `ejb-jar.xml` files. See Chapters 10 and 11 to learn about `web.xml` and the OC4J-specific `orion-web.xml` files, and Chapters 4 through 7 to learn about `ejb-jar .xml` files.
- **`RMIInitialContextFactory`** `ApplicationInitialContextFactory` and `ApplicationClientInitialContextFactory` are factories that can be used by most applications. However, use the `RMIInitialContextFactory` factory when looking up objects that are not part of your application; that is, objects that are part of another J2EE application.

Looking Up Resources in OC4J

Use JNDI to look up OC4J data sources, EJB remote and local home interfaces, and JMS services.

Using the InitialContext( ) Constructor

Use the `InitialContext()` constructor for application code that resides in OC4J. The steps to look up objects in OC4J are as follows:

1. Create a `Context` object:

```
Context context = new InitialContext();
```

2. Use the `lookup()` method of the `Context` object to locate the resource. You supply to `lookup()` the name of the object you want to look up, and it returns the object bound to that name:

```
Object myObject = context.lookup("MyObject");
```

Looking Up an OC4J Data Source

The following fragment of code illustrates how to locate an OC4J data source. For example, assume that you already created the `jdbc/MyDataSourceDS` OC4J data source and that you want to use it to connect to an Oracle or a non-Oracle database:

```
// Step 1: create a Context object
Context context = new InitialContext();

// Step 2: use the lookup() method of the context object
// to locate the jdbc/MyDataSourceDS data source
javax.sql.DataSource myDataSource =
  (javax.sql.DataSource)context.lookup("jdbc/MyDataSourceDS");

// Step 3: Use the getConnection() method of the
// myDataSource object to get a java.sql.Connection object
java.sql.Connection myConnection = myDataSource.getConnection();
```

Looking Up an OC4J EJB Local or Remote Home Interface

The following fragment of code illustrates how to locate the local or remote home interface of EJB components that reside in OC4J:

```
// Step 1: create a Context object
Context context = new InitialContext();

// Step 2: Locate the local home interface
// of the LineItemLocal CMP bean
LineItemLocalHome home = (LineItemLocalHome)
       context.lookup("java:comp/env/LineItemLocal");

// In Step 2, you can also use the following
// to locate the LineItemLocalHome
LineItemLocalHome home = (LineItemLocalHome)
       context.lookup("LineItemLocal");

// Locate the remote home interface of the PurchaseOrder CMP bean
PurchaseOrderHome aPurchaseOrderHome = (PurchaseOrderHome)
    context.lookup("java:comp/env/PurchaseOrderHome");
```

See Chapters 5 and 6 to learn more about locating EJB local and remote home interfaces.

NOTE
When using the OC4J default context, always use the java:comp/env notation.

Using the InitialContext(Hashtable env) Constructor

Use the `InitialContext(java.util.Hashtable env)` constructor for application code that does not reside in OC4J. For example, if you have a stand-alone Java application from which you want to look up objects that reside in OC4J, perform the following steps:

1. Create a `java.util.Hashtable` object.
2. Use the `java.util.Hashtable` object to store the JNDI properties.
3. Create a `Context` object using the properties that you stored in the `java.util.Hashtable` object.
4. Use the `lookup()` method of the `Context` object to locate the resource.

Looking Up an OC4J EJB Remote Home Interface

In this section, we present the step-by-step procedure that demonstrates how to look up an OC4J EJB remote home interface:

```
// Step 1: Create a Hashtable object
Hashtable env = new Hashtable();

// Step 2: Store the JNDI properties in the env object
env.put(Context.INITIAL_CONTEXT_FACTORY,
   "com.evermind.server.rmi.RMIInitialContextFactory");
// Set the OC4J administrator username
env.put(Context.SECURITY_PRINCIPAL, "admin");
// Set your OC4J administrator password
env.put(Context.SECURITY_CREDENTIALS, "Your_OC4J_password");
// For the URL, use your host name and your application name.
// For example:
// YourHostName: data-I or localhost
// Your application name: chapter6
env.put(Context.PROVIDER_URL, "ormi://YourHostName/chapter6");

// Step 3: Create a Context object
Context ctx = new InitialContext(env);

// Step 4: Use the lookup() method of the Context object
// to locate a reference to the VendorHome object
VendorHome vendorHome =
              (VendorHome)ctx.lookup("Vendor");
```

Next, we present an example that illustrates how to use the `lookup()` method of an initial context object and the `narrow()` method of the `javax.rmi.PortableRemoteObject` class to locate an OC4J EJB. The following fragment of code locates the remote `PurchaseOrderManagement` interface:

```
// Step 1: Create a Hashtable object
Hashtable env = new Hashtable();

// Step 2: Store the JNDI properties in the env object
env.put(Context.INITIAL_CONTEXT_FACTORY,
   "com.evermind.server.rmi.RMIInitialContextFactory");
// Set the OC4J administrator username
env.put(Context.SECURITY_PRINCIPAL, "admin");
// Set your OC4J administrator password
env.put(Context.SECURITY_CREDENTIALS, "Your_OC4J_password");
env.put(Context.PROVIDER_URL, "ormi://YourHostName/chapter6");

// Step 3: Create a Context object
Context ctx = new InitialContext(env);

// Step 4: Use the lookup() method
// of the ctx Context object to locate
// the PurchaseOrderManagement remote interface
Object homeObject = ctx.lookup("PurchaseOrderManagement");

// Step 5: Use the homeObject object and the narrow() method
// of the javax.rmi.PortableRemoteObject class to
// locate the PurchaseOrderManagementHome remote interface
PurchaseOrderManagementHome purchaseOrderManagementHome =
  (PurchaseOrderManagementHome)
    PortableRemoteObject.narrow(homeObject,
              PurchaseOrderManagementHome.class);
```

The `VendorHome` remote interface is part of the `Vendor` session bean, which is an EJB component that manipulates the `VENDOR` table that resides in the Oracle9*i* database. The `PurchaseOrderManagementHome` remote home interface is part of the `PurchaseOrderManagement` session bean, which is an EJB component that uses the `LineItemLocal` and `PurchaseOrderLocal` CMP (container-managed persistent) entity beans to manipulate the `LINE_ITEM` and `PURCHASE_ORDER` tables. See Chapter 5 to learn about CMP entity beans and Chapter 6 to learn more about session beans and specifically the `Vendor` and `PurchaseOrderManagement` EJB components.

OC4J and Data Sources

Applications deployed to OC4J use a data source object to connect to an Oracle database. A data source is a Java object that has the properties and methods specified by the `javax.sql.DataSource` interface. A `DataSource` object is a factory for `java.sql.Connection` objects. An object that implements the `DataSource` interface will typically be registered with a JNDI service. Refer to "Java Naming and Directory Interface," earlier in this chapter, to learn more about JNDI. Throughout this book, you will learn how to use data sources in EJB components (Chapters 5 through 7), and in servlets (Chapter 10), in JavaServer Pages (Chapter 11).

Connecting to Oracle via an OC4J J2EE Application

Use the OC4J `data-sources.xml` file to define the data sources for your application. You learned about the OC4J `data-sources.xml` file in Chapter 2. Recall that the `data-sources.xml` file is located in the `[OC4J-Root-Directory]/j2ee/home/config` directory. OC4J is distributed with a pre-installed data source. For most uses, this default is all you will need. However, you can also create your own data source. The default data source is an emulated data source.

An *emulated* data source is a wrapper around Oracle data source objects. Use an emulated data source for applications that need to access a single database or several databases. However, if your applications need to use true two-phase commit functionality to access several databases, you must use non-emulated data sources.

Creating Emulated OC4J Data Sources

Listing 3-2 demonstrates how to define the `jdbc/appDS` data source in the OC4J `data-sources.xml` file.

Listing 3-2: Data source definition

```
<data-source
     <! -- See Note 1. -- >
     class="com.evermind.sql.DriverManagerDataSource"
     name="appDS"
     <! -- See Note 2. -- >
     location="jdbc/appCoreDS"
     xa-location="jdbc/xa/appXADS"
     ejb-location="jdbc/appDS"
     <! -- See Note 3. -- >
     connection-driver="oracle.jdbc.driver.OracleDriver"
     <! -- See Note 4. -- >
     username="scott"
     password="tiger"
     url="jdbc:oracle:thin:@localhost:1521:oracle"
     inactivity-timeout="30"
/>
```

Notes on Listing 3-2:

1. The `class` attribute is whatever class is used to handle the retrieval of a `DataSource` object.
2. The `location`, `xa-location`, and `ejb-location` attributes are used to specify resource locations. Use these JNDI attribute names to bind the data source within the JNDI namespace. Oracle recommends that you use only the `ejb-location` JNDI name in the JNDI `lookup()` method to retrieve the data source.
3. The `connection-driver` attribute defines the type of connection you expect to be returned to you from the data source.
4. The `URL`, `username`, and `password` identify the database and its username and password.

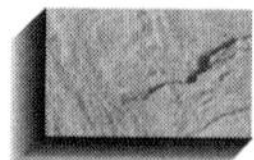

CAUTION
When you modify the `data-sources.xml` file, you must restart OC4J.

Acquiring a Database Connection via an OC4J Data Source

Use a `DataSource` object's method to retrieve a connection to your database. A `DataSource` object has the following methods:

- **`getConnection()`** Use this method to get a connection using the definition that you specify in the OC4J `data-sources.xml` file.
- **`getConnection(String username, String password)`** Use this method when you want to override the username and password specified in your data source definition.

The following statements demonstrate how to access the `jdbc/appDS` data source that you defined in Listing 3-2 and how to use the `jdbc/appDS` data source to connect to an Oracle database:

```
// Create a JNDI InitialContext object
javax.naming.InitialContext anInitialContext  =
             new javax.naming.InitialContext();
// Use the lookup() method of the anInitialContext object
// to locate "jdbc/appDS" data source
javax.sql.DataSource dataSource =
       (javax.sql.DataSource)anInitialContext.lookup("jdbc/appDS");
// Use the getConnection() method of the dataSource object
// to acquire a Connection
java.sql.Connection aConnection   = dataSource.getConnection();
```

Note that you can cast the `Connection` object returned from the `getConnection()` method to an `oracle.jdbc.OracleConnection` type and use all the Oracle extensions. Once you have an `OracleConnection` object, you can execute SQL statements against the database through either SQLJ or JDBC. The following statement illustrates how to cast a `Connection` object to an `OracleConnection` object:

```
oracle.jdbc.OracleConnection conn =
   (oracle.jdbc.OracleConnection) ds.getConnection();
```

Creating Non-Emulated OC4J Data Sources

Non-emulated data sources are used by applications that want to coordinate access to multiple sessions within the same database or to multiple databases within a global transaction. They provide XA and JTA global transactional support. Use non-emulated data sources when you want to coordinate modifications in a global transaction. Oracle recommends that you use these data sources for distributed database communications, recovery, and reliability. Non-emulated data sources share physical connections for several logical connections to the same database for the same user.

Listing 3-3 illustrates how to create an OC4J non-emulated data source.

Listing 3-3: Non-emulated data source definition

```
<data-source
   <! -- See Note 1. -- >
   class="com.evermind.sql.OrionCMTDataSource"
   name="OracleDS"
   <! -- See Note 2. -- >
   location="jdbc/OracleCMTDS1"
   <! -- See Note 3. -- >
   connection-driver="oracle.jdbc.driver.OracleDriver"
   <! -- See Note 4. -- >
   username="scott"
   password="tiger"
   url="jdbc:oracle:thin:@<hostname>:<TTC port number>:<DB SID>"
inactivity-timeout="30"
/>
```

Notes on Listing 3-3:

1. The `class` attribute defines what type of data source class to bind in the namespace. For example, you can define a non-emulated data source with the `com.evermind.sql.OrionCMTDataSource` class, as shown in Listing 3-3.

2. The `location` attribute specifies the location of the data source within the JNDI namespace. You use the location JNDI name in the JNDI lookup for retrieving this data source.

3. The `connection-driver` attribute defines the type of connection you expect to be returned to you from the data source.

4. The `URL`, `username`, and `password` identify the database and its username and password.

NOTE
Other non-emulated `DataSource` definitions can be found in the Oracle9i JDBC Developer's Guide *technical manual. This manual is part of the Oracle documentation CD-ROM that is distributed with the database.*

Next, we present the complete listing of the `DatabaseClient` class, a simple Java application that teaches how to look up an OC4J data source. Here, we assume that you have created the `jdbc/MyDatasourceDS` data source by modifying the OC4J `data-sources.xml` file.

```
/*
*     Program Name:   DatabaseClient.java
*     Purpose:        A simple class that uses the lookup()
*                     method to acquire an OC4J data source.
*
*/
package app;
import javax.naming.InitialContext;
import javax.naming.Context;
import javax.naming.NamingException;
import java.sql.Connection;
import java.sql.SQLException;
import javax.sql.DataSource;
import java.util.Hashtable;

public class DatabaseClient {
  public DatabaseClient()  {  }
  public static void main(String[] args)  {
    new DatabaseClient();
    try  {
      // Step 1:  Create the env Hashtable object
      Hashtable env = new Hashtable();
      // Step 2:  Set up the JNDI properties
```

```
        env.put(Context.INITIAL_CONTEXT_FACTORY,
           "com.evermind.server.rmi.RMIInitialContextFactory");
        env.put(Context.SECURITY_PRINCIPAL, "admin");
        env.put(Context.SECURITY_CREDENTIALS, "nirva");
        env.put(Context.PROVIDER_URL, "ormi://localhost:23791");
        // Step 3:  Create the ctx Context object using the env object
        Context ctx = new InitialContext(env);
        System.out.println("Got initial context: "+ctx);
        // Step 4:  Look up the OC4J jdbc/ MyDatasourceDS data source
        DataSource ds = (DataSource)ctx.lookup("jdbc/MyDatasourceDS");
        System.out.println("Got the datasource: "+ds);
        // Step 5:  Connect to the database via a java.sql.Connection
        Connection con = ds.getConnection();
        System.out.println("Got connection: "+con);
      }
      catch(SQLException e){System.out.println(e);}
      catch(NamingException ne){System.out.println(ne);}
    }
}  // End of DatabaseClient class
```

The following is the output from the `DatabaseClient` class:

```
Got initial context: javax.naming.InitialContext@4
Got the datasource:
   com.evermind.sql.OrionCMTDataSource/default/jdbc/MyDatasourceDS
Got connection: [Connection :
  com.evermind.sql.OrionCMTDataSource/default/jdbc/MyDatasourceDS
   connection]
```

NOTE
The `DatabaseClient` class can be useful when you want to test your newly created OC4J data sources.

RMI and OC4J

Remote Method Invocation was first introduced in JDK 1.1 and enables communication among Java programs running in different JVMs. The Java RMI API consists of several classes and interfaces. This Java API is essential for EJB, the core API in J2EE. RMI provides access to objects residing on remote virtual machines. Once a reference to a remote object has been obtained, it can be treated almost as a local object. RMI performs the marshalling, transportation, and garbage collection of remote objects in a manner that is transparent to the programmer, making it very easy to write distributed Java programs.

Oracle9*i*AS Containers For J2EE supports RMI over HTTP, a technique known as *RMI tunneling.* To get across firewalls, RMI uses HTTP tunneling by encapsulating the RMI calls within an HTTP POST request. HTTP tunneling is one of the methods that allows Java programs to make outgoing RMI calls through a local firewall. HTTP tunneling requires almost no setup, works quite well in firewalled environments, and permits HTTP to be handled via a proxy.

There are two forms of HTTP tunneling: `http-to-port` and `http-to-cgi`. In `http-to-port` tunneling, RMI attempts a HTTP POST request to an HTTP server. Sometimes, HTTP proxies may refuse to proxy requests to unusual port numbers. In this case, RMI will fall back to `http-to-cgi` tunneling.

Configuring RMI Tunneling

The steps to configure OC4J to support RMI tunneling are as follows:

1. Modify the JNDI `PROVIDER_URL`. Recall that the `PROVIDER_URL` is a JNDI property that is used to specify the URL that the application client uses to look up objects on an application server. The JNDI provider URL for accessing the OC4J is as follows:

```
ormi://<hostname>:<ormi_port>/<the_app>
// The following statement accesses
// the application that was developed in Chapter 5
// and has been deployed to OC4J
// on data-i.com host using the OC4J default
// ormi_port: 8888
ormi://data-i.com:8888/chapter5

// Modify the provider URL to locate objects,
// using the HTTP_port instead of the ormi_port.
// The following statement demonstrates the change:
http:ormi://<hostname>:<http_port>/<the_app>
```

2. If your HTTP traffic goes through a proxy server, you must specify the `http.proxyHost` property and (optionally) `http.proxyPort` in the command line when starting the EJB client. A proxy server is a server that sits between a client application, such as a web browser, and a real server. It intercepts all requests to the real server to see if it can fulfill the requests itself. If not, it forwards the request to the real server. Note that if you do not supply a value for the `http.proxyPort` property, it defaults to 80. Also, note that the argument port number is your HTTP port, *not* your ORMI port. At the command prompt, use the following statement before starting your EJB client:

```
-Dhttp.proxyHost=<proxy_host> -Dhttp.proxyPort=<proxy_port>
```

Configuring RMI in the OC4J server.xml and rmi.xml Files

To configure RMI in OC4J, modify the server.xml and rmi.xml files. These files are in the [OC4J_HOME]/j2ee/home/config directory. Modify the server.xml file by adding or uncomment the following entry:

```
<rmi-config path="<RMI_PATH>" />
// In OC4J, the <RMI_PATH> is "./rmi.xml"
<rmi-config path="./rmi.xml" />
```

Use the OC4J rmi.xml file to specify which hostname, port number, and user information will be used to connect to (and accept connections from) remote RMI servers. OC4J is distributed with the following rmi.xml file:

```
<?xml version="1.0" standalone='yes'?>
<!DOCTYPE rmi-server PUBLIC "Orion RMI-server"
      "http://xmlns.oracle.com/ias/dtds/rmi-server.dtd">
<!-- "23791" is the default RMI port#
<rmi-server port="23791" >
      <!-- A remote server connection example -->
      <!-- <server host="the.remote.server.com" username="adminUser"
                             password="123abc" /> -->
      <!-- path to the log-file where RMI-events/errors are stored -->
      <log>
            <file path="../log/rmi.log" />
      </log>
</rmi-server>
```

Use the <rmi-server> element to describe the following:

- The host and the port# attributes, where hostname is the name of the computer or IP name from which your server will accept RMI requests, and the port# is the port number on which your server listens for RMI requests. If you do not specify port#, the default is 23791. The following illustrates how to specify the host and port attributes:

  ```
  <rmi-server host="hostname" port="port">
  ```

- Use the <server> element to describe the hostname, username, port#, password, and the http-path attributes, where the username is a valid principal on the remote server (for example, the OC4J admin username), and the password is the password used by an OC4J principal. The host attribute is required, whereas the other attributes are optional. Each <server> element specifies a server that your application can contact over RMI. An

<rmi-server> element may contain zero or multiple <server> elements. Here is an example of how to define a <server> element:

```
<server host="hostname" username="username" port="port"
    password="password" http-path="pathname"/>
```

- The <log> element contains the pathname of a log file to which the server will write all RMI requests. In OC4J, the default name is rmi.log, as specified in the OC4J rmi.xml file. An <rmi-server> element can contain zero or one <log> element. Note that OC4J log files can be found in the [OC4J_HOME]\j2ee\home\log directory. Use the following entry to specify a log filename and its path:

```
<log>
  <file path="logfilepathname" />
</log>
<!-- OC4J default log file is: rmi.log -- >
```

JAAS, Oracle HTTP Server, and JMS

OC4J provides support for JAAS, Oracle HTTP server, and Java Message Service. In this section, we provide a brief description of each of these technologies.

JAAS

The Java Authentication and Authorization Service was firstly introduced as an optional package (extension) to the Java 2 SDK, Standard Edition (J2SDK), v 1.3. JAAS is now integrated into the J2SDK, v 1.4.

JAAS can be used to authenticate users and to determine, reliably and securely, who is currently executing Java code, regardless of whether the code is running as an application, an applet, a bean, or a Servlet. It can also be used to authenticate users to ensure that these users have the access control rights or the required permissions to perform specific operations.

OC4J supports the Java Authentication and Authorization Service. It does so by implementing a JAAS provider, which supplies application developers with user authentication, authorization, and delegation services to integrate into their application environments. To learn more about the JAAS implementation in OC4J, see Chapter 8, which covers security in OC4J using JAAS as well as Oracle HTTP Server.

Oracle HTTP Server

Hypertext Transfer Protocol Secure (HTTPS) is a web protocol developed by Netscape and built into its browser that encrypts and decrypts user page requests as well as the pages that are returned by the web server. You use HTTPS in a web address to indicate that the site uses a security protocol known as Secure Sockets Layer (SSL). The SSL security protocol provides data encryption, server authentication, message integrity, and optional client authentication. SSL is built into all major browsers and web servers. An industry-standard method for protecting web communications is to install a digital certificate in your browser and/or your web server. Digital certificates encrypt data using SSL technology.

Oracle HTTP Server provides an implementation of HTTPS that provides SSL functionality to client HTTP connections. It implements SSL using OSSL, which is a native module to Apache. The SSL implementation in Oracle HTTP Server makes secure communications possible for any client that is using HTTP as the transport protocol in a web browser. HTTPS is very important for securing client-server interactions. Java servlets that initiate connections to other web servers need their own HTTPS implementation to make requests and to receive information securely from the server. Java application developers can use Oracle HTTP Server to secure client interactions with a server.

JMS

Java Message Service, part of the J2EE (Java 2 Enterprise Edition) suite, provides standard APIs that allow Java applications to interact with messaging providers. This is similar to the approach taken with JDBC and JNDI APIs. Many vendors now offer JMS-compatible messaging systems, some stand-alone and some delivered as part of what J2EE vendors are offering.

OC4J supports JMS and is fully compliant with the JMS 1.0.2 specification. OC4J provides the necessary environment for you to build many different kinds of JMS message producers, message consumers, or message listeners. You can use servlets, JavaServer Pages, session beans, entity beans, or message-driven beans to be any kind of JMS message types. To learn more about OC4J JMS implementation, see Chapter 7.

Java Transaction API

The JTA specification was developed by Sun Microsystems in cooperation with leading industry partners in the transaction processing and database system arena. The JTA API allows you to demarcate transactions in a manner that is independent of the transaction manager implementation.

Enterprise JavaBeans use JTA 1.0.1 for managing transactions. In the EJB environment, the EJB server typically manages the transactional resources in use by the applications.

JTA specifies Java interfaces between a transaction manager, the resource manager, the application server, and the transactional applications:

- A transaction manager provides the services and management functions required to support transaction demarcation, transactional resource management, synchronization, and transaction context propagation.
- An application server (for example, an EJB server) provides the infrastructure to support the application runtime environment, which includes transaction state management.
- A resource manager (for example, a database server) provides the application access to resources.
- A component-based transactional application resides in the application server environment (for example, OC4J EJB server) and relies on the application server to provide transaction management support through declarative transaction attribute settings.
- A communication resource manager (CRM) supports transaction context propagation and access to the transaction service for incoming and outgoing requests.

NOTE
This section presents a brief overview of JTA and how to use JTA in OC4J. To learn more about JTA, see http://java.sun.com/products/jta/.

Enlisting Resources

JTA involves enlisting resources and demarcating the transaction. An application server provides the application runtime infrastructure that includes transactional resource management. Typically, an application server with some resource adapter and some connection pooling optimization manages transactional resources. In order for an external transaction manager to coordinate resource managers' transactional work, the application server must *enlist* and *delist* the resources used in the transaction.

When you are developing a transactional application, depending on the number of resources that your application requires, you can use the following:

- **Single-phase commit** Use single-phase commit if only a single resource (database) is enlisted in the transaction.
- **Two-phase commit** If more than one resource is enlisted, you are required to use two-phase commit.

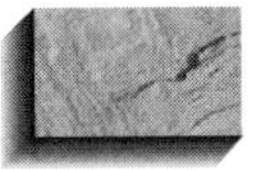

NOTE
OC4J supports both the single-phase commit and the two-phase commit. To learn more about OC4J data sources, see the Oracle9*i*AS Containers For J2EE (OC4J), Services Guide *technical manual.*

Java Connector Architecture

The concept of the Java Connector Architecture is similar to the JDBC concepts. Recall that JDBC technology defines a standard client API for accessing relational databases. The J2EE Connector Architecture defines an Enterprise Information Systems (EIS)-independent client API for EIS applications that are not relational databases, in particular legacy systems. Java Connector Architecture defines a standard architecture for connecting the J2EE platform to heterogeneous EIS. Examples of EIS include Enterprise Resource Planning (ERP), mainframe transaction processing, database systems, and legacy applications not written in the Java programming language. You can use Java Connector Architecture in OC4J to connect to EIS. To learn more about OC4J implementation of Java Connector Architecture, see Chapter 12 of the *Oracle9iAS Containers For J2EE, Services Guide* technical manual.

Oracle9*i*AS TopLink

One of the latest additions to the Oracle9*i*AS technology stack is Oracle9*i*AS TopLink. This well-known technology adds an industry-leading object-relational mapping and supporting architecture to Oracle9*i*AS that can help you overcome the object-relational impedance mismatch in all kinds of architectures, including JSP/servlet, classical two- or three-tier, and EJB architectures. As of the writing of this book, Oracle Corporation is still in the process of integrating certain TopLink features, such as EJB CMP support, into the OC4J container, but in future versions, TopLink will become the EJB container within OC4J for BMP and CMP EJB deployments.

This short overview of TopLink will merely focus on the generic object-relational mapping capabilities TopLink offers for regular Java objects, which could then, for example, be used in conjunction with a JSP/servlet architecture. While EJB entity beans address the issue of object-relational mappings for your business logic beans to your relational databases, they are often criticized as being "too heavy" for lightweight JSP/servlet architectures, which makes the TopLink usage described next an interesting alternative for such a scenario.

TopLink consists of two main pieces, the *TopLink Foundation Library* and the *TopLink Mapping Workbench.* The Foundation Library is used at runtime to provide the object-relational mapping functionality for the application, based on metadata that describes interactions, mappings and correlation between the Java objects and the relational structures. The Mapping Workbench is a developer/design environment that helps users in generating and managing metadata for the TopLink runtime engine. Even though users can also provide all necessary runtime metadata directly via Java code, the recommended and most productive approach is to use the TopLink Mapping Workbench to do so.

TopLink also provides a session console and other performance tuning and testing features, which are not covered in this short TopLink overview. Another set of functionality not covered is data-integration features for non-relational data sources, such as XML data stores, EIS, or mainframe data stores, as well as the TopLink Software Development Kit (SDK), which allows for customized mapping support for virtually any data source.

In this section, we present a short overview of functionality offered by the Foundation Library and the Mapping Workbench. Please refer to the TopLink manuals for more details.

The Foundation Library

The Foundation Library has the following capabilities:

- Uses non-intrusive metadata architecture that allows you to map existing objects/business logic to relational databases with almost no customization on your side. It also doesn't force you to use generated static code templates or other code generated at design time. SQL statements for database interaction get generated at runtime, based on design-time metadata. It uses standard JDBC drivers to connect and interact with the database.
- Provides comprehensive object-relational mapping support at runtime for diverse field and relationship mapping types, such as direct-to-field, type conversion, object type, serialized, transformation, one-to-one, one-to-many, many-to-many, and aggregate, among others. Please refer to the TopLink manuals for more details on the different mapping types.
- Offers diverse database session implementations for different architectures, supporting local, as well as distributed client/server, two- and three-tier architectures with thread-safe concurrent session access.

- Implements object caching and object identity via a comprehensive set of different caching policies, refresh policies, and cache synchronization across different server instances, among others.
- Provides comprehensive object querying support via the TopLink Query Framework (using very powerful query expressions), EJBQL, SQL, or stored procedures. Other query features include dynamic queries, in-memory queries, partial reads, batch reading, indirection/lazy reading, and others.
- Offers strong transactional support via JTA integration and object-level unit-of-work implementation.
- Provides application server integration at the JTA/JTS, JDBC connection pooling, and EJB container level.

The Foundation Library offers much more in addition to the preceding list, such as stored procedures support, diverse locking policies, parameterized SQL, statement caching, pre-allocation of sequence numbers, and scrolling cursors.

Mapping Workbench

The Mapping Workbench has the following capabilities:

- Provides an intuitive, easy-to-use graphical environment for generating and managing the metadata information needed by the TopLink Foundation Library runtime engine.
- Manages database schema information. You can read a schema and generate corresponding metadata, change database schema based on metadata changes via live a database connection, and generate schema DDL (data definition language) based on metadata for later processing.
- Manages object model information. Allows for object skeleton generation based on metadata and metadata generation based on existing object model information (via class file introspection).
- Graphically maps objects to database tables, object attributes to database columns, and object relationships to foreign key information and relation tables (in case of many-to-many relationships.)

The Mapping Workbench also offers much more, such as on-the-fly mapping and metadata validation, and comprehensive online help.

Next, we present a short object-relational mapping example for the same simple `Employee` object used in the SQLJ example earlier this chapter, but this time using Oracle9*i*AS TopLink.

Generating TopLink Object-Relational Mappings

Oracle9*i*AS TopLink provides three options to map an object model to a database schema:

- Let the Mapping Workbench auto-generate the object model for you based on an existing database schema.
- Generate a database schema based on your existing object model.
- Use the Mapping Workbench to manually or auto-map an existing object model to an existing database schema.

While the first two options usually result in either a non-optimal object model or database schema, the third option usually guarantees the best performance and design in both worlds and therefore is the recommended approach for more complex scenarios. It also keeps both models separate and independent from each other. The first two options provide their own benefits in easier scenarios and for "jump-starting" your project.

To keep this short introduction, and your first hands-on experience with TopLink, as simple as possible, we will use the first approach. This example assumes that the demo user SCOTT and the Purchase Order database schema including the `EMPLOYEE` table, as described in the Introduction of this book, already exist in the database. This example will merely focus on the step-by-step generation of the `Employee` object and the corresponding mapping to the `EMPLOYEE` table. As part of the examples provided with this book, you can also find in the `chapter03code.zip` file Ant build and execution scripts, a simple Java test client, a JSP/servlet-based test client using a custom tag library, as well as setup guidelines to run all examples in OC4J using Oracle9*i*AS TopLink. Recall that the source code for all the applications developed in this book can be downloaded from otn.oracle.com, www.data-i.com, and www.osborne.com.

Step-by-Step Employee Example

The steps to generate the object-relational mapping for the `EMPLOYEE` table are as follows:

1. Make sure your JDBC driver is set up on your system CLASSPATH variable or in the Mapping Workbench start script (see the TopLink manuals for details).
2. Start the TopLink Mapping Workbench.
3. Create a new project via File | New Project. Name the database **ORCL**. Make sure that the selected platform is Oracle, and then click OK.

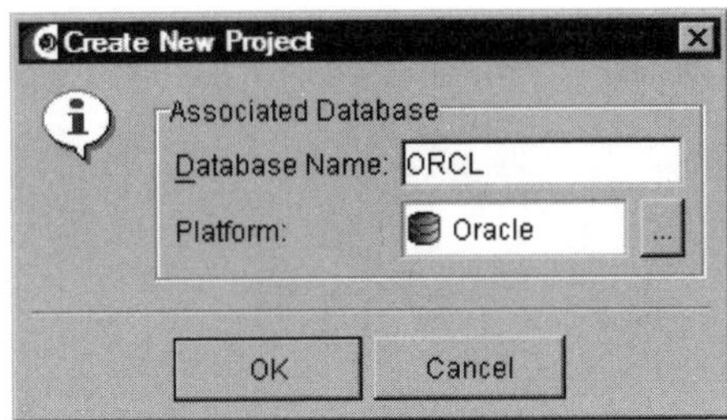

4. Save the project as **Employee**.
   Note that it is recommended to create an extra Mapping Workbench subfolder (that is, **mw**) in your project folder, since the Mapping Workbench creates several subfolders for storing its internal design-time metadata.
5. Expand the `Employee` project node in the left-side project navigator window and select the ORCL database node you created earlier. Click the Add button next to the Defined Logins box. In the Add New Login dialog box that opens, name the login **scott@orcl** and click OK.

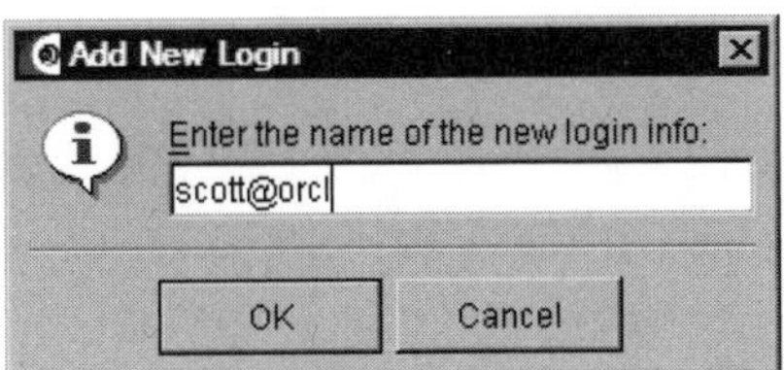

6. Provide the Driver Class, URL, Username, and Password information for the new login based on your JDBC driver and user account information. An example is shown in Figure 3-1 (the password is tiger).

7. Right-click the ORCL database node and select Log In.

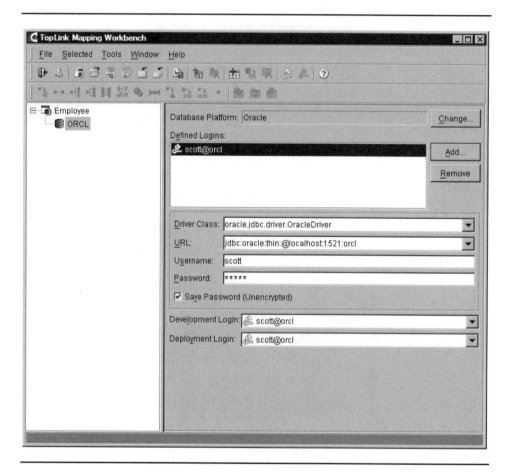

FIGURE 3-1. *Completing the driver class, URL, username, and password in the TopLink Mapping Workbench*

8. The ORCL database node will be overlaid with a green check mark indicating that you successfully logged in to the database.

9. Next you will import the table definition from the database. Right-click the ORCL database node and select Add/Update Existing Tables From Database.

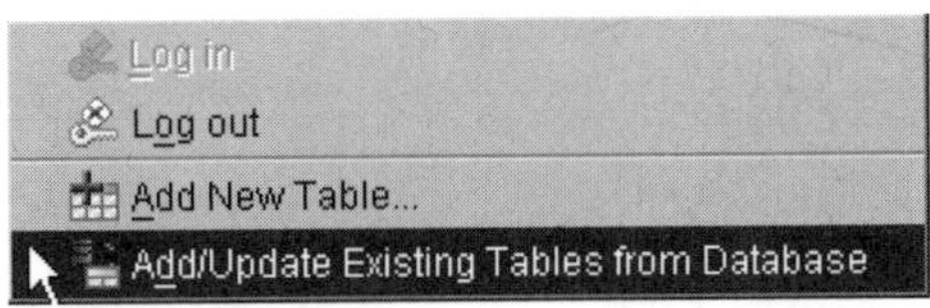

10. Search the database for the *EMPLOYEE* table and select it for import.

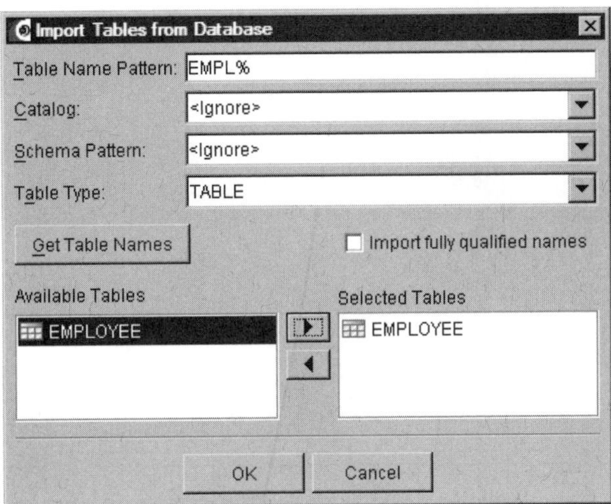

11. You can verify the imported metadata information for the `EMPLOYEE` table by selecting the `EMPLOYEE` table node beneath the ORCL database node. Figure 3-2 shows the result of this action.

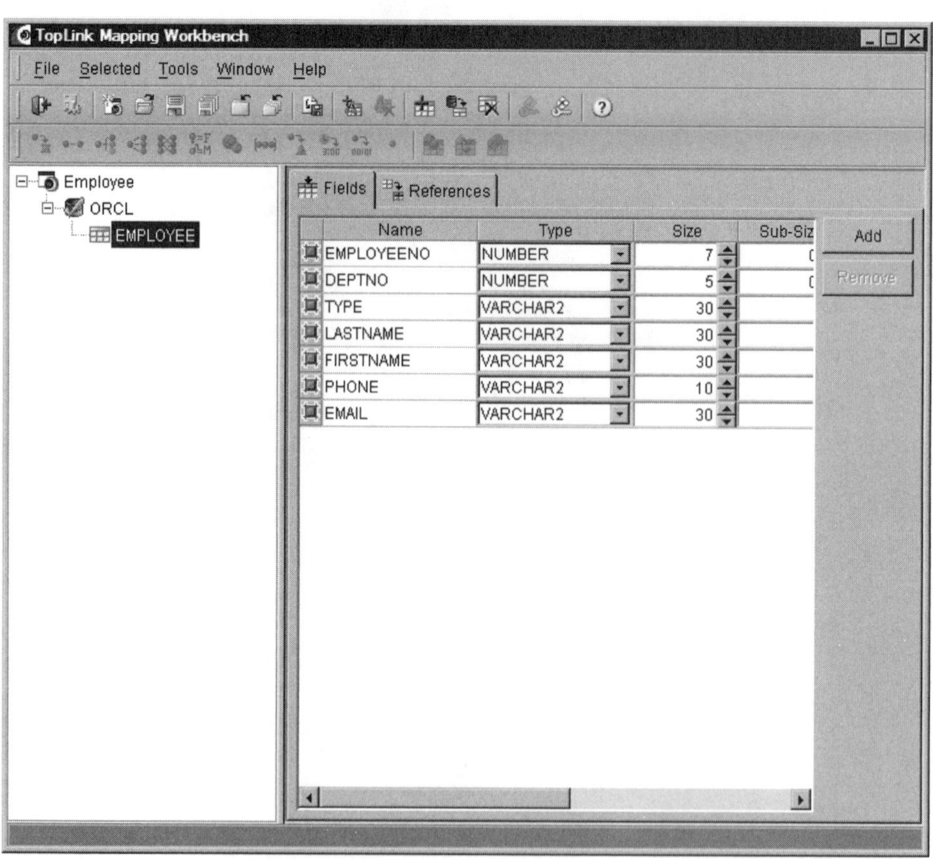

FIGURE 3-2. *Verifying the imported metadata information in the TopLink Mapping Workbench*

12. Once the EMPLOYEE table metadata is imported, you can create and auto-map the Employee object based on the table definition. Right-click the EMPLOYEE table node and select Generate Classes And Descriptors From | Selected Tables.

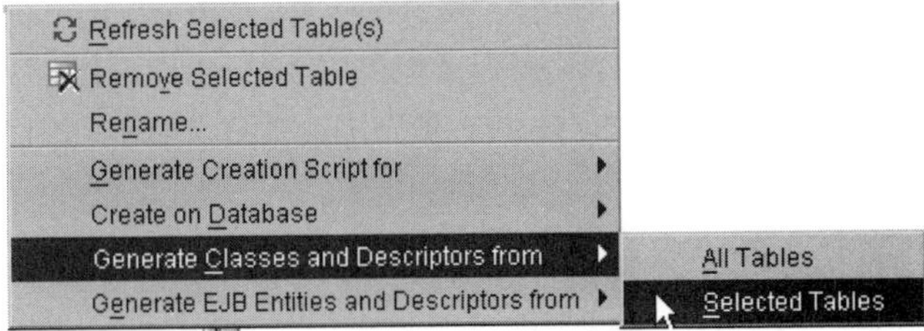

13. In the Generate Classes And Descriptors box, provide a package name, such as **purchase.model**. Click OK.

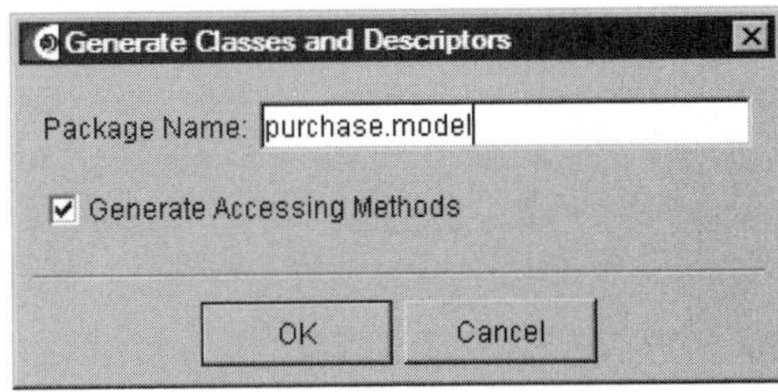

14. The Mapping Workbench will go ahead and auto-generate metadata information for the `Employee` class (descriptor). Select the `Employee` class node beneath the new `purchase.model` package node to browse the `Employee` class metadata information. Note that the `Employee` class has automatically been mapped to the `EMPLOYEE` table that it was derived from and that the primary key information has been automatically derived from the corresponding database constraints. An example is shown in Figure 3-3.

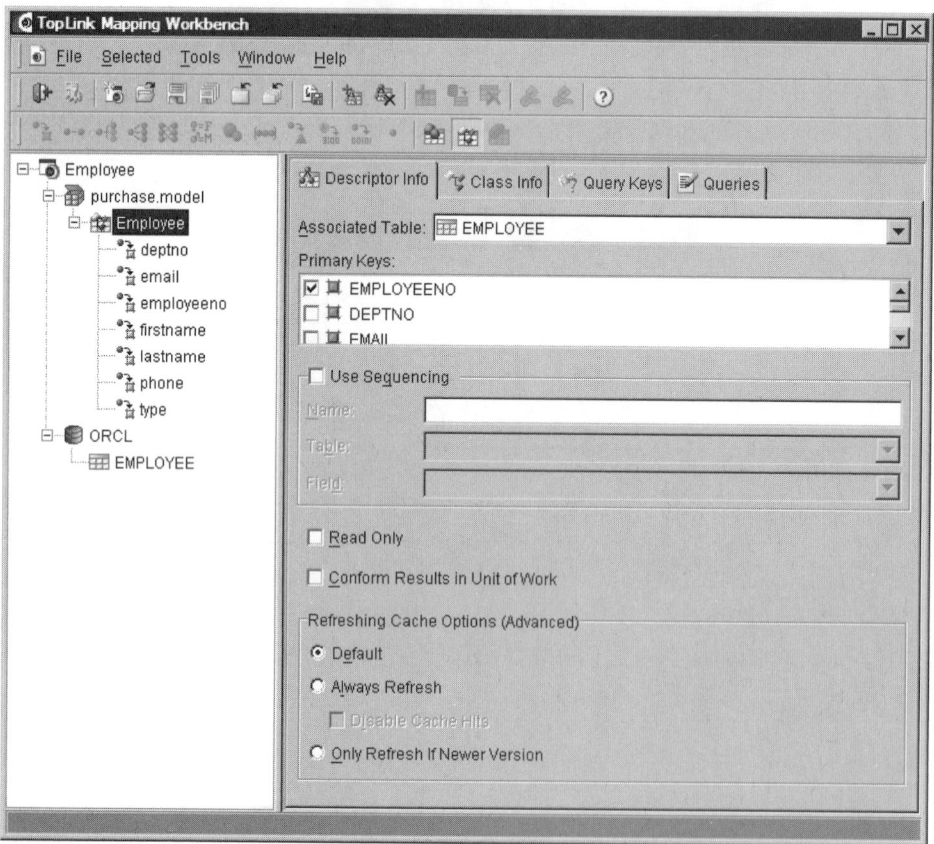

FIGURE 3-3. *Viewing the Mapping Workbench auto-generated metadata for the `Employee` class*

15. Also note that all class attributes have already been mapped to their corresponding table columns using so-called direct-to-field mappings (see Figure 3-4). Select, for example, the `employeeno` attribute to see how it is mapped to the `EMPLOYEENO` column of the `EMPLOYEE` table.

16. By default database columns of type *NUMBER* get mapped to *java.lang.Double* Java types (see Figure 3-5). In order to keep this example consistent with the SQLJ example earlier in this chapter, we will change the *employeeno* and

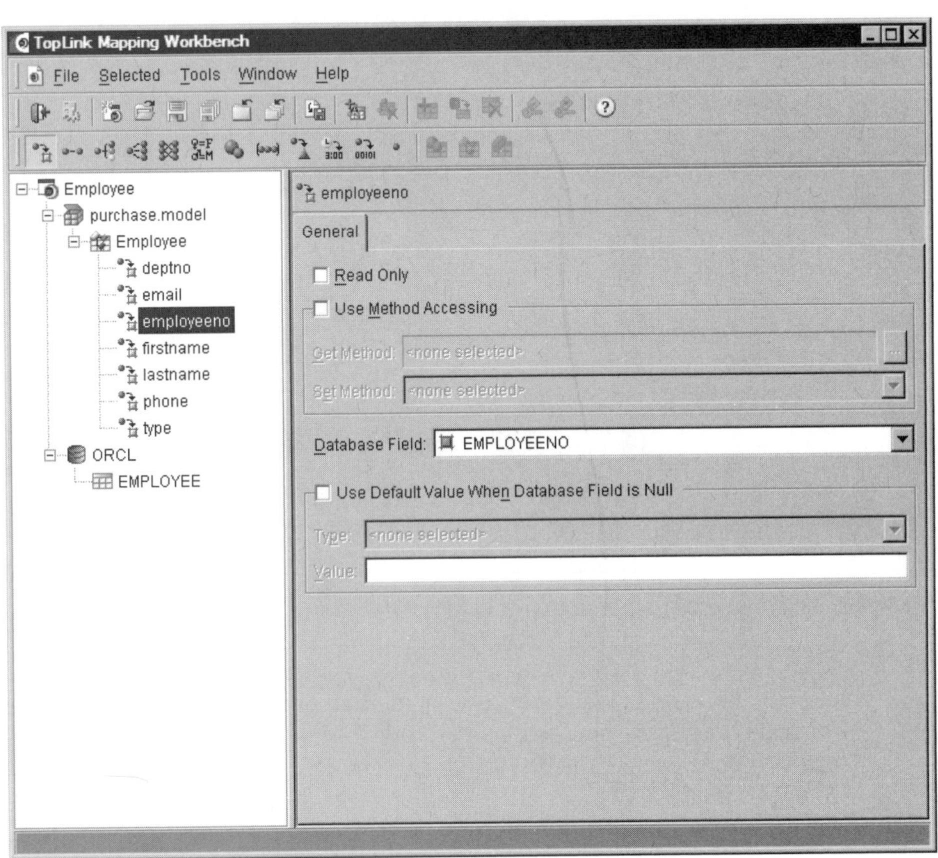

FIGURE 3-4. *Viewing the direct-to-field mapping of the* `employeeno` *attribute of the* `EMPLOYEE` *table*

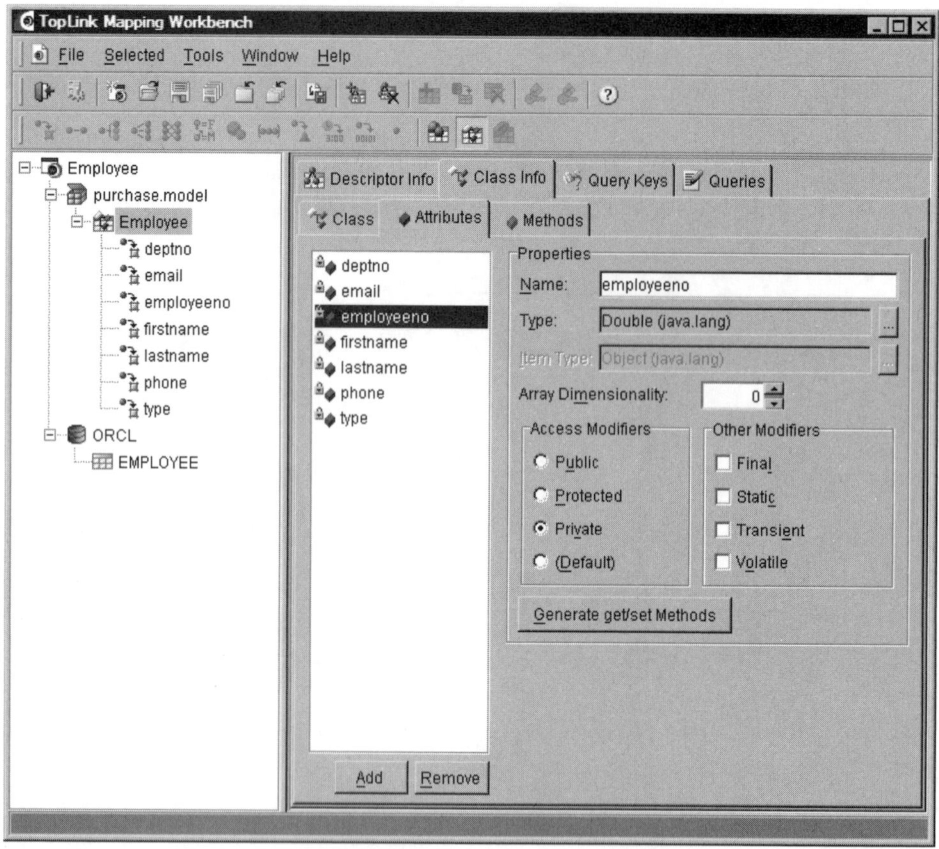

FIGURE 3-5. *Overriding the default value of the direct-to-field mapping for the* `employeeno` *attribute*

deptno attributes as well as the get/set method parameters and return values for both attributes from *java.lang.Double* to primitive Java *long* types. In order to do so, select the *Employee* class node and navigate to the *Class Info / Attributes* and *Class Info / Methods* tabs, respectively, to change the type from *java.lang.Double* to *long*. Use the class chooser to do so. Please

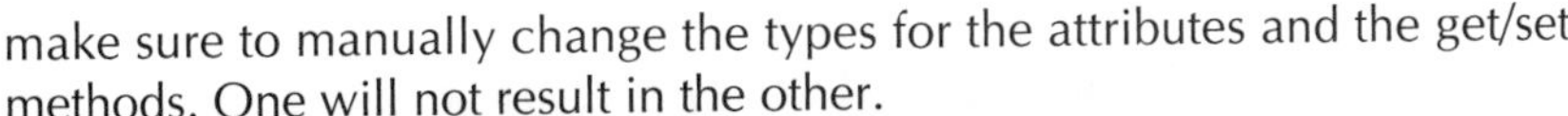
make sure to manually change the types for the attributes and the get/set methods. One will not result in the other.

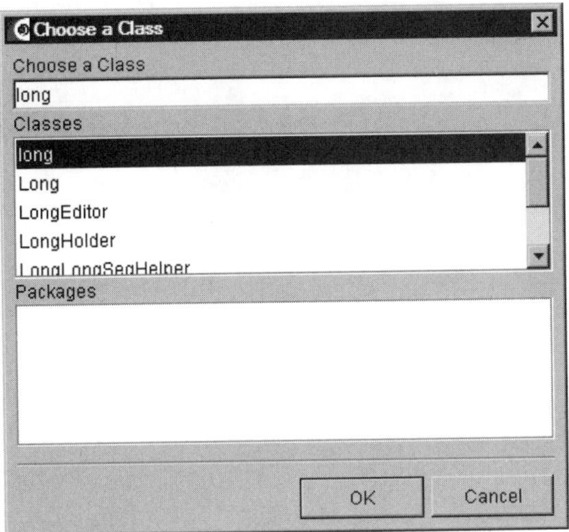

17. Next we will configure the sequencing information (shown in Figure 3-6) for the project. Select the Employee project node, then select the Sequencing tab on the right side of the window. Change the Sequencing Preallocation Size to 1 and select the Use Native Sequencing (Not Supported for DB2) option. Note that you can increase the pre-allocation size to improve performance. Refer to the TopLink technical manuals for more details.

18. After configuring the sequencing setup at the project level we will now configure the sequencing setup (shown in Figure 3-7) for the Employee descriptor. Select the Employee class node and enable the Use Sequencing checkbox. The exact sequencing information is as follows:
    Name: employeeno_SEQ
    Table: EMPLOYEE
    Field: EMPLOYEENO
    Note that employeeno_SEQ is a native sequence object in the database created during the PO schema setup.

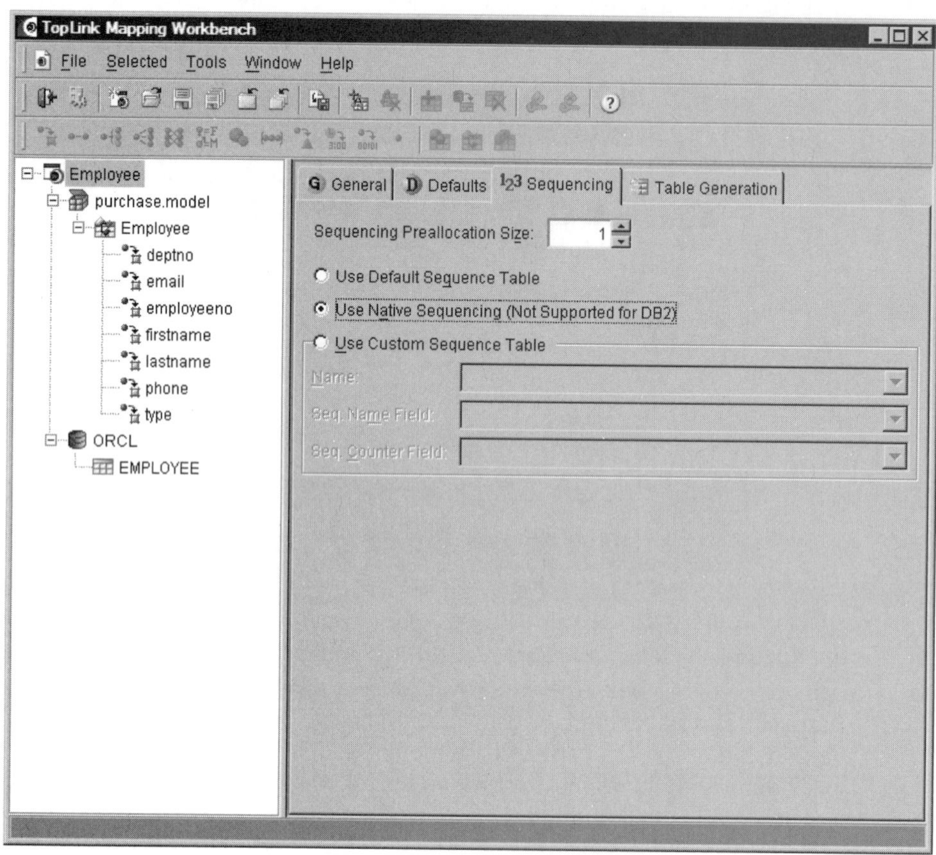

FIGURE 3-6. *Configuring the sequencing information*

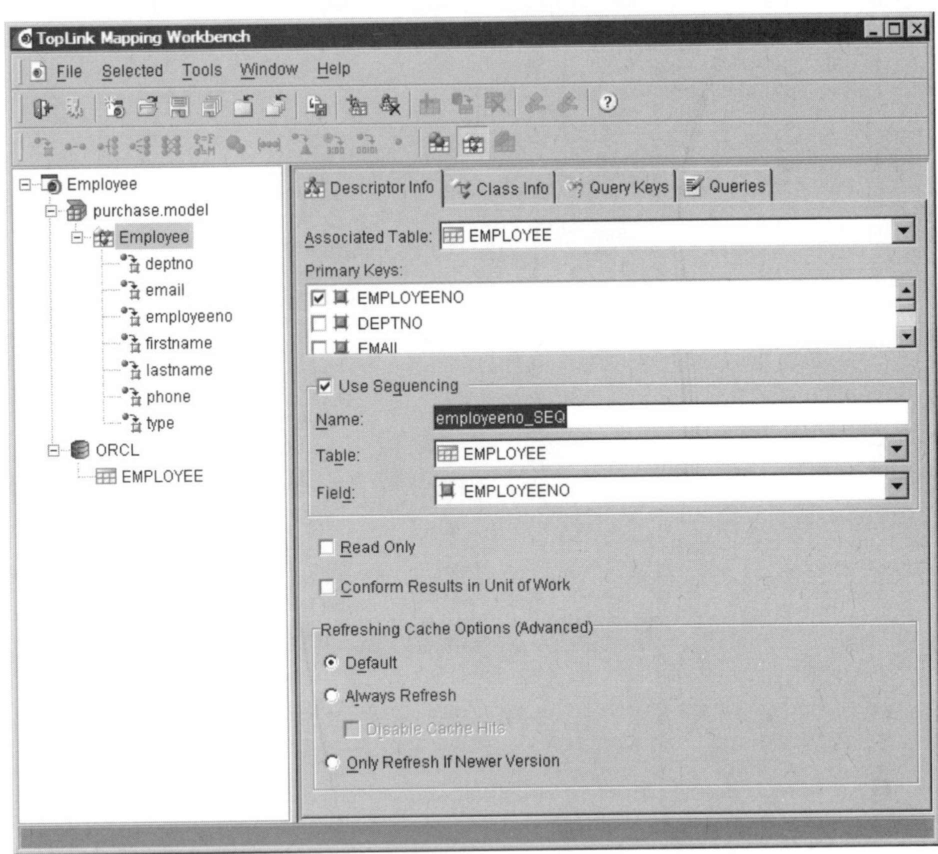

FIGURE 3-7. *Configuring the sequencing setup*

19. Next we will let the Mapping Workbench generate the Employee class skeleton code by right-clicking the Employee class node and selecting Generate Code.

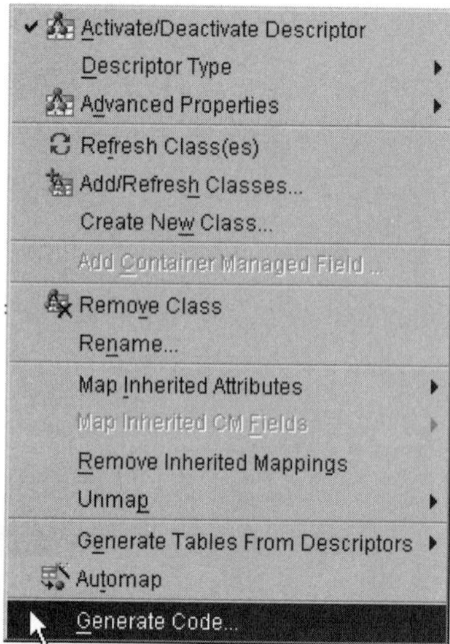

20. Choose or create an existing or new source/code directory in a location of your choice (e.g. *source*).

21. The Mapping Workbench will generate the corresponding Employee skeleton code at the location selected in the previous step. Note that it will generate subdirectories based on your package choice. The generated code for this example is shown in Listing 3-3.

22. Add the directory that your compile scripts will output the class code into (in the case of the provided Ant scripts for example *./web/WEB-INF/classes* or *./client*) to your Mapping Workbench project classpath. Select the *Employee* project node and click the Add Entry button under the Class Path section of the project information panel on the right side (under the General tab).

23. You should see a new project CLASSPATH entry based on your selection, as shown in Figure 3-8.

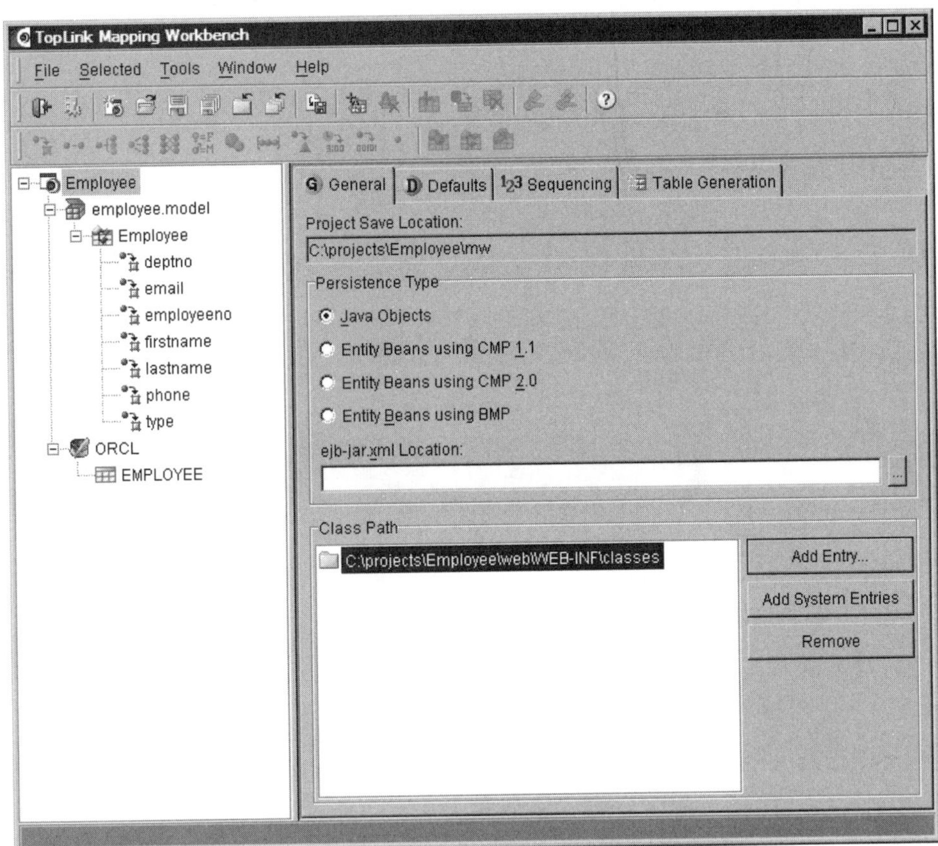

FIGURE 3-8. *The TopLink Mapping Workbench with a new project entry*

24. Next you will compile your model (in this simple case, only the Employee object) via your compiler of choice. The provided Ant scripts have corresponding tasks to do so. The final step before compiling and running your test client of choice will be to save the project metadata (class-database mapping information, runtime information, etc.) in the Mapping Workbench

as a project XML deployment definition. To do so right-click the Employee project node (shown in Figure 3-8) and select Generate Deployment XML.

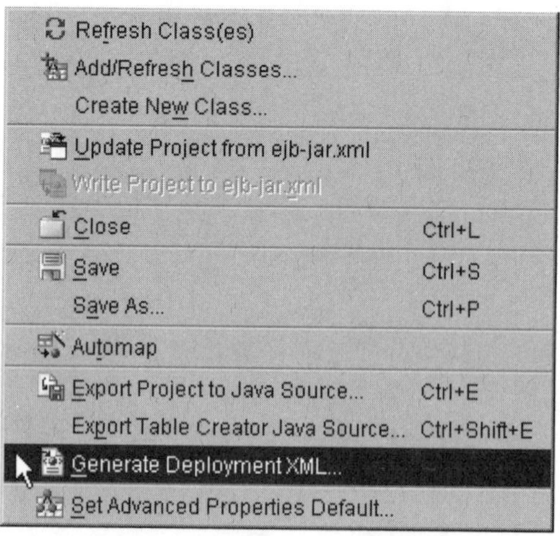

25. Choose a location to save the deployment XML file to. Note that the resulting project deployment XML file (that is, Employee.xml) needs to be located in the root directory of you runtime classpath in order to be located correctly by the TopLink Foundation Library runtime engine. The Employee class definition is shown in Listing 3-4.

Listing 3-4: The TopLink Employee definition

```
// ### TopLink Mapping Workbench 4.6.0 generated source code ###

package purchase.model;

public class Employee
{
      private java.lang.long deptno;

      private java.lang.String email;

      private java.lang.long employeeno;

      private java.lang.String firstname;

      private java.lang.String lastname;

      private java.lang.String phone;
```

```
private java.lang.String type;

public java.lang.long getDeptno()
{
      return deptno;
}

public java.lang.String getEmail()
{
      return email;
}

public java.lang.long getEmployeeno()
{
      return employeeno;
}

public java.lang.String getFirstname()
{
      return firstname;
}

public java.lang.String getLastname()
{
      return lastname;
}

public java.lang.String getPhone()
{
      return phone;
}

public java.lang.String getType()
{
      return type;
}

public void setDeptno(java.lang.long deptno)
{
      this.deptno = deptno;
}

public void setEmail(java.lang.String email)
{
      this.email = email;
```

```
        }

        public void setEmployeeno(java.lang.long employeeno)
        {
              this.employeeno = employeeno;
        }

        public void setFirstname(java.lang.String firstname)
        {
              this.firstname = firstname;
        }

        public void setLastname(java.lang.String lastname)
        {
              this.lastname = lastname;
        }

        public void setPhone(java.lang.String phone)
        {
              this.phone = phone;
        }

        public void setType(java.lang.String type)
        {
              this.type = type;
        }
} // End of Employee class
```

26. This will result in the following TopLink deployment XML definitions (shown in Listing 3-5 and Listing 3-6) reflecting all database login selections, object-database mapping settings, runtime information such as caching options, among others (see TopLink manuals for details on all the different tags and options.)

Listing 3-5: The TopLink deployment XML definition

```
<?xml version="1.0"?>

<project>
 <project-name>Employee</project-name>
 <login>
  <database-login>
   <platform>
       com.webgain.integrator.internal.databaseaccess.OraclePlatform
   </platform>
   <driver-class>oracle.jdbc.driver.OracleDriver</driver-class>
   <connection-url>
```

```
    jdbc:oracle:thin:@localhost:1521:orcl</connection-url>
 <user-name>scott</user-name>
 <password>78D969CF72A7FCAA504BA7E4FC</password>
 <uses-native-sequencing>true</uses-native-sequencing>
 <sequence-preallocation-size>1</sequence-preallocation-size>
 <sequence-table>SEQUENCE</sequence-table>
 <sequence-name-field>SEQ_NAME</sequence-name-field>
 <sequence-counter-field>SEQ_COUNT</sequence-counter-field>
 <should-bind-all-parameters>false</should-bind-all-parameters>
 <should-cache-all-statements>false</should-cache-all-statements>
 <uses-byte-array-binding>true</uses-byte-array-binding>
 <uses-string-binding>false</uses-string-binding>
 <uses-streams-for-binding>false</uses-streams-for-binding>
 <should-force-field-names-to-upper-case>
     false</should-force-field-names-to-upper-case>
 <should-optimize-data-conversion>
             true</should-optimize-data-conversion>
 <should-trim-strings>true</should-trim-strings>
 <uses-batch-writing>false</uses-batch-writing>
 <uses-jdbc-batch-writing>true</uses-jdbc-batch-writing>
 <uses-external-connection-pooling>
       false</uses-external-connection-pooling>
 <uses-external-transaction-controller>
       false</uses-external-transaction-controller>
 <type>com.webgain.integrator.sessions.DatabaseLogin</type>
</database-login>
</login>
<descriptors>
 <descriptor>
  <java-class>employee.model.Employee</java-class>
  <tables>
    <table>EMPLOYEE</table>
  </tables>
  <primary-key-fields>
    <field>EMPLOYEE.EMPLOYEENO</field>
  </primary-key-fields>
  <descriptor-type-value>Normal</descriptor-type-value>
  <sequence-number-field>EMPLOYEE.EMPLOYEENO</sequence-number-field>
  <sequence-number-name>employeeno_SEQ</sequence-number-name>
  <identity-map-class>
com.webgain.integrator.internal.identitymaps.SoftCacheWeakIdentityMap
  </identity-map-class>
  <remote-identity-map-class>
com.webgain.integrator.internal.identitymaps.SoftCacheWeakIdentityMap
  </remote-identity-map-class>
  <identity-map-size>100</identity-map-size>
  <remote-identity-map-size>100</remote-identity-map-size>
  <should-always-refresh-cache>false</should-always-refresh-cache>
  <should-always-refresh-cache-on-remote>
      false</should-always-refresh-cache-on-remote>
   <should-only-refresh-cache-if-newer-version>
```

```
    false</should-only-refresh-cache-if-newer-version>
<should-disable-cache-hits>false</should-disable-cache-hits>
<should-disable-cache-hits-on-remote>
        false</should-disable-cache-hits-on-remote>
<alias>Employee</alias>
<copy-policy>
  <descriptor-copy-policy>
    <type>
   com.webgain.integrator.internal.descriptors.CopyPolicy</type>
  </descriptor-copy-policy>
</copy-policy>
<instantiation-policy>
  <descriptor-instantiation-policy>
   <type>
  com.webgain.integrator.internal.descriptors.InstantiationPolicy
   </type>
   </descriptor-instantiation-policy>
 </instantiation-policy>
 <query-manager>
  <descriptor-query-manager>
  <existence-check>Check cache</existence-check>
  </descriptor-query-manager>
 </query-manager>
 <event-manager>
  <descriptor-event-manager emptyAggregate="true">
  </descriptor-event-manager>
 </event-manager>
 <mappings>
  <database-mapping>
    <attribute-name>deptno</attribute-name>
    <read-only>false</read-only>
    <field-name>EMPLOYEE.DEPTNO</field-name>
    <type>
   com.webgain.integrator.mappings.DirectToFieldMapping</type>
 </database-mapping>
 <database-mapping>
   <attribute-name>email</attribute-name>
   <read-only>false</read-only>
   <field-name>EMPLOYEE.EMAIL</field-name>
   <type>
    com.webgain.integrator.mappings.DirectToFieldMapping</type>
 </database-mapping>
 <database-mapping>
   <attribute-name>employeeno</attribute-name>
   <read-only>false</read-only>
   <field-name>EMPLOYEE.EMPLOYEENO</field-name
   <type>
     com.webgain.integrator.mappings.DirectToFieldMapping</type>
   </database-mapping>
   <database-mapping>
     <attribute-name>firstname</attribute-name>
```

```
          <read-only>false</read-only>
          <field-name>EMPLOYEE.FIRSTNAME</field-name>
          <type>
           com.webgain.integrator.mappings.DirectToFieldMapping</type>
         </database-mapping>
         <database-mapping>
           <attribute-name>lastname</attribute-name>
           <read-only>false</read-only>
           <field-name>EMPLOYEE.LASTNAME</field-name>
           <type>
           com.webgain.integrator.mappings.DirectToFieldMapping</type>
           </database-mapping>
           <database-mapping>
              <attribute-name>phone</attribute-name>
              <read-only>false</read-only>
              <field-name>EMPLOYEE.PHONE</field-name>
              <type>
           com.webgain.integrator.mappings.DirectToFieldMapping</type>
           </database-mapping>
           <database-mapping>
              <attribute-name>type</attribute-name>
              <read-only>false</read-only>
              <field-name>EMPLOYEE.TYPE</field-name>
              <type>
           com.webgain.integrator.mappings.DirectToFieldMapping</type>
           </database-mapping>
          </mappings>
          <type>com.webgain.integrator.publicinterface.Descriptor</type>
      </descriptor>
   </descriptors>
</project>
```

Listing 3-6: The TopLink `sessions.xml` session definition

```
<?xml version="1.0" encoding="US-ASCII"?>
<!DOCTYPE toplink-configuration PUBLIC
    "-//WebGain, Inc.//DTD TopLink for JAVA 4.6//EN"
      "http://www.webgain.com/dtd/toplink/sessions_4_6.dtd">
<toplink-configuration>
      <session>
            <name>default</name>
            <project-xml>Employee.xml</project-xml>
            <session-type>
                  <server-session/>
            </session-type>
            <login>
                  <user-name>scott</user-name>
                  <password>tiger</password>
            </login>
```

```
                <!--  log messages is disabled to get
                      a less confusing log ouput.
                      This can be turned on to get a much
                      more verbose log output.
                      The log content can be managed
                              with the <logging-options>  -->
                <enable-logging>false</enable-logging>
                <logging-options>
                      <log-debug>true</log-debug>
                      <log-exceptions>true</log-exceptions>
                      <log-exception-stacktrace>true</log-exception-stacktrace>
                      <print-thread>true</print-thread>
                      <print-session>true</print-session>
                      <print-connection>true</print-connection>
                      <print-date>true</print-date>
                </logging-options>
          </session>
    </toplink-configuration>
```

Note that all the source code for this chapter can be found in the `Chapter03Code.zip` file. Also, included in this file is a complete Oracle9*i*AS TopLink application. In Chapters 10 and 11, you will learn how to develop Oracle9*i*AS TopLink applications and deploy them to OC4J.

In this chapter, you learned about the following:

- How to use JDBC to connect to Oracle databases.
- How to use SQLJ to build stand-alone Java applications or helper classes to manipulate data in Oracle databases.
- How to use JNDI to look up resources such as data sources and references to EJB components.
- How to create OC4J data sources.
- How OC4J supports RMI, JAAS, Oracle HTTPS, JMS, JTA, and Java Connector Architecture.
- How to use Oracle9*i*AS TopLink to generate Java classes that you can use instead of EJBs.

This chapter marks the end of Part I. Chapter 4 begins Part II, which consists of Chapters 4 through 7, in which you will learn about the EJB technology. In Chapter 4, specifically, you will learn about the EJB 2.0 specification.

PART II

Building J2EE Business Tier Components

CHAPTER 4

Introduction to Enterprise JavaBeans (EJB)

n Part I of the book, you learned about the J2EE technology and the Oracle9*i*AS Containers For Java (OC4J). Part II of the book consists of four chapters, Chapters 4 through 7. In Part II, you will learn how to build J2EE business components and deploy them in OC4J.

Business components are made of business logic, which is logic that solves or meets the needs of a particular business domain, such as government, banking, retail, or finance. In J2EE, Enterprise JavaBeans (EJB) objects running in the business tier handle the business logic. EJB defines how server-side components are written. An enterprise bean is a component that contains the business logic of an application.

The EJB component model addresses issues that involve the management of distributed business objects in a multi-tier architecture. EJB components are Java components that run on an application server. They can run and execute anywhere, in any environment that has a Java interpreter (a Java Virtual Machine, or JVM) and an EJB container. An enterprise bean can be used alone or with other enterprise beans to execute business logic on the J2EE server. Enterprise JavaBeans allow applications to communicate across multi-tier client and server environments, and across Internet and intranet structures. To effectively use Enterprise JavaBeans, it is mandatory that you understand the EJB technology. The book includes four chapters on the subject. In this chapter, you will learn the overall architecture of EJB along with its major components; whereas in Chapters 5, 6, and 7 you will learn how to apply this knowledge while building EJB components that implement business rules. Although the material is quite theoretical, a good understanding of its substance is fundamental for any application developers who want to develop EJB applications.

In this chapter, you will learn the following:

- The elements of the Enterprise JavaBeans specification
- The components of the EJB architecture
- Types of Enterprise JavaBeans: session beans, entity beans, and message-driven beans
- Client views of Enterprise JavaBeans
- The components of an EJB application
- The EJB deployment descriptor (`ejb-jar` file)
- The transaction management for EJBs
- OC4J transactional support
- OC4J EJB support

The EJB specification defines the basic architecture of an EJB component, specifying the structure of its interfaces and the mechanisms by which it interacts with its container and with other components. An EJB container is a system that functions as the container for enterprise beans. The EJB specification provides guidelines to create and implement EJB components that can work together to form a larger application. Application builders can combine EJB components from different developers or different vendors to construct an application.

The Enterprise JavaBeans initiative was announced at the JavaOne 97 Conference and a draft was posted in December 1997. The EJB 1.0 formal specification was released on March 21, 1998. Enterprise JavaBeans 1.1 was posted on December 17, 1999. The final release of the most recent EJB specification, EJB 2.0, was posted on August 14, 2001. Thus, in this chapter, you will learn about the major elements of the most recent specification, EJB 2.0. To learn more about the EJB specification, see http://java.sun.com/products/ejb/.

Enterprise JavaBeans Specification

The Enterprise JavaBeans (Sun Microsystems) specification is a framework for Java server-side services that details services such as transactions, security, and naming. A *framework* is a set of classes that embodies an abstract design for solutions to a family of related problems. A *transaction* is an atomic unit of work consisting of one or more operations where all changes performed by these operations are executed as a whole and are either totally applied or totally undone. A transaction is committed or rolled back.

The EJB specification defines the major structures of the EJB framework. It defines the interfaces and general behavior of Enterprise JavaBeans components, including the three types of enterprise beans: session beans, which contain business-process models; entity beans, which can act as persistent data containers; and message-driven beans, which are stateless, server-side components for processing asynchronous Java Message Service (JMS) messages. Moreover, EJB defines the contract between the EJB components, which specifies their role, their responsibility, and the services that they must provide.

Vendors that want to create EJB server implementations must provide the required services as stated in the EJB specification. Today, many vendors such as BEA, GemStone, IBM, Netscape/Sun, Oracle, Borland, and Tandem support the EJB specification.

Enterprise JavaBeans Design Goals

The EJB specification has several design goals:

- **Operating-system independence** Enterprise JavaBeans can run on any platform, such as UNIX, Microsoft Windows, Hewlett-Packard UX (11.0 and 11i), and Mac OS.

- **Middleware independence** EJB components can run on any middleware solution that implements the EJB specification.
- **Interoperability between enterprise beans and other Java programming languages' APIs, non-Java programming language applications, and CORBA** CORBA and non-Java clients can use enterprise beans and vice versa. However, this is not true in most implementations. At the present time, only primitive types and remote object references are interoperable.
- **Ease of development and deployment of distributed applications** At the present time, this goal has not been reached, but will likely be reached in the future. For example, we would expect reuse of EJB technologies in a Web Services environment. There is some work in this direction in the Java community.
- **Component reusability and portability** Developers can reuse Enterprise JavaBeans, and they are portable from one EJB vendor to another.

EJB Releases 1.0 and 1.1

Release 1.0 focused on the following aspects of the EJB technology:

- Defined the distinct "EJB roles." The EJB specification clearly defines the following parties: Enterprise Bean Provider, Application Assembler, Deployer, EJB Server Provider, EJB Container Provider, and System Administrator. In the "Enterprise JavaBeans Roles" section of this chapter, you will learn more about the EJB roles.
- Defined the client's view of enterprise beans. A client of an enterprise bean can be another enterprise bean deployed in the same or a different container, or an arbitrary Java program, such as an application, applet, or servlet. The client view of an enterprise bean can also be CORBA clients that are not written in the Java programming language.
- Defined the format of the EJB's deployment descriptor file, called the `ejb-jar` file. An `ejb-jar` file is a standard format used by EJB tools for packaging enterprise beans with their declarative information. Application assembly and deployment tools process the `ejb-jar` file. In release 1.0, the `ejb-jar` file is an ASCII-based file. Starting with release 1.1, the `ejb-jar` file is XML based.

Release 1.1 extended 1.0 and provided the following:

- Defined an XML-based format of the EJB's deployment descriptor. Extensible Markup Language (XML) is the universal format for structured documents and data on the Web, data repositories, and data interchange in general.

- Specified in greater detail the responsibilities of the individual EJB roles.

EJB Release 2.0

The EJB 2.0 specification builds upon and extends the architecture and functionality defined by the EJB specification, releases 1.0 and 1.1. Additionally, release 2.0 provides the following:

- Defines the integration of EJB with the Java Message Service (JMS). JMS, designed by Sun and several partner companies, is a Java API that allows applications to create, send, receive, and read messages. The JMS API defines a common set of interfaces and associated semantics that allow programs written in the Java programming language to communicate with other messaging implementations. See Chapter 7 to learn more about JMS.
- Provides a local client's view to access enterprise beans from local clients. The local model avoids the performance overhead of the remote model.
- Provides improved support for the persistence of entity beans and the management of relationships among entity beans.
- Defines query syntax for entity bean finder methods. Release 2.0 defines the EJB QL: EJB Query Language for Container-Managed Persistence (CMP) query methods.
- Provides network interoperability among EJB servers.

Enterprise JavaBeans Roles

As stated earlier in the chapter, the EJB specification establishes six roles in the application development and deployment of EJB components. This section describes those roles in detail.

The *bean developer* is responsible for writing the required interfaces and classes as defined in the specification. If you are a Java developer, you can easily become a bean provider; that is, you can develop your own EJB components. Remember that EJB components are Java components. Enterprise JavaBeans are simple, portable, reusable, and deployable components for implementing business logic. You can also purchase existing Enterprise JavaBeans and plug them into your application, or you can combine your own EJB components with other vendors' EJB components to build your application. The interesting aspect of your job as a bean provider is that you no longer have to worry about complex issues such as multi-threaded, transactional, and distributed process computing. Consequently, you can concentrate on writing applications that deal strictly with the business logic rather than communication and network issues.

The *application assembler* gathers one or more beans developed by the bean providers to produce larger application units (new enterprise beans or non-EJB applications). This role was defined in both EJB 1.0 and 1.1 and extended in 2.0. Some of these roles are being automated through tools.

The *deployer,* an expert at a specific operational environment, is responsible for correctly installing the EJB classes and interfaces in the EJB server. The deployer takes one or more `ejb-jar` files created by the bean provider or the application assembler and deploys these files in a specific environment. In this book, you will acquire the skills to build enterprise beans that can run anywhere, but more importantly, you will learn how to deploy your beans in the OC4J environment. Note that, at deployment time, a deployer makes the EJB home interface object available for clients to use enterprise beans. To make the bean available, EJB server vendors must provide a namespace and a bean home reference name to clients that want to use the bean. A *namespace* is a hierarchical collection of objects and is analogous to a UNIX file system and directories. Oracle and other EJB server vendors provide a JNDI-accessible namespace in which to store the home object reference. Sun Microsystems, Inc. supplies the Java Naming and Directory Interface (JNDI) API in the `javax.naming` package. JNDI provides directory and naming functionality to Java applications. It is defined to be independent of any specific directory service implementation. JNDI allows Java applications to access a variety of directories in a uniform way. To learn more about the JNDI API, see Chapter 3 of this book and *Java Naming and Directory Interface Application Programming (JNDI API),* at http://java.sun.com/products/jndi/.

The *server provider,* a vendor (OS, middleware, or database), provides an EJB server that can implement a session and/or entity bean container. An EJB server is an application framework where EJB containers run. The server provider can include containers and deployment tools for their specific server and can publish their low-level interfaces so other vendors can develop containers and deployment tools that interoperate with theirs.

The *container provider* (an EJB container vendor) is responsible for providing software tools necessary to install EJB classes and interfaces into an EJB server; the EJB vendor also provides tools to monitor and manage the container, which in turn monitors and manages the beans at runtime. OC4J is part of the Oracle9*i* Application Server (Oracle9*i*AS), which offers a variety of solutions you can use to build your application server. Apart from OC4J, these solutions include portals, wireless support, caching, business intelligence features, security features, and management tools. Oracle provides several tools to manage and monitor OC4J and to deploy applications to OC4J. The primary tool for managing Oracle9*i*AS, as well as your entire Oracle environment, is Oracle Enterprise Manager (OEM). To manage multiple OC4J instances or to deploy applications to multiple OC4J instances, Oracle recommends that you use the Distributed Configuration Management (DCM) utility tool of the OEM, which provides a command-line alternative to using OEM for some management tasks. Use `admin.jar` or update the XML file manually only when you are executing OC4J in stand-alone mode. In this book, you will learn how to deploy applications to OC4J in a stand-alone mode. To learn more about the `admin.jar` tool and its options, see the *Oracle9iAS Containers For J2EE User's Guide* technical manual and Appendix A of this book.

The container providers also supply installation of references (pointers or addresses of EJB components) in a JNDI-accessible namespace and versioning support for installed EJB components. The integration and accessibility of services in a server using JNDI is addressed in more detail in the Java 2 Enterprise Edition (J2EE) specification and Chapter 3 of this book. Note that while an EJB server and container are two distinct components in an environment, the same vendor can provide both components. For example, OC4J includes an EJB server and an EJB container.

The *system administrator* uses runtime monitoring and management tools to oversee the system. The EJB server and container providers usually provide these tools. Also, note that the EJB architecture does not define the contracts for system management and administration. The system administrator typically uses runtime monitoring and management tools provided by the EJB server and container providers to accomplish these tasks. For example, the Oracle Enterprise Manager provides such system administrator tools.

Enterprise JavaBeans Architecture

Enterprise JavaBeans is an architecture designed for server-side components, particularly components of distributed transaction applications. To understand how an EJB application works, you need to understand the basic parts of the EJB system.

The EJB architecture consists of several components:

- The EJB server
- The EJB container that runs in the EJB server
- The Enterprise JavaBeans that run in the EJB container
- The EJB client application that uses the Enterprise JavaBeans
- Other auxiliary systems like JNDI and Java Transaction Service (JTS)

Enterprise JavaBeans Server

The EJB server (see Figure 4-1) is the high-level application that manages the EJB container and provides access to system services. Enterprise JavaBeans execute within an EJB container, which in turn executes within an EJB server. Any server that can

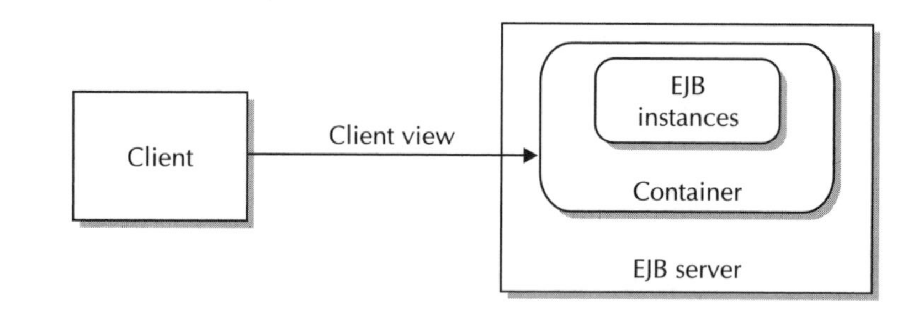

FIGURE 4-1. *Enterprise JavaBeans architecture*

host an EJB container and provides it with the necessary services can be an EJB server. Some examples of EJB servers are application and middleware servers.

The EJB server implements system services and provides the container with lower-level services such as network connectivity. In turn, the container provides services to the bean. In the EJB specification, the EJB server is required to provide an object's availability and accessibility via JNDI and transaction services.

Enterprise JavaBeans Container

Enterprise JavaBeans are components that live and operate in an EJB container. They do not operate in a vacuum. Container vendors are responsible for providing the necessary tools for the deployer to install Enterprise JavaBeans in an EJB container.

An EJB container is an abstraction that separates the business logic from the underlying implementations. There are a lot of interactions between the beans and the server. The container provides the appropriate services to the bean so it can access its environment. It presents a uniform interface that manages the interactions between enterprise beans and the server. It can manage many instances and many EJB components consisting of several EJB interfaces and classes. The container resides in an EJB server that can reside anywhere on a network. The EJB container provides to the enterprise bean it contains a set of services, such as transaction and resource management (security, cache management, and messaging management), versioning, scalability, mobility (that is, portability across all container implementations in which the entity bean might be deployed), persistence, and database connectivity. Since the EJB container handles all of these functions, the EJB component developer can concentrate on business rules, thus leaving service tasks to the container.

Two of the major responsibilities of the container are to make the EJB objects accessible to the clients and respond to client lookups. It does so by creating and/or activating Enterprise JavaBeans as required. The container accomplishes the former by *publishing* the "names" of its contained Enterprise JavaBeans with JNDI. The term "publish" refers to the act of storing in a namespace a reference to the EJB home and EJB objects. Remember that a namespace is analogous to a UNIX directory hierarchy. Clients using EJB locate a home reference object via the `lookup()` method of the `javax.naming.Context` interface. The reference to the home object allows clients to create new bean instances or use existing ones. Chapters 5, 6, and 7 include more information regarding clients' lookup mechanisms.

An EJB client never interacts directly with the EJB container. The EJB specification defines the contract between an enterprise bean and its container. An enterprise bean's container includes all the services (for example, security and transactional services) that a bean needs to perform the required business logic. Information regarding the container's services is stored in one object, called an EJB context. Each enterprise bean type has a specific context. A *context* is a set of properties and represents a way for beans to perform callbacks to the container. The EJB specification provides a context interface for each type of enterprise: `javax.ejb.SessionContext` for session beans; `javax.ejb.EntityContext` for entity beans; and `javax.ejb.MessageDrivenContext` for message-driven beans. See "Enterprise Beans Class," later in this chapter, for a detailed discussion on these interfaces.

The EJB container does not implement or extend a specific interface or class from the EJB specification, but it does have certain responsibilities to which it must adhere. Remember that the container's first responsibility is to publish the "names" of the contained Enterprise JavaBeans with a naming service and it must respond to JNDI lookups by creating and/or activating Enterprise JavaBeans when requested. Additionally, the container must give the bean its `javax.naming.Context` object, through which all other environmental objects can be retrieved. The notion of context is defined in the `javax.naming.Context` interface. This interface represents a naming context, which consists of a set of name-to-object bindings and contains methods for examining and updating these bindings.

Enterprise JavaBeans

There are three types of enterprise beans: session beans, entity beans, and message-driven beans. See the "Types of Enterprise JavaBeans" section of this chapter to learn more about these beans.

Client Applications

EJB clients make use of the EJB beans for their operations. They find the EJB container that contains the bean through the JNDI interface. They then make use of the EJB container to invoke EJB bean methods.

Other Auxiliary Systems

Other auxiliary systems that are available to EJB systems are the Java Naming and Directory Interface (JNDI), which allows EJB clients to find EJB beans, and the Java Transaction Service (JTS) that provides transaction support in an EJB environment. See Chapter 3 to learn more about JNDI and JTS.

Types of Enterprise JavaBeans

An enterprise bean is a building block that can be used alone or with other enterprise beans to build a larger application. The essential characteristics of enterprise beans are as follows:

- EJBs contain business logic.
- EJB instances are created dynamically at runtime. An EJB container at runtime manages these instances.
- EJBs can be customized at deployment time. This is done simply by editing some of the entries in the deployment descriptor file.

There are three types of enterprise beans:

- A session object
- An entity object
- A message-driven object

Session Beans

A *session* bean is an object that is used by a single client and is not shared between several clients. The EJB specification refers to a session bean as "... a logical extension of the client program that runs on the server." Session beans have the following characteristics:

- They represent a transient conversation with a single client and execute on behalf of this single client. Note that a client initiates a conversation with a session bean when it invokes a method of a bean class.
- They are relatively short-lived; that is, their life is associated with the life of the client that uses them.
- They can be transactional; that is, they can be used to manipulate data in a database. For example, the OC4J EJB server allows you to write session beans that can retrieve, insert, update, and remove data in relational tables as well as in tables of objects. Moreover, a bean's class that implements business logic can call Java stored procedures, SQLJ stored procedures, and PL/SQL procedures and functions, and execute embedded dynamic (JDBC) and static SQL (SQLJ) statements.

Types of Session Beans: STATELESS and STATEFUL

At deployment time, a session bean is specified as having either a `STATELESS` or a `STATEFUL` state management mode. A session bean is said to be `STATELESS` when the bean can be used by any client (moreover, its state is not retained across methods and transactions), or `STATEFUL` when the session bean does retain its state. A `STATELESS` session bean is referred to as a bean that contains no conversational state, whereas a `STATEFUL` session bean contains a conversational state. See Chapter 6 to learn how to build session beans and deploy them in OC4J.

Entity Beans

An *entity* bean is a long-lived object that can be accessed from session to session and can be shared by multiple clients. Entity beans have the following characteristics:

- They represent data from persistent storage devices such as a database. Since data in databases is sharable (that is, accessible at the same time by multiple concurrent users), entity beans allow shared access from multiple users.
- They are transactional. Entity beans allow developers to write applications that atomically update data that reside in databases. A nice feature of Enterprise JavaBeans (session or entity beans) is that transaction management is no longer a developer's concern. Note that Enterprise JavaBeans live in an EJB container, and a container runs in an EJB server. The EJB server and the EJB container control transaction management.
- They are persistent and therefore survive crashes of the EJB server and do not die when clients die or disconnect from the database. As long as the data remains in the database, the entity bean exists. The model can be used for relational, object-relational, or object-oriented databases.
- The entity, its primary key, and its remote reference survive the crash of the EJB container.

Types of Entity Beans: BMP and CMP

Recall that entity beans are server-side components that are persistent and transactional. The EJB specification defines two types of entity beans:

- **Bean-managed persistent (BMP) entity bean** A bean that can manage its own persistent state in a persistent storage (for example, in a database) and its own relationships.
- **Container-managed persistent (CMP) entity bean** A bean whose persistent data is managed by an EJB container. Note that container-managed persistence has changed significantly in EJB 2.0 from the earlier releases.

In EJB 2.0, multiple CMP entity beans can have container-managed relationships (CMRs) among themselves. The automatic management of relationships and the container management of the referential integrity of relationships allow developers to expose only an entity bean's instance state through its remote interface. The EJB 2.0 specification also introduces a query language called EJB Query Language, or EJB QL, which defines query methods (that is, `FINDER` and `SELECT` methods) for entity beans with container-managed persistence. For upward compatibility, EJB 2.0 also continues to support EJB 1.1-style entity beans. See Chapter 5 to learn how to build BMP and CMP entity beans and deploy them to OC4J.

Message-Driven Beans

A *message-driven* bean is a special EJB component that can receive JMS messages. It is an asynchronous message consumer. A message-driven bean consumes messages from queues or topics that are sent by JMS clients. Message queues retain all messages sent to them until the messages are consumed or until the messages expire. In a publish/subscribe (pub/sub) product or application, clients address messages to a topic. Topics retain messages only as long as it takes to distribute them to current subscribers. In Chapter 7, you'll learn how to develop message-driven beans.

A message-driven bean has the following characteristics:

- Executes upon receipt of a single client message.
- Is invoked asynchronously.
- Can be transaction-aware.
- May update shared data in an underlying database.
- Does not represent directly shared data in a permanent storage (for example, a database). Message-driven beans can access and update data residing in a database.
- Relatively short-lived.
- Stateless like a stateless session bean.
- Dies (that is, is removed) when the EJB container crashes.

The goal of this book is to teach you how to create simple enterprise beans and deploy them in the OC4J. To learn more about enterprise beans, see *Mastering Enterprise JavaBeans and the Java2 Platform Enterprise Edition* by Ed Roman (Wiley Computer Publishing, 2002) and *Enterprise JavaBeans*, Third Edition, by Richard Monson-Haefel (O'Reilly, 2001).

Client Views of Enterprise JavaBeans

Client programs access session or entity beans through the bean's home and component interfaces. In the EJB specification, releases 1.0 and 1.1, the client had to be a remote client. Starting with EJB 2.0, an EJB client may be a remote client or a local client.

Client View of Session and Entity Beans

The specification now separates clients that access an EJB into two types:

- **Remote clients** Can reside in a different virtual machine than the EJB container.
- **Local clients** Are collocated in the same virtual machine with the EJB container.

Note that the concepts of remote and local client views do not apply to message-driven beans. A client accesses a message-driven bean through JMS by sending messages to the JMS destination (queue or topic). A message-driven bean does not have a home interface, local home interface, remote interface, or local interface.

Remote Clients

EJB remote clients access an enterprise bean via the bean's remote interface and remote home interfaces. The remote interface and remote home interfaces are Java Remote Invocation Method (RMI) interfaces. At deployment time, the EJB container provides classes that implement the bean's remote and remote home interfaces.

One advantage of using remote clients is that the client view of remote Java objects is location independent. That is, clients running in JVMs can be distributed over any network and are able to invoke EJBs that are running in JVMs other than the clients that are using them. Remote objects are passed by remote reference. Other objects (arguments to methods) would be passed by value. A remote reference is a remote interface implemented by a distributed object stub. You will learn about stubs in the "Remote Calls vs. Local Calls" section of this chapter.

Local Clients

Unlike the remote clients, the local client view of enterprise beans is not location independent. Local enterprise beans can only be accessed by local clients—that is, beans that are running in the client's JVM.

EJB local clients access a session or an entity bean via the bean local interface and local home interface. Like the remote session or entity bean, the EJB container provides classes that implement the local interface and the local home interface. Note that local clients that access the local home or local interface of an EJB are granted optimized access by bypassing RMI semantics in favor of direct method invocation.

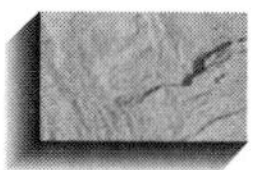

NOTE
Throughout this book, the terms "remote interface" and "home interface" refer to the RMI interfaces, whereas the terms "local interface" and "local home interface" refer to local enterprise beans (that is, beans that are running in the client's JVM).

Client View of Message-Driven Beans

To a client, a message-driven bean is simply a JMS message consumer. The concepts of remote/local interface or remote/local home interface no longer exist. JMS clients send messages to queues or topics (message destination), and then the message-driven bean, like any other JMS message consumer, handles the processing of the messages. Like session and entity beans, a client locates the JMS destination associated with a message-driven bean by using JNDI.

Components of an EJB Application

A component model defines a set of interfaces and classes (for example, in the form of Java packages) that must be used in a particular way. A component isolates and encapsulates a set of functionality. A component is developed for a specific purpose, not for a specific application, and once it is defined, it becomes an independent piece of software that can be distributed and used in other applications.

Session and Entity Bean Components

An enterprise bean (session or entity) consists of the following components:

- **The home interface or local home interface** A home interface extends the `javax.ejb.EJBHome` interface, whereas a local home interface extends the `javax.ejb.EJBLocalHome` interface. A remote home interface is a Java RMI interface. A remote client running in the same JVM as a bean instance uses the same API to access the bean as a client running in a different JVM on the same or different machine. Unlike the remote home, a local client can only access a local home interface; that is, both clients and local beans must reside in the same JVM.
- **The remote interface or local interface** A remote interface extends the `javax.ejb.EJBObject` interface. The remote and remote home interfaces are Java RMI interfaces. A local interface extends the `javax.ejb.EJBLocalObject` interface. The `javax.ejb.EJBObject` interface defines the operations that allow the client to access the EJB object's identity

and create a persistent handle for the EJB object. The `javax.ejb.EJBLocalObject` interface defines the operations that allow the local client to access the EJB object's identity.

- **The bean class** You may create one or more bean classes for your EJB application.
- **The primary key class** Every entity object has a unique identity within its home. The bean provider must provide the bean's unique identity or primary key. The primary key can be defined in a primary key class or in the `ejb-jar.xml` deployment descriptor file as a simple object using one of the persistent fields. The primary key class of the entity bean defines its identity. The primary key class may be specific to an entity bean class (in other words, each entity bean class may define a different class for its primary key, but it is possible that multiple entity beans may use the same primary key class).
- **The deployment descriptor (`ejb-jar.xml`) file** The deployment descriptor is part of the contract between the `ejb-jar` file producer and consumer. This contract covers both the passing of enterprise beans from the bean provider to the application assembler, and from the application assembler to the deployer.

Message-Driven Bean Components

A message-driven bean does not have a home interface, a local home interface, a remote interface, or a local interface. A message-driven bean does not have any return values and cannot send exceptions back to the client. For example, a message-driven bean must not throw application exceptions or the `java.rmi.RemoteException`.

A message-driven bean consists of the following components:

- A message-driven bean is a Java class that implements two interfaces: `javax.jms.MessageListener` and `java.ejb.MessageDrivenBean`. The message-driven bean class's implementation of the `javax.jms.MessageListener` interface distinguishes the message-driven bean as a JMS message-driven bean. All message-driven beans must implement the `MessageDrivenBean` interface. The container uses the `MessageDrivenBean` methods to notify the enterprise bean instances of the instance's life cycle events.
- A message-driven bean has a single business method, called `onMessage()`. This message accepts a JMS message.

Enterprise Bean Remote and Local Home Interface

When a client needs to use an enterprise bean, it does so via its remote home or local interface. Session or entity beans must have their own EJB remote/local home interface. The remote/local home interface lists methods for creating new beans, removing beans, and finding beans (entity beans, only).

The Remote Home Interface

An enterprise bean's home interface describes how a client program or another enterprise bean creates, finds, and removes an enterprise bean from its container. The EJB remote home interface is a Java RMI interface, whereas the local home interface is not. See Listing 4-1 for a partial definition of the `javax.ejb.EJBHome` interface.

EJB remote home interfaces are Java RMI interfaces. Hence, a remote home interface must follow RMI rules. Some of the RMI rules are as follows:

- Each method must declare `java.rmi.RemoteException` in its **`throws`** clause, in addition to any application-specific exceptions. Note that `java.rmi.RemoteException` is defined in the method signature to provide backward compatibility for enterprise beans written for the EJB 1.0 specification. Enterprise beans written for the EJB 1.1 specification and higher should throw `javax.ejb.EJBException` instead of this exception. `EJBException` extends `java.lang.RuntimeException` and is thrown by an enterprise bean instance to its container to report that the invoked business method or callback method could not be completed because of an unexpected error. A remote object of any Java *serializable* type can be used as an argument or a return value. Method parameters or return values can be Java primitive types, remote Java objects, and non-remote Java objects that implement the `java.io.Serializable` interface. Remember that the `java.io.Serializable` interface is a very important interface for marshaling and unmarshaling Java objects. According to *Oracle9*i *SQLJ Programming* (Oracle Press, 2001), "Marshaling packs a method call's parameters (at a client's space) or return values (at a server's space) into a standard format for transmission. Unmarshaling, the reverse operation, unpacks the standard format to an appropriate data presentation in the address space of a receiving process." Java objects defined as serialized objects are able to restore the contents of the objects that were saved to a new instance. The contents of serializable objects are stored in Java streams (that is, sequences of bytes) with sufficient information for the receiver process to restore the object to a compatible version of its class.

- A remote object passed as an argument or return value (either directly or embedded within a local object) must be declared as the remote interface, not the implementation class.

The home interface is defined as extending the `javax.ejb.EJBHome` interface, which in turn extends the `java.rmi.Remote` interface. Listing 4-1 presents the definition of the `javax.ejb.EJBHome` interface:

Listing 4-1

```
(See Note 1.)
public interface javax.ejb.EJBHome
extends java.rmi.Remote{
  public abstract EJBMetaData getEJBMetaData()
    throws RemoteException; // (See Note 2.)
public HomeHandle getHomeHandle()
    throws RemoteException; // (See Note 3.)
  public abstract void remove(Handle handle)
    throws RemoteException,RemoveException; // (See Note 4.)
public abstract void remove(Object primaryKey)
    throws RemoteException,RemoveException; // (See Note 5.)
}
```

Notes on Listing 4-1:

1. This statement defines the `javax.ejb.EJBHome` interface extending the `java.rmi.Remote` interface.
2. The `EJBMetaData` interface allows the client to obtain information about the enterprise bean. The information obtainable via the `EJBMetaData` interface is used by vendors' tools. All Java methods within a Java class that extends the `java.rmi.Remote` interface must use the `RemoteException` exception in their **`throws`** clause. This exception is thrown when the method fails due to a system-level failure.
3. This method returns a `HomeHandle` object. The `RemoteException` exception is thrown when the method fails due to a system-level failure.
4. This method gets rid of an EJB object identified by its `handle`. The first `RemoteException` exception is thrown if the enterprise bean or the container does not allow the client to delete the object. The second exception is triggered when the method fails due to a system-level failure.
5. This method deletes an EJB object identified by its primary key. The sequence of events to throw the `RemoteException` exception is the same as in Note 3, except that the EJB object is a primary key in a table stored in a database. This method is used only for entity beans.

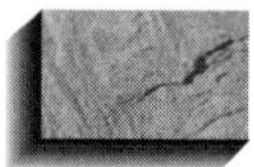

NOTE
See Appendix C for a complete definition of the `EJBHome` interface.

The Local Home Interface

Writing local home and local interfaces is very similar to writing remote and remote home interfaces. They follow the same rules with a few exceptions:

- The **throws** clause of all methods in the local home and local interfaces must not throw `java.rmi.RemoteException`. Local interfaces must throw `EJBException`.
- A local home interface must extend `EJBLocalHome`, unlike remote home interfaces, which extend `EJBHome`.
- A local interface must extend `EJBLocalObject` instead of `EJBObject`.

Listing 4-2 presents the definition of the `javax.ejb.EJBLocalHome` interface:

Listing 4-2

```
public interface javax.ejb.EJBLocalHome {
  // (See Note 1.)
  public void remove (Object primaryKey)
     throws javax.ejb.EJBException,
            javax.ejb.RemoveException;
}
```

Note on Listing 4-2:

1. The `remove()` method destroys an EJB local object based upon a given primary key. This applies only to entity beans. This will also remove the bean data (delete a row in the database) from the underlying persistent storage. Note that the local home interface does not throw `java.rmi.RemoteException`.

Remote Home Requirements

All EJB home interfaces must extend `javax.ejb.EJBHome`. Note that the container vendor must provide the home objects that implement the home and the local interfaces, since only the vendor can implement the code that can act as the factory to create the enterprise beans.

The requirements for an enterprise bean's home interface are as follows:

- The interface must extend the `javax.ejb.EJBHome` interface.

- The arguments and return values of the methods defined in this interface must be Java RMI valid types and their exception specification or **throws** clause must include the `java.rmi.RemoteException` exception. Remember, if you are writing EJB 2.0-compatible beans, you do not need to list `java.rmi.RemoteException` in the **throws** clause of your method. Sun recommends that you use `javax.ejb.EJBException` instead of `java.rmi.RemoteException`.
- A bean's home interface defines one or more `create(...)` methods.
- Each `create()` method must be named "create" and must match one of the `ejbCreate()` methods defined in your bean class. The matching `ejbCreate()` method must have the same number and types of its arguments.
- The return type for a `create()` method must be the enterprise bean's remote interface type.
- All the exceptions defined in the **throws** clause of an `ejbCreate()` method of the enterprise bean class must be defined in the **throws** clause of the matching `create()` method of the remote interface.
- The **throws** clause of the `create()` method must also include the `javax.ejb.CreateException` exception.
- The `findByPrimaryKey (SomePrimaryKeyClass primaryKey)` method is a standard method that all local and remote home interfaces for entity beans must support. This method applies only to entity beans. With container-managed persistence entity beans, implementations of the finder methods are generated automatically at deployment time. Developers of bean-managed persistence must provide the implementation for the finder method in the bean implementation class.

The EJB home interfaces that you define for your enterprise beans must extend the `javax.ejb.EJBHome` interface. Listing 4-3 and Listing 4-4 present a session bean home interface and an entity bean home interface, respectively.

Listing 4-3

```
// (See Note 1.)
public interface VendorHome extends javax.ejb.EJBHome {
  // (See Note 2.)
  Vendor create() throws CreateException, RemoteException;
}
```

Notes on Listing 4-3:

1. This statement declares the `VendorHome` interface that extends the `javax.ejb.EJBHome` interface. Remember that all developers' EJB interfaces must extend the `EJBHome` interface.
2. This statement declares a `create()` method that clients use to create new bean instances or access existing ones. In particular, this method will create an instance of the `Vendor` remote interface. See Chapter 6 for a complete definition of the `Vendor` session bean.

Listing 4-4

```
public interface PurchaseOrderHome extends EJBHome {
    public PurchaseOrder create( long requestNo,
           long employeeNo, long vendorNo )
          throws RemoteException, CreateException;
    // Find a PurchaseOrder using its primary key (PurchaseOrder id)
    public PurchaseOrder findByPrimaryKey(PurchaseOrderPK primaryKey)
          throws RemoteException, FinderException;

    // Optional method that returns a Collection
    // object consisting of a primary key objects
    public Collection findAllPurchases()
          throws RemoteException, FinderException;
 } // End of PurchaseOrderHome
```

Local Home Requirements

The requirements for an enterprise bean's local home interface are as follows:

- The interface must extend the `javax.ejb.EJBLocalHome` interface.
- The local home interface defines one or more `create(...)` methods.
- Each `create()` method must be named "create" and must match one of the `ejbCreate()` methods defined in your bean class. The matching `ejbCreate()` method must have the same number and types of arguments.
- The return type for a `create()` method must be the enterprise bean's local interface type.
- All the exceptions defined in the **throws** clause of an `ejbCreate()` method of the enterprise bean class must be defined in the **throws** clause of the matching `create()` method of the remote interface.
- The **throws** clause of the `create()` method must also include the `javax.ejb.CreateException` exception.

Listing 4-5 presents an example of a local home interface for an entity bean:

Listing 4-5

```
public interface PurchaseOrderLocalHome
     extends EJBLocalHome {
    // Note the absence of RemoteException in the
    // method signatures of the PurchaseOrderLocalHome interface
    public PurchaseOrderLocal create( long requestNo,
          long employeeNo, long vendorNo )
         throws CreateException;

    public PurchaseOrderLocal findByPrimaryKey(PurchaseOrderPK
primaryKey)
         throws FinderException;

    // Optional method that returns a Collection
    // object consisting of a primary key objects
    public Collection findAllPurchases()
         throws FinderException;
 } // End of PurchaseOrderLocalHome
```

See Chapter 5 for a complete definition of the `PurchaseOrderLocal` entity bean. Next, you will learn about EJB remote/local home methods.

Enterprise Bean's Home Interface Methods

The home (local or remote) interface of your enterprise bean (session or entity bean) will contain the following methods:

- One or more `create()` methods, which allow you to create enterprise bean instances. When you write the bean class, you need to define one or more `ejbCreate()` methods. You must declare corresponding `create()` methods with matching signatures to all `ejbCreate()` methods declared in the bean class.
- One or more finder methods (entity beans only). The container must be able to manipulate the primary key type. It does so via finder methods. When you write the bean class, as with the `create()` methods, you must provide corresponding `ejbFind` methods with matching signatures to all finder methods that you declare in the home interface. See Chapters 5 and 6 for complete examples demonstrating how to write a home interface for enterprise beans.

Remember that the EJB container implements the home (local or remote) interface of each enterprise bean installed in the container, and the container makes these interfaces available to the client through JNDI. Consequently, the OC4J EJB container will implement the home interfaces of all enterprise beans that you want to deploy to OC4J.

Enterprise Remote and Local Interface

An EJB remote or local interface advertises every business method that is callable by clients. That is, every method that your beans want to expose to clients. Like a Java interface, the EJB remote/local interface defines the behavior of the EJB component. The behavior is the contract that the object interface offers publicly. A client that wishes to access a bean class method would do so via the EJB remote/local interface.

Remote Interface Requirements

The requirements for the enterprise bean's remote interface are as follows:

- The interface must extend the `javax.ejb.EJBObject` interface.
- The methods defined in this interface must follow the rules for Java RMI interfaces.
- The **throws** clause must include the `java.rmi.RemoteException` exception.
- There must be a matching method for each method defined in the remote interface. The matching method must have:
  - The same name.
  - The same number and types of its arguments, and the same return type.

  All the exceptions defined in the **throws** clause of the matching method of the enterprise bean class must be defined in the **throws** clause of the same method listed in the remote interface.

Local Interface Requirements

The requirements for the enterprise bean's local interface are as follows:

- The interface must extend the `javax.ejb.EJBLocalObject` interface.
- There must be a matching method for each method defined in the remote interface. The matching method must have:
  - The same name.

- The same number and types of its arguments, and the same return type.

  All the exceptions defined in the **`throws`** clause of the matching method of the enterprise bean class must be defined in the **`throws`** clause of the same method listed in the remote interface.

When clients want to use an instance of an enterprise bean (session or entity) class, they never invoke the method directly on bean instances. A client's invocation is intercepted by the EJB container and then delegated to the bean instance. Thus, the EJB container acts as a layer of indirection (a proxy) between clients and beans. The `EJB object` is a network object that acts like a proxy between the client and a bean instance. Recall that EJB remote interfaces must extend the `javax.ejb.EJBObject` interface (see Listing 4-6 in the upcoming section), whereas EJB local interfaces must extend the `javax.ejb.EJBLocalObject` interface. The bean's methods are called indirectly via the `EJBObject` or the `EJBLocalObject` (see Listing 4-7 in the upcoming section).

Note that the container vendor provides the EJB container, `EJBObject`, and the `EJBLocalObject`. At deployment time, the container generates an `EJBObject` and the `EJBLocalObject` classes. The `EJBObject` implements the remote interface making the `EJBObject` class specific to the bean class, whereas `EJBLocalObject` implements the local interface.

Remote Calls vs. Local Calls

Communications between client-side objects and remote server-side objects are done via *stub* and *skeleton* classes. A *server object* is the business object that resides on the middle tier (for example, OC4J). Every instance of the remote server object is wrapped by an instance of its matching skeleton class. The stub resides on the client side and is connected to the network via the skeleton. Note that remote calls are very slow compared to local calls. But thanks to EJB 2.0, you can call enterprise beans in a faster and more efficient way by calling them via the local objects, provided that you stay in the same JVM.

When you deploy an enterprise bean, the vendor's tool will generate the client and server *stub* classes (see Figure 4-2) for you. In OC4J, the client stubs are automatically generated when you deploy your beans to the application server.

EJB clients use the client stub class to invoke remotely EJB objects. The client stub acts as a proxy to the server stub, and the server stub is a proxy to the actual object's method. A client first does a lookup for a home server object reference, gets a reference to the remote object, and then invokes methods on the bean object as if the bean object resided in the client's address space. At client lookup time, the client proxy packs the call parameters into a request message. The server proxy (server-side skeleton class) unpacks the message.

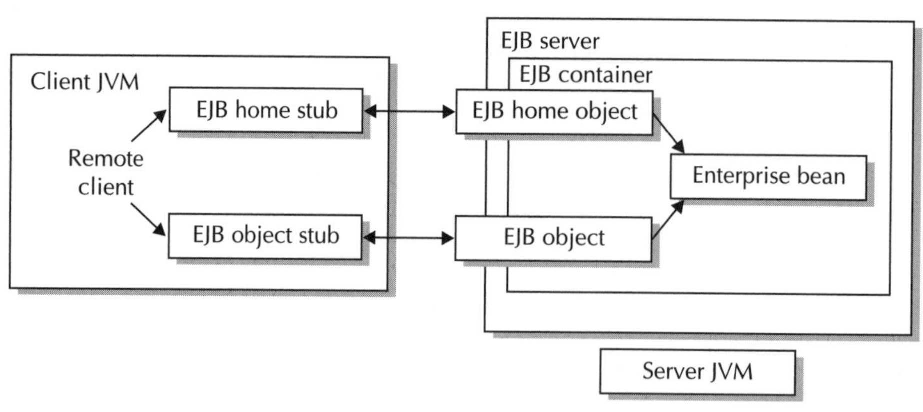

FIGURE 4-2. *Client's communication via client-side and server-side stub and classes*

In EJB 2.0, you can build Enterprise JavaBeans that are collocated in the same virtual machine with the EJB container. Recall that these types of beans are called local beans. Local beans are invoked via their *local objects* rather than via the *EJB objects*. No more client-side stub and server-side skeleton classes, no more marshalling/unmarshalling or serializing/deserializing of parameters. This results in a faster and more efficient way of invoking Enterprise JavaBeans. The local interfaces are optional. However, who would not want to use the local interfaces, specifically if you want to avoid the performance overhead associated with remote objects?

However, if you need to access your beans from clients that are not located in the same JVM as your beans, you may use a remote session bean facade that acts as a wrapper to your local beans. In Chapter 6, you will develop the `PurchaseOrderManagement` session bean, a session facade that can use your local or remote beans.

Listing 4-6 presents the definition of the `EJBObject` interface:

Listing 4-6

```
// (See Note 1.)
Public interface javax.ejb.EJBObject
  extends java.rmi.Remote {
    // (See Note 2.)
    public EJBHome getEJBHome() throws RemoteException;
    // (See Note 3.)
    public Object getHandle () throws RemoteException;
```

```
    // (See Note 4.)
    public void remove()() throws RemoteException;
}
```

Notes on Listing 4-6:

1. This statement defines the `javax.ejb.EJBObject` interface as extending the `java.rmi.Remote` interface. This is a very important interface in the EJB API. Remember that the `EJBObject` and the container work as a pair. Thankfully, the container vendor provides both the container and the `EJBObject` classes. At deployment time, the EJB container will automatically generate the `EJBObject` classes for you. Generating the `EJBObject` classes is a core function of the container.

2. This statement defines the `getEJBHome()` method that returns an `EJBHome` object to the caller. In the "Enterprise Bean Remote and Local Home Interface" section of this chapter, you learned that clients needing the use of Enterprise JavaBeans create them through their home interface. More importantly, a reference to the home object must be placed in a naming service that is accessible from clients using JNDI. At deployment time, OC4J reads the deployment descriptors of the beans and puts the references to the home object of these beans into the JNDI namespace.

3. This statement defines the `getHandle()` method and returns a Java `Object` object to the caller. A `Handle` is an object that identifies an EJB object. Clients that have a reference to an `EJBObject` object can obtain the object's handle by invoking the `getHandle()` method on the reference.

4. This statement defines a `remove()` method that clients and the EJB container use to remove an EJB object.

The container and `EJBObject/EJBLocalObject` objects (see Figure 4-3) collaborate and work together to implement the services required by a container. For example, the container is responsible for transaction management and knows which transaction attributes to apply to a bean's methods, but it is through the `EJBObject/EJBLocalObject` objects that these methods are invoked. See "Transaction Management for EJBs," later in this chapter, to learn more about EJB transaction attributes. In turn, the `EJBObject/EJBLocalObject` objects must communicate with the container to determine in which transaction context to call the business method.

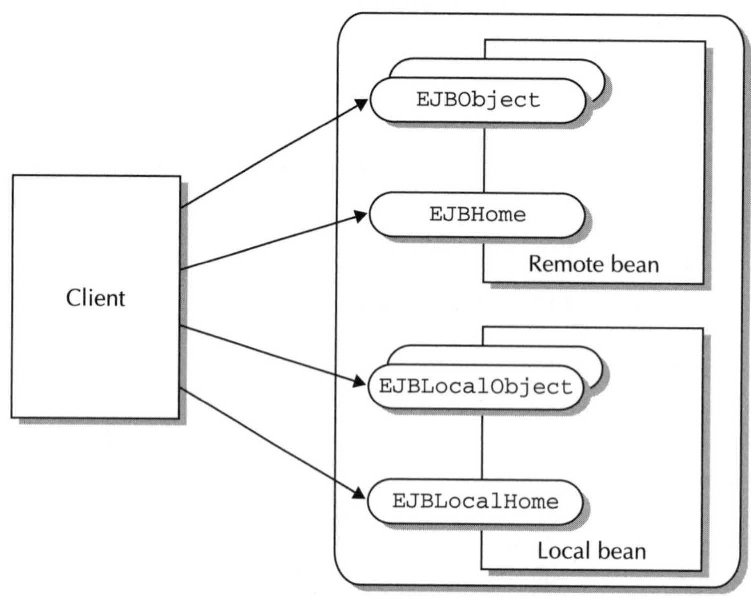

FIGURE 4-3. *EJB container and `EJBObject/EJBLocalObject` collaborate*

Listing 4-7 presents the definition of the `EJBLocalObject` interface:

Listing 4-7

```
public interface EJBLocalObject {
    // Get the enterprise Bean's local home interface.
    public EJBLocalHome getEJBLocalHome()
        throws EJBException;
    // Get the primary key of the EJB local object.
    public java.lang.Object getPrimaryKey()
        throws EJBException;
    // Remove the EJB local object.
    public void remove()
        throws RemoveException,EJBException;
    // Check if a given EJB local object is identical
    // to the invoked EJB local object.
    public boolean isIdentical(EJBLocalObject obj)
        throws EJBException;
} // End of EJBLocalObject interface
```

The `EJBObject` interface must be extended by all session and entity bean remote interfaces, whereas all local entity bean and session bean interfaces must extend the `EJBLocalObject` interface. Consequently, remote interfaces that you develop will extend the `EJBObject` interface and local interfaces will extend the `EJBLocalObject` interface. Listing 4-8 presents a partial listing of the `PurchaseOrder` EJB remote interface:

Listing 4-8

```
// (See Note 1.)
public interface PurchaseOrder extends javax.ejb.EJBObject {
  // (See Note 2.)
  long getRequestNo() throws RemoteException;
  ...
}
```

Notes on Listing 4-8:

1. This statement declares the **`public`** `PurchaseOrder` interface that extends the `javax.ejb.EJBObject` interface.
2. This statement declares a method that returns a Java `long` object to the caller. This method must match exactly the bean class method.

Enterprise Bean's Remote Interface Methods

Method signatures, whose implementations reside in an enterprise bean class, must be listed in the EJB remote interface if you want clients to be able to invoke them. These methods match exactly the methods implemented in the bean class. Clients that use Enterprise JavaBeans do not have direct access to the bean object. That is, the methods of your bean will never be invoked directly from the client.

Enterprise Beans Class

A bean class is a body of code with fields and methods that implements some enterprise business logic. A bean class lives in an EJB container and runs on the server (application or database server). It is a Java class that conforms to a well-defined interface and obeys certain rules. These rules allow your beans to run in any EJB container.

The EJB specification defines several standards that a bean class must implement. All EJB implementation classes implement the `javax.ejb.EnterpriseBean` interface, shown in Listing 4-9. Additionally, session beans, entity beans, and message-driven beans each have more specific interfaces that extend the `javax.ejb.EnterpriseBean` interface. Session beans must implement the `javax.ejb.SessionBean` interface; entity beans must implement the `javax.ejb.EntityBean` interface; and message-driven beans must implement the `javax.ejb.MessageDrivenBean` and the `javax.MessageListener` interfaces. Recall that EJB context contains callbacks useful for session beans, entity beans, and message-driven beans. There is a different context interface for each EJB type. However, all EJB context interfaces implement `javax.ejb.EJBContext`. For example:

- The `javax.ejb.SessionContext` interface is a specific EJB context used only for session beans.
- The `javax.ejb.EntityContext` interface is a specific EJB context used only for entity beans.
- The `javax.ejb.MessageDrivenContext` interface is a specific EJB context used only for message-driven beans.

Although there are no hard-written rules in EJB, session bean, entity bean, and message-driven bean classes are typically used in different ways, as described next.

A session bean class contains business-process-flow logic. For example, session bean classes model business logic that performs a purchase order entry or raises an employee salary. A session bean class must fill some standard callback methods. For example, developers of session beans need to implement the EJB container callbacks defined in the `javax.ejb.SessionBean` interface, and optionally the `javax.ejb.SessionSynchronization` interfaces. The EJB container will call these methods appropriately to manage the session bean.

An entity bean class contains data-related logic. It maps to an entity definition in a database schema. Recall that an entity bean is a long-lived object that resides in a persistent storage. For example, entity bean classes model logic that manipulates data in a database. Another important feature to all entity beans is the primary key class. Recall that the primary key of a record in a database table uniquely identifies that record. Like a primary key of a table in a database, the primary class of an entity bean uniquely identifies that bean. Also, note that the primary class of an entity bean maps the primary key of a record in a persistent storage. Like a session bean class, the EJB specification also requires that an entity bean class provide some standard callback methods. For example, developers of entity beans must implement the EJB container callbacks defined in the `javax.ejb.EntityBean` interface. In Chapter 6, you will build entity beans to insert, update, and delete data that resides in an Oracle9*i* database.

A message-driven bean class contains message-oriented logic. For example, a message-driven bean will receive messages and may call session beans to perform specific tasks.

Listing 4-9 presents the definition of the `javax.ejb.EnterpriseBean` interface:

Listing 4-9

```
Public interface javax.ejb.EnterpriseBean
     extends java.io.Serializable (
}
```

Listing 4-10 shows the definition of the `javax.ejb.SessionBean` interface:

Listing 4-10

```
// (See Note 1.)
public interface javax.ejb.SessionBean
  extends javax.ejb.EnterpriseBean {
    // (See Note 2.)
    public void ejbActivate()
       throws EJBException, java.rmi.RemoteException;
    // (See Note 3.)
    public void ejbPassivate()
       throws EJBException, java.rmi.RemoteException;
    // (See Note 4.)
    public void ejbRemove()
       throws EJBException, java.rmi.RemoteException;
    // (See Note 5.)
    public void setSessionContext(SessionContext ctx)
       throws EJBException, java.rmi.RemoteException;
}
```

Notes on Listing 4-10:

1. This statement declares the Java public `javax.ejb.SessionBean` interface that extends the `javax.ejb.EnterpriseBean` interface. Every bean class must implement the `EnterpriseBean` interface, which extends the `java.io.Serializable` interface, a very important interface for transporting (marshaling and unmarshaling) Java objects over networks.

2. This statement declares the `ejbActivate()` method. This method is called when the instance is activated from its "passive" state. Note that the temporary transfer of the state of an idle session bean to some form of secondary storage is called *passivation,* and the transfer back is called *activation.* At activation time, the EJB instance will acquire any resource that it had released earlier with the `ejbPassivate()` method.

3. This statement declares the `ejbPassivate()` method. This method is called before the instance enters the "passive" state. It will release any resource that it can reacquire later in the `ejbActivate()` method.

4. This statement declares the `ejbRemove()` method. A container invokes this method before it ends the life of a session object to release system resources and destroy a bean instance at the client's request.

5. This statement declares the `setSessionContext (SessionContext ctx)` method. The container uses this method to store a reference to the context object in a variable. This method is called at a bean's creation.

Listing 4-11 provides the definition of the `javax.ejb.SessionContext` interface:

Listing 4-11

```
// (See Note 1.)
public interface javax.ejb.SessionContext
  extends javax.ejb.EJBContext {
    public abstract EJBObject getEJBObject();
}
```

Note on Listing 4-11:

1. The EJB container provides the bean instances with a `SessionContext` interface class that consists of several methods that allow a client to manipulate `SessionContext` instances maintained by the container. JNDI contexts and EJB `SessionContexts` have no relation with each other; the session context is used to interact with the EJB container, and the JNDI context represents the nodes (directories) in the JNDI namespace. The notion of a context (JNDI), defined by the Context package, is the core interface for clients to look up, bind, unbind, and rename EJB objects, as well as create and destroy sub-contexts.

The definition of the `EntityBean` interface is shown in Listing 4-12:

Listing 4-12

```
public interface javax.ejb.EntityBean
     extends javax.ejb.EnterpriseBean{
   public void ejbActivate()
      throws EJBException, java.rmi.RemoteException;
   public void ejbLoad()
      throws EJBException, java.rmi.RemoteException;
   public void ejbPassivate()
```

```
      throws EJBException, java.rmi.RemoteException;
   public void ejbRemove()
      throws EJBException, java.rmi.RemoteException;
   public void ejbStore()
      throws EJBException, java.rmi.RemoteException;
   public void setEntityContext(EntityContext ctx)
      throws EJBException, java.rmi.RemoteException;
   public void unsetEntityContext()
      throws EJBException, java.rmi.RemoteException;
}
```

Listing 4-13 presents the definition of the `javax.ejb.MessageDrivenBean` interface:

Listing 4-13

```
public interface javax.ejb.MessageDrivenBean
     extends java.ejb.EnterpriseBean {
   public void ejbRemove() throws EJBException;
   public setMessageDrivenContext
     (MessageDrivenContext ctx) throws EJBException;
}
```

The definition of the `javax.jms.MessageListener` is shown in Listing 4-14:

Listing 4-14

```
Public interface java.jms.MessageListener {
   // The only business method that a
   // message-driven bean must implement
   public void onMessage(Message message);
}
```

Listing 4-15 provides the definition of the `MessageDrivenBean` interface:

Listing 4-15

```
public interface javax.ejb.MessageDrivenBean
     extends javax.ejb.EnterpriseBean{

   // The container invokes this method
   // before it removes a message-driven bean
   public void ejbRemove() throws EJBException;

   // Set the associated messaged-driven context
   public void setMessageDrivenContext(MessageDrivenContext ctx)
       throws EJBException;
}
```

Enterprise JavaBeans Deployment Descriptor

In the earlier "Enterprise JavaBeans Roles" section of this chapter, you learned about the deployer's role. Remember that the deployer is responsible for taking the EJB interfaces, classes, and their supporting classes and installing them in the EJB server. A deployer addresses issues such as runtime linkage information (for example, the EJB server namespace and the name of your database server) that clients use to access the database. As a bean developer, you may be required to deploy the Enterprise JavaBeans that you develop. In this book, you will acquire the skills to do so through a good understanding of Enterprise JavaBeans and the characteristics of their runtime environment.

Deployment descriptors allow you to describe and customize runtime attributes—runtime behaviors of server-side components (for example, security, transactional context, and so on)—without having to change the bean class or its interfaces. A deployment descriptor can define one or multiple enterprise beans. In EJB 1.0, the deployment descriptor was a text-based file. Starting with EJB 1.1, the descriptor is XML based.

After you create the interface classes and the bean class for your enterprise bean, you need to create a deployment descriptor file for it. The deployment descriptor acts as a property sheet (a file) in which you list the runtime and security requirements of the bean as well as transaction management associated with your bean.

Use a deployment descriptor to specify the following:

- **Bean management and lifecycle requirements** These requirements indicate how the EJB container should manage the beans.
- **Persistence requirements** These requirements apply only to entity beans and inform the container whether the bean handles its persistence on its own or needs the container to handle the persistence for the bean.
- **Transaction requirements** When you build an EJB application, you can define the transaction requirements of the beans in the code itself or you can specify transaction settings in the deployment descriptor.
- **Security requirements** Deployment descriptor files contain access control entries that the beans and container use to enforce access to certain operations. Here, you can specify who is allowed to use the beans, the methods of the beans, and security roles.

At deployment time, additional classes are generated and are needed internally by the EJB container. The container vendor will provide you with the correct tool to deploy your Enterprise JavaBeans. The additional classes generated at deployment time allow the EJB container to manage enterprise beans at runtime. In the

"Transaction Management for EJBs" section of this chapter, you will learn how an EJB container controls transaction management via transaction attributes specified in a deployment descriptor file. Deployment of a bean consists of the installation of one or more `ejb-jar` files as well as the assignment of properties, runtime parameters, and security constraints for the beans. These additional classes are generated automatically by OC4J.

Throughout this book, as you develop more EJB components, you will learn how to list your bean's transaction and security requirements in the deployment descriptor file. Your vendor may provide the tool to create this file or you may use another vendor's tool to do so. For example, the Oracle9*i* JDeveloper tool allows you to create Enterprise JavaBeans through its EJB wizard. When you use the tool to create your EJB component, it will automatically create a deployment descriptor file for you.

ejb-jar File

Once the deployment descriptor is complete and saved to a file, the bean can be packaged in a JAR (Java archive) file for deployment. The JAR file, called `ejb-jar`, consists of the EJB interfaces (remote or local home and remote or local interface), classes, their dependent classes, the primary key class if the bean is an entity bean, the environment properties, and the deployment descriptor for Enterprise JavaBeans. The EJB specification defines the format of the `ejb-jar` file. The `ejb-jar` file is a standard format used by the EJB tool to "package" Enterprise JavaBeans. EJB files are packaged for deployment. Note that the bean provider or the application assembler is responsible for creating the `ejb-jar` file. You can create the `ejb-jar` file using the `jar` command-line tool or any J2EE-compliant tool such as Oracle9*i* JDeveloper, Rational Rose, or TogetherSoft.

Transaction Management for EJBs

One of the nice features of the EJB framework is that transaction management is no longer a developer's responsibility. The burden of managing transactions is shifted from the beans' providers to the EJB server and container. Therefore, the EJB server and container vendors (vendors that implement the EJB specification) provide transaction management. The EJB container and server implement the necessary low-level transaction protocols, such as the two-phase commit protocol between a transaction manager and a database system or JMS provider, transaction context propagation, and distributed two-phase commit. When you develop enterprise beans for the Oracle9*i* Application Server, the OC4J EJB server and container will manage the beans' transactions for you.

Support for Transaction

Enterprise JavaBeans allow bean providers to develop applications that access and manipulate data in a single database and distributed databases (multiple databases that live anywhere on a network). More importantly, the site location may use EJB servers and containers from several different vendors implementing the same EJB specification. In EJB 2.0, the EJB architecture requires that the EJB container support the JTA API and the connector APIs. To learn more about JTA, see Chapter 3 and http://java.sun.com/products/jta/.

The Java Transaction API (JTA) is a specification of the interfaces between a transaction manager and the other parties involved in a distributed transaction processing system, such as the application programs, the resource managers, and the application server.

A JTA transaction is a transaction managed and coordinated by the J2EE platform. A J2EE product is required to support JTA transactions according to the transaction requirements defined in the J2EE specification. Consequently, J2EE-compliant application servers must support JTA.

The Java Transaction Service (JTS) specifies the implementation of a transaction manager that supports JTA and implements the Java mapping of the OMG Object Transaction Service (OTS) 1.1 specification. JTS propagates transactions using IIOP. Note that the EJB architecture does not require the EJB container to support the JTS interfaces. The JTS API is intended for vendors who implement transaction-processing infrastructure for enterprise middleware. For example, an EJB server vendor may use a JTS implementation as the underlying transaction manager.

The connector architecture is a standard API for connecting the J2EE platform to enterprise information systems, such as enterprise resource planning, mainframe transaction processing, and database systems. The architecture defines a set of scalable, secure, and transactional mechanisms that describe the integration of enterprise information systems with an EJB server and enterprise applications. Refer to Chapters 1 and 2 to learn more about the J2EE connector architecture and OC4J connector support, respectively.

With bean-managed transaction demarcation, the enterprise bean code demarcates transactions using the `javax.transaction.UserTransaction` interface. However, with container-managed transaction demarcation, the container demarcates transactions per instructions provided by the application assembler in the deployment descriptor. These instructions, called *transaction attributes,* tell the container how to handle the beans' transaction environment.

The Enterprise JavaBeans architecture supports flat transactions. A flat transaction cannot have any child (nested) transactions. A flat transaction is a series of operations that are performed atomically as a single unit of work. A successful transaction is committed, while a failed transaction is aborted. The EJB architecture does not support nested transactions.

When you write the deployment descriptor for an enterprise bean, you can specify the transaction attribute value to instruct the container how to manage the bean's transactions. The EJB specification defines the following transaction attribute values:

- `NOTSUPPORTED`
- `REQUIRED`

- SUPPORTS
- REQUIREDNEW
- MANDATORY
- NEVER

Note that, for message-driven beans, only the REQUIRED and NOTSUPPORTED transaction attributes may be used. See Chapters 5, 6, and 7 to learn how to list transaction attributes in deployment descriptor files. In the remainder of this chapter, you will learn how OC4J supports transactions and, more importantly, how OC4J supports EJB.

OC4J Transactional Support

OC4J supports different types of transactions:

- **Declarative transactions** Used in container-managed persistent beans and called container-managed transactions.
- **Programmatic transactions** Used in bean-managed persistent beans and called bean-managed transactions.
- **EJB transactional attributes** Such as REQUIRED, REQUIREDNEW, SUPPORTS, NOTSUPPORTED, and NEVER.
- **Transaction isolation** Such as READ_COMMITTED and SERIALIZABLE are directly supported in the Oracle database.
  - **READ_UNCOMMITTED** No isolation but guarantees better performance.
  - **READ_COMMITTED** Solves dirty read problems.
  - **REPEATABLE_READ** Solves dirty read and repeatable-read problems.
  - **SERIALIZABLE** Solves dirty read, repeatable-read, and phantom problems
- **Concurrency control** Pessimistic and optimistic concurrency control. In optimistic concurrency control, lock is acquired only at the time of committing the transaction, whereas in pessimistic concurrency control, lock is acquired for the entire duration of the transaction. Concurrency control can be specified in the <entity-deployment> tag of the orion-ejb-jar.xml file.

OC4J J2EE EJB Support

The OC4J EJB container provides the following:

- **Support for EJB 1.1 and 2.0** Full support for session beans, entity beans (BMP and CMP), message-driven beans, and object-relational (O-R) mapping. Object-relational mapping products integrate object programming language capabilities with relational databases. OC4J supports one-to-one and one-to-many object-relational mappings. OC4J contains the following features:
  - **Simple O-R mapping** Mapping fields of an entity bean to a corresponding database table. Additionally, users can specify O-R mappings between EJBs.
  - **Complex O-R mappings** OC4J includes an O-R mapping system that allows complex object models to be mapped to database tables. Specifically, it allows the following types of fields to be mapped within entity beans:
    - Simple objects and primitives such as `INT` or `CHAR`.
    - Compound objects.
    - Serializable objects such as `BLOB` and `CLOB`.
    - Entity references. For example, references to another entity bean.
    - Collections.
    - An isolation layer that captures the SQL that is automatically code-generated. This feature allows the CMP facilities to target Oracle and non-Oracle databases.
    - Toplink certification for CMP O-R mapping.
- **Dynamic EJB stub generation for remote beans** At deployment time, the OC4J EJB container generates EJB stubs for you.
- **Full EAR file-based deployment** OC4J provides the following tools to:
  - Deploy the EAR file, using a deployment tool, to one or more OC4J instances. This tool supports cluster deployment as well.

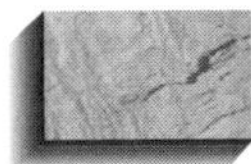

NOTE
For OC4J stand-alone, Oracle provides the `admin.jar` tool, which does not support clustering. In any other installation of Oracle9i Application Server (Oracle9iAS), Oracle provides the Oracle Enterprise Manager tool and the command-line tool `dcmctl` for deployment. Oracle9iAS supports cluster deployment as well.

- **Simplified and automatic deployment of EJB applications** OC4J supports application server-specific deployment information in the following ways:
  - **Auto-deployment** The Oracle-specific deployment information is automatically generated when the EAR file is deployed on the server.
  - **Simplified configuration customizing** Any Oracle-specific configuration information can be customized by manually editing a set of XML configuration files. These include settings for auto-create and auto-delete tables for CMP, security role mappings, JNDI namespace access, session persistence and time-out settings, transaction-retry settings, CMP and O-R mappings, buffering, character sets, locales, virtual directories, cluster configuration, session-tracking, and development and debugging mode settings.
  - **Hot deployment** Once an application has been deployed, module changes do not require redeployment or the restart of OC4J. The user simply edits the `server.xml` configuration file. The next time a user accesses the application, the server reads the file and automatically picks up the changes.

In this chapter, you learned the following:

- The elements of the Enterprise JavaBeans specification.
- The components of the EJB architecture.
- The types of Enterprise JavaBeans: session beans, entity beans, and message-driven beans.
- Client views of Enterprise JavaBeans.
- The components of an EJB application.
- The EJB deployment descriptor.
- The `ejb-jar` file.

- The transaction management for EJBs.
- OC4J transactional support.
- OC4J EJB support.

In Chapter 5, you will learn how to create entity beans that manipulate data stored in Oracle8*i* and Oracle9*i* databases.

CHAPTER 5

Developing Entity Beans

In the Introduction of this book, we presented two use case specifications: the Purchase Order System and the Manage Employee use cases. In this chapter, you will build three entity beans that implement the business logic requirements of these use cases.

In Chapter 4, you learned the elements of the EJB specification, the definition of session beans, entity beans, and message-driven beans. That chapter was meant to give you a good foundation in EJB programming concepts. You may want to review it before proceeding. In this chapter, you will learn how to develop and code two types of EJB components: bean-managed persistent (BMP) entity beans and container-managed persistent (CMP) entity beans. Specifically, you will learn the following:

- How to design the application.
- How to write the components that define an entity bean application.
- How to develop CMP entity beans.
- How to develop BMP entity beans. In this section, you will build a BMP entity bean that uses the `EmployeeTool` SQLJ class to manipulate data in the `EMPLOYEE` table. Refer to Chapter 3 to learn more about the `EmployeeTool` SQLJ class.
- How to write the `ejb-jar.xml` deployment descriptor for entity beans.
- How to write the `orion-ejb-jar.xml` OC4J-specific deployment descriptor for entity beans.
- How to deploy EJB components to OC4J.

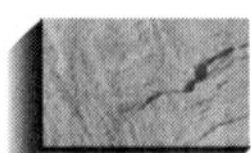

NOTE
In this chapter and in the remainder of the book, we will deploy and run applications in OC4J stand-alone mode. A stand-alone installation of OC4J provides a single instance of the application server.

The Application Design

In this chapter, you will build three entity beans: the `LineItemLocal` CMP bean, the `PurchaseOrderLocal` CMP bean, and the `EmployeeLocal` BMP bean. The high-level view of the `LineItemLocal` CMP bean and the `PurchaseOrderLocal` CMP bean is shown in Figure 5-1, and the high-level view of the `EmployeeLocal` BMP bean is shown in Figure 5-2.

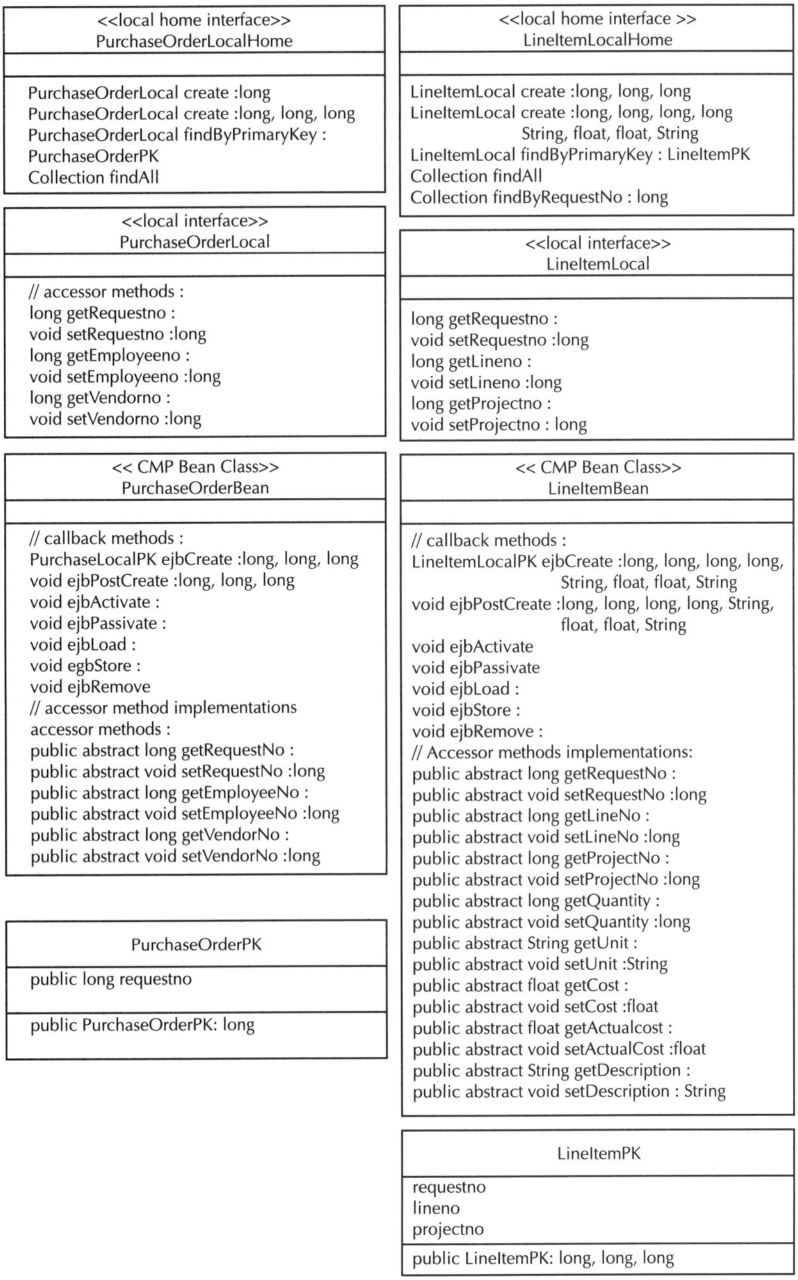

<<local home interface>>
PurchaseOrderLocalHome

PurchaseOrderLocal create :long
PurchaseOrderLocal create :long, long, long
PurchaseOrderLocal findByPrimaryKey :
PurchaseOrderPK
Collection findAll

<<local interface>>
PurchaseOrderLocal

// accessor methods :
long getRequestno :
void setRequestno :long
long getEmployeeno :
void setEmployeeno :long
long getVendorno :
void setVendorno :long

<< CMP Bean Class>>
PurchaseOrderBean

// callback methods :
PurchaseLocalPK ejbCreate :long, long, long
void ejbPostCreate :long, long, long
void ejbActivate :
void ejbPassivate :
void ejbLoad :
void egbStore :
void ejbRemove
// accessor method implementations
accessor methods :
public abstract long getRequestNo :
public abstract void setRequestNo :long
public abstract long getEmployeeNo :
public abstract void setEmployeeNo :long
public abstract long getVendorNo :
public abstract void setVendorNo :long

PurchaseOrderPK

public long requestno

public PurchaseOrderPK: long

<<local home interface >>
LineItemLocalHome

LineItemLocal create :long, long, long
LineItemLocal create :long, long, long, long
String, float, float, String
LineItemLocal findByPrimaryKey : LineItemPK
Collection findAll
Collection findByRequestNo : long

<<local interface>>
LineItemLocal

long getRequestno :
void setRequestno :long
long getLineno :
void setLineno :long
long getProjectno :
void setProjectno : long

<< CMP Bean Class>>
LineItemBean

// callback methods :
LineItemLocalPK ejbCreate :long, long, long, long,
String, float, float, String
void ejbPostCreate :long, long, long, long, String,
float, float, String
void ejbActivate
void ejbPassivate
void ejbLoad :
void ejbStore :
void ejbRemove :
// Accessor methods implementations:
public abstract long getRequestNo :
public abstract void setRequestNo :long
public abstract long getLineNo :
public abstract void setLineNo :long
public abstract long getProjectNo :
public abstract void setProjectNo :long
public abstract long getQuantity :
public abstract void setQuantity :long
public abstract String getUnit :
public abstract void setUnit :String
public abstract float getCost :
public abstract void setCost :float
public abstract float getActualcost :
public abstract void setActualCost :float
public abstract String getDescription :
public abstract void setDescription : String

LineItemPK

requestno
lineno
projectno

public LineItemPK: long, long, long

FIGURE 5-1. *High-level view of the `LineItemLocal` and `PurchaseOrderLocal` CMP beans*

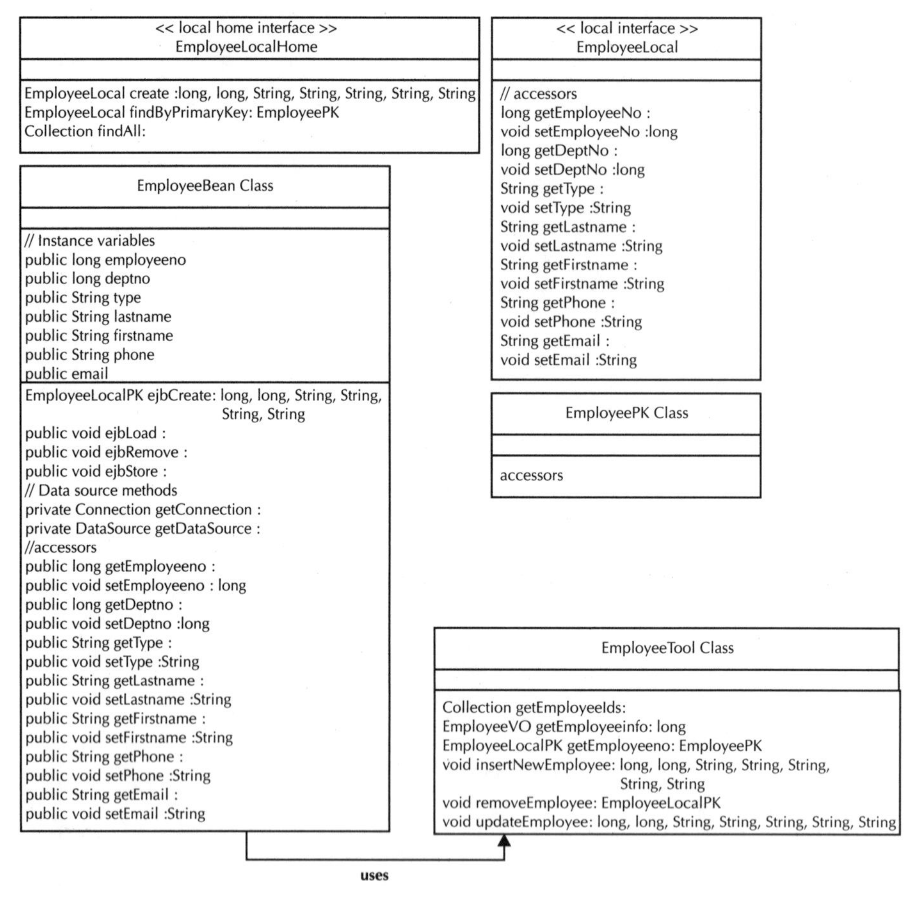

FIGURE 5-2. *High-level view of the `EmployeeLocal` BMP bean*

Defining Entity Bean Components

Entity beans are persistent, allow shared access, have primary keys, and can participate in relationships with other entity beans. The enterprise bean class of an entity bean typically contains data-related logic.

There are two types of entity beans: bean-managed persistent (BMP) entity beans and container-managed persistent (CMP) entity beans. In the first part of this chapter, you will develop two CMP entity beans. In the second part, you will develop one BMP bean. Specifically, you will learn how to build EJB 2.0-compliant entity beans. The EJB 2.0 specification, released in August 2001, is the most recent EJB specification.

Entity Bean Characteristics

Entity beans have the following characteristics:

- They represent data from persistent storage devices, such as a database.
- They are sharable; that is, they allow shared access from multiple users.
- They are transactional. They allow developers to write applications that atomically update data that resides in databases.
- They are persistent and therefore survive. As long as the data remains in the database, the entity bean exists. The model can be used for relational, object-relational, or object-oriented databases. At runtime, the EJB container automatically synchronizes this state with the database. During deployment, the container typically maps the entity bean to a database table and maps the persistent fields to the columns of the table.
- The entity bean, its primary key, and its remote reference survive the crash of the EJB container.

Types of Entity Beans: BMP and CMP

The EJB specification defines two types of entity beans:

- **Bean-managed persistent (BMP) entity bean** A bean that manages its own persistent state in a persistent storage (for example, in a database) and its own relationships.
- **Container-managed persistent (CMP) entity bean** A bean whose persistent data is managed by an EJB container.

The EJB specification provides client-view contracts for entity beans. The client-view contracts are contracts between a client and an EJB container. They provide a uniform development model for applications using enterprise beans as components. The EJB 2.0 specification provides a local client's view to access enterprise beans from local clients. Recall that the remote and remote home interfaces are Java RMI interfaces and thus are accessible from a client through the standard Java RMI APIs. Remote clients reside in a different virtual machine than the EJB container, whereas local clients are collocated in the same virtual machine with the EJB container. When you are developing an entity bean, both the local and remote clients' views must include the following:

- **Interfaces** The remote and home interfaces are required for remote access. For local access, the local and local home interfaces are required.
- **Enterprise bean class** Implements all the methods defined in the remote or local interfaces and the local or remote home interfaces.
- **The primary key class** This class uniquely identifies an entity bean object and is required if the primary key is not made up of a single, simple bean property.
- **Other classes** Additional classes needed by the enterprise bean class, such as value object, JavaBean, exception, and utility classes.
- **Deployment descriptor** An XML file that specifies information about the bean. Recall that deployment descriptors allow you to describe and customize runtime attributes—runtime behaviors of server-side components (for example, security, transactional context, and so on)—without having to change the bean class or its interfaces.

The J2EE application that you will develop in this chapter consists of the following:

- **`LineItemLocal` CMP entity bean** Maps the `LINE_ITEM` table that consists of line item elements for the purchase order requisitions. This CMP bean, along with the `PurchaseOrderLocal` and `EmployeeLocal` CMP beans, consists of code to manipulate business logic.
- **`PurchaseOrderLocal` CMP entity bean** Maps the `PURCHASE_ORDER` table that consists of elements relating to purchase order requisitions.
- **`EmployeeLocal` BMP entity bean** Maps the `EMPLOYEE` table that consists of elements relating to employees.
- **`EmployeeTool` SQLJ class** Implements the business logic that manipulates the `EMPLOYEE` table. This class is tightly coupled with the `EmployeeLocal` BMP entity bean. The `EmployeeTool` object is a dependent object of the `EmployeeLocal` object. Its lifecycle is completely managed by the `EmployeeLocal` object and it can only be accessed indirectly through that object. The `EmployeeTool` SQLJ class provides the necessary methods that an `EmployeeLocal` object uses to insert, update, remove, and query data of the `EMPLOYEE` table.

- **`EmployeeVO` class** A value object (VO)—that is, a business object that is passed by value as a serializable Java object—used by the `EmployeeTool` SQLJ class and the `EmployeeLocal` BMP bean to ship data between themselves. In this chapter, we present a brief discussion on what is a value object. Detailed descriptions of value objects and their use are presented in the "The J2EE Value Object Pattern" section of Chapter 6.

The J2EE Value Object Pattern

As developers design and build different applications, they come across the same or similar problem domains. This leads them to find a solution for the same or similar problem over and over again. Using design patterns can diminish the process of reinventing the wheel.

A design pattern prescribes a proven solution for a recurring design problem. Patterns focus on the context of a problem and a solution, thereby guiding the designer in using the design knowledge. *Core J2EE Patterns: Best Practices and Design Strategies,* by Deepak Alur, John Crupi, and Dan Malks, contains a catalog of J2EE patterns. To learn more about J2EE patterns, see http://java.sun.com/blueprints/patterns/j2ee_patterns/index.html. This web site provides a list of useful patterns that you can use when you are designing J2EE applications. The patterns at this Sun site are specifically targeted for use in J2EE.

Use a value object class to group a set of attributes that are "always" used together. The `EmployeeVO` class aggregates the employee information–related attributes of the `EmployeeBean` class into an instance of the `EmployeeVO` class. At the server side, the bean will create instances of the `EmployeeVO` class, serialize the instance, and send it over the network to a requesting client. At the client side, the client object will deserialize instances of the `EmployeeVO` class in order to retrieve information that your server objects would have sent.

NOTE
When using local client interfaces and local calls, there is no real reason to employ this pattern.

When developing a J2EE application, it is recommended that you create a development directory, name it after your application, and develop your application as modules within that directory. All the subdirectories under this directory need to be consistent with the structure for creating JAR, WAR, and EAR archive files. When your development directory is in the required archive format, it is easy to archive the source code and the class files. You can create your development directory structure manually or you can use any J2EE-compliant tool to do so. Some of the J2EE-compliant tools are Oracle9*i* JDeveloper, Rational Rose, and TogetherSoft.

Next, you will create the development directory structure for the J2EE application that you will develop in this chapter.

Creating the Development Directory

The development directory for the application is as follows:

- **chapter05** Root directory of your J2EE application.
    - **META-INF** Directory where your `application.xml` file (and possibly your `orion-application.xml` file) is located, which defines the modules you have in your J2EE application.
    - **src** Directory where all the source files are located.
        - **META-INF** Directory where the `ejb-jar.xml` deployment descriptor file and the `orion-ejb-jar.xml` OC4J-specific deployment descriptor file are located.
        - **purchase** Package indicating the starting point of the `Purchase` application.
            - **ejb** Package consisting of the source code of your EJB components.
                - **bmp** Package consisting of the source code of all your bean-managed persistent (BMP) entity beans.
                - **cmp** Package consisting of the source code of all your container-managed persistent (CMP) entity beans.
            - **util** Package consisting of the source code of your utility classes.
            - **vo** Package consisting of the source code of your value object classes.
        - **webapps** Package consisting of the source code of the testing servlet program.
                - **test** Package.
    - **classes** Root directory for your EJBs: the EJB module.
        - **META-INF** Directory where the `ejb-jar.xml` deployment descriptor file and the `orion-ejb-jar.xml` OC4J-specific deployment descriptor file are located.
        - **purchase** Package indicating the starting point of the Java class files of the `Purchase` application.
            - **ejb** Package consisting of the class files of your EJB components.

        - **bmp** Package consisting of the class files of all your bean-managed persistent (BMP) entity beans.
        - **cmp** Package consisting of the class files of all your container-managed persistent (CMP) entity beans.
      - **util** Package consisting of the class files of your utility classes.
      - **vo** Package consisting of the class files of your value object classes.
- **web** Root directory for your Web module, containing your .jsps, .html pages, and tag libraries.
  - **WEB-INF** Directory where your `web.xml` file is located (and possibly your `orion-web.xml` file).
    - **classes** Starting point for your Web module's classes.
      - **webapps** Package.
        - **test** Package consisting of the class files of your servlets.

Regarding the development directory structure, note the following:

- All Java source code for the EJB module of the Purchase application is located under the `chapter05/src/purchase` directory.
- All Java class files for the EJB module are located under the `chapter05/classes/purchase` directory.
- The Java class file for the Web module is located under the `chapter05/web/WEB-INF/classes/` directory. Remember that you can create the development directory structure manually or use a J2EE-compliant tool. Also, to set up your class files properly at deployment time, you can use the ANT tool from http://jakarta.apache.org/.
- You cannot change the following directory names: `META-INF` and `WEB-INF`. Nor can you change the following XML filenames: `application.xml`, `ejb-jar.xml`, `web.xml`, and `application-client.xml`.
- In Chapter 2, we presented a generic development directory structure. Recall that the directories may contain several separate modules, such as an EJB `<ejb_module>`, a Web `<web_module>`, a client `<client_module>`, or a combination of the three. These modules can have arbitrary names. For example, in the development directory that we presented in the previous section, we named the `<ejb_module>` as follows: `purchase`.

- The top of the module (for example, `chapter05`) represents the start of a search path for classes. Consequently, classes belonging to packages are expected to be located in a nested directory structure beneath this point. For example, the purchase order application that you will develop later in this chapter has the `purchase.ejb.cmp` and `purchase.ejb.bmp` directories. Thus, a reference to the EJB `purchase.ejb.cmp.PurchaseOrderLocal` class is expected to be located in the `purchase/ejb/cmp/ directory`.

For basic applications, you configure the following four XML files:

- **application.xml** This is the manifest for the application. This file must be properly configured and you must include it in the J2EE EAR file that you will create before deploying your application.
- **server.xml and default-web-site.xml** The `server.xml` file contains the configuration for the OC4J application server. It is the root configuration file and contains references to other OC4J configuration files. You register your EJB applications in the OC4J's `server.xml` file, whereas you register your Web application and its context in the OC4J's `http-web-site.xml` file. In the "Deploying EJB Components to OC4J" section of this chapter, you will learn how to register your applications in the `server.xml` file, and then you bind the Web modules of your J2EE application in `http-web-site.xml`. Note that the `server.xml`, `http-web-site.xml`, and `data-sources.xml` files are located under the *`your_OC4J_home_directory`*`/j2ee/home/config` directory. See Chapter 2 and Appendix A to learn about the elements of the `server.xml` and `http-web-site.xml` files.
- **data-sources.xml** J2EE-based applications use `DataSource` objects to access a database. Consequently, if your application needs to access a database, you must configure its `DataSource` objects. You do so by adding the elements specific to your application in the OC4J's `data-sources.xml` file.

Developing Entity Beans: Basic Steps

The basic steps to develop an EJB component are as follows:

- Create the remote/local interface.
- Create the remote/local home interface.
- Create the bean implementation class.

- Create the primary key class.
- Create helper classes, exception classes, and other classes that your application may need.
- Create the deployment descriptor. The `ejb-jar.xml` file is specific to your beans. If your application consists of several beans, you may create one `ejb-jar.xml` file for each of your beans or you may create a single `ejb-jar.xml` file in which you list all beans.
- Create the OC4J-specific deployment descriptor. If you are developing applications to be deployed to OC4J, then you may want to provide an `orion-ejb-jar.xml` file. At deployment time, if you do not create that file, OC4J will generate it for you.

Developing Container-Managed Persistent Beans

A CMP bean is an entity bean that handles all database access required by an entity bean. In contrast to a JDBC program that contains database access code, such as SQL statements, the code that you provide for a CMP bean does not contain any database access. However, code that is created automatically on your behalf by the container (and that is considered part of the container) typically will. The EJB container handles all database storage and retrieval calls and manages the relationships between the entity beans. In the CMP approach, developers do not code the database access calls in the entity bean. Instead, they specify settings in the deployment descriptor of the bean. This approach not only saves development time but, more importantly, also makes the bean portable across various database servers and EJB servers.

The additions in EJB 2.0 over EJB 1.1 principally concern container-managed persistence (CMP). Along with CMP, the EJB 2.0 specification introduces container-managed relationships (CMRs), a query language called EJB Query Language (EJB QL), a new type of enterprise bean, called a message-driven bean, and the notion of local interfaces in addition to the remote interfaces defined in EJB 1.0 and 1.1.

The EJB specification, releases 1.0 and 1.1, defines a remote model that uses remote interfaces. The EJB 2.0 specification builds upon and extends the architecture and functionality defined by the earlier specifications. It offers some significant advantages, especially in terms of greater flexibility. EJB 2.0 allows multiple entity beans to have CMRs among themselves. It does so by introducing a local model, which uses local interfaces. In contrast to the remote model, the local model avoids the performance overhead of the remote model. In this chapter, you will develop entity beans using local interfaces. In Chapter 6, you will convert the local interfaces to remote interfaces.

Next, we present the cardinality in container-managed relationships.

Cardinality in Container-Managed Relationships

Relationships in EJB are implemented differently for CMP and for BMP. In BMP, developers must provide the code to manage relationships. In CMP, you declare relationships in the deployment descriptor. At deployment time, the EJB container generates all the relationship code for you. With CMP, you use cardinality to specify how many instances of data can participate in each side of a relationship. There are three types of cardinality:

- **One-to-one (1:1)** Each entity bean instance is related to a single instance of another entity bean.
- **One-to-many (1:N)** An entity bean instance may be related to multiple instances of the other entity bean.
- **Many-to-many (M:N)** The entity bean instances may be related to multiple instances of each other.

Use the `orion-ejb-jar.xml` OC4J-specific deployment descriptor file to define EJB relationships and cardinality. To learn how to describe the relationships, see the "OC4J Object-Relational Mapping of Persistent Fields and Relationships" section later in this chapter.

Next, you will code the `LineItemLocal` CMP entity bean. This bean maps the `LINE_ITEM` table of the *Purchase Order* database schema presented in the Introduction of this book.

Coding the LineItemLocal CMP Bean

Developing EJB components is rather simple. You can write all the Java source code yourself or you can use a J2EE-compliant tool to generate some of the code for you. For example, we use the Oracle9*i* JDeveloper tool to generate some of the code for the application that we present in this chapter. Next, you will develop the `LineItemLocal` CMP bean.

The `LineItemLocal` CMP entity bean consists of the following:

- The `LineItemLocal` local interface.
- The `LineItemLocalHome` local home interface.
- The `LineItemPK` primary key class.
- The `LineItemBean` EJB implementation class.
- The deployment descriptor. In this chapter, we present a single `ejb-jar.xml` file comprised of all the beans that you will develop. See the "The ejb-jar.xml Deployment Descriptor File" section of this

chapter to learn how to write the `ejb-jar.xml` file for the `LineItemLocal` CMP bean.

Next, you will code the `LineItemLocal` local interface. The local interface of a CMP bean advertises the business methods callable by EJB clients. A CMP local interface has the following characteristics:

- It must extend the `javax.ejb.EJBLocalObject` interface. You do not implement the `javax.ejb.EJBLocalObject` interface. At deployment time, the EJB container will generate a local EJB object that implements this interface.
- It defines getter and setter method signatures corresponding to the persistent fields.

The LineItemLocal Local Interface

Here is the definition of the `LineItemLocal` local interface:

```
/*
** Program Name: LineItemLocal.java
**
** Purpose: The Local interface
** of the LineItemLocal CMP bean.
*/
package purchase.ejb.cmp;
import javax.ejb.EJBLocalObject;

public interface LineItemLocal
    extends EJBLocalObject {

  long getRequestNo();

  void setRequestNo(long newRequestNo);

  long getLineNo();

  void setLineNo(long newLineNo);

  long getProjectNo();

  void setProjectNo(long newProjectNo);

  long getQuantity();

  void setQuantity(long newQuantity);

  String getUnit();
```

```
  void setUnit(String newUnit);

  float getCost();

  void setCost(float newCost);

  float getActualCost();

  void setActualCost(float newActualCost);

  String getDescription();

  void setDescription(String newDescription);

} // End of LineItemLocal interface
```

Next, you will code the LineItemLocalHome local home interface. A CMP bean's local home interface has the following characteristics:

- It must extend the `javax.ejb.EJBLocalHome` interface.
- It includes one or more `create()` methods.
- It has the same number and types of arguments as its matching `ejbCreate()` method in the entity bean class.
- It returns the local interface type of the entity bean.
- Its **`throws`** clause includes the exceptions specified by the **`throws`** clause of the corresponding `ejbCreate()` method.
- Its **`throws`** clause contains the `javax.ejb.CreateException` interface.

These rules apply to a finder method:

- Its name begins with find.
- Its return type is the entity bean's local interface type, or a collection of primary key types.
- Its **`throws`** clause contains the `javax.ejb.FinderException` interface.
- Its `findByPrimaryKey` method must be defined in the local home interface. A local home interface may also include other *finder* methods.

For example, the `LineItemLocalHome` local home interface includes the `findByPrimaryKey()`, `findAll()`, and `findByRequestNo()` methods. One of the nice things about OC4J is that the server will automatically generate the finder methods for you. The `findByPrimaryKey()` and `findAll()` methods are two basic finder methods that you will always get when developing your CMP entity beans. However, if you specify a `findBy`*`XX`* in your home interface, where the *`XX`* corresponds to a field in your CMP bean, OC4J will generate that finder method for you. For example, in the `LineItemLocalHome` interface, when you define the `findByRequestNo()` accessor method, OC4J will create that finder method for you. The `findByRequestNo()` accessor method is called an advanced finder method, in contrast to the `findByPrimaryKey()` and `findAll()` methods. In the "Advanced Configuration for Finder Methods" section of this chapter, you will learn how OC4J defines advanced finder methods in CMP entity beans.

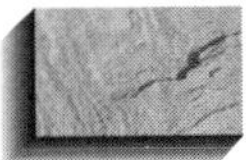

NOTE
You do not *provide the implementation code of the finder methods in your bean implementation class. At deployment time, the EJB container will generate it for you. For example, the EJB container will provide the implementation for the `findByPrimaryKey()`, `findAll()`, and `findByRequestNo()` methods.*

The LineItemLocalHome Local Home Interface

Here is the definition of the `LineItemLocalHome` local home interface:

```
/*
** Program Name: LineItemLocalHome.java
**
** Purpose: The Local Home interface
** of the LineItemLocal CMP bean.
*/
package purchase.ejb.cmp;
import javax.ejb.EJBLocalHome;
import javax.ejb.CreateException;
import javax.ejb.FinderException;
import java.util.Collection;

public interface LineItemLocalHome
   extends EJBLocalHome {
```

```
  LineItemLocal create(long requestNo, long lineNo, long projectNo)
    throws CreateException;

  LineItemLocal create(long requestNo, long lineNo, long projectNo,
                        long quantity, String unit, float cost,
                        float actualCost, String description)
    throws CreateException;

  LineItemLocal findByPrimaryKey(LineItemPK primaryKey)
    throws FinderException;

  Collection findAll() throws FinderException;

  Collection findByRequestNo(long requestNo) throws FinderException;

}  // End of the LineItemLocalHome interface
```

The EJB specification requires that you provide a *primary key* class for all entity beans. The primary key class is a unique identifier that enables the client to locate a specific entity bean. It is possible to use a Java class, such as String or Integer, if that captures the primary key of your bean (which is not possible here, since the primary key in this example consists of three components). See http://otn.oracle.com/docs/products/ias/doc_library/90200doc_otn/web.902/a95881/cmp.htm#1026995 to learn more on how to define primary key classes.

The LineItemPK Primary Key Class

Here is the definition of the `LineItemPK` primary key class:

```
/*
** Program Name: LineItemPK.java
**
** Purpose: The primary key class
** of the LineItemLocal CMP bean.
*/
package purchase.ejb.cmp;
import java.io.Serializable;

public class LineItemPK implements Serializable
{
  public long projectNo;
  public long lineNo;
  public long requestNo;

  public LineItemPK()
  {
  }
```

```
  public LineItemPK(long requestNo, long lineNo, long projectNo)
  {
    this.requestNo = requestNo;
    this.lineNo = lineNo;
    this.projectNo = projectNo;
  }

  public boolean equals(Object other)
  {
    return (other instanceof LineItemPK &&
            this.requestNo==((LineItemPK)other).requestNo &&
            this.lineNo==((LineItemPK)other).lineNo &&
            this.projectNo==((LineItemPK)other).projectNo);
  }

  public int hashCode()
  {
    return (new Long(projectNo)).hashCode()
      ^ (new Long(lineNo)).hashCode()
      ^ (new Long(requestNo)).hashCode();
  }
} // End of LineItemPK class
```

In the EJB 2.0 specification for CMP entity beans, the bean implementation class must be defined as public and abstract. A CMP bean implementation class has the following characteristics:

- It implements the `javax.ejb.EntityBean` interface.
- It includes zero or more `ejbCreate()` and `ejbPostCreate()` methods.
- It includes getter and setter methods for the persistent and relationship fields, which must be defined as `abstract`.
- It may include select methods, which must be defined as `abstract`.
- It includes the home methods.
- It includes the business methods.

The entity bean class must not implement the finder methods or the finalize method.

Defining Getter and Setter Methods

A CMP entity bean has persistent fields and relationships. You do not define class instance variables corresponding to the persistent fields. To allow access to the persistent fields, you define abstract getter and setter methods in the entity bean class. The EJB container automatically performs the database storage and retrieval of the bean's persistent fields. In the LineItemLocal CMP bean, the persistent fields correspond to the attributes of the LINE_ITEM table stored in the Oracle9*i* database. This table is part of the *Purchase Order* schema that we defined in the Introduction of this book. Each instance of the LineItemLocal CMP bean represents a row in the LINE_ITEM table.

The LINE_ITEM Table

Here is the definition of the LINE_ITEM table:

```
CREATE TABLE LINE_ITEM (
requestno NUMBER(10),
lineno NUMBER(5),
projectno NUMBER(5),
quantity NUMBER(5),
unit VARCHAR2(2),
cost NUMBER(8,2),
actualcost NUMBER(8,2),
description VARCHAR2(30))
```

In the deployment descriptor of the LineItemLocal bean, you need to declare the persistent fields of your CMP bean, as shown in the following example. Remember that these persistent fields map one-to-one to the attributes of the LINE_ITEM table. Use the <cmp-field> and the <field-name> elements of the deployment descriptor to define the persistent fields.

Declaring the LineItemLocal CMP Persistent Fields

```
<cmp-field>
<field-name>requestNo</field-name>
</cmp-field>
<cmp-field>
<field-name>lineNo</field-name>
</cmp-field>
<cmp-field>
<field-name>projectNo</field-name>
</cmp-field>
<cmp-field>
<field-name>quantity</field-name>
</cmp-field>
<cmp-field>
<field-name>unit</field-name>
</cmp-field>
<cmp-field>
```

```
<field-name>cost</field-name>
</cmp-field>
<cmp-field>
<field-name>actualCost</field-name>
</cmp-field>
<cmp-field>
<field-name>description</field-name>
</cmp-field>
```

In the `LineItemBean` class, you need to define the access methods for the persistent fields as follows:

Defining CMP Accessor Methods

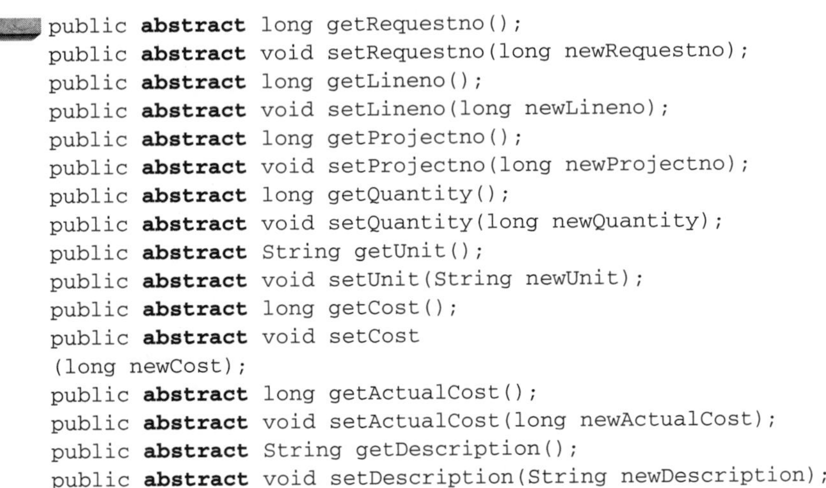

```
public abstract long getRequestno();
public abstract void setRequestno(long newRequestno);
public abstract long getLineno();
public abstract void setLineno(long newLineno);
public abstract long getProjectno();
public abstract void setProjectno(long newProjectno);
public abstract long getQuantity();
public abstract void setQuantity(long newQuantity);
public abstract String getUnit();
public abstract void setUnit(String newUnit);
public abstract long getCost();
public abstract void setCost
(long newCost);
public abstract long getActualCost();
public abstract void setActualCost(long newActualCost);
public abstract String getDescription();
public abstract void setDescription(String newDescription);
```

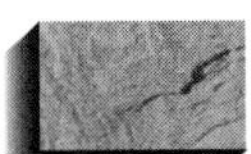

NOTE
In addition to access methods, you may also define select methods for the persistent relationships.

Defining Other Mandatory Methods

In this section, we present a list of the callback methods required by the EJB container. To learn how the EJB container invokes the callback methods on a session bean instance, see the "Life Cycle of an Entity Bean" section of this chapter.

- `public void ejbCreate() { }` A client creates a CMP instance using the `create()` method defined in the `LineItemLocalHome` local home interface.

- `public void ejbActivate() { }` A developer provides no implementation code for this method. That is, the developer provides an *empty* implementation method. You must also provide an *empty* implementation method for the `ejbLoad()`, `ejbPassivate()`, `ejbRemove()`, and `ejbStore()` methods.
- `public void ejbLoad() { }` Empty implementation method.
- `public void ejbPassivate() { }` Empty implementation method.
- `public void ejbRemove() { }` Empty implementation method.
- `public void ejbStore() { }` Empty implementation method.
- `public void setSessionContext(EntityContext ctx) { }` This method is used by the container to associate a context to a specific entity.

Note that you did not write any JDBC or other persistent logic code. At deployment time, the EJB container will generate the JDBC code for you. The EJB container does so by *subclassing* your entity bean class.

Life Cycle of an Entity Bean

Figure 5-3 shows how an EJB container interacts with entity beans. The steps are as follows:

1. The Does Not Exist state represents entity beans that have not been instantiated.
2. The EJB container invokes the `newInstance()` method, which calls the default constructor on the entity bean. Then, the container uses the `setEntityContext(EntityContext ctx)` callback method to associate an entity bean with an entity context object. Remember that you implemented this callback method in the bean implementation class.
3. After instantiation, the container moves the entity bean to a pool of available instances. While in the Pooled state, the instance is not associated with any particular EJB object identity. All instances in the pool are identical. The EJB container assigns an identity to an instance when moving it to the Ready state.
4. When a client invokes the `create()` method of the home interface, the EJB container gets an entity bean instance from the pool and calls the `ejbCreate()` method, which initializes the bean instance to a specific data set. The bean is now in the Ready state, in which the bean is tied to specific data and, therefore, to a specific EJB object.

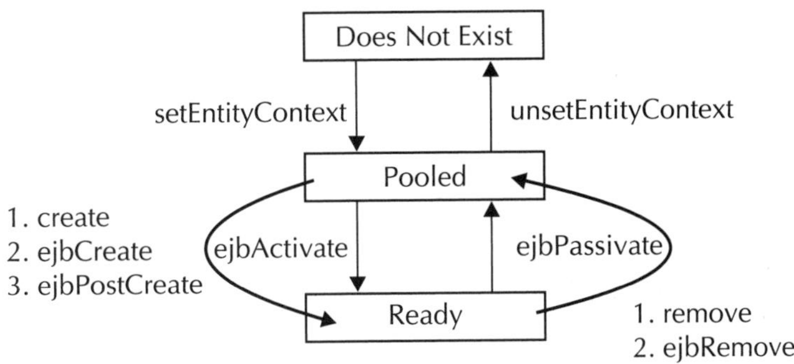

FIGURE 5-3. *Life cycle of entity beans*

5. When a client calls the `remove()` method on the home object, the EJB container calls the `ejbRemove()` method of the bean class to put back the bean instance in the pool. The record at this time is removed (deleted) from the underlying database.
6. If the client has timed out, or the container needs to use the bean to service another request, or the container is running out of resources, the container may kick back a bean instance to the pool. In this scenario, your bean is passivated and the EJB container calls the `ejbStore()` method to store your data in the database. After storing the data, the EJB container calls the `ejbPassivate()` method to release held resources.
7. At the end of the life cycle, the EJB container removes the instance from the pool and invokes the `unsetEntityContext()` method.

Next, we present the complete definition of the `LineItemBean` class:

The LineItemBean EJB Class

```
/*
** Program Name: LineItemBean.java
**
** Purpose: The EJB class
** of the LineItemLocal CMP bean.
*/
package purchase.ejb.cmp;
import javax.ejb.EntityBean;
import javax.ejb.EntityContext;
```

```
public abstract class LineItemBean
   implements EntityBean {

  public EntityContext entityContext;

  public LineItemPK ejbCreate(long requestNo, long lineNo,
                    long projectNo)  {
    setRequestNo(requestNo);
    setLineNo(lineNo);
    setProjectNo(projectNo);
    return new LineItemPK(requestNo, lineNo, projectNo);
  }

  public void ejbPostCreate(long requestNo, long lineNo,
                    long projectNo)  {
  }

  public LineItemPK ejbCreate(long requestNo, long lineNo,
                 long projectNo, long quantity, String unit,
                 float cost, float actualCost, String description) {

        setRequestNo(requestNo);
        setLineNo(lineNo);
        setProjectNo(projectNo);
        setQuantity(quantity);
        setUnit(unit);
        setCost(cost);
        setActualCost(actualCost);
        setDescription(description);
    return new LineItemPK(requestNo, lineNo, projectNo);
  }

  public void ejbPostCreate(long requestNo, long lineNo,
                 long projectNo, long quantity, String unit,
                 float cost, float actualCost, String description) {

  }

  public void ejbActivate()
  {
  }

  public void ejbLoad()
  {
  }

  public void ejbPassivate()
  {
```

```
  }

  public void ejbRemove()
  {
  }

  public void ejbStore()
  {
  }

  public void setEntityContext(EntityContext ctx)
  {
    this.entityContext = ctx;
  }

  public void unsetEntityContext()
  {
    this.entityContext = null;
  }

  public abstract long getRequestNo();
  public abstract void setRequestNo(long newRequestNo);
  public abstract long getLineNo();
  public abstract void setLineNo(long newLineNo);
  public abstract long getProjectNo();
  public abstract void setProjectNo(long newProjectNo);
  public abstract long getQuantity();
  public abstract void setQuantity(long newQuantity);
  public abstract String getUnit();
  public abstract void setUnit(String newUnit);
  public abstract float getCost();
  public abstract void setCost(float newCost);
  public abstract float getActualCost();
  public abstract void setActualCost(float newActualCost);
  public abstract String getDescription();
  public abstract void setDescription(String newDescription);
} // End of the LineItemBean class
```

Next, you will code the `PurchaseOrderLocal` CMP bean.

Coding the PurchaseOrderLocal CMP Entity Bean

The design of the `PurchaseOrderLocal` CMP bean is similar to the design of the `LineItemLocal` CMP bean. The `LineItemLocal` CMP bean defines the persistent fields that map the attributes of the `LINE_ITEM` table, whereas

PurchaseOrderLocal CMP bean defines the persistent fields that map the attributes of the PURCHASE_ORDER table. Each instance of the PurchaseOrderLocal CMP bean represents a purchase order requisition.

Here is the definition of the PURCHASE_ORDER table:

The PURCHASE_ORDER Table

```
CREATE TABLE  PURCHASE_ORDER (
requestno NUMBER(10),
employeeno NUMBER(7),
vendorno NUMBER(6))
```

Next, you will code the PurchaseOrderLocal local interface:

The PurchaseOrderLocal Local Interface

```
/*
** Program Name: PurchaseOrderLocal.java
**
** Purpose: The Local interface
** of the PurchaseOrderLocal CMP bean.
*/
package purchase.ejb.cmp;
import javax.ejb.EJBLocalObject;

public interface PurchaseOrderLocal
    extends EJBLocalObject {

  long getRequestNo();

  void setRequestNo(long newRequestNo);

  long getEmployeeNo();

  void setEmployeeNo(long newEmployeeNo);

  long getVendorNo();

  void setVendorNo(long newVendorNo);

}  // End of  the PurchaseOrderLocal interface
```

Here is the listing of the PurchaseOrderLocalHome local home interface:

The PurchaseOrderLocalHome Local Home Interface

```
/*
** Program Name: PurchaseOrderLocalHome.java
**
** Purpose: The Local Home interface
** of the PurchaseOrderLocal CMP bean.
*/
package purchase.ejb.cmp;
import javax.ejb.EJBLocalHome;
import javax.ejb.CreateException;
import javax.ejb.FinderException;
import java.util.Collection;

public interface PurchaseOrderLocalHome extends EJBLocalHome
{
  PurchaseOrderLocal create(long requestNo) throws CreateException;

  PurchaseOrderLocal create(long requestNo, long employeeNo,
         long vendorNo)  throws CreateException;

  PurchaseOrderLocal findByPrimaryKey(PurchaseOrderPK primaryKey)
    throws FinderException;

  Collection findAll() throws FinderException;
}  // End of PurchaseOrderLocalHome interface
```

Here is the listing of the `PurchaseOrderPK` primary key class:

The PurchaseOrderPK Primary Key Class

```
/*
** Program Name: PurchaseOrderPK.java
**
** Purpose: The primary key class
** of the PurchaseOrderLocal CMP bean.
*/
package purchase.ejb.cmp;
import java.io.Serializable;

public class PurchaseOrderPK implements Serializable
{
  public long requestNo;

  public PurchaseOrderPK()
  {
```

```
  }

  public PurchaseOrderPK(long requestNo)
  {
    this.requestNo = requestNo;
  }

  public boolean equals(Object other)
  {
    return (other instanceof PurchaseOrderPK &&
            this.requestNo==((PurchaseOrderPK)other).requestNo);
  }

  public int hashCode()
  {
    return (new Long(requestNo)).hashCode();
  }
}  // End of the PurchaseOrderPK class
```

As you do with the LineItemLocal CMP bean, you need to define the persistent fields of the PurchaseOrderLocal CMP bean in the deployment descriptor file. The persistent fields of the PurchaseOrderLocal CMP bean map the attributes of the PURCHASE_ORDER table:

Declaring the PurchaseOrderLocal CMP Persistent Fields

```
<cmp-field>
<field-name>requestNo</field-name>
</cmp-field>
<cmp-field>
<field-name>employeeNo</field-name>
</cmp-field>
<cmp-field>
<field-name>vendorNo</field-name>
</cmp-field>
```

In the PurchaseOrderBean implementation class, you need to define the access methods for the persistent fields that you define in the deployment descriptor file:

Defining CMP Accessor Methods

```
public abstract long getRequestNo();
public abstract void setRequestNo(long newRequestNo);
public abstract long getEmployeeNo();
public abstract void setEmployeeNo(long newEmployeeNo);
public abstract long getVendorNo();
public abstract  setVendorNo (long newVendorNo);
```

Here is the listing of the `PurchaseOrderBean` bean class:

The PurchaseOrderBean EJB Class

```
/*
** Program Name: PurchaseOrderBean.java
**
** Purpose: The EJB class
** of the PurchaseOrderLocal CMP bean.
*/
package purchase.ejb.cmp;
import javax.ejb.EntityBean;
import javax.ejb.EntityContext;

public abstract class PurchaseOrderBean
  implements EntityBean {

  public EntityContext entityContext;

  public PurchaseOrderPK ejbCreate(long requestNo)
  {
    setRequestNo(requestNo);
    return new PurchaseOrderPK(requestNo);
  }

  public void ejbPostCreate(long requestNo)
  {
  }

  public PurchaseOrderPK ejbCreate(long requestNo, long employeeNo,
                                   long vendorNo)
  {
      setRequestNo(requestNo);
        setEmployeeNo(employeeNo);
        setVendorNo(vendorNo);
      return new PurchaseOrderPK(requestNo);
  }

  public void ejbPostCreate(long requestNo, long employeeNo, long vendorNo)
  {
  }

  public void ejbActivate()
  {
  }

  public void ejbLoad()
  {
  }
```

```
  public void ejbPassivate()
  {
  }

  public void ejbRemove()
  {
  }

  public void ejbStore()
  {
  }

  public void setEntityContext(EntityContext ctx)
  {
    this.entityContext = ctx;
  }

  public void unsetEntityContext()
  {
    this.entityContext = null;
  }

  public abstract long getRequestNo();
  public abstract void setRequestNo(long newRequestNo);
  public abstract long getEmployeeNo();
  public abstract void setEmployeeNo(long newEmployeeNo);
  public abstract long getVendorNo();
  public abstract void setVendorNo(long newVendorNo);
} // End of  the PurchaseOrderBean class
```

In the "The LocalClientServlet Class" section of this chapter, you will write an EJB client, a simple servlet that will use the `LineItemLocal` and `PurchaseOrderLocal` CMP beans. In Chapters 10 and 11, you will develop servlets and JavaServer Pages programs that use the entity beans that you create in this chapter.

In the following section, you will learn how to develop BMP entity beans. You will do so while writing the `EmployeeLocal` BMP bean.

Developing Bean-Managed Persistent Beans

Unlike CMP entity beans, the BMP entity bean code that you write contains the calls that access the database. Developers can use straight JDBC to code database access or they can use SQLJ to do so. In this chapter, we use Oracle9*i* SQLJ to code the BMP database access. Recall that you learned about Oracle9*i* SQLJ in Chapter 3. You may want to review that chapter before proceeding.

A BMP bean's local interface has the following characteristics:

- It must extend the `javax.ejb.EJBLocalObject` interface. You do not implement the `javax.ejb.EJBLocalObject` interface. At deployment time, the EJB container will generate a local EJB object that implements this interface.
- It defines getter and setter method signatures corresponding to the persistent fields.

Next, you will learn how to code a BMP entity bean.

Coding BMP Entity Beans

We first present the `EmployeeLocal` local interface.

The EmployeeLocal Local Interface

```
/*
** Program Name: EmployeeLocal.java
**
** Purpose: The Local interface
** of the EmployeeLocal BMP bean.
*/

package purchase.ejb.bmp;
import javax.ejb.EJBLocalObject;

public interface EmployeeLocal extends EJBLocalObject
{
  long getEmployeeNo();

  void setEmployeeNo(long newEmployeeNo);

  long getDeptNo();

  void setDeptNo(long newDeptNo);

  String getType();

  void setType(String newType);

  String getLastName();
```

```
  void setLastName(String newLastName);

  String getFirstName();

  void setFirstName(String newFirstName);

  String getPhone();

  void setPhone(String newPhone);

  String getEmail();

  void setEmail(String newEmail);
} // End of EmployeeLocal interface
```

Like a CMP bean's local home interface, a BMP bean's local interface has the following characteristics:

- It must extend the `javax.ejb.EJBLocalHome` interface.
- It includes one or more `create()` methods.
- It has the same number and types of arguments as its matching `ejbCreate()` method in the entity bean class.
- It returns the local interface type of the entity bean.
- Its **`throws`** clause includes the exceptions specified by the **`throws`** clause of the corresponding `ejbCreate()` method.
- Its **`throws`** clause contains the `javax.ejb.CreateException` interface.

These rules apply to a finder method:

- Its name begins with find.
- Its return type is the entity bean's local interface type, or a collection of those types.
- Its **`throws`** clause contains the `javax.ejb.FinderException` interface.
- Its `findByPrimaryKey` method must be defined in the local home interface. A local home interface may also include other finder methods. The `EmployeeLocalHome` local home interface includes the `findByPrimaryKey()`, `findAll()`. Unlike a CMP bean, developers

must provide the implementation code for all methods defined in the local home interface. In this section, you will learn how to write the implementation code in Oracle9*i* SQLJ.

Here is the definition of the `EmployeeLocalHome` local home interface:

The EmployeeLocalHome Local Home Interface

```
/*
** Program Name: EmployeeLocalHome.java
**
** Purpose: The Local home interface
** of the EmployeeLocal BMP bean.
*/
package purchase.ejb.bmp;

import javax.ejb.EJBLocalHome;
import javax.ejb.CreateException;
import javax.ejb.FinderException;
import java.util.Collection;

public interface EmployeeLocalHome extends EJBLocalHome
{
  EmployeeLocal create(long employeeNo,long deptNo,
                       String type, String lastName,
                       String firstName, String phone,
                       String email)
      throws CreateException;

  EmployeeLocal findByPrimaryKey(EmployeePK primaryKey)
      throws FinderException;

  Collection findAll()
       throws FinderException;
} // End of EmployeeLocalHome interface
```

Here is the definition of the `EmployeePK` primary key class:

The EmployeePK Primary Key Class

```
/*
** Program Name: EmployeePK.java
**
** Purpose: The primary key class
** of the EmployeeLocal BMP bean.
```

```
*/
package purchase.ejb.bmp;
import java.io.Serializable;

public class EmployeePK implements Serializable
{
  public long employeeNo;

  public EmployeePK(long employeeNo)
  {
    this.employeeNo = employeeNo;
  }

  public boolean equals(Object other)
  {
    return (other instanceof EmployeePK
            &&
            this.employeeNo==((EmployeePK)other).employeeNo);
  }

  public int hashCode()
  {
    return (new Long(employeeNo)).hashCode();
  }

}  // End of EmployeePK class
```

The `EmployeeBean` implementation class consists of the following:

- **Class instance variables** Persistent fields in BMPs are represented as class instance variables.
- **The** `public EmployeePK ejbCreate( ... )` **method** This method corresponds to the `create()` method defined in the `EmployeeLocalHome` interface. To implement the JDBC code, we call the `insertNewEmployee()` method of the `EmployeeTool` SQLJ class. This method is defined in the "The insertNewEmployee( ) Method" section of this chapter. (Remember that you defined that class in Chapter 3.)
- **The** `public void ejbLoad( )` **method** You need to provide the JDBC code to load data into memory. This method invokes the `getEmployeeInfo(anEmployee)` method of the `EmployeeTool` SQLJ class to do the job. This method is defined in the "The getEmployeeInfo( ) Method" section of this chapter.

- **The** `public void ejbRemove( )` **method** The `removeEmployee(...)` method of the `EmployeeTool` class provides the logic to remove permanently data from the `EMPLOYEE` table.
- **The** `public void ejbStore( )` **method** The `updateEmployee(...)` method of the `EmployeeTool` class provides the logic to update data in the `EMPLOYEE` table.
- **The** `public EmployeePK ejbFindByPrimaryKey( ... )` **method** The `getEmployeeno(...)` method of the `EmployeeTool` class provides the logic to get the employee number of an employee in the `EMPLOYEE` table. This method is defined in the "The getEmployeeNo( ) Method" section of this chapter.
- **The** `public Collection ejbFindAll()` **method** The `getEmployeeIds(...)` method of the `EmployeeTool` class returns a list of employee numbers to the EJB container.
- **The** `private Connection getConnection()` **method** This method uses a data source object to connect to the database.

Here is the definition of the `insertNewEmployee()` method:

The insertNewEmployee( ) Method

```
public void insertNewEmployee (long employeeno,long deptno,
String type,String lastname,
String firstname,String phone, String email)
throws SQLException {
       System.out.println("Inside insertNewEmployee()!!");
       try {
       // Get an employeeno
       #sql { INSERT INTO EMPLOYEE
       VALUES(:employeeno,:deptno,
              :type, :lastname,
              :firstname, :phone, :email)
       };
       System.out.println("I insertNewEmployee()-- Record!!");
       } // End try
       catch( SQLException e ) {
       throw new SQLException ("EmployeeTool: "
            +"Unable to insert new employee"
             +e.getMessage());
       } // End catch
...
...
} // End of insertNewEmployee()
```

Here is the definition of the `getEmployeeInfo(anEmployee)` method:

The getEmployeeInfo( ) Method

```
public EmployeeVO getEmployeeInfo(long anEmployeeno)
throws SQLException {
System.out.println("Inside getEmployeeInfo()!!");
EmployeeVO employeeVO = null;
long employeeno;
long deptno;
String type;
String lastname;
String firstname;
String phone;
String email;
try {
     #sql { SELECT employeeno ,deptno,
          type,lastname,firstname, phone INTO
          :employeeno,:deptno,:type,
          :lastname,:firstname,:phone, :email
      FROM EMPLOYEE
      WHERE employeeno = :anEmployeeno
     };
employeeVO =
    new EmployeeVO(employeeno,deptno,type,
    lastname,firstname,phone, email);
System.out.println("Inside getEmployeeInfo()-- Record!!");
return employeeVO;
} // End try
       catch( SQLException e ) {
       throw new SQLException ("EmployeeTool: "
       +"Unable to get employee info "
       +e.getMessage());
        } // End catch
...
...
```

Here is the definition of the `getEmployeeNo()` method of the EmployeeTool SQLJ class:

The getEmployeeNo( ) Method

```
public EmployeePK getEmployeeNo(Connection conn,
                                    EmployeePK employeeNoPK)
    throws SQLException    {
    long anEmployeeNo = employeeNoPK.employeeNo;
```

```
    System.out.println("Inside getEmployeeNo()!!" +anEmployeeNo);

    DefaultContext ctx = null;
    try {
      ctx = getDefaultContext(conn);
      // Get an employeeNo
      #sql [ctx] { SELECT employeeNo INTO :anEmployeeNo
              FROM EMPLOYEE
              WHERE employeeNo =
                  :(employeeNoPK.employeeNo)
       };
      System.out.println("Inside getEmployeeNo()-- Record!!");

    }  // End try
    catch( SQLException e ) {
      …
      …
    return employeeNoPK;
  } // End of the getEmployeeNo() method
```

Next, we present the definition of the `EmployeeBean` implementation class:

The EmployeeBean EJB Class

```
/*
** Program Name: EmployeeBean.java
**
** Purpose: The EJB class
** of the EmployeeLocal BMP bean.
*/
package purchase.ejb.bmp;
import javax.ejb.EntityBean;
import javax.ejb.EntityContext;
import javax.ejb.EJBException;
import javax.naming.NamingException;
import javax.naming.Context;
import javax.naming.InitialContext;

// Package to manipulate database objects
import javax.sql.DataSource;
import java.sql.SQLException;
import javax.ejb.FinderException;
import javax.ejb.CreateException;
import javax.ejb.RemoveException;

import java.sql.Connection;
```

```
import purchase.util.EmployeeTool;
import purchase.vo.EmployeeVO;

import java.util.Collection;


public class EmployeeBean implements EntityBean {

  private transient Connection aConnection = null;

  public EntityContext entityContext;

  public long employeeNo; // Primary key
  public long deptNo;
  public String type;
  public String lastName;
  public String firstName;
  public String phone;
  public String email;

  public EmployeePK ejbCreate(long employeeNo, long deptNo,
                  String type, String lastName,
                  String firstName, String phone,
                  String email)
      throws CreateException
  {
    System.out.println("ejbCreate employeeNo = " +employeeNo);
        try {
          aConnection = getConnection();
      EmployeeTool employeeTool = new EmployeeTool();

      employeeTool.insertNewEmployee(aConnection,
                                     employeeNo, deptNo,
                                     type, lastName,
                                     firstName, phone, email);
        } // End try
        catch(SQLException e) {
          throw new CreateException("Unable to create a new employee!! "
                                  + e.getMessage());
        } // End catch
        finally {
          try {
            if (aConnection != null) aConnection.close();
          } catch (Exception e) {}
    } // End finally()

    this.employeeNo = employeeNo;
    this.deptNo = deptNo;
```

```
    this.type = type;
    this.lastName = lastName;
    this.firstName = firstName;
    this.phone = phone;
    this.email = email;

    return new EmployeePK(employeeNo);
  }  // End of ejbCreate()

  public void ejbPostCreate(long employeeNo, long deptNo,
                            String type, String lastName,
                            String firstName, String phone,
                            String email)
  {
  }

  public void ejbActivate()
  {
  }

  public void ejbLoad()
  {
        EmployeePK pk = (EmployeePK)entityContext.getPrimaryKey();

        long anEmployeeNo = pk.employeeNo;
        System.out.println("ejbLoad employeeNo = " + anEmployeeNo);

        try {
          aConnection = getConnection();
            EmployeeTool employeeTool = new EmployeeTool();

      EmployeeVO employeeVO =
              employeeTool.getEmployeeInfo(aConnection,
                                           anEmployeeNo);

      System.out.println("ejbLoad employeeVO.getEmployeeNo() = "
              +employeeVO.getEmployeeNo());
      employeeNo = employeeVO.getEmployeeNo();
      deptNo     = employeeVO.getDeptNo();
      type       = employeeVO.getType();
      lastName   = employeeVO.getLastName();
      firstName  = employeeVO.getFirstName();
      phone      = employeeVO.getPhone();
      email      = employeeVO.getEmail();
        } // End try
        catch (SQLException e) {
          throw new EJBException("Unable to load employee info !! "
                            + e.getMessage());
```

```
        } // End catch
        finally {
            try {
        if  (aConnection != null) aConnection.close();
            } catch (Exception e) {}
        } // End finally()
}  // End of ejbload()

public void ejbPassivate()
{
}

public void ejbRemove() throws RemoveException {

        EmployeePK pk = (EmployeePK)entityContext.getPrimaryKey();

        System.out.println("ejbRemove employeeNo = " + pk.employeeNo);

        try {
      aConnection = getConnection();
      EmployeeTool employeeTool = new EmployeeTool();
      employeeTool.removeEmployee(aConnection,pk);
        } // End try
        catch (SQLException e) {
      throw new RemoveException("Unable to remove a new employee!! "
                                  + e.getMessage());
        } // End catch
        finally {
      try {
        if  (aConnection != null) aConnection.close();
          } catch (Exception e) {}
  } // End finally()
} // End of ejbRemove()

public void ejbStore()
{
        /* EmployeePK pk =
                 (EmployeePK)entityContext.getPrimaryKey();
        */
        System.out.println("ejbStore employeeNo = " +employeeNo);

        try {
          aConnection = getConnection();
            EmployeeTool employeeTool = new EmployeeTool();

        employeeTool.updateEmployee(aConnection,
                                      employeeNo,deptNo,
                                              type, lastName,
```

```
                                    firstName, phone, email);
      } // End try
      catch (SQLException e) {
        throw new EJBException("Unable to update employee info!! "
                               + e.getMessage());
      } // End catch
      finally {
    try {
            if  (aConnection != null) aConnection.close();
        } catch (Exception e) {}
      } // End finally()
}

public void setEntityContext(EntityContext ctx)
{
  this.entityContext = ctx;
}

public void unsetEntityContext()
{
  this.entityContext = null;
}

public long getEmployeeNo()
{
  return employeeNo;
}

public void setEmployeeNo(long newEmployeeNo)
{
  employeeNo = newEmployeeNo;
}

public long getDeptNo()
{
  return deptNo;
}

public void setDeptNo(long newDeptNo)
{
  deptNo = newDeptNo;
}

public String getType()
{
  return type;
}
```

```
public void setType(String newType)
{
  type = newType;
}

public String getLastName()
{
  return lastName;
}

public void setLastName(String newLastName)
{
  lastName = newLastName;
}

public String getFirstName()
{
  return firstName;
}

public void setFirstName(String newFirstName)
{
  firstName = newFirstName;
}

public String getPhone()
{
  return phone;
}

public void setPhone(String newPhone)
{
  phone = newPhone;
}
public String getEmail()
{
    return email;
  }

  public void setEmail(String newEmail)
  {
    phone = newEmail;
}

// Business logic
public EmployeePK ejbFindByPrimaryKey(EmployeePK primaryKey)
     throws FinderException
{
```

```
        System.out.println("ejbFindByPrimaryKey employeeNo = "
             +primaryKey.employeeNo);

    try {
      aConnection = getConnection();
      EmployeeTool employeeTool = new EmployeeTool();

       return employeeTool.getEmployeeno(aConnection,
                                          primaryKey);
    } // End try
    catch (SQLException e) {
      throw new FinderException(e.getMessage());
    } // End catch
    finally {
      try {
        if  (aConnection != null) aConnection.close();
      } catch (Exception e) {}
    } // End finally()
}  // End of ejbFindByPrimaryKey()

public Collection ejbFindAll() throws FinderException
{
      System.out.println("ejbFindAll ");

  try {
    aConnection = getConnection();
    EmployeeTool employeeTool = new EmployeeTool();

    return employeeTool.getEmployeeIds(aConnection);
  } // End try
  catch (SQLException e) {
    throw new FinderException(e.getMessage());
  } // End catch
  finally {
    try {
      if  (aConnection != null) aConnection.close();
    } catch (Exception e) {}
  } // End finally()
}  // End of ejbFindAll()

private Connection getConnection() throws SQLException {
  // Get datasource
  DataSource ds = getDataSource();
  return ds.getConnection();
} // End of getConnection()

private DataSource getDataSource() throws EJBException
{
```

```
    DataSource ds = null;
    try {
      Context ic = new InitialContext();
      ds = (DataSource) ic.lookup("jdbc/OracleDS");
    } catch (NamingException e) {
      e.printStackTrace();
      throw new EJBException(
      "EmployeeBean Cannot Connect!!! " + e.getMessage());
    }
    return ds;
  } // End of getDataSource()
} // End of EmployeeBean class
```

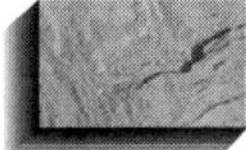

NOTE
*In Oracle9*i *SQLJ release 9.0.2, we have SQLJ-specific data sources that permit you to get either (or both) a SQLJ connection or a JDBC connection and that ensure that you can either close the SQLJ connection or the JDBC connection with the same semantics. See http://otn.oracle.com/docs/products/oracle9i/doc_library/release2/java.920/a96655/alangfea.htm#1015992.*

Next, you will write the `LocalClientServlet` class, a simple servlet to test your beans. To learn how to develop servlet and JavaServer Pages programs, see Chapters 10 and 11, respectively. Here is the definition of the `LocalClientServlet` class:

The LocalClientServlet Class

```
/* Program Name: LocalClientServlet.java
**
** Purpose: Test the LineItemLocal and
** PurchaseOrderLocal CMP beans and
** the EmployeeLocal BMP bean.
*/
package webapps.web.test;
import javax.servlet.ServletConfig;
import javax.servlet.ServletException;
import javax.servlet.http.HttpServletResponse;
import javax.servlet.http.HttpServletRequest;
import javax.servlet.http.HttpServlet;
import java.io.PrintWriter;
import java.io.IOException;
import javax.naming.Context;
import javax.naming.InitialContext;
```

```
import purchase.ejb.cmp.PurchaseOrderLocalHome;
import purchase.ejb.cmp.LineItemLocalHome;
import purchase.ejb.bmp.EmployeeLocal;
import purchase.ejb.bmp.EmployeeLocalHome;
import purchase.ejb.bmp.EmployeePK;

public class LocalClientServlet extends HttpServlet
{
  private static final String CONTENT_TYPE =
            "text/html; charset=windows-1252";

  public void init(ServletConfig config) throws ServletException
  {
    super.init(config);
  }

  public void doGet(HttpServletRequest request,
                    HttpServletResponse response)
          throws ServletException, IOException  {
  try
    {
    //Create a Context object
    Context ctxLineItem = new InitialContext();
    //Look up the local interface
    LineItemLocalHome home = (LineItemLocalHome)
          ctxLineItem.lookup("java:comp/env/LineItemLocal");
    System.out.println("Got LineItemlocalHome: "+ home);
    Context ctxPurchase = new InitialContext();
    PurchaseOrderLocalHome home1 = (PurchaseOrderLocalHome)
         ctxPurchase.lookup("java:comp/env/PurchaseOrderLocal");
    System.out.println("Got PurchaseOrderLocalHome: "+ home1);
    Context ctxEmployee = new InitialContext();
    EmployeeLocalHome home2 = (EmployeeLocalHome)
    ctxEmployee.lookup("java:comp/env/EmployeeLocal");
    System.out.println("Got EmployeeLocalHome: "+ home2);

    //Create a Primary key object
    EmployeePK pk = new EmployeePK(101);
    //Create an EmployeeLocal object
    EmployeeLocal employeeLocal = home2.findByPrimaryKey(pk);

    System.out.println();
    response.setContentType(CONTENT_TYPE);
    PrintWriter out = response.getWriter();
    out.println("<html>");
    out.println("<head><title>LocalClientServlet</title></head>");
    out.println("<body>");
    out.println("<pre>");
    //Retrieve Employee's data
    //whose primary key is 101.
```

```
      out.println("Got EmployeeLocal: "+ employeeLocal);
      out.println("employeeNo = " + employeeLocal.getEmployeeNo());
          out.println("deptNo = " + employeeLocal.getDeptNo());
          out.println("type = " + employeeLocal.getType());
          out.println("lastName = " + employeeLocal.getLastName());
          out.println("firstName = " + employeeLocal.getFirstName());
          out.println("phone = " + employeeLocal.getPhone());
     out.println("email = " + employeeLocal.getEmail());
     out.println("</pre>");
     out.println("</body></html>");
     out.close();
     }
   catch(Exception e){System.out.println(e);}
   }
}  // End of the LocalClientServlet class
```

Compile all the beans, their dependent classes, and the LocalClientServlet class. In the "Testing Your Application" section of this chapter, you will use a Web browser to test your beans.

Next, you will write the deployment descriptor file. After implementing and compiling your classes, you must create the standard J2EE EJB deployment descriptor for all beans in the EJB module. The XML deployment descriptor, defined in the `ejb-jar.xml` file, describes the application components and provides additional information to enable the container to manage the application. The structure for this file is mandated in the DTD file, which is provided at http://java.sun.com/dtd/ejb-jar_2_0.dtd.

If your application consists of several beans, you may write a deployment descriptor file for each bean or write a single one comprising all the beans of your application. The J2EE specification defines how enterprise beans and other application components contained in multiple `ejb-jar` files can be assembled into an application. To learn more about the EJB specification, download the `ejb-2_0-fr2-spec.pdf` file at http://java.sun.com/products/ejb/docs.html.

In the following section, we present a single deployment descriptor file that includes all the entity beans that you created in the previous sections.

The ejb-jar.xml Deployment Descriptor File

In this section, you will define the deployment descriptor file for your beans. Remember that this file is part of the `ejb-jar` archive file. The EJB specification defines the structure of the `ejb-jar.xml` file. Developers use this file to provide information for each enterprise bean. Also, use the `ejb-jar.xml` file to specify fields that define simple or complex primary keys. The `ejb-jar.xml` file consists of information common to all entity beans as well as information specific to particular types of entity beans.

For CMP and cmp-version 2.x, note the following:

- You must specify the abstract schema name of the entity bean using the `abstract-schema-name` element. The *abstract schema* defines the bean's persistent fields and relationships. The term *abstract* distinguishes this schema from the physical Purchase Order schema of the Oracle9*i* database. You specify the abstract schema name of the entity bean using the `abstract-schema-name` element.
- You must specify CMP's persistent fields using the `cmp-field` elements.
- You must define the Enterprise JavaBeans Query Language (EJB QL) for every finder method except for the `findByPrimaryKey()` method. The name of the abstract schema is referenced by queries written in EJB QL. The EJB QL query determines the query that is executed by the EJB container when the finder method is invoked. Note that for CMP beans that you want to deploy to OC4J, you should define EJB QL in the `orion-ejb-jar.xml` file instead of the `ejb-jar.xml` file. Always remember that, at deployment time, if you do not provide an `orion-ejb-jar.xml` file, OC4J will generate one for you. One of the nice things about OC4J is that the server will automatically generate all the finder methods (basic and advanced) for you.
- You must specify the CMP relationships of the entity bean using the `<relationships>` element.
- Use the <query> element to specify any EJB QL finder or select query for the entity bean other than a query for the `findByPrimaryKey()` method.

Here is the `ejb-jar.xml` file:

The ejb-jar.xml File

```
<?xml version = '1.0' encoding = 'windows-1252'?>
<!DOCTYPE ejb-jar PUBLIC "-//Sun Microsystems, Inc.//DTD
Enterprise JavaBeans 2.0//EN"
"http://java.sun.com/j2ee/dtds/ejb-jar_2_0.dtd">
<ejb-jar>
<enterprise-beans>
<entity>
<description>
Entity Bean ( Container-managed Persistence )
</description>
<display-name>LineItemLocal</display-name>
<ejb-name>LineItemLocal</ejb-name>
```

```
<!-- Use <local-home> and <remote-home> elements
for local and remote home, respectively. -- >
<local-home>purchase.ejb.cmp.LineItemLocalHome</local-home>
<!-- Use <local> and <remote> elements
for local and remote interface, respectively. -- >
<local>purchase.ejb.cmp.LineItemLocal</local>
<ejb-class>purchase.ejb.cmp.LineItemBean</ejb-class>
<persistence-type>Container</persistence-type>
<prim-key-class>
purchase.ejb.cmp.LineItemPK</prim-key-class>
<reentrant>False</reentrant>
<cmp-version>2.x</cmp-version>
<abstract-schema-name>LineItemLocal</abstract-schema-name>
<cmp-field>
<field-name>requestnNo</field-name>
</cmp-field>
<cmp-field>
<field-name>lineNo</field-name>
</cmp-field>
<cmp-field>
<field-name>projectNo</field-name>
</cmp-field>
<cmp-field>
<field-name>quantity</field-name>
</cmp-field>
<cmp-field>
<field-name>unit</field-name>
</cmp-field>
<cmp-field>
<field-name>cost</field-name>
</cmp-field>
<cmp-field>
<field-name>actualCost</field-name>
</cmp-field>
<cmp-field>
<field-name>description</field-name>
</cmp-field>
</entity>
<entity>
<description>
Entity Bean ( Container-managed Persistence )
</description>
<display-name>PurchaseOrderLocal</display-name>
<ejb-name>PurchaseOrderLocal</ejb-name>
<local-home>purchase.ejb.cmp.PurchaseOrderLocalHome</local-home>
<local>purchase.ejb.cmp.PurchaseOrderLocal</local>
<ejb-class>epurchase.ejb.cmp.PurchaseOrderBean</ejb-class>
<!-- Specify Container CMP. -- >
```

```
<persistence-type>Container</persistence-type>
<prim-key-class>purchase.ejb.cmp.PurchaseOrderPK</prim-key-class>
<reentrant>False</reentrant>
<cmp-version>2.x</cmp-version>
<abstract-schema-name>PurchaseOrderLocal</abstract-schema-name>
<cmp-field>
<field-name>requestNo</field-name>
</cmp-field>
<cmp-field>
<field-name>employeeNo</field-name>
</cmp-field>
<cmp-field>
<field-name>vendorNo</field-name>
</cmp-field>
</entity>
<entity>
<description>
Entity Bean ( Bean-managed Persistence )</description>
<display-name>EmployeeLocal</display-name>
<ejb-name>EmployeeLocal</ejb-name>
<local-home>purchase.ejb.bmp.EmployeeLocalHome</local-home>
<local>purchase.ejb.bmp.EmployeeLocal</local>
<ejb-class>purchase.ejb.bmp.EmployeeBean</ejb-class>
<!-- Specify Bean BMP. -- >
<persistence-type>Bean</persistence-type>
<prim-key-class>
purchase.ejb.bmp.EmployeePK</prim-key-class>
<reentrant>False</reentrant>
<resource-ref>
       <res-ref-name>jdbc/OracleDS</res-ref-name>
       <res-type>javax.sql.DataSource</res-type>
       <res-auth>Application</res-auth>
</resource-ref>
</entity>
</enterprise-beans>
<assembly-descriptor>
<container-transaction>
<method>
<ejb-name>LineItemLocal</ejb-name>
<method-name>*</method-name>
</method>
<method>
<ejb-name>PurchaseOrderLocal</ejb-name>
<method-name>*</method-name>
</method>
<method>
       <ejb-name>EmployeeLocal</ejb-name>
       <method-name>*</method-name>
```

```
</method>
<!-- Use the trans-attribute element to indicate
how you want the EJB container to
perform transaction management -->
<trans-attribute>Required</trans-attribute>
</container-transaction>
</assembly-descriptor>
</ejb-jar>
```

Next, you will write the `orion-ejb-jar.xml` OC4J-specific deployment descriptor file. The nice thing about Oracle9*i*AS Containers For J2EE is that you do not have to provide the `orion-ejb-jar.xml` file. At deployment time, OC4J will generate it for you.

Note that the first time you deploy your application to OC4J, OC4J automatically generates a new OC4J-specific XML file for you, using its default elements. However, if you have provided an OC4J-specific XML file within your application, OC4J will merge your configuration with the one that gets generated to produce a new OC4J-specific deployment descriptor for you. For example, if you do not specify any finders in your `orion-ejb-jar.xml` file (that is, the one that you provide with your application) or any application-specific data source settings within your deployment descriptor, but you have finder methods defined in your home interface, OC4J will generate a deployment descriptor with the automatically generated finder methods defined in your home interface and also merge in your application-specific data source settings. If you do not store an `orion-ejb- jar.xml` server-specific deployment descriptor in your application, OC4J will generate one for you.

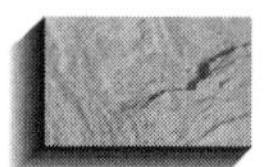

CAUTION
If you want to edit this deployment descriptor, we recommend that you take the generated one and store it within your application, edit it, and, more importantly, delete the generated one under your application deployment directory. Then, restart the server.

Advanced Configuration for Finder Methods

Use the local or remote home interface of your CMP entity bean to define finder methods other than the `findByPrimaryKey()` and `findAll()` methods. The following code demonstrates how to define the `findByRequestNo()` method in the `LineItemLocalHome` interface:

```
// This method is specified in the
// LineItemLocalHome interface
LineItemLocal findByRequestNo(requestno)
  throws FinderException;
```

At deployment time, OC4J generates the following entries in the `orion-ejb-jar.xml` file:

```
<finder-method query="$requestno = $1">
<!-- Generated SQL: "select LINE_ITEM.LINENO,
                            LINE_ITEM.PROJECTNO,
                            LINE_ITEM.REQUESTNO,
                            LINE_ITEM.QUANTITY,
                            LINE_ITEM.UNIT,
                            LINE_ITEM.COST,
                            LINE_ITEM.ACTUALCOST,
                            LINE_ITEM.DESCRIPTION
            from LINE_ITEM
                  where LINE_ITEM.REQUESTNO = ?" -->
<method>
  <ejb-name>LineItemLocal</ejb-name>
  <method-name>findByRequestNo</method-name>
  <method-params>
    <method-param>long</method-param>
  </method-params>
</method>
```

Note that the **Where** clause refers to passed-in parameters using the $ symbol, where the first parameter is denoted by "$1". If you have more than one method parameter, each parameter type is defined in successive `<method-param>` elements and referred to in the query statement by successive "$*n*" parameters, where *n* represents the position number of the parameter. For example, the first parameter is denoted by "$1", the second by "$2", and so on.

Here is the complete listing of the `orion-ejb-jar.xml` file:

The orion-ejb-jar.xml File

```
<?xml version="1.0" encoding="utf-8"?>
<!DOCTYPE orion-ejb-jar PUBLIC
"-//Evermind//DTD Enterprise JavaBeans 1.1 runtime//EN"
"http://xmlns.oracle.com/ias/dtds/orion-ejb-jar.dtd">
<orion-ejb-jar deployment-version="9.0.3.0.0"
deployment-time="edc70f30bd">
<enterprise-beans>
 <entity-deployment name="LineItemLocal" max-instances="10"
              location="LineItemLocal"
```

```
            wrapper="LineItemLocalHome_EntityHomeWrapper5"
            table=" LINE_ITEM "
            data-source="jdbc/OracleDS"
            exclusive-write-access="false"
            locking-mode="optimistic"
            update-changed-fields-only="true"
            min-instances-per-pk="0"
             max-instances-per-pk="50" disable-wrapper-cache="true">
 <primkey-mapping>
  <cmp-field-mapping>
   <fields>
    <cmp-field-mapping name="lineNo"
       persistence-name="LINENO"
       persistence-type="NUMBER(5)" />
    <cmp-field-mapping name="projectNo"
       persistence-name="PROJECTNO"
       persistence-type="NUMBER(5)" />
    <cmp-field-mapping name="requestNo"
       persistence-name="REQUESTNO"
       persistence-type="NUMBER(10)" />
   </fields>
  </cmp-field-mapping>
   </primkey-mapping>
     <cmp-field-mapping name="quantity"
        persistence-name="QUANTITY"
        persistence-type="NUMBER(5)" />
     <cmp-field-mapping name="unit"
        persistence-name="UNIT"
        persistence-type="VARCHAR2(2)" />
     <cmp-field-mapping name="cost"
        persistence-name="COST"
        persistence-type="NUMBER(8,2)" />
     <cmp-field-mapping name="actualCost"
        persistence-name="ACTUALCOST"
        persistence-type="NUMBER(8,2)" />
     <cmp-field-mapping name="description"
        persistence-name="DESCRIPTION"
        persistence-type="VARCHAR2(30)" />
  <finder-method query="$requestno = $1">
    <!-- Generated SQL: "select LINE_ITEM.LINENO,
         LINE_ITEM.PROJECTNO, LINE_ITEM.REQUESTNO,
         LINE_ITEM.QUANTITY, LINE_ITEM.UNIT,
        LINE_ITEM.COST, LINE_ITEM.ACTUALCOST,
        LINE_ITEM.DESCRIPTION
    from LINE_ITEM
    where LINE_ITEM.REQUESTNO = ?" -->
<method>
   <ejb-name>LineItemLocal</ejb-name>
```

```
    <method-name>findByRequestNo</method-name>
    <method-params>
    <method-param>long</method-param>
    </method-params>
 </method>
 </finder-method>
   <finder-method query="">
      <!-- Generated SQL: "select LINE_ITEM.LINENO,
         LINE_ITEM.PROJECTNO, LINE_ITEM.REQUESTNO,
         LINE_ITEM.QUANTITY, LINE_ITEM.UNIT,
         LINE_ITEM.ESTIMATEDCOST, LINE_ITEM.ACTUALCOST,
         LINE_ITEM.DESCRIPTION
      from LINE_ITEM " -->
 <method>
   <ejb-name>LineItemLocal</ejb-name>
   <method-name>findAll</method-name>
   <method-params>
     </method-params>
 </method>
 </finder-method>
   </entity-deployment>
   <entity-deployment name="PurchaseOrderLocal" max-instances="10"
      location="PurchaseOrderLocal"
      wrapper="PurchaseOrderLocalHome_EntityHomeWrapper6"
      table="PURCHASE_ORDER" data-source="jdbc/OracleDS"
      exclusive-write-access="false"
      locking-mode="optimistic"
      update-changed-fields-only="true"
      min-instances-per-pk="0" max-instances-per-pk="50"
  disable-wrapper-cache="true">
<primkey-mapping>
 <cmp-field-mapping>
  <fields>
    <cmp-field-mapping name="requestNo"
       persistence-name="REQUESTNO"
       persistence-type="NUMBER(10)" />
  </fields>
 </cmp-field-mapping>
</primkey-mapping>
 <cmp-field-mapping name="employeeNo"
      persistence-name="EMPLOYEENO"
      persistence-type="NUMBER(7)" />
 <cmp-field-mapping name="vendorNo"
      persistence-name="VENDORNO"
      persistence-type="NUMBER(6)" />
    <finder-method query="">
    <!-- Generated SQL: "select PURCHASE_ORDER.REQUESTNO,
       PURCHASE_ORDER.EMPLOYEENO, PURCHASE_ORDER.VENDORNO
```

```
            from PURCHASE_ORDER" -->
      <method>
       <ejb-name>PurchaseOrderLocal</ejb-name>
       <method-name>findAll</method-name>
       <method-params>
       </method-params>
      </method>
      </finder-method>
    </entity-deployment>
      <entity-deployment name="EmployeeLocal" max-instances="10"
         location="EmployeeLocal"
         wrapper="EmployeeLocalHome_EntityHomeWrapper7"
         table="EmployeeLocal" exclusive-write-access="false"
         locking-mode="optimistic"
         update-changed-fields-only="true"
         min-instances-per-pk="0"
         max-instances-per-pk="50" disable-wrapper-cache="true">
       <resource-ref-mapping name="jdbc/OracleDS" />
      </entity-deployment>
     </enterprise-beans>
     <assembly-descriptor>
      <default-method-access>
        <security-role-mapping
                   name="&lt;default-ejb-caller-role&gt;"
                   impliesAll="true" />
      </default-method-access>
  </assembly-descriptor>
</orion-ejb-jar>
```

CMP's persistent data can be automatically mapped to a database table by the container. However, if you do not want the defaults that OC4J provides for you or you find that the data represented by your bean is more complex, you can map the CMP permanent fields to an existing database table by modifying the `orion-ejb-jar.xml` file. Once mapped, the container provides the persistence storage of the CMP data to the specified table and rows.

NOTE
There is no need for you to write this file. At deployment time, OC4J automatically generates the `orion-ejb-jar.xml` file for you. If you use the Oracle9i JDeveloper tool, it will also generate this file for you.

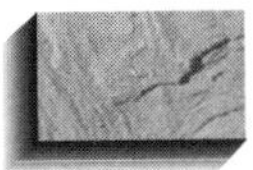

CAUTION
Before configuring the object-relational mapping, add the `DataSource` used for the destination within the `<resource-ref>` element in the `ejb-jar.xml` file.

OC4J Object-Relational Mapping of Persistent Fields and Relationships

To map CMP persistent fields to a database table and its columns, do the following in the `orion-ejb-jar.xml` file:

1. Configure the `<entity-deployment>` element for every CMP entity bean that contains persistent fields that you need to map.
2. Configure a `<cmp-field-mapping>` element for every field within the bean that is mapped. Each `<cmp-field-mapping>` element must contain the name of the field to be persisted.
   A. Configure the primary key in the `<primkey-mapping>` element contained within its own `<cmp-field-mapping>` element.
   B. Configure simple data types (such as a primitive, simple object, or serializable object) that are mapped to a single field within a single `<cmp-field-mapping>` element. The name and database field are fully defined within the element attributes.
   C. Configure complex data types using one of the many subelements of the `<cmp-field-mapping>` element. These can be one of the following:
      - If you define an object as your complex data type, then specify each field or property within the object in the `<fields>` or `<properties>` element.
      - If you specify a field defined in another entity bean, then define the home interface of this entity bean in the `<entity-ref>` element.
      - If you define a `List`, `Collection`, `Set`, or `Map` of fields, then define these fields within the `<list-mapping>`, `<collection-mapping>`, `<set-mapping>`, or `<map-mapping>` elements, respectively.

Your enterprise application comprises also a web application consisting of the `LocalClientServlet` class. Consequently, you need to provide a `web.xml` file for the servlet. We present here a simple example of the `web.xml` file. To learn more about the elements of this file, see Chapters 10 and 11, and Appendix A.

Here is the `web.xml` file that we use for the application:

The web.xml File

```
<?xml version = '1.0' encoding = 'windows-1252'?>
<!DOCTYPE web-app PUBLIC
"-//Sun Microsystems, Inc.//DTD Web Application 2.2//EN"
"http://java.sun.com/j2ee/dtds/web-app_2_2.dtd">
<web-app>
<description>Simple web.xml file for Web Application</description>
<servlet>
<servlet-name>LocalClientServlet</servlet-name>
<servlet-class>test.LocalClientServlet</servlet-class>
</servlet>
<servlet-mapping>
<servlet-name>LocalClientServlet</servlet-name>
<url-pattern>/</url-pattern>
</servlet-mapping>
<session-config>
<session-timeout>30</session-timeout>
</session-config>
<mime-mapping>
<extension>html</extension>
<mime-type>text/html</mime-type>
</mime-mapping>
<mime-mapping>
<extension>txt</extension>
<mime-type>text/plain</mime-type>
</mime-mapping>
<welcome-file-list>
<welcome-file>index.jsp</welcome-file>
<welcome-file>index.html</welcome-file>
</welcome-file-list>
<ejb-local-ref>
<ejb-ref-name>LineItemLocal</ejb-ref-name>
<ejb-ref-type>Entity</ejb-ref-type>
<local-home>purchase.ejb.cmp.LineItemLocalHome</local-home>
<local>purchase.ejb.cmp.LineItemLocal</local>
</ejb-local-ref>
<ejb-local-ref>
<ejb-ref-name>PurchaseOrderLocal</ejb-ref-name>
<ejb-ref-type>Entity</ejb-ref-type>
<local-home>purchase.ejb.cmp.PurchaseOrderLocalHome</local-home>
<local>purchase.ejb.cmp.PurchaseOrderLocal</local>
</ejb-local-ref>
```

```
<ejb-local-ref>
<ejb-ref-name>EmployeeLocal</ejb-ref-name>
<ejb-ref-type>Entity</ejb-ref-type>
<local-home>purchase.ejb.bmp.EmployeeLocalHome</local-home>
<local>purchase.ejb.bmp.EmployeeLocal</local>
</ejb-local-ref>
</web-app>
```

In the previous sections, you created your application, you compiled all the Java classes, and you wrote the deployment descriptor. The next step is to archive your EJB application into a JAR file. The JAR file should include all bean class files, their dependent class files, and the `ejb-jar.xml` deployment descriptor file. You have also created a web application consisting of one servlet. You also need to package your web application in a WAR file. Archive the JAR and WAR files that belong to an enterprise Java application into an EAR file for deployment to OC4J.

Deploying EJB Components to OC4J

Deploying EJB components to OC4J is rather simple. In Chapter 2, you learned how to deploy a J2EE application to the Oracle9*i*AS Containers For J2EE server and how to bind that application to the server so that you can access the application from OC4J. In this section, we will revisit the necessary steps in order to refresh your memory.

Recall that a J2EE application can contain the following modules:

- **Web applications** The Web applications module (WAR files) can consist of servlets, JSPs, HTML pages, tag libraries, and utility classes.
- **EJB applications** The EJB applications module (`ejb-jar` files) includes Enterprise JavaBeans (EJBs).
- **Client applications** The Client applications module includes client application programs and is contained within a JAR file.

Archiving the EJB Application

The very first step in archiving the EJB application is to package your application. You do so when you create the J2EE EAR file.

Packaging the Application: Creating the EAR File

This application consists of a *Web module,* containing the `LocalClientServlet`, and an *EJB module,* containing two CMP beans and one BMP bean.

Let's start by creating the WAR file:

1. Open a command prompt, and position yourself in the web directory (chapter05/web).
2. Type the following:

```
jar cvf chapter05-web.war WEB-INF
```

3. Copy chapter05-web.war to the root directory, chapter05.
4. Position yourself in the classes directory.
5. Type the following:

```
jar cvf chapter05-ejb.jar META-INF purchase
```

6. Copy chapter05-ejb.jar to the root directory, chapter05.
7. Modify the application.xml file in the chapter05/META-INF directory. For example:

```
<?xml version="1.0"?>
<!DOCTYPE application PUBLIC "-//Sun Microsystems,
      Inc.//DTD J2EE Application 1.2//EN"
     "http://java.sun.com/j2ee/dtds/application_1_2.dtd">
<!-- The application element is the root element of a
      J2EE application deployment descriptor.  -->
<application>
      <display-name>Chapter5</display-name>
      <module>
            <web>
                  <web-uri>chapter05-web.war</web-uri>
                  <context-root>/</context-root>
            </web>
      </module>
      <module>
            <ejb>chapter05-ejb.jar</ejb>
      </module>
</application>
```

8. Position yourself in the root directory, chapter05.
9. Type the following:

```
jar cvf chapter05.ear chapter05-web.war
  chapter05-ejb.jar META-INF
```

You now have your chapter05.ear file and are ready to deploy.

If your application will access a database, then you need to define an OC4J data source. You do so by modifying the OC4J `data-sources.xml` XML file.

Modifying the OC4J data-sources.xml File

Before deploying your application, you need to register your data source with OC4J. You do that by modifying the OC4J `data-sources.xml` file. This file is located in the OC4J's .../`config` directory. All the beans that you created in this chapter use a data source called `jdbc/OracleDS`. You need to specify that data source in the OC4J `data-sources.xml` file. Recall that you used the `jdbc/OracleDBDS` data source in the `EmployeeBean` class:

```
// Method from the EmployeeBean class
private DataSource getDataSource()
throws EJBException {
DataSource ds = null;
try {
Context ic = new InitialContext();
// jdbc/OracleDS is the name of your data source
ds = (DataSource) ic.lookup("jdbc/OracleDS");
} catch (NamingException e) {
e.printStackTrace();
throw new EJBException(
"EmployeeBean Cannot Connect!!! " + e.getMessage());
}
```

In the OC4J's `data-sources.xml` file, Oracle provides an example default `DataSource` that uses Oracle's JDBC driver to create the connections. Modify the file as follows:

```
<!-- Original source from Oracle -->
<data-source
            class="com.evermind.sql.DriverManagerDataSource"
            name="OracleDS"
            location="jdbc/OracleCoreDS"
            xa-location="jdbc/xa/OracleXADS"
            ejb-location="jdbc/OracleDS"
            connection-driver="oracle.jdbc.driver.OracleDriver"
            username="scott"
            password="tiger"
            url="jdbc:oracle:thin:@localhost:5521:oracle"
            inactivity-timeout="30"
      />

<!-- Your datasource -->
<data-source
```

```
        class="com.evermind.sql.DriverManagerDataSource"
        name="OracleDS"
        location="jdbc/OracleCoreDS"
        xa-location="jdbc/xa/OracleXADS"
        ejb-location="jdbc/OracleDS"
        connection-driver="oracle.jdbc.driver.OracleDriver"
        username="scott"
        password="tiger"
        url="jdbc:oracle:thin:@yourhost:your-port-no:your-sid"
        inactivity-timeout="30"
/>
```

Next, you will deploy the application. OC4J supports deployment of both EAR files as well as deploying an exploded directory conforming to the J2EE standard (as does our `chapter05` directory structure). We will show you both ways, starting with the EAR file.

Deploying an EAR File to OC4J

The steps to deploy an EAR file to OC4J are as follows:

1. Copy the `Chapter05.ear` file to your OC4J installation's `applications` directory; if you have unzipped OC4J under the `d:\OC4J` directory, then this will be `d:\OC4J\j2ee\home\applications`. The EAR file can be placed anywhere, but in this example, you will use the OC4J `applications` directory.

2. Edit the OC4J `server.xml` file, found under your `OC4J\j2ee\home\config` directory. Add the following entry as shown in Listing 5-1:

   Listing 5-1

   ```
   <application name="chapter5" path="../applications/ chapter05.ear"
   auto-start="true" />
   ```

3. Edit **`http-web-site.xml`** to bind your Web module to this J2EE application. Add the following entry:

   ```
   <web-app application="chapter5" name="chapter05-web"
       root="/chapter5" load-on-startup="true" />
   ```

CAUTION
The name must correspond to whatever name you gave the WAR file; the root will be your virtual path where OC4J can reach your application.

Recall that OC4J supports hot deployment. Therefore, if OC4J is running, it will immediately pick up and deploy this application. If OC4J is not running, position yourself in the `OC4J/j2ee/home` directory and start OC4J by typing the following:

```
java -jar oc4j.jar -verbosity 10
```

Output from OC4J

You should see something like this as output from OC4J:

```
Auto-unpacking .....\applications\chapter05.ear... done.
Auto-unpacking .....\applications\chapter05\chapter05-web.war... done.
Auto-deploying chapter5 (New server version detected)...
Application default (default) initialized...
Copying default deployment descriptor from .....
Auto-deploying chapter05-ejb.jar(No previous deployment found).. done.
Application chapter5 (Chapter5) initialized...
Web-App default:defaultWebApp (0.0.0.0/0.0.0.0:80) started...
Auto-deploying file.....applications/chapter05/chapter 05-web/
    (New server version detected)...
Oracle9iAS Containers For J2EE initialized
```

Next, you will test your application.

Testing Your Application

Open a Web browser and type the following URL:

```
http://localhost:port/chapter5
```

where *localhost* is your machine, *port* is the port the Web server is listening on, and chapter5 is the name that you defined in the <name> element of the `<application>` tag in the OC4J `server.xml` file (refer back to Listing 5-1). Note that the default port for the standalone OC4J is 8888. The port can be found and changed in the OC4J `http-web-site.xml` XML file. The OC4J `http-web-site.xml` XML file can be found in the `OC4J_HOME/j2ee/home/config` directory.

Next, we present the output displayed in the Web browser and the OC4J console.

Web Browser Output from the LocalClientServlet

```
Got EmployeeLocal: EmployeeLocal
  purchase.ejb.bmp.EmployeePK@65
employeeNo = 101
```

```
deptNo = 200
type = Registered Nurse
lastName = Jewel
firstName = Missy
phone = 1001
email = Missy@acme-hospital.com
```

OC4J Console: Output from the LocalClientServlet

```
Web-App chapter5:web (0.0.0.0/0.0.0.0:80/chapter5) started...
Got LineItemlocalHome: LineItemLocal EJBHome
Got PurchaseOrderLocalHome: PurchaseOrderLocal EJBHome
Got EmployeeLocalHome: EmployeeLocal EJBHome
ejbFindByPrimaryKey employeeno = 101
Inside getEmployeeno()!!
Inside getEmployeeno()-- Record!!
ejbLoad employeeno = 101
Inside getEmployeeInfo()!!
Inside getEmployeeInfo()-- Record!!
ejbLoad employeeVO.getEmployeeno() = 101
ejbStore employeeno = 101
Inside UpdateEmployee()!!
I UpdateEmployee()-- Record!!
Got EmployeeLocal: EmployeeLocal purchase.ejb.bmp.EmployeeLocalPK@78144
```

Next, you will learn how to deploy an exploded directory.

Deploying an Exploded Directory

OC4J also supports deployment of an exploded directory structure. If you have your chapter05 code unzipped in the d:\chapter05 directory, do the following:

1. Make sure the application.xml file is correct in your chapter05/META-INF directory. For an exploded directory, it should look like the following:

```
<?xml version="1.0"?>
<!DOCTYPE application PUBLIC "-//Sun Microsystems,
     Inc.//DTD J2EE Application 1.2//EN"
    "http://java.sun.com/j2ee/dtds/application_1_2.dtd">
<!-- The application element is the root
     element of a J2EE application deployment descriptor.  -->
<application>
      <display-name>Chapter5</display-name>
      <module>
            <web>
```

```
                        <web-uri>web</web-uri>
                        <context-root>/</context-root>
                  </web>
            </module>
            <module>
                  <ejb>classes</ejb>
            </module>
      </application>
```

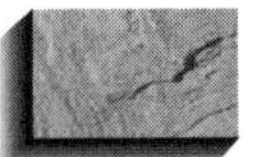

NOTE
The attribute `web` *inside* `<web-uri>` *points to the root directory of your Web module; the attribute* `ejb` *points to the root directory of your EJB module.*

2. Edit the OC4J `server.xml` file; for an exploded deployment, add the following entry:

   ```
   <application name="chapter5" path="file:///d:/chapter05"
       auto-start="true" />
   ```

   Note that the "file:///" prefix takes care of the forward slash (/) and backslash (\).

3. Edit the OC4J `http-web-site.xml` file and add the following entry:

   ```
   <web-app application="chapter5" name="web"
             root="/chapter5" auto-start="true" />
   ```

If your OC4J instance is still running, you might need to restart it if you're using the same names again.

Note that if you want a clean deployment of an application deployed to OC4J, do the following:

1. Stop OC4J.
2. Delete the `chapter05-prebuilt.ear` file and the `chapter05-prebuilt` directory under the OC4J `applications` directory.
3. Delete the application directory under the OC4J `application-deployments` directory.
4. Start OC4J again. OC4J will then do a clean install of the application.

NOTE
We have provided the application.xml file for the exploded approach under `chapter05/META-INF`*, called* `application-exploded.xml`*, and also the prebuilt* `chapter05.ear` *file, called* `chapter05-prebuilt.ear`*.*

In this chapter, you learned the following:

- How to design a J2EE application.
- How to define entity bean components.
- How to develop CMP and BMP entity beans.
- How to write the `ejb-jar.xml` deployment descriptor for entity beans.
- How to write the `orion-ejb-jar.xml` OC4J-specific deployment descriptor for entity beans.
- How to deploy EJB components to OC4J.

In Chapter 6, you will learn how to write session beans and how to code them to use BMP and CMP entity beans.

CHAPTER 6

Developing Session Beans

Session beans are reusable business components that can be used to implement business logic, business rules, algorithms, and workflow. They extend the reach of clients into remote and local servers. For a client, a session object is a non-persistent object that implements some business logic. In this chapter, you will learn how to develop session beans that implement business logic and workflow. Specifically, you will learn how to do the following:

- Design the application.
- Define session bean components.
- Create the `Vendor` application.
- Create the `PurchaseOrderManagement` application.
- Write the `ejb-jar.xml` deployment descriptor file.
- Write or generate the OC4J-specific `orion-ejb-jar.xml` deployment descriptor file.
- Deploy Enterprise JavaBeans (EJB) components to OC4J.

Application Design

In this chapter, you will build two session beans: the `Vendor` session bean (Figure 6-1) and the `PurchaseOrderManagement` session bean (Figure 6-2).

The `Vendor` session bean contains logic to manipulate the `VENDOR` table. While coding the `Vendor` EJB component, you will learn how to develop value objects to ship the data from a server-side object to a client-side object using the J2EE value object pattern.

The `PurchaseOrderManagement` session bean contains logic to manage purchase order requisitions. In this section of the chapter, you will learn how to build a session bean façade using the J2EE session façade pattern. The `PurchaseOrderManagement` application satisfies the requirements of the *Maintain Purchase Order System* use case specification presented in the Introduction of this book. The application consists of the `PurchaseOrderManagement` session bean, which uses the local `PurchaseOrderLocal`, the `LineItemLocal`, and the `ApprovalLocal` CMP entity beans. In Chapter 5, you created the local `PurchaseOrderLocal` and the `LineItemLocal` CMP entity beans. In Chapter 7, you will develop the `ApprovalLocal` CMP bean. Note that, in addition to the Java classes for these three beans, we also provide the `PurchaseOrder`, `LineItem`, and the `Approval` CMP beans, which are the remote versions of the `PurchaseOrderLocal`, `LineItemLocal`, and the `ApprovalLocal` local CMP beans. Figure 6-3 shows the high-level view of the local `PurchaseOrderLocal` and `LineItemLocal` CMP entity beans.

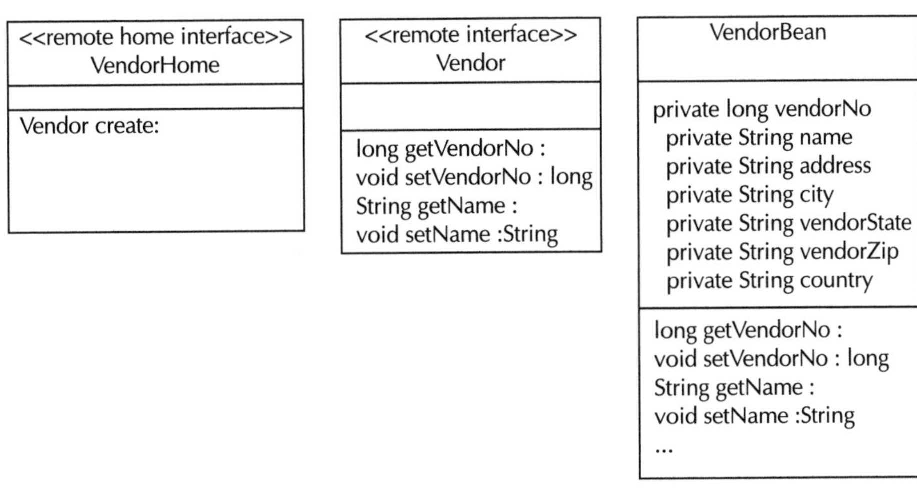

FIGURE 6-1. *High-level view of the `Vendor` session bean*

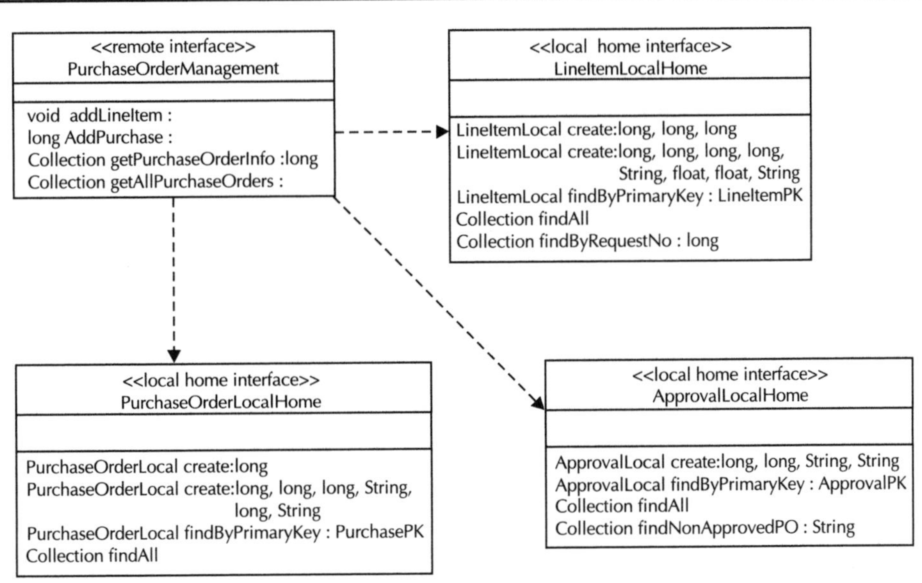

FIGURE 6-2. *High-level view of the `PurchaseOrderManagement` session bean*

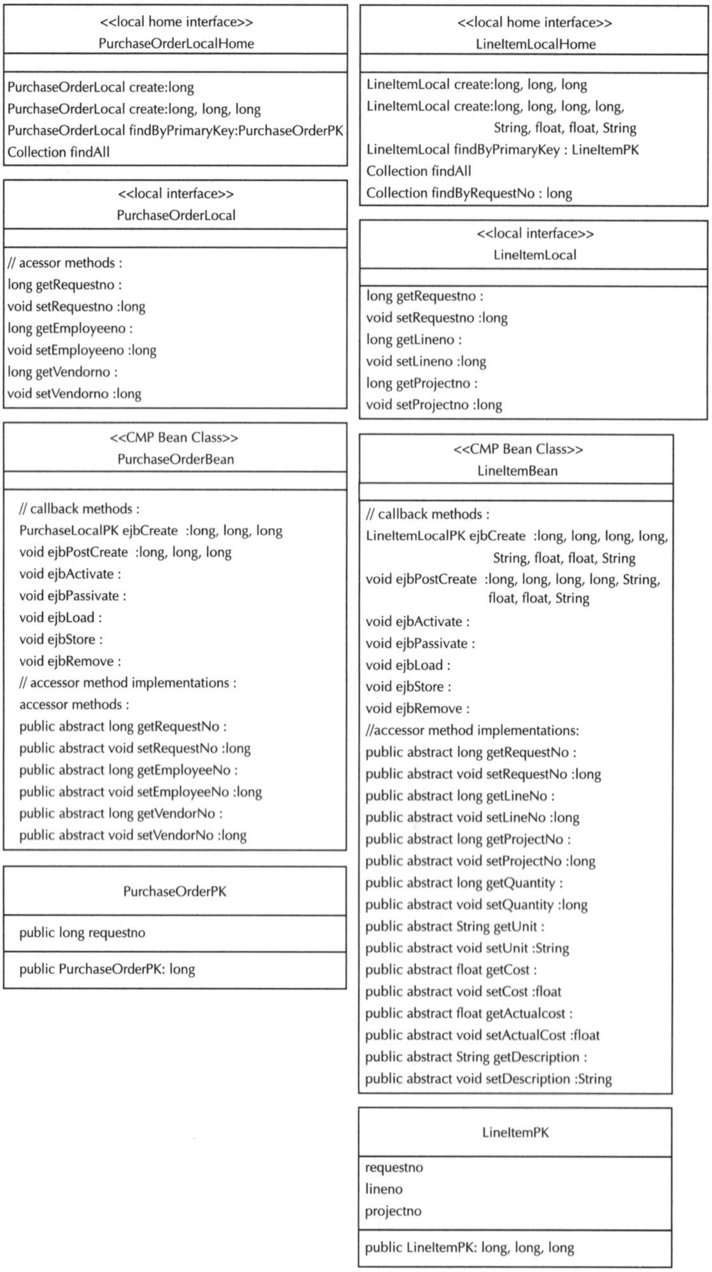

<<local home interface>>
PurchaseOrderLocalHome

PurchaseOrderLocal create:long
PurchaseOrderLocal create:long, long, long
PurchaseOrderLocal findByPrimaryKey:PurchaseOrderPK
Collection findAll

<<local interface>>
PurchaseOrderLocal

// acessor methods :
long getRequestno :
void setRequestno :long
long getEmployeeno :
void setEmployeeno :long
long getVendorno :
void setVendorno :long

<<CMP Bean Class>>
PurchaseOrderBean

// callback methods :
PurchaseLocalPK ejbCreate :long, long, long
void ejbPostCreate :long, long, long
void ejbActivate :
void ejbPassivate :
void ejbLoad :
void ejbStore :
void ejbRemove :
// accessor method implementations :
accessor methods :
public abstract long getRequestNo :
public abstract void setRequestNo :long
public abstract long getEmployeeNo :
public abstract void setEmployeeNo :long
public abstract long getVendorNo :
public abstract void setVendorNo :long

PurchaseOrderPK

public long requestno

public PurchaseOrderPK: long

<<local home interface>>
LineItemLocalHome

LineItemLocal create:long, long, long
LineItemLocal create:long, long, long, long,
String, float, float, String
LineItemLocal findByPrimaryKey : LineItemPK
Collection findAll
Collection findByRequestNo : long

<<local interface>>
LineItemLocal

long getRequestno :
void setRequestno :long
long getLineno :
void setLineno :long
long getProjectno :
void setProjectno :long

<<CMP Bean Class>>
LineItemBean

// callback methods :
LineItemLocalPK ejbCreate :long, long, long, long,
String, float, float, String
void ejbPostCreate :long, long, long, long, String,
float, float, String
void ejbActivate :
void ejbPassivate :
void ejbLoad :
void ejbStore :
void ejbRemove :
//accessor method implementations:
public abstract long getRequestNo :
public abstract void setRequestNo :long
public abstract long getLineNo :
public abstract void setLineNo :long
public abstract long getProjectNo :
public abstract void setProjectNo :long
public abstract long getQuantity :
public abstract void setQuantity :long
public abstract String getUnit :
public abstract void setUnit :String
public abstract float getCost :
public abstract void setCost :float
public abstract float getActualcost :
public abstract void setActualCost :float
public abstract String getDescription :
public abstract void setDescription :String

LineItemPK

requestno
lineno
projectno

public LineItemPK: long, long, long

FIGURE 6-3. *High-level view of the `PurchaseOrderLocal` and `LineItemLocal` CMP entity beans*

Defining Session Bean Components

The EJB specification provides client-view contracts for session beans. The client-view contracts are contracts between a client and an EJB container. They provide a uniform development model for applications using enterprise beans as components. When you are developing a session bean, both the local and remote client views must include the following:

- **Interfaces** The remote and home interfaces are required for remote access. For local access, the local and local home interfaces are required.
- **Enterprise bean class** Implements the methods defined in the remote or local interfaces.
- **Other classes** Additional classes needed by the enterprise bean class, such as value object, JavaBean, exception, and utility classes.
- **Deployment descriptor** An XML file that specifies information about the bean. Recall that deployment descriptors allow you to describe and customize runtime attributes—runtime behaviors of server-side components (for example, security, transactional context, and so on)—without having to change the bean class or its interfaces. Chapter 5 presents detailed information regarding EJB deployment descriptor files. To refresh your memory, you may want to review that chapter before delving into this one.

Creating the Development Directory

The root of the development directory for the applications developed in this chapter is `chapter06`. The structure of the development directory is as follows:

- **chapter06** Root directory of your J2EE application.
  - **META-INF** Directory where your `application.xml` file is located (and possibly your `orion-application.xml` file), which defines the modules you have in your J2EE application.
  - **src** Directory where all the source files are located.
    - **META-INF** Directory where the `ejb-jar.xml` deployment descriptor file and the `orion-ejb-jar.xml` OC4J-specific deployment descriptor file are located.
    - **client** Directory consisting of the source code of the `VendorClient` and `PurchaseClient` Java classes.
    - **purchase** Package indicating the starting point of the `Purchase` application.

- **ejb** Package consisting of the source code of your EJB components.
    - **bmp** Package consisting of the source code of all your bean-managed persistent (BMP) entity beans.
    - **cmp** Package consisting of the source code of all your container-managed persistent (CMP) entity beans.
    - **slsb** Package consisting of the source code of the `Vendor` EJB `STATELESS` session bean.
    - **sfsb** Package consisting of the source code of the `PurchaseOrderManagement` `STATEFUL` session bean.
- **vo** Package consisting of the source code of your value object classes.

- **classes** Root directory for your EJBs: the EJB module.
  - **META-INF** Directory where the `ejb-jar.xml` deployment descriptor file and the `orion-ejb-jar.xml` OC4J-specific deployment descriptor file are located.
  - **client** Package consisting of the class files of the `VendorClient` and `PurchaseClient` Java applications.
  - **purchase** Package indicating the starting point of the Java class files of the Purchase application.
    - **ejb** Package consisting of the class files of your EJB components.
      - **bmp** Package consisting of the class files of all your bean-managed persistent (BMP) entity beans.
      - **cmp** Package consisting of the class files of all your container-managed persistent (CMP) entity beans.
      - **slsb** Package consisting of the class files of the `Vendor` EJB `STATELESS` session bean.
      - **sfsb** Package consisting of the class files of the `PurchaseOrderManagement` `STATEFUL` session bean.
    - **vo** Package consisting of the class files of your value object classes.

A session bean is an object that is used by a single client and is not shared between several clients. In Chapter 4, you learned that there are two types of session beans: `STATELESS` session beans and `STATEFUL` session beans. More importantly, you learned that session beans have specific characteristics, as follows:

- They represent a transient conversation with a single client and execute on behalf of this single client. Note that a client initiates a conversation with a session bean when it invokes a method of a bean class.
- They are relatively short-lived; that is, their life is associated with the life of the client that uses them.
- They can be transactional; that is, they can be used to manipulate data in a database. For example, the OC4J EJB server allows you to write session beans that can retrieve, insert, update, and remove data in relational tables as well as in tables of objects. The `Vendor` session bean that you will develop in subsequent sections of this chapter is an example of an enterprise bean that contains business logic that manipulates vendor data that resides in an Oracle9*i* database. In Chapter 4, you learned that bean classes that implement business logic can call Java stored procedures, SQLJ stored procedures, and PL/SQL procedures and functions, and can execute dynamic (JDBC) and SQLJ embedded (dynamic and static) statements.

Types of Session Beans: STATELESS and STATEFUL

At deployment time, a session bean is specified as having either a `STATELESS` or a `STATEFUL` state management mode. A session bean is said to be `STATELESS` when the bean can be used by any client (moreover, its state is not retained across methods and transactions), and is said to be `STATEFUL` when the session bean does retain its state. A `STATELESS` session bean is referred to as a bean that contains no conversational state, whereas a `STATEFUL` session bean contains a conversational state.

In the following section, you will learn how to code the `Vendor` session bean.

Creating the Vendor Session Bean

In this section, you will build the `Vendor` `STATELESS` session bean, which will manipulate data that resides in the `VENDOR` table. Developing local client views is similar to developing remote client views. In this chapter, you will learn how to develop remote client views. We provide a local view of the `Vendor` session bean in the `chapter06code.zip` file. Remember that source code for all the applications developed in this book can be downloaded from otn.oracle.com, www.data-i.com, and www.osborne.com.

The components of the `Vendor` session bean are as follows:

- **The `Vendor` remote interface** Duplicates every business method that you want to expose to clients.
- **The `VendorHome` remote home interface** Requires a single `create()` method with no arguments. Clients invoke the `create()` method to create EJB objects.
- **The `VendorBean` class** Provides implementation code for all the business methods advertised in the `Vendor` remote interface.
- **The `VendorVO` class** A Java class that the `Vendor` application uses to ship data from EJB instances and clients' objects.
- **The `ejb-jar.xml` file** The deployment descriptor specific to the `Vendor` session bean.
- **The `orion-ejb-jar.xml` file** The OC4J-specific deployment descriptor file. At deployment time, OC4J will generate this file for you.

The Vendor Remote Interface

Like the remote interface of an entity bean, the remote interface of a session bean advertises the business method callable by your EJB clients. The `Vendor` remote interface includes the following, as dictated by the EJB specification:

- A session bean's remote interface must extend `javax.ejb.EJBObject`. A session bean's local interface must extend `javax.ejb.EJBLocalObject`. This means that, at deployment time, the OC4J EJB container will generate an EJB object or local object, which implements the remote/local interface and also contains every method that the `javax.ejb.EJBObject` or `javax.ejb.EJBLocalObject` interface defines. See Appendix C to learn about the specific methods that the EJB container will implement for you.
- The `Vendor` remote interface contains several getter and setter method signatures and one business method that the corresponding `VendorBean` class must implement. The `getAllVendorInfo()` business method returns a `Collection` object consisting of several `ArrayList` objects that map data from the `VENDOR` table store in the Oracle9*i* database. Also, notice that because the `Vendor` remote interface is an RMI-IIOP remote interface, it must throw `java.rmi.RemoteException`. Recall that remote interfaces and remote home interfaces are RMI-IIOP interfaces, which must follow RMI-IIOP rules. One of these rules is that the methods

of RMI-IIOP interfaces must include `java.rmi.RemoteException` in their **`throws`** clause. A `RemoteException` is thrown by the underlying system (that is, the EJB object) when a communication error or system failure occurs.

Here is the listing of the `Vendor.java` remote interface program:

```
/*
      ** Program Name:    Vendor.java
      **
      ** Purpose:         The remote interface of
      **                  the Vendor session bean.
*/
package purchase.ejb.slsb;
import javax.ejb.EJBObject;
import java.util.ArrayList;
import java.rmi.RemoteException;
import java.util.Collection;

// All EJB remote session beans are RMI-IIOP
// interfaces. All must extend EJBObject
public interface Vendor extends EJBObject {

  // All getter and setter methods must
  // include java.rmi.RemoteException in
  // their throws clause
  long getVendorNo() throws RemoteException;
  void setVendorNo(long newVendorNo)
        throws RemoteException;
  String getName()
        throws RemoteException;
  void setName(String newName)
        throws RemoteException;
  String getAddress()
        throws RemoteException;
  void setAddress(String newAddress)
        throws RemoteException;
  String getCity()
        throws RemoteException;
  void setCity(String newCity)
        throws RemoteException;
  String getVendorState()
        throws RemoteException;
  void setVendorState(String newVendorState)
        throws RemoteException;
  String getVendorZip()
```

```
        throws RemoteException;
  void setVendorZip(String newVendorZip)
        throws RemoteException;
  String getCountry()
        throws RemoteException;
  void setCountry(String newCountry)
       throws RemoteException;

  // All business methods must
  // include java.rmi.RemoteException in
  // their throws clause
  Collection getAllVendorInfo()
       throws RemoteException,
              javax.ejb.EJBException;
} // End of the Vendor interface
```

The VendorHome Remote Home Interface

Like the `Vendor` remote interface, the `VendorHome` remote home interface is an RMI-IIOP interface. Consequently, methods listed in the remote home interface must include `java.rmi.RemoteException` in their **`throws`** clause. Remember that the remote or local home interface has methods to create and destroy EJB objects or local objects, respectively. At deployment time, the EJB container will generate the local or remote home object, which implements the local or remote home interface.

Notice the following:

- The `VendorHome` home remote home interface consists of a single `create()` method. Like the entity bean, the `create()` method is a factory method that clients use to acquire a reference to EJB objects or local objects. The `create()` method is also used to initialize a bean. Recall that the `VendorHome` remote home interface is an RMI-IIOP interface and as such its methods must include java.rmi.RemoteException in their **`throws`** clause. Additionally, `create()` methods must also include `javax.ejb.CreateException` in their **`throws`** clause.
- The EJB specification mandates that a session bean's remote home extend the `javax.ejb.EJBHome` and that a session bean's local home extend the `javax.ejb.EJBLocalHome`.

Here is the listing of the `VendorHome` remote home interface:

```
/*
    ** Program Name:    VendorHome.java
    **
```

```
    ** Purpose:          The remote home interface
    **                   the Vendor session bean.
*/
package purchase.ejb.slsb;
import javax.ejb.EJBHome;
import java.rmi.RemoteException;
import javax.ejb.CreateException;

public interface VendorHome extends EJBHome {
  Vendor create()
      throws RemoteException, CreateException;
}  // End of the VendorHome interface
```

Next, you will learn about value objects while developing the `VendorVO` class.

The J2EE Value Object Pattern

As developers design and build different applications, they come across the same or similar problem domains. This leads them to find a solution for the same or similar problem over and over again. Using design patterns can diminish the process of reinventing the wheel.

A design pattern prescribes a proven solution for a recurring design problem. Patterns focus on the context of a problem and solution, thereby guiding the designer in using the design knowledge. *Core J2EE Patterns: Best Practices and Design Strategies*, by Deepak Alur, John Crupi, and Dan Malks (Prentice Hall PTR, 2001) contains a catalog of J2EE patterns. To learn more about J2EE patterns, see http://java.sun.com/blueprints/patterns/j2ee_patterns/index.html. This web site provides a list of useful patterns that you can use when you are designing J2EE applications. The patterns at the Sun site are specifically targeted for use in J2EE.

The VendorVO Class

In this section, you will learn about the value object pattern while creating the `VendorVO` class, as shown in Figure 6-4. Note that when using local client interfaces and local calls, there is no real reason to employ this pattern. Use a value object class to group a set of attributes that are "always" used together. The `VENDOR` table consists of a set of eight attributes that represent the contact information of a vendor. To access the attributes of the `VENDOR` table, you will need to create eight `getXXXX` and `setXXXX` methods. This means that every time a vendor's information is requested, clients accessing this information will need to invoke eight remote `getXXX` calls on the `Vendor` interface, one for each attribute. The remote calls can incur heavy costs in network traffic.

You can reduce these costs by using a class that groups the vendor information-related attributes. The `VendorVO` class aggregates the vendor information-related

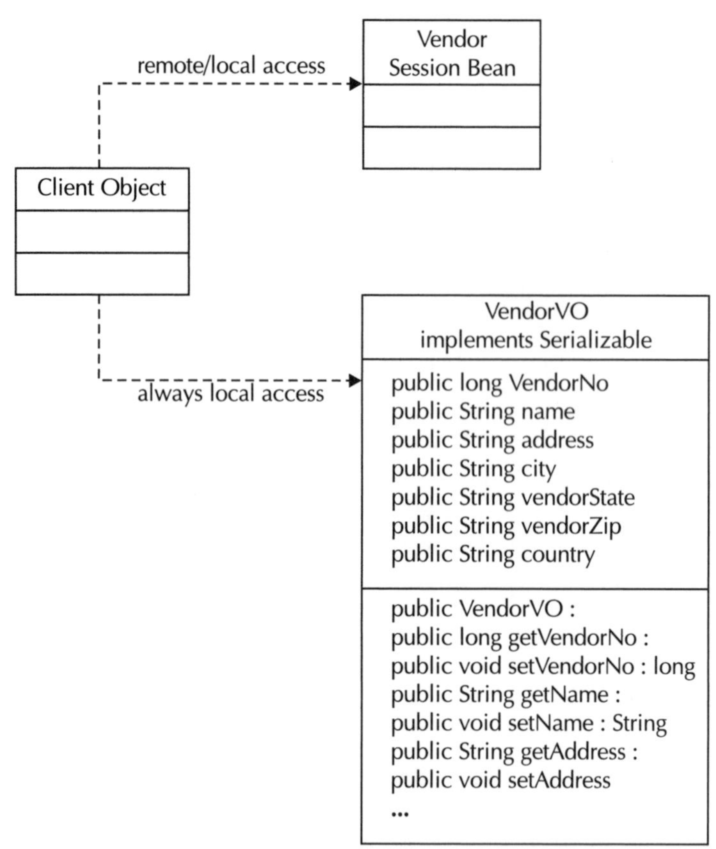

FIGURE 6-4. *Structure of `Vendor` session bean and `VendorVO` value object*

attributes of the `VendorBean` into an instance of the `VendorVO` class. At the server side, the bean will create instances of the `VendorVO` class, serialize the instance, and send it over the network to a requesting client. At the client side, the client object will deserialize instances of the `VendorVO` class in order to retrieve information that your server objects would have sent. As you can see, subsequent attribute accesses would go through the value object rather than the remote entity object. In this scenario, since these accesses are local, they require no server communication and use fewer resources.

The `VendorVO` object is a property of a session bean or entity bean. With enterprise beans, objects are passed by value. Notice that the `VendorVO` class implements the `java.io.Serializable` interface. A *serializable* object is an immutable object.

A VendorVO object is a copy, not a remote reference. A serialized object represents a copy of the original value and any changes to it are not reflected in the original. To change the fields of a VendorVO object, a client must remove (destroy) the VendorVO object and create a new one with the changes.

Here is the listing of the VendorVO class:

```
/*
      ** Program Name:     VendorVO.java
      **
      ** Purpose:          A Java class used to ship
      **                   data between EJB clients and
      **                   bean instances.
*/
package purchase.vo;
import java.io.*;
public class VendorVO implements Serializable {
  public long vendorNo;
  public String name;
  public String address;
  public String city;
  public String vendorState;
  public String vendorZip;
  public String country;

  public VendorVO()  {
  }
  public long getVendorNo()  {
    return vendorNo;
  }
  public void setVendorNo(long newVendorNo)  {
    VendorNo = newVendorNo;
  }
  public String getName()  {
    return name;
  }
  public void setName(String newName)  {
    name = newName;
  }
  public String getAddress()  {
    return address;
  }
  public void setAddress(String newAddress)  {
    address = newAddress;
  }
  public String getCity()  {
    return city;
  }
```

```
  public void setCity(String newCity)  {
    city = newCity;
  }
  public String getVendorState()  {
    return vendorState;
  }
  public void setVendorState(String newVendorState)  {
    vendorState = newVendorState;
  }
  public String getVendorZip()  {
    return vendorZip;
  }
  public void setVendorZip(String newVendorZip)  {
    vendorZip = newVendorZip;
  }
  public String getCountry()  {
    return country;
  }
  public void setCountry(String newCountry)  {
    country = newCountry;
  }
} // End of VendorVO
```

Next, you will code the `VendorBean` class.

The VendorBean Class

An EJB bean class must be declared **public**; it must contain a public, empty, default constructor and must not include a `finalize()` method; it must implement all business methods published in the EJB remote/local interface and provide callback methods required by EJB containers. Refer to the "Life Cycles of STATEFUL Session Beans" section of this chapter to learn how the EJB container invokes the callback methods on a session bean instance.

The `VendorBean` class consists of the following:

- **`public void ejbCreate() { }`** A client creates a session bean instance using the `create()` method defined in the `VendorHome` remote home interface. `STATELESS` session beans do not implement this method. However, `STATEFUL` session beans can initiate state in this method. Your code does not control the `ejbCreate()` method. The EJB container controls it. The EJB container invokes this method when a client calls the `create()` method of an EJB remote/local home interface.

- **`public void ejbActivate() { }`** In the case of a `STATELESS` session bean, the EJB container does not use the `ejbActivate()` and `ejbPassivate()` methods. See the "Life Cycles of STATELESS Session Beans" section of this chapter to learn more about these methods.

- **`public void ejbPassivate() { }`** Developers must provide an *empty* implementation method.
- **`public void ejbRemove() { }`** The `ejbRemove()` method signals that the container is in the process of removing a bean's instance. Developers must provide an *empty* implementation method.
- **`public void setSessionContext(SessionContext ctx) { }`** The EJB container maintains a session bean instance with its specific context. The bean's container calls the `setSessionContext()` method to associate a session bean instance with its context. The container calls this method after the bean creation. A session bean class must implement all business methods advertised in its remote or local interface. The business methods of the `VendorBean` consist of getter and setter methods and the `getAllVendorInfo()` method, which returns an `ArrayList` object consisting of `VendorVO` objects. Importantly, note that the `getAllVendorInfo()` method does not have the `java.rmi.RemoteException` in its **`throws`** clause. Instead, it throws a `javax.ejb.RemoteException`. Remember that `java.rmi.RemoteException` is defined in the method signatures of remote interfaces to provide backward compatibility for enterprise beans written for the EJB 1.0 specification. Enterprise beans written for the EJB 1.1 specification and higher should throw the `javax.ejb.EJBException` instead of `java.rmi.RemoteException`.

- Three private methods that are not callable by EJB clients:
  - **`private VendorVO populateData (ResultSet rset)`** Creates a `VendorVO` object and populates into it the data from the database.
  - **`private Connection getConnection()`** Gets the JDBC connection from the connection pool and returns a `Connection` object to the caller.
  - **`private DataSource getDataSource()`** Uses the Java Naming and Directory Interface (JNDI) to locate the data source, named `jdbc/OracleDS`.

In the following section, you will learn about the life cycles of session beans.

Life Cycles of STATELESS Session Beans

An enterprise bean goes through various stages during its lifetime, or life cycle. Each type of enterprise bean has a different life cycle. In Chapter 5, you learned about the life cycles of entity beans. Here, you will learn about the life cycle of session beans. The life cycle of a `STATELESS` session bean has two stages: nonexistent and ready for the invocation of business methods (see Figure 6-5).

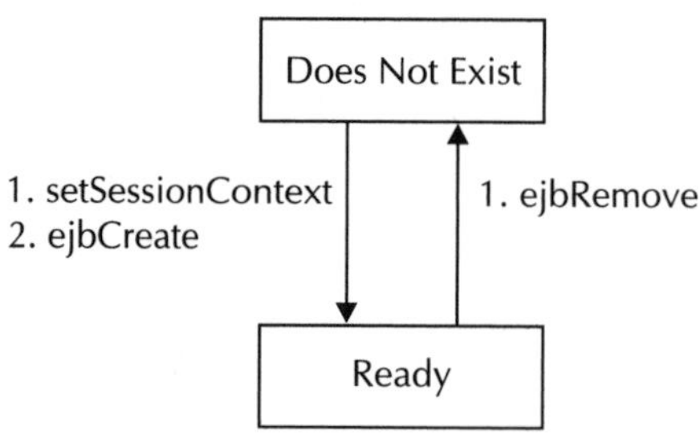

FIGURE 6-5. *Life cycle of `STATELESS` session beans*

NOTE
The EJB container controls the invocation of the callback methods, such as the `ejbCreate( )`, `ejbActivate( )`, `ejbPassivate( )`, and `setSessionContext(SessionContext ctx)` methods. Your client code does not have access to these methods.

Note that we also provide a *local* `Vendor` session bean. You can download the source code for all the examples presented in the book from the following sites: http://otn.oracle.com, www.osborne.com, and www.data-i.com.

Next, you will learn how to develop session beans that control the process workflow of the purchase order requisition system. In the following section, you will build the `PurchaseOrderManagement STATEFUL` session bean.

A session bean implements the `javax.ejb.SessionBean` interface, the definition of which was provided in Chapter 4 and is shown here to refresh your memory:

```
public interface javax.ejb.SessionBean
    extends javax.ejb.EnterpriseBean {
  public void setSessionContext
               (SessionContext ctx)
     throws EJBException,
            java.rmi.RemoteException;
  public void ejbRemove()
     throws EJBException,
            java.rmi.RemoteException;
  public void ejbActivate()
     throws EJBException,
```

```
           java.rmi.RemoteException;
  public void ejbPassivate()
     throws EJBException,
           java.rmi.RemoteException;
}  // End of SessionBean
```

Next, we present the definition of the `VendorBean` session bean class:

```
/*
      ** Program Name:    VendorBean.java
      **
      ** Purpose:         The bean class that implements
      **                  the business methods advertised
      **                  in the Vendor remote interface.
*/
package purchase.ejb.slsb;
import javax.ejb.SessionBean;
import javax.ejb.SessionContext;
import java.util.Collection;
import java.util.ArrayList;

// Exception classes to handle exceptions
import java.rmi.RemoteException;
import javax.ejb.EJBException;
import java.sql.SQLException;
// Package to manipulate database objects
import java.sql.*;
import javax.sql.*;
import java.sql.Connection;
import java.sql.PreparedStatement;
// JNDI package to locate objects
import javax.naming.*;

// Import VendorVO
import purchase.vo.VendorVO;
public class VendorBean implements SessionBean {
  private long vendorNo;
  private String name;
  private String address;
  private String city;
  private String vendorState;
  private String vendorZip;
  private String country;

  // Mandatory callback methods for all EJBs
  public void ejbCreate()  {  }
  public void ejbActivate()  {  }
```

```
public void ejbPassivate()  {  }
public void ejbRemove()  {  }
public void setSessionContext(SessionContext ctx)  {  }

// End of mandatory EJB methods

public long getVendorNo()  {
  return vendorNo;
}
public void setVendorNo(long newVendorNo)  {
  vendorNo = newVendorNo;
}
public String getName()  {
  return name;
}
public void setName(String newName)  {
  name = newName;
}
public String getAddress()  {
  return address;
}
public void setAddress(String newAddress)  {
  address = newAddress;
}
public String getCity()  {
  return city;
}
public void setCity(String newCity)  {
  city = newCity;
}
public String getVendorState()  {
  return vendorState;
}
public void setVendorState(String newVendorState)  {
  vendorState = newVendorState;
}
public String getVendorZip()  {
  return vendorZip;
}
public void setVendorZip(String newVendorZip)  {
  vendorZip = newVendorZip;
}
public String getCountry()  {
  return country;
}
public void setCountry(String newCountry)  {
  country = newCountry;
}
```

```
public Collection getAllVendorInfo()
      throws EJBException {
   System.out.println("Inside getAllVendorInfo()!!!");
   Connection conn = null;
   // Need a Java ArrayList to store the
   // table rows since you do not know
   // how many rows are being retrieved.
   ArrayList vendorList = null;
   // Declare a Java ResultSet object
   ResultSet rset = null;
   // Declare a PreparedStatement variable
   PreparedStatement pstmt = null;
   // Prepare the SQL SELECT statement
   String sql =
     "SELECT vendorno,name, "
     + "address, city, "
     + "state, zip, country "
     + "FROM VENDOR";
   try {
      // get a Connection from the
      // data source
      conn = getConnection();
      System.out.println("I connected to the database!!!");
      pstmt = conn.prepareStatement(sql);
      // Execute the query and store
      // the result in a Java ResultSet.
      rset = pstmt.executeQuery();
      System.out.println("I got rset!!!");
       // Instantiate the vendorList ArrayList
       vendorList = new ArrayList();
       while (rset.next()) {
           VendorVO oneVendor = populateData(rset);
           // Insert oneVendor object into the Java
           // vendorList ArrayList
           vendorList.add(oneVendor);
     }  // End while

     vendorList.trimToSize();
     // Get the size of the vendorList ArrayList
     return vendorList;
  } // End try
  catch (SQLException e) {
     throw new EJBException("Cannot select vendor info: "
                     + e.getMessage());
  }  // End catch
  catch (java.lang.Exception e) {
     throw new EJBException("ArrayList error in Select "
       + " Vendors: " + e.getMessage());
```

```
 }  // End catch
 // Clean up
 finally {
    try {
              if  ( rset  != null ) rset.close();
    }catch (Exception e) {}
    try {
              if  ( pstmt  != null ) pstmt.close();
     }catch (Exception e) {}
     try {
              if  ( conn  != null ) conn.close();
     }catch (Exception e) {}
 } // End finally
}  // End of getAllVendorInfo()

// This method populates the result set data
// to a VendorVO object.
private VendorVO populateData (ResultSet rset)
  throws SQLException {
  try {
          // Declare a VendorVO object
          // using the default constructor.
          VendorVO oneVendor = new VendorVO();

         // Set the member variables of the
         // VendorVO object.
         oneVendor.setVendorNo(rset.getInt(1));
         oneVendor.setName(rset.getString(2));
         oneVendor.setAddress(rset.getString(3));
         oneVendor.setCity(rset.getString(4));
         oneVendor.setVendorState(rset.getString(5));
         oneVendor.setVendorZip(rset.getString(6));
         oneVendor.setCountry(rset.getString(7));

         System.out.println("Inside populate()!!!");
         return oneVendor;
 } // End try
 catch (SQLException e) {
    throw new SQLException("Error in populateData");
 }  // End catch
 catch (java.lang.NullPointerException e) {
     throw new EJBException (e.getMessage());
 }
} // End populateData()

private Connection getConnection()
     throws SQLException, RemoteException  {
```

```
    // DataSource ds = getDataSource(DSName);
    DataSource ds = getDataSource();
    return ds.getConnection();

  } // End of getConnection()

  private DataSource getDataSource()
       throws RemoteException  {

    DataSource ds = null;
    try {
      Context ic = new InitialContext();
      ds = (DataSource) ic.lookup("jdbc/OracleDS");
    }
    catch (NamingException e) {
      e.printStackTrace();
       throw new EJBException( "VendorBean Cannot"
           +" Connect!!! " + e.getMessage());
    }
    return ds;
  } // End of getDataSource()

} // End of VendorBean
```

Note that the Vendor session bean that you built in the previous sections of this chapter does not use any of the new EJB 2.0 features. Therefore, we can use any EJB-compliant (1.0, 1.1, or 2.0) tool to generate the ejb-jar.xml deployment descriptor file for the Vendor session bean.

The ejb-jar.xml File for Session Beans

The ejb-jar.xml file consists of the following tags:

```
</enterprise-beans>
      <session>
        <!-- Use the <description> element to describe your bean -- >
         <description>Session Bean ( Stateless )</description>
         <display-name>Vendor</display-name>
         <!-- Use the <ejb-name> element to name your bean -- >
         <ejb-name>Vendor</ejb-name>
        <!-- Use the <home> element for the name of the
             remote home interface and its complete path -- >
         <home>purchase.ejb.slsb.VendorHome</home>
       <!-- Use the <remote> element for the name of
            the remote interface and its complete path -- >
         <remote>purchase.ejb.slsb.Vendor</remote>
       <!-- Use the <ejb-class> element for the name of the bean class
```

```
            and its complete path -- >
          <ejb-class>purchase.ejb.slsb.VendorBean</ejb-class>
        <!-- Use the < session-type > element for the type of beans
            (stateless or stateful) -- >
<session-type>Stateless</session-type>
        <!-- Use the < transaction-type > element to indicate
            how the EJB container should manage transactions -- >
          <transaction-type>Container</transaction-type>
      </session>
   </enterprise-beans>
```

In this chapter, as in Chapter 5, we wrote a single `ejb-jar.xml` deployment descriptor file that comprises all the Enterprise JavaBeans developed in this chapter. In the "Writing the ejb-jar.xml Deployment Descriptor File" and "Writing or Generating the orion-ejb-jar.xml Deployment Descriptor File" sections of this chapter, we will present the elements of the `ejb-jar.xml` and `orion-ejb-jar.xml` files that relate to the `Vendor` and the `PurchaseOrderManagement` session beans.

For completeness, we present also the `VendorClient` Java application.

The VendorClient Application

A client may access a session or an entity bean only through the methods defined in the bean's interfaces. These interfaces define the client's view of a bean. The `VendorClient` class is a simple EJB client, specifically a Java RMI-IIOP-based client that uses the `Vendor` bean. As a Java RMI-IIOP-based client, the `VendorClient` Java application uses JNDI to look up objects over the network. Recall that a Java RMI-IIOP-based client uses the Java Transaction API (JTA) to control transactions. To learn more about JNDI and JTA, refer to Chapter 3. Note that CORBA (Common Object Request Broker Architecture) clients can also access your enterprise beans. CORBA clients can be written in C/C++. In Chapters 10 and 11, you will learn how to build EJB clients in the form of Java servlets and JavaServer Pages programs.

The `VendorClient` Java application does the following:

1. Creates a `Hashtable` object and stores in it the OC4J environment properties to run the `VendorClient` Java application. For example:

```
Hashtable env = new Hashtable();
env.put(Context.INITIAL_CONTEXT_FACTORY,
   "com.evermind.server.rmi.RMIInitialContextFactory");
// Set the OC4J administrator user name
env.put(Context.SECURITY_PRINCIPAL, "admin");
// Set your OC4J administrator password
env.put(Context.SECURITY_CREDENTIALS, "Your_OC4J_password");
env.put(Context.PROVIDER_URL, "ormi://YourHostName/chapter6");
```

2. Creates a `Context` object and sets up the environment. For example:

```
Context ctx = new InitialContext(env);
```

3. Looks up the home object. For example:

```
// Use the lookup() method of the Context
// to locate a reference to the VendorHome object
VendorHome vendorHome =
             (VendorHome)ctx.lookup("Vendor");
```

4. Uses the home object to create an EJB object. For example:

```
// Use the create() method
// below to create a new instance of
// the Vendor object
Vendor vendor = vendorHome.create(  );
```

5. Calls business methods on the EJB object. For example:

```
// Once you have the Vendor object,
// use that object to invoke the
// business methods that implement
// the business logic of your application.
// The following statement calls the
// getAllVendorInfo(  ) method to
// Get vendors' info
Collection arrayOfVendors =
             vendor.getAllVendorInfo(  );
```

6. Removes the EJB object. The client can only indirectly destroy the bean instance. When the client terminates, then the EJB container will remove the EJB object. A container may also remove the session object automatically when the session object's lifetime expires.

   Here is the listing of the `VendorClient` application:

```
/*
      ** Program Name:    VendorClient.java
      **
      ** Purpose:         The client application that
      **                  uses the Vendor session bean.
*/
package client;
import java.util.Hashtable;
import javax.naming.Context;
import javax.naming.InitialContext;
import purchase.ejb.slsb.Vendor;
import purchase.ejb.slsb.VendorHome;
```

```
import java.util.Collection;
import java.util.Iterator;
import purchase.vo.VendorVO;
public class VendorClient {
  public static void main(String [] args)  {
    VendorClient vendorClient = new VendorClient();
    try {
      String password = System.getProperty("password");
      if  (password != null) {
          if(password.length()<2) password = "manager";
      }
      String host = System.getProperty("host");
      if  (host != null) {
          if(host.length()<2) host = "localhost";
      }
      String port = System.getProperty("port");
      if  (port != null){
           if(port.length()<2) port = "23791";
      }
      String name = System.getProperty("name");
      if  (name != null) {
          if  (name.length()<2) name = "chapter6";
      }
      Hashtable env = new Hashtable();
      env.put(Context.INITIAL_CONTEXT_FACTORY,
           "com.evermind.server.rmi.RMIInitialContextFactory");
      env.put(Context.SECURITY_PRINCIPAL, "admin");
      env.put(Context.SECURITY_CREDENTIALS, password);
      env.put(Context.PROVIDER_URL, "ormi://"+host+":"
                                        +port+"/"+name);
      env.put("dedicated.connection" ,"true");
      System.out.println("password: "+password+" ,
                    application: "+name+" ,host: "+host);
      System.out.println("Setting up env!!!");
      Context ctx = new InitialContext(env);
      System.out.println("Get IC!!!");
      VendorHome vendorHome = (VendorHome)ctx.lookup("Vendor");
      System.out.println("Get VendorHome!!!");
      Vendor vendor = null;
      // Use one of the create methods below to create a new instance
      vendor = vendorHome.create(  );
      // Call any of the Remote methods below to access the EJB
      // vendor.getVendorNo(  );
      // vendor.setVendorNo( long newVendorNo );
      // vendor.getName(  );
```

```
        // vendor.setName( java.lang.String newName );
        // vendor.getAddress(  );
        // vendor.setAddress( java.lang.String newAddress );
        // vendor.getCity(  );
        // vendor.setCity( java.lang.String newCity );
        // vendor.getVendorState(  );
        // vendor.setVendorState( java.lang.String newVendorState );
        // vendor.getVendorZip(  );
        // vendor.setVendorZip( java.lang.String newVendorZip );
        // vendor.getCountry(  );
        // vendor.setCountry( java.lang.String newCountry );
        System.out.println("Before while!!!");
        // Get vendors' info
        Collection arrayOfVendors = vendor.getAllVendorInfo(  );
        System.out.println("Got a Collection of vendors!!!");
        Iterator iter = arrayOfVendors.iterator();
        System.out.println("Created an Iterator object!!!");
        while (iter.hasNext()){
            VendorVO oneVendor = (VendorVO)iter.next();
            System.out.println("vendorno = " + oneVendor.getVendorNo());
            System.out.println(" ");
        } // End while
      }
      catch(Throwable ex)    {
        ex.printStackTrace();
      }
    }
  }  // End of VendorClient
```

Once you have completed your application, the next steps are to compile, archive, and deploy your enterprise bean. In the "Deploying EJB Components to OC4J" section, you will learn how to package your application and deploy it to OC4J.

Next, you will create the `PurchaseOrderManagement` `STATEFUL` session bean.

Creating the PurchaseOrderManagement Session Bean

In this section, you will develop the `PurchaseOrderManagement` session bean that acts as a mediator between the client and the `PurchaseOrderLocal` and `LineItemLocal` CMP entity beans. As shown earlier in Figure 6-2, all access to the CMPs is done through the `PurchaseOrderManagement` session bean, which functions as a façade for the authentication system.

The J2EE Session Façade

The intent of a session façade is to provide a "unified, workflow-oriented interface to a set of enterprise beans" (*Core J2EE Patterns,* http://java.sun.com/blueprints/corej2eepatterns/Patterns/SessionFacade.html). The J2EE session façade pattern is also known as *Session Entity Façade.* You can implement a session façade as a `STATELESS` session bean or as a `STATEFUL` session bean, depending upon your needs.

The idea behind this pattern is to decouple clients and entity beans. Thus, instead of communicating directly with entity beans, clients communicate only with the façade. In the EJB application that you will build in this section, instead of communicating directly with the `PurchaseOrderLocal` and `LineItemLocal` entity beans, clients will access the `PurchaseOrderManagement` session bean, a much simpler interface that has all the necessary methods to process purchase order requisitions.

Recall that you developed the `PurchaseOrderLocal` and `LineItemLocal` entity beans in Chapter 5. You used the `PurchaseOrderLocal` and `LineItemLocal` entity beans to manipulate data in the `PURCHASE_ORDER` and `LINE_ITEM` tables, respectively. You may want to review Chapter 5 before delving in this section.

It is important to note that, since the `PurchaseOrderManagement` session bean resides in the same server as the `PurchaseOrderLocal` and `LineItemLocal` entity beans, only the remote calls of the `PurchaseOrderManagement` session bean are needed to carry out a purchase order workflow. Once the `PurchaseOrderManagement` façade session bean receives a call, it coordinates its enterprise beans on the same server, thereby using less network communication. Note that network performance could be reduced further if you were to use the local CMP entity beans that you created in Chapter 5.

The Components of the PurchaseOrderManagement Session Bean

The `PurchaseOrderManagement` session bean consists of the following components:

- The `PurchaseOrderManagement` remote interface
- The `PurchaseOrderManagementHome` remote home interface
- The `PurchaseOrderManagementBean` bean class

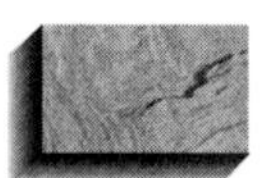

NOTE
We provide also a client view of the `PurchaseOrderManagement` *session bean. The source code for the local* `PurchaseOrderManagement` *session bean is in the* `chapter06code.zip` *file for this chapter.*

Here is the definition of the PurchaseOrderManagement remote interface:

The PurchaseOrderManagement Remote Interface

```
/*
      ** Program Name: PurchaseOrderManagement.java
      **
      ** Purpose:          The remote interface
      **
*/

package purchase.ejb.sfsb;
import javax.ejb.EJBObject;
import java.rmi.RemoteException;
import javax.ejb.EJBException;


public interface PurchaseOrderManagement
     extends EJBObject {
    // Add a line item for a specific requestno
    void addLineItem(long requestno, long lineno,
                     long projectno, long quantity, String unit,
                     float cost, float actualcost,
                     String description)
         throws EJBException, RemoteException;
    // Add a collection of line items
    void addLineItem(Collection lineItems)
         throws RemoteException;
    // Add a purchase order requisition
    long AddPurchase(long requestno, long employeeno,
                  long vendorno)
         throws RemoteException;
    // Get all the line items for a specific purchase order
    // and the associated attributes for that purchase order
    Collection getPurchaseOrderInfo(long requestno)
         throws RemoteException;
    // Get all the purchase order requisitions
    Collection getAllPurchaseOrders()
         throws RemoteException;

} // End PurchaseOrderManagement
```

Next, you will code the PurchaseOrderManagementHome remote home interface.

The PurchaseOrderManagementHome Remote Home Interface

Here is the definition of the `PurchaseOrderManagementHome` remote home interface:

```
/*
      ** Program Name: PurchaseOrderManagementHome.java
      **
      ** Purpose:         The remote home interface
      **
*/
package purchase.ejb.sfsb;
import javax.ejb.EJBHome;
import java.rmi.RemoteException;
import javax.ejb.CreateException;

public interface PurchaseOrderManagementHome
     extends EJBHome {
  PurchaseOrderManagement create()
    throws RemoteException, CreateException;
}  // End of PurchaseOrderManagementHome
```

The PurchaseOrderManagementBean Class

In this section, you will code the `PurchaseOrderManagementBean` class, which consists of the following:

- A list of the callback methods required by EJB containers. See the "Life Cycles of STATEFUL Session Beans" section of this chapter for a detailed description of how the EJB container creates instances of `STATEFUL` session beans and manages their life cycle.
- **`public void ejbCreate() { }`** A client creates a session bean instance using the `create()` method defined in the `PurchaseOrderManagementHome` remote home interface. The instances of `STATEFUL` session beans contain a conversational state, which must be retained across methods and transactions. The conversational state of a `STATEFUL` session object is defined as the session bean instance's field values, plus the transitive closure of the objects from the instance's fields reached by following Java object references. Note that, when a client invokes the `create()` method, the EJB container calls this method before creating the bean's instance. At creation time, the program automatically locates the `PurchaseOrderLocalHome` and `LineItemLocalHome` interfaces of the `PurchaseOrderBean` and `LineItemBean`, respectively.
- **`public void ejbActivate() { }`** The `ejbActivate` notification signals the instance that it has just been reactivated.

- **public void ejbPassivate() { }** The `ejbPassivate` notification signals the intent of the container to *passivate* the instance. Because containers automatically maintain the conversational state of a session bean instance when it is passivated, most session beans can ignore these notifications. The purpose of the `ejbPassivate()` method is to allow a session bean to maintain open resources that need to be closed prior to an instance's passivation and then reopened during an instance's activation.
- **public void ejbRemove() { }** The `ejbRemove` notification signals that the instance is in the process of being removed by the container. In the `ejbRemove()` method, the instance typically releases the same resources that it releases in the `ejbPassivate()` method.
- **public void setSessionContext(SessionContext ctx) { }** The EJB container calls the `setSessionContext()` method to associate a session bean instance with its context maintained by the container. Typically, a session bean instance retains its session context as part of its conversational state.
- Several business logic methods callable by EJB clients:
  - **public void addLineItem(long requestno, long lineno, long projectno, long quantity, String unit, float cost, float actualcost, String description)** The `addLineItem()` method creates an instance of the `LineItemLocal` CMP bean, which in turn creates a row in the `LINE_ITEM` table.
  - **void addLineItem(Collection lineItems)** Use this method to insert a collection of line items for a specific `requestno` (purchase order requisition number). This method is empty. We leave the implementation code as an exercise for the reader.
  - **public void addPurchase(long requestno, long employeeno, long vendorno)** The `addPurchase()` method creates an instance of the `PurchaseOrderLocal` CMP bean, which in turn creates a row in the `PURCHASE_ORDER` table. Additionally, the `addPurchase()` method creates an instance of the `ApprovalLocal` CMP bean, which in turn creates a row in the `APPROVAL` table.
  - **Collection getPurchaseOrderInfo(long requestno)** Use this method to get detailed data for a specific `requestno`.
  - **Collection getAllPurchaseOrders()** Use this method to get all purchase order requisitions from the database. We provide no code implementation for this method. It is left as an exercise for the reader.

- Three private methods not callable by EJB clients:
  - **private LineItemLocalHome getLineItemLocalHome()** This method acquires a reference to the LineItemLocalHome object of the LineItemLocal CMP entity bean.
  - **private PurchaseOrderLocalHome getPurchaseOrderLocalHome()** This method acquires a reference to the PurchaseOrderLocalHome object of the PurchaseOrderLocal CMP entity bean.
  - **private ApprovalLocalHome getApprovalLocalHome()** This method acquires a reference to the ApprovalLocalHome object of the ApprovalLocal CMP entity bean. Refer to Chapter 7 for a complete definition of the ApprovalLocal bean.

Life Cycles of STATEFUL Session Beans

The life cycle for a STATELESS session bean is very similar to the life cycle of a STATEFUL session bean, but some fundamental differences exist between the types of session beans. The life cycle of a STATELESS session beans was shown earlier in the chapter, in Figure 6-5. The life cycle of STATEFUL session beans is shown in Figure 6-6. The client initiates the life cycle by invoking the create() method.

The container creates an instance of a session bean in three steps:

1. The container calls the bean class's newInstance() method to create a new session bean instance.
2. The container calls the setSessionContext() method to pass the Context object to the instance.
3. The container calls the instance's ejbCreate() method whose signature matches the signature of the create() method of the home interface that the client invoked. The input parameters sent from the client are passed to the ejbCreate() method.

The session bean instance is now ready for the client's business methods. While in the Ready state, the EJB container may decide to *deactivate* (or passivate) the bean by moving it from memory to secondary storage. The EJB container invokes the bean's ejbPassivate() method immediately before passivating it. If a client invokes a business method on the bean while it is in the passive stage, the EJB container activates the bean, moving it back to the Ready state, and then calls the bean's ejbActivate() method. At the end of the life cycle, the client invokes the remove() method, and

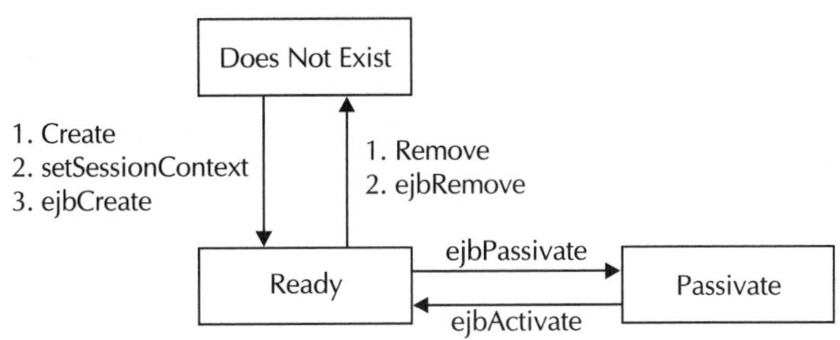

FIGURE 6-6. *Life cycle of `STATEFUL` session beans*

the EJB container calls the bean's `ejbRemove()` method. The bean's instance is ready for garbage collection. Note that your application code controls the invocation of only two life-cycle methods: the `create()` and `remove()` methods in the client.

NOTE
The EJB container controls the invocation of the callback methods, such as the `ejbCreate( )`, `ejbActivate( )`, `ejbPassivate( )`, and `setSessionContext(SessionContext ctx)` methods. Your client code does not have access to these methods.

Here is the definition of the `PurchaseOrderManagementBean` class:

```
/*
    ** Program Name:     PurchaseOrderManagementBean.java
    **
    ** Purpose:          The bean class of
    **                   the PurchaseOrderManagement
    **                   stateful session bean.

*/
package purchase.ejb.sfsb;
import javax.ejb.SessionBean;
import javax.ejb.SessionContext;

import purchase.ejb.cmp.LineItemLocal;
import purchase.ejb.cmp.LineItemLocalHome;
```

```
import purchase.ejb.cmp.PurchaseOrderLocal;
import purchase.ejb.cmp.PurchaseOrderLocalHome;
import purchase.ejb.cmp.ApprovalLocal;
import purchase.ejb.cmp.ApprovalLocalHome;

import javax.naming.Context;
import javax.naming.InitialContext;

import javax.ejb.CreateException;
import javax.ejb.RemoveException;
import java.rmi.RemoteException;
import javax.ejb.EJBException;
import javax.naming.NamingException;
import javax.ejb.FinderException;

import purchase.vo.PurchaseVO;
import purchase.vo.LineItemVO;
import java.util.ArrayList;
import java.util.Collection;
import java.util.Iterator;


public class PurchaseOrderManagementBean
    implements SessionBean {

  public SessionContext sessionContext;

  private LineItemLocalHome lineItemLocalHome;
  private PurchaseOrderLocalHome purchaseOrderLocalHome;
  private ApprovalLocalHome approvalLocalHome;

  public PurchaseOrderManagementBean() {
  }

  public void ejbCreate() throws CreateException
  {
    // Get LineItemLocalHome
    try {
        lineItemLocalHome = getLineItemLocalHome();
        System.out.println("Inside POCreate: "
                       +"I got LineItemLocalHome!!!");
    }  // End try
    catch (NamingException no_item) {
       throw new CreateException (
           "Unable to find LineItemLocalHome in "
           + " ejbCreate " +no_item.getMessage());
```

```
    } // End catch

    // Get PurchaseOrderLocalHome
    try {
        purchaseOrderLocalHome = getPurchaseOrderLocalHome();
        System.out.println("Inside POCreate: "
                             +"I got PurchaseOrderHome!!!");
    }  // End try
    catch (NamingException no_purchase) {
       throw new CreateException (
           "Unable to find PurchaseOrderHome in "
           + " ejbCreate " +no_purchase.getMessage());
    } // End catch

    // Get ApprovalLocalHome
    try {
        approvalLocalHome = getApprovalLocalHome();
        System.out.println("Inside POCreate: "
               +"I got ApprovalLocalHome!!!");
    }  // End try
    catch (NamingException no_approval) {
       throw new CreateException (
           "Unable to find ApprovalLocalHome in "
           + " ejbCreate " +no_approval.getMessage());
    } // End catch

  } // End of ejbCreate()

  public void ejbActivate()
  {
  }

  public void ejbPassivate()
  {
  }

  public void ejbRemove()
  {
  }

  public void setSessionContext(SessionContext ctx)
  {
    this.sessionContext = ctx;
  }

  private LineItemLocalHome getLineItemLocalHome()
     throws javax.naming.NamingException {
```

```
  Context ic = new InitialContext();
  return (LineItemLocalHome)
        ic.lookup("java:comp/env/LineItemLocal");
}

private PurchaseOrderLocalHome getPurchaseOrderLocalHome()
   throws javax.naming.NamingException {
  Context ic = new InitialContext();
  return (PurchaseOrderLocalHome)
       ic.lookup("java:comp/env/PurchaseOrderLocal");
}

private ApprovalLocalHome getApprovalLocalHome()
   throws javax.naming.NamingException {
  Context ic = new InitialContext();
  return (ApprovalLocalHome)
       ic.lookup("java:comp/env/ApprovalLocal");
}

public void  addLineItem(long requestno, long lineno,
     long projectno, long quantity, String unit,
     float cost, float actualcost,
     String description) {

     try {
          // Add a LineItemLocal
          LineItemLocal lineItemLocal =
              lineItemLocalHome.create(requestno,lineno,
                        projectno, quantity, unit,
                        cost, actualcost,
                        description);
    } // End try
    catch (CreateException e) {
       throw new EJBException
         ("Unable to create lineitem " +requestno);
    }  // End catch

}  // End of addLineItem

public void addLineItem(Collection lineItems)
{
}

public long AddPurchaseOrder(long requestno, long employeeno,
                             long vendorno)
{
   long officerNo = 100;
```

```
      String approved ="N";
      String reasons = null;
          try {
                  // Add a purchase
          PurchaseOrderLocal purchaseOrderLocal =
              purchaseOrderLocalHome.create(requestno, employeeno,
                                           vendorno);
          } // End try
          catch (CreateException pec) {
                throw new EJBException
                  ("Unable to create PurchaseOrderLocal "
                         +requestno +" " +pec.getMessage());
          }  // End catch
    try {
                  // Add an ApprovalLocal
          ApprovalLocal approvalLocal =
              approvalLocalHome.create(requestno, officerNo,
                                          approved, reasons);
          } // End try
          catch (CreateException aec) {
                throw new EJBException
                  ("Unable to create ApprovalLocal "
                      +requestno +" " +aec.getMessage());
          }  // End catch

    return requestno;

}  // End of addPurchase()

public Collection getPurchaseOrderInfo(long requestno)
{
    // Need a Java ArrayList to store the
     // table rows since you do not know
     // how many rows are being retrieved.
     ArrayList purchaseOrderLocal = new ArrayList();
     // An LineItemLocal object
     LineItemLocal lineItemLocal;
     try {
          Collection purchaseLineItem =
                lineItemLocalHome.findByRequestNo(requestno);
          Iterator items = purchaseLineItem.iterator();

          while (items.hasNext()) {
             lineItemLocal = (LineItemLocal)items.next();
             LineItemVO oneLineItem =
               new LineItemVO(lineItemLocal.getRequestNo(),
                           lineItemLocal.getLineNo(),
```

```
                              lineItemLocal.getProjectNo(),
                              lineItemLocal.getQuantity(),
                              lineItemLocal.getUnit(),
                              lineItemLocal.getCost(),
                              lineItemLocal.getActualCost(),
                              lineItemLocal.getDescription() );
              // Insert oneLineItem object into the Java
               // purchaseLocalOrder ArrayList
               purchaseOrderLocal.add(oneLineItem);
          }  // End while

          purchaseOrderLocal.trimToSize();

          return purchaseOrderLocal;
      } // End try
      catch (FinderException fe) {
        throw new EJBException("Cannot select PurchaseOrderLocal info: "
                        + fe.getMessage());
      }  // End catch
      catch (java.lang.Exception le) {
      throw new EJBException("ArrayList error in Select "
          + " Line Items: " + le.getMessage());
      }  // End catch

    } // End getPurchaseInfo

    public Collection getAllPurchaseOrders() {
      return null;
    }

}  // End of PurchaseOrderManagementBean class
```

Next, you will write a Java application, a simple client that will use the `PurchaseOrderManagement` session bean. In Chapters 10 and 11, you will develop more elaborate EJB clients that use this bean.

The PurchaseOrderManagementClient Class

Here is the `PurchaseOrderManagementClient` application:

```
/*
      ** Program Name: PurchaseOrderManagementClient.java
      **
      ** Purpose:         The EJB client
      **
*/

package client;
```

```
import java.util.Hashtable;
import javax.naming.Context;
import javax.naming.InitialContext;
import purchase.ejb.sfsb.PurchaseOrderManagement;
import purchase.ejb.sfsb.PurchaseOrderManagementHome;
import javax.rmi.PortableRemoteObject;
import java.util.ArrayList;
import purchase.vo.LineItemVO;

public class PurchaseOrderManagementClient
{
  public static void main(String [] args)
  {
    PurchaseOrderManagementClient
        purchaseOrderManagementClient =
             new PurchaseOrderManagementClient();
    try
    {
      String password = System.getProperty("password");
      if(password != null)
        {
        if(password.length()<2) password = "manager";
        }
      String host = System.getProperty("host");
      if(host != null)
        {
        if(host.length()<2) host = "localhost";
        }
      String port = System.getProperty("port");
      if(port != null)
        {
        if(port.length()<2) port = "23791";
        }
      String name = System.getProperty("name");
      if(name != null)
        {
        if(name.length()<2) name = "chapter6";
        }
      Hashtable env = new Hashtable();
      env.put(Context.INITIAL_CONTEXT_FACTORY,
         "com.evermind.server.rmi.RMIInitialContextFactory");
      env.put(Context.SECURITY_PRINCIPAL, "admin");
      env.put(Context.SECURITY_CREDENTIALS, password);
      env.put(Context.PROVIDER_URL, "ormi://"+host+":"+port+"/"+name);
      env.put("dedicated.connection" ,"true");
      System.out.println("Running with host: "+host+"
            ,port: "+port+" ,appname: "+name+" ,password: "+password);
```

```
Context ctx = new InitialContext(env);
/*
PurchaseOrderManagementHome
   purchaseOrderManagementHome =
     (PurchaseOrderManagementHome)
            ctx.lookup("PurchaseOrderManagement");
*/
Object homeObject =
   ctx.lookup("PurchaseOrderManagement");

PurchaseOrderManagementHome
    purchaseOrderManagementHome =
    (PurchaseOrderManagementHome)
       PortableRemoteObject.narrow(homeObject,
                  PurchaseOrderManagementHome.class);

PurchaseOrderManagement purchaseOrderManagement;

// Use one of the create() methods
// below to create a new instance
// purchaseOrderManagement =
      purchaseOrderManagementHome.create(  );
 purchaseOrderManagement = (PurchaseOrderManagement)
      PortableRemoteObject.narrow(
            purchaseOrderManagementHome.create(),
            PurchaseOrderManagement.class);

System.out.println("I Got a PurchaseOrderManagementHome!!!");
long requestno = 500;

// Call any of the Remote methods below to access the EJB
// purchaseOrderManagement.addLineItem( long requestno,
   long lineno, long projectno,
   long quantity, java.lang.String unit,
   float cost, float actualcost,
   java.lang.String description );
// purchaseOrderManagement.addLineItem
//     ( java.util.Collection lineItems );
// purchaseOrderManagement.AddPurchase( long requestno,
//                      long employeeno, long vendorno );
// purchaseOrderManagement.getPurchaseOrderInfo(long requestno);
// purchaseOrderManagement.getAllPurchaseOrders(  );
System.out.println("I Got a PurchaseOrderManagement!!!");
//System.out.println("PurchaseOrderInfo: "
//    "+purchaseOrderManagement.getPurchaseOrderInfo( requestno ));
ArrayList a = new ArrayList
 (purchaseOrderManagement.getPurchaseOrderInfo(requestno));
```

```
      for(int i=0;i<a.size();i++)
      {
        LineItemVO item = (LineItemVO)a.get(i);
        System.out.println("Item: "+item.description+"
             cost: "+item.cost);
      }
    }
    catch(Throwable ex)
    {
      ex.printStackTrace();
    }

  }
} // End of the PurchaseOrderManagementClient class
```

Compile all the Java classes and the dependent classes for the `Vendor` `STATELESS` session bean, the `PurchaseOrderManagement` `STATEFUL` session beans, and the `VendorClient` and the `PurchaseOrderManagementClient` Java applications.

Next, you will write the deployment descriptor file. After implementing and compiling your classes, you must create the standard J2EE EJB deployment descriptor for all beans in the EJB module. The XML deployment descriptor, defined in the `ejb-jar.xml` file, describes the application components and provides additional information to enable the container to manage the application. The structure for this file is mandated in the DTD file, which is provided at http://java.sun.com/dtd/ejb-jar_2_0.dtd.

If your application consists of several beans, you may write a deployment descriptor file for each bean or you may write a single one comprising all the beans of your application. The J2EE specification defines how enterprise beans and other application components contained in multiple `ejb-jar` files can be assembled into an application. To learn more about the EJB specification, download the `ejb-2_0-fr2-spec.pdf` file at http://java.sun.com/products/ejb/docs.html.

In the following section, we present a single deployment descriptor file that includes the `Vendor` `STATELESS` session bean, the `PurchaseOrderManagement` `STATEFUL` session bean, the `PurchaseOrderLocal`, `LineItemLocal`, and the `ApprovalLocal` CMP entity beans.

Writing the ejb-jar.xml Deployment Descriptor File

In this section, you will define the deployment descriptor file for your beans. Remember that this file is part of the `ejb-jar` archive file. The EJB specification defines the structure of the `ejb-jar.xml` file. Developers use this file to provide information for each enterprise bean that comprises the application. In this section, we will only present the elements relating to session beans (STATELESS or STATEFUL). Recall that the PurchaseOrderManagement STATEFUL session bean uses the PurchaseOrderLocal and LineItemLocal CMP beans. Thus, we will also present the elements of the ejb-jar.xml file that indicate to the EJB container the relationships between PurchaseOrderManagement, PurchaseOrderLocal, LineItemLocal, and the ApprovalLocal Enterprise JavaBeans.

The ejb-jar.xml File

Here is a partial listing of the ejb-jar.xml file:

```
<?xml version = '1.0' encoding = 'windows-1252'?>
<!DOCTYPE ejb-jar PUBLIC "-//Sun Microsystems,
    Inc.//DTD Enterprise JavaBeans 1.1//EN"
    "http://java.sun.com/j2ee/dtds/ejb-jar_1_1.dtd">
<ejb-jar>
   <enterprise-beans>
      <entity>
       <-- Use an <entity>…</entity> for each of the entity beans -->
       <description>Entity Bean ( Container-managed Persistence )
       </description>
       <display-name>LineItemLocal</display-name>
…
…
     </entity>
     <entity>
       <-- Use an <entity>…</entity> for each of the entity beans -->
       <description>Entity Bean ( Container-managed Persistence )
       </description>
       <display-name>PurchaseOrderLocal</display-name>
…
…
     </entity>
     <entity>
       <-- Use an <entity>…</entity> for each of the entity beans -->
       <description>Entity Bean ( Container-managed Persistence )
       </description>
       <display-name>ApprovalLocal</display-name>
…
…
     </entity>
     <session>
      <description>Session Bean ( Stateful )</description>
      <display-name>PurchaseOrderManagement</display-name>
         <ejb-name>PurchaseOrderManagement</ejb-name>
```

```
<home>purchase.ejb.sfsb.PurchaseOrderManagementHome</home>
<remote>purchase.ejb.sfsb.PurchaseOrderManagement</remote>
<ejb-class>purchase.ejb.sfsb.PurchaseOrderManagementBean
</ejb-class>
<session-type>Stateful</session-type>
<transaction-type>Container</transaction-type>
<!-- Use the <resource-ref> element to
     specify your OC4J data source -- >
<resource-ref>
       <res-ref-name>jdbc/OracleDS</res-ref-name>
       <res-type>javax.sql.DataSource</res-type>
       <res-auth>Application</res-auth>
</resource-ref>
<!-- Use the <ejb-local-ref> element to
     specify other local beans (session or entity)
     that your bean will use -- >
<ejb-local-ref>
   <description>
        This EJB reference indicates that
        the PurchaseOrderManagement stateful
        session bean uses the LineItemLocal CMP
        entity bean
   </description>
   <ejb-ref-name>LineItemLocal</ejb-ref-name>
   <ejb-ref-type>Entity</ejb-ref-type>
   <local-home>
      purchase.ejb.cmp.LineItemLocalHome</local-home>
   <local>purchase.ejb.cmp.LineItemLocal</local>
</ejb-local-ref>
<ejb-local-ref>
   <description>
        This EJB reference indicates that
        the PurchaseOrderManagement stateful
        session bean uses the PurchaseOrderLocal CMP
        entity bean
   </description>
   <ejb-ref-name>PurchaseOrderLocal</ejb-ref-name>
   <ejb-ref-type>Entity</ejb-ref-type>
   <local-home>
      purchase.ejb.cmp.PurchaseOrderLocalHome</local-home>
   <local>purchase.ejb.cmp.PurchaseOrderLocal</local>
</ejb-local-ref>
<ejb-local-ref>
      <description>
              This EJB reference indicates that
              the PurchaseOrderManagement stateful
              session bean uses the ApprovalLocal CMP
              entity bean
```

```
                </description>
                <ejb-ref-name>ApprovalLocal</ejb-ref-name>
                <ejb-ref-type>Entity</ejb-ref-type>
                <local-home>
                    purchase.ejb.cmp.ApprovalLocalHome</local-home>
                <local>purchase.ejb.cmp.ApprovalLocal</local>
          </ejb-local-ref>
      </session>
      <session>
       <description>Session Bean ( Stateless )</description>
          <display-name>Vendor</display-name>
          <ejb-name>Vendor</ejb-name>
          <home> purchase.ejb.slsb.VendorHome</home>
          <remote> purchase.ejb.slsb.Vendor</remote>
          <ejb-class> purchase.ejb.slsb.VendorBean</ejb-class>
          <session-type>Stateless</session-type>
          <transaction-type>Container</transaction-type>
          <resource-ref>
                 <res-ref-name>jdbc/OracleDS</res-ref-name>
                 <res-type>javax.sql.DataSource</res-type>
                 <res-auth>Application</res-auth>
          </resource-ref>
      </session>
   </enterprise-beans>
   <assembly-descriptor>
       <container-transaction>
          <method>
                 <ejb-name>LineItemLocal</ejb-name>
                 <method-name>*</method-name>
          </method>
          <method>
                 <ejb-name>PurchaseOrderLocal</ejb-name>
                 <method-name>*</method-name>
          </method>
          <method>
                 <ejb-name>ApprovalLocal</ejb-name>
                 <method-name>*</method-name>
          </method>
          <trans-attribute>Required</trans-attribute>
       </container-transaction>
     </assembly-descriptor>
</ejb-jar>
```

Next, you will write the `orion-ejb-jar.xml` OC4J-specific deployment descriptor file. The nice thing about Oracle9*i*AS Containers For J2EE is that you do not have to provide the `orion-ejb-jar.xml` file. At deployment time, OC4J will generate it for you.

Note that the first time you deploy your application to OC4J, OC4J automatically generates a new OC4J-specific XML file for you, using its default elements. However, if you have provided an OC4J-specific XML file within your application, OC4J will merge your configuration with the one that gets generated to produce a new OC4J-specific deployment descriptor for you. If you do not store an `orion-ejb-jar.xml` server-specific deployment descriptor in your application, OC4J will generate one for you.

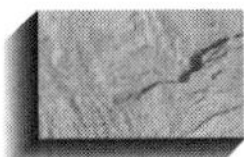

CAUTION
If you want to edit this deployment descriptor, we recommend that you take the generated one and store it within your application, edit it, and, more importantly, delete the generated one under your application deployment directory. Then, restart the server.

Writing or Generating the orion-ejb-jar.xml File

In this section, we will only present the elements relating to the `Vendor` and `PurchaseOrderManagement` session beans.

Here is a partial listing of the `orion-ejb-jar.xml` file:

```
<?xml version = '1.0' encoding = 'windows-1252'?>
<!DOCTYPE orion-ejb-jar PUBLIC
   "-//Evermind//DTD Enterprise JavaBeans 1.1 runtime//EN"
   "http://xmlns.oracle.com/ias/dtds/orion-ejb-jar.dtd">
<orion-ejb-jar>
   <enterprise-beans>
     <entity-deployment name="LineItemLocal" data-source="jdbc/OracleDS" … >
     </entity-deployment>
     <session-deployment name="PurchaseOrderManagement"/>
     <session-deployment name="Vendor"/>
   </enterprise-beans>
   <assembly-descriptor>
      <default-method-access>
         <security-role-mapping name="&lt;default-ejb-caller-role>"
                           impliesAll="true"/>
      </default-method-access>
   </assembly-descriptor>
</orion-ejb-jar>
```

In the previous sections, you created your application, compiled all the Java classes, and wrote the deployment descriptor. The next step is to archive your EJB application into a JAR file. The JAR file should include all bean class files, their dependent class files, and the `ejb-jar.xml` deployment descriptor file.

The application that you developed in this chapter consists of an EJB module, containing one remote `STATELESS` session bean, `Vendor`, one remote `STATEFUL` session bean, the session façade `PurchaseOrderManagement`, and two remote CMP beans, `LineItemLocal` and `PurchaseOrderLocal`. Next, you will learn how to deploy your application to OC4J.

Deploying EJB Components to OC4J

Deploying EJB components to OC4J is rather simple. In Chapters 2 and 5, you learned how to deploy a J2EE application to the Oracle9*i*AS Containers For J2EE server and how to bind that application to the server so that you can access the application from OC4J. In this section, we will revisit the necessary steps, to refresh your memory.

Archiving the EJB Application

The very first step is to package your application. You do so when you create the J2EE EAR file.

Packaging the Application: Creating the EAR File

The steps are as follows:

1. Open a command prompt, and position yourself in the classes directory (`chapter06/classes`).
2. Create the JAR file. Type the following:

   ```
   jar cvf chapter06-ejb.jar META-INF ejbapps vo
   ```

3. Copy the `chapter06-ejb.jar` file to the root development directory: `chapter06`.
4. Modify the `application.xml` file in the `chapter06/META-INF` directory to look like this:

   ```
   <?xml version="1.0"?>
   <!DOCTYPE application PUBLIC "-//Sun Microsystems,
       Inc.//DTD J2EE Application 1.2//EN"
       "http://java.sun.com/j2ee/dtds/application_1_2.dtd">
   <!-- The application element is the root element
        of a J2EE application deployment descriptor.  -->
   ```

```
<application>
      <display-name>Chapter6</display-name>
      <module>
            <ejb>chapter06-ejb.jar</ejb>
      </module>
</application>
```

5. Position yourself in the root directory, `chapter06`.
6. Create the EAR file. Type the following:

```
jar cvf chapter06.ear chapter06-ejb.jar META-INF
```

You now have your `chapter06.ear` file and are ready to deploy the application. If your application will access a database, then you need to define an OC4J data source. You do so by modifying the OC4J `data-sources.xml` XML file.

Modifying the OC4J data-sources.xml File

Before deploying your application, you need to register your data source with OC4J. You do that by modifying the OC4J `data-sources.xml` file. This file is located in the OC4J's .../`config` directory.

In the OC4J's `data-sources.xml` file, Oracle provides a default `DataSource` example that uses Oracle's JDBC driver to create the connections. Modify the file as follows:

```
<!-- Original source from Oracle -->
<data-source
            class="com.evermind.sql.DriverManagerDataSource"
            name="OracleDS"
            location="jdbc/OracleCoreDS"
            xa-location="jdbc/xa/OracleXADS"
            ejb-location="jdbc/OracleDS"
            connection-driver="oracle.jdbc.driver.OracleDriver"
            username="scott"
            password="tiger"
            url="jdbc:oracle:thin:@localhost:5521:oracle"
            inactivity-timeout="30"
      />

<!-- Your datasource -->
<data-source
            class="com.evermind.sql.DriverManagerDataSource"
            name="OracleDS"
            location="jdbc/OracleCoreDS"
            xa-location="jdbc/xa/OracleXADS"
            ejb-location="jdbc/OracleDS"
```

```
        connection-driver="oracle.jdbc.driver.OracleDriver"
        username="scott"
        password="tiger"
        url="jdbc:oracle:thin:@yourhost:your-port-no:your-sid"
        inactivity-timeout="30"
/>
```

Next, you will deploy the application. OC4J supports deployment of both EAR files and an exploded directory conforming to the J2EE standard (as does our `chapter05` directory structure). We will show you both ways, starting with the EAR file.

Deploying an EAR File to OC4J

The steps for deploying an EAR file to OC4J are as follows:

1. Copy the `chapter06.ear` file to your OC4J installation `applications` directory. If you have unzipped OC4J under `d:\OC4J`, then this will be `d:\OC4J\j2ee\home\applications`. The EAR file can be placed anywhere, but in this example, we'll use the OC4J `applications` directory.
2. Edit the OC4J `server.xml` file, found under your `OC4J\j2ee\home\config` directory. Add the following entry:

   ```
   <application name="chapter6" path="../applications/chapter06.ear"
           auto-start="true" />
   ```

Recall that OC4J supports hot deployment; therefore, if OC4J is running, it will immediately pick up and deploy this application. If OC4J is not running, position yourself in the `OC4J/j2ee/home` directory and start OC4J by typing the following:

```
java -jar oc4j.jar -verbosity 10
```

Output from the OC4J Console

Standing in the `OC4J/j2ee/home` directory, you should see something like this as output from the OC4J console:

```
Auto-unpacking …chapter06.ear... done.
Auto-deploying chapter6 (New server version detected)...
Application default (default) initialized...
Application chapter6 initialized...
Copying default deployment …
Auto-deploying chapter06-ejb.jar(No previous deployment found)...done.

Binding EJB PurchaseOrderManagement to PurchaseOrderManagement...
```

```
Binding EJB Vendor to Vendor...
Application chapter6 (Chapter6) initialized...
Web-App default:defaultWebApp (0.0.0.0/0.0.0.0:80) started...
Oracle9iAS Containers for J2EE initializedOracle9iAS Containers
                                              for J2EE initialized
```

Next, let us test the application.

Testing the Application

Use the `VendorClient` and `PurchaseOrderManagementClient` Java applications to test your application. For convenience, we have provided two BAT files, `runVendor.bat` and `runPurchaseClient.bat`, to set up the environment and run the test clients. Those files are located in the classes (`chapter06/classes`) directory.

Running the Clients

The steps to run the clients are as follows:

1. Open a command prompt in the `classes` directory.
2. Set up the two environment variables `OC4J_HOME` and `JAVA_HOME`. If you have installed OC4J at `d:\OC4J`, type **set OC4J_HOME=d:\OC4J**. If you have Java installed at `d:\java13`, type **set JAVA_HOME=d:\java13**.
3. If you have the following values for your environment, `host=localhost`, `applicationname=chapter6` (the name you gave your application in the OC4J `server.xml` file), `port=23791` (the OC4J default RMI port is listed in the `OC4J/config/rmi.xml` file), and `password=manager` (the password for the admin user is listed in the `OC4J/config/ principals.xml` file), you can run the client by just typing the following:

   ```
   runVendorClient.bat
   ```

   Note that, if any of the parameters in Step 3 do not match your setup, you can pass them to the `runVendorClient` program at the command prompt. For example:

   ```
   runVendorClient.bat myHost myPassword chapter6 23791
   ```

Output from the VendorClient Class

The output from `VendorClient` is as follows:

```
#######################################################
# if you are running
# this client with any other
```

```
# settings than the defaults which
# are host=localhost, rmi-port=23791
# admin-password=manager, application-name=
# chapter6, you have to pass those variables
# like runVendorClient hostname password appname 23781
# e.g runVendorClient myhost mypassword mychapter6 23781
########################################################
Running with host: localhost ,port: 23791 ,
appname: chapter6 ,password: manager
Setting up env!!!
Get IC!!!
Get VendorHome!!!
Before while!!!
Got a Collection of vendors!!!
Created an Iterator object!!!
vendorno = 400
vendorno = 401
```

Output from the OC4J Console

From the OC4J console, you will see the following output:

```
Inside getAllVendorInfo()!!!
I connected to the database!!!
I got rset!!!
Inside populate()!!!
Inside populate()!!!
```

Next, you will run the `PurchaseOrderManagementClient` Java application. Follow the steps just described in the "Running the Clients" section. If your environment parameters match the ones listed in Step 3 of that section, then type the following:

```
runPurchaseClient.bat
```

If your environment parameters do not match the ones listed in Step 3, then type the following:

```
runPurchaseClient.bat myhost mypassword chapter6 myRMI-port
```

Output from the PurchaseOrderManagementClient Class

The output from `PurchaseOrderClient` is as follows:

```
########################################################
# if you are running
# this client with any other
# settings than the defaults which
```

```
# are host=localhost, rmi-port=23791
# admin-password=manager, application-name=
# chapter6, you have to pass those variables
# like runPurchaseClient hostname password appname 23781
# e.g runPurchaseClient myhost mypassword mychapter6 23781
########################################################
Running with host: localhost ,port: 23791 ,
  appname: chapter6 ,password: manager
I Got a PurchaseOrderManagementHome!!!
I Got a PurchaseOrderManagement!!!
Item: OFFICE DESK Estimated cost: 14850
Item: OFFICE DESK Estimated cost: 9900
Item: COMPUTER SHELVES Estimated cost: 500
Item: COMPUTER SHELVES Estimated cost: 1000
```

Output from the OC4J Console

From the OC4J console, you will see the following output:

```
Inside POCreate: I got LineItemLocalHome!!!
Inside POCreate: I got PurchaseOrderLocalHome!!!
```

Next, you will learn how to deploy an exploded directory.

Deploying an Exploded Directory

OC4J also supports deployment of an exploded directory structure. If you have your `chapter06` code unzipped in the `d:\chapter06` directory, do the following:

1. Make sure the `application.xml` file is correct in your `chapter06/META-INF` directory. For an exploded directory, it should look something like this:

```
<?xml version="1.0"?>
<!DOCTYPE application PUBLIC "-//Sun Microsystems,
   Inc.//DTD J2EE Application 1.2//EN"
   "http://java.sun.com/j2ee/dtds/application_1_2.dtd">
<!-- The application element is the root element of
      a J2EE application deployment descriptor.  -->
<application>
      <display-name>Chapter6</display-name>
      <module>
            <ejb>classes</ejb>
      </module>
</application>
```

2. Edit the OC4J `server.xml` file, for an exploded deployment add the following entry:

```
<application name="chapter6" path="file:///d:/chapter06"
          auto-start="true" />
```

   Note that the "file:///" prefix takes care of forward slashes (/) and backslashes (\).

If your OC4J instance is still running, you might need to restart it if you're using the same names again.

Note that if you want a clean deployment of an application deployed to OC4J, do the following:

1. Stop OC4J.
2. Delete the `chapter06-prebuilt.ear` file and the `chapter05-prebuilt` directory under the OC4J `applications` directory.
3. Delete the `application` directory under the OC4J `application-deployments` directory.
4. Start OC4J again:

```
java -jar oc4j.jar -verbosity 10
```

OC4J will then do a clean install of the application.

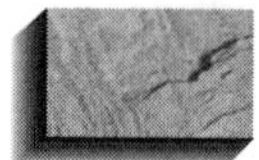

NOTE
We have provided the `application.xml` file for the exploded approach under `chapter06/META-INF`, called `application-exploded.xml`, and also the prebuilt `chapter06.ear file`, called `chapter06-prebuilt.ear`.

In this chapter, you learned the following:

- How to design an EJB application.
- How to define session bean components.
- How to create the `Vendor` session bean and how to develop value objects using the J2EE value object pattern.

- How to create the `PurchaseOrderManagement` session bean and use the J2EE session façade pattern.
- How to write the `ejb-jar.xml` and the OC4J-specific `orion-ejb-jar.xml` files.
- How to deploy enterprise beans to OC4J.

In Chapter 7, you will learn how to build message-driven beans, and in Chapters 10 and 11, you will learn how to code EJB clients using the Servlet API and JavaServer Pages API.

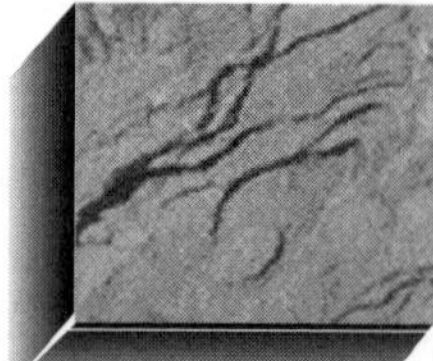

CHAPTER 7

Developing EJB Message-Driven Beans

In Chapters 5 and 6, you learned how to develop entity beans and session beans. In this chapter, you will learn how to write message-driven beans (MDBs). You will do so while coding the Approval application. A message-driven bean is an enterprise bean that allows J2EE applications to process messages asynchronously. It acts as a Java Message Service (JMS) listener that consumes messages asynchronously. It is a new type of enterprise bean that was introduced in the EJB 2.0 specification.

In this chapter, you will build the Approval application, which consists of two MDBs and three entity beans that implement the business logic requirements of the *Purchase Order Approval* use case. We presented the Purchase Order Approval use case in the Introduction of the book.

Specifically, you will learn about:

- Java Message Service.
- J2EE application design.
- Defining message-driven beans.
- Creating message-driven beans. You will set up Oracle Advanced Queuing (AQ) as a JMS provider and code the Approval application.
- Writing the `ejb-jar.xml` deployment descriptor for message-driven beans.
- Writing or generating the `orion-ejb-jar.xml` OC4J-specific deployment descriptor for message-driven beans.
- Coding JMS clients to use `Queue` and `Topic` message implementations supplied by Oracle AQ.
- Writing the application-specific `web.xml` and OC4J-specific `orion-web.xml` XML files.
- Deploying EJB components and message-driven beans to OC4J.

Introduction to Java Message Service

In this section, you will learn some basic concepts that will facilitate the assimilation of the contents of this chapter. Specifically, you will learn about the following:

- What is messaging?
- What is a message queue?
- What are message system types?

- What is JMS?
- How do you construct JMS messages and what is the format of a JMS body message?
- What is a JMS client?
- How does OC4J implement JMS?
- What kind of message providers does OC4J support?

What Is Messaging?

Messaging is a method of communication between software components. Messaging makes it easy for application developers to communicate with application programs by sending and receiving messages. Messaging products allow distributed application components to communicate and coordinate their activity (via messages) by providing services, such as message queuing, guaranteed once-and-only-once delivery, priority delivery, and transaction support.

What Is a Message Queue?

A *message* is a unit of data sent between two computers. It is a lightweight object consisting of a header and a body. The header contains identification and routing information. The body contains application data.

A message can be very simple, consisting of just a string of text, or more complex, possibly involving embedded objects. Messages are sent to queues. A *message queue* is a container that holds messages while they are in transit. The message queue manager acts as the middleman in relaying a message from its source to its destination. A queue's main purpose is to provide routing and guarantee the delivery of messages; if the recipient is not available when a message is sent, the queue holds the message until it can be successfully delivered.

Queue communication is inherently *asynchronous,* meaning that messages are sent to a queue and received from a queue in separate processes. This is very different from what is known as *synchronous communication,* in which the sender of a request must wait for a response from the intended receiver before performing other tasks. The amount of time that the sender must wait depends entirely on the amount of time it takes for the receiver to process the request and send a response.

Message System Types

There are two different messaging paradigms or domains: point-to-point and publish/subscribe. The type of destination for message delivery and the pattern of interaction between destination and client characterize both domains.

Point-to-Point

The destination in the point-to-point (PTP) domain is called a queue. One client sends messages to the queue, and the other receives messages from the queue. In PTP messaging systems, messages are routed to an individual consumer who maintains a queue of "incoming" messages. More importantly, messages are sent to one consumer only.

Publish/Subscribe

The destination in the publish/subscribe (pub/sub) domain is called a topic. The pub/sub messaging system supports an event-driven model in which information consumers and producers participate in the transmission of messages. In the pub/sub model, messages are broadcast to all registered listeners. Messaging systems based on the pub/sub model provide asynchronous delivery of messages. This means that in pub/sub messaging systems, the sender does not wait for the intended consumer before processing other tasks.

What Is JMS?

Java Message Service, part of the J2EE (Java 2 Enterprise Edition) suite, provides standard APIs that allow Java applications to interact with messaging providers. This is similar to the approach taken with Java Database Connectivity (JDBC) and Java Naming and Directory Interface (JNDI) APIs. Many vendors now offer JMS-compatible messaging systems, some stand-alone and some delivered as part of what J2EE vendors are offering. Probably the best-known messaging system is MQSeries written by IBM, which has JMS support.

The JMS specification supports both PTP and pub/sub models. Whether using PTP or pub/sub, the object model is very similar. A JMS client has to establish a connection to the provider and establish an association with a destination to either consume or produce messages. The destination will be either a `Topic` or a `Queue`. JMS, like many of the J2EE APIs, makes use of JNDI to discover needed resources. (See Chapter 3 for a discussion of JNDI.)

JMS brings asynchronous messaging services to Java applications developers. The integration of JMS and EJB allows enterprise beans to participate fully in loosely connected systems. For example, a message-driven bean can receive and act upon JMS messages. With the integration of asynchronous messaging services, any EJB can now send asynchronous messages via the JMS API.

JMS Messages

A JMS message consists of three parts:

- A message header is used for message identification.
- The properties are used for application-specific, provider-specific, and optional header fields.
- The body holds the content of the message.

JMS Body Message Format

The `javax.jms` package defines five message body formats, as described in Table 7-1.

The following sections provide some examples of how to use the `TextMessage`, `MapMessage`, and `ObjectMessage` JMS message types.

TextMessage Format

Use an object of type `TextMessage` if you want to send a simple text message. Use the `createMessage()` method of a session object to create a message of

Message Type	Body Contains
`TextMessage`	`String` or XML file.
`MapMessage`	Set of name/value pairs with name as `String` objects and values as Java primitive types.
`BytesMessage`	A stream of uninterpreted bytes.
`StreamMessage`	A stream of primitive values.
`ObjectMessage`	A `Serializable` object.
`Message`	Only composed of header fields and properties; no body.

TABLE 7-1. *JMS Message Types*

TextMessage type. See the "Sessions" section of this chapter to learn about session objects. The following code fragment demonstrates how to use a TextMessage object:

```
TextMessage message = session.createMessage();
message.setText("hello world");
```

MapMessage Format

Use a MapMessage object if you want to send a set of value pairs. For example:

```
// Use a Topic or a Queue session to send a MapMessage
MapMessage message = topicSession.createMapMessage();
message.setInt("requestno", 500);
message.setInt("employeeno", 100);
message.setString("reasons", "");
```

ObjectMessage Format

Use an object of type ObjectMessage if you want to send a Java object. Any serializable Java object can be used as an ObjectMessage. Use a Java Collection object to send multiple objects in a single message. The following code fragment demonstrates how to use a ObjectMessage object:

```
ObjectMessage message = session.createObjectMessage();
message.setObject(myObject);
```

JMS Clients

A JMS client has two parts: connection factory objects and destination factory objects. JMS clients use JNDI to access these objects. Clients do so via interfaces provided by the JMS API.

Connection Factory Objects

JMS clients use a *connection factory* to create a connection with a provider. A connection factory encapsulates a set of connection configuration parameters that are usually defined by an administrator.

Before creating a message, your JMS client program must establish a connection with the provider. Use JNDI to locate the connection factory. Recall that PTP is a messaging paradigm whose destination is a Queue. The following code fragment demonstrates how to locate the PTP QueueConnectionFactory and the TopicConnectionFactory:

```
Context ctx = new InitialContext();
// Look up a QueueConnectionFactory object
```

```
QueueConnectionFactory queueConnectionFactory =
        (QueueConnectionFactory)ctx.lookup("QueueConnectionFactory");

// Look up a TopicConnectionFactory
TopicConnectionFactory topicConnectionFactory =
        (TopicConnectionFactory)ctx.lookup("TopicConnectionFactory");
```

Destination Factory Objects

A *destination* is the object a JMS client uses to specify the target message that it wants to produce and possibly the source of messages that it wants to consume. Use the following code fragment to specify the target of messages that your JMS client may produce or consume:

```
// Look up a PTP queue
Queue myQueue = (Queue)ctx.lookup("MyQueueDestination");
// Look up a Topic
Topic myTopic =(Topic)ctx.lookup("MyTopicDestination");
```

Connections

A *connection* encapsulates a connection to a JMS provider. Connections come in the form of `XxxxConnection`, and are produced by `XxxxConnectionFactory` factories. There are two kinds of connections: `QueueConnectionFactory` and `TopicConnectionFactory`. Use the following code fragment to acquire a connection to your JMS provider:

```
// Create a PTP queue connection
QueueConnection queueConnection =
     queueConnectionFactory.createQueueConnection();

// Create a Topic connection
TopicConnection topicConnection =
     topicConnectionFactory.createTopicConnection();
```

Please, release resources after using the connection. You do so by calling the `close()` method of a `QueueConnection` or `TopicConnection` object:

```
// Close the connections
queueConnection.close();
topicConnection.close();
```

Note that before your application can consume messages, you must call the connection's `start()` method. There exists also a `stop()` method that allows your program to stop consuming messages. Use the following code fragment to start or stop consuming messages:

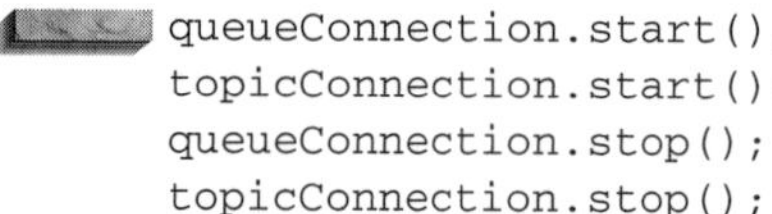

```
queueConnection.start();
topicConnection.start();
queueConnection.stop();
topicConnection.stop();
```

Sessions

A session is a single-threaded context for producing or consuming messages. Use sessions to create message producers, message consumers, and messages. For example:

```
// Create a TopicConnection
TopicConnection topicConnection =
     topicConnectionFactory.createTopicConnection();
// Use the topicConnection to create a Topic session
TopicSession topicSession =
   topicConnection.createTopicSession(false,
                              Session.AUTO_ACKNOWLEDGE);
// Create a PTP queue connection

QueueConnection queueConnection =
     queueConnectionFactory.createQueueConnection();
// Use the queueConnection to create a Queue session
QueueSession queueSession =
   queueConnection.createQueueSession(true, 0);
```

The next concepts that you need to know are as follows:

- **Message producer** An object created by a session. Use a message producer to send messages to a destination (`Queue` or `Topic`). In the "Creating Message-Driven Beans" section of this chapter, you will write the `LocalClientServlet` JMS client, in which you will create a message producer to send messages to the `ProcessApprovalMessageBean` MDB. You create a message producer as follows:

```
// Use a the createPublisher() method of
// a TopicSession to create a Topic producer
TopicPublisher topicPublisher =
   topicSession.createPublisher(myTopic1);
// Use the createSender() method of
// a QueueSession to create a Queue producer
QueueSender queueSender =
   queueSession.createSender (myQueue1);
```

- **Message consumer** An object created by a session. Use a message consumer to consume messages from a destination (`Queue` or `Topic`), as follows:

```
// Use the createSubscriber() method of
// a TopicSession to create a Topic receiver (consumer)
TopicSubscriber topicSubscriber =
   topicSession.createSubscriber(myTopic1);

// Use the createReceiver() method of
// a QueueSession to create a Queue producer
QueueReceiver queueReceiver =
   queueSession.createReceiver (myQueue1);
```

- **Message listener** An object that acts as an event handler and consumes asynchronous messages. This object implements the `MessageListener` interface, which contains one method, `onMessage()`. A message-driven bean is a special kind of message listener. You will learn about message-driven beans in the "Defining Message-Driven Beans" section of this chapter.

OC4J and JMS

The OC4J implementation is fully compliant with the JMS 1.0.2 specification. OC4J message producers, message consumers, or message listeners can access `Queues` and `Topics` using the JMS API. OC4J applications can also use an OC4J-specific JNDI namespace to look up JMS connection factories and destinations. Recall that a *connection factory* encapsulates a set of connection configuration parameters, and that JMS clients use a connection factory to create a connection with a provider. A *destination* is the object a JMS client uses to specify the target message that it wants to produce or consume.

OC4J provides the necessary environment for you to build many different kinds of JMS message producers, message consumers, or message listeners. You can use servlets, JavaServer Pages, session beans, entity beans, or message-driven beans to be any kind of JMS message types. In this chapter, you will learn how to develop JMS clients in the form of servlets and message-driven beans that will produce messages and JMS message listeners in the form of message-driven beans that will consume messages. In Chapters 10 and 11, you will learn how to build servlets and JMS JavaServer Pages clients, respectively.

OC4J and Message Providers

OC4J defines a `ResourceProvider` interface that allows you to plug in message providers and third-party messaging systems, such as Oracle Advanced Queuing (AQ), IBM MQSeries, Sonic Software's SonicMQ, and SwiftMQ (swiftmq.com). Oracle Corporation has an integrated message queuing feature in the Oracle database. With this functionality, message queuing operations can be performed similarly to SQL operations from the Oracle database. Message queuing functionality allows applications on the Oracle database to communicate asynchronously via messages in AQ queues. Oracle AQ has additional features, such as e-mail notifications and transformation useful for Internet applications. AQ operations can also be performed over the Internet via HTTP(s) and e-mail. To learn more about Oracle AQ, see the *Oracle9*i *Application Developer's Guide – Advanced Queuing, Release 1 (9.0.2)* technical manual and http://otn.oracle.com/products/aq/content.html. In the "Writing the ejb-jar.xml Deployment Descriptor" section of this chapter, you will learn how to configure JMS for the Approval application that you will develop here.

This concludes our discussion on JMS. To learn more about the subject, get the JMS specification at http://java.sun.com/products/jms/index.html and the JMS tutorial at http://java.sun.com/products/jms/tutorial/. This is an excellent tutorial on JMS and MDBs.

In the following sections, you will learn how to develop MDBs. You will do so while building the J2EE Approval application. In addition, you will learn how to use Oracle AQ as a JMS provider to produce messages to be consumed by EJB MDBs.

Application Design

In this chapter, you will develop the J2EE Approval application, which consists of several enterprise beans:

- The `ProcessApprovalMessageBean` and the `EmailMessageBean` MDBs. The high-level views of these MDBs are shown in Figure 7-1.
- The `ApprovalLocal` and `PurchaseOrderLocal` CMP beans and the `EmployeeLocal` BMP bean. You developed the `PurchaseOrderLocal` and the `EmployeeLocal` beans in Chapter 5. In this chapter, you will code the `ApprovalLocal` CMP bean. This chapter assumes that you have some basic understanding of BMP and CMP entity beans. You may want to review Chapter 5 or any other documents relating to entity beans before proceeding.
- The `LocalClientServlet` JMS client, a simple servlet that produces messages to be consumed by the `ProcessApprovalMessageBean` MDB.

The basic steps of the Approval application are as follows:

1. The `LocalClientServlet` JMS client publishes a message containing the `requestno` of the purchase order requisition, the budget officer `employeeno`, and the `reasons` for approving or not approving the purchase order requisition.

2. The `ProcessApprovalMessageBean` MDB processes the message. To process the message, the `ProcessApprovalMessageBean` bean creates three entity bean instances:

   - The `ApprovalLocal` CMP that updates the `APPROVAL` table using the `requestno`, the budget officer's `employeeno`, and the `reasons`. The high-level view of the `ApprovalLocal` CMP entity bean is shown in Figure 7-2.

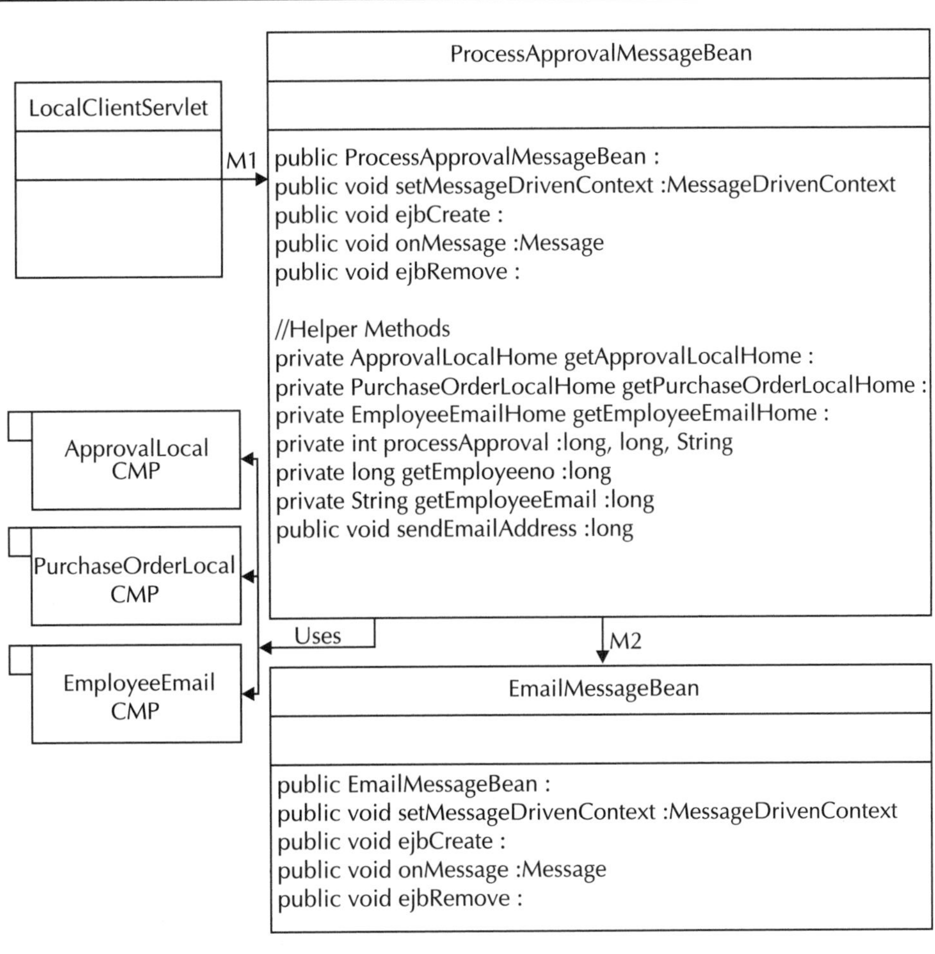

FIGURE 7-1. *High-level view of the MDBs*

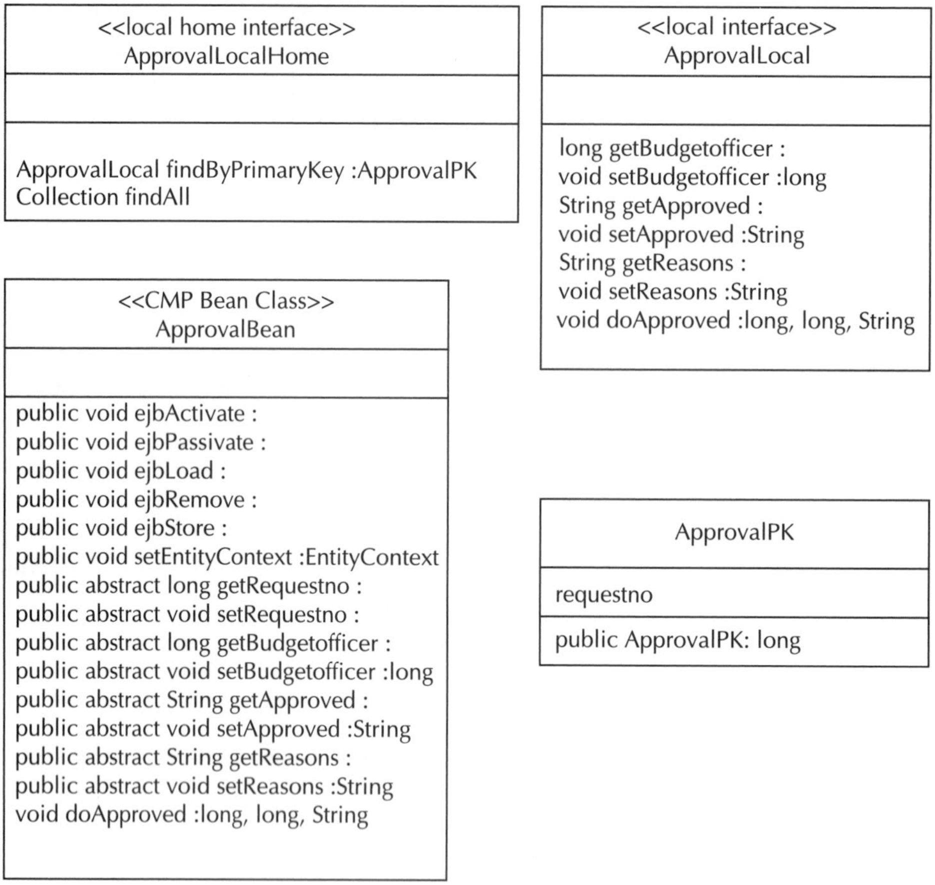

<<local home interface>>
ApprovalLocalHome

ApprovalLocal findByPrimaryKey :ApprovalPK
Collection findAll

<<local interface>>
ApprovalLocal

long getBudgetofficer :
void setBudgetofficer :long
String getApproved :
void setApproved :String
String getReasons :
void setReasons :String
void doApproved :long, long, String

<<CMP Bean Class>>
ApprovalBean

public void ejbActivate :
public void ejbPassivate :
public void ejbLoad :
public void ejbRemove :
public void ejbStore :
public void setEntityContext :EntityContext
public abstract long getRequestno :
public abstract void setRequestno :
public abstract long getBudgetofficer :
public abstract void setBudgetofficer :long
public abstract String getApproved :
public abstract void setApproved :String
public abstract String getReasons :
public abstract void setReasons :String
void doApproved :long, long, String

ApprovalPK

requestno

public ApprovalPK: long

FIGURE 7-2. *High-level view of the `ApprovalLocal` CMP bean*

- The `PurchaseOrderLocal` CMP that returns to the `ProcessApprovalMessageBean` MDB the `employeeno` of the employee who generated the purchase order requisition. The high-level view of the `PurchaseOrderLocal` CMP entity bean is shown in Figure 7-3.
- The `EmployeeLocal` BMP that returns to the `ProcessApprovalMessageBean` MDB the employee's e-mail address. The high-level view of the `EmployeeLocal` BMP entity bean is shown in Figure 7-4.

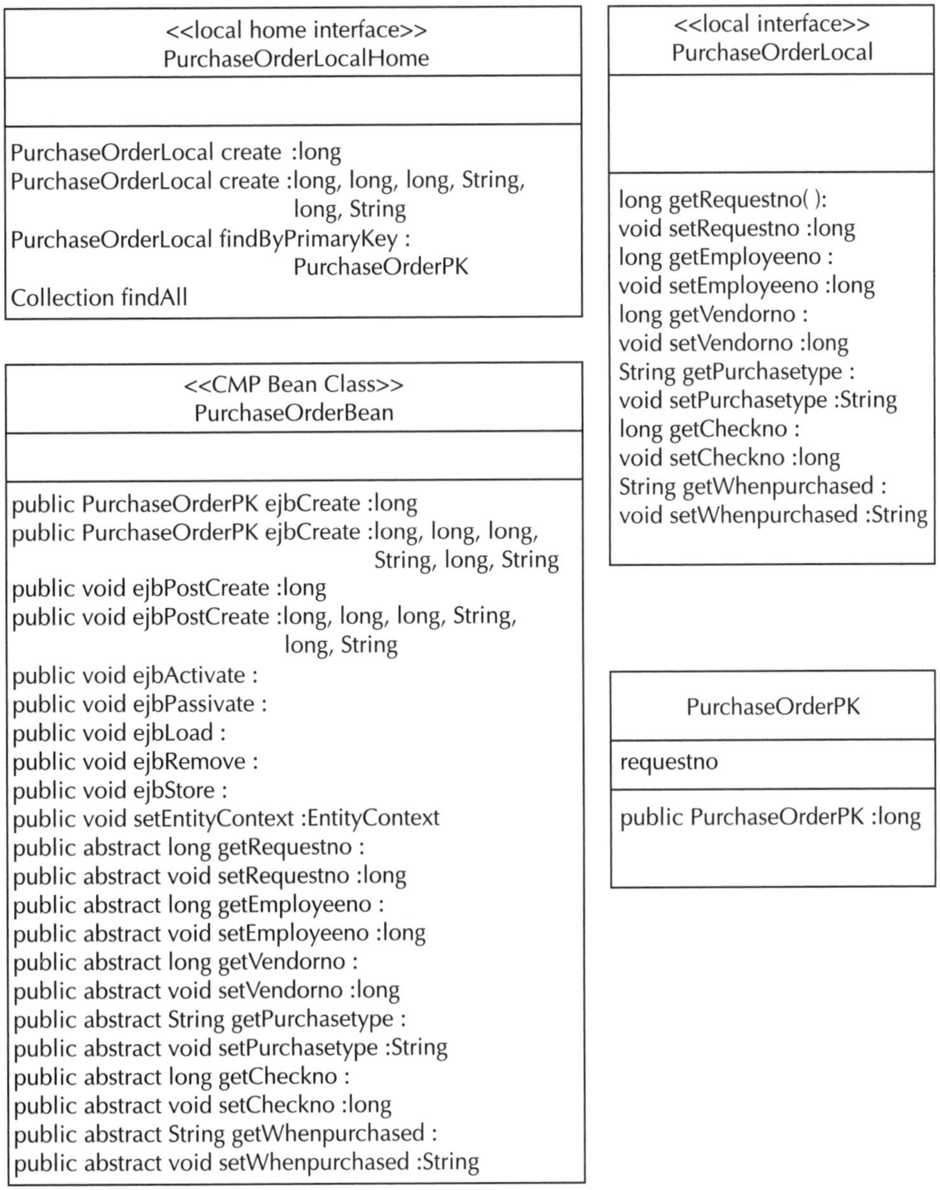

<<local home interface>>
PurchaseOrderLocalHome

PurchaseOrderLocal create :long
PurchaseOrderLocal create :long, long, long, String, long, String
PurchaseOrderLocal findByPrimaryKey : PurchaseOrderPK
Collection findAll

<<CMP Bean Class>>
PurchaseOrderBean

public PurchaseOrderPK ejbCreate :long
public PurchaseOrderPK ejbCreate :long, long, long, String, long, String
public void ejbPostCreate :long
public void ejbPostCreate :long, long, long, String, long, String
public void ejbActivate :
public void ejbPassivate :
public void ejbLoad :
public void ejbRemove :
public void ejbStore :
public void setEntityContext :EntityContext
public abstract long getRequestno :
public abstract void setRequestno :long
public abstract long getEmployeeno :
public abstract void setEmployeeno :long
public abstract long getVendorno :
public abstract void setVendorno :long
public abstract String getPurchasetype :
public abstract void setPurchasetype :String
public abstract long getCheckno :
public abstract void setCheckno :long
public abstract String getWhenpurchased :
public abstract void setWhenpurchased :String

<<local interface>>
PurchaseOrderLocal

long getRequestno( ):
void setRequestno :long
long getEmployeeno :
void setEmployeeno :long
long getVendorno :
void setVendorno :long
String getPurchasetype :
void setPurchasetype :String
long getCheckno :
void setCheckno :long
String getWhenpurchased :
void setWhenpurchased :String

PurchaseOrderPK

requestno

public PurchaseOrderPK :long

FIGURE 7-3. *High-level view of the* `PurchaseOrderLocal` *CMP bean*

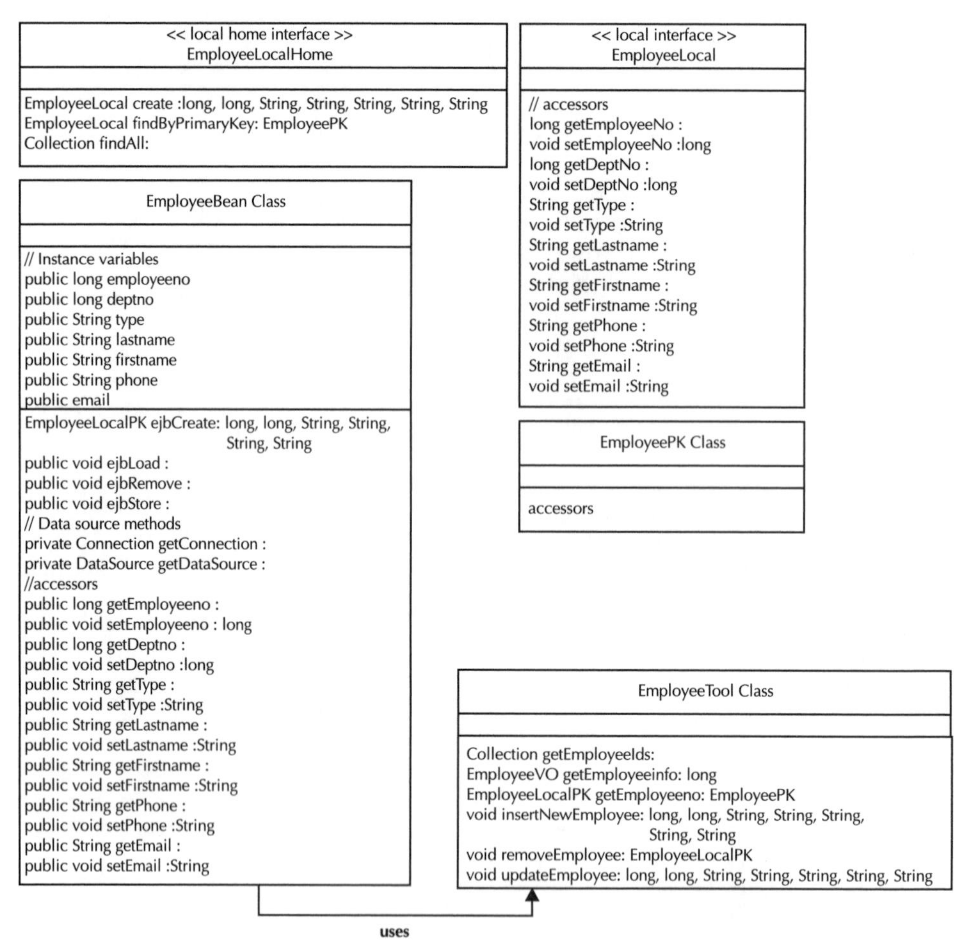

FIGURE 7-4. *High-level view of the `EmployeeLocal` CMP bean*

3. The `ProcessApprovalMessageBean` MDB publishes a message containing the purchase order requisition number and the employee's e-mail address.

4. The `EmailMessageBean` MDB processes the message produced by the `ProcessApprovalMessageBean`.

The interactions between all the components of the Approval application are shown in Figure 7-5.

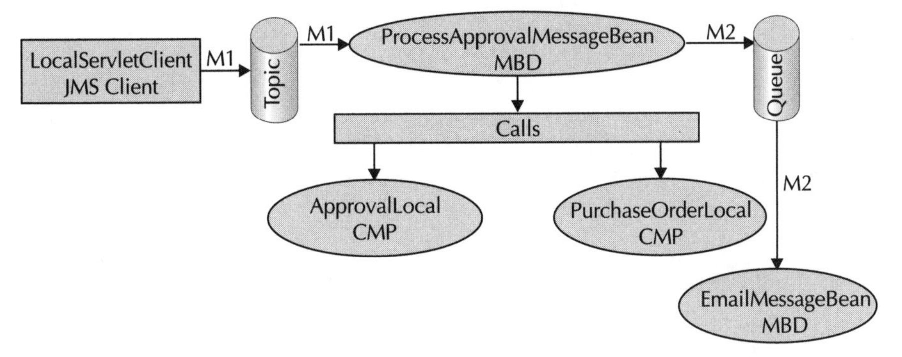

FIGURE 7-5. *The approval J2EE application: client to MDB to CMP and MDB*

Defining Message-Driven Beans

Unlike session beans and entity beans that process messages synchronously, a message-driven bean is a server-side transaction-aware component that processes asynchronous messages delivered via JMS. The messages may be sent by any J2EE component or from an application or a system that does not use the J2EE technology. An MDB is a JMS message listener that can consume messages from a queue or a durable subscription. Recall that an asynchronous message leaves senders independent of receivers. That is, the sender sends its message and does not have to wait for the receiver to receive or process that message. From its creation until its destruction, like session bean and entity bean instances, an MDB instance lives in a container and the container controls its lifetime. The EJB container automatically manages the entire environment of MDBs. The MDB's main responsibility is to consume messages.

Message-Driven Bean Characteristics

An MDB has the following characteristics:

- Unlike session and entity beans, MDBs do not have local interfaces, local home interfaces, remote interfaces, or remote home interfaces.
- An MDB consists of one implementation bean class.
- An MDB instance is an instance of an MDB class.

- Like stateless session beans, MDBs have no conversational state. This implies that all bean instances are equivalent when they are not involved in servicing a client message.
- An MDB class must implement the `javax.ejb.MessageDrivenBean` interface, which contains the `setMessageDrivenContext()` method, and the `javax.jms.MessageListener` interface, which contains the `onMessage()` method.
- An MDB class must provide implementation code for the `onMessage()` method of the `javax.jms.MessageListener` interface. The EJB container invokes this method to process incoming asynchronous messages produced by JMS clients. When you write the `onMessage()` method, you may also provide helper methods that the `onMessage()` method can invoke to aid in message processing. For example, in the `ProcessApprovalMessageBean` MDB class that you will code in this chapter, you will create several helper methods to help your MDB consume the message.
- An MDB must use the Java `instanceof` operator to determine what type of message (`TextMessage`, `MapMessage`, and so on) that an MDB needs to process. Recall that the `instanceof` operator allows you to check at runtime whether or not an object is of a particular type.
- An MDB class must also implement EJB container callback methods. Recall that each type of enterprise bean must implement a set of container callback methods. To learn which callback methods entity beans and session beans must implement, see Chapters 5 and 6, respectively. Usually, callback methods in a bean implementation class match methods in an EJB home interface. Although MDBs have no local/remote interface components, you are still required to list in an MDB class the following callback methods:
    - **`ejbCreate()`** You can provide empty implementation code or you can use this method to look up JMS API connection factories and destinations in order to create a JMS API connection, acquire database connections, or acquire object references to EJB objects. For example, in the following code fragment, when the container creates an instance of the MDB, the `approvalLocalHome`, `purchaseOrderLocalHome`, and `employeeLocalHome` instance variables of this instance will contain references to the `ApprovalLocalHome`, `PurchaseOrderLocalHome`, and `EmployeeLocalHome` interfaces:

```
public void ejbCreate()   {
     System.out.println("In ProcessApprovalMessageBean." +
                       "ejbCreate()");
```

```
        // Locate ApprovalLocalHome, PurchaseOrderLocalHome,
        // and EmployeeEmailHome interfaces.
        try {
            approvalLocalHome = getApprovalLocalHome();
            purchaseOrderLocalHome = getPurchaseOrderLocalHome();
            employeeLocalHome = getEmployeeLocalHome();
        } // End of try
        catch (Exception e) {
            System.err.println("Unable to get BMP/CMP Homes: "
                                      +e.getMessage());
        }  // end catch

    }  // End of ejbCreate()
```

- **`ejbRemove()`** You must provide an empty implementation code. The container invokes this method to destroy the instance of an MDB.

- MDBs are anonymous; therefore, they have no client-visible identity. Although an MDB instance does not contain a state for a specific client, the instance variables of the instance can contain the state of an open database connection or an object reference to EJB objects or local EJB objects. In the "Creating Message-Driven Beans" section of this chapter, you will write the `ProcessApprovalMessageBean` class, which demonstrates how to declare instance variables in a message-driven class that contains the state of object references to local EJB objects.
- Access to an MDB is done via JMS clients, any J2EE components, or systems that do not use the J2EE technology.

Message-Driven Beans and the EJB Container

The container provides security, concurrency, transactions, and other services for the MDB. An MDB exists as long as its EJB container exists. The container manages the life cycle of the MDB instances, notifies the instances when bean action may be necessary, and provides a full range of services to ensure that the MDB implementation is scalable and can support the concurrent processing of a large number of messages.

Unlike a stand-alone client's message listener that needs to do all the setup tasks, the EJB container automatically performs several setup tasks for your MDB. The EJB container performs the following tasks:

- **Creates a message consumer** The EJB container uses the elements specified in the MDB's deployment descriptor file to create message consumers of a `QueueReceiver` type or a `TopicSubscriber` type. At deployment time, use the deployment descriptor file to associate your

MDB with a destination and a connection factory or to specify a JMS API *message selector*. A message selector allows a message consumer to specify the message that it is interested in processing.

- **Registers the message listener** Your code must not call the `setMessageListener()` method.
- **Specifies a message acknowledgement mode** To learn more about a message acknowledgement mode, refer to the earlier "Connections" section of this chapter and the JMS specification.

The Approval J2EE Application

The Approval application that you will develop in this chapter consists of the following:

- The `LocalClientServlet` JMS client that produces messages to be consumed by the `ProcessApprovalMessageBean` MDB.
- The `ProcessApprovalMessageBean` MDB consists of one implementation class that bears the same name. This bean does the following:
    - Consumes messages produced by the `LocalClientServlet` JMS client.
    - Calls the `ApprovalLocal`, the `PurchaseOrderLocal`, and the `EmployeeLocal` entity beans to manipulate data residing in the Oracle9*i* database.
    - Produces a message to be consumed by the `EmailMessageBean` MDB.
- The `EmailMessageBean` MDB consists of one implementation class that also bears the same name. It consumes messages from the `ProcessApprovalMessageBean` MDB.
- The `ApprovalLocal` CMP entity bean. This bean maps the `APPROVAL` table and provides the methods to manipulate the table's data.
- The `PurchaseOrderLocal` CMP entity bean. This bean maps the `PURCHASE_ORDER` table that consists of elements relating to purchase order requisitions and provides the methods to manipulate the table's data. Recall that you developed this CMP bean in Chapter 5. You may want to go to that chapter to review the source code for the `PurchaseOrderLocal` CMP.
- The `EmployeeLocal` BMP entity bean. This bean maps the `EMPLOYEE` table that consists of elements relating to employees and provides the methods to manipulate the table's data.

Next, you will create the development directory structure for the Approval application that you will develop in this chapter.

Creating the Development Directory

The development directory for the application is as follows:

- **chapter07** Root directory of your J2EE application.
    - **META-INF** Directory where your `application.xml` file is located (and possibly your `orion-application.xml` file), which defines the modules you have in your J2EE application.
    - **src** Directory where all the source files are located.
        - **META-INF** Directory where the `ejb-jar.xml` deployment descriptor file and the `orion-ejb-jar.xml` OC4J-specific deployment descriptor file are located.
        - **webapps** Root package of the `LocalClientServlet` class.
            - **web** Package.
                - **test** Package where the `LocalClientServlet` class resides.
        - **purchase** Package indicating the starting point of the `Purchase` application.
            - **ejb** Package consisting of the source code of your EJB components.
                - **bmp** Package consisting of the source code of all your bean-managed persistent (BMP) entity beans.
                - **cmp** Package consisting of the source code of all your container-managed persistent (CMP) entity beans.
                - **mdb** Package consisting of the source code of all the message-driven beans.
            - **util** Package consisting of the source code of the `EmployeeTool` SQLJ program that manipulates the data of the `EMPLOYEE` table.
            - **vo** Package consisting of the source code of your value object classes.
    - **classes** Root directory for your EJBs: the EJB module.
        - **META-INF** Directory where the `ejb-jar.xml` deployment descriptor file and the `orion-ejb-jar.xml` OC4J-specific deployment descriptor file are located.

- **purchase** Package indicating the starting point of the Java class files of the `Purchase` application.
  - **ejb** Package consisting of the class files of your EJB components.
    - **bmp** Package consisting of the class files of all your bean-managed persistent (BMP) entity beans
    - **cmp** Package consisting of the class files of all your container-managed persistent (CMP) entity beans.
    - **mdb** Package consisting of the source code of all the message-driven beans.
  - **util** Package consisting of the class files of the `EmployeeTool` class.
  - **vo** Package consisting of the class files of your value object classes.

- **web** Root package of your `LocalClientServlet` testing class.
  - **WEB-INF** Directory consisting of the `web.xml` and `orion-web.xml` files.
    - **classes** Root directory for your web applications: the Web module.
      - **webapps** Root package of the `LocalClientServlet` class
        - **web** Package.
          - **test** Package in which the class file of the `LocalClientServlet` class resides.
      - **purchase** Root package of the EJB and their dependent classes.
        - **ejb/bmp** Class files for BMP.
        - **ejb/cmp** Class files for CMPs.
        - **ejb/mdb** Class files for MDBs.
        - **util, vo** Class files for `util` and `value` objects.

Creating Message-Driven Beans

Creating message-driven beans to deploy to OC4J is fairly easy. Recall that you can use third-party messaging systems as JMS providers in your J2EE applications that you want to deploy to OC4J. In the Approval application that you will develop in subsequent sections of this chapter, you will use Oracle Advanced Queuing as your JMS provider. When you want to use third-party JMS providers, before you code your application, Oracle recommends that you first set up and configure the JMS provider. So, in the step-by-step procedure that we will describe in this section, we will first set up and configure Oracle AQ.

The basic steps are as follows:

1. Set up Oracle Advanced Queuing as the JMS provider. This involves setting up the `Queues` and `Topics` to be used.
2. Write the message-driven implementation class. This class must be defined `public` and must implement the `javax.ejb.MessageDrivenBean` and `javax.jms.MessageListener` interfaces, list the `ejbCreate()` and the `ejbRemove()` callback methods, and provide implementation code for the `setMessageDrivenContext()` method of the `MessageDrivenBean` interface and the `onMessage()` method of the `MessageListener` interface.
3. Create the MDB deployment descriptor. In this step, you will create the `ejb-jar.xml` deployment descriptor.
4. Define the resource provider used to "talk" to AQ in the OC4J `application.xml` (this is the OC4J "global" `application.xml` file in the `[OC4J_HOME]/j2ee/home/config` directory).
5. Map the JMS destination type to the MDB in the OC4J-specific deployment descriptor `orion-ejb-jar.xml`. Recall that this file is specific to your application. Note that Steps 2 and 3 can be performed at any time during the development of the application.
6. Create a WAR file containing the Web module and its deployment descriptors.
7. Create an `ejb-jar` file containing the bean and the deployment descriptor.
8. Configure the application-specific `application.xml` file. Note that this is not the OC4J `application.xml` as described in Step 4. To learn how to define an application-specific `application.xml` file, see the "Deploying an Exploded Directory" section at the end of the chapter.

9. Create an EAR file.
10. Deploy the Approval application to OC4J.

Before coding the Approval application, you will learn how to set up a JMS provider. You will use Oracle AQ as the JMS provider for your application.

Setting Up Oracle Advanced Queuing as a JMS Provider

In this section, you will learn how to create `Queues` and `Topics` in Oracle AQ. The steps to set up Oracle AQ as a JMS provider are as follows:

1. Create the database user who will own the `Queues` and `Topics`. You can either use an existing user or create a new one. To use an existing one you only have to grant the Oracle `AQ_USER_ROLE` role. Note that in order for you to create a user in the Oracle database, you must have been granted the Oracle `CREATE USER` privilege. If you do not have this privilege, consult your Oracle Database Administrator. The Oracle `system` user has that privilege. To manage users in the Oracle database, you can use Oracle Enterprise Manager (OEM) or Oracle SQLPLUS. In this section, we elect to use SQLPLUS. Thus, invoke Oracle SQLPLUS:

```
-- Using the existing SCOTT database user
-- Just grant that user the AQ_USER_ROLE:
GRANT "AQ_USER_ROLE" TO "SCOTT";
ALTER USER "SCOTT" DEFAULT ROLE  ALL;

-- Creating the AQUSER database user
CREATE USER "AQUSER"  PROFILE "DEFAULT"
    IDENTIFIED BY "x" DEFAULT TABLESPACE "USERS"
    TEMPORARY TABLESPACE "TEMP"
    QUOTA UNLIMITED
    ON USERS
    ACCOUNT UNLOCK;

-- Grant the following Oracle system privileges to AQUSER
GRANT "AQ_USER_ROLE" TO "AQUSER";
GRANT "CONNECT" TO "AQUSER";
```

2. Create the `Queues` and `Topics` in AQ that you need. For the Approval application, you need one Topic destination that handles `MapMessage` messages and one `Queue` destination that handles `TextMessage` messages. Here, we will set up a `Topic` destination called `PROCESSTOPIC` and a `Queue` destination called `EMAILQUEUE`:

- Invoke SQLPLUS
- Use the CREATE_QUEUE_TABLE() procedure of the internal DBMS_AQADM Oracle PL/SQL package to create the queue table. To instruct Oracle AQ that you need to create a table that corresponds to a Topic destination, set the multiple_consumers flag of the CREATE_QUEUE_TABLE() procedure to true. When the multiple_consumers flag is set to false, the table corresponds to a Queue destination.
- Use the CREATE_QUEUE() procedure of the internal DBMS_AQADM Oracle PL/SQL package to create the actual Topic or Queue destination.
- Start the Topic or the Queue destination.

```
-- Setting up the PROCESSTOPIC Topic

-- 1. Create the queue table
BEGIN
  DBMS_AQADM.CREATE_QUEUE_TABLE ( queue_table=> 'AQUSER.PROCESSTOPIC',
   queue_payload_type=> 'SYS.AQ$_JMS_MAP_MESSAGE',
   sort_list=> '', comment=> '',
   multiple_consumers=> TRUE, message_grouping=> DBMS_AQADM.NONE,
   non_repudiation => DBMS_AQADM.NONE,
   storage_clause=> '', compatible=> '8.1',
   primary_instance=> '0', secondary_instance=> '0');
  COMMIT;
END;

-- 2. Create the actual Topic destination
BEGIN
  DBMS_AQADM.CREATE_QUEUE(queue_name=> 'AQUSER.PROCESSTOPIC',
   queue_table=> 'AQUSER.PROCESSTOPIC',
   queue_type=> DBMS_AQADM.NORMAL_QUEUE,
   max_retries=> '0', retry_delay=> '0',
   retention_time=> '0', comment=> '');
  COMMIT;
END;

-- 3. Start the Topic destination
BEGIN
  DBMS_AQADM.START_QUEUE('AQUSER.PROCESSTOPIC', TRUE, TRUE);
  COMMIT;
END;

-- ################## --
```

```
-- Setting up the EMAILQUEUE Queue

-- 1. Create the queue table
BEGIN
  DBMS_AQADM.CREATE_QUEUE_TABLE ( queue_table=> 'AQUSER.EMAILQUEUE',
   queue_payload_type=> 'SYS.AQ$_JMS_TEXT_MESSAGE', sort_list=> '',
   comment=>'', multiple_consumers=> FALSE,
   message_grouping=> DBMS_AQADM.NONE,
   non_repudiation => DBMS_AQADM.NONE, storage_clause=> '',
   compatible=> '8.1', primary_instance=> '0',
   secondary_instance=> '0');
  COMMIT;
END;

-- 2. Create the actual Queue destination
BEGIN
  DBMS_AQADM.CREATE_QUEUE(queue_name=> 'AQUSER.EMAILQUEUE',
   queue_table=> 'AQUSER.EMAILQUEUE',
   queue_type=> DBMS_AQADM.NORMAL_QUEUE,
   max_retries=> '0', retry_delay=> '0',
   retention_time=> '0', comment=> '');
  COMMIT;
END;

-- 3. Start the Queue destination
BEGIN
  DBMS_AQADM.START_QUEUE('AQUSER.EMAILQUEUE', TRUE, TRUE);
  COMMIT;
END;
-- 4. Grant the following privileges to AQUSER
GRANT "AQ_ADMINISTRATOR_ROLE" TO "AQUSER";
ALTER USER "AQUSER" DEFAULT ROLE ALL;
COMMIT;
```

3. If you create the queues in another schema (for example, `AQUSER`), like we did in this example, and you want to access them from another schema (for example, `SCOTT`) using the data source definition associated to the `SCOTT` user as specified in the OC4J-specific `datasources.xml` file, then you will need to grant the `enqueue` and `dequeue` object privileges to `SCOTT`. In the "Modifying the OC4J application.xml File" section of this chapter, you will learn how to configure a resource provider and associate to that resource provider the `jdbc/OracleDS` data source, which is associated to the `SCOTT` schema. If you want the SCOTT user to access the `PROCESSTOPIC` and `EMAILQUEUE` destinations, grant to `SCOTT` the following Oracle privileges:

```
connect aquser/x
/
-- Grant privilege to the AQUSER.PROCESSTOPIC Topic
BEGIN
DBMS_AQADM.GRANT_QUEUE_PRIVILEGE (privilege=>'DEQUEUE',
   queue_name=>'AQUSER.PROCESSTOPIC', grantee=>'SCOTT',
   grant_option=>FALSE);
   COMMIT;
END;
BEGIN
DBMS_AQADM.GRANT_QUEUE_PRIVILEGE (privilege=>'ENQUEUE',
     queue_name=>'AQUSER.PROCESSTOPIC', grantee=>'SCOTT',
     grant_option=>FALSE);
COMMIT;
END;
-- Grant privilege to the AQUSER.EMAILQUEUE Queue
BEGIN
DBMS_AQADM.GRANT_QUEUE_PRIVILEGE (privilege=>'DEQUEUE',
    queue_name=>'AQUSER.EMAILQUEUE', grantee=>'SCOTT',
    grant_option=>FALSE);
COMMIT;
END;
BEGIN
DBMS_AQADM.GRANT_QUEUE_PRIVILEGE (privilege=>'ENQUEUE',
   queue_name=>'AQUSER.EMAILQUEUE', grantee=>'SCOTT',
   grant_option=>FALSE);
COMMIT;
END;
```

Now Oracle AQ is ready to be used as the JMS provider. Next, you will code the Approval application.

Coding the Approval Application

In the following section, we will code the `ProcessApprovalMessageBean` MDB. This MDB plays two roles: a JMS message listener that consumes messages, and a JMS message producer that produces messages. Message-driven beans can receive messages from a `Queue` or `Topic`. Recall that there are two types of messaging systems: point-to-point (PTP) and publish/subscribe (pub/sub). PTP uses a `Queue` destination, whereas pub/sub uses a Topic destination. You learned about `Queues` and `Topics` in the "Message System Types" section of this chapter.

Next, you will code the ProcessApprovalMessageBean class.

The ProcessApprovalMessageBean Bean

The `ProcessApprovalMessageBean` class consists of the following:

- It is defined `public` and implements `javax.ejb.MessageDrivenBean` and `javax.jms.MessageListener` interfaces.
- It implements the `ProcessApprovalMessageBean()` constructor.
- It implements the `setMessageDrivenContext()` method.
- It implements the `ejbCreate()` method. In this method, when the EJB container creates an instance of the `ProcessApprovalMessageBean` class, this instance will contain references to the `ApprovalLocal`, `PurchaseOrderLocal`, and `EmployeeLocal` local EJB objects.
- It implements the `onMessage()` method. In this method, the bean instance processes the message and calls several methods:
  - **`processApproval(requestno, officerno, reasons)`** Invokes the `doApproved(requestno, officerno, reasons)` method of the `ApprovalLocal` CMP bean to update the data in the `APPROVAL` table.
  - **`getEmployeeno(requestno)`** Invokes the `getEmployeeno()` method of the `PurchaseOrderLocal` CMP bean to get the `employeeno` of the employee who generated the purchase order requisition. This bean uses the `PURCHASE_ORDER` table to get the data.
  - **`getEmployeeEmail(employeeno)`** Calls the method of the `EmployeeLocal` BMP that manipulates data in the `EMPLOYEE` table and returns the employee's e-mail address.
  - **`sendEmailAddress(queuemsg)`** Produces a message consisting of the purchase order requisition number and the employee's e-mail address that will be consumed by the `EmailMessageBean` MDB. In the "Writing Point-to-Point JMS Clients" section of this chapter, you will learn step-by-step how JMS clients produce messages to `queue` destinations.
- It implements the `ejbRemove()` method. No implementation code is necessary for this method.
- It implements the `onMessage()` method of the `javax.jms.MessageListener` interface. The `onMessage()` method invokes the following helper methods to aid message processing:
  - **`processApproval()`** Uses the `ApprovalLocal` CMP bean to update the `APPROVAL` table.

- **getEmployeeno()** Uses the PurchaseOrderLocal CMP bean to get the employeeno of the employee that generated the purchase order requisition.
- **getEmployeeEmail()** Uses the EmployeeLocal BMP bean to get the e-mail address of the employee.
- **sendEmailAddress(queuemsg)** Produces a TextMessage message to be consumed by the EmailMessageBean MDB.

Here is the complete definition of the ProcessApprovalMessageBean class:

```
/**
**   Program Name:  ProcessApprovalMessageBean.java
**
**   Purpose:
**          This message-driven bean does the following:
**          1. Processes a message
**          2. Calls the ApprovalLocal CMP bean
**             to update the APPROVAL table
**          3. Calls the PurchaseOrderLocal CMP bean
**             to query the Purchase-Order table and
**             get the employeeno associated to a requestno.
**          4. Calls the EmployeeLocal BMP bean
**             to get the e-mail address of the employee.
**          5. Sends the requestno and the e-mail address to the
**             EmailMessageBean MDB.
**
**
*/
package purchase.ejb.mdb;

import javax.ejb.*;
import javax.naming.*;
import javax.jms.*;
import purchase.ejb.cmp.*;
import purchase.ejb.bmp.*;
import javax.ejb.FinderException;


public class ProcessApprovalMessageBean
  implements MessageDrivenBean, MessageListener {

  private MessageDrivenContext mdc = null;
  private ApprovalLocalHome approvalLocalHome = null;
  private PurchaseOrderLocalHome purchaseOrderLocalHome = null;
  private EmployeeLocalHome employeeLocalHome = null;
```

```
private Context context;

public ProcessApprovalMessageBean()
{
    System.out.println("In "
        +"ProcessApprovalMessageBean."
        +"ProcessApprovalMessageBean()");
}
/**
* setMessageDrivenContext method, declared as
* public not final or static, with a return type void,
* and with one argument of type javax.ejb.MessageDrivenContext.
*
*/
public void setMessageDrivenContext(MessageDrivenContext mdc)
{
  System.out.println("In "
     +"ProcessApprovalMessageBean.setMessageDrivenContext()");
  this.mdc = mdc;
}

 /**
* ejbCreate method, declared as public not final or static,
* with a return type void, and with no argument
*/

 public void ejbCreate()
 {
   System.out.println("In ProcessApprovalMessageBean." +
                  "ejbCreate()");
   // Locate ApprovalLocalHome, PurchaseOrderLocalHome,
   // and EmployeeLocalHome interfaces.
   try {
       approvalLocalHome = getApprovalLocalHome();
       purchaseOrderLocalHome = getPurchaseOrderLocalHome();
       employeeLocalHome = getEmployeeLocalHome();
       System.out.println("got approvallocalhome: "
                            +approvalLocalHome);
       System.out.println("got approvallocalhome: "
                            +purchaseOrderLocalHome);
       System.out.println("got approvallocalhome: "
                            +employeeLocalHome);
   } // End of try
   catch (Exception e) {
       System.err.println("Unable to get CMP/BMP Homes: "
           +e.getMessage());
   }  // end catch
```

```
} // End of ejbCreate()


private ApprovalLocalHome getApprovalLocalHome()
     throws javax.naming.NamingException {
     Context ic = new InitialContext();
     return (ApprovalLocalHome)
             ic.lookup("java:comp/env/ApprovalLocal");
} // End of getApprovaleLocalHome()

private PurchaseOrderLocalHome getPurchaseOrderLocalHome()
       throws javax.naming.NamingException {
     Context ic = new InitialContext();
     return (PurchaseOrderLocalHome)
             ic.lookup("java:comp/env/PurchaseOrderLocal");
} // End of getPurchaseOrderLocalHome()

private EmployeeLocalHome getEmployeeLocalHome()
       throws javax.naming.NamingException {
     Context ic = new InitialContext();
     return (EmployeeLocalHome)
             ic.lookup("java:comp/env/EmployeeLocal");
} // End of getEmployeeLocalHome()

/**
* onMessage method, declared as public not final or static,
* with a return type void, and with one argument
* of type javax.jms.Message.
*
* Casts the incoming Message to a MapMessage, retrieves
* its contents and does the following:
*   1. calls the processApproval() to update the APPROVAL table
*   2. calls the getEmployeeno() to get the employeeno
*      associated to the requestno
*   3. calls the getEmployeeEmail()
*   4. calls the sendEmailAddress() to send a
*      message consisting of the requestno
*      and employee's email address.
*/

public void onMessage(Message inMessage)
{
System.out.println("onMessage called");


   MapMessage msg = null;
   long requestno;
```

```
        long officerno;
        String reasons = null;
        long employeeno = 0;
        String email = null;
        int successful = 0;

        try {
            if  (inMessage instanceof MapMessage) {
                 msg = (MapMessage)inMessage;
                 requestno = msg.getInt("requestno");
                 officerno = msg.getInt("officerno");
                 reasons = msg.getString("reasons");

                 System.out.println("ProcessApprovalMessageBean: " +
                 "Message received: ");

                 successful = processApproval(requestno,
                                         officerno, reasons);
                 if  (successful == 0)
                      employeeno = getEmployeeno(requestno);
                 if  (employeeno > 0)
                      email = getEmployeeEmail(employeeno);

                 if (email != null) {
                     String queuemsg = email+", "+requestno;
                      sendEmailMessage(queuemsg);
                 }

            } else {
                 System.out.println("Message of wrong type: "
                         +inMessage.getClass().getName());
            }
            System.out.println("onMessage in processorder returned");
        } // End try
        catch (JMSException e) {
           System.err.println("ProcessApprovalMessageBean."
              +"onMessage: "
                 + "JMSException: " +e.toString());
           mdc.setRollbackOnly();
        } // End catch
        catch (Throwable te) {
           System.err.println("ProcessApprovalMessageBean."
           +"onMessage: "
                 + "Exception: " +te.toString());
           mdc.setRollbackOnly();
        } // End catch

    } // End onMessage()
```

```
private int processApproval(long requestno, long officerno,
                      String reasons) {

      ApprovalLocal approvalLocal = null;
  int sucessful = 0;

      try {
        ApprovalPK ApprovalPK = new ApprovalPK(requestno);
            approvalLocal =
                approvalLocalHome.findByPrimaryKey(ApprovalPK);

            System.out.println("I got the ApprovalPK");

            approvalLocal.doApproved(requestno, officerno, reasons);

    }
    catch (FinderException e) {
           System.err.println("Cannot find data from "
             + "APPROVAL info: " + e.getMessage());
       sucessful = 1;
       mdc.setRollbackOnly();
  }  // End catch

  return sucessful;

} // End of processApproval()

private long getEmployeeno(long requestno) {

      PurchaseOrderLocal purchaseOrderLocal = null;
  long employeeno = 0;
      try {
              PurchaseOrderPK purchasePK =
                          new PurchaseOrderPK(requestno);
              purchaseOrderLocal =
                purchaseOrderLocalHome.findByPrimaryKey(purchasePK);

                  System.out.println("I got the PurchasePK");

        employeeno = purchaseOrderLocal.getEmployeeNo();

      }
       catch (FinderException e) {
              System.err.println("Cannot select "
                  +"PurchaseOrderLocal info: " +e.getMessage());
         mdc.setRollbackOnly();
  }  // End catch
```

```
    return employeeno;

  }  // End of getEmployeeno()

  private String getEmployeeEmail(long employeeno) {

        EmployeeLocal employeeLocal = null;
      String email = null;
        try {
                EmployeePK employeePK =
                         new EmployeePK(employeeno);
                employeeLocal =
                   employeeLocalHome.findByPrimaryKey(employeePK);

                System.out.println("I got the EmployeePK");

                email = employeeLocal.getEmail();

         }
         catch (FinderException e) {
              System.err.println("Cannot select PurchaseOrder info: "
                                   + e.getMessage());
              mdc.setRollbackOnly();
      }  // End catch

      return email;

    }  // End of getEmployeeEmail()

    private void sendEmailMessage(String msg)
    {
    /* The ProcessApprovalMessageBean is a PTP client producer
    ** The program uses this private method to produce messages
    ** to Queue destinations
    */

    QueueConnectionFactory factory = null;
    QueueConnection queueConnection = null;
    QueueSender queueSender = null;
    QueueSession queueSession = null;
    try {

        /* Steps to produce messages to a Queue destination

        // Step 1: Create an InitialContext object
        InitialContext ic = new InitialContext();

        // Step 2: Use the emailMessageQueueConnectionFactory
```

```
    // user-defined name to look up a queue connection factory
    factory = (QueueConnectionFactory)
    ic.lookup(
      "java:comp/env/jms/emailMessageQueueConnectionFactory");

    // Step 3: Create a QueueConnection object
    queueConnection = factory.createQueueConnection();

    // Step 4: Start the connection so we can use it
    queueConnection.start();

    // Step 5: Create a QueueSession object
    queueSession =
      queueConnection.createQueueSession(false,
                                Session.AUTO_ACKNOWLEDGE);

    // Step 6: Use the emailMessageQueue user-defined
    // name to look up the Queue destination. This name
    // maps to actual JNDI location
    Queue queue = (Queue)
       ic.lookup("java:comp/env/jms/emailMessageQueue");

    // Step 7: Create a QueueSender object
    queueSender = queueSession.createSender(queue);

    // Step 8: Create a TextMessage object
    TextMessage message = queueSession.createTextMessage(msg);

    // Step 9: Send the message to the Queue destination
    queueSender.send(message);
  System.out.println("Emailmessage sent to the Queue");

}
catch(JMSException e) {
    System.err.println("Communication error: " + e.getMessage());
}
catch(NamingException e) {
    System.err.println("Error looking up objects: "
                 + e.getMessage());
}
finally {
  if (queueSender != null) {
    try {
      queueSender.close();
    } catch (JMSException e) {}
  }
  //added a close on session object
  if (queueSession != null) {
```

```
          try {
            queueSession.close();
          } catch (JMSException e) {}
        }
        if (queueConnection != null) {
          try {
            queueConnection.close();
          } catch (JMSException e) {}
        }
      }
    }
  }  // End sendEmailMessage() method


  /**
  * ejbRemove method, declared as public not final or static,
  * with a return type void, and with no argument
  */
  public void ejbRemove()
  {
    System.out.println("EmailMessage: ejbRemove() ");
  }

}  // End of ProcessApprovalMessageBean
```

Next, you will write the `ApprovalLocal` CMP entity bean. Before delving into the source code, let us understand how the EJB container handles an MDB by looking at its life cycle.

Life Cycle of a Message-Driven Bean

Figure 7-6 shows how an EJB container interacts with MDBs. The EJB container does the following:

1. Creates a new instance of an MDB.
2. Calls the `setMessageDrivenContext (MessageDrivenContext mdc)` method to pass the context object to the instance.
3. Calls the instance's `ejbCreate()` method.
4. Calls the `ejbRemove()` method at the end of the life cycle. The bean instance is then ready for garbage collection.

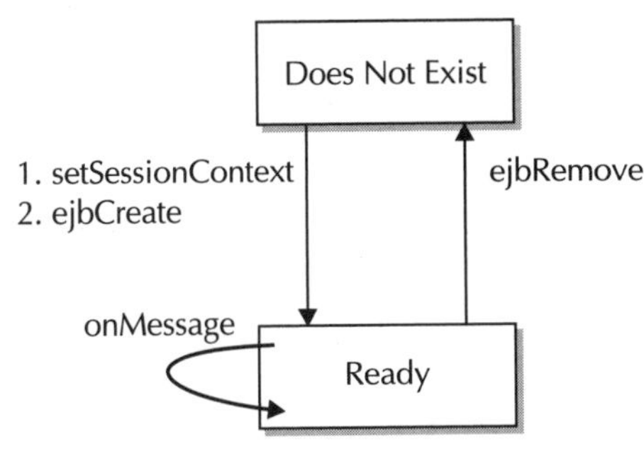

FIGURE 7-6. *Life cycle of an MDB*

Coding the CMP Entity Beans

In this section, you will write the `ApprovalLocal` CMP entity bean. Recall that the `ProcessApprovalMessageBeanMDB` uses the `PurchaseOrderLocal` CMP and `EmployeeLocal` BMP entity beans to aid in processing messages. You developed these CMP beans in Chapter 5. As a refresher, we present again the definitions of these beans.

The ApprovalLocal Local CMP

The `ApprovalLocal` CMP entity bean maps the `APPROVAL` table in the Oracle9*i* database. It consists of several components:

- The `ApprovalLocal` interface, like any CMP local interface, contains several getter and setter methods. Additionally, it contains the `doApproved(long requestno, long officerno, String reason)` method that sets up the persistent fields that the EJB container uses to update the `APPROVAL` table. The `ProcessApprovalMessageBean` MDB will call the `doApproved(…)` method when the EJB container invokes the MDB's `onMessage()` method.
- The `ApprovalLocalHome` interface.
- The `ApprovalPK` primary class.
- The `ApprovalBean` bean class.

The ApprovalLocal Interface Here is the definition of the `ApprovalLocal` interface:

```
/**
**    Program Name:  ApprovalLocal.java
**
**    Purpose:      This CMP bean maps the APPROVAL table.
**
*/
package purchase.ejb.cmp;
import javax.ejb.EJBLocalObject;

public interface ApprovalLocal
    extends EJBLocalObject {

  long getRequestNo();

  void setRequestNo(long newRequestno);

  long getBudgetofficer();

  void setBudgetofficer(long newBudgetofficer);

  String getApproved();

  void setApproved(String newApproved);

  String getReasons();

  void setReasons(String newReasons);

  void doApproved(long requestno, long officerno, String reason);

}  // End of ApprovalLocal local interface
```

The ApprovalLocalHome Local Home Interface Here is the definition of the `ApprovalLocalHome` interface:

```
/**
**    Program Name:  ApprovalLocalHome.java
**
**    Purpose:
**
*/
package purchase.ejb.cmp;
import javax.ejb.EJBLocalHome;
```

```
import javax.ejb.CreateException;
import javax.ejb.FinderException;
import java.util.Collection;
import java.rmi.RemoteException;

public interface ApprovalLocalHome extends EJBLocalHome
{

  ApprovalLocal create(long requestNo, long officerNo,
            String approved, String reasons) throws CreateException;

  ApprovalLocal findByPrimaryKey(ApprovalPK primaryKey)
             throws FinderException;

  Collection findAll() throws FinderException;

  Collection findNonApprovedPO(String approved)
             throws FinderException;
}  // End of ApprovalLocalHome local home interface
```

The ApprovalPK Primary Key Class Here is the definition of the `ApprovalPK` primary key class:

```
/**
**   Program Name:  ApprovalPK.java
**
**   Purpose:
**
*/
package purchase.ejb.cmp;
import java.io.Serializable;

public class ApprovalPK implements Serializable
{
  public long requestNo;

  public ApprovalPK() { }

  public ApprovalPK(long requestNo)
  {
    this.requestNo = requestNo;
  }

  public boolean equals(Object other)
  {
    return (other instanceof ApprovalPK &&
```

```
            this.requestNo==((ApprovalPK)other).requestNo);
  }

  public int hashCode()
  {
    return (new Long(requestNo)).hashCode();
  }
}  // End of ApprovalPK primary key class
```

The ApprovalBean Bean Class Here is the definition of the `ApprovalBean` bean class:

```
/**
**   Program Name:  ApprovalBean.java
**
**   Purpose:       CMP bean class to manipulate
**                  data in the Approval database table
**
*/
package purchase.ejb.cmp;
import javax.ejb.EntityBean;
import javax.ejb.EntityContext;
import javax.ejb.CreateException;
import javax.ejb.EJBException;
import javax.naming.NamingException;
import javax.ejb.FinderException;

import javax.naming.Context;
import javax.naming.InitialContext;

public abstract class ApprovalBean
    implements EntityBean {

  public EntityContext entityContext;

  public ApprovalPK ejbCreate(long requestNo, long officerNo,
            String approved, String reasons) throws CreateException
  {
     setRequestNo(requestNo);
     setBudgetofficer(officerNo);
     setReasons(reasons);
     setApproved("N");
     return new ApprovalPK(requestNo);
  }
```

```
public void ejbPostCreate(long requestNo, long officerNo,
            String approved, String reasons) throws CreateException
{
}

public void ejbActivate()
{
}

public void ejbLoad()
{
}

public void ejbPassivate()
{
}

public void ejbRemove()
{
}

public void ejbStore()
{
}

public void setEntityContext(EntityContext ctx)
{
  this.entityContext = ctx;
}

public void unsetEntityContext()
{
  this.entityContext = null;
}

public abstract long getRequestNo();

public abstract void setRequestNo(long newRequestno);

public abstract long  getBudgetofficer();

public abstract void setBudgetofficer(long newBudgetofficer);

public abstract String getApproved();

public abstract void setApproved(String newApproved);
```

```
  public abstract String getReasons();

  public abstract void setReasons(String newReasons);

  public void doApproved(long requestno,
           long officerno, String reason) {

     setRequestNo(requestno);
     setBudgetofficer(officerno);
     setReasons(reason);
     if  (reason == null)
         setApproved("N");
     else
         setApproved("Y");

  }  // End of doApproved()

}  // End of ApprovalBean class
```

The PurchaseOrderLocal CMP and the EmployeeLocal BMP Entity Beans

Next, let us revisit the `PurchaseOrderLocal` CMP and the `EmployeeLocal` BMP entity beans. You created those beans in Chapter 5. The `ProcessApprovalMessageBean` uses the `PurchaseOrderLocal` CMP bean to retrieve the `employeeno` of the employee who generated the purchase order requisition. To allow you to deploy this application as a unit, we copied the source code from Chapter 5 into the development directory of this chapter. The `PurchaseOrderLocal` CMP bean, which maps the `PURCHASE_ORDER` table of the Oracle9*i* database, consists of the following components:

- The `PurchaseOrderLocal` interface
- The `PurchaseOrderLocalHome` interface
- The `PurchaseOrderPK` primary class
- The `PurchaseOrderBean` bean class

The `ProcessApprovalMessageBean` uses the `EmployeeLocal` BMP entity bean to retrieve the e-mail address of the employee who generated the purchase order requisition. The `EmployeeLocal` BMP, which maps the `EMPLOYEE` table of the Oracle9*i* database, consists of the following components:

- The `EmployeeLocal` interface
- The `EmployeeLocalHome` interface

- The EmployeePK primary class
- The EmployeeBean bean class

Next, you will code the EmailMessageBean MDB class.

Coding the EmailMessageBean MDB

The ProcessApprovalMessageBean MDB produces messages that EmailMessageBean will consume. The EmailMessageBean class consists of a simple onMessage() method that consumes a TextMessage message. We would like this bean, upon consuming the message, to send an e-mail notifying the employee that his/her purchase order requisition has been approved. Sending an e-mail in Java is rather simple. You can use the JavaMail API to do so. There are numerous examples available over the Web. Thus, we leave this exercise for the readers.

Here is the complete definition of the EmailMessageBean class:

```
**   ProgramName:   EmailMessageBean.java
**
**   Purpose:       This bean only consumes the
**                  message from a Queue destination.
**                  The implementation code to send
**                  an email message is left to the reader.
**
*/
package purchase.ejb.mdb;
import javax.ejb.*;
import javax.naming.*;
import javax.jms.*;
public class EmailMessageBean
  implements MessageDrivenBean, MessageListener {
  private transient MessageDrivenContext mdc = null;
  private Context context;
  public EmailMessageBean()  {
     System.out.println("In EmailMessageBean.EmailMessageBean()");
  }
  /**
  * setMessageDrivenContext method, declared as
  * public not final or static, with a return type void,
  * and with one argument of type javax.ejb.MessageDrivenContext.
  *
  */
  public void setMessageDrivenContext(MessageDrivenContext mdc) {
    System.out.println("In EmailMessageBean."
               +"setMessageDrivenContext()");
    this.mdc = mdc;
  }
```

```
 /**
* ejbCreate method, declared as public not final or static,
* with a return type void, and with no argument
*/

 public void ejbCreate() {
   System.out.println("In EmailMessageBean.ejbCreate()");
 }

 /**
* onMessage method, declared as public not final or static,
* with a return type void, and with one argument
* of type javax.jms.Message.
*
* Casts the incoming Message to a TextMessage, display
* the text and send the email.
*/
public void onMessage(Message inMessage)    {
   TextMessage msg = null;
   try {
        if  (inMessage instanceof TextMessage) {
             msg = (TextMessage)inMessage;
             System.out.println("EmailMessage: Message "
                 + "received: " +msg.getText());
        } else {
             System.out.println("Message of wrong type: "
                     +inMessage.getClass().getName());
        }
   }  // End try
   catch (JMSException e) {
      System.err.println("EmailMessageBean.onMessage: "
            + "JMSException: " +e.toString());
      mdc.setRollbackOnly();
   }  // End catch
   catch (Throwable te) {
      System.err.println("EmailMessageBean.onMessage: "
            + "Exception: " +te.toString());
      mdc.setRollbackOnly();
   }  // End catch
}  // End onMessage()

/**
* ejbRemove method, declared as public not final or static,
* with a return type void, and with no argument
*/
public void ejbRemove()  {
  System.out.println("EmailMessage: ejbRemove() ");
```

```
    }
} // End of EmailMessageBean class
```

Next, you will write the ejb-jar.xml deployment descriptor for the Approval application.

Writing the ejb-jar.xml Deployment Descriptor

In this chapter, we created a single deployment descriptor file in which we specify all the enterprise beans of the Approval application. Note that we will only explain the elements applicable to message-driven beans. To learn more about the elements regarding the entity and session beans, see Chapters 5 and 6.

In this section, you will accomplish two tasks:

- You will create the ejb-jar.xml MDB deployment descriptor: In this file, you will specify whether you are using a Queue (PTP messaging system) destination or Topic (pub/sub messaging system) destination.
- You will configure the resource provider in the OC4J-specific application.xml file. Recall that the OC4J application.xml file is located in the [OC4J_HOME]/j2ee/home/config directory.

Message-Driven Elements in the ejb-jar.xml File

MDBs that you want to deploy to OC4J can use either a Queue or a Topic destination. Normally, you create JMS destinations administratively (by listing the destination in the ejb-jar.xml file) rather than programmatically (by coding the destination in the program itself). Recall that the ProcessApprovalMessageBean MDB is a JMS listener that processes messages from a Topic destination and a PTP client that produces messages to a Queue destination. Recall also that the EJB container is aware of resources (data sources or JMS connections) when you declare these resources in the ejb-jar.xml file. Since Topic and Queue destinations are resources (JMS resources), you will also declare them in the ejb-jar.xml file.

Use the <message-driven-destination><destination-type> element of the ejb-jar.xml file to specify the JMS destination. Use javax.jms.Topic or javax.jms.Queue to specify a JMS API of type Topic or Queue. Note that, if it is intended for a topic destination, you can use the <message-driven-destination><subscription-durability> element to specify whether the subscription is durable or nondurable. Durable topic subscriptions can receive messages published while the subscriber is not active. Durable subscriptions offer the reliability of queues to the publish/subscribe message domain. A nondurable subscriber can only receive messages that are published while it is active. The following entries demonstrate how to specify a topic JMS destination and a durable topic subscription:

```
<message-driven-destination>
 <!-- The <destination-type> element
     (J2EE 1.3 Specification) replaces
     the <jms-destination-type> element -->
   <destination-type>
       javax.jms.Topic
   </destination-type>
   <subscription-durability>
       Durable
   </subscription-durability>
</message-driven-destination>
```

Next, you will create the Queue destination. Like the Topic JMS destination, you will create a Queue JMS destination administratively by listing the Queue destination in the ejb-jar.xml file. Recall that the ProcessApprovalMessageBean MDB is also a JMS producer that produces messages to a Queue destination. Use the EJB <resource-ref> element to declare any J2EE resource (database resources or JMS connections). The EJB container manages these resources.

The <resource-ref> elements allow the ejb-jar consumer (that is, EJB *application assembler* or *deployer*) to discover all the resource manager connection factory references used by an enterprise bean. Recall that an application assembler gathers one or more beans developed by the bean providers to produce larger application units (new enterprise beans or non-EJB applications), whereas a deployer is responsible for correctly installing the EJB classes and interfaces in the EJB server. Note that the <resource-ref> element must be within the <message-driven> tag.

Each <resource-ref> element describes a single resource manager connection factory reference. The <resource-ref> element consists of the description element and the mandatory <res-ref-name>, <res-type>, and <res-auth> elements. To learn more about the <resource-ref> element, see the EJB 2.0 specification.

Use the <res-type> element to specify the type of resource. In this section, we use <res-type> to declare a resource reference of type Queue, identified by javax.jms.Queue, and QueueConnectionFactory, identified by javax.jms.QueueConnectionFactory.

Use the <res-ref-name> element for the name of the resource that your EJB or JMS client code will use to access resources. These names will be used by the ProcessApprovalMessageBean MDB when looking up these objects and sending a message to the EMAILQUEUE destination.

In the following code fragment, the jms/emailMessageQueue name is associated to the javax.jms.Queue JMS destination, whereas the jms/emailMessageQueueConnectionFactory name is associated to the javax.jms.QueueConnectionFactory connection factory:

```
<resource-ref>
  <description>The queue for EmailMessage</description>
  <res-ref-name>jms/emailMessageQueue</res-ref-name>
  <res-type>javax.jms.Queue</res-type>
  <res-auth>Container</res-auth>
</resource-ref>
<resource-ref>
  <description>The Factory used </description>
  <res-ref-name>jms/emailMessageQueueConnectionFactory</res-ref-name>
  <res-type>javax.jms.QueueConnectionFactory</res-type>
  <res-auth>Container</res-auth>
</resource-ref>
```

To indicate how your transaction management should be performed, use the <transaction-type> element. The following entry indicates that the EJB container will manage transactions for you:

```
<transaction-type>Container</transaction-type>
```

Recall that the ProcessApprovalMessageBean MDB is using three entity beans. You also need to inform the EJB container that your MDB will access other EJB components. Use the <ejb-ref> element for remote beans or the <ejb-local-ref> element for local beans. The following entries in the ejb-jar.xml file indicate that your MDB is using the local ApprovalLocal CMP entity bean:

```
<ejb-local-ref>
          <ejb-ref-name>ApprovalLocal</ejb-ref-name>
          <ejb-ref-type>Entity</ejb-ref-type>
          <local-home>purchase.ejb.cmp.ApprovalLocalHome</local-home>
          <local>purchase.ejb.cmp.ApprovalLocal</local>
</ejb-local-ref>
```

Here is a partial listing of the ejb-jar.xml deployment descriptor that relates to MDBs:

```
<ejb-jar>
   <enterprise-beans>
```

```
<message-driven>
  <!-- Information relating to
    the ProcessApprovalMessageBean MDB -->
    <description></description>
    <ejb-name>ProcessApprovalMessageBean</ejb-name>
    <ejb-class>
       purchase.ejb.mdb.ProcessApprovalMessageBean</ejb-class>
    <transaction-type>Container</transaction-type>
    <!-- Information relating to
      the JMS Topic destination -->
    <message-driven-destination>
      <destination-type>javax.jms.Topic</destination-type>
      <subscription-durability>Durable</subscription-durability>
    </message-driven-destination>
    <!-- Information relating to
      the local entity beans that the MDB uses -->
    <ejb-local-ref>
      <ejb-ref-name>ApprovalLocal</ejb-ref-name>
      <ejb-ref-type>Entity</ejb-ref-type>
      <local-home>purchase.ejb.cmp.ApprovalLocalHome</local-home>
      <local>purchase.ejb.cmp.ApprovalLocal</local>
    </ejb-local-ref>
    <ejb-local-ref>
      <ejb-ref-name>PurchaseOrderLocal</ejb-ref-name>
      <ejb-ref-type>Entity</ejb-ref-type>
      <local-home>
           purchase.ejb.cmp.PurchaseOrderLocalHome</local-home>
      <local>purchase.ejb.cmp.PurchaseOrderLocal</local>
    </ejb-local-ref>
    <ejb-local-ref>
      <ejb-ref-name>EmployeeLocal</ejb-ref-name>
      <ejb-ref-type>Entity</ejb-ref-type>
      <local-home>purchase.ejb.bmp.EmployeeLocalHome</local-home>
      <local>purchase.ejb.bmp.EmployeeLocal</local>
    </ejb-local-ref>
    <!-- Information relating to
      the JMS Queue destination -->
    <resource-ref>
     <description>The queue for EmailMessage</description>
     <!-- User-defined name that the PTP client uses
       to locate the JMS Queue destination -->
     <res-ref-name>jms/emailMessageQueue</res-ref-name>
     <res-type>javax.jms.Queue</res-type>
     <res-auth>Container</res-auth>
   </resource-ref>
   <!-- Information relating to
     the QueueConnectionFactory used -->
```

```
        <resource-ref>
            <description>The Factory used </description>
            <!-- User-defined name that the PTP client uses
              to locate the JMS Queue connection factory -->
            <res-ref-name>
                 jms/emailMessageQueueConnectionFactory</res-ref-name>
            <res-type>javax.jms.QueueConnectionFactory</res-type>
            <res-auth>Container</res-auth>
          </resource-ref>
          <!-- End of information relating to
            the ProcessApprovalMessageBean MDB -->
    </message-driven>
    <!-- Information relating to
      the EmailMessageBean MDB -->
    <message-driven>
      <description>EmailMessageBean</description>
         <ejb-name>EmailMessageBean</ejb-name>
         <ejb-class>purchase.ejb.mdb.EmailMessageBean</ejb-class>
         <transaction-type>Container</transaction-type>
         <!-- Information relating to
           the JMS Queue destination from which
           the EmailMessageBean MDB will consume messages -->
         <message-driven-destination>
         <!-- Like for the Topic destination, use this element
           to specify the Queue destination -->
           <destination-type>javax.jms.Queue</destination-type>
         </message-driven-destination>
      </message-driven>
      <!-- Information relating to
        the entity beans -->
      <entity>
         <description>
           Entity Bean ( Container-managed Persistence )</description>
         <display-name>ApprovalLocal</display-name>
...
         <display-name>PurchaseOrderLocal</display-name>
...
         <display-name>EmployeeLocal</display-name>
...
</ejb-jar>
```

Modifying the OC4J application.xml File

Modify the OC4J `application.xml` file to configure the resource provider. Recall that Oracle Advanced Queuing is our JMS provider. The OC4J `application.xml` file is located in the `[OC4J-HOME]/j2ee/home/config` directory. Use the `<resource-provider>` tag to configure the resource provider. Add the following entries at the end of OC4J `application.xml` file but before the `</orion-application>` tag:

```
<resource-provider class="oracle.jms.OjmsContext" name="ojms">
  <property name="datasource" value="jdbc/OracleDS"/>
  <property name="username" value="aquser"/>
  <property name="password" value="x"/>
</resource-provider>
```

We have now configured the resource provider for Oracle AQ with the context name `ojms`. This name will be used when looking up connection factories and destinations through JNDI.

To learn how to configure OC4J to use third-party providers including Oracle AQ, see Appendix A of this book and the *Oracle9iAS Containers For J2EE, Services Guide* technical manual.

Next, you will create the `orion-ejb-jar.xml` file. Use this file to inform the OC4J EJB container of which JMS destination it should associate with your MDBs.

Writing or Generating the orion-ejb-jar.xml Deployment Descriptor

Once you have created the `ejb-jar.xml` deployment descriptor for your EJB components, you need to create or modify the `orion-ejb-jar.xml` OC4J-specific deployment descriptor. The nice thing about Oracle9*i*AS Containers For J2EE is that you do not have to provide the `orion-ejb-jar.xml` file. At deployment time, OC4J generates a new OC4J-specific XML file for you, using its default elements. However, if you have provided an OC4J-specific XML file within your application, OC4J will merge your configuration with the one that gets generated to produce a new OC4J-specific deployment descriptor for you. If you do not store an `orion-ejb-jar.xml` server-specific deployment descriptor in your application, OC4J will generate one for you.

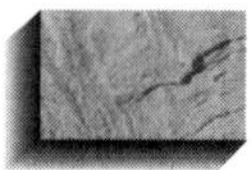

CAUTION

If you want to edit this deployment descriptor, we recommend that you take the generated one and store it within your application, edit it, and, more importantly, delete the generated one under your application deployment directory. Then, restart the server.

In order to identify the JMS destination that is to be associated with an MDB, you need to map the JMS destination location and connection factory to the MDB through the `<message-driven-deployment>` element in the `orion-ejb-jar.xml` file.

The `orion-ejb-jar.xml` file maps JMS resources to the `ProcessApprovalMessageBean` and `EmailMessageBean` MDBs. The `orion-ejb-jar.xml` file derives from the `orion-ejb-jar.dtd` OC4J-specific EJB deployment descriptor file. In this section, we present the definition of some of the elements contained within `orion-ejb-jar.dtd`. To learn more about the elements of this file, see Appendix D of the book and Appendix A of the *Oracle9iAS Containers For J2EE, Enterprise JavaBeans Developer's Guide and Reference* technical manual.

To the `ProcessApprovalMessageBean` MDB, the `orion-ejb-jar.xml` file provides the following:

- The MDB name, `ProcessApprovalMessageBean`, as defined in the `<ejb-name>` in the EJB deployment descriptor, is specified in the `name` attribute.
- The `java:comp/resource/ojms/Topics/aquser.processtopic` JNDI location of the Topic destination is specified in the `<destination-location>` attribute. Recall that you created the `aquser.processtopic` JMS destination in the "Setting Up Oracle Advanced Queuing as a JMS Provider" section of the chapter. This location, as you can see, uses the name `ojms` that you defined in the OC4J-specific `application.xml` file as the context name for the resource provider.
- The `java:comp/resource/ojms/TopicConnectionFactories/aqTcf` JNDI location of the connection factory is specified in the `<connection-factory-location>` attribute.
- The `<resource-ref-mapping>` element is used for the declaration of a reference to an external resource (data source or JMS queue). It consists of two attributes: `name` and `location`. The `name` attribute is used to specify the `resource-ref` name. It matches the name of a `resource-ref` specified in the `ejb-jar.xml` file. When deploying the application, the `<resource-ref-mapping>` element ties the JMS resource to a JNDI-location. The `location` attribute is used to specify the JNDI location from which to look up the resource factory. In the `orion-ejb-jar.xml` file of the Approval application, you use the `name` attribute to specify the name of the `jms/emailMessageQueue` resource (Queue) and the `location` attribute to specify the `java:comp/resource/ojms/Queues/aquser.emailqueue` JNDI location from which to look up the resource factory.

Recall that a JMS destination works in pair with a connection factory. Thus, you will use the `<resource-ref-mapping>` element and its attributes to specify the `jms/emailMessageQueueConnectionFactory` name of the connection factory and its JNDI location, `java:comp/resource/ojms/QueueConnectionFactories/qcf`.

To the `EmailMessageBean` MDB, the `orion-ejb-jar.xml` file provides the `<destination-location>` attribute to specify the `java:comp/resource/ojms/Queue/aquser.emailqueue` JNDI location of the `Queue` destination, and the `<connection-factory>` attribute to specify the `java:comp/resource/ojms/Queue/QueueConnectionFactories/aqQcf` JNDI location of the `Queue` connection factory to use.

Here is a partial listing of the `orion-ejb-jar.xml` file:

```
<?xml version = '1.0' encoding = 'windows-1252'?>
<!DOCTYPE orion-ejb-jar PUBLIC
  "-//Evermind//DTD Enterprise JavaBeans 1.1 runtime//EN"
 "http://xmlns.oracle.com/ias/dtds/orion-ejb-jar.dtd">
<orion-ejb-jar>
   <enterprise-beans>
   <!-- Information relating to the ProcessApprovalMessageBean,
        the Oracle AQ PROCESSTOPIC and EMAILQUEUE resources that
        you defined in the Oracle9i database, the entity beans and
        the EmailMessageBean MDB that the Approval application
        is using. -->
     <message-driven-deployment name="ProcessApprovalMessageBean"
         destination-location=
           "java:comp/resource/ojms/Topics/aquser.processtopic"
         connection-factory-location=
           "java:comp/resource/ojms/TopicConnectionFactories/aqTcf"
         subscription-name="topicSubscriber" >
        <ejb-ref-mapping name="ApprovalLocal" />
          <ejb-ref-mapping name="PurchaseOrderLocal" />
        <resource-ref-mapping name="jms/emailMessageQueue"
         location=
            "java:comp/resource/ojms/Queues/aquser.emailqueue" />
     <resource-ref-mapping
           name="jms/emailMessageQueueConnectionFactory"
           location=
             "java:comp/resource/ojms/QueueConnectionFactories/qcf" />
   </message-driven-deployment>
   <message-driven-deployment name="EmailMessageBean"
       destination-location=
           "java:comp/resource/ojms/Queues/aquser.emailqueue"
       connection-factory-location=
```

```
            "java:comp/resource/ojms/QueueConnectionFactories/aqQcf">
    </message-driven-deployment>
      <entity-deployment name="ApprovalLocal"
          data-source="jdbc/OracleDS" table="APPROVAL">
...
...
</orion-ejb-jar>
```

Next, you will code JMS clients that produce and consume messages using the PROCESSTOPIC and EMAILQUEUE destinations that you set up in the Oracle9*i* database. Recall that in the "Setting Up Oracle Advanced Queuing as a JMS Provider" section, you learned how to use Oracle AQ as the JMS provider for the Approval application. Note that the JMS implementation supplied by Oracle AQ complies with the JMS specification, and thus the code is portable and will run in any environment that hosts a Java Virtual Machine.

Coding JMS Clients

A JMS client is a Java program that can send and receive messages. JMS clients use the message implementations supplied by their JMS provider. Recall that a JMS provider is the entity that implements JMS for a messaging product. JMS providers must be written in 100 percent pure Java so they can run in any environment where there is a JVM and work across architectures and operating systems. The JMS implementation supplied by Oracle AQ complies with the JMS specification, and thus is portable and platform-independent.

In this section, we will delve into the code of the sendEmailAddress() method of the ProcessApprovalMessageBean MDB and you will code the LocalClientServlet servlet. Recall that the ProcessApprovalMessageBean MDB is a JMS producer that uses the PTP messaging system. In a PTP product or application, clients address messages to a Queue destination. You use PTP messaging when you want every message you send to be processed successfully by one consumer. The LocalClientServlet class is a JMS message producer that publishes messages to a Topic (pub/sub) destination.

Next, you will learn how to write PTP JMS clients that produce messages to Queue destinations.

Writing Point-to-Point JMS Clients

In this section, you will learn how to code JMS client programs that use PTP messaging systems. In the sendEmailAddress() method of the ProcessApprovalMessageBean MDB, the program produces an asynchronous TextMessage message to the EMAILQUEUE Queue destination. Recall that you set up the EMAILQUEUE Queue destination in the Oracle9*i* database. The EmailMessageBean MDB consumes messages produced by the ProcessApprovalMessageBean MDB.

The sendEmailAddress() method performs the following steps:

1. Creates an InitialContext object:

```
InitialContext ic = new InitialContext();
```

2. Uses the lookup() method of the InitialContext object to locate a Queue connection factory. In this example, you use the emailMessageQueueConnectionFactory user-defined name to get back the javax.jms.QueueConnectionFactory connection factory object, which you defined in the ejb-jar.xml XML file. This user-defined name, emailMessageQueueConnectionFactory, will then be mapped, in the orion-ejb-jar.xml file, to java:comp/resource/ojms/QueueConnectionFactories/qcf, the actual JNDI location for a Queue connection factory. See the "Writing the ejb-jar.xml Deployment Descriptor" and the "Writing or Generating the orion-ejb-jar.xml Deployment Descriptor" sections of the chapter to learn more about the above elements. Remember that you use the lookup() method of an InitialContext object to locate any J2EE resource. Thus, in the following code fragment, you will use the lookup() method to locate the Queue connection factory:

```
// Define a QueueConnectionFactory object
QueueConnectionFactory factory = null;
// Get queue connection factory
factory =
(QueueConnectionFactory) ic.lookup(
       "java:comp/env/jms/emailMessageQueueConnectionFactory");
```

3. Uses the createQueueConnection() method of the QueueConnectionFactory object to create a Queue connection:

```
queueConnection = factory.createQueueConnection();
```

4. Uses the start() method of the QueueConnection object to start the connection, so you can use it:

```
queueConnection.start();
```

5. Creates a Queue session using the createQueueSession() method of the Queue connection:

```
queueSession =
    queueConnection.createQueueSession(false,
                                       Session.AUTO_ACKNOWLEDGE);
```

6. Uses the `lookup()` method of the `InitialContext` object to locate a `Queue` destination. In this example, you use the `emailMessageQueue` user-defined name to get back the `javax.jms.Queue` destination object, which you defined in the `ejb-jar.xml` XML file. You will use the `lookup()` method of an `InitialContext` object, in a similar manner as you did to locate the `Queue` connection factory object, to locate the `Queue` destination. The following code fragment locates the `javax.jms.Queue` destination:

```
Queue queue =
   (Queue)ic.lookup("java:comp/env/jms/emailMessageQueue");
```

7. Uses the `createSender()` method of the `Queue` session to create a `Queue` sender:

```
queueSender = queueSession.createSender(queue);
```

8. Uses the `createTextMessage()` method of the `Queue` session to create a `TextMessage` message:

```
TextMessage message = queueSession.createTextMessage(msg);
```

9. Uses the `send()` method of the `Queue` sender to send the message to the `Queue` destination:

```
queueSender.send(message);
```

Next, you will write the `LocalClientServlet`, a simple JMS message producer that publishes messages to a Topic destination that the `ProcessApprovalMessageBean` consumes.

Writing Publish/Subscribe JMS Clients

In this section, you will learn how to code JMS client programs that use pub/sub messaging systems. In a pub/sub product or application, clients address messages to a Topic destination. The `LocalClientServlet` JMS client will publish messages to the `PROCESSTOPIC` Topic destination. You set up the `PROCESSTOPIC` Topic destination earlier in the "Setting Up Oracle Advanced Queuing as a JMS Provider" section of the chapter.

The steps to produce topic messages are as follows:

1. Create an `InitialContext` object:

```
InitialContext ic = new InitialContext();
```

2. Use the `lookup()` method of the `InitialContext` object to locate a `Topic` connection factory. In this example, you use the `processApprovalTopicConnectionFactory` user-defined name to get back the `javax.jms.TopicConnectionFactory` connection

factory object, which you will define in the `web.xml` XML file. This user-defined name, `processApprovalTopicConnectionFactory`, will then be mapped, in the `orion-web.xml` file, to `java:comp/resource/ojms/TopicConnectionFactories/tcf`, the actual JNDI location for a `Topic` connection factory. The following code fragment locates the `Topic` connection factory:

```
TopicConnectionFactory factory =
   (TopicConnectionFactory)ic.lookup
   ("java:comp/env/jms/processApprovalTopicConnectionFactory");
```

3. Use the `createTopicConnection()` method of the connection factory to create a `TopicConnection` object:

```
TopicConnection topicConnection =
   factory.createTopicConnection();
```

4. Use the `start()` method of the `TopicConnection` object to start the connection, so you can use it:

```
topicConnection.start();
```

5. Use the `createTopicSession()` method of the `TopicConnection` object to create a `TopicSession` object:

```
TopicSession topicSession =
  topicConnection.createTopicSession(false,
                                     Session.AUTO_ACKNOWLEDGE);
```

6. Use the `lookup()` method of the `InitialContext` object to locate a `Topic` destination. In this example, you use the `processApprovalTopic` user-defined name to get back the `javax.jms.Topic` destination object, which you defined in the `ejb-jar.xml` XML file. You will use the `lookup()` method of an `InitialContext` object, in a similar manner as you did to locate the Topic connection factory object, to locate the Topic destination. The following code fragment locates the `javax.jms.Topic` destination:

```
Topic topic =
(Topic)ic.lookup("java:comp/env/jms/processApprovalTopic");
```

7. Use the `createPublisher()` method of the `TopicSession` object to create a `TopicPublisher` object:

```
topicPublisher = topicSession.createPublisher(topic);
```

8. Use the method specific to your JMS message type to create the message. Here, we are using the `createMapMessage()` method of the JMS `MapMessage` message:

```
MapMessage message = topicSession.createMapMessage();
```

9. Use the setters of the `MapMessage` object to format your message:

```
// Setting the requestno of the
// purchase order requisition
message.setInt("requestno", 500);
// Setting the budget officer's employee number
message.setInt("officerno", 101);
// Setting the reasons to approve or reject
// the purchase order requisition
message.setString("reasons", "");
```

10. Use the `publish()` method of the `TopicPublisher` object to send the message:

```
topicPublisher.publish(message);
```

11. Release resources by closing the `TopicPublisher` and the `TopicConnection` objects:

```
finally {
 if (topicPublisher != null) {
    try {
        topicPublisher.close();
    } catch (JMSException e) {}
  }
  if (topicConnection != null) {
    try {
        topicConnection.close();
    } catch (JMSException e) {}
  }
}
```

Here is the complete listing of the `LocalClientServlet` class:

```
/**
**   Program Name:  LocalClientServlet.java
**
**   Purpose:      A JMS client that produces
**                 messages to a Topic destination
**                 using Oracle AQ.
**
*/
/**
package webapps.web.test;
import javax.servlet.*;
import javax.servlet.http.*;
import java.io.*;
import java.util.*;
import javax.naming.*;
```

```
import javax.jms.*;
import java.net.*;


public class LocalClientServlet extends HttpServlet
{
  private static final String CONTENT_TYPE = "text/html";

  public void init(ServletConfig config) throws ServletException
  {
    super.init(config);
  }

  public void doGet(HttpServletRequest request,
    HttpServletResponse response) throws ServletException, IOException
  {
    TopicConnectionFactory factory = null;
    TopicConnection topicConnection = null;
    TopicPublisher topicPublisher = null;
    //added a topicSession variable
    TopicSession topicSession = null;
    try {
      InitialContext ic = new InitialContext();

      factory = (TopicConnectionFactory)
        ic.lookup(
           "java:comp/env/jms/processApprovalTopicConnectionFactory");
      topicConnection = factory.createTopicConnection();

      // Start the connection so we can use it
      topicConnection.start();

      topicSession =
          topicConnection.createTopicSession(false,
                              Session.AUTO_ACKNOWLEDGE);

      Topic topic = (Topic)
          ic.lookup("java:comp/env/jms/processApprovalTopic");

      topicPublisher = topicSession.createPublisher(topic);

      MapMessage message = topicSession.createMapMessage();

      message.setInt("requestno", 500);
      message.setInt("officerno", 101);
      message.setString("reasons", "");
```

```
      topicPublisher.publish(message);

      System.out.println("MapMessage sent to the Topic");

      response.setContentType(CONTENT_TYPE);
      PrintWriter out = response.getWriter();
      out.println("<html>");
      out.println("<head><title>LocalClientServlet</title></head>");
      out.println("<body>");
      out.println("<p>A MapMessage containing: requestno,
          officerno and reasons has been sent your Topic...</p>");
      out.println("</body></html>");
      out.close();
    }
    catch(JMSException e) {
                System.err.println("Communication error: "
                          + e.getMessage());
    }
    catch(NamingException e) {
                System.err.println("Error looking up objects: "
                     + e.getMessage());
    }
    finally {
      if (topicPublisher != null) {
        try {
          topicPublisher.close();
        } catch (JMSException e) {}
      }
      //added a close on session object
      if (topicSession != null) {
        try {
          topicSession.close();
        } catch (JMSException e) {}
      if (topicConnection != null) {
        try {
          topicConnection.close();
        } catch (JMSException e) {}
      }
    }
  }
 }
} // End of LocalClientServlet class
```

Next, you will write the application-specific `web.xml` file and the OC4J-specific `orion-web.xml` file.

Writing the web.xml and orion-web.xml XML Files

Your enterprise application comprises also a web application consisting of the LocalClientServlet class. Consequently, you need to provide a web.xml file for the servlet. We present here an example of the web.xml file. To learn more about the elements of this file, see Chapters 10 and 11 and Appendix A.

Earlier, in the "Writing or Generating the orion-ejb-jar.xml Deployment Descriptor" section of the chapter, we presented detailed information regarding the EJB <resource-ref> element. Recall that the <resource-ref> element is used to declare database resources and JMS connections. You use the <resource-ref> element and its attributes for two purposes:

- To specify the javax.jms.Queue and the javax.jms.QueueConnectionFactory JMS resources.
- To associate the jms/emailMessageQueue name to the javax.jms.Queue JMS destination and the jms/emailMessageQueueConnectionFactory name to the javax.jms.QueueConnectionFactory connection factory.

In order for a web application to use a Topic destination and connection factory, you need to provide the information in the web.xml deployment descriptor. In the "Message-Driven Elements in the ejb-jar.xml File" section of the chapter, your learned how to specify a JMS API of type Topic. Recall that you used the javax.jms.Topic interface to do so.

In this section, you will write the web.xml deployment descriptor file. As in an EJB ejb-jar.xml file, you will use the <resource-ref> element and its attributes to associate user-defined names to the javax.jms.Topic and the javax.jms.TopicConnectionFactory JMS resources. The following code fragment demonstrates how to do so:

```
<! -- Use the <resource-ref> element to map
    the jms/processApprovalTopic user-defined name
    to the javax.jms.Topic destination.  -->
 <resource-ref>
         <description>
         The topic for ProcessApprovalMessageBean</description>
         <res-ref-name>jms/processApprovalTopic</res-ref-name>
         <res-type>javax.jms.Topic</res-type>
         <res-auth>Container</res-auth>
   </resource-ref>
  <! -- Use the <resource-ref> element to map
```

```
        the jms/processApprovalTopicConnectionFactory
        user-defined name to the
        javax.jms.TopicConnectionFactory connection factory.  -->
    <resource-ref>
          <description>The Factory used </description>
          <res-ref-name>
            jms/processApprovalTopicConnectionFactory</res-ref-name>
          <res-type>javax.jms.TopicConnectionFactory</res-type>
          <res-auth>Container</res-auth>
    </resource-ref>
```

Here is the definition of the `web.xml` file that we use for the application:

```
<?xml version = '1.0' encoding = 'windows-1252'?>
<!DOCTYPE web-app PUBLIC
"-//Sun Microsystems, Inc.//DTD Web Application 2.2//EN"
"http://java.sun.com/j2ee/dtds/web-app_2_2.dtd">
<web-app>
   <description>Simple web.xml file for Web Application
         </description>
   <servlet>
     <servlet-name>LocalClientServlet</servlet-name>
     <servlet-class>test.LocalClientServlet</servlet-class>
   </servlet>
   <servlet-mapping>
      <servlet-name>LocalClientServlet</servlet-name>
      <url-pattern>/</url-pattern>
   </servlet-mapping>
   <session-config>
      <session-timeout>30</session-timeout>
   </session-config>
   <mime-mapping>
      <extension>html</extension>
      <mime-type>text/html</mime-type>
   </mime-mapping>
   <mime-mapping>
      <extension>txt</extension>
      <mime-type>text/plain</mime-type>
   </mime-mapping>
   <welcome-file-list>
      <welcome-file>index.jsp</welcome-file>
      <welcome-file>index.html</welcome-file>
   </welcome-file-list>
   <! -- Use the <resource-ref> element to map
      the jms/processApprovalTopic user-defined name
      to the javax.jms.Topic destination.  -->
   <resource-ref>
```

```
            <description>
            The topic for ProcessApprovalMessageBean</description>
            <res-ref-name>jms/processApprovalTopic</res-ref-name>
            <res-type>javax.jms.Topic</res-type>
            <res-auth>Container</res-auth>
    </resource-ref>
    <! -- Use the <resource-ref> element to map
       the jms/processApprovalTopicConnectionFactory
       user-defined name to the
       javax.jms.TopicConnectionFactory connection factory.  -->
    <resource-ref>
          <description>The Factory used </description>
          <res-ref-name>
              jms/processApprovalTopicConnectionFactory</res-ref-name>
          <res-type>javax.jms.TopicConnectionFactory</res-type>
          <res-auth>Container</res-auth>
    </resource-ref>
</web-app>
```

Next, we provide the definition of the `orion-web.xml` OC4J-specific XML file. Like the OC4J-specific `orion-ejb-jar.xml` EJB deployment descriptor file, the `orion-web.xml` file maps user-defined names to actual JMS resource locations. In the `orion-web.xml` file, use the `<resource-ref-mapping>` element to tie the topic JMS resource to a JNDI location. Here is the complete definition of the `orion-web.xml` file:

```
<?xml version="1.0"?>
<!DOCTYPE orion-web-app PUBLIC
"-//Evermind//DTD Orion Web Application 2.3//EN"
"http://xmlns.oracle.com/ias/dtds/orion-web.dtd">
<orion-web-app>
    <! -- Tie the jms/processApprovalTopic user-defined name
       to the actual Topic destination -- >
    <resource-ref-mapping
         name="jms/processApprovalTopic"
      <! -- This location is specified in orion-ejb-jar.xml -- >
       location="java:comp/resource/ojms/Topics/aquser.processtopic" />
      <! -- Tie the jms/processApprovalTopicConnectionFactory
      user-defined name to the actual topic connection factory -- >
    <resource-ref-mapping
        name="jms/processApprovalTopicConnectionFactory"
      <! -- This location is specified in orion-ejb-jar.xml -- >
       location="java:comp/resource/ojms/TopicConnectionFactories/tcf" />
</orion-web-app>
```

Next, you will learn how to deploy the Approval application.

Deploying EJB Components and Message-Driven Beans to OC4J

Deploying EJB applications consisting of message-driven beans is similar to deploying EJB applications consisting of entity beans, session beans, or a combination of both. You learned how to deploy to OC4J entity beans and session beans in Chapters 5 and 6. Please refer to the "Deploying EJB Components to OC4J" section of either Chapter 5 or 6 for a detailed description on how to deploy EJB components to OC4J.

In Chapter 2, you learned how to deploy a J2EE application to the Oracle9*i*AS Containers For J2EE server and how to bind that application to the server so that you can access the application from OC4J. In this section, we will revisit the necessary steps to refresh your memory. Recall that a J2EE application can contain the following modules:

- **Web applications** The Web applications module (WAR files) can consist of servlets, JSPs, HTML pages, tag libraries, and utility classes.
- **EJB applications** The EJB applications module (`ejb-jar` files) includes Enterprise JavaBeans (EJBs).
- **Client applications** The Client applications module includes client application programs and is contained within a JAR file.

Archiving the EJB Application

In the previous sections, you created your application, compiled all the Java classes, and wrote the deployment descriptor. The next step is to archive your EJB application into a JAR file. The JAR file should include all bean class files, their dependent class files, and the `ejb-jar.xml` deployment descriptor file. You have also created a web application consisting of one servlet. You also need to package your web application in a WAR file, and archive the JAR and WAR files that belong to an enterprise Java application into an EAR file for deployment to OC4J. The very first step in archiving the EJB application is to package your application. You do so when you create the J2EE EAR file.

Packaging the Application: Creating the EAR File

This application consists of an EJB module, containing three CMP beans, two message-driven beans, and a Web module containing one servlet.

Let's start by creating the WAR file:

1. Open a command prompt, and position yourself in the web directory (`chapter07/web`).

2. Type the following:

```
jar cvf chapter07-web.war WEB-INF
```

3. Copy `chapter07-web.war` to the root directory, `chapter07`.
4. Position yourself in the classes directory.
5. Type the following:

```
jar cvf chapter07-ejb.jar META-INF purchase
```

6. Copy `chapter07-ejb.jar` to the root directory, `chapter07`.
7. Modify the `application.xml` file in the `chapter07/META-INF` directory to look like the following:

```
<?xml version="1.0"?>
<!DOCTYPE application PUBLIC "-//Sun Microsystems,
      Inc.//DTD J2EE Application 1.2//EN"
     "http://java.sun.com/j2ee/dtds/application_1_2.dtd">
<!-- The application element is the root element of a
      J2EE application deployment descriptor.  -->
<application>
      <display-name>Chapter7</display-name>
      <module>
            <web>
                  <web-uri>chapter07-web.war</web-uri>
                  <context-root>/</context-root>
            </web>
      </module>
      <module>
            <ejb>chapter07-ejb.jar</ejb>
      </module>
</application>
```

8. Position yourself in the root directory, `chapter07`.
9. Type the following:

```
jar cvf chapter07.ear chapter07-web.war chapter07-ejb.jar META-INF
```

10. You now have your `chapter07.ear` file and are ready to deploy the application.

Modifying the OC4J data-sources.xml File

Before deploying your application, you need to register your data source with OC4J. You do that by modifying the OC4J `data-sources.xml` file. This file is located in the OC4J's .../`config` directory.

In the OC4J's data-sources.xml file, Oracle provides an example default DataSource that uses the Oracle JDBC driver to create the connections. Modify the file as follows:

```
<!-- Your data source definition -->
<data-source
            class="com.evermind.sql.DriverManagerDataSource"
            name="OracleDS"
            location="jdbc/OracleCoreDS"
            xa-location="jdbc/xa/OracleXADS"
            ejb-location="jdbc/OracleDS"
            connection-driver="oracle.jdbc.driver.OracleDriver"
            username="scott"
            password="tiger"
            url="jdbc:oracle:thin:@yourhost:yourport:oracle_sid"
            inactivity-timeout="30"
    />
```

Next, you will deploy the application. OC4J supports deployment of both EAR files as well as deploying an exploded directory conforming to the J2EE standard (as does our chapter07 directory structure). We will show you both ways, starting with the EAR file.

Deploying an EAR File to OC4J

The steps to deploy an EAR file to OC4J are as follows:

1. Copy the chapter07.ear file to your OC4J installation applications directory; if you have unzipped OC4J under the d:\OC4J directory, then this will be d:\OC4J\j2ee\home\applications. The EAR file can be placed anywhere, but in this example, we will use the OC4J applications directory.
2. Edit the OC4J server.xml file, found under your OC4J\j2ee\home\config directory. Add the following entry to the OC4J server.xml file:

   ```
   <application name="chapter7"
      path="../applications/chapter07.ear" auto-start="true" />
   ```

3. Edit the OC4J http-web-site.xml file to bind your Web module to this J2EE application. Add the following entry to the OC4J http-web-site.xml file:

   ```
   <web-app application="chapter7" name="chapter07-web"
                  root="/chapter7" load-on-startup="true" />
   ```

CAUTION
The name must correspond to whatever name you gave the WAR file; the root will be your virtual path where you can reach your application.

Recall that OC4J supports hot deployment. Therefore, if OC4J is running, it will immediately pick up and deploy this application. If OC4J is not running, position yourself in the `OC4J/j2ee/home` directory and start OC4J by typing the following:

```
java -jar oc4j.jar -verbosity 10
```

Output from OC4J

You should see something like this as output from OC4J:

```
Auto-unpacking .....\applications\chapter07.ear... done.
Auto-unpacking .....\applications\chapter07\chapter07-web
.war... done.
Auto-deploying chapter7 (New server version detected)...
Application default (default) initialized...
Copying default deployment descriptor from .....
Auto-deploying chapter07-ejb.jar
(No previous deployment found)... done.
Application chapter7 (Chapter7) initialized...
Web-App default:defaultWebApp (0.0.0.0/0.0.0.0:80) started...
Auto-deploying file.....applications/chapter07/chapter 07-web/
(New server version detected)...
Oracle9iAS Containers For J2EE initialized
```

NOTE
We have provided the `application.xml` file for the exploded approach under `chapter07/META-INF`, called `application-exploded.xml`, and also the prebuilt `chapter07.ear` file, called `chapter07-prebuilt.ear`.

Testing Your Application

Now, test the application by going to

```
http://localhost:port/chapter7
```

where *localhost* is your machine, *port* is the port the web server is listening on, and *chapter7* is the name that you defined in the <name> element of the <application> tag in the OC4J `server.xml` file. Note that the default for the stand-alone OC4J port is 8888. The port can be found and changed in the OC4J `http-web-site.xml` XML file, which can be found in the `OC4J_HOME/j2ee/home/config` directory.

Next, we present the output displayed in the web browser and the OC4J console.

Web Browser Output from the LocalClientServlet

```
A MapMessage containing: requestno, officerno
    and reasons has been sent your Topic...
```

OC4J Console: Output from the LocalClientServlet

```
MapMessage sent to the Topic
In ProcessApprovalMessageBean.ProcessApprovalMessageBean()
In ProcessApprovalMessageBean.setMessageDrivenContext()
In ProcessApprovalMessageBean.ejbCreate()
got approvallocalhome: ApprovalLocal EJBHome
got approvallocalhome: PurchaseOrderLocal EJBHome
got approvallocalhome: EmployeeLocal EJBHome
onMessage called
ProcessApprovalMessageBean: Message received:
I got the ApprovalPK
I got the PurchasePK
ejbFindByPrimaryKey employeeno = 104
Inside getEmployeeno()!!
Inside getEmployeeno()-- Record!!
ejbLoad employeeno = 104
Inside getEmployeeInfo()!!
Inside getEmployeeInfo()-- Record!!
ejbLoad employeeVO.getEmployeeno() = 104
ejbStore employeeno = 104
Inside UpdateEmployee()!!
I UpdateEmployee()-- Record!!
Emailmessage sent to the Queue
onMessage in processorder returned
In EmailMessageBean.EmailMessageBean()
In EmailMessageBean.setMessageDrivenContext()
In EmailMessageBean.ejbCreate()
EmailMessage: Message received: Pam@acme-hospital.com, 500
```

Deploying an Exploded Directory

OC4J also supports deployment of an exploded directory structure. If you have your `chapter07` code unzipped in the `d:\chapter07` directory, do the following:

1. Make sure the `application.xml` file is correct in your `chapter07/META-INF` directory. For an exploded directory, it should look like the following:

```
<?xml version="1.0"?>
<!DOCTYPE application PUBLIC "-//Sun Microsystems,
     Inc.//DTD J2EE Application 1.2//EN"
    "http://java.sun.com/j2ee/dtds/application_1_2.dtd">
<!-- The application element is the root
     element of a J2EE application deployment descriptor.  -->
<application>
      <display-name>Chapter7</display-name>
      <module>
            <web>
                  <web-uri>web</web-uri>
                  <context-root>/</context-root>
            </web>
      </module>
      <module>
            <ejb>classes</ejb>
      </module>
</application>
```

NOTE
The attribute `web` *inside* `<web-uri>` *points to the root directory of your Web module; the attribute* `ejb` *points to the root directory of your EJB module.*

2. Edit the OC4J `server.xml` file; for an exploded deployment, add the following entry:

```
<application name="chapter7" path="file:///d:/chapter07"
    auto-start="true" />
```

   Note that the "file:///" prefix takes care of the forward slash (/) and backslash (\).

3. Edit the OC4J `http-web-site.xml` file and add the following entry:

```
<web-app application="chapter7" name="web"
          root="/chapter7" auto-start="true" />
```

   If your OC4J instance is still running, you might need to restart it if you're using the same names again.

Note that if you want a clean deployment of an application deployed to OC4J, do the following:

1. Stop OC4J.
2. Delete the `chapter07-prebuilt.ear` file and the `chapter07-prebuilt` directory under the OC4J `applications` directory.
3. Delete the application (`chapter07`) directory under the OC4J `application-deployments`.
4. Start OC4J again.

OC4J will then do a clean install of the application.

Note that the Java source code and class files for the Approval application that you built in this chapter are included in the `chapter07code.zip` file. Included in that file are also the `chapter07-ejb.jar`, `chapter07-web.war`, and `chapter07-ejb.ear` files.

In this chapter, you learned about the following:

- The Java Message Service (JMS) and how it is implemented in OC4J.
- Writing EJB applications consisting of message-driven beans (MDB).
- Writing the `ejb-jar.xml` file for MDBs.
- Configuring the OC4J-specific `orion-ejb-jar.xml` file for MDBs.
- Writing JMS message producers, message consumers, and special kinds of message listeners.

This chapter concludes Part II of the book. In Part III, you will learn about OC4J security, Web services, servlets, and JavaServer Pages. Part III begins with Chapter 8, which presents OC4J security. In that chapter, you will learn about OC4J security and the Java Authentication and Authorization Service (JAAS).

PART III

Building J2EE Web and Presentation Tier Components

CHAPTER 8

OC4J Security

Security has always been a major concern for those involved in the software world. With the advent of the Internet era, the need for security in software systems has become increasingly heightened. Growing awareness with respect to conducting Internet-based business with a secure approach has accelerated the adoption of security as an integral part of software architectures. In the wake of such advancements, the inclusion of an entire chapter dedicated to security is a given.

In Chapters 5, 6, and 7, you learned about developing J2EE business-tier components, such as entity beans, session beans, and message-driven beans. In this chapter, you will learn about OC4J security.

Specifically, you will learn the following:

- Challenges in architecting secure Internet systems
- Java security models
- Components of Java security
- Java Authentication and Authorization Service (JAAS)
- Components of J2EE security
- Security components of the Oracle9*i*AS suite
- The OC4J implementation of JAAS
- Integrated and switchable user managers
- Using JAAS in OC4J applications; coding security in OC4J applications
- Deploying the application to OC4J

The concepts that you learn in this chapter will enable you to develop security mechanisms for the other modules in this book, such as JavaServer Pages (JSP), Java servlets, Enterprise JavaBeans (EJB), and Web Services.

Challenges in Architecting Secure Internet Systems

What does it mean to architect secure Internet systems? This involves protection for data, processes, and transmission against malicious, unauthorized, or otherwise inappropriate use, access, corruption, or even misrepresentation. This chapter deals with all such undesirable factors.

In today's Internet-enabled world, security concerns are of paramount importance, because the number and complexity of such undesirable possibilities have multiplied with every new Internet user and business connection. While databases, applications, operating systems, and communication methods have grown ever more complicated and interwoven, so too have the number and sophistication of attackers. Whatever the source of such undesirable actions, the result is that the security will be compromised, thus leading to a failure of the system.

Keeping in mind the limitation of resources, the design goals of security systems and methods should be based on the achievement of the following objectives:

- Denial of undesirable system access, so that someone requesting access who cannot prove legitimacy cannot act as a user.
- Denial of undesirable access to databases and system resources so that even validated users can access only the resources for which they have permission.
- If undesirable access is gained to databases, changes to critical or sensitive data can be made only by users with permissions specific to the sensitive data, or by using additional knowledge not contained in the database and not derivable from the same validation that granted access (that is, the original password).
- If undesirable access to data occurs, the following protections are active:
  - Data is unusable without special knowledge.
  - Operations on the data are constrained by links to other data regulated by rules or relationships within the database.
  - Undesirable communication of the data is difficult or impossible.
  - Undesirable communication of data will not be believed, used, or relied upon.

If undesirable access to system resources occurs, limitations are in place that restrict their undesirable use, such as erasing files not owned, communicating over restricted lines, or avoiding firewall-type barriers. Data and web security also involve the accessibility of information to authorized users, as needed. While system security by itself does not ensure availability, availability may not be possible without security.

Most denial-of-service (DoS) attacks prevent legitimate users from getting serviced, by overwhelming a site with an extremely high volume of repetitive requests. The results can include much slower service for legitimate users or actual site shutdown due to resource overload. Security of the attacked site has little to do with such an attack.

On the other hand, many such attacks begin by exploiting security flaws in other systems, which are not targets of DoS attacks. The intent is to acquire rights and resources that can later be used to generate some of those repetitive phony requests that do build a DoS attack.

In addition to protecting the site itself, appropriate security measures prevent exposing any vulnerabilities that could be exploited by a malicious intruder to mount an attack elsewhere. Individual user profiles that limit the system resources available to each user can help. Examples include limiting usable disk space, the allowable number of concurrent sessions, the permissible CPU processing time, and the amount of logical I/O available to the user.

The intention is to make each layer as impenetrable and incorruptible as possible, within constraints of time, money, staff, and "user convenience." But this layered defense also requires each layer to contain defenses against undesirable actions by users who, though validated for entry to this level, might accidentally or intentionally act to compromise the previously mentioned objectives.

Protecting against such misuse is made more complex by the diversity and sheer size of the user communities that can access business systems over the Internet. Business and security systems designed to cope with this level of risk and complexity need to be:

- **Scalable** The system needs to handle far more users and transactions than non-Internet systems.
- **Manageable** The system needs to automate reliably and securely administrative tasks such as assigning each user an account and password and handling all associated information the user may supply or want.
- **Interoperable** The system needs to communicate or even integrate with the proprietary systems of customers, suppliers, partners, and others, enabling outsourcing to acquire supplies and collaboration to provide services.

The security needs of systems within a web environment are as follows:

Confidentiality Confidentiality refers to not revealing or exposing critical or sensitive information. Confidentiality ensures encrypted communications. OC4J is preconfigured to run behind Oracle HTTP Server. In this manner, Oracle HTTP Server ensures confidentiality. For example, you can configure Oracle HTTP Server to use Secure Sockets Layer (SSL).

Authentication Authentication ensures that users are who they claim to be. Some authentication methods require the user to be known in advance, by name and password, but other methods can employ the use of certificates that cannot be forged.

Authorization Authorization guards against misuse of systems, applications, or data after access has already been granted; it controls what objects and actions can be used. Authorization generally refers to the process that determines what a user can access. The enforcement of that authorization is called *access control,* which can require an additional password or validate a request for resources against lists of approved users or permissible activities.

Nonrepudiation The intent of nonrepudiation is to preserve accountability and prevent misrepresentation. Nonrepudiation means that when someone actually sends a message, the sender cannot later disclaim responsibility for sending it.

To ensure against false claims, a message must include a digital signature, usable only by the true sender, that any recipient can verify. A *digital signature* is an encrypted compression of the message that proves that the person signing the electronic transmission is that person, since no one else can create the unique digital signature supplied. A digital signature also solves the parallel problem of someone sending a message claiming falsely that the message is being sent by a third party.

Network Attacks The various types of network attacks are data corruption, loss of display of confidential information, and denial of service. Distributed environments bring with them the possibility that a malicious third party can perpetrate a computer crime by tampering with data. The damage can be done to messages as they move between sites on the network or, more seriously, to the sites themselves.

In a data-modification attack, an unauthorized party on the network intercepts data in transit and changes parts of that data before retransmitting it. An example of this is changing the dollar amount of a banking transaction from $100 to $10,000.

In a replay attack, an entire set of valid data is interjected again onto the network. An example would be to repeat 1,000 times (or even just once) an initially valid $100 bank account transfer transaction.

Levels of authentication and authorization are your primary defenses in preventing a hacker's access and use of administrative or database functions to corrupt, falsify, or otherwise misuse site data. Auditing mechanisms can ensure that data tampering is detected. Nonrepudiation mechanisms can help to identify perpetrators.

Data in transit must not be modified or viewed, and database data must not be accessible for unauthorized copying or sharing. No unauthorized party should be able to intercept, display, or otherwise misuse confidential information while it is being transmitted over the network or available online for legitimate users.

Fault Containment Among the best ways to lessen security risk on the Internet is to provide multiple layers of security mechanisms. Each layer's independent security measures prevent a single security failure. This concept, referred to as *deep data protection,* ensures well-formed, comprehensive security from client to application server to data server, as well as throughout the layers of an application.

OC4J provides fault containment through access control, data encryption, and extensive auditing.

Complex User Management Requirements Security mechanisms must remain effective and easy to administer even when the number of transactions, simultaneous users, and size of the databases become huge.

Overview of Java Security Models

To better understand the safety features of OC4J, it is important to understand the evolution of the security models provided by the Java platform. This will be followed by an overview of the components of Java security, thus providing you with a solid understanding of how the Java platform handles security, and an introduction to the various terms associated with the world of security.

Java 1.0 Sandbox

The original security model provided by the Java platform, known as the *sandbox*, consisted of a restricted environment in which to run untrusted code obtained from the open network, such as applets. As shown in Figure 8-1, local code is trusted to have full access to critical system resources, but downloaded remote code (an applet) is not trusted and can access only the limited resources inside the sandbox. A security manager is responsible for determining which resource accesses are allowed.

The Java 1.0 sandbox has the following components:

- **Verifier** Traverses the bytecodes, constructs the type state information, and verifies the types of the parameters to all the bytecode instructions
- **Class loader** Loads classes on request from the running Java application
- **Security Manager** Defines the outer boundaries of the sandbox

Further details on the preceding components are discussed in the upcoming section "Components of Java Security."

Java 1.1 Security Model

JDK 1.1 introduced the concept of a *signed applet,* as illustrated in Figure 8-2. A digitally signed applet is treated like local code, with full access to resources, if the public key used to verify the signature is trusted. Unsigned applets are still run in the sandbox. Signed applets are delivered, with their signatures, in signed JAR files.

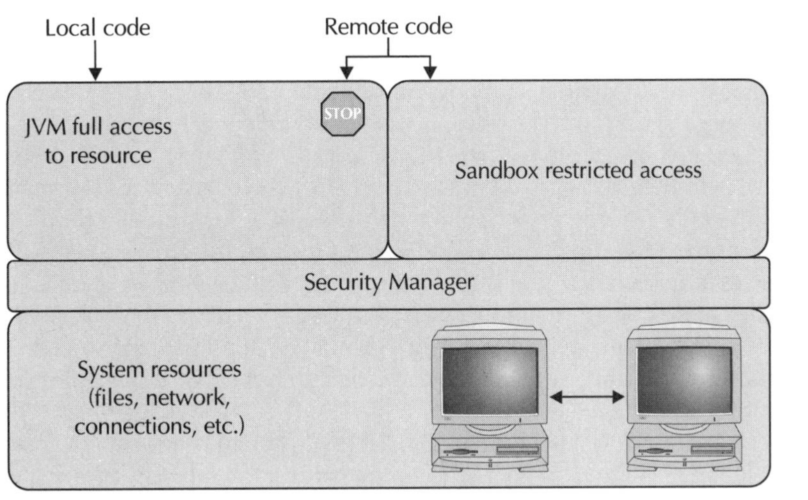

FIGURE 8-1. *Java 1.0 sandbox*

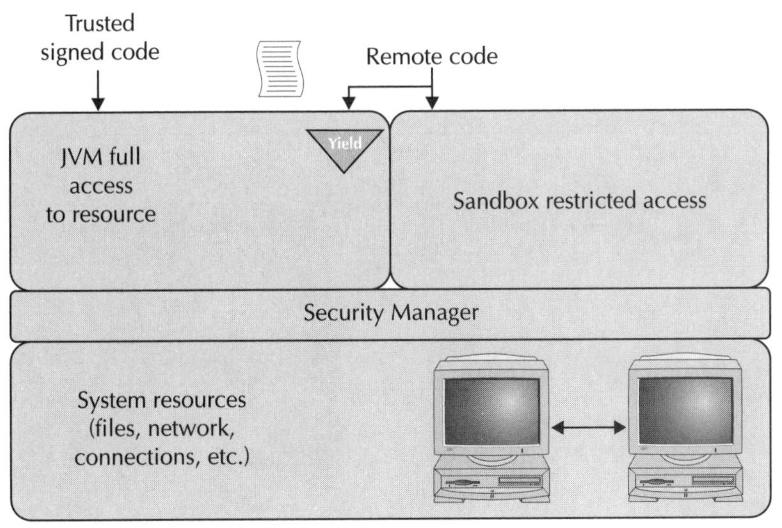

FIGURE 8-2. *Java 1.0 security model*

Java 1.2 Security Model

JDK 1.2 introduces a number of improvements over JDK 1.1. Code, regardless of whether it is local or remote, can now be subject to a *security policy*. The security policy defines the set of permissions available for code from various signers or locations and can be configured by a user or a system administrator. Each permission specifies a permitted access to a particular resource, such as read and write access to a specified file or directory or connect access to a given host and port.

The runtime system organizes code into individual domains, each of which encloses a set of classes whose instances are granted the same set of permissions. A domain can be configured to be equivalent to the sandbox, so applets can still be run in a restricted environment if the user or the administrator so chooses. Applications run unrestricted, as before, by default but can optionally be subject to a security policy.

The new security architecture in JDK 1.2 is illustrated in Figure 8-3. The arrow on the left end refers to a domain whose code is granted full access to resources; the arrow on the right refers to the opposite extreme: a domain restricted exactly the same as the original sandbox. The domains in between have more accesses allowed than the sandbox but less than full access.

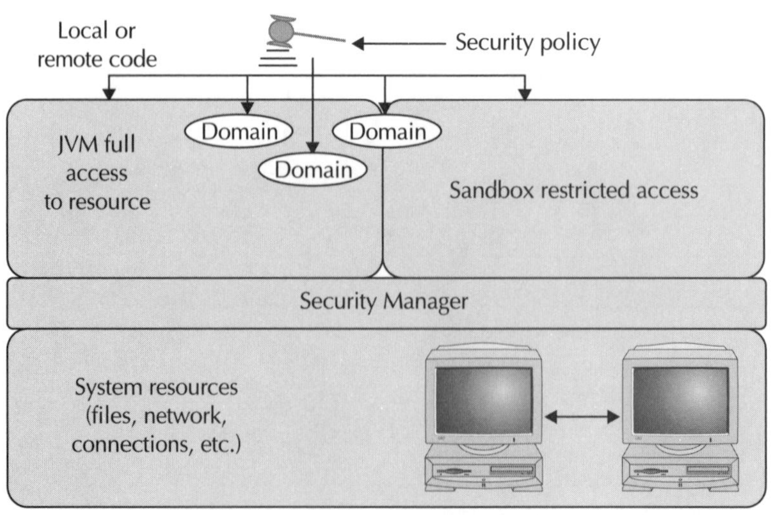

FIGURE 8-3. *Java 1.2 security model*

Components of Java Security

In this section, we take a brief look at the following components of Java security:

- Java language safety
- Java Virtual Machine security
- Message digests
- Digital signatures
- Public key cryptography
- Authentication and certificates

Java Language Safety

The Java programming language is often declared to be a *secure* language, but what does that really mean? Code *safety* refers to the property that the Java programming language allows you to generate bug-free code that doesn't crash the program or the user's machine. This can also be referred to as *robustness.* The Java programming language helps to prevent you from writing programs that are accidentally harmful. When you compile your programs with the Java compiler `javac`, the only compile-time warning is for using deprecated methods. Every other detected problem is an error that must be corrected.

The following constitute the components of Java Language Safety:

Valid Memory Access The Java programming language does not let you perform pointer arithmetic. This is perhaps the most important language feature that contributes to the Java language's safety, since it is pointer arithmetic that leads to accessing inappropriate memory areas, which leads to runtime crashes.

However, in the Java programming language, pointers are called *references,* and are fully supported. Reference variables allow the creation of data structures such as linked lists, binary trees, and so forth.

Also, the Java language specification clearly defines the behavior of uninitialized variables. All heap-based memory is automatically initialized. However, all stack-based memory isn't. So, all class and instance variables are never set to undefined values, and all local variables must definitely be assigned before use or the source compiler is obligated to give you an error.

Garbage Collection Garbage collection is the runtime environment's ability to automatically release memory that is no longer referenced. Since all dynamic memory requests are allocated from the heap, the garbage collector only needs to monitor references to places within it. When an area of memory no longer has any references to it, the garbage collector releases the memory. In effect, this places the freed memory block into the free storage pool, to be reallocated by another part of the program.

With the help of the garbage collector, a Java programmer no longer needs to determine when, or if, it is safe to release memory. The garbage collector will release memory only when it is safe and no longer referenced.

Compile-Time Type Checking Strong type checking ensures a programmer can't interpret a block of memory as anything other than what it is.

Access Modifiers The Java language access modifiers—`public`, `protected`, `default`, and `private`—contribute to robustness by controlling visibility of members. By properly using the modifiers, you can restrict access to data members, methods, and inner classes. In addition, the `final` modifier disallows subclassing in class definitions and overriding in method definitions.

Java Virtual Machine Security

The Java Virtual Machine (JVM) depends on software systems to provide a secure sandbox, as described earlier, so that programs can run in a secure environment. The sandbox verifies all classes and does runtime checks, to ensure that these programs do not perform invalid actions. The JVM thus provides a safe place for Java programs to run.

The machine language of the JVM is Java bytecode, as defined in the JVM specification. A Java bytecode-generating compiler takes a source file and converts the appropriate input to Java bytecode instructions in a class file format.

With this background in mind, the following constitute the components of JVM security:

Bytecode Verification When each Java class file is loaded, before anything else can happen, the JVM inspects the file to verify the validity of the Java bytecode.

Why all this verification? When class files are loaded (possibly over the network or from an untrusted source) into a JVM, there is no way of telling how its bytecode was generated. Basically, in most cases, you can't trust the source of the Java class files. In fact, the default verification setting in JRE 1.1 is to only verify classes loaded from over the network.

As in JRE 1.1, in JDK 1.2, the default setting for verification, again, is to only verify classes loaded over the network. The system classes are specified by either the system property `sun.boot.class.path` or the command-line option `-Xbootclasspath`: directories and JAR files.

With regard to verification, to manually control the level of verification, the following options to the `java` command with JRE 1.2 are possible:

Option	Verifies
`-Xverify:remote`	Only the classes loaded over network (default)
`-Xverify:all`	Everything
`-Xverify:none`	Nothing

By performing these checks once at class-loading time, as opposed to repeatedly during execution, runtime efficiency can be improved.

Class Loading It is the `ClassLoader` that finds and loads the bytecode for the class definitions. Once loaded, they are verified before the `ClassLoader` can create actual classes. The `ClassLoader` also performs many other security-related duties. The `ClassLoader` will not attempt to load any classes in `java.*` packages from over the network. The `ClassLoader` also provides separate namespaces for classes loaded from different locations. So, classes with the same name loaded from different hosts will not clash. And, classes loaded from different hosts will not communicate within the JVM, which prohibits untrusted programs from getting information from trusted ones.

Runtime Checking The JVM's next level of security is its runtime checking. Because of the late binding provided by the JVM, additional late (runtime) type checking is done with assignments and array bounds. When the specific type of an object is not determinable until runtime, the JVM ensures that only properly assignable operations are performed. While you can access subclasses as a superclass, the reverse is not allowed. Also, the JVM makes sure that something that isn't part of the class hierarchy is passed off as one of its own. Array-bounds checking is processed as a runtime check. In the Java language, if an invalid position in an array is specified, `ArrayIndexOutOfBoundsException` is thrown, thus denying access to memory space not belonging to the array.

Managing Security The Security Manager, available in all the JDK versions, allows you to establish a security policy such that you can trust or restrict the operations of a Java program. Each running JVM has at most one Security Manager installed. `SecurityManager` is a class in the `java.lang` package, so you can subclass this and establish your own `SecurityManager` manager using the `System.setSecurityManager()` method. Once a `SecurityManager` is installed, it cannot be replaced. So, once a program has set the `SecurityManager`, a `SecurityException` will be thrown if another attempt is made. No one can maliciously alter its function by replacing it.

The `SecurityManager` provides fine-grained control over what operations can be performed by code running within the JVM. Whenever a Java program (applet, application, or otherwise) attempts to do an operation that may be restricted, it checks with the `SecurityManager` to see whether the operation is allowable or denied. If permissions are granted, then the operation is performed. Each check throws a `SecurityException` if it fails. This is a `RuntimeException`, so it does not need to be within a `try/catch` block.

When creating your own `SecurityManager`, you normally do not directly subclass `SecurityManager`. Instead, most people tend to create a `NullSecurityManager` that extends `SecurityManager` but opens access to everything. Then, you subclass this manager, overriding the checks you wish to restrict.

Message Digests

A message digest is the fixed-length result of a one-way hash of the contents in the message, similar to a cryptographic checksum or cyclic redundancy check (CRC). Because this is a one-way hash, you cannot recover the original message contents from its digest.

A message digest is typically attached to the end of a clear-text message, or sent separately. While this does not provide secrecy for the message content, it does provide verification of the original content of the message. The recipient will recompute the message digest and compare it to the digest that was created by the sender. If the recomputed digest is the same, the message was not tampered with; if it were, then a new digest would have been inserted (making it undetectable that the message was altered).

Since there is nothing to prevent anyone from changing the message *and* the hash, the message digest is encrypted with the sender's private key. This way, anyone can decrypt the digest to verify that the message is authentic, and the message arrived unaltered.

Digital Signatures

To authenticate a message and its sender, you need to use digital signatures. Using digital signatures is a way to categorize messages or objects so that the creator of that message or object may be positively identified to the recipient or user, and also to verify that the contents are not altered.

A digital signature is basically a message digest. It does not alter the original message contents. Instead, the digital signature digest is encrypted. The signing algorithms to generate this digest are public. However, they rely on a pair of keys to encrypt and decrypt the signature. At the sending side, a private key is used to encrypt the digest. At the receiving side, a public key is used to decrypt the digest, based on the algorithm and the message contents. As long as you trust the means of receiving the public key, you are then assured of the identity of the message originator and that the contents have not been altered.

Public Key Cryptography

There are two forms of cryptography: symmetric and asymmetric. With *symmetric cryptography,* the sender and recipient share the same key used to encrypt and decrypt messages. If a third party intercepts the key, they can encrypt messages and pose as the sender, or decrypt messages and see what only the recipient is supposed to see. This type of cryptography requires you to control *who* has the keys. Symmetric cryptography offers neither identification of who is accessing something nor authentication of any specific identity.

Asymmetric cryptography, on the other hand, uses different keys for encryption and decryption. In fact, every person involved in a transaction has his or her own key pair. Each individual has a private key, which only that person knows, and a public key, which everyone can know. To verify that someone is the sender of a message, that person would use his or her private key to encrypt the message or its digest. Then, the recipient can decrypt the message with the sender's public key. If the only thing encrypted is the digest, this truly just verifies the sender, but the world can read the message. This in fact is a digital signature.

Public key cryptography goes further if you encrypt the message, too. If you are sending a message, you can encrypt the message with the *public* key of the recipient. Then, only the recipient would be able to decrypt it. Encrypting it only with the recipient's public key doesn't authenticate the sender, so you would need to encrypt it with the sender's *private* key, too. This provides both security of the data and verification of the sender. The recipient would then need to decrypt the message twice, once with the sender's public key and once with the recipient's private key.

Authentication and Certificates

With the public and private key scheme, the issue of public key distribution is a problem. A message can be authenticated only if you are sure the public key you received for the sender is really that sender's public key. A *certificate* is used to ensure that someone isn't providing a false public key or impersonating someone else. It consists of a public key, detailed information about the certificate owner (such as name, e-mail address, and so on), and other, application-specific data. To ensure the integrity of the certificate, it is signed by a *certification authority (CA),* a trusted entity whose public key is widely known and distributed, which vouches for the validity of the public key contained in the certificate, and ensures that the identity of the certificate owner reflects the actual person or entity.

Java Authentication and Authorization Service (JAAS)

JAAS can be used for *authentication* of users, to reliably and securely determine who is currently executing Java code, regardless of whether the code is running as an application, an applet, a bean, or a servlet. JAAS can be used for *authorization* of users to ensure they have the access control rights or permissions required to do the actions performed.

Traditionally, Java 2 provided access controls based on where the code originated from and who signed the code. It did not have the ability to additionally enforce access controls based on who runs the code. JAAS provides a framework that augments the Java 2 security architecture with such support.

JAAS authentication is performed in a pluggable fashion, thus permitting applications to remain independent from underlying authentication technologies. New or updated authentication technologies can be plugged under an application without requiring modifications to the application itself. Applications enable the authentication process by instantiating a `LoginContext` object, which in turn references a `Configuration` object to determine the authentication technology, or `LoginModule` to be used in performing the authentication. Typical `LoginModules` may prompt for and verify a username and password. Others may read and verify a voice or fingerprint.

Once the user or service executing the code has been authenticated, the JAAS authorization component works in conjunction with the core Java 2 access control model to protect access to sensitive resources. The `Subject` is updated by a `LoginModule`, with relevant `Principals` and credentials if authentication succeeds.

The basic concepts used in JAAS are as follows:

- **Subjects and Principals** JAAS uses the term `Subject` to refer to any user of a computing service. Both users and computing services, therefore, represent a `Subject`. A computing service has a name for each `Subject`, but a `Subject` might not have the same name for each service. The term `Principal` represents a name associated with a `Subject`. Since a `Subject` may have multiple names (potentially one for each service with which it interacts), a `Subject` comprises a set of `Principals`. The following code fragment illustrates this concept:

```
public interface Principal {
public String getName();
}
public final class Subject {
```

```
public Set getPrincipals() {
}
```

Principals can become associated with a Subject upon successful authentication to a service. Authentication typically involves the Subject demonstrating some form of evidence to prove its identity. Such evidence may be information only the Subject would likely know or have (a password or fingerprint), or it may be information only the Subject could produce (signed data using a private key).

- **Credentials** A Credential may contain information used to authenticate the Subject to new services. Such Credentials may include passwords, Kerberos tickets, and public key certificates (X.509, PGP, and so forth), and are used in environments that support single sign-on. Credential implementations including third-party implementations can be easily incorporated into JAAS. JAAS divides each Subject's Credentials into two sets. One set contains the Subject's public credentials (public key certificates, Kerberos tickets, and so forth), and the second set stores the Subject's private Credentials (private keys, encryption keys, passwords, and so forth). To access a Subject's public Credentials, no permissions are required. However, access to a Subject's private Credential set is security checked.

  The following code fragment shows an implementation of Subject:

```
public final class Subject {
// not security checked
public Set getPublicCredentials() { }
// security checked
public Set getPrivateCredentials() { }
}
```

Once authentication has successfully completed, JAAS enables you to enforce access controls upon the Principals associated with the authenticated Subject. The JAAS Principals-based access controls supplement the existing Java 2 access controls based on where code came from and who signed it.

JAAS defines a security policy to specify what resources are accessible to authorized Principals. The JAAS policy extends the existing default Java 2 security policy and, in fact, the two policies, together, form a single logical access control policy for the entire Java runtime.

The following code fragment depicts an example codesource-based policy entry currently supported by the default policy provided with Java 2. This entry grants code loaded from foo.com, and signed by foo, permission to read all files in the cdrom directory and its subdirectories. Since no Principal information is included with this policy entry, the code will always be able to read files from the `cdrom` directory, regardless of who executes it, as the following fragment of code shows:

```
grant Codebase "http://foo.com", Signedby "foo" {
  permission java.io.FilePermission "/cdrom/-", "read";
}
```

The following code fragment depicts an example `Principal`-based policy entry supported by JAAS. This example entry grants code loaded from `bar.com`, signed by `bar`, and executed by `duke`, permission to read only those files located in the `/cdrom/duke` directory. To be executed by `duke`, the `Subject` affiliated with the current access control context must have an associated `Principal` of class `bar.Principal` whose `getName()` method returns `duke`.

```
// JAAS principal-based policy
grant Codebase "http://bar.com, Signedby "bar",
 Principal bar.Principal "duke" {
permission java.io.FilePermission "/cdrom/duke/-", "read";
}
```

JAAS treats roles and groups simply as named `Principals`. Therefore, access control can be imposed upon roles and groups just as they are with any other type of principal, as shown in the following code fragment:

```
// an administrator role can access user passwords
grant Principal foo.Role "administrator" {
permission java.io.FilePermission "/passwords/-", "read, write";
}
// A basketball team (group) can read its directory
grant Principal foo.Team "SlamDunk" {
permission java.io.FilePermission "/teams/SlamDunk/-", "read";
}
```

The Java 2 runtime enforces access controls via the `java.lang.SecurityManager`, and is consulted any time untrusted code attempts to perform a sensitive operation, such as accepting a socket connection from a specified host and port, modifying a thread, deleting a specific file, causing the application to exit, and so on. Code in the Java library consults the `SecurityManager` whenever a potentially dangerous operation is attempted. The `SecurityManager` can veto the operation by generating a `SecurityException`. Decisions made by the `SecurityManager` take into account the origin of the requesting class. Obviously, built-in classes are usually given more privilege than classes loaded across the Internet. The `SecurityManager` makes the final decision as to whether a particular operation is permitted or rejected. To check whether the code has sufficient permissions, the `SecurityManager` implementation delegates responsibility to the `java.security.AccessController`, which first obtains an image of the current `AccessControlContext`, and then ensures that the retrieved `AccessControlContext` contains sufficient permissions for the operation to be permitted.

JAAS supplements this architecture by providing the method `Subject.doAs()` to dynamically associate an authenticated subject with the current `AccessControlContext`. Hence, as subsequent access control checks are made, the `AccessController` can base its decisions upon both the executing code itself and the `Principals` associated with the `Subject`.

With the JAAS framework, the JVM can be used to provide a general login facility for users. This enables the JVM itself to impose access controls based on who logged in and impose access controls based on the identity of the user. Special `UserPermissions` may allow code running as a particular user to permit access to particular resources.

Overview of J2EE Security

The J2EE platform defines declarative contracts between those who develop and assemble application components and those who configure applications in operational environments. Application providers are required to declare the security requirements of their applications in such a way that these requirements can be satisfied during application configuration. The declarative security mechanisms used in an application are expressed in a declarative syntax in a document called a *deployment descriptor.* An application deployer then employs container-specific tools`to map the application requirements that are in a deployment descriptor to security mechanisms that are implemented by J2EE containers. The J2EE SDK provides this functionality with the `deploytool` utility, which simplifies packaging applications. This utility has two modes: command-line and GUI. To start the `deploytool` GUI, open a command-line window and type **deploytool**.

Programmatic security refers to security decisions that are made by security-aware applications. Programmatic security is useful when declarative security alone is not sufficient to express the security model of an application.

J2EE applications are made up of components that can be deployed into different containers. These components are used to build a multi-tier enterprise application. The goal of the J2EE security architecture is to achieve end-to-end security by securing each tier.

The tiers can contain both protected and unprotected resources. Often, you need to protect resources to ensure that only authorized users have access. Authorization provides controlled access to protected resources. Authorization is based on identification and authentication. Identification is a process that enables recognition of an entity by a system, and authentication is a process that verifies the identity of a user, device, or other entity in a computer system, usually as a prerequisite to allowing access to resources in a system.

Authorization is not required to access unprotected resources. Because authorization is built upon authentication, authentication is also not needed to access unprotected resources. Accessing a resource without authentication is referred to as unauthenticated or anonymous access.

Security Roles

When you design an Enterprise JavaBean or web component, you should always think about the kinds of users who will access the component. Each of these user categories is called a *security role,* an abstract logical grouping of users that is defined by the person who assembles the application. When an application is deployed, the deployer will map the roles to security identities in the operational environment.

A J2EE group also represents a category of users, but it has a different scope from a role. A J2EE group is designated for the entire J2EE server, whereas a role covers only a specific application in a J2EE server.

To create a role using `deploytool` for a J2EE application, you declare it for the `ejb-jar` file or for the WAR file that is contained in the application.

Declaring and Linking Role References

As you have learned, a security role reference allows an enterprise bean or web component to reference an existing security role. A security role is an application-specific logical grouping of users, classified by common traits such as customer profile or job title. When an application is deployed, roles are mapped to security identities, such as `Principals` (identities assigned to users as a result of authentication) or groups, in the operational environment. Based on this, a user with a certain security role has associated access rights to a J2EE application. The link is the actual name of the security role that is being referenced.

During application assembly, the assembler creates security roles for the application and associates these roles with available security mechanisms. The assembler then resolves the security role references in individual servlets and JSPs by linking them to roles defined for the application.

The security role reference defines a mapping between the name of a role that is called from a web component using `isUserInRole(String name)` or from an enterprise bean using `isCallerInRole(String name)` and the name of a security role that has been defined for the application.

Mapping Roles to J2EE Users and Groups

When you are developing a J2EE application, you should know the roles of your users, but you probably won't know exactly who the users will be. That's taken care of in the J2EE security architecture, because after your component has been deployed, the administrator of the J2EE server will map the roles to the J2EE users (or groups) of the default realm. An administrator can map roles to J2EE users and groups by using `deploytool`.

Security in J2EE Web Tier

You can protect web resources by specifying a *security constraint.* A security constraint determines who is authorized to access a web resource collection, which is a list of URL patterns and HTTP methods that describe a set of resources to be protected. Security constraints can be defined using `deploytool`.

When you try to access a protected web resource, the web container activates the authentication mechanism that has been configured for that resource. The following authentication mechanisms can be configured for a web resource:

- **Basic authentication** The web server authenticates a user by using the username and password obtained from the web client. This form of authentication, which uses base 64 encoding, is not particularly secure, because it sends usernames and passwords over the Internet as text that is uuencoded, but not encrypted. This can expose your usernames and passwords unless all connections are over SSL. If someone can intercept the transmission, the username and password information can easily be decoded.
- **`FORM`-based authentication** Enables you to customize the login screen and error pages that are presented to the end user by an HTTP browser. This method also is not particularly secure, because the content of the user dialog box is sent as plain text, and the target server is not authenticated. In this chapter, the sample code provided uses this authentication method.
- **Client-certificate authentication** A more secure method of authentication than either basic or `FORM`-based authentication. It uses HTTP over SSL (HTTPS), in which the server and, optionally, the client authenticate each other with public key certificates. SSL provides data encryption, server authentication, message integrity, and optional client authentication for a TCP/IP connection. You can think of a *public key certificate* as the digital equivalent of a passport. It is issued by a trusted organization, called a *certification authority (CA),* and provides identification for the bearer. If you specify client-certificate authentication, the web server will authenticate the client using an *X.509 certificate,* a public key certificate that conforms to a standard that is defined by X.509 Public Key Infrastructure (PKI).

Programmatic security is used by security-aware applications when declarative security alone is not sufficient to express the security model of the application. Programmatic security consists of the following methods of the `HttpServletRequest` interface, as per the Java servlet specification:

- **`getRemoteUser()`** Used to determine the username with which the client authenticated
- **`isUserInRole()`** Used to determine whether a user is in a specific security role
- **`getUserPrincipal()`** Returns a `java.security.Principal` object

These APIs allow servlets to make business logic decisions based on the logical role of the remote user. They also allow the servlets to determine the principal name of the current user.

Security in J2EE EJB Tier

After you've defined the roles, you can define the method permissions of an enterprise bean. Method permissions indicate which roles are allowed to invoke which methods. Mapping roles to J2EE users and groups can be done by using `deploytool` to specify method permissions by mapping roles to methods.

Programmatic security in the EJB tier consists of the `getCallerPrincipal` and the `isCallerInRole` methods. You can use the `getCallerPrincipal` method to determine the caller of the enterprise bean, and the `isCallerInRole` method to get the caller's role.

The `getCallerPrincipal` method of the `EJBContext` interface returns the `java.security.Principal` object that identifies the caller of the enterprise bean. (In this case, a `Principal` is the same as a user.) In the following example, the `getUser` method of an enterprise bean returns the name of the J2EE user that invoked it:

```
public String getUser() {
   return context.getCallerPrincipal().getName();
}
```

You can determine whether an enterprise bean's caller belongs to a particular role by invoking the `isCallerInRole` method:

```
boolean result = context.isCallerInRole("Customer");
```

Propagating Security Identity

When you deploy an enterprise bean or a web component, you can specify the security identity that will be propagated to enterprise beans invoked from within that component. You can choose one of the following propagation styles:

- The caller identity of the component is propagated to the target enterprise bean. This is when the target container trusts the intermediate container.
- A specific identity is propagated to the target enterprise bean. This technique is used when the target container expects access via a specific identity.

Trust Between Containers

When an enterprise bean is designed so that either the original caller identity or a designated identity is used to call a target bean, the target bean will receive the propagated identity only. It will not receive any authentication data.

There is no way for the target container to authenticate the propagated security identity. However, since the security identity is used in authorization checks (for example, method permissions or with the `isCallerInRole()` method), it is vitally important that the security identity be authentic. Since there is no authentication data available to authenticate the propagated identity, the target must trust that the calling container has propagated an authenticated security identity.

By default, the J2EE SDK server is configured to trust identities that are propagated from different containers.

J2EE Users, Realms, and Groups

A J2EE user is similar to an operating system user. However, these two types of users belonging to different realms are not the same and the J2EE authentication service has no knowledge of the username and password provided to the OS. Also, the security mechanisms are not connected.

A *realm* is a collection of users controlled by the same authentication policy. The J2EE authentication service has users in two realms, certificate and default.

Certificates are used with the HTTPS protocol to authenticate web browser clients. To verify the identity of a user in the certificate realm, the authentication service verifies an X.509 certificate, for which the common name field is `Principal` name. In most cases, the J2EE authentication service verifies user identity by checking the default realm. This realm is used for the authentication of all clients except for web browser clients that use the HTTPS protocol and certificates.

A J2EE user of the default realm can belong to a J2EE group. A user in the certificate realm cannot. A J2EE *group* is a category of users classified by common traits. This makes it easier to control the access of large numbers of users.

Security Components of the Oracle9*i*AS Suite

The OC4J that we are using throughout this book is the stand-alone container of the Oracle9*i*AS suite of products. The Oracle9*i*AS suite additionally consists of a number of products forming a solid framework for building and deploying web and J2EE applications. Some of the components of the suite are the Apache-based Oracle HTTP Server, Oracle9*i*AS Containers For J2EE, which is the platform used throughout this book, and Oracle9*i*AS Portal, which uses advanced security functionality provided by Oracle9*i*AS.

As shown in Figure 8-4, the Oracle9*i*AS suite consists of Oracle9*i*AS Metadata Repository, Oracle Internet Directory (OID), and Oracle9*i*AS Single Sign-On (SSO).

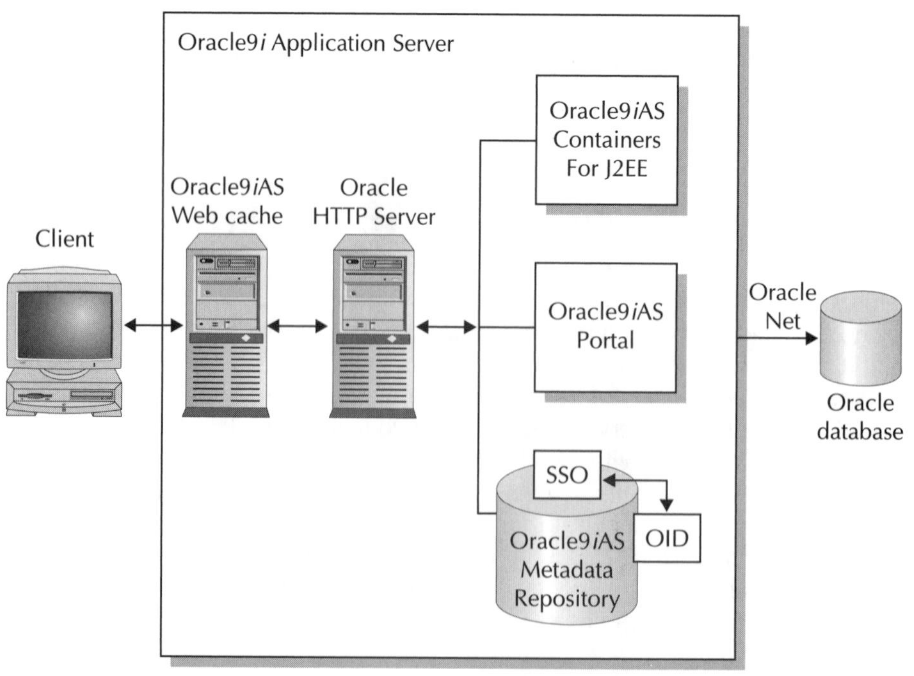

FIGURE 8-4. *Security components of the Oracle9iAS suite*

The Oracle9*i*AS suite security starts from well-tested and highly configurable web security services provided by Oracle HTTP Server, adds a comprehensive set of web single sign-on services, and centralized user provisioning that is available in OID, an LDAP version 3–compliant directory service. The Oracle9*i*AS suite also provides Oracle's implementation of JAAS for J2EE application security, as was discussed in this chapter for OC4J, and extensive portal authorization and application integration mechanisms. The Oracle9*i*AS suite also supports secure access to Oracle database systems using Oracle Advanced Security.

Additional details regarding the security components of the Oracle9*i*AS suite can be found at: http://otn.oracle.com/docs/products/ias/doc_library/90200doc_otn/core.902/a90146/toc.htm.

The OC4J Implementation of JAAS

OC4J supports JAAS by implementing a JAAS provider, also called JAZN (Java AuthoriZatioN). The JAAS provider provides application developers with user authentication, authorization, and delegation services to integrate into their application environments. It also supports JAAS policies. Policies contain the rules (permissions) that authorize a user to use resources, such as reading a file, and so forth.

The JAAS provider uses the capability model of access control. In this model, authorization information is associated with the subjects or users (in other words, what permissions does a user have) and not with the resources or objects (who can access this resource) as in the access control list model.

By default, OC4J uses a `principals.xml` file to configure and store authentication and authorization information. JAZN has the ability to store sensitive information, such as passwords, in an encrypted format in the `jazn-data.xml` file.

Configuring JAZN for Use with OC4J

To configure your application to use JAZN, you need to add either the `<jazn>` or `<user-manager>` tag to your OC4J-specific deployment descriptor, `orion-application.xml` or `application.xml`.

Configuring JAZN for Use with LDAP

To configure JAZN to use an LDAP directory service, use the `<jazn>` element:

```
<jazn provider="LDAP" default-realm="my_realm"
location="ldap://myhost:389" />
```

Alternatively, you can use the <user-manager> element, like this:

```
<user-manager class="oracle.security.jazn.oc4j.JAZNUserManager">
    <property name="provider.type" value="LDAP" />
    <property name="realm.default" value="my_realm" />
    <property name="ldap.service" value="ldap://myhost:389" />
</user-manager>
```

Configuring JAZN for Use with jazn-data.xml

To configure JAZN to use the `jazn-data.xml` file with the <jazn> element, the following line should be included in the file:

```
<jazn provider="XML" location="./jazn-data.xml" />
```

To use the alternative <user-manager> element, do the following:

```
<user-manager class="oracle.security.jazn.oc4j.JAZNUserManager">
    <property name="provider.type" value="XML" />
    <property name="xml.store.fs.jazn" value="./jazn-data.xml" />
</user-manager>
```

Note that the default realm in OC4J is `jazn.com`.

`JAZNUserManager` is essentially a client application of JAZN and can be used seamlessly with either JAZN-LDAP or JAZN-XML.

Using jazn.jar

The `jazn.jar` utility is a command-line administration tool for JAZN. It provides the ability to add, remove, list, and modify user, role, and permission information in JAZN. To invoke the JAZN administration tool, execute the following command from your `%J2EE_HOME%` directory:

```
java -jar jazn.jar
```

This command will display the help/usage contents and is the same as executing `java -jar jazn.jar -help`. The contents of the help screen are as follows:

```
Admintool usage:

 java -jar jazn.jar

-listusers [<realm> [-role <role>|-perm <permission>]] |
-listroles [<realm> [<user>|-role <role>]] |
-listrealms |
```

```
-listperms [<realm> { <user> |-role <role>}] |
-listperm <permission_name> |
-listprncpls |
-listprncpl <principal_name> |
-adduser <realm> <username> <password> |
-addrole <realm> <role> |
-addrealm <realm> <admin> {<adminpwd> <adminrole> |
          <adminrole> <userbase> <rolebase> <realmtype>}
-addperm <perm_name> <perm_class> <action> <target> [<description>] |
-addprncpl <prncpl_name> <prncpl_class> <params> [<description>] |
-remuser <realm> <user> |
-remrole <realm> <role> |
-remrealm <realm> |
-remperm <permission_name> |
-remprncpl <principal_name> |
-grantperm <realm> {user|-role <role>} <permission_class>
<permission_params> |
-grantrole <role> <realm> {user|-role <to_role>} |
-revokeperm <realm> {user|-role <role>} <permission_class>
<permission_params> |
-revokerole <role> <realm> {user|-role <from_role>} |
-setpasswd <realm> <user> <old_pwd> <new_pwd> |
-checkpasswd <realm> <user> [-pw <password>] |
-getconfig <default_realm> <admin> <password> |
-convert <filename> <realm> |
-shell
-help
```

To add a new user to JAZN, execute the following command from the OC4J home directory:

```
java -jar jazn.jar -adduser <realm> <myuser> <password>
```

Once you have created a user, you need to add the user to a specific role, which can be done with the following command:

```
java -jar jazn.jar -grantrole <role> <realm> <myuser>
```

Authentication Environments

The JAAS provider integrates with different login authentication environments in J2EE applications as follows:

- **Basic authentication** Prompts the user directly for a username and password.

- **Single sign-on** Lets a user access multiple accounts and applications with a single set of login credentials. JAZN uses Oracle9*i*AS Single Sign-On to authenticate logins.
- **SSL** Uses this industry-standard protocol for managing the security of message transmission on the Internet. JAZN uses a login module (for example, `RealmLoginModule`) to authenticate logins.

JAAS can then be integrated with the type of authentication method selected; for example, if the authentication method to be used is `FORM`, then the `web.xml` file is modified as follows:

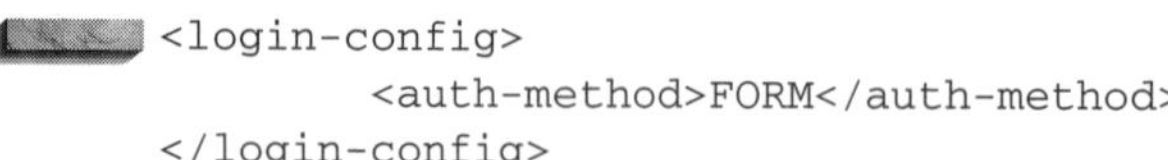

```
<login-config>
        <auth-method>FORM</auth-method>
</login-config>
```

Integrated and Switchable User Managers

As shown in Figure 8-5 and as discussed earlier, the JAAS provider supports the following two types of repository providers, referred to as provider types. These provider types are repositories for secure, centralized storage, retrieval, and administration of provider data. This data consists of realm (users and roles) and JAAS policy (permissions) information.

- **JAZN-XML** The default fast, lightweight implementation of the JAAS provider API. It uses XML to store usernames and encrypted passwords. The user repository is file-based and stored in the `jazn-data.xml` file.
- **JAZN-LDAP** More scalable, secure, enterprise-ready, and integrated with SSO. You can only support SSO with JAZN-LDAP. The user repository is an Oracle Internet Directory, which necessitates that the application server instance is associated with an infrastructure. If it is not associated with an OID, JAZN-LDAP is not a security option.

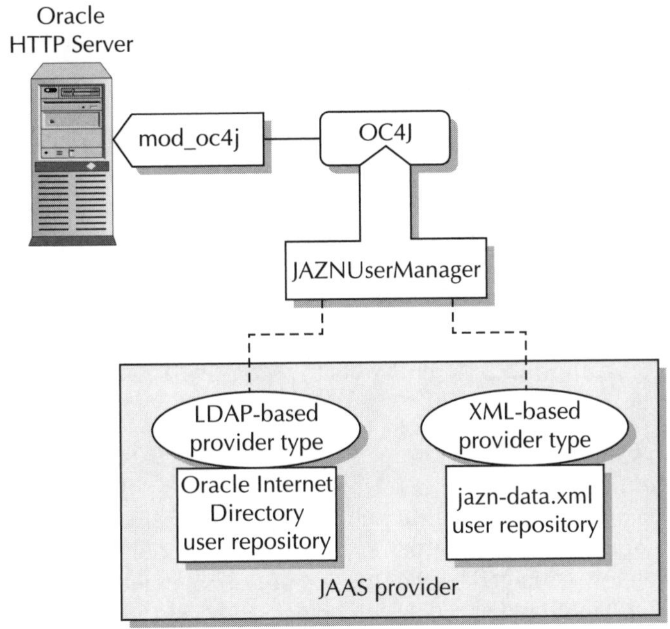

FIGURE 8-5. *Security architecture using the* `JAZNUserManager` *class*

Using OC4J in Applications; Coding Security in OC4J Applications

After completing this section, you should be able to do the following:

- Configure Oracle's JAAS provider for use on your OC4J container.
- Use the `jazn.jar` command-line administration tool.
- Test that Oracle's JAAS provider works correctly with the application developed in Chapter 5.

The Application Design

The J2EE application developed in Chapter 5, which we will reuse in this chapter, consists of the following:

- **`LineItemLocal` CMP entity bean** Maps the `LINE_ITEM` table that consists of line-item elements for the purchase order requisitions. This CMP bean, along with the `PurchaseOrderLocal` and `EmployeeLocal` CMP beans, consists of code to manipulate business logic.
- **`PurchaseOrderLocal` CMP entity bean** Maps the `PURCHASE_ORDER` table that consists of elements relating to purchase order requisitions.
- **`EmployeeLocal` BMP entity bean** Maps the `EMPLOYEE` table that consists of elements relating to employees.
- **`EmployeeTool` SQLJ class** Implements the business logic that manipulates the `EMPLOYEE` table. This class is tightly coupled with the `EmployeeLocal` BMP entity bean. The `EmployeeTool` object is a dependent object of the `EmployeeLocal` object. Its life cycle is completely managed by the `EmployeeLocal` object and it can only be accessed indirectly through that object. The `EmployeeTool` SQLJ class provides the necessary methods that an `EmployeeLocal` object uses to insert, update, remove, and query data of the `EMPLOYEE` table.
- **`EmployeeVO` class** A value object (VO)—that is, a business object that is passed by value as a serializable Java object—used by the `EmployeeTool` SQLJ class and the `EmployeeLocal` BMP bean to ship data between themselves. This chapter briefly discusses value objects. Detailed descriptions of value objects and their use are presented in the "The J2EE Value Object Pattern" section of Chapter 6.

Creating the Development Directory

The development directory for the application is as follows:

- **chapter08** Root directory of your J2EE application (for example, `c:\chapter08`)
  - **META-INF** Directory where your `application.xml` file is located (and possibly your `orion-application.xml` file), which defines the modules you have in your J2EE application
  - **src** Directory where all the source files are located

- **META-INF** Directory where the `ejb-jar.xml` deployment descriptor file and the `orion-ejb-jar.xml` OC4J-specific deployment descriptor file are located
- **purchase** Package indicating the starting point of the `Purchase` application
    - **ejb** Package consisting of the source code of your EJB components
        - **bmp** Package consisting of the source code of all your bean-managed persistent (BMP) entity beans
        - **cmp** Package consisting of the source code of all your container-managed persistent (CMP) entity beans
    - **util** Package consisting of the source code of your utility classes
    - **vo** Package consisting of the source code of your value object classes
- **webapps** Package consisting of the source code of the testing Java Servlet program
    - **test** Package

- **classes** Root directory for your EJB module
    - **META-INF** Directory where the `ejb-jar.xml` deployment descriptor file and the `orion-ejb-jar.xml` OC4J-specific deployment descriptor file are located
    - **purchase** Package indicating the starting point of the Java class files of the `Purchase` application
        - **ejb** Package consisting of the class files of your EJB components
            - **bmp** Package consisting of the class files of all your BMP entity beans
            - **cmp** Package consisting of the class files of all your CMP entity beans
        - **util** Package consisting of the class files of your utility classes
        - **vo** Package consisting of the class files of your value object classes

- **web** Root directory for your Web module, which includes your JSPs, HTML pages, and tag libraries
  - **WEB-INF** Directory where your `web.xml` file is located (and possibly your `orion-web.xml` file)
    - **classes** Starting point for your Web module's classes
      - **webapps** Package
        - **test** Package consisting of the class files of your servlets

The application developed and used in this chapter is based on the code developed in Chapter 5. Refer to Chapter 5 for a detailed discussion on developing the application. The high-level views of the CMP and BMP entity beans developed in Chapter 5 are shown in Figures 8-6, 8-7, and 8-8.

Specifying Users and Groups in jazn-data.xml

As described earlier in the chapter, the JAZN-XML users, roles, and groups are defined in the `jazn-data.xml` file. When you add users, roles, and groups, these are stored in the `jazn-data.xml` file. The passwords are obfuscated.

For example, you may use the `jazn.jar` command-line tool to create a user as follows, if the user does not already exist:

```
java -jar jazn.jar -adduser jazn.com admin welcome
```

The following `jazn-data.xml` code fragment is an example of a JAZN-XML group named `administrators` and a user named `admin`:

```
<role>
  <name>administrators</name>
  <members>
   <member>
    <type>user</type>
    <name>admin</name>
   </member>
  </members>
</role>
```

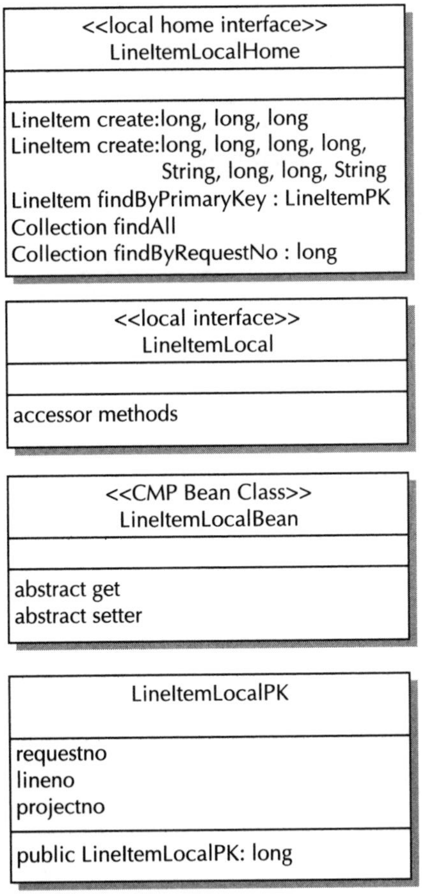

<<local home interface>>
LineItemLocalHome

LineItem create:long, long, long
LineItem create:long, long, long, long, String, long, long, String
LineItem findByPrimaryKey : LineItemPK
Collection findAll
Collection findByRequestNo : long

<<local interface>>
LineItemLocal

accessor methods

<<CMP Bean Class>>
LineItemLocalBean

abstract get
abstract setter

LineItemLocalPK

requestno
lineno
projectno

public LineItemLocalPK: long

FIGURE 8-6. *High-level view of the* `LineItemLocal` *CMP bean*

Unlike the XML from the `XMLUserManager` user repository, the password is encrypted under `JAZNUserManager`:

```
<user>
  <name>admin</name>
  <description>The admin user</description>
  <credentials>NVgOIAV2Xe0Is+t+Q1xhU/3G5glW/KH8</credentials>
</user>
```

These elements define a role of `administrators` with a member of `user/admin` as its credentials on the Security page.

NOTE
*See the Oracle9*i*AS JAAS API specification provided in Appendix B for further details on the Oracle9*i*AS implementation of JAAS.*

<<local home interface>>
PurchaseOrderLocalHome

PurchaseOrderLocal create :long
PurchaseOrderLocal create :long, long, long
PurchaseOrderLocal findByPrimaryKey:
PurchaseOrderPK
Collection findAll

<<local interface>>
PurchaseOrderLocal

// accessor methods :
long getRequestNo :
void setRequestNo :long
long getEmployeeNo :
void setEmployeeNo :long
long getVendorNo :
void setVendorNo :long

<<CMP Bean Class>>
PurchaseOrderBean

public EntityContext entityContext

// callback methods :
PurchaseLocalPK ejbCreate :long, long, long
void ejbPostCreate :long, long, long
void ejbActivate :
void ejbPassivate :
void ejbLoad :
void ejbStore :
void ejbRemove :
// accessor method implementations :
accessor methods :
public abstract long getRequestNo :
public abstract void setRequestNo :long
public abstract long getEmployeeNo :
public abstract void setEmployeeNo :long
public abstract long getVendorNo :
public abstract void setVendorNo :long

PurchaseOrderPK

public long requestno

public PurchaseOrderPK :long

FIGURE 8-7. *High-level view of the `PurchaseOrderLocal` CMP bean*

<<local home interface>>
EmployeeLocalHome

EmployeeLocal create: long, long, String, String, String, String, String
EmployeeLocal findByPrimaryKey: EmployeePK
Collection findAll:

EmployeeBean Class

//Instance variables
public long employeeno
public long deptno
public String type
public String lastname
public String firstname
public String phone
public email

EmployeeLocalPK ejbCreate: long, long, String, String, String, String
public void ejbLoad :
public void ejbRemove :
public void ejbStore :
//Data source methods
private Connection getConnection :
private DataSource getDataSource :
//accessors
public long getEmployeeno :
public void setEmployeeno :long
public long getDeptno :
public void setDeptno :long
public String getType :
public void setType :String
public String getLastname :
public void setLastname :String
public String getFirstname :
public void setFirstname :String
public String getPhone :
public void setPhone :String
public String getEmail :
public void setEmail :String

<<local interface>>
EmployeeLocal

//accessors
long getEmployeeNo :
void setEmployeeNo :long
long getDeptNo :
void setDeptNo :long
String getType :
void setType :String
String getLastname :
void setLastname :String
String getFirstname :
void setFirstname :String
String getPhone :
void setPhone :String
String getEmail :
void setEmail :String

EmployeePKClass

accessors

EmployeeToolClass

Collection getEmployeeIds:
EmployeeVO getEmployeeInfo: long
EmployeeLocalPK getEmployeeno: EmployeePK
void insertNewEmployee: long, long, String, String, String, String, String
void removeEmployee: EmployeeLocalPK
void updateEmployee: long, long, String, String, String, String, String

Uses

FIGURE 8-8. *High-level view of the `EmployeeLocal` CMP bean*

Configuring an Authentication Method

The following integrates JAAS with the type of authentication method FORM in the web.xml file:

```
<login-config>
        <auth-method>FORM</auth-method>
</login-config>
```

As discussed in the next section, we can then specify FORM as the auth-method (instead of BASIC, DIGEST, or CLIENT-CERT), and then we tell the system that the JSP login.jsp file has the <FORM> element that will authenticate a user. If our authentication fails (we do not log in correctly as the system user), then we will be sent to retryLogin.jsp.

Extending the web.xml File to Include OC4J Security Mechanisms

The following code fragment shows the changes to the web.xml file, used with the application developed for Chapter 5, to include the security mechanisms that we have discussed in this chapter. The modifications to note are the login-config, form-login-config, security-role, and security-constraint elements. You will notice from the file that there are the web components such as the LocalClientServlet that you have used in Chapter 5, and the new JSP login.jsp and retryLogin.jsp files, all of which will be discussed after the next section on the web.xml file, which follows.

```
<?xml version = '1.0' encoding = 'windows-1252'?>
<!DOCTYPE web-app PUBLIC
"-//Sun Microsystems, Inc.//DTD Web Application 2.2//EN"
"http://java.sun.com/j2ee/dtds/web-app_2_2.dtd">
<web-app>
.
.
.
<servlet>
  <servlet-name>LocalClientServlet</servlet-name>
  <servlet-class>webapps.web.test.LocalClientServlet</servlet-class>
</servlet>
<servlet-mapping>
  <servlet-name>LocalClientServlet</servlet-name>
  <url-pattern>/</url-pattern>
</servlet-mapping>
<login-config>
```

```
  <auth-method>FORM</auth-method>
    <form-login-config>
      <form-login-page>/login.jsp</form-login-page>
      <form-error-page>/retryLogin.jsp</form-error-page>
    </form-login-config>
</login-config>
.
.
.
<security-role>
  <role-name> administrators</role-name>
</security-role>
<!-- Login Constraint -->
<security-constraint>
  <web-resource-collection>
    <web-resource-name>localClientServlet</web-resource-name>
    <url-pattern>/</url-pattern>
  </web-resource-collection>
  <auth-constraint>
    <!-- This is the server admin: "admin/welcome" the password when
you installed OC4J or any other username/password combination that
you created using the jazn.jar tool -->
    <role-name>administrators</role-name>
  </auth-constraint>
</security-constraint>
.
.
.
  <welcome-file-list>
    <welcome-file>login.jsp</welcome-file>
    <welcome-file>index.html</welcome-file>
  </welcome-file-list>
.
.
.
</web-app>
```

The following list describes the functions of the various key tags in the preceding code:

- **<servlet-mapping>** Defines a mapping between a servlet and a URL pattern.
- **<servlet-name>** Defines the canonical name of the Java servlet, used to reference the Java servlet definition elsewhere in the deployment descriptor.

- **<servlet-class>** Defines the fully qualified class name of the Java servlet.
- **<url-pattern>** Describes a pattern used to resolve URLs. The portion of the URL after `http://host:port + ContextPath` is compared to the `<url-pattern>`.
- **<login-config>** Used to configure how the user is authenticated, and the attributes that are needed by the form login mechanism (optional element).
- **<auth-method>** Describes the method used to authenticate the user. Possible values are `BASIC` (uses browser authentication), `FORM` (uses a user-written HTML form), and `CLIENT-CERT`, as discussed earlier in the chapter.
- **<form-login-config>** Used to configure the `<auth-method>` to `FORM`.
- **<form-login-page>** Describes the URI of a web resource relative to the document root, used to authenticate the user. This can be an HTML page, JSP, or HTTP servlet, and must return an HTML page containing a FORM that conforms to a specific naming convention.
- **<form-error-page>** Describes the URI of a web resource relative to the document root, sent to the user in response to a failed authentication login.
- **<security-constraint>** Defines the access privileges to a collection of resources defined by the `<web-resource-collection>` element.
- **<web-resource-collection>** Defines the components of the web application to which this security constraint is applied. Use one or more of the `<url-pattern>` elements to declare to which URL patterns this security constraint applies.
- **<auth-constraint>** Defines which groups or principals have access to the collection of web resources defined in this security constraint.
- **<role-name>** Defines which security roles can access resources defined in this security constraint.
- **<welcome-file-list>** Contains an ordered list of `<welcome-file>` elements (optional element). We will use the `login.jsp` file introduced later in the chapter as the default welcome file.

As the preceding code fragment shows, the security role is detailed by the `<security-role>` element. The user `admin`, as mentioned before, is used to log in to the application.

Reusing the LocalClientServlet Class

The `LocalClientServlet` class developed in Chapter 5 is now modified to use the `getUserPrincipal()` method that was discussed earlier, and will be referenced in the JSP files `login.jsp` and `retryLogin.jsp`, the code for which follows this section. Refer to "Deploying the Application to OC4J," later in this chapter, for instructions on how to package and deploy these web components. Methods like `request.getRemoteUser()`, `request.isUserInRole("admin")`, and `request.getUserPrincipal()`, discussed earlier in the chapter, have been used in the `LocalClientServlet` class, shown here:

```
/* Program Name: LocalClientServlet.java
**
** Purpose: Test the LineItemLocal and
** PurchaseOrderLocal CMP beans and
** the EmployeeLocal BMP bean.
*/
package webapps.web.test;
.
.
.
public class LocalClientServlet extends HttpServlet
{
  public void doGet(HttpServletRequest request,
                    HttpServletResponse response)
          throws ServletException, IOException  {
  try
    {
    .
    .
    .
      out.println("request.getRemoteUser = " +
request.getRemoteUser() + "<br>");
      out.println("request.isUserInRole('admin') = " +
request.isUserInRole("admin") + "<br>");
      out.println("request.getUserPrincipal = " +
request.getUserPrincipal() + "<br>");
      .
      .
      .
```

```
    }
  catch(Exception e)
  {
      System.out.println(e);}
  }
}  // End of the LocalClientServlet class
```

Creating the login.jsp File

As mentioned earlier, the JSP `login.jsp` and `retryLogin.jsp` files, as specified in the updated `web.xml`, are used as the front end to the application developed. The `<form>` element, discussed earlier, in the `web.xml` file is configured for `FORM` authentication. The following is the code for the `login.jsp` file:

```
<%@ page contentType="text/html"%>
<HTML>
<HEAD>
<TITLE>
Please Login
</TITLE>
<META HTTP-EQUIV="Content-Type" CONTENT="text/html">
</HEAD>
<body bgcolor="#FFFFCC" text="#000000" link="#009900"
vlink="#666666" alink="#FF0000" style="font-family: Jenson,
Garamond, serif">
<div><img src="./web/psynex-logo.gif" width="333" height="110"
border=0 alt="Psynex Pharmaceutical" align="left"></div>
<h1 align="center">Login to the<br>
Psynex Management System</h1>
<form method="post" action="j_security_check" focus="j_username">
<H2>
Please Login to view the LocalClientServlet:
<p>
Login:
<input type="text" name="j_username" size="15"/>
</p>
<p>
Password <font class="required">*</font>
<input type="password" name="j_password" size="15"/>
</p>
<p>
<input type="submit" name="submit" value="Login">
<input type="reset"/>
```

```
</p>
</H2>
<P>
The time is: <% out.println((new java.util.Date()).toString()); %>
</P>
</FORM>
</body>
</HTML>
```

Creating the retryLogin.jsp File

On authentication error, the user is presented with a `retryLogin.jsp` file. The following is the code for the `retryLogin.jsp` file:

```
<!doctype html public "-//W3C//DTD HTML 4.01 Transitional//EN"
"http://www.w3.org/TR/html4/loose.dtd">

<html>
  <head>
    <title>
      Retry Login Page!!
    </title>
    <meta http-equiv="Content-Type" content="text/html; charset=iso-8859-1">
  </head>
  <body bgcolor="#FFFFCC" text="#000000" link="#009900"
vlink="#666666" alink="#FF0000" style="font-family: Jenson,
Garamond, serif">
    <div><img src="C:\Documents and Settings\Ashish
Parikh\Desktop\chapter08code\psynex-logo.gif" width="333"
height="110" border=0 alt="Psynex Pharmaceutical" align="left"></div>
    <h1 align="center">Login to the<br>
Psynex Management System</h1>
    <form method="post" action="j_security_check" focus="j_username">
      <H2>
          Please Login to view the LocalClientServlet (Try Again):
           <p>
          Username <font class="required">*</font>
          <input type="text" name="j_username" size="16"/>
        </p>
        <p>
          Password <font class="required">*</font>
          <input type="password" name="j_password" size="16"/>
        </p>
```

```
        <p>
          <input type="submit" name="submit" value="Login">
          <input type="reset"/>
        </p>
      </H2>
    </form>
    <p> </p>
  </body>
</html>
```

The high-level view of `LocalClientServlet`, `login.jsp`, and the entity beans developed in Chapter 5 are shown in Figure 8-9.

Deploying the Application to OC4J

In Chapter 2, you learned how to deploy a J2EE application to the OC4J server, and how to bind that application to the server so that you can access the application from OC4J. In this section, we will revisit the necessary steps, to refresh your memory.

Recall that a J2EE application can contain the following modules:

- **Web applications** The Web applications module (WAR files) can consist of servlets, JSPs, HTML pages, tag libraries, and utility classes. This is where `LocalClientServlet`, `login.jsp`, and `retryLogin.jsp` will be packaged.
- **EJB applications** The EJB applications module (`ejb-jar` files) includes Enterprise JavaBeans.
- **Client applications** The Client applications module includes client application programs and is contained within a JAR file.

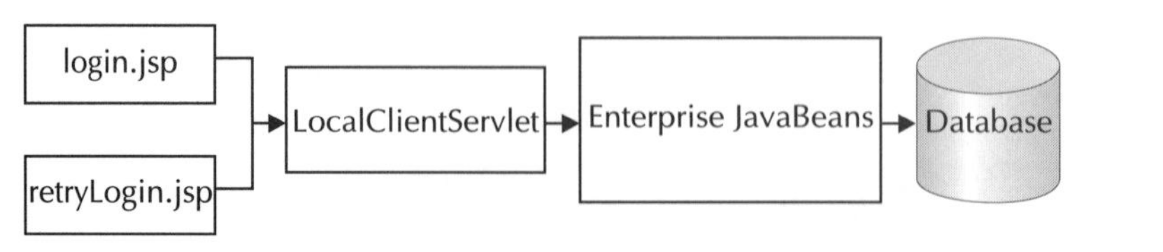

FIGURE 8-9. *High-level view of `LocalClientServlet`, `login.jsp`, and the EJBs*

Archiving the EJB Application

The very first step in archiving the EJB application is to package your application. You do so when you create the J2EE EAR file.

Packaging the Application: Creating the EAR File

This application consists of a Web module, containing `LocalClientServlet`, `login.jsp`, and `retryLogin.jsp`, and an EJB module, containing two CMP beans and one BMP bean. The following list shows the steps you would need to follow to create the EAR file.

1. Let's start by creating the WAR file. Open a command prompt, and position yourself in the web directory (for example, `c:\chapter08\web`).
2. Type the following:

   ```
   jar cvf chapter08-web.war *
   ```
3. Copy `chapter08-web.war` to the root directory, `chapter08`.
4. Position yourself in the `classes` directory.
5. Type the following:

   ```
   jar cvf chapter08-ejb.jar *
   ```
6. Copy `chapter08-ejb.jar` to the root directory, `chapter08`.
7. Position yourself in the root directory, `chapter08`.
8. Type the following:

   ```
   jar cvf chapter08.ear chapter08-web.war chapter08-ejb.jar META-INF\
   application.xml
   ```

   You now have your `chapter08.ear` file and are ready to deploy.

If your application will access a database, then you need to define an OC4J data source. You do so by modifying the OC4J `data-sources.xml` file.

Modifying the OC4J data-sources.xml File

If you have not already defined the data source `jdbc/OracleDS`, you need to do this now. Before deploying your application, you need to register your data source with OC4J. You do that by modifying the OC4J `data-sources.xml` file, located in the OC4J's `.../config` directory. All the beans that you created in this chapter use a data source called `jdbc/OracleDS`. You need to specify that data source in the OC4J `data-sources.xml` file.

In the OC4J's `data-sources.xml` file, Oracle provides an example default `DataSource` that uses Oracle JDBC driver to create the connections. Modify the file as follows:

```
<!-- Original source from Oracle -->
<data-source
            class="com.evermind.sql.DriverManagerDataSource"
            name="OracleDS"
            location="jdbc/OracleCoreDS"
            xa-location="jdbc/xa/OracleXADS"
            ejb-location="jdbc/OracleDS"
            connection-driver="oracle.jdbc.driver.OracleDriver"
            username="scott"
            password="tiger"
            url="jdbc:oracle:thin:@localhost:5521:oracle"
            inactivity-timeout="30"
      />
<!-- Your datasource -->
<data-source
            class="com.evermind.sql.DriverManagerDataSource"
            name="OracleDS"
            location="jdbc/OracleCoreDS"
            xa-location="jdbc/xa/OracleXADS"
            ejb-location="jdbc/OracleDS"
            connection-driver="oracle.jdbc.driver.OracleDriver"
            username="scott"
            password="tiger"
            url="jdbc:oracle:thin:@yourhost:your-port-no:your-sid"
            inactivity-timeout="30"
      />
```

Next, you will deploy the application. OC4J supports deployment of both EAR files and an exploded directory conforming to the J2EE standard (as does our `chapter08` directory structure). We will show you both ways, starting with the EAR file.

Deploying an EAR File to OC4J

The steps to deploy an EAR file to OC4J are as follows:

1. Copy the `Chapter08.ear` file to your OC4J installation's `applications` directory; if you have unzipped OC4J under the `c:\OC4J` directory, then this will be `c:\OC4J\j2ee\home\applications`. The EAR file can be placed anywhere, but in this example, you will use the OC4J `applications` directory.

2. Edit the OC4J `server.xml` file, found under your `OC4J\j2ee\home\config` directory. Add the following entry as shown below:

```
<application name="chapter8" path="../applications/chapter08.ear"
auto-start="true" />
```

3. Edit `http-web-site.xml` to bind your Web module to this J2EE application. Add the following entry:

```
<web-app application="chapter8" name="chapter08-web" root="/chapter8"
load-on-startup="true" />
```

CAUTION
The name must correspond to whatever name you gave the WAR file; the root will be your virtual path where OC4J can reach your application.

Recall that OC4J supports hot deployment. Therefore, if OC4J is running, it will immediately pick up and deploy this application. If OC4J is not running, position yourself in the `OC4J/j2ee/home` directory and start OC4J by typing the following:

```
java -jar oc4j.jar -verbosity 10
```

Next, you will test your application.

Testing Your Application

Open a web browser and type the URL

```
http://localhost:8888/chapter8/login
```

where *localhost* is your machine, 8888 is the port the web server is listening on, and chapter8 is the name that you defined in the <name> element of the `<application>` tag in the OC4J `server.xml` file. Note that the default for the stand-alone OC4J is 8888. The port can be found and changed in the OC4J `http-web-site.xml` XML file, found in the `OC4J_HOME/j2ee/home/config directory`.

The login page for the sample application is shown in Figure 8-10.

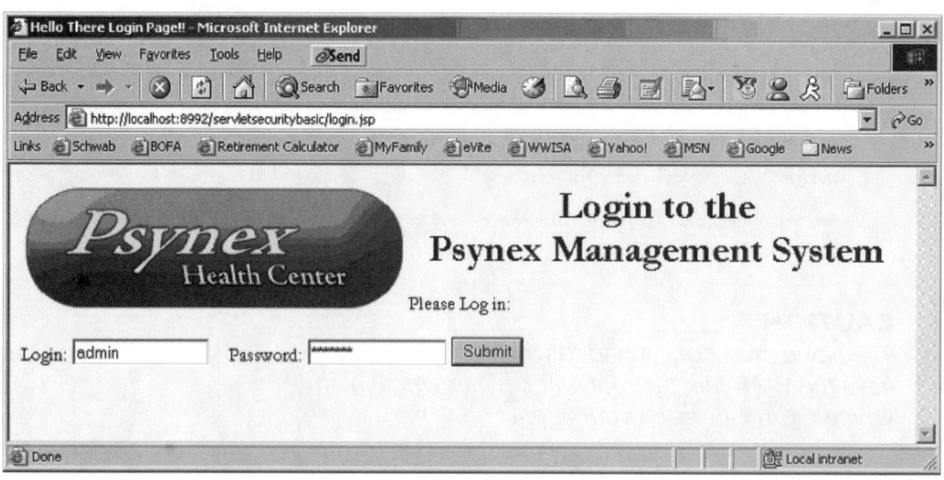

FIGURE 8-10. *Login page to the application*

Output from Testing Your Application

The following fragment shows the output that you will see when you run the application:

```
request.getRemoteUser = jazn.com/admin
request.isUserInRole('admin') = true
request.getUserPrincipal = [JAZNUserAdaptor: user=RealmUser: jazn.com/
admin]
Got EmployeeLocal: EmployeeLocal purchase.ejb.bmp.EmployeePK@65
employeeNo = 101
deptNo = 200
type = Registered Nurse
lastName = Jewel
firstName = Missy
phone = 1001
```

Deploying an Exploded Directory

OC4J also supports deployment of an exploded directory structure. If you have your `chapter08` code unzipped in the `c:\chapter08` directory, do the following:

1. Make sure the application.xml file is correct in your chapter08/META-INF directory. For an exploded directory, it should look like the following:

```
<?xml version="1.0"?>
<!DOCTYPE application PUBLIC "-//Sun Microsystems,
     Inc.//DTD J2EE Application 1.2//EN"
    "http://java.sun.com/j2ee/dtds/application_1_2.dtd">
<!-- The application element is the root
     element of a J2EE application deployment descriptor.  -->
<application>
      <display-name>Chapter8</display-name>
      <module>
            <web>
                  <web-uri>web</web-uri>
                  <context-root>/</context-root>
            </web>
      </module>
      <module>
            <ejb>classes</ejb>
      </module>
</application>
```

NOTE
The attribute web inside <web-uri> points to the root directory of your Web module; the attribute ejb points to the root directory of your EJB module.

2. Edit the OC4J server.xml file; for an exploded deployment, add the following entry:

```
<application name="chapter8" path="file:///c:/chapter08"
    auto-start="true" />
```

Note that the "file:///" prefix takes care of the forward slash (/) and backslash (\ ).

3. Edit the OC4J http-web-site.xml file and add the following entry:

```
<web-app application="chapter8" name="web"
          root="/chapter8" auto-start="true" />
```

If your OC4J instance is still running, you might need to restart it if you're using the same names again.

Note that if you want a clean deployment of an application deployed to OC4J, do the following:

1. Stop OC4J.
2. Delete the `chapter08.ear` file and the `chapter08` directory under the OC4J `application` directory.
3. Delete the `chapter8` application directory under the OC4J `application-deployments` directory.
4. Start OC4J again. OC4J will then do a clean install of the application.

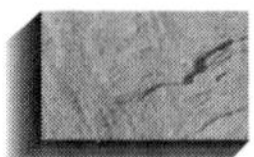

NOTE
We have provided the `application.xml` file for the exploded approach under `chapter08/META-INF`, called `application.xml`, and also the prebuilt `chapter08.ear` file, called `chapter08.ear`.

In this chapter, you learned about OC4J security concepts, such as the challenges faced in architecting secure Internet systems, the evolution of Java Security Models, components of Java Security, Java Authentication and Authorization Service (JAAS), components of J2EE Security, the security architecture built into Oracle9*i*AS, components of Oracle9*i*AS Security, Oracle9*i*AS's implementation of JAAS, and integrated and switch-able User Managers.

In the next chapter, you will learn how to create and deploy Web Services in the OC4J environment. The section "Providing Secure Web Services" will briefly discuss the security mechanisms used in Web Services, and will allow you to reuse the concepts learned in this chapter.

CHAPTER 9

Web Services: SOAP, WSDL, and UDDI

eb Services have become a hot topic. Enterprise software vendors and programmers—irrespective of whether they belong to the J2EE or the .NET camp—expect to use Web Services technologies to open up individual applications—regardless of platform or language technology choice—to be composed or "orchestrated" into coherent intra- and inter-enterprise computing solutions. Three components of Web Services provide the underpinning for this vision: SOAP specifies the protocol with which Web Services communicate, while WSDL provides a language for fully describing Web Services, and UDDI complements these two by permitting cataloging and advertising of Web Services to users.

The OC4J Web Services implementation is fully based on J2EE functionality. Web Services can be defined and deployed similar to other J2EE components. For example, what you will learn in Chapter 10 about servlet deployment is directly applicable to Web Services. (If you want to first learn about the J2EE technology that forms the underpinning of OC4J Web Services, you may want to turn to Chapter 10 before continuing here.) Also, the OC4J security mechanisms that were explained in Chapter 8 can be put to immediate use for securing Web Services. What is more, you have lots of flexibility in creating Web Services: They can be based on a stateless or a stateful Java class instance, on a PL/SQL package with procedures and functions defined in an Oracle database, or on a stateless session bean (such as you would have encountered in Chapter 7). The scalability, reliability, and security that you expect from OC4J also extend to the Web Services deployed into it.

This chapter covers the following:

- A brief introduction to the basics of Web Services, including:
  - Simple Object Access Protocol (SOAP), a Web Services communication protocol
  - Web Services Description Language (WSDL), a description for deployed Web Services
  - Universal Description, Discovery, and Integration (UDDI), an API for cataloging, advertising, and retrieving Web Services definitions
  - Representational State Transfer (REST), a simplified, "alternative view" of Web Services
- How to write, deploy, and test a Web Service implemented from the following:
  - A Java class
  - A PL/SQL package
  - A stateless session bean

- How to write a Web Services client:
  - Using static client-proxy code
  - Using a dynamic client proxy that consumes WSDL

A Brief Web Services Primer

Web Services are an application architecture for enterprise and business applications with the following properties:

- It describes application-to-application communication that is platform and language independent and thus supports interoperable, distributed applications.
- It is based on self-describing services (or business functions) that can be accessed via a messaging protocol.
- It is standards-based, using preexisting and emerging standards (HTTP, SMTP, XML Schema, SOAP, WSDL, and UDDI).
- It provides a component-based distributed computing model. Some would even argue that Web Services are ushering in a new era of distributed computing inside the enterprise as well as between businesses that will supersede traditional Internet computing.

OC4J provides you with full support for this new architecture with a solid foundation in OC4J's J2EE roots. Let us first look in more detail at some of the Web Services components before delving into programming with them.

SOAP

SOAP (formerly known as the "Simple Object Access Protocol," though now this acronym just stands for itself) defines the message format for Web Services. This in turn is based on XML and XML Schema standards. Let us consider an invocation of a remote procedure call (RPC)-style Web Service and take a peek at the SOAP request message (Listing 9-1) and the SOAP response message (Listing 9-2) that are flying over the wire in order to see what is going on in the SOAP protocol. Line numbers have been added to both listings so that we can better highlight the various components.

The purpose of this SOAP request is to obtain a current date in a particular format from a Web Service located on some host, say `wshost` on port 8888, accessed with the URL http://wshost:8888/chapter09/JavaWS. The operation invoked on the service is called `getCurrentDate`. It takes a string argument named `Format` that characterizes the format in which the local date should be returned to the requester. We can discern the following components in this message, which is transported via HTTP POST to `wshost:8888`.

Listing 9-1: A SOAP request message

```
01  POST /chapter09/JavaWS HTTP/1.1
02  Content-type: text/xml; charset="utf-8"
03  Content-length: nnnn
04  SOAPAction "http://www.acme.com/webservices/getCurrentDate"
05
06  <?xml version = '1.0' encoding = 'utf-8'?>
07  <soap:Envelope
08       xmlns:soap="http://schemas.xmlsoap.org/soap/envelope/"
09       xmlns:xsi="http://www.w3.org/2001/XMLSchema-instance"
10       xmlns:xsd="http://www.w3.org/2001/XMLSchema"
11       soap:encodingStyle=
12                 "http://schemas.xmlsoap.org/soap/encoding/">
13     <soap:Body>
14       <m:getCurrentDate
15            xmlns:m="http://www.acme.com/webservices">
16         <Format xsi:type="xsd:string">YYMMMDD</Format>
17       </m:getCurrentDate>
18     </soap:Body>
19  </soap:Envelope>
```

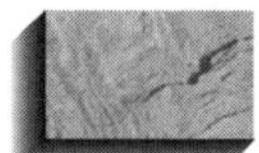

NOTE

The spaces and line breaks make this example easier to read. In practice, SOAP implementations often dispose of such niceties in favor of performance. You may have to use an XML-capable editor or browser when looking at such real-life SOAP messages.

Notes on Listing 9-1:

- **HTTP-specific information (lines 1–5)** This information identifies the URL at the target host, and it also adds a `SOAPAction` entry (line 4) to the HTTP header to identify this message as a SOAP message. (Note that with the SOAP 1.2 specification, this header is no longer required.) The actual message is an XML document.
- **SOAP envelope (lines 7–12 and 19)** The SOAP `Envelope` is the top element in the document. XML namespaces are used to ensure that SOAP-specific elements remain distinct from application-specific elements. They

could also distinguish different versions of the SOAP protocol. In lines 9 and 10, you can see that the XML document is also based on the XML Schema definition.

- **SOAP headers** These are optional, and are not present in this example. If present, a header would have to be the first node placed in the envelope. In our example, the header would appear as follows: `<soap:Header>...</soap:Header>`. Headers are employed for additional processing, such as routing, caching, encrypting, or signing of the SOAP message.
- **SOAP body (lines 13–18)** This is the part of the message that we want the recipient to act upon. The actual payload is in lines 14–17.
- **XML request payload** This describes the operation and its argument values (if any) as follows:
  - **SOAP operation** In our examples, Web Services provide synchronous RPC-like functionality. By convention, the operation that is to be invoked is characterized by the name of the payload element (line 14), and the arguments of the operation (if any) are provided—as named elements and in order—as children nodes of the operation element (line 16).
  - **Argument values** The SOAP `encodingStyle` attribute (line 11) states that values are to be encoded according to a simple encoding scheme defined in the SOAP specification. While this is typically used for RPC-style Web Services interactions, such as ours, it is also possible to reference an XML Schema that describes a representation and use that. Here we will not talk further about such document-style Web Services.

Now that we have seen how the HTTP request encodes an RPC, Listing 9-2 shows how the result of this call would be represented in the HTTP response.

Listing 9-2: A SOAP response message

```
HTTP/1.1 200 OK
Content-Type: text/xml; charset="utf-8"
Content-Length: nnnn

<?xml version = '1.0' encoding = 'utf-8'?>
<soap:Envelope
      xmlns:soap="http://schemas.xmlsoap.org/soap/envelope/"
      xmlns:xsi="http://www.w3.org/2001/XMLSchema-instance"
      xmlns:xsd="http://www.w3.org/2001/XMLSchema">
  <soap:Body>
```

```
11         <getCurrentDateResponse
12              xmlns="http://www.acme.net/webservices">
13            <getCurrentDateResult>
14              22JUL2002
15            </getCurrentDateResult>
16         </getCurrentDateResponse>
17      </soap:Body>
18   </soap:Envelope>
```

Notes on Listing 9-2:

- **HTTP-specific information (lines 1–4)** This is standard HTTP fare.
- **SOAP envelope (lines 6–9 and 18); SOAP headers (none); SOAP body (lines 10 and 17)** The SOAP response has the same structure as the SOAP request: it is composed of an envelope, optional headers, and the body that actually carries the XML payload.
- **XML response payload** Now we have to represent the response of the underlying RPC.
  - **Response node (lines 11 and 16)** This is the top-level node in the payload. By convention, its name is `*Operation*Response`. In our example, it is `getCurrentDateResponse`.
  - **Result node(s)** A remote procedure or function invocation can have a return (or result) value and/or one or more output argument values. If there is a return value, it needs to come first and—by convention—it will have the name `*Operation*Result`. The output argument values (if any) will come next, in order, and will be tagged with their argument name.

    One additional note: In our example, the result was not encoded using the SOAP encoding style; it was just returned as an XML literal.
- **Errors and the SOAP Fault element** If the execution of our RPC Web Service is successful, we will receive back the response and the result embedded in it. But what happens if that is not the case? Different scenarios are possible:
  - **HTTP error** You may be connecting to the wrong host, or the wrong URL, or there may be no Web Service running at the endpoint that you specified. In this case, you would expect to receive an HTTP error directly from the HTTP server.
  - **SOAP error** An error may be encountered when processing a SOAP header, or the SOAP body. In this case, you will receive a SOAP response whose `Body` contains a SOAP `Fault` element. The children of this element—`faultCode`, `faultString`, `faultActor`, and `detail`—will describe further the error that has occurred.

So, what should we take home from this excursion? While we have obtained some insight into how SOAP message communication works, we also hope that you agree that it does not make sense to compose or decompose these kinds of messages by hand. Rather, we would prefer to start with the underlying "provider" pieces (such as Java classes, PL/SQL packages, and session beans) that do the actual work, and have the Web Services part added quasi-automatically for us. Before we can get there, we need to understand the technology that is used to fully describe our Web Services: WSDL.

WSDL

Web Services Description Language is based on XML and provides a standard way for describing everything about our Web Service down to a tee. Well, that is, everything that a client would need to know in order to talk with the Web Service—we will leave aspects of semantics to UDDI and other layers, such as ebXML (*electronic business XML,* a project to standardize XML business specifications). Instead of presenting a sample WSDL file and explaining it (which is more on the dreary side), we prefer to talk about *what* type of information you would find in a WSDL file. Later, we will see how OC4J can even generate WSDL automatically from our deployed Web Services.

Imagine that there were no WSDL, but you needed to tell us how to get to your Web Service—for example, by writing it on the back of an envelope or giving it over the phone. You would have to provide information along the following lines:

- **The nature of the service** In the examples, we are using the *response-request* model (the most common one). However, there might just be a *one-way* message that your client submits (asynchronously) to your Web Service. Or, what if the Web Service itself initiates the communication, either *notifying* us with a message, or *soliciting* us for a response to the Web Service?
- **The transport** We have used HTTP POST in the example. For more secure communication, you may prefer HTTPS. Some might like a simpler access to Web Services with HTTP GET (see also the section on REST in "The REST of the Web Services Story," later in this chapter). Or you may want to send or receive e-mail; or use a messaging service, such as Oracle's Java Message Service (JMS); or even have different transports for the different directions of a request-response or solicit-response interaction.
- **The network address** How do you get to the Web Service? What are its host, port, and endpoint?
- **The operations that make up a Web Service** What are the operation names? What are the names and types of input, result, and output arguments?

What encodings are being used? Are any type definitions (in XML Schema format, for example) needed to encode particular argument types?

Other folks thought much harder about these requirements and came up with more abstract and reusable elements for describing Web Services: the WSDL specification. Its elements are as follows.

- **Types** Provide definitions of types using XML Schema or similar
- **Message** An abstract, typed definition of the data being communicated
- **Operation** Describes an exposed method
- **PortType** A set of operations
- **Binding** Protocol and data format for a PortType
- **Port** A single endpoint created from relating a binding and a network address
- **Service** A collection of endpoints

Do you still want to see a WSDL specification corresponding to our SOAP messages? Well, here it is in Listing 9-3—but do not say that you have not been warned!

Listing 9-3: WSDL specification of a Web Service

```
<?xml version="1.0" encoding="UTF-8"?>
<wsdl:definitions targetNamespace="http://www.acme.com/webservices"
     xmlns="http://schemas.xmlsoap.org/wsdl/"
     xmlns:soap="http://schemas.xmlsoap.org/soap/encoding/"
     xmlns:intf="http://www.acme.com/webservices"
     xmlns:wsdl="http://schemas.xmlsoap.org/wsdl/"
     xmlns:wsdlsoap="http://schemas.xmlsoap.org/wsdl/soap/"
     xmlns:xsd="http://www.w3.org/2001/XMLSchema">
  <wsdl:message name="getCurrentDateRequest">
    <wsdl:part name="format" type="xsd:string"/>
  </wsdl:message>
  <wsdl:message name="getCurrentDateResponse">
    <wsdl:part name="return" type="xsd:string"/>
  </wsdl:message>
  <wsdl:portType name="JavaWS">
    <wsdl:operation name="getCurrentDate" parameterOrder="format">
      <wsdl:input message="intf:getCurrentDateRequest"/>
      <wsdl:output message="intf:getCurrentDateResponse"/>
    </wsdl:operation>
  </wsdl:portType>
  <wsdl:binding name="JavaWSSoapBinding" type="intf:JavaWS">
```

```
    <wsdlsoap:binding style="rpc"
                      transport="http://schemas.xmlsoap.org/soap/http"/>
    <wsdl:operation name="getCurrentDate">
      <wsdlsoap:operation soapAction="http://www.acme.com/webservices"/>
      <wsdl:input>
        <wsdlsoap:body
           encodingStyle="http://schemas.xmlsoap.org/soap/encoding/"
           namespace="getCurrentDate" use="encoded"/>
      </wsdl:input>
      <wsdl:output>
        <wsdlsoap:body
           encodingStyle="http://schemas.xmlsoap.org/soap/encoding/"
           namespace="http://www.acme.com/webservices"
           use="encoded"/>
      </wsdl:output>
    </wsdl:operation>
  </wsdl:binding>
  <wsdl:service name="JavaWSService">
    <wsdl:port binding="intf:JavaWSSoapBinding" name="JavaWS">
      <wsdlsoap:address
         location="http://wshost:8888/chapter09/JavaWS"/>
    </wsdl:port>
  </wsdl:service>
</wsdl:definitions>
```

Let us take stock once more. Clearly, you do not want to be in a business of writing your WSDL specifications by hand. And you would not want to read these just so you can write a Web Service client, either. No need to worry—computers are made to deal with these kinds of things. We will cover later how you can extract the WSDL from the Web Services that you deploy in OC4J, as well as how to easily program your Web Service clients based on WSDL information.

Now we have all of these Web Services with all of their associated WSDL definitions. Given the WSDL, we can get to the service, but how do you get to the WSDL in the first place? Is there some sort of repository or "phone book" to look this up? You bet, and that is what we will look at next.

UDDI

Universal Description, Discovery, and Integration is an electronic registry and repository for Web Services descriptions (through a publishing API) and for Web Services discovery (through an inquiry API). Essentially, you can view UDDI as a set of phone books for Web Services with the following elements:

- **White pages** Contain the address, provider, and contact information of Web Services

- **Yellow pages** Permit searches for specific businesses and services by product, geographic location, service type, and other contextual information
- **Green pages** Contain technical information on the Web Services provided by a business, including the provided interfaces, URL-based discovery, and other technical details

In many simple use cases, such as if you interact with a known Web Service, the WSDL specification of the service will give you all the information you need to interact with the service. Thus, in this chapter we will not cover UDDI any further. However, the OC4J product does provide you with a UDDI registry. Please consult the "Discovering and Publishing Web Services" chapter in *Oracle9iAS Web Services Developer's Guide* to get all the information on how to utilize the UDDI inquiry and the publishing APIs in OC4J.

The REST of the Web Services Story

The Web Services view of the Internet and intranets is one of interconnected, self-describing computing resources. The more traditional notion has been one of data resources that are addressable via URL. Some folks argue that the traditional view, coupled with HTTP POST, PUT, GET, and DELETE operations and with proper decomposition into states and into transitions between these states, provides just as much capability as Web Services—this is the REST (Representational State Transfer) approach. Take online ordering as an example: As you add items to your shopping basket and then proceed to checkout and payment, you transition through a series of states, each of which is represented by a URL, including the final state with your order confirmation. You can inspect or even save these states with your browser.

The REST philosophy points out some limitations of Web Services: While endpoints are directly addressable via URL, individual operations are not. This makes it harder, for example, to cache Web Services results in web caches. Also, one can argue that direct addressability allows one to compose and combine Web Services much more easily. SOAP-style Web Services, on the other hand, require additional orchestration tools and infrastructure in order to combine them. Finally, the REST attitude essentially encapsulates practices that have been around for a while, and thus does not require retooling and relearning.

A Web Services counterargument would be that SOAP, WSDL, and UDDI provide a standard protocol, a standard type representation, as well as definition, discovery, and registry capabilities for Web Services. In REST, these issues need to be addressed ad hoc. For example, try to represent some complex object as an argument in an HTTP URL, never using more than 8,000 characters. Obviously, this approach will break down at some point and is not as conducive for linking different representations into a coherent whole.

Some of the REST criticisms leveraged against Web Services have been addressed in the SOAP 1.2 specification through a new GET binding definition for SOAP.

What is more, SOAP tools are recognizing that, despite its XML roots, SOAP is fundamentally a computer-computer protocol, and not a computer-human one. This means that when you are asked to test a Web Service, you do *not* want to start out decoding WSDL and writing SOAP-compliant XML messages from scratch. Rather, you prefer to use a human-readable form that you fill out in your browser to check out a Web Service. This is exactly what tools will provide you with. Stay tuned, because we revisit this topic when we talk about how you want to verify the Web Services that you have written and deployed.

In summary, if you are holding a hammer in your hand, an awful lot of things may look like a nail. We would like to encourage you to step back and reflect on your situation first. There may be cases where a Web Service may not be called for, but rather a simple servlet that just displays some state in XML or HTML format will do the job. However, if you expect that your component will eventually be linked up with other components and the world at large, by all means, go ahead and turn it into a Web Service.

Next, we will be looking at exactly this problem: how you take a component (some piece of code) and create a Web Service out of it.

Writing Web Services

In OC4J, all Web Services are deployed similarly to other J2EE components. Apache-style Web Services in OC4J are deprecated and only supported for backward compatibility. In the following discussion, we describe creation, deployment, and testing of OC4J J2EE Web Services. Even though Oracle9*i* JDeveloper supports both kinds of Web Services, you may want to ensure that, going forward, you will be using the OC4J J2EE Web Service style.

What Do You Want to Serve Up Today?

We promised that we would show you how to expose Java classes, stateless PL/SQL code, and stateless session beans as Web Services.

Let us first define what it is that we would like to expose as a Web Service. We shall provide three different Web Services based on the three underlying provider concepts: a Java class, a PL/SQL package, and a session bean.

Directory and Sample File Layout

Before starting to write code, let us briefly review the directory layout for this chapter's code.

- **chapter09** Root directory for Web Services examples for Chapter 9 with SH and BAT scripts
  - **src** Source files for Web Services examples

- **META-INF** Deployment info for the `Vendor2` Session Bean
- **purchase** Web Service examples are part of the `Purchase` application
  - **ejb/slsb** Definition of the `Vendor2` Session Bean that is published as a Web Service
  - **ws** Java source code for the Web Service based on a Java class
    - **client** Test code for static and dynamic Web Service clients
    - **proxy** Generated proxy code from client proxy jars

The top-level directory holds all the Windows, UNIX, and SQL scripts and configuration files to run the three sample Web Services:

- **`java_ws*`** Web Service based on a Java class
- **`plsql_ws*`** Web Service based on a PL/SQL package
- **`ejb_ws*`** Web Service based on a stateless session bean

Java code that implements a Web Service is found under `src` in the `purchase.ws` package. Code that is used on the client for Web Service testing is found in `purchase.ws.client`. The client-proxy code generated by OC4J is in the `purchase.ws.proxy` package: the Java files here are provided for reference. They have been extracted from client-side proxy source jars but are not incorporated into the build process for Web Service clients, since we will use the generated client proxy jars directly. Compiled class files are also placed under the `src` hierarchy, whereas generated EAR, JAR, or WSDL files are placed in the `chapter09` top-level directory. We will also be using special names for two absolute directory paths. We use `$CHAPTER09` to describe the location of the `chapter09` directory, and use `$OC4JHOME` for the top-level directory of the unzipped OC4J stand-alone distribution. Depending on your platform, you need to edit either the BAT or the corresponding SH files in order to properly initialize these absolute path locations. Once you have accomplished this, you can automatically run the examples described in this chapter via the batch scripts.

A Java Class

Listing 9-4 defines a Java class `JavaWS` that returns the current date as well as unique sequence numbers.

Listing 9-4: Java class `JavaWS`

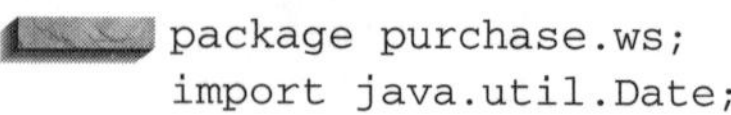

```
package purchase.ws;
import java.util.Date;
```

```
public class JavaWS
{
  public JavaWS() { }  // class must have a public
                       // no-argument constructor, either
                       // explicit or implicit

  public String getCurrentDate(String format)
  { Date d = new Date();
    if (format == null)
       return d.toString();
    else if (format.equalsIgnoreCase("DDMMMYYYY"))
       return getDay(d) + getNameOfMonth(d) + getYear(d);
    else if (format.equalsIgnoreCase("MM/DD/YYYY"))
       return getMonth(d) + "/" + getDay(d) + "/" + getYear(d);
    else if (format.equalsIgnoreCase("DD-MM-YYYY"))
       return getDay(d) + "-" + getMonth(d) + "-" + getYear(d);
    else return d.toString();
  }

  // The following are helper functions that
  // we do not want to expose as Web Services
  public String getMonth(Date d)
  { String m = "0"+ (1 + d.getMonth());
    return m.substring(m.length()-2); }
  public String getNameOfMonth(Date d)
  { return month[d.getMonth()]; }
  private static String[] month =
             {"Jan","Feb","Mar","Apr","May","Jun",
              "Jul","Aug","Sep","Oct","Nov","Dec"};
  public String getYear(Date d)
  { String y = "000" + (1900 + d.getYear());
    return y.substring(y.length()-4); }
  public String getDay(Date d)
  { String t = "0" + (d.getDate());
    return t.substring(t.length()-2); }
  // End of helper functions

   public synchronized  long nextSeq()
   { return m_lastSeq++; }
   private static long m_lastSeq= System.currentTimeMillis();
} // End of JavaWS class
```

Notes on Listing 9-4:

- Using the `getCurrentDate(String)` method, you can implement the Web Service operation `getCurrentDate` that we employed as an example in our discussion on SOAP messages earlier.

- This class contains a number of `public` auxiliary functions: `getDay()`, `getMonth()`, `getNameOfMonth()`, and `getYear()`. We do not want to expose these functions in our Web Service. Since we wrote these functions from scratch, we could of course have given them accessibility other than `public`. However, you may not always have such flexibility: Your class may implement specific interfaces, forcing certain of its methods to be `public`. Or, you may just have been given the class and not its source. Or, your class may not specifically define a method, but rather inherit it from its superclass, and it is that method you want to publish. In all of these cases, the solution is to provide an interface that contains the methods that you want to publish.

In our example, we define the `JavaWSInterface` interface in Listing 9-5.

Listing 9-5: Java interface `JavaWSInterface`

```
package purchase.ws;

public interface JavaWSInterface
{
  public abstract String getCurrentDate(String format);
  public abstract long nextSeq();
} // End of JavaWSInterface
```

Note on Listing 9-5:

- The `nextSeq()` method actually uses the `static` class state. However, this does not mean that we must treat instances of this class as stateful. Statefulness implies that the same class instance is to be reused during the same HTTP session. In our case, we have state on the class and not on the instance. Thus, we will deploy this class as a stateless Web Service.

NOTE
Can you think of reasons why using this Web Service would not guarantee unique sequence numbers? How could you write a Web Service that would give you unique sequence numbers? (Hint: assume that you can utilize a database connection.) How could you reduce the number of database round trips if this Web Service gets invoked rather frequently? What would you expect to happen if `m_lastSeq` is redefined as a nonstatic field, and the Java class `JavaWS` is published as a stateful Web Service implementation?

A PL/SQL Package for Looking Up a Phone Number

Next, we write a PL/SQL package that permits us to look up employee phone numbers based on different criteria, such as employee ID or employee name. The following lookup functions should be implemented by our package.

- If we provide the employee ID, we should get back the employee's phone number, or an error if no employee was found.
- If we provide a last name and a first name, we should get back the employee's phone number, or an error if no employee was found.
- We can also provide a last name and/or a first name with wildcards. If more than one employee was found, we get back a list of last name, first name of matching employees. If none was found, we get back an error.

Listing 9-6 contains the PL/SQL package PHONENO with its package declaration and its package implementation. The name of this file is `phoneno.sql`.

Listing 9-6: PL/SQL package PHONENO

```
/* Recall that employee info is stored in the following table:
   CREATE TABLE EMPLOYEE(
     employeeno   NUMBER(7),
     deptno  NUMBER(5),
     type   VARCHAR2(30),
     lastname      VARCHAR2(30),
     firstname  VARCHAR2(30),
     phone         VARCHAR2(10),
     email         VARCHAR2(30))
 */

create or replace package phoneno as

-- Lookup by employee number.
   function get_employee_by_id(id number) return varchar2;

-- Lookup by last name and first name
   function get_employee_by_name(lname varchar2, fname varchar2)
                return varchar2;
-- Wildcard lookup by last name and first name
   function get_employee_like(lname varchar2, fname varchar2)
               return varchar2;

   type ecurs is ref cursor;
end phoneno;
/

create or replace package body phoneno is
```

```
    function get_employee_by_id(id number) return varchar2 is
       ret varchar2(2000);
       begin
          SELECT 'Phone: ' || phone
            INTO ret
            FROM employee
            WHERE id = employeeno;
          return ret;
       end get_employee_by_id;

    function get_employee_by_name(lname varchar2, fname varchar2)
                return varchar2 is
       ret varchar2(2000);
       begin
          SELECT 'Phone: ' || phone
            INTO ret
            FROM employee
            WHERE lastname = lname AND firstname = fname;
          return ret;
       end get_employee_by_name;

    function get_employee_like(lname varchar2, fname varchar2)
                return varchar2 is
       ret varchar2(2000);
       r   varchar2(255);
       c ecurs;
       begin
         begin
          SELECT 'Phone: ' || phone
            INTO ret
            FROM employee
            WHERE lastname LIKE lname AND firstname LIKE fname;
          return ret;
         end;
         exception
          WHEN TOO_MANY_ROWS
          THEN
          begin
            ret := 'More than one employee matches search.\n';
            OPEN c FOR SELECT '    ' || lastname || ', ' || firstname
                           || ' [' || employeeno || ']\n'
                       FROM employee
                       WHERE lastname LIKE lname AND firstname LIKE fname;
            LOOP
               FETCH c INTO r;
               EXIT WHEN c%NOTFOUND;
               ret := ret || r;
            END LOOP;
            return ret;
          end;
       end get_employee_like;
end phoneno;
/
```

NOTE
If you have not yet installed the sample schema, then go to the directory with the code that was shown in the Introduction of this book and run the `poexample.sql` *and the* `LoadPO.SQL` *scripts as per the instruction given in these scripts. In this chapter, we assume that you have installed these into the schema SCOTT using the password TIGER. If you have chosen a different user and password, you will have to replace these with your own in the sample command lines.*

From the `chapter09` directory, start the Oracle SQL*Plus utility and connect to SCOTT with the password TIGER, load the SQL script `phoneno.sql` to create the PHONENO package, and then quit SQL*Plus:

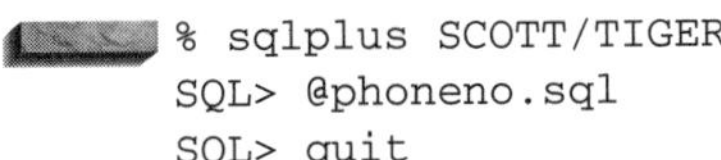

```
% sqlplus SCOTT/TIGER
SQL> @phoneno.sql
SQL> quit
```

A Stateless Session Bean—Vendor2

We slightly modify the `Vendor` stateless session bean from Chapter 6. Our variant is called `Vendor2`. We would like to publish this session bean as a Web Service. Listing 9-7 gives the remote interface for the `Vendor2` bean.

Listing 9-7: Stateless session bean `Vendor2`

```
package purchase.ejb.slsb;
import javax.ejb.EJBObject;
import java.rmi.RemoteException;

public interface Vendor2 extends EJBObject
{

  void createVendor(int vendorNo,
                    String name, String address,
                    String city, String state,
                    String zip, String country) throws RemoteException;

  String getName(int vendorNo) throws RemoteException;
  String getAddress(int vendorNo) throws RemoteException;
  String getCity(int vendorNo) throws RemoteException;
  String getState(int vendorNo) throws RemoteException;
  String getZip(int vendorNo) throws RemoteException;
  String getCountry(int vendorNo) throws RemoteException;
}  // End of Vendor2 remote interface
```

Please see under `chapter09/src/purchase/ejb/slsb` for the home interface and the implementation of this bean. Consult your operating system–specific `ejb_ws` script file for the specifics on compiling and jarring up the bean components and their associated deployment descriptors. Before proceeding further, you may also want to ensure that you have run the `poexample.sql` and `LoadPO.SQL` scripts and that the `jdbc/OracleDS` data source is set up. If you have already run the PL/SQL example successfully, you are ready to go.

It is time to step back and reflect for a second. We have three pieces of code: a Java class, a PL/SQL package, and a session bean (with an additional interface). How do we now transform each one of these into a Web Service?

The basic idea is that we use a tool called the Web Services Assembler to turn these into J2EE components that can be deployed like other web applications. Thus, we will have to provide information to the Web Services Assembler that describes *what* should be exposed as a Web Service, and *how*. For example, in the case of our PL/SQL package, an additional required piece of information is the database connection that the Web Service should use to connect and properly invoke the requested PL/SQL function or procedure. The Web Services Assembler packages everything up into EAR files that can be deployed into OC4J just like any other J2EE web application.

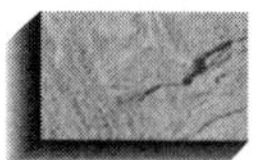

NOTE

We are demonstrating how Web Services are built with OC4J version 9.0.3. The 9.0.3 release uses the Web Services Assembler tool to directly create deployable EAR files for Web Services. Before 9.0.3, the Java `ant` tool was used for building EAR files. Another limitation was that in order to expose PL/SQL Web Services, a Java interface always had to be provided manually. We strongly suggest you use OC4J 9.0.3 or later for writing Web Services—it will simplify your task considerably.

Java Class as a Web Service

The `java_ws_config.xml` file in the `chapter09` directory controls the operation of the Web Service Assembler tool for this Web Service. Let us take a look at Listing 9-8 to see how the Java class `JavaWS` is to be turned into a Web Service.

Listing 9-8: Configuration file for Java class Web Service

```
<web-service>

<display-name>Java Class as a Web Service</display-name>
```

```
<description>
Exposing the Java class purchase.ws.JavaWS as a Web Service
under the endpoint:  /chapter09/JavaWS.

This will result in the generation of java_ws.ear, which can be
deployed in OC4J.
</description>

<!-- The full name of the .ear file that is to be generated.
     This .ear file contains the Web Service archive (.war)
     file that will be deployed. -->
<destination-path>./java_ws.ear</destination-path>

<!-- A directory for the assembler tool to create temporary files -->
<temporary-directory>./tmp</temporary-directory>

<!-- The servlet context under which the Web Service is accessed -->
<context>/chapter09</context>

<!-- Our Java-based Web Service is stateless
     Use the tag  <stateful-java-service>  instead if you need to
     define a stateful Web Service -->
<stateless-java-service>
   <!-- The URL under the servlet context defined above
        where the Web Service can be accessed.  -->
   <uri>/JavaWS</uri>

   <!-- the interface defines the methods that are exposed. -->
   <interface-name>purchase.ws.JavaWSInterface</interface-name>
   <!-- The Java class that is to be accessed as a Web Service -->
   <class-name>purchase.ws.JavaWS</class-name>

   <!-- Location of the Java class files for this Web Service -->
   <java-resource>./src</java-resource>

</stateless-java-service>

<!-- define additional Web Services as required -->

</web-service>
```

Before we can invoke the Web Services Assembler tool, we need to compile the Java classes and interfaces that are used by the Web Service. Here we do this from the `chapter09` directory:

```
javac -d src/  src/purchase/ws/JavaWS*.java
```

This results in the `JavaWS` class, as well as the `JavaWSInterface` class that controls the visible methods. Now we can use the Web Services Assembler tool to create a deployable EAR file:

```
java -jar $OC4JHOME/webservices/lib/WebServicesAssembler.jar \
    -config java_ws_config.xml
```

The resulting `java_ws.ear` file contains the following files and directories:

- **java_ws.ear** Java Web Service, ready to be deployed
  - **META-INF** Contains descriptions of application modules
    - **application.xml** Describes the J2EE application that is based on the Web Service
  - **java_ws_web.war** Web application that comprises the Web Service
    - **index.html** Index page for deployed services at `http://<host>:8888/chapter09`
    - **WEB-INF** Contains the web application
      - **web.xml** Defines web application as a Web Service implemented by a Java class
      - **classes/purchase/ws** Package that implements the Java class Web Service

Now all that remains to be done is to deploy `java_ws.ear` to OC4J:

```
java -jar $OC4JHOME/j2ee/home/admin.jar                     \
      ormi://localhost:23791 admin <your_oc4j_admin_password> \
      -deploy  -file java_ws.ear   -deploymentName java_ws
```

Finally, you bind the web application to a port:

```
java -jar $OC4JHOME/j2ee/home/admin.jar                     \
      ormi://localhost:23791 admin <your_oc4j_admin_password> \
     -bindWebApp java_ws java_ws_web http-web-site /chapter09
```

You can test your Web Service now by connecting your browser to http://localhost:8888/chapter09/JavaWS.

You may want to skip forward to the "Testing Web Services" section for a description of what you can find on this page.

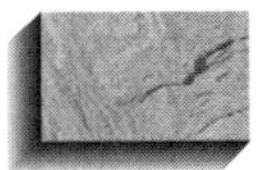

NOTE
In a full iAS installation, you need to use Oracle Enterprise Manager or the `dcmctl` command-line utility to deploy EAR files.

Let us now turn to the remaining usage cases. Next, we will examine how we can turn a PL/SQL package into a Web Service—again with the help of the Web Service Assembler tool.

PL/SQL Package as a Web Service

We assume you have installed the PHONENO PL/SQL package into the SCOTT schema. The `plsql_ws_config.xml` file (see Listing 9-9) is available in the `chapter09` directory. We use it to control the creation of a Web Service based on a PL/SQL package.

Listing 9-9: Configuration file for a PL/SQL Web Service

```
<web-service>

<!-- The following is the same boilerplate that we used for
     the Java class Web Service. The only difference is the
     name of the .ear file and location of the service. -->

<display-name>PL/SQL package as a Web Service</display-name>
<description>
Exposing the PL/SQL package PHONENO as a Web Service
under the endpoint:  /chapter09/PlsqlWS.

This will result in the generation of plsql_ws.ear, which can be
deployed in OC4J.
</description>

<destination-path>./plsql_ws.ear</destination-path>
<temporary-directory>./tmp</temporary-directory>
<context>/webservices</context>

<!-- The service is stateless and based on a PL/SQL package. -->
<stateless-stored-procedure-java-service>

  <!-- We also have seen this before: The URL under the
       servlet context defined above where the Web Service
       can be accessed.  -->
  <uri>/PlsqlWS</uri>
```

```
  <!-- The following information is required during Web Services
       assembly for being able to properly invoke the JPublisher
       tool.  We need to define:
        - the PL/SQL "part": connection information, package name
        - the Java "part": package name (JPublisher can automatically
                           generate a Java class name based on the
                           PL/SQL package name) -->
  <jar-generation>

    <!-- Connection information - adjust this for your database. -->
    <schema>scott/tiger</schema>
    <db-url>jdbc:oracle:thin:@localhost:1521:orcl</db-url>
    <!-- PL/SQL package information.  By default, this is
         also used for the Java class name -->
    <db-pkg-name>PhoneNo</db-pkg-name>

    <!-- Java package information -->
    <prefix>purchase.ws</prefix>
  </jar-generation>

  <!-- We also need to access the database at runtime.
       We specify the connection in form of a JNDI data source. -->
  <database-JNDI-name>/jdbc/OracleDS</database-JNDI-name>

</stateless-stored-procedure-java-service>

</web-service>
```

Ensure that the information in the `<schema>` and `<db-url>` tags reflects your configuration. Specifically, you need to be able to connect to the database schema that contains the PHONENO package using the username/password and the JDBC URL you provide here.

If the JNDI data source specified in `<database-JNDI-name>` is not yet available in OC4J, you need to define it. Refer to "Configuring the OC4J data-sources.xml File" in Chapter 2 for more information.

Here we assume that the data source `jdbc/OracleDS` has been properly set up (in particular, if this data source is emulated, it has to be defined in an `ejb-location`) and also connects to the same schema into which you have installed the PHONENO package.

As before, you run the Web Services Assembler tool against the configuration file (here `plsql_ws_config.xml`) in order to create a deployable EAR file:

```
java -jar $OC4JHOME/webservices/lib/WebServicesAssembler.jar \
     -config plsql_ws_config.xml
```

Now you can deploy the generated `plsql_ws.ear` file into OC4J. The following two steps accomplish deployment and binding to an HTTP endpoint:

```
java -jar $OC4JHOME/j2ee/home/admin.jar                  \
      ormi://localhost:23791 admin <your_oc4j_admin_password> \
      -deploy  -file plsql_ws.ear   -deploymentName plsql_ws
```

```
java -jar $OC4JHOME/j2ee/home/admin.jar                  \
      ormi://localhost:23791 admin <your_oc4j_admin_password> \
     -bindWebApp plsql_ws plsql_ws_web http-web-site /chapter09
```

Similarly to before, you can now test the Web Service by connecting your browser to http://localhost:8888/chapter09/PlsqlWS.

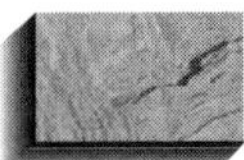

NOTE

When we bound the PL/SQL Web Service, we removed our previous `JavaWS` Web Service, since we are specifying the same context root `/chapter09` for both. To avoid this, you can either rename this root context for each sample or assemble all services at the same time—see the file `all_ws_config.xml` and its corresponding batch scripts.

Session Bean as a Web Service

Deploying a stateless session bean as a Web Service is also a cinch. For convenience, we have provided a variant of the stateless session bean `Vendor` from Chapter 6 in the file `Vendor2.jar` in the `chapter09` sample directory. If you want to compile and jar this bean from scratch, you need to first set up your environment, as described in the "Static Web Services Client-Side Proxy" section of this chapter.

The configuration file `ejb_ws_config.xml` is provided in Listing 9-10. It accounts for the fact that we are turning a session bean into a Web Service. Other entries should look rather familiar to you by now.

Listing 9-10: Configuration file for session bean `web-service`

```
<web-service>

<!-- More of the same boilerplate... -->
<display-name>Session Bean as a Web Service</display-name>
<description>
Exposing the stateless Session Bean purchase.ejb.slsb.Vendor2
as a Web Service under the endpoint:  /chapter09/EjbWS.
```

```
This will result in the generation of ejb_ws.ear, which can be
deployed in OC4J.
</description>

<destination-path>./ejb_ws.ear</destination-path>
<temporary-directory>./tmp</temporary-directory>
<context>/chapter09</context>

<!-- This service is based on a stateless session bean. -->
<stateless-session-ejb-service>

  <!-- As before: the Web Service URL under the servlet context -->
  <uri>/EjbWS</uri>

  <!-- Location and name of the session bean that is to be
       deployed as a Web Service -->
  <path>./Vendor2.jar</path>
  <ejb-name>Vendor2</ejb-name>
</stateless-session-ejb-service>

<!-- define additional Web Services as required -->

</web-service>
```

Once more we invoke the Web Services Assembly tool to generate an `ejb_ws .ear` file:

```
java -jar $OC4JHOME/webservices/lib/WebServicesAssembler.jar \
     -config $CHAPTER09/ejb_ws_config.xml
```

You are now rather familiar with the deployment of the generated `ejb_ws.ear` file to OC4J:

```
java -jar $OC4JHOME/j2ee/home/admin.jar                    \
      ormi://localhost:23791 admin <your_oc4j_admin_password> \
      -deploy  -file ejb_ws.ear   -deploymentName ejb_ws

java -jar $OC4JHOME/j2ee/home/admin.jar                    \
      ormi://localhost:23791 admin <your_oc4j_admin_password> \
     -bindWebApp ejb_ws ejb_ws_web http-web-site /chapter09
```

In the next section, you will learn how to test your Web Service from its home page: http://localhost:8888/chapter09/EjbWS.

Testing Web Services

How can you quickly test your Web Service after deploying it? You could write and run a client for your Web Service (we will get to that in a minute). The quickest way is to use the Web Service GET binding that is provided in OC4J release 9.0.3 and later. This is yet another reason why you may want to use a 9.0.3 or later OC4J distribution.

The Web Services Assembler tool automatically creates a context root page when we deploy a Web Service. In our case, this page is called `/chapter09`. From this page you can get to individual Web Service endpoints or "home" pages, such as: `/chapter09/JavaWS`, `/chapter09/PlsqlWS`, or `/chapter09/EjbWS`. When you POST a SOAP message to the endpoint, you are invoking the Web Service. If you issue a GET request to the same page, you retrieve the Web Service's home page.

From this home page, you can reach a method invocation page for operation of Web Services. In the `JavaWS` example, you can get to the following invocation pages:

http://<host name>:8888/chapter09/JavaWS?operation=getCurrentDate

http://<host name>:8888/chapter09/JavaWS?operation=nextSeq.

The invocation pages contain a form with the names and types of the various parameters. Enter the parameter values in the provided fields and click the Invoke button to test your Web Service. You will see the result of your invocation in a new window. That's all there is to it!

You can also directly invoke a particular Web Service through HTTP GET. In this case, you must provide the operation name as well as the parameter values in the URL. The following is an example:

```
http://<host>:8888/chapter09/JavaWS?invoke=getCurrentDate&param0=DDMMMYYYY
```

Web Service invocation through HTTP GET resembles the REST philosophy. However, it has its limitations: At this point, neither arrays nor complex arguments are supported. Also note that you may see many arguments of type `java.math.BigDecimal`, since the Oracle NUMBER type is mapped in your PL/SQL Web Services to `BigDecimal` by default.

The Web Service home page also gives you options to retrieve the WSDL for the particular Web Service, as well as a JAR file with client-side proxy code. These are just the things we will make use of next when writing the Web Service client.

Writing a Web Services Client

If you know all the information for your Web Service ahead of time, you can write a static Web Service client. If the information is only known at runtime, you need to utilize dynamic capabilities for invoking the Web Service. We will start out writing static clients. For all of our examples, the Web Service information is known statically ahead of time. What is more, given one of our Web Service's endpoints, we can retrieve the WSDL specification as follows:

```
http://<host name>:8888/chapter09/JavaWS?WSDL
```

You can either save the WSDL to a file, such as java_ws.wsdl in this example, or just remember the URL and point to it. More interestingly—and immediately useful—you can retrieve a JAR file containing complete client-side proxy code, including a stub for invoking the OC4J Web Service as follows:

```
http://<host name>:8888/chapter09/JavaWS?proxy_jar
```

Save the client-proxy JAR to the file java_ws_proxy.jar. You may be curious about what the name of the proxy class is. If the Web Service is defined in a class foo.bar.Baz, then the generated proxy class to access this service is, by default, foo.bar.**proxy.**Baz**Proxy**. In our Java class Web Service example, the class defining the service is actually the *interface* purchase.ws.JavaWSInterface. Consequently, the proxy class in our JAR file is purchase.ws.proxy .JavaWSProxy.

Now consider our PL/SQL sample for a moment. The Java class that implements the service wraps the PL/SQL wrapper class. We specified the package purchase .ws and the name PhoneNo for it. Thus, according to our logic, we will now end up with the proxy class purchase.ws.proxy.PhoneNoProxy.

Finally, you can also obtain the corresponding source code JAR for the client proxy with the following:

```
http://<host name>:8888/chapter09/JavaWS?proxy_source
```

Java sources for the proxies can also be admired in the src/purchase/ws/ proxy directory (slightly renamed). Next, we will see how easy it is to write Java clients using these proxies.

Static Web Services Client-Side Proxy

The client-side proxy file contains everything you need for connecting to the Web Service and for interacting with it via SOAP. Using it is as easy as creating an instance of the proxy—for example purchase.ws.proxy.JavaWSInterfaceProxy— and then calling the methods on this instance. You may already have guessed that in this case the methods are the same as on purchase.ws.JavaWSInterface. The client test code in Listing 9-11 demonstrates this for the sample JavaWS Web Service.

Listing 9-11: Test code for JavaWS client-side proxy

```
package purchase.ws.client;
import purchase.ws.proxy.JavaWSInterfaceProxy;

public class JavaWSTest
{
  public static void main(String[] args) throws Exception
```

```
  { JavaWSInterfaceProxy proxy = new JavaWSInterfaceProxy();
    System.out.println("getCurrentDate(\"DDMMMYYYY\") = "+
                       proxy.getCurrentDate("DDMMMYYYY"));
    System.out.println("getCurrentDate(\"MM/DD/YYYY\") = "+
                       proxy.getCurrentDate("MM/DD/YYYY"));
    System.out.println("getCurrentDate(\"No format.\") = "+
                       proxy.getCurrentDate("No format."));
    for (int i=0; i<4; i++) {
      System.out.println("nextSeq() = " + proxy.nextSeq());
    }
  }
}
```

Before compiling and running the client code, you want to set up your CLASSPATH to contain the following locations and libraries:

- **Under `$CHAPTER09`** `src` (JavaWSTest source) and `java_ws_proxy.jar` (client-side proxy class)
- **Under `$OC4JHOME/soap/lib`** `wsdl.jar` and `soap.jar`
- **Under `$OC4JHOME/lib`** `xmlparserv2.jar`, `jsse.jar`, `tools.jar`, and `dsv2.jar`
- **Under `$OC4JHOME/jlib`** `javax-ssl-1_1.jar` and `jssl-1_1.jar`
- **Under `$OC4JHOME/j2ee/home/lib`** `http_client.jar`, `ejb.jar`, `jasper.jar`, `mail.jar`, `activation.jar`, `jnet.jar`, and `jndi.jar`

This should comprise all the libraries that you may need for compiling or running Web Services client code, whether in conjunction with proxy jars or if you are working with dynamic clients. If you are using a client proxy other than `java_ws_proxy.jar`, do not forget to include it with the preceding libraries.

Now compiling and running the Web Services client code is straightforward:

```
javac  -d src  src/purchase/ws/client/JavaWSTest.java
java   purchase.ws.client.JavaWSTest
```

Using WSDL for Creating Web Services Clients

If the Web Service you want to invoke does not originate from OC4J, our trick for getting the client-proxy JAR will not work. In this case, you need to work off of the WSDL specification for the service. Given the WSDL, the Oracle 9.0.3 Web Services Assembler tool can generate a client proxy for you (see Chapter 8 in *Oracle9iAS Web Services Developer's Guide Release 3 (9.0.3)*). Alternatively, you can utilize Oracle9*i* JDeveloper for generating a client based on WSDL. Or, you may be able to invoke your service dynamically. This is described next.

Dynamic Web Services Clients

If you do not know your Web Service's WSDL ahead of time, your Web Services client needs to utilize dynamic invocation. The good news is that Oracle J2EE and SOAP libraries provide you with the capabilities to create such a dynamic client based on the WSDL information.

The following code permits you to dynamically invoke a Web Service. You need to provide the URL to the service's WSDL information. The additional arguments to the `JavaWSDynamicTest` client are the name of the operation you want to invoke and the input arguments for the service. After successfully invoking the Web Service dynamically, you should see the SOAP return message from the service. The following is the invocation line:

```
java purchase.ws.client.JavaWSDynamicTest   \
     <wsdl-url> <operation> <param_1> ... <param_n>
```

The Java resource /`purchase/ws/client/java_ws_dynamic.properties` contains general properties for the dynamic client. For example:

```
http.proxyHost=<name-of-HTTP-proxy>
http.proxyPort=<port-for-HTTP-proxy>
```

Listing 9-12 contains the code for the dynamic client.

Listing 9-12: Dynamic `JavaWS` client code

```
package purchase.ws.client;
import java.util.*;
import java.io.*;
import java.net.*;
import oracle.j2ee.ws.client.*;
import oracle.j2ee.ws.client.wsdl.*;
import org.apache.soap.util.xml.QName;
import org.apache.soap.util.xml.XMLJavaMappingRegistry;

/***
  Invocation:
    java purchase.ws.client.JavaWSDynamicTest \
         <wsdl-url> <operation> <param1> ... <paramn>

  The java resource:
    purchase/ws/client/java_ws_dynamic.properties
  contains general properties for this dynamic client, for example:
    http.proxyHost=<name-of-HTTP-proxy>
    http.proxyPort=<port-for-HTTP-proxy>
***/
```

```
public class JavaWSDynamicTest
{
  public static void main(String[] args) throws Exception
  { URL wsdlURL = new URL(args[0]);
    String operation = args[1];
    Object[] params = new Object[args.length-2];
    String[] pNames = new String[params.length];
    for (int i=0; i<params.length; i++) params[i]=args[i+2];

    WebServiceProxyFactory wspf= new WebServiceProxyFactory();
    InputStream ps = JavaWSDynamicTest.class
      .getResourceAsStream("java_ws_dynamic.properties");
    Properties props = new Properties();
    props.load(ps);
    ps.close();
    wspf.setProperties(props);

    WebServiceProxy wsp = wspf.createWebServiceProxy(wsdlURL);
    List ol = wsp.getPortType().getOperations();
    Operation op = null;
    for (int i=0; i<ol.size(); i++) {
        Operation o = (Operation) ol.get(i);
        if (o.getName().equals(operation))
        { op=o; break; }
    }
    if (op==null)
       throw new
         IllegalArgumentException("Operation "+operation+" not found.");

    String opName = op.getName();
    Iterator it = op.getInput().getMessage()
                  .getParts().values().iterator();
    int count = 0;
    while (it.hasNext())
      pNames[count++] =  ((Part) it.next()).getName();

    WebServiceMethod wsm = wsp.getMethod(opName);
    Object res = wsm.invoke(pNames, params);
    System.out.println("WSDL is taken from: " + wsdlURL);
    System.out.print  ("Invoking operation: " + opName + "(");
    for (int i=0; i<params.length; i++) {
      System.out.print(pNames[i] + "=\"" + params[i] + "\"");
      if (i<params.length-1) System.out.print(", ");
      }
    System.out.println(")");
    System.out.println("Returned value    : " + res);
  }
}
```

Before compiling and running this program, set up your CLASSPATH as explained in the previous section, "Static Web Services Client-Side Proxy." Now you can compile as follows:

```
javac  -d src  src/purchase/ws/client/JavaWSDynamicTest.java
```

You are now ready to test the dynamic client. In the first invocation, we use the WSDL description that you have previously saved to the local file `java_ws.wsdl`.

```
java purchase.ws.client.JavaWSDynamicTest         \
     file:java_ws.wsdl    getCurrentDate DDMMMYYYY
```

In the second invocation, we obtain the WSDL directly from the Web Service's WSDL page:

```
java purchase.ws.client.JavaWSDynamicTest         \
     http://<host name>:8888/chapter09/JavaWS?WSDL   nextSeq
```

Of course, the `JavaWSDynamicTest` class has quite a few shortcomings at this point. The biggest is that it only works with Web Services that expect `String` input parameters. Moreover, it does not detect a mismatch either in type or in number between actual and expected input arguments. You may want to try your hand at improving these shortcomings. For further information, see Chapter 11 of *Oracle9iAS Web Services Developer's Guide Release 3 (9.0.3).*

More on Writing Web Services

Let us briefly consider a couple of topics related to Web Services that we have not touched upon but that you will likely encounter.

Dealing with Complex Types

Primitive and basic Java types, such as `int`, `Integer`, `String`, `float`, `Double`, and so on, can be used in the code that we intend to turn into Java Web Services. In addition, a complex Java type is supported if it fits the JavaBean pattern, meaning:

- It contains a public no-argument constructor.
- It exposes bean properties (or attributes) either as public fields or as public get*Xxx* and set*Xxx* methods. Moreover, the order of setting properties on a bean instance should not matter. Methods that do not represent properties should not use this naming pattern.

If the Web Service uses such "complex" types, then the generated client-side proxy code will also contain corresponding Java bean classes for arguments of these types.

If your Java type is neither a basic type nor a JavaBean, nor an array of such a type, you have to write your own custom *serializer* and *deserializer* classes for your Java type and register them with your service application.

Providing Secure Web Services

Since your Web Services are J2EE applications, you will be using the same mechanisms for security. In addition, you need to set corresponding properties in your Web Services, such as the password and username for basic HTTP authentication, and so forth, depending on the security mechanism that you have specified for the service you are accessing. You can set these properties as Java system properties, or you can call the `_setTransportProperties` method on the client-side proxy class to establish them. For a full list of these properties, see Chapter 8 of *Oracle9iAS Web Services Developer's Guide Release 3 (9.0.3)*.

Widening the Gamut of Web Services

You learned how to convert Java classes, PL/SQL packages, and stateless session beans into Web Services. Note that this does not cover all of the possibilities that you have. You are also able to accomplish the following:

- Write a document-style Web Service instead of an RPC-style Web Service (see Chapter 6 of *Oracle9iAS Web Services Developer's Guide Release 3 (9.0.3)*).
- Write a JMS Web Service that is based on a message-driven bean (see Chapter 7 of *Oracle9iAS Web Services Developer's Guide Release 3 (9.0.3)*).
- Access Oracle Advanced Queuing. While AQ is not fully exposed as a Web Service, you can access AQ functionality by sending SOAP messages to the AQ servlet (see *Oracle9i Application Developer's Guide – Advanced Queuing* for more information).

It is easy to expose your own code—both Java and PL/SQL—as a Web Service. You should expect an increasing number of Oracle's APIs and services to become available as Web Services also, permitting you to fully exploit the new paradigm of distributed computing services for the applications and components that you are creating right now and in the future.

This chapter has introduced you to Web Services, including the SOAP, WSDL, and UDDI specifications. You have learned how to program, test, and deploy Web Services based on Java classes, PL/SQL packages, and stateless session beans. And you have seen how to write static as well as dynamic Web Service clients.

Fundamentally, OC4J Web Services are based on the OC4J servlet technology, which serves up HTTP pages. We saw how communication is choreographed by the SOAP protocol and how services can be identified through WSDL and called via client proxies. Have you become curious about the underpinnings of Web Services in OC4J? Read on—Chapter 10 has all the good stuff on OC4J servlets!

CHAPTER 10

Developing Web Applications

In Part II, you learned how to build J2EE business-tier components and deploy them to Oracle9*i*AS Containers For J2EE (OC4J). Recall that business components are made of business logic. In J2EE, Enterprise JavaBeans (EJBs) handle the business logic. You developed EJBs in Chapters 5, 6, and 7. In this chapter, you will develop Java servlets and deploy them to OC4J.

OC4J enables you to develop standard J2EE-compliant applications. Applications are packaged in standard Enterprise Archive (EAR) deployment files, which include standard Web Archive (WAR) files to deploy the Web modules, and JAR files for any EJB and client application modules in the application.

The most important thing to understand about Java servlet development under OC4J is how the web application is built and deployed. A web application is a dynamic extension of a web server. A web application can consist of dynamic web pages containing various types of markup language (HTML, XML, and so on) as well as static resources such as images. A web application can also be the endpoint of a fine-grained Web Service that is used by the dynamic web pages, about which you learned in Chapter 9.

This chapter introduces servlets, provides examples of servlets, and reuses the applications and concepts developed earlier in this book. A servlet is a Java program that runs in a J2EE application server, such as OC4J. A servlet is the server-side counterpart of a Java applet. Servlets are one of the four application component types of a J2EE application, the others being applets and client application programs on the client side, and EJBs on the server side. Servlets are managed by the OC4J servlet container, whereas EJBs are managed by the OC4J EJB container. These containers, together with the JSP container, form the core of OC4J. We also briefly discuss how you can use servlets in a J2EE application to address some server-side programming issues.

Specifically, you will learn about the following:

- Using servlets in web applications
- Basic servlet concepts, including the servlet architecture; the servlet container; filtering; the servlet context, request, and response objects; and the servlet's life cycle
- Servlet sessions
- Designing a web applications using servlets
- Developing servlets containing EJBs
- Configuring Oracle9*i*AS TopLink and servlets to run on OC4J
- Deploying applications to OC4J

The concepts that you learn in this chapter will enable you to develop web applications that can also be applied to the other modules in this book, such as JavaServer Pages, Enterprise JavaBeans, and Web Services.

Servlets in Web Applications

A few years ago, the most popular way to create dynamic web content was with Common Gateway Interface (CGI) programs. CGI is a gateway between a web server and a CGI script; however, CGI programs can degrade system performance on high-volume web sites since the web server must spawn a new process each time a CGI program is invoked. In early 1997, Sun Microsystems introduced a standard API called Java Servlets, for developing server-side Java components. One of the greatest advantages of a servlet over a CGI program, is that a servlet can be launched once to service many clients. Upon new requests, a servlet does not spawn a new process, thus processor overhead is much lower.

Servlets have additional advantages over CGI and other earlier models of server-side web application development:

- A servlet stays in memory and does not spawn a new process. Therefore, the overhead of creating a new process for each request is removed.
- A single instance of a servlet can answer many requests concurrently.
- A servlet runs in a servlet container, a restrictive sandbox that allows secure use of untrusted and potentially harmful servlets.
- Servlets are fully integrated into the J2EE framework.
- Java servlets are supported natively by most web servers such Netscape, Sun, IBM, and Apache. Because servlets are written in Java, they are portable to any platform that has a Java Virtual Machine (JVM) and a web server that supports servlets.

Basic Servlet Concepts

Servlet technology provides developers a consistent mechanism for extending the functionality of a web server and for accessing business systems. Servlets have access to the entire family of Java APIs, including the JDBC API to access enterprise databases. Servlets can also access a library of HTTP-specific calls and receive all the benefits of the mature Java language, including portability, performance, reusability, and crash protection.

As mentioned earlier, the OC4J servlet container, OC4J EJB container, and OC4J JSP container form the core of OC4J. JSPs are another server-side component type. JSP pages also involve the servlet container, because the JSP container itself is a servlet and is therefore executed by the servlet container. The JSP container translates JSP pages into page implementation classes, which are executed by the JSP container but function similarly to servlets.

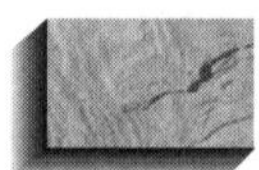

NOTE
Refer to Chapter 11 of this book, the Oracle9iAS Containers For J2EE User's Guide, and the Oracle9iAS Containers For J2EE Support for JavaServer Pages Reference, for more information about JavaServer Pages.

Most servlets render HTML text, which is then sent back to the client for display by the web browser, or is sent on to other components in the application. Servlets can also generate XML, to encapsulate data, and send this to the client or to other components.

HTTP Essentials

Before we can start discussing servlets in further detail, you need to know some basics of Hypertext Transfer Protocol (HTTP), the protocol that is used by a World Wide Web client (for example, a browser) to send a request to a web server.

HTTP is request-response oriented. An HTTP request consists of a request method, a uniform resource identifier (URI), header fields, and a body (which can be empty). Most web clients use HTTP to communicate with a J2EE server. HTTP defines the requests that a client can send to a server and responses that the server can send in reply. Each request contains a uniform resource locator (URL), which is a string that identifies a web component or a static object such as an HTML page or image file.

The J2EE server converts an HTTP request to an HTTP request object and delivers it to the web component identified by the request URL. An HTTP response contains a result code as well as header fields and a body.

Basic Servlet Architecture

A servlet is a Java class that implements the `javax.servlet.Servlet` interface. Most servlets, however, extend one of the standard implementations of that interface, namely `javax.servlet.GenericServlet` and `javax.servlet.http.HttpServlet`, as shown in Figure 10-1.

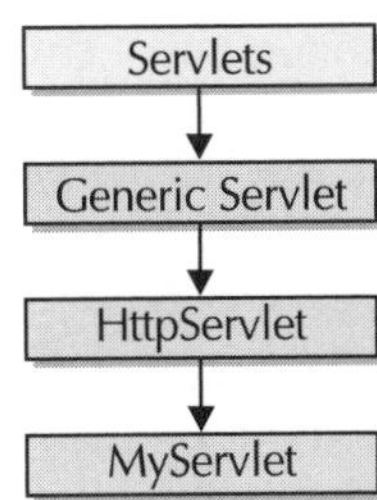

FIGURE 10-1. *Standard servlet interfaces*

There are two main types of servlets:

- **Generic servlets** Extend `javax.servlet.GenericServlet`. Generic servlets are protocol independent and do not contain any support for HTTP or any other transport protocol.
- **HTTP servlets** Extend `javax.servlet.HttpServlet`. HTTP servlets have built-in support for the HTTP protocol and are usually used in browser environments. Servlets that extend `HttpServlet` are designed for an HTTP environment.

For both types of servlets, use the *constructor* method `init()` to initialize resources and the *destructor* method `destroy()` to deallocate resources.

All servlets (generic or HTTP) must implement a `service()` method, which handles requests made to the servlet. For generic servlets, you simply override the `service()` method to provide routines for handling requests. HTTP servlets provide a `service()` method that automatically routes the request to another method in the servlet based on which HTTP transfer method is used. HTTP servlets extend `HttpServlet` and override the `doGet()` or `doPost()` method (or both), depending on whether the data are sent by `GET()` requests or by `POST()` requests.

The following are the methods of a servlet:

- `init(ServletConfig config)`
- `service(ServletRequest req, ServletResponse res)`
- `destroy()`

To initialize a servlet, a server application loads the particular servlet's class and creates an instance by calling the no argument constructor. Then, it calls the servlet's `init(ServletConfig config)` method. The servlet should perform one-time setup procedures in this method and store the `ServletConfig` object so that it can be retrieved later by calling the servlet's `getServletConfig()` method. The implementation provided in `GenericServlet` handles this automatically. Servlets that extend `GenericServlet` (or its subclass `HttpServlet`) should call `super.init(config)` at the beginning of the `init()` method to make use of this feature. The `ServletConfig` object contains servlet parameters and a reference to the servlet's `ServletContext`. The `init()` method is guaranteed to be called only once during the servlet's life cycle. It does not need to be thread-safe because the `service()` method will not be called until the call to `init()` returns.

When the servlet is initialized, its `service(ServletRequest req, ServletResponse res)` method is called for every request to the servlet. The method is called concurrently (that is, multiple threads may call this method at the same time), so it should be implemented in a thread-safe manner.

When the servlet needs to be unloaded, the `destroy()` method is called. There may still be threads that execute the `service()` method when the `destroy()` method is called, so the `destroy()` method has to be thread-safe. All resources that were allocated in `init()` should be released in the `destroy()` method. This method is guaranteed to be called only once during the servlet's life cycle.

The `service()` method of `HttpServlet` dispatches a request to different Java methods for different HTTP request methods. It recognizes the standard HTTP/1.1 methods and should not be overridden in subclasses unless you need to implement additional methods. The recognized methods are `GET()`, `HEAD()`, `PUT()`, `POST()`, `DELETE()`, `OPTIONS()`, and `TRACE()`. Other methods are answered with a `Bad Request` HTTP error. An HTTP method *XXX* is dispatched to a Java method `do`*`Xxx`*; for example, `GET -> doGet`. All of these servlet methods expect the parameters `HttpServletRequest req, HttpServletResponse res`. The methods `doOptions()` and `doTrace()` have suitable default implementations and are usually not overridden. The `HEAD()` method, which returns the same header lines that a `GET()` method would return, but doesn't include a body, is performed by calling `doGet()` and ignoring any output that is written by this Java method into the servlet response. That leaves us with the methods `doGet()`, `doPut()`, `doPost()`, and `doDelete()`, whose default implementations in `HttpServlet` return a `Bad Request` HTTP error. A user-written subclass of `HttpServlet` overrides one or more of these methods to provide a meaningful implementation.

The request data is passed to all methods through the first argument of type `HttpServletRequest`, which is a subclass of the more general `ServletRequest` class. The response can be created with methods of the second argument of type `HttpServletResponse` (a subclass of `ServletResponse`).

When you request a URL in a web browser, the `GET()` method is used for the request. A `GET()` request does not have a body (in other words, the body is empty). The response should contain a body with the response data and header fields that describe the body (especially `Content-Type` and `Content-Encoding`). When you send an HTML form, either `GET()` or `POST()` can be used. With a `GET()` request, the parameters are encoded in the URL, and with a `POST()` request, they are transmitted in the body. HTML editors and upload tools use `PUT()` requests to upload resources to a web server and use `DELETE()` requests to delete resources.

Servlet Containers

Unlike a Java client application program, a servlet has no static `main()` method. A servlet must execute under the control of a servlet container, because it is the container that creates and destroys the servlet instance, calls servlet methods, and provides services that the servlet needs when executing.

The servlet container provides the servlet easy access to properties of the HTTP request, such as its headers and parameters. Also, a servlet can use other Java APIs, such as JDBC or SQLJ to access a database, RMI to call remote objects, JMS for asynchronous messaging, or many other Java and J2EE services.

Figure 10-2 shows how a servlet relates to the servlet container and to a client, such as a web browser. When the web listener is the Oracle HTTP Server (powered by Apache), then the connection to the OC4J servlet container goes through the `mod_oc4j` module. See the *Oracle HTTP Server Administration Guide* for details.

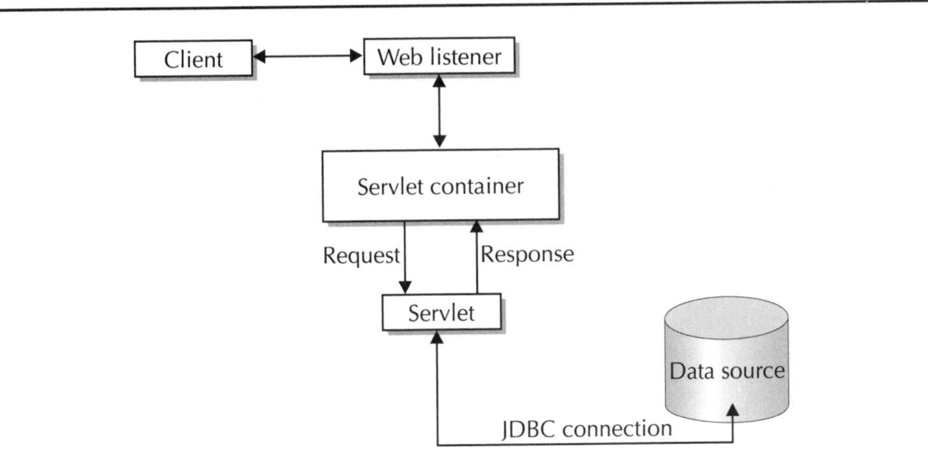

FIGURE 10-2. *Interaction with the servlet container*

Servlet Life Cycle

Java servlets have a predictable and manageable life cycle:

1. The container creates a new instance of a Java servlet when either the Java servlet is first invoked by a client or OC4J starts. This depends upon whether a `<load-on-startup>` element is declared for the Java servlet in the application `web.xml` file. A `web.xml` file is a deployment descriptor in which you specify the configuration information of your web application.
2. When the Java servlet is loaded, its configuration details are read from `web.xml`. These can include initialization parameters.
3. There is only one instance of a Java servlet. Client requests share Java servlet instances.
4. Client requests invoke the `service()` method of the generic Java servlet, which then delegates the request to the `doGet()` or `doPost()` methods, depending on the information in the request headers.
5. Filters can be interposed between the container and the Java servlet to modify the Java servlet behavior, during either the request or the response. A filter is an object that can transform the header or content or both of a request or response.
6. A Java servlet can forward requests to other Java servlets.
7. The Java servlet creates a response object, which the container passes back to the client in HTTP response headers. Java servlets can write to the response using a `java.io.PrintWriter` or `javax.servlet.ServletOutputStream` object.
8. The container calls the `destroy()` method before the servlet is unloaded.

Filters and Chaining

When the servlet container calls a method in a servlet on behalf of the client, the HTTP request from the client is, by default, passed directly to the servlet. The response that the servlet generates is, by default, passed directly back to the client, with its content unmodified by the container. So, normally, the servlet must process the request and generate as much of the response as the application requires.

But, in many cases, some preprocessing of the request for servlets is useful. In addition, it is sometimes useful to modify the response from a class of servlets. One example is encryption. A servlet, or a group of servlets in an application, might generate response data that is sensitive and should not go out over the network in clear-text form, especially when the connection has been made using a nonsecure protocol such as HTTP. A filter can encrypt the responses.

A common case for a filter is where you want to apply pre-processing or post-processing to requests and responses for a group of servlets versus a single servlet. If you need to modify the request or response for just one servlet, there is no need to create a filter—just do what is required directly in the servlet itself.

Note that filters are not servlets. They do not implement and override `HttpServlet` methods such as `doGet()` and `doPost()`. Rather, a filter implements the methods of the `javax.servlet.Filter` interface. The filtering API is defined by the `Filter`, `FilterChain`, and `FilterConfig` interfaces in the `java.servlet` package. You define a filter by implementing the `doFilter()` method, which takes the parameters `ServletRequest`, `ServletResponse`, and `FilterChain`. It is called by the container each time a request/response pair is passed through the chain due to a client request for a resource at the end of the chain.

A `FilterChain` is an object provided by the servlet container to the developer that gives a view into the invocation chain of a filtered request for a resource. The methods of the `FilterChain` interface are:

- `init()`
- `destroy()`
- `doFilter()`

Servlet Context

A servlet context is an object containing servlet information. A web component executes in a context that implements the `ServletContext` interface, which defines the methods that a servlet uses to communicate with the servlet container. Using the context, a servlet can log events, obtain URL references to resources, and set and store context attributes for other servlets in the same context.

A `ServletContext` object represents a complete web application within a JVM. There is one context per web application. Your web application may consist of servlets, JSP pages, JavaBeans, and other class files. However, all these application components run inside a single context called `ServletContext`. This `ServletContext` allows all application components to get application-level initialization parameters, set and get application attributes, get hold of the `RequestDispatcher` object to forward requests to other application components within the server or to include responses from certain components within the servlet, and to log messages to the application log file.

The `ServletContext` interface allows application components to interact with each other and to get application-level information from the servlet container. The methods of this interface are `getAttribute()`, `getAttributeNames()`, `setAttribute()`, and `removeAttribute()`. These methods are used to set, get, or remove application-level objects.

Request Object

The `ServletRequest` interface defines an object that provides client request information to a servlet. It provides the servlet access to the following:

- Client's parameters, protocol (scheme), and the names of the remote host that made the request and the server that received it.
- The input stream `ServletInputStream`, which Java servlets use to get data from clients that use application protocols such as the HTTP `POST()` and `PUT()` methods.

Interfaces that extend the `ServletRequest` interface allow the servlet to retrieve more protocol-specific data. For example, the `HttpServletRequest` interface contains methods for accessing HTTP-specific header information.

Response Object

The `ServletResponse` interface gives the Java servlet methods for replying to the client. It does the following:

- Allows the Java servlet to set the content length and MIME type of the reply.
- Provides an output stream, `ServletOutputStream`, and a writer through which the Java servlet can send the reply data.

Interfaces that extend the `ServletResponse` interface give the Java servlet more protocol-specific capabilities. For example, the `HttpServletResponse` interface contains methods that allow the Java servlet to manipulate HTTP-specific header information.

Servlet Behavior

A servlet typically receives information from one or more sources, including the following:

- Parameters from the request object
- The `HttpSession` object

- The `ServletContext` object
- Data sources outside the servlet (for example, databases, file systems, or external sensors)

The servlet adds information to the response object, and the container sends the response back to the client.

Thread Safety

Because a servlet can be invoked from more than one thread, you must ensure that servlet code is thread-safe. Critical sections of code must be synchronized, although you must do this selectively and carefully, because it can affect performance. The Java Servlet specification provides that a servlet can implement the `javax.servlet.SingleThreadModel` interface to guarantee synchronized access to the whole servlet.

The implementation of the `SingleThreadModel` interface in the servlet engine is similar to maintaining a pool of serially reusable servlet instances, where each servlet instance can be used by only one thread at a time. Therefore, any servlet that implements the `SingleThreadModel` interface is considered to be thread-safe, and no synchronization is needed when accessing any servlet instance variables or objects. This is effectively getting the support of a managed pool without the overhead of having to implement it yourself.

Servlet Sessions

Servlets provide convenient ways to keep the client and a server session in synchronization, enabling stateful servlets to maintain session state on the server over the whole duration of a client browsing session. Many server-side applications must keep some state information and maintain a dialogue with the client. The most common example of such application is a shopping cart application. The techniques to maintain the session state involve cookies, URL rewriting, and the `javax.servlet.http.HttpSession` object.

In a shopping cart application, a client may access the server several times from the same browser and from several web pages. In this instance, there is a need to maintain the client's identification for each transaction that is being performed. You do so via the session state.

Cookies

A number of approaches have attempted to add a measure of state to the HTTP protocol. One technique is to use cookies that let the client transmit an identifier to the server. In combination with stateful servlets that maintain session state, cookies permit you to keep conversational state. Session objects are simply dictionaries that store a value (a Java object) together with a key (a Java string).

When a client first connects to a stateful servlet, the server (container) sends a cookie that contains a session identifier back to the client, often along with a small amount of other useful information (all less than 4KB). Then, on each subsequent request from the same web client session, the client sends the cookie back to the server. Cookies are sent and updated by the container in the response header. The servlet code does not need to do anything to send a cookie. Similarly, cookies are sent back to the server by the web browser. A browser user only has to enable cookies on the browser to get cookie functionality. The container uses the cookie for session maintenance.

URL Rewriting

An alternative to using cookies is URL rewriting, through the `encodeURL()` method of the response object. You can append some extra data on the end of each URL that identifies the session, and the server can associate that session identifier with data it has stored about that session. This is also an excellent solution, and even has the advantage that it works with browsers that don't support cookies or where the user has disabled cookies. However, it has most of the same problems as cookies, namely that the server-side program has a lot of straightforward but tedious processing to do. See the code for the `MySessionServlet`, later in the chapter in "Coding the MySessionServlet Servlet," for an example of URL rewriting. A fragment of this code is shown here:

```
    // to activate URL rewriting. It is not done by default.
    out.println("Click <a href=" +
res.encodeURL(HttpUtils.getRequestURL(req).toString()) + ">here</a>");
```

Other Session Tracking Methods

Other techniques have been used in the past to relate client and server sessions. These include server hidden form fields and user authentication mechanisms to store additional information. In a hidden form field, an HTML form will have an entry that looks like the following:

```
<INPUT TYPE="HIDDEN" NAME="session" VALUE="...">.
```

This means that, when the form is submitted, the specified name and value are included in the `GET` or `POST` data. This can be used to store information about the session. However, it has the major disadvantage that it only works if every page is dynamically generated, since the whole point is that each session has a unique identifier.

Session Cancellation

HttpSession objects persist for the duration of the server-side session. A session either is terminated explicitly by the servlet or experiences a timeout after a certain period and is cancelled by the container, as described here:

- **Cancellation through a timeout** The default session timeout for the OC4J server is 20 minutes. You can change this for a specific application by setting the <session-timeout> subelement in the <session-config> element of web.xml. For example, to reduce the session timeout to five minutes, add the following lines to the application web.xml:

```
<session-config>
  <session-timeout>5</session-timeout>
</session-config>
```

- **Cancellation by the servlet** A servlet explicitly cancels a session by invoking the invalidate() method on the session object. You must obtain a new session object by invoking the getSession() method of the HttpServletRequest object.

Session Events

An event occurs when a new HttpSession object is created for a user. An event occurs also when an HttpSession object is destroyed. In addition, events are triggered when an attribute in a HttpSession object is added, deleted, or modified.

The javax.servlet.http package provides two interfaces that you can implement to listen to HttpSession events: HttpSessionListener and HttpSessionAttributeListener. The first enables you to listen to a session's life-cycle events, such as the event that is triggered when an HttpSession object is created and the event that is raised when an HttpSession object is destroyed.

The HttpSessionListener interface has two methods, sessionCreated() and sessionDestroyed():

```
public void sessionCreated(HttpSessionEvent se);
public void sessionDestroyed(HttpSessionEvent se);
```

The sessionCreated() method is called automatically when an HttpSession object is created. The sessionDestroyed() method is called when an HttpSession object is invalidated. Both methods will be passed an HttpSessionEvent class that you can use from inside the method. The HttpSessionEvent class is derived from the java.util.EventObject class. The HttpSessionEvent class defines one new method called getSession() that you can use to obtain the HttpSession object that changed.

Coding the MySessionServlet Servlet

The following `MySessionServlet` program implements a servlet that establishes an `HttpSession` object and prints some interesting data held by the request and session objects:

```
import java.io.*;
import javax.servlet.*;
import javax.servlet.http.*;
import java.util.Date;

public class MySessionServlet extends HttpServlet
{
  public void doGet (HttpServletRequest req, HttpServletResponse res)
     throws ServletException, IOException
  {
    // Get the session object. Create a new one if it doesn't exist.
    HttpSession session = req.getSession(true);
    res.setContentType("text/html");
    PrintWriter out = res.getWriter();
    out.println("<head><title> " + "MySessionServlet Output " +
       "</title></head><body>");
    out.println("<h1> MySessionServlet Output </h1>");

    // Set up a session hit counter. "mysessionservlet.counter" is just
    // the conventional way to create a key for the value to be
    // stored in the session object "dictionary".
    Integer ival = (Integer)
      session.getAttribute("mysessionservlet.counter");
    if (ival == null)
    {
      ival = new Integer(1);
    }
    else
    {
      ival = new Integer(ival.intValue() + 1);
    }
    // Save the counter value.
    session.setAttribute("mysessionservlet.counter", ival);
    // Report the counter value.
    out.println(" You have hit this page <b>" + ival +
                "</b> times.<p>");
```

```
    // This statement provides a target that the user can click on
    // to activate URL rewriting. It is not done by default.
    out.println("Click <a href=" +
          res.encodeURL(HttpUtils.getRequestURL(req).toString()) +
          ">here</a>");
    out.println(" to ensure that session tracking is working even " +
                "if cookies aren't supported.<br>");
    out.println("Note that by default URL rewriting is not enabled" +
                " due to its large overhead.");

    // Report data from request.
    out.println("<h3>Request and Session Data</h3>");
    out.println("Session ID in Request: " +
                req.getRequestedSessionId());
    out.println("<br>Session ID in Request is from a Cookie: " +
                 req.isRequestedSessionIdFromCookie());
    out.println("<br>Session ID in Request is from the URL: " +
                 req.isRequestedSessionIdFromURL());
    out.println("<br>Valid Session ID: " +
                req.isRequestedSessionIdValid());
    // Report data from the session object.
    out.println("<h3>Session Data</h3>");
    out.println("New Session: " + session.isNew());
    out.println("<br> Session ID: " + session.getId());
    out.println("<br> Creation Time: " +
                new Date(session.getCreationTime()));
    out.println("<br>Last Accessed Time: " +
                new Date(session.getLastAccessedTime()));
    out.println("</body>");
    out.close();
  }  // End of doGet()

  public String getServletInfo()
  {
    return "A simple session servlet";
  }  // End of getServletInfo()
}  // End of MySessionServlet class
```

Designing a Web Application Using a Servlet

It is important at this juncture to understand the design of the application that will be employed in this chapter. The J2EE application developed in this chapter reuses to some extent the application developed in Chapter 6, and consists of the following:

- **`PurchaseOrderManagement` session bean** Contains logic to manage purchase order requisitions and uses the local `PurchaseOrderLocal`, `LineItemLocal`, and `ApprovalLocal` CMP entity beans.
- **`LineItemLocal` CMP entity bean** Maps the `LINE_ITEM` table that consists of line item elements for the purchase order requisitions. This CMP bean, along with the `PurchaseOrderLocal` and `EmployeeLocal` CMP beans, consists of code to manipulate business logic.
- **`PurchaseOrderLocal` CMP entity bean** Maps the `PURCHASE_ORDER` table that consists of elements relating to purchase order requisitions.
- **`ApprovalLocal` CMP entity bean** Maps the `APPROVAL` table that consists of elements relating to the approval process.

Creating the Development Directory

The development directory for the application is as follows:

- **chapter10** Root directory of your J2EE application (for example, `c:\chapter10`).
  - **classes** Root directory for your EJBs: the EJB module.
    - **META-INF** Directory where the `ejb-jar.xml` deployment descriptor file and the `orion-ejb-jar.xml` OC4J-specific deployment descriptor file are located.
    - **purchase** Package indicating the starting point of the Java class files of the `Purchase` application.
      - **ejb** Package consisting of the class files of your EJB components.

        - **cmp** Package consisting of the class files of all your container-managed persistent (CMP) entity beans.
        - **sfsb** Package consisting of the class files of the stateful session bean.
    - **vo** Package consisting of the class files of your value object classes.
- **src** Directory where all the source files are located.
    - **META-INF** Directory where the `ejb-jar.xml` deployment descriptor file and the `orion-ejb-jar.xml` OC4J-specific deployment descriptor file are located.
    - **purchase** Package indicating the starting point of the `Purchase` application.
        - **bean** Package consisting of the helper beans.
        - **ejb** Package consisting of the source code of your EJB components.
            - **cmp** Package consisting of the source code of all your CMP entity beans.
            - **sfsb** Package consisting of the source code for all your stateful session beans.
        - **model** Package consisting of the generated source code from TopLink.
        - **servlets** Package consisting of the source code for all your servlets.
        - **vo** Package consisting of the source code of your value object classes.
- **web** Root directory for your Web module.
    - **WEB-INF** Directory where your `web.xml` file (and possibly your `orion-web.xml` file) is located.
        - **classes** Root directory for your servlets and their dependent classes: the Web module.

- **purchase** Package indicating the starting point of the Java class files of the Purchase application.
    - **bean** Package consisting of the class files of the helper beans.
    - **model** Package consisting of the class files of the Java classes generated by Oracle9*i*AS TopLink.
    - **servlets** Package consisting of the class files of the servlets.
- **images** Directory where your image files are located.

Using EJBs with Servlets

In Chapter 6, you learned how to use Enterprise JavaBeans from a client Java application. In this section, you will learn how to use EJBs from servlets. You will do so while building the `ViewPurchaseOrder` class, a servlet that uses the `PurchaseOrderManagement` session bean that you developed in Chapter 6. Here is a quick reminder of the steps necessary to call an EJB:

1. Import the EJB package for the bean home and remote interfaces into the program that makes the EJB calls.
2. Use JNDI to look up the EJB home interface.
3. Create the EJB remote object from the home.
4. Invoke business methods on the remote object.

Use the `ViewPurchaseOrder` servlet to view the details of a purchase order based on the purchase order number given by a user. The high-level view of the `ViewPurchaseOrder` servlet and its interaction with the `PurchaseOrderManagement` session bean and the `PurchaseOrderLocal`, `LineItemLocal`, and `Approval` CMP entity beans developed in Chapter 6 is shown in Figure 10-3. Figure 10-4 shows the interaction between the web browser and the OC4J objects.

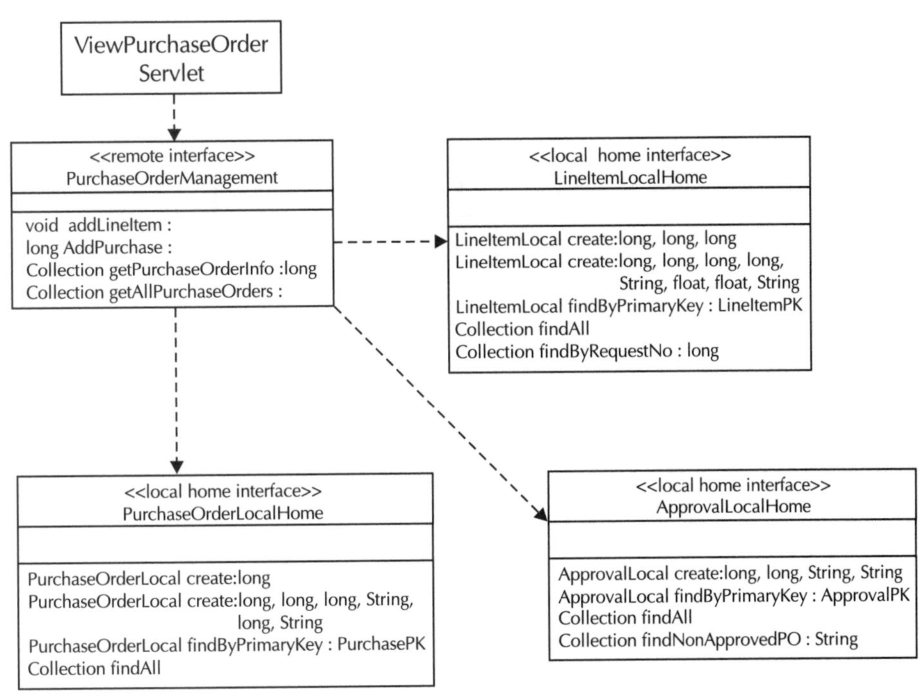

FIGURE 10-3. *High-level view of the `ViewPurchaseOrder` servlet and the EJBs*

Here is the definition of the `ViewPurchaseOrder` servlet:

```
/*
** Program Name: ViewPurchaseOrder.java
**
** Purpose: A Servlet that uses the PurchaseOrderManagement
**          session bean to display the details of
**          Purchase Order based on a purchase order number
**          given by a user.
*/
package purchase.servlets;

// Basic imports
import java.io.*;
import java.util.List;
```

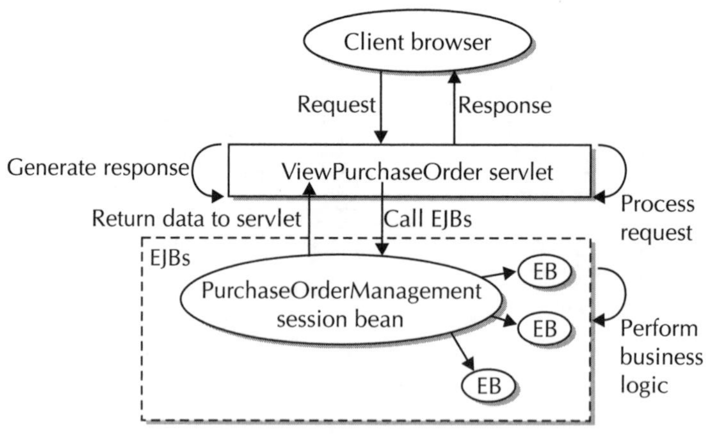

FIGURE 10-4. *Calls to OC4J objects from a web browser*

```
// J2EE imports
import javax.servlet.*;
import javax.servlet.http.*;
import javax.rmi.PortableRemoteObject;
import javax.naming.NamingException;
import javax.naming.InitialContext;
import javax.ejb.CreateException;
import java.rmi.RemoteException;

//  Step 1: Import the EJB home and remote interfaces
import purchase.ejb.sfsb.PurchaseOrderManagement;
import purchase.ejb.sfsb.PurchaseOrderManagementHome;
import purchase.vo.LineItemVO;

public class ViewPurchaseOrder extends HttpServlet {

  PurchaseOrderManagement purchaseOrderManagement;

  public void init() throws ServletException
  {
    try {
      // Step 2: Use JNDI to look up the EJB home interface
      InitialContext ctx = new InitialContext();
      PurchaseOrderManagementHome  purchaseOrderManagementHome =
        (PurchaseOrderManagementHome)
```

```
            ctx.lookup("PurchaseOrderManagement");

      // Step 3: Create the EJB remote object from the home
      purchaseOrderManagement = purchaseOrderManagementHome.create();
    } catch(NamingException e) {
      throw new ServletException("Error: NamingException", e);
    } catch(CreateException e) {
      throw new ServletException("Error: CreateException", e);
    } catch(RemoteException e) {
      throw new ServletException("Error: RemoteException", e);
    }
  } // End of init()

  protected void service(HttpServletRequest request,
                         HttpServletResponse response)
          throws ServletException, java.io.IOException {

    long requestno = 0L;
    String poNumber = request.getParameter("purchaseorder");

    if (poNumber != null && !poNumber.equals("")) {
      requestno = Long.parseLong(poNumber);
    }

    // Step 4: Invoke business methods on the remote object.
    // Get the line items of a selected purchase order.
    List po  =
     (List)purchaseOrderManagement.getPurchaseOrderInfo(requestno);

    printPage(po, request, response);

      } // End of service()

  public void printPage(List purchaseOrders,
                        HttpServletRequest request,
                        HttpServletResponse response)
    throws ServletException, IOException {

    response.setContentType("text/html");
    ServletOutputStream out = response.getOutputStream();

    out.println("<html>");
    out.println("<head>");
    out.println("<title>View Purchase Order</title>");
    out.println("</head>");

    out.println("<body bgcolor=\"#FFFFCC\" text=\"#000000\" ");
```

```
out.println("link=\"#009900\" vlink=\"#666666\" alink=" );
out.println(" \"#FF0000\" style=\"font-family: ");
out.println(" Jenson, Garamond, serif\">");

out.println("<h1 align=\"center\">View Purchase Order</h1>");
out.println("<h4 align=\"left\"> ");

out.println("<hr align=\"center\" size=4 width=\"65%\">");
out.println("<form name=\"purchase_form\" method=\"post\">");
out.println("  <p>Order Number: ");
out.println("    <input type=\"text\" name=\"purchaseorder\"");
out.println("           size=\"10\">");
out.println("    <input type=\"submit\" name=\"View\">");
out.println("  </p>");
out.println("</form>");

// Don't show header if there are no purchase orders
if (purchaseOrders.size() > 0) {
  out.println("<h3>Purchases Detail:</h3>");
  out.println("<table>");
  out.println("<tr>");
  out.println(" <th valign=\"bottom\">Project<br>Number</th>");
  out.println(" <th valign=\"bottom\">Quantity</th>");
  out.println(" <th valign=\"bottom\">Unit of Issue</th>");
  out.println(" <th valign=\"bottom\">Estimated<br>Cost</th>");
  out.println(" <th valign=\"bottom\">Total Cost</th>");
  out.println(" <th valign=\"bottom\">Description</th>");
  out.println("</tr>");

  for (int i=0; i < purchaseOrders.size(); i++) {

   // Get the line items of the purchase
     LineItemVO lo = (LineItemVO)purchaseOrders.get(i);

    out.println("<tr>");
    out.println("  <td>");
    out.print("    <input type=\"text\" name=\"po_num\"");
    out.print("       size=\"10\" value=\"");
    out.println(        lo.projectno + " \" readonly>");
    out.println("  </td>");
    out.println("  <td align=\"center\">");
    out.print("    <input type=\"text\" name=\"quantity\" ");
    out.print("       size=3 value=\"" );
    out.println(        lo.quantity + "\" readonly>");
    out.println("  </td>");
    out.println("  <td>");
    out.print("      <input type=\"text\" name=\"unit\" ");
    out.print("         size=6 value=\"" + lo.unit +  "\"");
```

```
        out.println("           readonly>");
        out.println("  </td>");
        out.println("  <td align=\"center\">");
        out.print("    $<input type=\"text\" name=\"est\" ");
        out.print("       size=12 value=\"" + lo.cost );
        out.println("        \" readonly>");
        out.println("  </td>");
        out.println("  <td align=\"center\">");
        out.print("    $<input type=\"text\" name=\"total\"  ");
        out.print("       size=12 value=\"" );
        out.println(       lo.cost*lo.quantity + "\" readonly>");
        out.println("  </td>");
        out.println("  <td>");
        out.print("    <input type=\"text\" name=\"desc\"");
        out.print("       size=60 value=\"" );
        out.println(       lo.description + "\" readonly>");
        out.println("  </td>");
        out.println("</tr>");
      }//end for loop

      out.println("</table>");

    } // End if
    out.println("</body>");
    out.println("</html>");
    out.close();

  } // End of printPage()
}  // End of ViewPurchaseOrder class
```

The "Configuring TopLink and Servlets to Run on OC4J" section later in this chapter shows you how to configure, package, and run the servlet applications of this chapter, including the `ViewPurchaseOrder` servlet.

Developing a Basic Servlet with Oracle9*i*AS TopLink

Oracle9*i*AS TopLink integrates the object and relational data worlds, allowing applications to transparently store and retrieve Java objects using relational databases, and is one of the latest additions to the Oracle9*i*AS technology stack.

In this section, you will code the `EmployeeTopLinkServlet` class, which is a servlet that uses the `Employee` class definition generated by Oracle9*i*AS TopLink, as described in Chapter 3. The `EmployeeTopLinkServlet` servlet class will call an Oracle9*i*AS TopLink JavaBean (`EmployeeToplinkBean`) that will be responsible for all communications to the database. The interactions between `EmployeeTopLinkServlet` servlet, `EmployeeToplinkBean` JavaBean, and the Oracle database are shown in Figure 10-5. The servlet also uses an `Employee` class that maps to the `EMPLOYEE` table stored in the Oracle9*i* database. The `EMPLOYEE` table is part of the Purchase Order database schema presented in the Introduction of the book. As a reminder, the following shows the definition of the `EMPLOYEE` table:

```
CREATE TABLE EMPLOYEE(
  employeeno     NUMBER(7),
  deptno         NUMBER(5),
  type           VARCHAR2(30),
  lastname       VARCHAR2(30),
  firstname      VARCHAR2(30),
  phone          VARCHAR2(10),
  email          VARCHAR2(20))
/
```

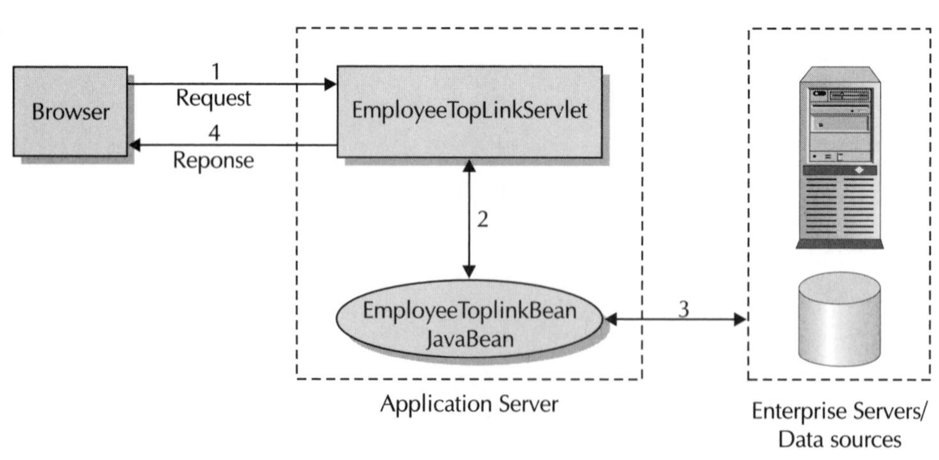

FIGURE 10-5. *High-level view of the* `EmployeeServlet` *class*

The EmployeeTopLinkServlet Class

The `EmployeeTopLinkServlet` class consists of the following methods:

- **`protected void service(HttpServletRequest request, HttpServletResponse response)`** The `HttpServlet` class breaks this `service()` method into more useful `doGet()`, `doPost()`, `doDelete()`, `doOptions()`, `doPut()`, and `doTrace()` methods, depending on the type of HTTP request it receives. So, in order to generate a response, you have to override the `doGet()` or `doPost()` methods as required.
- **`private getEmployee(String empNo, EmployeeToplinkBean eteb)`** This method gets an employee of the supplied employee number.
- **`private getEmployeesSelectList(EmployeeToplinkBean eteb)`** This method returns a string of HTML that contains all employees in a select drop-down list.

Here is the complete definition of the `EmployeeTopLinkServlet` class:

```
package purchase.servlets;

// Basic imports
import java.io.*;
import java.util.List;

// J2EE imports
import javax.servlet.*;
import javax.servlet.http.*;

// Model import
import purchase.bean.EmployeeToplinkBean;
import purchase.vo.EmployeeVO;
import purchase.model.Employee;

/**
 * This servlet provides diverse facilities to create, update and delete
 * employees using TopLink and employee data provided by the request
 */
```

```
public class EmployeeTopLinkServlet extends HttpServlet {

  public void service( HttpServletRequest request,
                       HttpServletResponse response)
  throws ServletException, IOException {

    ServletOutputStream out = response.getOutputStream();

    out.println("<html>");
    out.println("<head>");
    out.println("<title>View Employees</title>");
    out.println("</head>");

    out.println
     ("<body bgcolor=\"#FFFFCC\" text=\"#000000\" link=\"#009900\" ");
    out.println
     ("  vlink=\"#666666\" alink=\"#FF0000\" style=\"font-family: ");
    out.println("  Jenson, Garamond, serif\">");

    out.println("<h1 align=\"center\">View an Employee</h1>");


    out.println("<hr align=\"left\" size=4 width=\"65%\">");

    String empNo = request.getParameter("employeeno");

    // Get JavaBean
    EmployeeToplinkBean eteb = new EmployeeToplinkBean();

    out.println("<form name=\"form1\" method=\"post\"");
    out.println("action=\"EmployeeTopLinkServlet\">");

    // Get the select list of all employees
    out.println(getEmployeesSelectList( eteb));
    out.println("  </form>");

    out.println("  <h3>Employee Information</h3>");
    out.println(getEmployee(empNo, eteb));

    out.println("</body>");
    out.println("</html>");
  }

      /**
       * Method to get the list of all employees as a select list
       */
  private String getEmployeesSelectList(EmployeeToplinkBean eteb) {
```

```
  StringBuffer empstb = new StringBuffer();

  List employees = (List)eteb.readEmployees();

  empstb.append("<h3>Employees</h3>");
  empstb.append("<p>");
  empstb.append("<select name=\"employeeno\">");
  empstb.append("<option value=\"0\">Select an Employee</option>");

  Employee emp = null;

  // iterate though all employees and put them in a drop-down list
  for (int i=0; i < employees.size(); i++) {
    emp = (Employee)employees.get(i);
    empstb.append("<option value=\"" + emp.getEmployeeno());
    empstb.append("\"> ");
    empstb.append(emp.getFirstname() + " " );
    empstb.append(emp.getLastname() + "</option>\n");
  }

  empstb.append("</select>");
  empstb.append("<input type=\"submit\" name=\"View\">");
  empstb.append("</p>");

  return empstb.toString();
}

    /**
     * Get and return the HTML for an employee
     */
    private String getEmployee(String empNo,
                          EmployeeToplinkBean eteb) {

  if (empNo==null) empNo = "0";

  Employee empr = (Employee)eteb.readEmployee(empNo);

  if (empr == null)
    empr = new Employee();

  StringBuffer empstb = new StringBuffer();

  empstb.append("<h3>Employees</h3>");
  empstb.append("  <table border=\"0\" cellspacing=\"2\" ");
  empstb.append("     cellpadding=\"2\">");
  empstb.append("   <tr>");
  empstb.append("      <td align=\"right\">Title:</td>\n");
  empstb.append("      <td><input type=\"text\"");
```

```
        empstb.append("            value=\"");
        empstb.append( empr.getType()==null?"":empr.getType());
        empstb.append("\"          size=\"45\" readonly></td>\n");
        empstb.append("     </tr>");
        empstb.append("     <tr>");
        empstb.append("       <td align=\"right\">First Name:</td>\n");
        empstb.append("       <td><input type=\"text\"");
        empstb.append("            value=\"");
        empstb.append( empr.getFirstname()==null?"":empr.getFirstname());
        empstb.append("\"          size=\"30\" readonly></td>\n");
        empstb.append("     </tr>");
        empstb.append("     <tr>");
        empstb.append("       <td align=\"right\">Last Name:</td>\n");
        empstb.append("       <td><input type=\"text\" value=\"");
        empstb.append( empr.getLastname()==null?"":empr.getLastname());
        empstb.append("\"           size=\"45\" readonly></td>\n");
        empstb.append("     </tr>");
        empstb.append("     <tr>");
        empstb.append("       <td align=\"right\">Telephone: </td>\n");
        empstb.append("       <td><input type=\"text\" ");
        empstb.append("            value=\"");
        empstb.append( empr.getPhone()==null?"":empr.getPhone());
        empstb.append("\"           size=\"20\" readonly></td>\n");
        empstb.append("     </tr>");
        empstb.append("     <tr>");
        empstb.append("       <td align=\"right\">Email:</td>\n");
        empstb.append("       <td><input type=\"text\"");
        empstb.append("            value=\"");
        empstb.append( empr.getEmail()==null?"":empr.getEmail());
        empstb.append("\"           size=\"45\" readonly></td>\n");
        empstb.append("     </tr>");
        empstb.append("     <tr>");
        empstb.append("       <td align=\"right\">Department:</td>\n");
        empstb.append("       <td><input type=\"text\"");
        empstb.append("            value=\"");
        empstb.append( empr.getDeptno());
        empstb.append("\"          size=70 readonly></td>\n");
        empstb.append("     </tr>");

        empstb.append("  </table>");

        return empstb.toString();
    }
}
```

The EmployeeToplinkBean JavaBean Class

The following `EmployeeToplinkBean` JavaBean was create from the TopLink application from Chapter 3. Refer to Chapter 3 to learn more about how to program using TopLink. This JavaBean is responsible for all the communication with the database using TopLink. The `EmployeeToplinkBean` JavaBean contains methods to read, create, delete, and update employees. In this chapter, you will only use the read method. In Chapter 11, you will use all the methods of this JavaBean.

The `EmployeeToplinkBean` JavaBean contains the `private UnitOfWork getUnitOfWork()` method that retrieves a TopLink `UnitofWork` object. `UnitofWork` handles all reads from the database, and registers clean objects whenever they are read. Rather than marking objects as dirty, the `UnitofWork` takes a copy at read time, and then compares the object at commit time. Here is a complete definition of the `EmployeeToplinkBean` class:

```
/*
** Program Name: EmployeeToplinkBean.java
**
** Purpose: A JavaBean that is responsible to read, create, delete,
** and update an employee using Oracle9iAS TopLink
*/
package purchase.bean;

// Basic imports
import java.io.Serializable;
import java.util.Vector;

// TopLink imports
import com.webgain.integrator.sessions.UnitOfWork;
import com.webgain.integrator.threetier.Server;
import com.webgain.integrator.threetier.ClientSession;
import com.webgain.integrator.tools.sessionmanagement.SessionManager;
import com.webgain.integrator.queryframework.ReadObjectQuery;
import com.webgain.integrator.expressions.ExpressionBuilder;
import com.webgain.integrator.queryframework.ReadAllQuery;
import com.webgain.integrator.sessions.Session;
import com.webgain.integrator.queryframework.QueryByExamplePolicy;
import com.webgain.integrator.expressions.ExpressionBuilder;

// Model import
import purchase.model.Employee;
import purchase.vo.EmployeeVO;
/**
 * This JavaBean provides diverse facilities to create, update
 * and delete employees using TopLink and employee data provided
 * by the request
 */
```

```
public class EmployeeToplinkBean implements Serializable {

  /**
   * Use the SessionManager to read the "default" ServerSession
   * defined in sessions.xml. Then acquire ClientSession and
   * UnitOfWork.
   */
  private UnitOfWork getUnitOfWork() {
    //Get ServerSession from SessionManager (using sessions.xml).
    //Use class loader of this class to do so.
    Server serverSession =
      (Server)SessionManager.getManager().getSession("default",
               this.getClass().getClassLoader());
    //Acquire ClientSession from thread-safe ServerSession.
    ClientSession clientSession =
       serverSession.acquireClientSession();
    //Acquire and return UnitOfWork from ClientSession.
    //See TopLink manuals for more details.
    return clientSession.acquireUnitOfWork();
  }

  /**
   * Read the employee based on employeeno
   */
  public Employee readEmployee(String employeeno) {

    // Get the unit of Work
    UnitOfWork uow = getUnitOfWork();

    //Create and execute a ReadObjectQuery object and set selection
    //criteria using a TopLink expression.
    ReadObjectQuery readObjectQuery =
                          new ReadObjectQuery(Employee.class);
    ExpressionBuilder builder = new ExpressionBuilder();
     readObjectQuery.setSelectionCriteria(
                builder.get("employeeno").equal(employeeno));
    return (Employee)uow.executeQuery(readObjectQuery);
  }

  /**
   * Read the employee based on employeeno and UnitOfWork
   */
  public Employee readEmployee(String employeeno, UnitOfWork uow) {
    //Create and execute a ReadObjectQuery object and set selection
    //criteria using a TopLink expression.
    ReadObjectQuery readObjectQuery =
                              new ReadObjectQuery(Employee.class);
    ExpressionBuilder builder = new ExpressionBuilder();
```

```
    readObjectQuery.setSelectionCriteria(
        builder.get("employeeno").equal(employeeno));
  return (Employee)uow.executeQuery(readObjectQuery);
}

/**
 * Populate the employee with employee data from request
 */
public void populateEmployee(EmployeeVO employeeVO,
                             Employee employee) {
  //Get employee data from request
  String firstname = employeeVO.getFirstName();
  String lastname = employeeVO.getLastName();
  String deptno = Long.toString(employeeVO.getDeptNo());
  String type = employeeVO.getType();
  String phone = employeeVO.getPhone();
  String email = employeeVO.getEmail();

  //Populate employee
  employee.setFirstname((firstname != null) ? firstname : "");
  employee.setLastname((lastname != null) ? lastname : "");
  //If no deptno is specified, use deptno = 200 in order
  //to satisfy integrity constraint (SCOTT.EMP_DEPTNO_FK)
  employee.setDeptno((deptno != null && deptno.length()>0) ?
                    Long.parseLong(deptno) : 200L);
  employee.setType((type != null) ? type : "");
  employee.setPhone((phone != null) ? phone : "");
  employee.setEmail((email != null) ? email : "");
}

/**
 * Create a new employee based on employee data from request
 */
public long createEmployee(EmployeeVO employeeVO) {

  //Create and populate employee
  Employee employee = new Employee();
  populateEmployee(employeeVO, employee);

  //Register the new employee with UnitOfWork and commit.
  UnitOfWork uow = getUnitOfWork();
  uow.registerNewObject(employee);
  uow.commit();

  return employee.getEmployeeno();
}

/**
```

```
 * Update an existing employee based on employee data from request
 */
public void updateEmployee(EmployeeVO employeeVO) {
  String employeeno = Long.toString(employeeVO.getEmployeeNo());

  //Read employee, update it and commit.
  UnitOfWork uow = getUnitOfWork();
  Employee employee = readEmployee(employeeno, uow);
  populateEmployee(employeeVO, employee);
  uow.commit();
}


/**
 * Delete an existing employee
 */
public void deleteEmployee(String employeeno) {

  //Delete employee and commit using UnitOfWork.
  UnitOfWork uow = getUnitOfWork();
  Employee employee = readEmployee(employeeno, uow);
  uow.deleteObject(employee);
  uow.commit();
}
/**
 * First get ServerSession from sessions.xml, then
 * acquire ClientSession from ServerSession.
 */
public Session getClientSession() {
  // Get ServerSession from SessionManager (using sessions.xml).
  // Use class loader of this class to do so.
  Server serverSession =
    (Server)SessionManager.getManager().getSession("default",
     this.getClass().getClassLoader());
  //Acquire ClientSession from thread-safe ServerSession.
  //See TopLink manuals for more details.
  return serverSession.acquireClientSession();
}

  /**
 * Read all employees using the given first- & lastname.
 * Use a query-by-example to do so.
 */
public Vector readEmployees() {
  //Create and execute a ReadAllQuery object.
  ReadAllQuery readAllQuery = new ReadAllQuery(Employee.class);
  //Use an example employee object to run a query-by-example
```

```
    Employee exampleEmployee = new Employee();
    readAllQuery.setExampleObject(exampleEmployee);
    //Use a QueryByExamplePolicy in order to allow for a "like" query
    exampleEmployee.setFirstname("%");
    exampleEmployee.setLastname("%");
    QueryByExamplePolicy policy = new QueryByExamplePolicy();
    policy.addSpecialOperation(String.class, "like");
    readAllQuery.setQueryByExamplePolicy(policy);
    return (Vector)getClientSession().executeQuery(readAllQuery);
  }

}
```

The following section shows you how to configure, package, and run the servlet applications of this chapter, including the `EmployeeTopLinkServlet` servlet.

Configuring TopLink and Servlets to Run on OC4J

You learned in Chapter 2 how to deploy a J2EE application to the Oracle9*i*AS Containers For J2EE server and how to bind that application to the server so that you can access the application from Oracle9*i*AS Containers For J2EE. You also learned in Chapter 3 how to use Oracle9*i*AS TopLink to generate Java classes for tables stored in the Oracle database. In this section, we will configure TopLink in OC4J, and we will go through the steps to configure and run all the servlets that you created for this chapter. Also, we will examine the `web.xml` file.

Configuring OC4J to Run Oracle9*i*AS TopLink

In order for OC4J to run TopLink, OC4J needs to have access to the TopLink runtime Foundation Library, which is provided in the TopLink `wdiall.jar` and `xerces.jar` files (you can download and install TopLink from OTN).

To make the TopLink runtime Foundation Library available to all applications running in your OC4J instance, copy the `wdiall.jar` and `xerces.jar` files to the `$OC4J_HOME/j2ee/home/lib` directory. However, if you want to make TopLink available to only one application, copy the `wdiall.jar` and `xerces.jar` files to the `WEB-INF/lib` directory of your web application. Next, you will modify the Oracle9*i*AS TopLink `sessions.xml` file.

Edit Your sessions.xml File

Next, make sure to modify the `<login>` information in the `web/WEB-INF/classes/sessions.xml` file to reflect your database setup. Recall that you developed the sessions.xml file in Chapter 3. The following code fragment demonstrates how to modify the sessions.xml file:

```
<login>
   <! -- Use the <platform-class>, <driver-class>, and
       <connection-url> elements to set up your data source -- >
   <platform-class>
      com.webgain.integrator.internal.databaseaccess.OraclePlatform
   </platform-class>
   <driver-class>oracle.jdbc.driver.OracleDriver</driver-class>
   <! -- Using the Oracle thin JDBC driver -- >
   <connection-url>
         jdbc:oracle:thin:@localhost:1521:orcl
   </connection-url>
   <user-name>scott</user-name>
   <password>tiger</password>
</login>
```

The web.xml Deployment Descriptor File

The web.xml file is the web application deployment descriptor for your application. This XML file describes servlets and other components that make up your application, along with any initialization parameters and container-managed security constraints that you want the server to enforce.

The following fragment of code shows the web.xml file that is used for the MySessionServlet, EmployeeTopLinkServlet, and ViewPurchaseOrder servlet applications of this chapter and the EJB application developed for Chapter 6:

```
<?xml version = '1.0' encoding = 'windows-1252'?>
<!DOCTYPE web-app PUBLIC "-//Sun Microsystems, Inc.
  //DTD Web Application 2.3//EN"
  "http://java.sun.com/dtd/web-app_2_3.dtd">
<web-app>
  <description>Purchase web.xml file for Web Application</description>
  <servlet>
    <servlet-name>MySessionServlet</servlet-name>
    <servlet-class>purchase.servlets.MySessionServlet</servlet-class>
  </servlet>
  <servlet-mapping>
    <servlet-name>MySessionServlet</servlet-name>
    <url-pattern>/MySessionServlet</url-pattern>
  </servlet-mapping>
  <servlet>
    <servlet-name>EmployeeTopLinkServlet</servlet-name>
    <servlet-class>purchase.servlets.EmployeeTopLinkServlet
    </servlet-class>
  </servlet>
  <servlet-mapping>
```

```
    <servlet-name>EmployeeTopLinkServlet</servlet-name>
    <url-pattern>/EmployeeTopLinkServlet</url-pattern>
  </servlet-mapping>
  <servlet>
    <servlet-name>ViewPurchaseOrder</servlet-name>
    <servlet-class>purchase.servlets.ViewPurchaseOrder</servlet-class>
  </servlet>
  <servlet-mapping>
    <servlet-name>ViewPurchaseOrder</servlet-name>
    <url-pattern>/ViewPurchaseOrder</url-pattern>
  </servlet-mapping>
  <ejb-ref>
    <ejb-ref-name>ejb/PurchaseOrderManagement</ejb-ref-name>
    <ejb-ref-type>Session</ejb-ref-type>
    <home>purchase.ejb.sfsb.PurchaseOrderManagementHome</home>
    <remote>purchase.ejb.sfsb.PurchaseOrderManagement</remote>
    <ejb-link>PurchaseOrderManagement</ejb-link>
  </ejb-ref>
  <ejb-local-ref>
    <ejb-ref-name>ejb/local/LineItemLocal</ejb-ref-name>
    <ejb-ref-type>Entity</ejb-ref-type>
    <ejb-ref-type>Entity</ejb-ref-type>
    <local-home>purchase.ejb.cmp.LineItemLocalHome</local-home>
    <local>purchase.ejb.cmp.LineItemLocal</local>
    <ejb-link>LineItemLocal</ejb-link>
  </ejb-local-ref>
  <ejb-local-ref>
    <ejb-ref-name>ejb/local/PurchaseOrderLocal</ejb-ref-name>
    <ejb-ref-type>Entity</ejb-ref-type>
    <local-home>purchase.ejb.cmp.PurchaseOrderLocalHome</local-home>
    <local>purchase.ejb.cmp.PurchaseOrderLocal</local>
    <ejb-link>PurchaseOrderLocal</ejb-link>
  </ejb-local-ref>
  <ejb-local-ref>
    <ejb-ref-name>ejb/local/ApprovalLocal</ejb-ref-name>
    <ejb-ref-type>Entity</ejb-ref-type>
    <local-home>purchase.ejb.cmp.ApprovalLocalHome</local-home>
    <local>purchase.ejb.cmp.ApprovalLocal</local>
    <ejb-link>ApprovalLocal</ejb-link>
  </ejb-local-ref>
</web-app>
```

As you learned in Chapter 8, the `<servlet-mapping>` tag defines a mapping between a servlet and a URL pattern. The `<servlet-name>` tag defines the canonical name of the Java servlet, used to reference the Java servlet definition elsewhere in the deployment descriptor. The `<servlet-class>` tag is the fully qualified class name of the Java servlet.

Deploying the Application to OC4J

In Chapter 2, you learned how to deploy a J2EE application to the Oracle9*i*AS Containers For J2EE server and how to bind that application to the server so that you can access the application from OC4J. In this section, we revisit the necessary steps, to refresh your memory.

Recall that a J2EE application can contain the following modules:

- **Web applications** The Web applications module (WAR files) can consist of servlets, JSPs, HTML pages, tag libraries, and utility classes. This is where the `PurchaseOrderServlet`, `ViewPurchaseOrder`, `MySessionServlet`, `EmployeeTopLinkServlet` and supporting classes (`purchase.model.Employee`, `purchase.bean.EmployeeToplinkBean`) will be packaged.
- **EJB applications** The EJB applications module (`ejb-jar` files) includes Enterprise JavaBeans (EJBs).
- **Client applications** The Client applications module includes client application programs and is contained within a JAR file.

Archiving the EJB Application

The very first step in *archiving* the EJB applications is to package your application. You do so when you create the J2EE EAR file.

Creating the EAR File

This application consists of a Web module, containing the `PurchaseOrderServlet`, `ViewPurchaseOrder`, `MySessionServlet`, `EmployeeTopLinkServlet` servlets; the `purchase.model.Employee` utility class; the `purchase.bean.EmployeeToplinkBean` JavaBean class; and an EJB module, consisting of two CMP beans and one BMP bean. Let's start by creating the WAR file:

1. Open a command prompt, and position yourself in the web directory (for example `c:\chapter10\web`).
2. Type the following:

   ```
   jar cvf chapter10-web.war *
   ```

3. Copy `chapter10-web.war` to the root directory, `chapter10`.
4. Position yourself in the `classes` directory (for example `c:\chapter10\classes`).
5. Type the following:

   ```
   jar cvf chapter10-ejb.jar *
   ```

6. Copy `chapter10-ejb.jar` to the root directory, `chapter10`.
7. Position yourself in the root directory, `chapter10`.
8. Type the following:

```
jar cvf chapter10.ear chapter10-web.war chapter10-ejb.jar
  META-INF\application.xml
```

You now have your `chapter10.ear` file and are ready to deploy.

If your application will access a database, then you need to define an OC4J data source. You do so by modifying the OC4J `data-sources.xml` file.

Modifying the OC4J data-sources.xml File

If you have not already defined the data source `jdbc/OracleDS`, you need to do this now. Before deploying your application, you need to register your data source with OC4J. You do that by modifying the OC4J `data-sources.xml` file and restarting OC4J. This file is located in the OC4J's …`/config` directory. All the beans that you created in this chapter use a data source called `jdbc/OracleDS`. You need to specify that data source in the OC4J `data-sources.xml` file. Modify the file as follows:

```
<!-- Your datasource -->
<data-source
          class="com.evermind.sql.DriverManagerDataSource"
          name="OracleDS"
          location="jdbc/OracleCoreDS"
          xa-location="jdbc/xa/OracleXADS"
          ejb-location="jdbc/OracleDS"
          connection-driver="oracle.jdbc.driver.OracleDriver"
          username="scott"
          password="tiger"
          url="jdbc:oracle:thin:@yourhost:your-port-no:your-sid"
          inactivity-timeout="30"
     />
```

Deploying the Applications

Next, you will deploy the application. OC4J supports deployment of both EAR files as well as deploying an exploded directory conforming to the J2EE standard (as does our `chapter10` directory structure). We will show you both ways, starting with the EAR file.

Deploying an EAR File to OC4J

The steps to deploy an EAR file to OC4J are as follows:

1. Copy the `chapter10.ear` file to your OC4J installation's `applications` directory; if you installed OC4J under the `c:\OC4J` directory, then this will be `c:\OC4J\j2ee\home\applications`. The EAR file can be placed anywhere, but in this example, you will use the OC4J `applications` directory.

2. Edit the OC4J `server.xml` file, found under your `OC4J\j2ee\home\config` directory. Add the following entry:

   ```
   <application name="chapter10"
   path="../applications/chapter10.ear"
   auto-start="true" />
   ```

   The previous command tells OC4J the location of the `chapter10.ear` file.

3. Edit `http-web-site.xml` to bind your Web module to this J2EE application. Add the following entry:

   ```
   <web-app application="chapter10" name="chapter10-web"
   root="/chapter10" load-on-startup="true" />
   ```

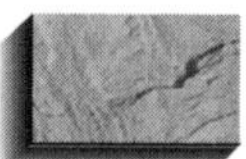

CAUTION
The name must correspond to whatever name you gave the WAR file; the root will be the virtual path where OC4J can reach your application.

Recall that OC4J supports hot deployment. Therefore, if OC4J is running, it will immediately pick up and deploy this application. If OC4J is not running, position yourself in the `OC4J/j2ee/home` directory and start OC4J by typing the following:

```
java -jar oc4j.jar -verbosity 10
```

Next, you will test the servlet applications of this chapter.

Testing the MySessionServlet Servlet

Open a web browser and type the following URL:

```
http://localhost:port/chapter10/MySessionServlet
```

where *localhost* is your machine, *port* is the port the web server is listening on, and `chapter10` refers to the root element of the `<application>` tag in the OC4J `server.xml` file. The output in the browser is shown in Figure 10-6.

Note that the default port for the stand-alone OC4J is 8888. The port can be found and changed in the OC4J `http-web-site.xml` file. The OC4J `http-web-site.xml`

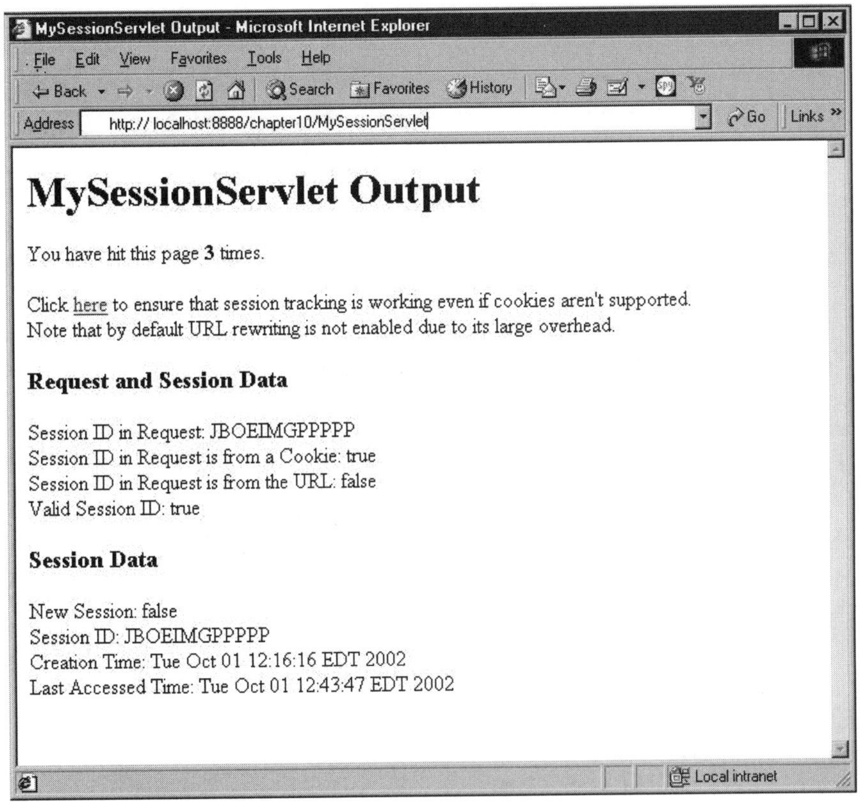

FIGURE 10-6. *Output for `MySessionServlet`*

file can be found in the `OC4J_HOME/j2ee/home/config` directory. Therefore, if you use the default port, you would enter into your web browser the following:

```
http://localhost:8888/chapter10/MySessionServlet
```

Testing the ViewPurchaseOrder Servlet

Open a web browser and type the following URL:

```
http://localhost:8888/chapter10/ViewPurchaseOrder
```

You will get a screen that has a purchase order input field as shown in Figure 10-7. You can enter purchase order 500, 501, or 502. These purchase orders were preloaded with the SQL script that came with this book.

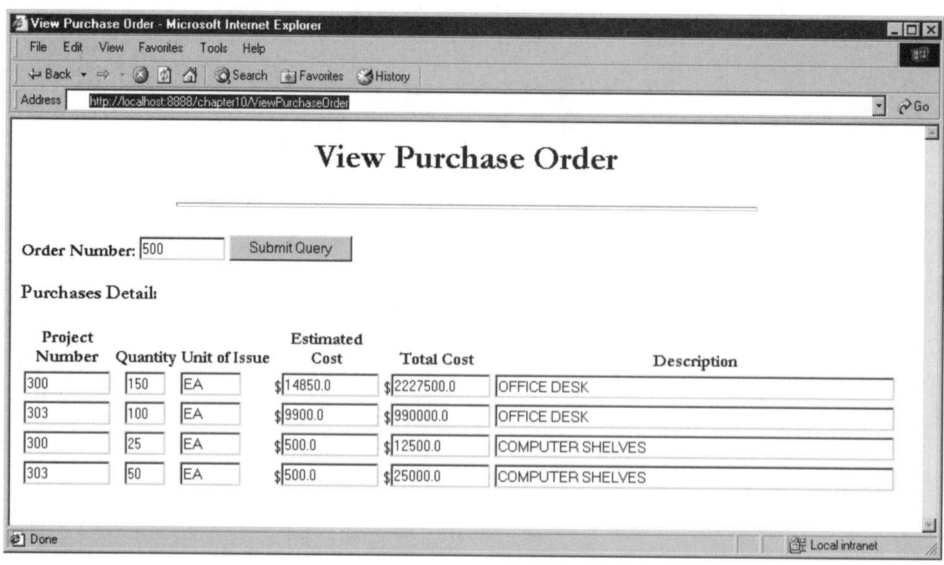

FIGURE 10-7. *Output for `ViewPurchaseOrder`*

Testing the EmployeeTopLinkServlet Servlet

Lastly, to test the `EmployeeTopLinkServlet` servlet application, enter the following in your browser to execute it:

```
http://localhost:8888/chapter10/EmployeeTopLinkServlet
```

The output generated by this URL is shown in Figure 10-8.

In this chapter, you learned the basic concepts behind servlets (servlet container, filter, chaining, context, and so on), how to build servlets and use them in web applications, how to create servlets that access EJB components, and how to use Java mapping classes generated by Oracle9*i*AS TopLink.

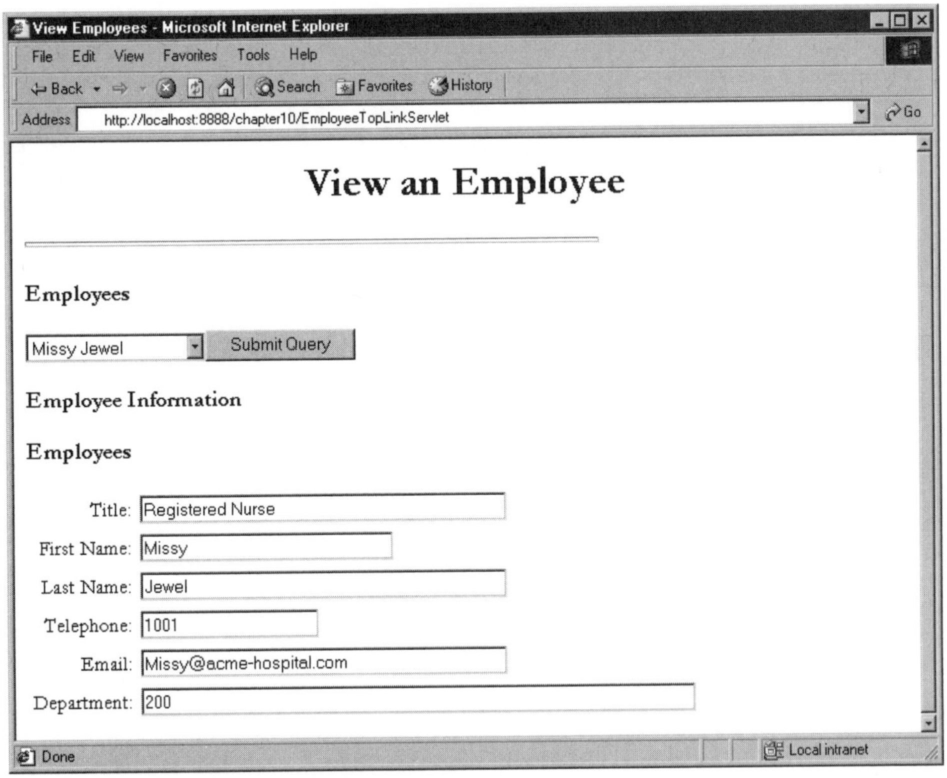

FIGURE 10-8. *Output for `EmployeeTopLinkServlet`*

In Chapter 11, you will learn how to create and deploy JSPs in the OC4J environment. You will also learn that JSPs are based on the Java Servlets API, and that JSPs are first compiled into servlets. This will give you an opportunity to reuse many of the concepts you learned in this chapter.

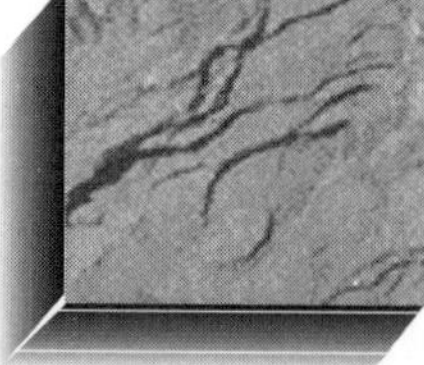

CHAPTER 11

Introduction to JavaServer Pages (JSP)

In J2EE, web components are either servlets or JavaServer Pages (JSPs), which provide the dynamic extension capabilities for a web server. In Chapter 10, you learned how to build web applications using servlets. In this chapter, you will learn how JSP can be leveraged to take advantage of your knowledge of servlets. More importantly, you will learn how to create J2EE applications consisting of JSP and other J2EE components and deploy them to Oracle9*i*AS Containers For J2EE (OC4J), which is fully compliant with the Sun Microsystems JSP specification.

Introduced by Sun Microsystems, the JSP technology allows web developers to mix regular static HTML with dynamically generated HTML into a `*.jsp` file and to directly insert Java code into files on the local file system. JSP pages are very appropriate for generating text-based markup such as HTML, Scalable Vector Graphics (SVG), Wireless Markup Language (WML), and XML. SVG is an XML grammar for describing 2-D graphics. WML pages are pages that wireless devices can read. The WML page is delivered over the Wireless Application Protocol (WAP), and the network configuration requires a gateway to translate WAP to HTTP and back again.

The JSP technology is closely coupled with the servlet technology. As you will see in the "JSP Architecture" section of this chapter, a JSP page is compiled into a servlet. Remember that servlets are Java classes that dynamically process requests and construct responses, while JSPs are text-based documents that execute as servlets.

In this chapter, you will learn about the following topics:

- The basic JSP syntax
- JSP architecture
- Configuring OC4J JSP
- The development directory structure
- Implicit objects
- Error handling
- OC4J support for Oracle SQLJ
- Calling EJB from JSP
- Building an application with TopLink using the MVC pattern
- Configuring and deploying JSPs to OC4J

JSP Syntax Basics

The JSP technology provides a text-based document language that describes how to process a request and construct a response, a set of constructs for accessing server-side objects, and a mechanism for defining extensions to the JSP language. The JSP technology also contains an API that is used by developers of Web containers. The JSP syntax is straightforward, and can be classified into the following categories:

- Directives
- Scripting elements
- Standard actions

Directives

JSP directives do not produce any output to your browser. Their purpose is to provide you with a way to pass messages to the JSP translator. Directives are enclosed with the <%@ ... %> tag and have the following form:

```
<%@ directive attribute="value" %>
```

You can also combine multiple attributes in one directive call:

```
<%@ directive attribute1="value1"
              attribute2="value2"
              ...
              attributeN="valueN" %>
```

There are three types of directives that you can have in your JSP file:

- The `page` directive lets you control various JSP page executions such as importing classes and specifying error pages.
- The `include` directive lets you insert a file into a JSP file at translation time.
- The `taglib` directive lets you specify the uniform resource identifier (URI) or uniform resource locator (URL) of custom JSP libraries.

Directives, with the exception of the `include` directive, should normally be placed at the beginning of the page. We will discuss the first two directives in more detail in the following two sections.

Page Directive

The page directive allows you to pass to the JSP runtime environment or the OC4J JSP translator the instructions that will apply to the entire JSP page that contains the directive. Even though you can place the page directive anywhere in the JSP file, it is good coding practice for you to include it in the beginning of the file.

With the exception of the `import` attribute, each attribute of the page directive can be called only once in a JSP page. The syntax to call a page directive follows:

```
<%@ page attribute1="value1"
         attribute2="value2"
         ...
         attributeN="valueN" %>
```

Now you will learn the different page directives that are frequently used:

- **import** Specifies the packages/classes/interfaces that you wish to import into your package. Note that just like Java source files, `java.lang.*` is implicitly imported; `javax.servlet.*` and `javax.servlet.http.*` are also implicitly imported in JSP files.
- **language** Specifies the scripting language to be used in the scriptlets of the JSP page. The default language that OC4J uses is `java`. Therefore, you do not have to specify this attribute. As you will see later in this chapter, OC4J supports the use of the value of `sqlj` as a scripting language. Here is an example of the directive call:

  ```
  <%@ page language ="sqlj" %>
  ```

When the JSP translation engine encounters the previous statement, it will allow the use of the embedded SQL statements (`#sql`) within the JSP scriptlet. The `#sql` is used to define SQLJ executable statements, as well as SQLJ declarations.

- **buffer** Instructs OC4J of the size of the JSP page output stream. The default size specified by OC4J is 8KB. The size may be increased or decreased; for example:

  ```
  <%@ page buffer="30kb" %>
  ```

  specifies a buffer size of 30kb. The buffer automatically flushes when it is full. You can put a value of none if you do not want any buffering to be done:

  ```
  <%@ page buffer="none" %>
  ```

- **autoFlush** Instructs the JSP engine to automatically flush when the `boolean` value is set to `true` and the buffered output is set to `true`. The `autoFlush` attribute takes a `boolean` as its value. The default is set to `false`. Note that an exception is raised when the value is set to `false` and the `buffer` attribute is set to `none`.

- **`isErrorPage`** Tells OC4J that the current JSP page will be the target of another JSP page's `errorPage` when the value of this attribute is set to `true`. This attribute takes a `boolean` as its value. The default is set to `false`.
- **`errorPage`** Defines the `errorPage` URL of another JSP page that will handle errors when an uncaught `Exception` occurs. OC4J processing will be forwarded to the specified URL. The URL of the forwarded JSP page should contain a `page` directive with the attribute `isErrorPage` defined to `true`. An exception will be thrown on the called JSP page if the `isErrorPage` is not defined.
- **`contentType`** Defines the character encoding for the JSP page. The value of the `contentType` attribute can be of the form `TYPE` or `TYPE; charset=CHARSET`, where `TYPE` is a MIME type. The default value for TYPE is `text/html`, and the default value for the character encoding is ISO-8859-1, also known as Latin-1. See the IANA (http://www.iana.org/numbers.htm) registry for more information on useful values.

Include Directive

The `include` directive allows you to separate your JSP files into components, to do such things as include a common header and footer into your JSP files. The file included into your JSP file can be an ASCII file, such as a static HTML file, or other JSP files. The JSP files will be included into the main JSP file at the time of translation/compilation, and once the JSP file is compiled, any changes in the included file may not be reflected in the main JSP file. The syntax for the include `directive` follows:

```
<%@ include file="/TheNameOfTheFile.xxx" %>
```

The file included must use a relative URL from the context root. The following JSP file, `manage-main-include.jsp`, is an example of how you can use one JSP file to include another:

```
<%-- Program name: manage-main-include.jsp
  -- Purpose: to illustrate how to use the include tag.
  -->

<HTML>
  <HEAD>
    <title>Main Page</title>
  </HEAD>

  <BODY bgcolor="#FFFFCC" text="#000000" link="#009900"
        vlink="#666666" alink="#FF0000">
    <img src="psynex-logo.gif" width="333" height="110"
         border=0 align="left">
```

```
    <H1 align="center">Psynex Management System</H1>
    <p>The current time and date is <%= new java.util.Date() %> </p>
    <BR>
    <!-- This is a file that will be included into this JSP file-->
    <%@ include file="./header.jsp " %>
    <BR>
  </BODY>
</HTML>
```

The manage-main-include.jsp file will include the static header.jsp file:

```
<%-- Program name: header.jsp
  -- Purpose: header that will be included in jsp files
  -->
<H4 align="center">
  <a href="./manage-dept.jsp">Manage Departments
  </a> &#149;
  <a href="./manage-project.jsp">Manage Projects
  </a> &#149;
  <a href="./manage-empl.jsp">Manage Employees
  </a> &#149;
  <a href="./purchase-order.jsp">Purchase Order
  </a>
</H4>
```

To run and test the manage-main-include.jsp page, you have to put the manage-main-include.jsp and header.jsp file in the web/jsp/include directory, as specified later in the "Development Directory Structure" section of this chapter. You then have to deploy the application and start OC4J. The instructions on how to deploy applications and start OC4J can be found in "Configuring and Deploying JSPs to OC4J," later in this chapter.

To test the manage-main-include.jsp page, open your web browser and type:

```
http://localhost:8888/chapter11/jsp/include/manage-main-include.jsp
```

where localhost is the name of the computer running OC4J; 8888 is the port number of the web listener as defined in $OC4J_HOME/j2ee/home/config/http-web-site.xml; and chapter11 is the servlet context root as defined in the http-web-site.xml file.

Scripting Elements

There are four types of scripting elements that you can use in JSP files:

- Comments
- Declarations

- Expressions
- Scriptlets

You will learn about each of the scripting elements next, as well as how to use them in a JSP file.

Comments

JSP comments are intended for the JSP developers to comment their code the same way they would comment their Java source. Comments are stripped out before the page is rendered to the browser. JSP comments are very useful when you want to block out scriptlet code from compiling.

The syntax for a JSP comment is as follows:

```
<%-- JSP comment text goes here --%>
```

You can use HTML comments and they will be rendered as hidden text to the HTML page. The syntax for HTML comments follows:

```
<!-- This is an HTML comment -->
```

Declarations

Declarations allow you to define Java member variables and methods that you will use in JSP files. An example of declarations follows:

```
<%!
    private int orderNumber = 0;
    String department;
    String vendorName;
 %>
```

Scripting elements have XML equivalents. You can also use the XML equivalent, if you wish, for the declaration scripting element:

```
<jsp:declaration>
    private int orderNumber = 0;
    String department;
    String vendorName;
</jsp:declaration>
```

Expressions

Expression in JSP is the result of evaluating Java expressions within a JSP file where the Java expressions are converted to a `String` and are rendered to an output page.

You typically use expressions to show variables. If you have defined a variable called `firstName`, the syntax for an expression would be:

```
<%= firstName %>
```

The following is the XML syntax for the expression:

```
<jsp:expression>
  firstName
</jsp:expression>
```

Note that a JSP expression does *not* end in a semicolon.

Scriptlets

JSP scriptlets are embedded within `<% ... %>` tags and are used to contain code fragments that are valid for the scripting language used in a page. The following is the syntax for a scriptlet:

```
<%
 the scriptlet code goes here
%>
```

The scriptlet is based on the language that you set for the `language` attribute of the page directive. Remember that, by default, the `language` attribute is set to `java`. Therefore, you can place any valid Java statement within the scriptlet tags. As discussed earlier, if you specify `sqlj` as the language, then you will be able to use any valid `sqlj` statement within the scriptlet tags. You will see an example of using `sqlj` in the "OC4J Support for Oracle SQLJ" section of this chapter.

The following is an example of how to use scriptlets. The code assumes that a variable named `numberOfItems` has been defined:

```
<% if (numberOfItems == 0) {%>
     There are no items in your cart<br>
<%} else {%>
     You have <%=numberOfItems%> in your cart<br>
<%}%>
```

You can use scriptlets as well as expressions with HTML code. The equivalent XML representation of the previous code follows:

```
<jsp:scriptlet> if (numberOfItems == 0) {</jsp:scriptlet>
     There are no items in your cart<br>
<jsp:scriptlet>} else {</jsp:scriptlet>
     You have <%=numberOfItems%> in your cart<br>
<jsp:scriptlet> } </jsp:scriptlet>
```

Standard Actions

JSP provides standard action elements that will result in some action to occur at request time while the JSP is being executed. There are three types of action elements:

- **Control tags** Used for flow and plug-in control
- **Bean tags** Used with JavaBeans inside of JSP pages
- **Custom tags** Used to define and provide custom JSP tags

In this section, we look at the following control tags, which allow you to pass information or control to another file or servlet:

- `jsp:param` action tag
- `jsp:include` action tag
- `jsp:forward` action tag

Notice that all three action tags begin with the `jsp:` syntax.

The jsp:param Action Tag

The `jsp:param` tag allows you to pass information to JSP pages that are being included into the JSP file or are being forwarded to other JSP pages. You will see how to include and forward JSP pages in the next two sections. The following is the syntax for you to pass parameters:

```
<jsp:param name="someName" value="someValue" >
```

An example of how to use this in your code follows:

```
<jsp:param name="username" value="scott">
<jsp:param name="password" value="tiger">
```

Now you can access these values from a forwarded or an included page by using the `request` object, which is an instance of `javax.servlet.http.HttpServletRequest`. You can access the parameters in the receiving page by calling `request.getParameter("name")`. Therefore, you can call the previous two parameters in a scriptlet as follows:

```
<%
  String username = request.getParameter("username");
    String password = request.getParameter("password");
%>
```

which would result in the username and password variables, respectively, to contain scott and tiger.

The jsp:include Action Tag

The jsp:include tag allows you to include into your JSP file both static and dynamic resources, where the static resource can be an HTML file and the dynamic resource can be a servlet. Each resource must be a valid URL that can be page-relative or application-relative to the application root. Since you are calling a valid URL, you can include JSP pages as well as servlets. However, the jsp:include action tag can be used only between pages in the same servlet context. The syntax for using the jsp:include tag follows:

```
<jsp:include page="/someJSPFile.jsp" flush="true" />
```

The resource for this syntax is application-relative.

The flush attribute is a mandatory boolean attribute. If the value is true, the buffer is flushed. A false value is not valid in JSP 1.1.

You can pass parameters to the page that the include tag is calling by using the jsp:param tag. The syntax to do this follows:

```
<jsp:include page="chapter11/loginpage.jsp" flush="true" >
   <jsp:param name="username" value="scott" />
   <jsp:param name="password" value="tiger" />
</jsp:include>
```

The preceding code snippet is equivalent to passing the parameters as part of the URL, as follows:

```
<jsp:include
 page="/chapter11/loginpage.jsp?username=scott&password=tiger"
 flush="true" />
```

The jsp:forward Action Tag

The jsp:forward tag allows you to stop execution of the current page and transfer control to another JSP page. Just like the jsp:include tag, the resource has to be a valid URL, which can be page-relative or application-relative of the same servlet context. You can forward control to another JSP page or servlet. The syntax for using the jsp:forward tag follows:

```
<jsp:forward page="/chapter11/loginpage.jsp" />
```

You can also pass parameters to the page that the include is calling by using the jsp:param tag. The syntax to do this follows:

```
<jsp:forward page="/chapter11/loginpage.jsp" >
   <jsp:param name="username" value="scott" />
   <jsp:param name="password" value="tiger" />
</jsp:forward >
```

The buffer will be cleared when the `jsp:forward` action is encountered in a JSP page. You cannot set the page directive of `buffer="none"`. An `IllegalStateException` exception will be thrown if there is no buffer.

JSP Architecture

Since you have seen the basics and syntax of JSP, the next step is for you to learn the life cycle of JSPs. It is very important that you understand the life cycle and what happens behind the scenes when a user makes a JSP request to OC4J. In Figure 11-1, you can see what happens when a user calls a JSP page.

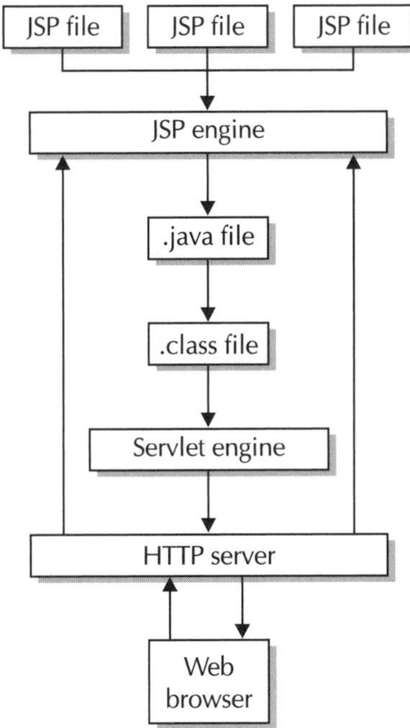

FIGURE 11-1. *OC4J handling of JSP requests*

Here are the steps that OC4J uses by default for JSPs:

1. The client sends a request to the HTTP server requesting a JSP page.
2. OC4J receives the request. If the request is a `*.jsp` file, OC4J sends the request to the JSP engine. The default maps for JSP are files that end with `.jsp`. The default map can be found in the `global-web-application.xml` file located in the $OC4J_HOME/config directory.
3. The JSP engine sees if the requested JSP file has been translated to a `*.java` file. If it has not, OC4J will translate the JSP file. OC4J also checks to see if the JSP file has been updated since it was last translated. The engine will translate the JSP file if it has changed. A translation error will be sent to the browser if the JSP file is not syntactically correct. Note that this *on-demand translation* is the default behavior of OC4J. These settings are configurable. See the following "Configuring OC4J JSP" section to see how to change the way JSP is translated in OC4J.
4. OC4J compiles the `*.java` file into a servlet. A compilation error will be sent to the browser if there are any compilation errors. This step is skipped if the JSP file has been compiled into a servlet and the file has not changed since it was last compiled. Note that this *on-demand compilation* is the default behavior of OC4J. You can configure this default option. See the following "Configuring OC4J JSP" section.
5. The class file or the servlet is loaded into the servlet engine.
6. The servlet engine executes the servlet and sends the response back to the browser.

As described in all the preceding chapters, when developing a J2EE application, it is recommended that you create a development directory, name it after your application, and develop your application as modules within that directory.

Configuring OC4J JSP

The JSP container is preconfigured in OC4J to run JSP pages when you start it. The following settings appear in the OC4J `global-web-application.xml` file to map the name of the front-end JSP servlet, and to map the appropriate filename extensions for JSP pages:

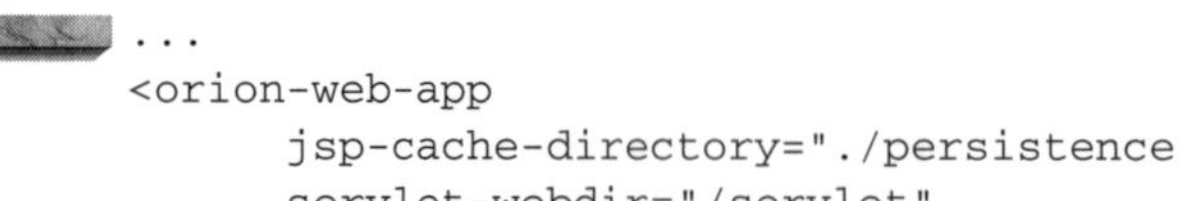

```
...
<orion-web-app
      jsp-cache-directory="./persistence"
      servlet-webdir="/servlet"
```

```
      development="false"
      jsp-timeout="0" >
...
      <web-app>

            <servlet>
                  <servlet-name>jsp</servlet-name>
                  <servlet-class>
                       oracle.jsp.runtimev2.JspServlet
                  </servlet-class>
                  <load-on-startup>0</load-on-startup>
                  <!-- you can disable page scope listener if you
                       don't need this function. -->
                  <init-param>
                        <param-name>check_page_scope</param-name>
                        <param-value>true</param-value>
                  </init-param>
                  <!-- you can set main_mode to "justrun" to speed up
                       JSP dispatching, if you don't need to recompile
                       your JSP anymore. You can always switch your
                       main_mode. Please see our doc for details -->
                  <!--
                  <init-param>
                        <param-name>main_mode</param-name>
                        <param-value>justrun</param-value>
                  </init-param>
                  -->
            </servlet>

...
            <servlet-mapping>
                  <servlet-name>jsp</servlet-name>
                  <url-pattern>/*.jsp</url-pattern>
            </servlet-mapping>
            <servlet-mapping>
                  <servlet-name>jsp</servlet-name>
                  <url-pattern>/*.JSP</url-pattern>
            </servlet-mapping>
            <servlet-mapping>
                  <servlet-name>jsp</servlet-name>
                  <url-pattern>/*.sqljsp</url-pattern>
            </servlet-mapping>
            <servlet-mapping>
                  <servlet-name>jsp</servlet-name>
                  <url-pattern>/*.SQLJSP</url-pattern>
            </servlet-mapping>
...
</orion-web-app>
```

You have the option of changing the JSP settings of OC4J in this file by putting `init-param` element tags in the `global-web-application.xml` file. The example and syntax for the `init-param` element follows:

```
</servlet>
  ...
  <init-param>
    <param-name>main_mode</param-name>
    <param-value>justrun</param-value>
  </init-param>
  ...
 </servlet>
```

When you are going through the development process, you may want to adjust some parameters to help you with debugging. The following is a list of a few parameters that may help you while you are in the development process:

- **`main_mode`** Can be set for the compilation behavior of OC4J. The default mode is `recompile`. This flag can be set for automatic recompilation of JSP pages and reloading of Java classes that have changed. Here are the supported settings:
  - **`justrun`** The container will not do any timestamp checking, so there is no recompilation of JSP pages or reloading of Java classes. This mode should be used in a production environment.
  - **`reload`** The container will check if any classes have been modified since loading, including translated JSP pages, JavaBeans invoked from pages, and any other dependency classes.
  - **`recompile`** The container will check the timestamp of JSP pages to see if they have been modified.
- **`precompile_check`** Set to `true` when you want to check the HTTP request to see if a `jsp_precompile` has been passed as a parameter. If this value is set to `true`, when a page is executed with the `precompile_check` as its parameter, the container will recompile the JSP page without executing it.
- **`debug_mode`** Use the default `true` setting to print a stack trace whenever a runtime exception occurs. A `false` setting disables this feature. The default mode for `debug_mode` is `false`. Note that when this mode is set to `false`, the filename is not displayed when a file is not found.

Refer to the *Oracle9iAS Containers For J2EE Support for JavaServer Pages Developer's Guide* for a complete listing of all the parameter options for the `init-param` element.

Precompilation

You learned OC4J's default behavior for handling JSP pages in the "JSP Architecture" section of this chapter. Recall that OC4J retranslates and recompiles JSP pages the first time the container encounters a JSP page. It also recompiles a JSP page every time the JSP page has been modified. Fortunately, OC4J provides you with ways to precompile JSP files to binary files so that the first end user to execute the page is saved the translation and compilation time.

JSP Precompilation

The JSP specification provides a way for containers to precompile JSP files. You can configure OC4J to precompile JSP files by using `jsp_precompile` as a request parameter of the JSP pages that you want to precompile. OC4J will pretranslate and precompile the JSP pages without executing them when it encounters the `jsp_precompile` request parameter. The steps necessary to invoke precompilation follow:

1. Enable the JSP `precompile_check` parameter in your `global-web-application.xml` file as follows:

   ```
   ...
   <init-param>
     <param-name>precompile_check</param-name>
     <param-value>true</param-value>
   </init-param>
   ...
   ```

   You should not set the `precompile_check` in a production environment, so that performance is not degraded.

2. Make a call to each JSP page that you want to precompile by including the `jsp_precompile` parameter as part of the request. The syntax follows:

   ```
   http://host[:port]/someJSPFile.jsp?jsp_precompile=true
   or:
   http://host[:port]/someJSPFile.jsp?jsp_precompile
   ```

   where the `true` value is optional.

Development Directory Structure

The development directory for the applications in this chapter follows:

- **chapter11** Root directory of your J2EE application.
  - **META-INF** Directory where your `application.xml` file is located, which defines the modules you have in your J2EE application.
  - **src** Root directory where all the source files are located.
    - **META-INF** Directory that contains the `ejb-jar.xml` deployment descriptor file and the `orion-ejb-jar.xml` OC4J-specific deployment descriptor file.
    - **purchase** Package indicating the starting point of the `Employee` Servlets application.
      - **bean** Package consisting of the source code JavaBeans for TopLink.
      - **model** Package consisting of the source code containing the `Employee` class used by TopLink.
      - **servlets** Package consisting of the source code containing the servlet controller used by this chapter.
      - **vo** Package consisting of the source code of your value object classes.
      - **ejb** Package consisting of the source code of your EJB components.
        - **cmp** Package consisting of the source code of all your container-managed persistent (CMP) entity beans.
        - **sfsb** Package containing all the source code for your session beans.
  - **web** Root package containing files necessary for the application.
    - **WEB-INF** Directory consisting of the `web.xml` file.
      - **classes** Root directory for your web applications; contains the `Employee.xml` and `Sessions.XML` used by TopLink.
        - **purchase** Root package of classes.
          - **bean** Class files for JavaBeans.

        - **model** Class files for TopLink classes.
        - **servlets** Class files for servlets.
        - **vo** Class files for value objects.
- **jsp** Contains the JSP files used in this chapter.
    - **ejb** Directory containing the JSP files for the EJB example.
    - **exception** Directory containing JSP file for exception handling example.
    - **include** Directory containing JSP file for include example.
    - **sqlj** Directory containing JSP file for sqlj example.
    - **toplink** Directory containing JSP file for the TopLink example.
- **images** Directory containing image files.

Implicit Objects

The JSP specification provides *implicit* or *default* objects, which are the following named objects that you can use in JSP files without having to explicitly create an object:

- **`request`** The HTTP request object that is an instance of the `javax.servlet.http.HttpServletRequest` servlet class.
- **`response`** The HTTP request object that is an instance of the `javax.servlet.http.HttpServletResponse` servlet interface.
- **`session`** The HTTP session object that is an instance of the `javax.servlet.http.HttpSession` class.
- **`application`** The servlet context of OC4J. It is an instance of the `javax.servlet.ServletContext` class. The `application` object is accessible from multiple sessions running within a single JVM.
- **`out`** An object that is an instance of the `javax.servlet.jsp.JspWriter` class. It is used to write content to the output stream that will eventually render the page.
- **`exception`** An object that is created only if the `isErrorPage="true"` page directive is in the JSP page. It is an instance of `java.lang.Throwable`.

Error Handling

Now that you have seen how to use the syntax of JSP to develop applications, the next step is to see how you can handle errors and exceptions in JSPs. So, what do you do when an exception is thrown in JSP? You can certainly put `try-catch` blocks in your scriptlet code to handle errors. However, JSP provides a convenient and clean way to handle runtime exceptions in your application.

The JSP specification provides developers an easy way to handle runtime exceptions. Exceptions are stored in the implicit object named `exception`. As you will see in the next example, you can use the `exception` implicit object in a special type of JSP page called an *error page*.

The following JSP file is a simple JSP page that looks for a remote `java.security.Principal` from the request. A new `Exception` will be thrown stating that the user from the `Principal` object is not found.

```
<%-- Program name: getPrincipal.jsp
  -- Purpose: Looks for a Principal object.
  --          Throw an exception if not found.
  --%>
<%@ page import ="java.security.Principal" %>

<HTML>
  <HEAD>
    <title>Get Principal Page</title>
  </HEAD>

  <BODY bgcolor="#FFFFCC" text="#000000" link="#009900"
        vlink="#666666" alink="#FF0000">
    <img src="/chapter11/images/psynex-logo.gif" width="333"
         height="110" border=0 align="left">
    <% // Scriptlet gets the user principal
      Principal user = request.getUserPrincipal();
      if (user == null) {
        throw new Exception("User was not found. " +
                            " Possible login error");
      }
      else {
        out.println("Welcome " + user.getName());
      }
     %>
  </BODY>
</HTML>
```

To run and test the `getPrincipal.jsp`, you have to put the `getPrincipal.jsp` in the `web/jsp/exception` directory, as specified earlier in the "Development

Directory Structure" section of this chapter. You then have to deploy the application and start OC4J. The instructions on how to deploy applications and start OC4J can be found later in this chapter in "Configuring and Deploying JSPs to OC4J."

To test the `getPrincipal.jsp` JSP page, open your web browser and type the following:

```
http://localhost:8888/chapter11/jsp/exception/getPrincipal.jsp
```

Figure 11-2 shows the error that is thrown when the `getPrincipal.jsp` page is called. You can tell the container to automatically redirect a different JSP page by specifying a `page` directive with the `errorPage` attribute. The following code snippet is a modification of the `getPrincipal.jsp` file, which adds an `errorPage` page directive that tells the JSP page where to redirect when an exception is raised:

```
<%-- Program name: getPrincipal.jsp
  -- Purpose: Looks for a Principal object.
  --          Throw an exception if not found.
  --%>
<%@ page import ="java.security.Principal" %>
<%@ page errorPage ="ErrorPage.jsp" %>

<HTML>
...
```

FIGURE 11-2. *Output of calling the `getPrincipal.jsp` page*

You now have to create the ErrorPage.jsp file, with a page directive with isErrorPage="true", that will handle and report an error message if the Principal object is not found:

```
<%-- Program name: ErrorPage.jsp
  -- Purpose: Handles and reports exceptions
  --%>
<%@ page isErrorPage ="true" %>

<HTML>
  <HEAD>
    <title>Error Page</title>
  </HEAD>

  <BODY bgcolor="#FFFFCC" text="#000000" link="#009900"
        vlink="#666666" alink="#FF0000">
    <IMG src="/chapter11/images/psynex-logo.gif" width="333"
       height="110" border=0 align="left">
    <BR>
    <H2>Error Page Handler</H2>
    <BR>
    <B>An Error occurred with the message:</B>
        <%=exception.getMessage()%>
    <BR>
    <B>The exception raised was:</B>
        <%=exception.toString()%>
  </BODY>
</HTML>
```

Now, when you open your web browser and rerun the following, you should see the page displayed in Figure 11-3:

```
http://localhost:8888/chapter11/jsp/exception/getPrincipal.jsp
```

You can provide a default error page in your web.xml file with the following syntax:

```
...
<error-page>
  <error-code>404</error-code>
  <location>/error404.html</location>
</error-page>
...
```

For more information on default error pages, see the Sun Microsystems Java Servlet Specification.

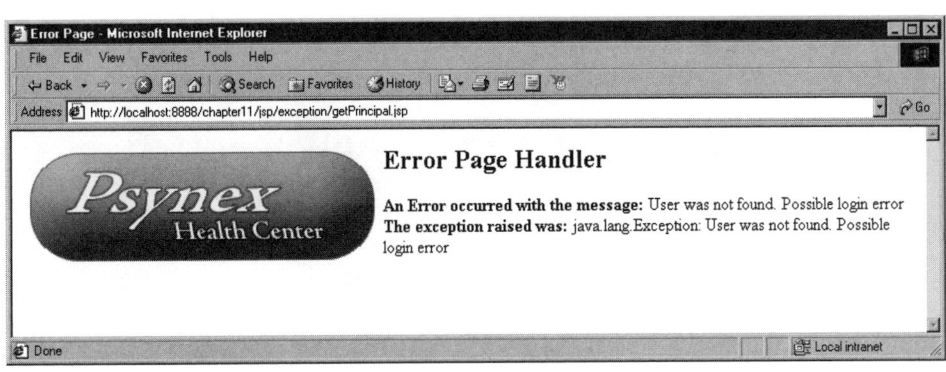

FIGURE 11-3. *Error page called by `getPrincipal.jsp`*

OC4J Support for Oracle SQLJ

SQLJ provides a way for Java developers to write static embedded SQL code, whereas JDBC provides a dynamic SQL interface for Java. Chapter 3 discusses how to use SQLJ statements with Java. The "SQLJ" section of Chapter 3 also provides you with an application example called `EmployeeTool.sqlj` that illustrates how to use SQLJ in an application. Note that even though OC4J provides you with the facility to use SQLJ in your JSP, using SQLJ in your JSP is not recommended. It is better programming practice to use SQLJ in JavaBean components or JSP custom tags to communicate with the database.

The OC4J JSP engine fully supports SQLJ within JSP. In this section, you will learn how to use SQLJ in your JSP file to communicate with the Oracle database. Figure 11-4 shows what happens behind the scenes when a JSP page contains SQLJ.

In the next example, you will call a JSP page that will use SQLJ to dynamically create a drop-down list consisting of departments. You will then be able to select a department number from the list and submit a query that will return to the selected department.

You will start by creating a department value object called `DepartmentVO`, and then you will create a JSP file containing SQLJ statements. Let us first create a value object that the JSP file will use. Remember that value objects are used to group a set of class attributes that are used together. Value objects provide

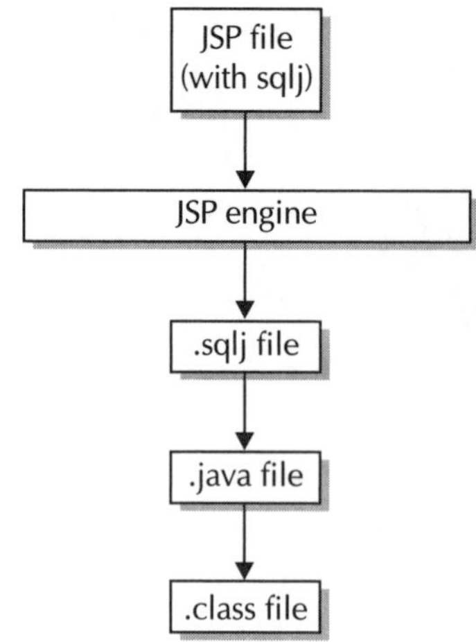

FIGURE 11-4. *JSP-SQLJ translation compilation process*

a convenient way to access the class attributes by providing getter and setter methods. The following code contains the `DepartmentVO` value object:

```
package purchase.vo;

import java.io.Serializable;

public class DepartmentVO implements Serializable {

  private long deptNo;
  private String shortName;
  private String name;

  public DepartmentVO() { }

  public DepartmentVO(long deptNo, String shortName,
                      String name)
  {
        this.deptNo = deptNo;
        this.name = name;
        this.shortName = shortName;
  }

  public long getDeptNo()
  {
    return deptNo;
```

```
  }

  public void setDeptNo(long newDeptNo)
  {
    deptNo = deptNo;
  }

  public String getName()
  {
    return name;
  }

  public void setName(String newName)
  {
    name = newName;
  }

  public String getShortName()
  {
    return shortName;
  }

  public void setShortName(String newShortName)
  {
    shortName = newShortName;
  }
}  // End of DepartmentVO()
```

Now, you need to know how to tell OC4J that your JSP file contains SQLJ code in one of two ways:

- End your JSP source files with the `.sqljsp` extension instead of the `.jsp` extension.
- Use the attribute `language ="sqlj"` page directive. Refer to the "Directives" section earlier in this chapter for information on the page directive.

The following JSP file named `view-dept.jsp` shows you how to use SQLJ in a JSP page. The JSP page contains:

- A page directive of `language ="sqlj"` that tells the OC4J translating engine that the JSP file may contain SQLJ statements.
- A declaration scriptlet element that has a `DeptIter` SQLJ iterator and a `getDepartments()` private method that uses the `DeptIter` iterator to create and return an `ArrayList` of `DepartmentVO` objects.

```
<%-- Program name: view-dept.jsp
  -- Purpose: This is an example of how to use SQLJ within
  --          OC4J's JSP.
  --%>

<%@ page language="sqlj"%>
<%@ page import="sqlj.runtime.ref.DefaultContext%>
<%@ page import="oracle.sqlj.runtime.Oracle"%>
<%@ page import="purchase.vo.DepartmentVO"%>
<%@ page import="java.util.ArrayList"%>

<%! //jsp declarations
  #sql iterator DeptIter( long deptno, String shortName, String name );

  private ArrayList getDepartments()throws java.sql.SQLException {

    DeptIter deptIter = null;
    DefaultContext dctx = null;
    DepartmentVO dept = null;
    ArrayList depts = new ArrayList();

    try {
      dctx = Oracle.getConnection(
               "jdbc:oracle:thin:@localhost:1521:orcl",
               "scott", "tiger");

      #sql [dctx] deptIter = {
        SELECT deptno, shortname, name
        FROM department
      };

      while (deptIter.next()) {
        dept = new DepartmentVO(deptIter.deptno(),
                                deptIter.shortName(),
                                deptIter.name());
        depts.add(dept);
      }  // End of while
      return depts;

     } catch (java.sql.SQLException e) {

     } finally {
     if (dctx!= null) dctx.close();
     }
    return depts;
```

```
  }
%>

<html>
  <head>
    <title>View a Department</title>
    <meta http-equiv="Content-Type" content="text/html;
      charset=iso-8859-1">
  </head>

  <body bgcolor="#FFFFCC" text="#000000" link="#009900"
    vlink="#666666" alink="#FF0000">
    <img src="/chapter11/images/psynex-logo.gif" width="333"
             height="110" border=0 alt="Psynex Pharmaceutical"
             align="left">

    <h1 align="center">View a Department</h1>
    <h4 align="center">
      <a href="manage-dept.jsp">Manage Departments</a> &#149;
      <a href="create-dept.jsp">Create a department</a><br>
      <a href="modify-dept.jsp">Modify a department</a> &#149;
      <a href="delete-dept.jsp">Delete a department</a> &#149;
      <a href="manage-main.jsp">Management Home</a>
    </h4>

    <hr align="left" size=4 width="65%">
    <% // Scriptlet
        String deptNo = request.getParameter("deptno");
        String shortName = "";
        String name = "";
     %>

    <form method="get">
      <h3>Department Numbers</h3>
      <p>
      <select name="deptno">
        <% // Scriptlet
          ArrayList depts = getDepartments();
          DepartmentVO dept = null;

          out.print("<option>Select a department</option>");
          // loop through list of departments and display departments
          for (int i=0; i<depts.size(); i++) {
            String deptStr = null;
            dept = (DepartmentVO)depts.get(i);
```

```
            // get the string dept number to make it the selected
            //  dept of the list
            deptStr = Long.toString(dept.getDeptNo());

            out.print("<option ");
            if( deptNo != null && deptNo.equals(deptStr)) {
              out.print(" selected ");
              shortName = dept.getShortName();
              name = dept.getName();
            }
            out.print("> "); // close <option> tag
            out.println(dept.getDeptNo() + "</option>");
          }
        %>
      </select>

      <input type="submit" value="View Department">
      </p>
    </form>
    <p>
      Department name: <input type="text" name="deptName" size="55"
                              value="<%=name%>" readonly><br>
      Department short name: <input type="text" name="shortName"
                                    value="<%=shortName%>" size="25"
                                    readonly>
    </p>
    <p> </p>
  </body>
</html>
```

To run and test the `view-dept.jsp` page, you have to put it in the `web/jsp/sqlj` directory, as specified earlier in the "Development Directory Structure" section of this chapter. You then have to deploy the application and start OC4J. The instructions on how to deploy applications and start OC4J can be found later in the chapter in "Configuring and Deploying JSPs to OC4J."

To run the `view-dept.jsp` page, open your web browser and type the following:

```
http://localhost:8888/chapter11/jsp/sqlj/view-dept.jsp
```

Figure 11-5 shows the output of your web browser after selecting and submitting Department 201.

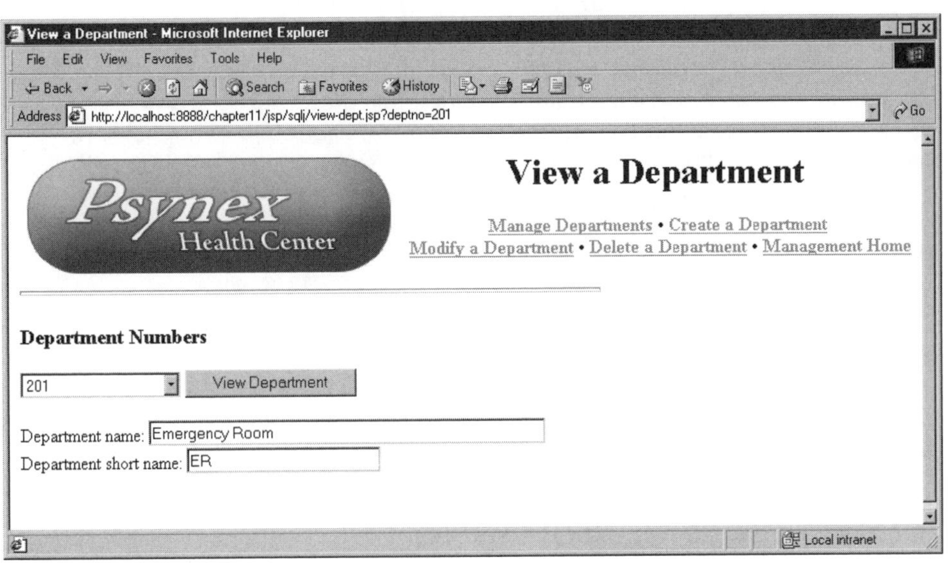

FIGURE 11-5. *Output screen of* `view-dept.jsp`

Calling EJB from JSP Pages

Just as you can make a call to EJB from a servlet, you can also make calls to EJB from JSP pages. In this section, you will build the `view-order.jsp` page that uses the `PurchaseOrderManagement` session bean that you developed in Chapter 6. You can make calls to EJBs from a JSP page the same way you do it from an application. Here is a reminder of the steps necessary to call an EJB:

1. Import the EJB package for the bean home and remote interfaces into each JSP page that makes EJB calls.
2. Use JNDI to look up the EJB home interface.
3. Create the EJB remote object from the home.
4. Invoke business methods on the remote object.

The next example, `view_order.jsp`, is a JSP page in which a user enters a purchase order number and then is shown the line item of the purchase order. The `view-order.jsp` page uses the preceding four steps to call and invoke an EJB: import packages; use JNDI to look up the `PurchaseOrderManagement` home interface; create the `PurchaseOrderManagement` EJB remote object; and invoke the `getPurchaseOrderInfo()` business method of the `getPurchaseOrderManagement` remote object.

```
<%-- Program name: /jsp/ejb/view-order.jsp
  -- Purpose: This is an example of how to use EJB within
  --          OC4J's JSP.
  --%>

<%@ page import="java.util.Hashtable" %>
<%@ page import="javax.naming.InitialContext" %>
<%@ page import="purchase.ejb.sfsb.PurchaseOrderManagement"%>
<%@ page import="purchase.ejb.sfsb.PurchaseOrderManagementHome"%>
<%@ page import="javax.rmi.PortableRemoteObject"%>
<%@ page import="java.util.List"%>
<%@ page import="purchase.vo.LineItemVO"%>

<%  //scriptlet
  List po = null;
  // Get the Initial context
  InitialContext ctx = new InitialContext();
  PurchaseOrderManagementHome  purchaseOrderManagementHome =
    (PurchaseOrderManagementHome)ctx.lookup("PurchaseOrderManagement");

  // Use one of the create() methods below to create a new instance
  PurchaseOrderManagement purchaseOrderManagement =
       purchaseOrderManagementHome.create();

  String poNumber = request.getParameter("purchaseorder");
  long requestno = (poNumber == null || phoNumber.equals(""))?
                  0:Long.parseLong(poNumber);

  // Get the line items of a selected purchase order.
  po = (List)purchaseOrderManagement.getPurchaseOrderInfo(requestno);

%>

<html>
<head>
<title>View Purchase Order</title>
<meta http-equiv="Content-Type" content="text/html; charset=iso-8859-1">
</head>
```

```
<body bgcolor="#FFFFCC" text="#000000" link="#009900"
      vlink="#666666" alink="#FF0000" style="font-family:
      Jenson, Garamond, serif">

<div><img src="/chapter11/images/psynex-logo.gif" width="333"
      height="110" border=0 alt="Psynex Pharmaceutical" align="left">
</div>

<h1 align="center">View Purchase Order</h1>
<h4 align="center">
  <a href="purchase-order.html">Purchase Order</a> &#149;
  <a href="create-order.html">Create a purchase order</a> &#149;
  <a href="modify-order.html">Modify a purchase order</a> &#149;
  <a href="delete-order.html">Delete a purchase order</a> &#149;
  <a href="approve-order.html">Purchase Approval</a> &#149;
  <a href="manage-main.html">Management Home</a></h4>

<hr align="left" size=4 width="65%">
<form name="purchase_menu_form" method="post">
  <h3>Purchase Orders</h3>
  <p>Order Number:
    <input type="text" name="purchaseorder" size="25">
    <input type="submit" name="View" value="View">
  </p>
</form>

  <% // Don't show header if there is no purchase order
     if (po.size() > 0) {%>
  <h3>Purchases Detail:</h3>
  <table>
  <tr>
    <th valign="bottom">Project<br>Number</th>
    <th valign="bottom">Quantity</th>
    <th valign="bottom">Unit of Issue</th>
    <th valign="bottom">Estimated<br>Cost</th>
    <th valign="bottom">Total Cost</th>
    <th valign="bottom">Description</th>
  </tr>
  <%}%>

  <% // Loop and print all the LineItemVO objects of the Arraylist
     // that the getPurchaseOrderInfo() method returned.
     for (int i=0; i < po.size(); i++) {

     // Get the line items of the purchase
     LineItemVO lo = (LineItemVO)po.get(i); %>
```

```
  <tr>
    <td>
      <input type="text" name="project_number1" size="10"
         value="<%=lo.projectno%>" readonly>
    </td>
    <td align="center">
      <input type="text" name="quantity" size=3
         value="<%=lo.quantity%>" readonly>
    </td>
    <td>
      <input type="text" name="unit" size=6
         value="<%=lo.unit%>" readonly>
    </td>
    <td align="center">
      $<input type="text" name="est" size=12
          value="<%=lo.cost%>" readonly>
    </td>
    <td align="center">
      $<input type="text" name="total" size=12
         value="<%=lo.cost*lo.quantity%>"readonly>
    </td>
    <td>
      <input type="text" name="description1" size=60
         value="<%=lo.description%>"readonly>
    </td>
  </tr>
 <%}%>

</table>

</body>
</html>
```

Now, you can configure the web.xml and application.xml files to make the EJB work with the view-order.jsp page. The following is a code snippet of web.xml that contains references to the EJB components by using the ejb-local-ref element:

```
...
  <ejb-ref>
    <ejb-ref-name>ejb/PurchaseOrderManagement</ejb-ref-name>
    <ejb-ref-type>Session</ejb-ref-type>
    <home>purchase.ejb.sfsb.PurchaseOrderManagementHome</home>
    <remote>purchase.ejb.sfsb.PurchaseOrderManagement</remote>
    <ejb-link>PurchaseOrderManagement</ejb-link>
```

```
  </ejb-ref>
  <ejb-local-ref>
    <ejb-ref-name>ejb/local/LineItemLocal</ejb-ref-name>
    <ejb-ref-type>Entity</ejb-ref-type>
    <local-home>purchase.ejb.cmp.LineItemLocalHome</local-home>
    <local>purchase.ejb.cmp.LineItemLocal</local>
    <ejb-link>LineItemLocal</ejb-link>
  </ejb-local-ref>
  <ejb-local-ref>
    <ejb-ref-name>ejb/local/PurchaseOrderLocal</ejb-ref-name>
    <ejb-ref-type>Entity</ejb-ref-type>
    <local-home>purchase.ejb.cmp.PurchaseOrderLocalHome</local-home>
    <local>purchase.ejb.cmp.PurchaseOrderLocal</local>
    <ejb-link>PurchaseOrderLocal</ejb-link>
  </ejb-local-ref>
  <ejb-local-ref>
    <ejb-ref-name>ejb/local/ApprovalLocal</ejb-ref-name>
    <ejb-ref-type>Entity</ejb-ref-type>
    <local-home>purchase.ejb.cmp.ApprovalLocalHome</local-home>
    <local>purchase.ejb.cmp.ApprovalLocal</local>
    <ejb-link>ApprovalLocal</ejb-link>
  </ejb-local-ref>
...
```

The following is the application.xml code snippet:

```
...
  <module>
    <ejb>chapter11-ejb.jar</ejb>
  </module>
...
```

To run and test the /jsp/ejb/view-order.jsp file, you have to first make the modifications to the web.xml and application.xml files, as described previously. You then have to put the view-dept.jsp file in the web/jsp/ejb directory, as specified in the "Development Directory Structure" section of this chapter. You then have to deploy the application and start OC4J. The instructions for how to deploy applications and start OC4J are provided later in the chapter in "Configuring and Deploying JSPs to OC4J."

To run the view-order.jsp page, open your web browser and type the following:

```
http://localhost:8888/chapter11/jsp/ejb/view-order.jsp
```

Building an Application with TopLink Using the MVC Pattern

Using JSPs with servlets is an excellent way to implement the model-view-controller (MVC) model 2 architecture design pattern. The MVC architecture pattern is the interaction between the model, view, and controller where:

- The model can be a number of different resources, such as a JavaBean or session bean.
- The view is the JSP page that contains no processing logic.
- The controller is responsible for receiving information from the view and communicates with the model.

In this section, you will develop an Employee MVC application that uses Java servlets, JavaServer Pages, and JavaBeans using Oracle9*i*AS TopLink to effectively deliver dynamic web content of the Employee application. Figure 11-6 shows all the moving parts of the application.

Because of space constraints, the JSP pages for this application are not provided here. However, you can download the entire source code and JSP files from http://shop.osborne.com/cgi-bin/oraclepress/downloads.html.

The EmployeeServlet Servlet Controller Class

The servlet that is the controller for the Employee application is the `EmployeeServlet` servlet controller. All interaction with the model must go through this controller. Refer to Chapter 10 for a full discussion of servlets.

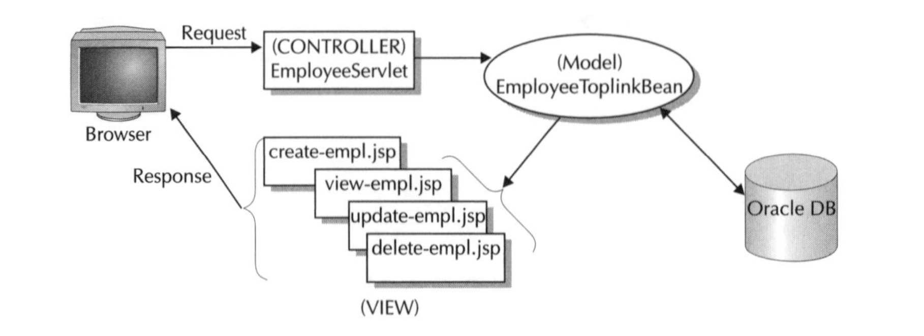

FIGURE 11-6. *MVC Employee application architecture*

Here is the description of some methods of the `EmployeeServlet` that describes the different methods of the the `EmployeeServlet` class:

- **`service(HttpServletRequest request, HttpServletResponse response)`** All incoming requests, including `GET` and `POST` requests, to this servlet come through this method. This method in the `EmployeeServlet` application gets a `mode` request parameter that is used to decide the action that should be taken next.
- **`forwardToPage( String forwardToUrl, HttpServletRequest request, HttpServletResponse response)`** This method uses the `RequestDispatcher`, which is used to stop the current thread of execution and redirects/forwards the next rendered JSP page to the browser. Therefore, use the `RequestDispatcher` to forward control to another servlet/JSP page or redirect the web browser to a new URL.
- The other methods of the class are used to create, update, and delete an employee. Each of these methods creates a new `EmployeeToplinkBean` TopLink JavaBean instance, which communicates with the database; calls the appropriate methods of the bean; and then redirects to the next appropriate JSP page.

```
/*
** Program Name: EmployeeServlet.java
 * This servlet controller provides diverse facilities to view,
 * create, update, and delete employees using TopLink and employee
 * data provided by the request
*/

package purchase.servlets;

// Basic imports
import java.io.*;

// J2EE imports
import javax.servlet.*;
import javax.servlet.http.*;

// Model import
import purchase.model.Employee;
import purchase.bean.EmployeeToplinkBean;
import purchase.vo.EmployeeVO;
```

```
public class EmployeeServlet extends HttpServlet {

  // requests will be redirected to the following JSP pages
  private static String MAIN_PAGE = "/jsp/toplink/manage-empl.jsp";
  private static String VIEW_PAGE = "/jsp/toplink/view-empl.jsp";
  private static String CREATE_PAGE = "/jsp/toplink/create-empl.jsp";
  private static String MODIFY_PAGE = "/jsp/toplink/modify-empl.jsp";
  private static String DELETE_PAGE = "/jsp/toplink/delete-empl.jsp";

  private static int VIEW = 1;
  private static int CREATE = 2;
  private static int MODIFY = 3;
  private static int DELETE = 4;
  private static int CREATE_EMP = 10;
  private static int UPDATE_EMP = 11;
  private static int DELETE_EMP = 12;

  protected void service(HttpServletRequest request,
                         HttpServletResponse response)
    throws ServletException, java.io.IOException {

    // Get JavaBean
    EmployeeToplinkBean etb = new EmployeeToplinkBean();

    //Use the mode switch to decide which operation to execute
    String modeStr = request.getParameter("mode");

    // set mode switch to 0 if mode was not found in the request
    int mode = 0;
    if (modeStr != null)
      mode = (new Integer(modeStr)).intValue();

      if (mode == VIEW) { //Action 1: redirect to the main page
        // put the list of employees in the session
        forwardToPage(VIEW_PAGE,request, response);
      } else //  redirect to the create employee page
      if (mode == CREATE) {
        forwardToPage(CREATE_PAGE,request, response);
      } else //  redirect to the modify employee page
      if (mode == MODIFY) {
        // put the list of employees in the session
        forwardToPage(MODIFY_PAGE,request, response);
      } else // redirect to the delete employee page
      if (mode == DELETE)  {
        forwardToPage(DELETE_PAGE,request, response);
      } else // Create a new employee
      if (mode == CREATE_EMP) {
        createEmployee(request, response);
```

```
    } else //Update an existing employee
    if (mode == UPDATE_EMP) {
      updateEmployee(request, response);
    } else // Delete an existing employee
    if (mode == DELETE_EMP) {
      deleteEmployee(request, response);
    } else { // Go to Main Page
      forwardToPage(MAIN_PAGE, request, response);
    }

}

private void  forwardToPage( String forwardToUrl,
                             HttpServletRequest request,
                             HttpServletResponse response)
  throws ServletException, IOException {
   // use the RequestDispatcher to forward the JSP page
    RequestDispatcher dispatcher =
      getServletContext().getRequestDispatcher(forwardToUrl);
    dispatcher.forward(request, response);
}

/**
 * Populate the employee with employee data from request
 */
private EmployeeVO populateEmployee(HttpServletRequest request) {

  //Get employee data from request
  String employeeno = request.getParameter("employeeno");
  String firstname = request.getParameter("firstname");
  String lastname = request.getParameter("lastname");
  String deptno = request.getParameter("deptno");
  String type = request.getParameter("type");
  String phone = request.getParameter("phone");
  String email = request.getParameter("email");

  EmployeeVO employee = new EmployeeVO();

  //Populate employee
  employee.setEmployeeno((employeeno != null) ?
                        Long.parseLong(employeeno) : 0L);
  employee.setFirstName((firstname != null) ? firstname : "");
  employee.setLastName((lastname != null) ? lastname : "");
  //If no deptno is specified, use deptno = 200 in order
  //to satisfy integrity constraint (SCOTT.EMP_DEPTNO_FK)
  employee.setDeptno((deptno != null && deptno.length()>0) ?
                    Long.parseLong(deptno) : 200L);
  employee.setType((type != null) ? type : "");
```

```
      employee.setPhone((phone != null) ? phone : "");
      employee.setEmail((email != null) ? email : "");

      return employee;
    }

    /**
     * Create a new employee based on employee data from request
     */
    private void createEmployee(HttpServletRequest request,
                                HttpServletResponse response)
      throws ServletException, IOException {

      // Get JavaBean
      EmployeeToplinkBean etb = new EmployeeToplinkBean();

      //Get employee from request
      EmployeeVO employee = populateEmployee(request);

      long employeeNo = etb.createEmployee(employee);

      //Redirect to employee details page
      forwardToPage(MODIFY_PAGE + "?employeeno=" + employeeNo,
                    request, response);
    }

    /**
     * Update an existing employee based on employee data from request
     */
    private void updateEmployee(HttpServletRequest request,
                                  HttpServletResponse response)
      throws ServletException, IOException {

      // Get JavaBean
      EmployeeToplinkBean etb = new EmployeeToplinkBean();

      //Get employee from request
      EmployeeVO employee = populateEmployee(request);

      // Do nothing if employee number not given
      if (employee.employeeNo == 0) {
       forwardToPage(MODIFY_PAGE, request, response);
      }
      else {
       etb.updateEmployee(employee);

        //Redirect to employee details page
        forwardToPage(MODIFY_PAGE + "?employeeno=" +
```

```
                    employee.getEmployeeNo(),
                    request, response);
      }
    }


    /**
     * Delete an existing employee based on employeeno from request
     */
    private void deleteEmployee(HttpServletRequest request,
                                HttpServletResponse response)
      throws ServletException, IOException {

      // Get JavaBean
      EmployeeToplinkBean etb = new EmployeeToplinkBean();

      //Get employeeno from request
      String employeeno = request.getParameter("employeeno");

      // Do nothing if employee number not given
      if (employeeno == null) {
       forwardToPage(DELETE_PAGE, request, response);
      }
      else {
        etb.deleteEmployee(employeeno);

        //Redirect to main page
        forwardToPage(MAIN_PAGE, request, response);
      }
    }

  }
```

The EmployeeToplinkBean JavaBean Class

This section presents the `EmployeeToplinkBean` JavaBean class that is responsible for communicating with the database. The following JavaBean was created by using the methods of the TopLink application from Chapter 3. Refer to Chapter 3 to learn more about how to program using TopLink. The `EmployeeToplinkBean` contains methods that use TopLink to read, create, update, and delete employees from the database.

```
/*
** Program Name: EmployeeToplinkBean.java
**
** Purpose: A JavaBean that is responsible to read, create, delete,
** and update an employee using Oracle9iAS Toplink
```

```
*/
package purchase.bean;

// Basic imports
import java.io.Serializable;
import java.util.Vector;

// TopLink imports
import com.webgain.integrator.sessions.UnitOfWork;
import com.webgain.integrator.threetier.Server;
import com.webgain.integrator.threetier.ClientSession;
import com.webgain.integrator.tools.sessionmanagement.SessionManager;
import com.webgain.integrator.queryframework.ReadObjectQuery;
import com.webgain.integrator.expressions.ExpressionBuilder;
import com.webgain.integrator.queryframework.ReadAllQuery;
import com.webgain.integrator.sessions.Session;
import com.webgain.integrator.queryframework.QueryByExamplePolicy;
import com.webgain.integrator.expressions.ExpressionBuilder;

// Model import
import purchase.model.Employee;
import purchase.vo.EmployeeVO;
/**
 * This JavaBean provides diverse facilities to create, update,
 * and delete employees using TopLink and employee data provided
 * by the request
 */
public class EmployeeToplinkBean implements Serializable {

  /**
   * Use the SessionManager to read the "default" ServerSession
   * defined in sessions.xml. Then acquire ClientSession and
   * UnitOfWork.
   */
  private UnitOfWork getUnitOfWork() {
    //Get ServerSession from SessionManager (using sessions.xml).
    //Use class loader of this class to do so.
    Server serverSession =
      (Server)SessionManager.getManager().getSession("default",
                this.getClass().getClassLoader());
    //Acquire ClientSession from thread-safe ServerSession.
    ClientSession clientSession =
       serverSession.acquireClientSession();
    //Acquire and return UnitOfWork from ClientSession.
    //See TopLink manuals for more details.
    return clientSession.acquireUnitOfWork();
  }
```

```
/**
 * Read the employee based on employeeno
 */
public Employee readEmployee(String employeeno) {

  // Get the unit of Work
  UnitOfWork uow = getUnitOfWork();

  //Create and execute a ReadObjectQuery object and set selection
  //criteria using a TopLink expression.
  ReadObjectQuery readObjectQuery =
                        new ReadObjectQuery(Employee.class);
  ExpressionBuilder builder = new ExpressionBuilder();
   readObjectQuery.setSelectionCriteria(
               builder.get("employeeno").equal(employeeno));
  return (Employee)uow.executeQuery(readObjectQuery);
}

/**
 * Read the employee based on employeeno and UnitOfWork
 */
public Employee readEmployee(String employeeno, UnitOfWork uow) {
  //Create and execute a ReadObjectQuery object and set selection
  //criteria using a TopLink expression.
  ReadObjectQuery readObjectQuery =
                            new ReadObjectQuery(Employee.class);
  ExpressionBuilder builder = new ExpressionBuilder();
   readObjectQuery.setSelectionCriteria(
       builder.get("employeeno").equal(employeeno));
  return (Employee)uow.executeQuery(readObjectQuery);
}

/**
 * Populate the employee with employee data from request
 */
public void populateEmployee(EmployeeVO employeeVO,
                            Employee employee) {
  //Get employee data from request
  String firstname = employeeVO.getFirstName();
  String lastname = employeeVO.getLastName();
  String deptno = Long.toString(employeeVO.getDeptNo());
  String type = employeeVO.getType();
  String phone = employeeVO.getPhone();
  String email = employeeVO.getEmail();

  //Populate employee
  employee.setFirstname((firstname != null) ? firstname : "");
```

```
    employee.setLastname((lastname != null) ? lastname : "");
    //If no deptno is specified, use deptno = 200 in order
    //to satisfy integrity constraint (SCOTT.EMP_DEPTNO_FK)
    employee.setDeptno((deptno != null && deptno.length()>0) ?
                        Long.parseLong(deptno) : 200L);
    employee.setType((type != null) ? type : "");
    employee.setPhone((phone != null) ? phone : "");
    employee.setEmail((email != null) ? email : "");
  }

  /**
   * Create a new employee based on employee data from request
   */
  public long createEmployee(EmployeeVO employeeVO) {

    //Create and populate employee
    Employee employee = new Employee();
    populateEmployee(employeeVO, employee);

    //Register the new employee with UnitOfWork and commit.
    UnitOfWork uow = getUnitOfWork();
    uow.registerNewObject(employee);
    uow.commit();

    return employee.getEmployeeno();
  }

  /**
   * Update an existing employee based on employee data from request
   */
  public void updateEmployee(EmployeeVO employeeVO) {
    String employeeno = Long.toString(employeeVO.getEmployeeNo());

    //Read employee, update it and commit.
    UnitOfWork uow = getUnitOfWork();
    Employee employee = readEmployee(employeeno, uow);
    populateEmployee(employeeVO, employee);
    uow.commit();
  }


  /**
   * Delete an existing employee
   */
  public void deleteEmployee(String employeeno) {
```

```
    //Delete employee and commit using UnitOfWork.
    UnitOfWork uow = getUnitOfWork();
    Employee employee = readEmployee(employeeno, uow);
    uow.deleteObject(employee);
    uow.commit();
  }
  /**
   * First get ServerSession from sessions.xml, then
   * acquire ClientSession from ServerSession.
   */
  public Session getClientSession() {
    // Get ServerSession from SessionManager (using sessions.xml).
    // Use class loader of this class to do so.
    Server serverSession =
      (Server)SessionManager.getManager().getSession("default",
       this.getClass().getClassLoader());
    //Acquire ClientSession from thread-safe ServerSession.
    //See TopLink manuals for more details.
    return serverSession.acquireClientSession();
  }

    /**
   * Read all employees using the given first- & lastname.
   * Use a query-by-example to do so.
   */
  public Vector readEmployees() {
    //Create and execute a ReadAllQuery object.
    ReadAllQuery readAllQuery = new ReadAllQuery(Employee.class);
    //Use an example employee object to run a query-by-example
    Employee exampleEmployee = new Employee();
    readAllQuery.setExampleObject(exampleEmployee);
    //Use a QueryByExamplePolicy in order to allow for a "like" query
    exampleEmployee.setFirstname("%");
    exampleEmployee.setLastname("%");
    QueryByExamplePolicy policy = new QueryByExamplePolicy();
    policy.addSpecialOperation(String.class, "like");
    readAllQuery.setQueryByExamplePolicy(policy);
    return (Vector)getClientSession().executeQuery(readAllQuery);
  }

}
```

You need to follow the directions in the next section to configure, deploy, and run the `EmployeeServlet` controller.

Configuring and Deploying JSPs to OC4J

You learned in Chapter 2 how to deploy a J2EE application to the Oracle9*i*AS J2EE server and how to bind that application to the server so that you can access the application from Oracle9*i*AS J2EE. In this section, you will revisit the necessary steps to deploy a J2EE application. You will also learn how to configure OC4J for TopLink, update the `web.xml` file, and add a JSP file for deployment.

Recall that a J2EE EAR (Enterprise Archive) package can contain the following modules:

- **Web applications** The Web applications module (WAR files) can consist of servlets, JSPs, HTML pages, tag libraries, and utility classes.
- **EJB applications** The EJB applications module (`ejb-jar` files) includes Enterprise JavaBeans (EJBs).
- **Client applications** The Client applications module includes client application programs and is contained within a JAR file.

You will go through the steps to configure and run all the JSPs and applications in this chapter. You will first configure TopLink.

Configuring OC4J to Run Oracle9*i*AS TopLink

In order for OC4J to run TopLink, OC4J needs to have access to the TopLink runtime Foundation Library, which is provided in the TopLink `wdiall.jar` and `xerces.jar` files (you can download and install TopLink from OTN to get these two files).

To make the TopLink runtime Foundation Library available to all applications running in your OC4J instance, copy the `wdiall.jar` and `xerces.jar` files to the `$OC4J_HOME/j2ee/home/lib` directory. However, if you want to make TopLink available to your web application, copy the `wdiall.jar` and `xerces.jar` files to the `WEB-INF/lib` directory of your web application.

Next, make sure to modify the `<login>` information in the `web/WEB-INF/classes/sessions.xml` file to reflect your database setup. The `sessions.xml` file was developed in Chapter 3. The following code fragment demonstrates how to modify the `sessions.xml` file:

```
<login>
   <! -- Use the <platform-class>, <driver-class>, and
        <connection-url> elements to set up your data source -- >
   <platform-class>
      com.webgain.integrator.internal.databaseaccess.OraclePlatform
```

```
    </platform-class>
    <driver-class>oracle.jdbc.driver.OracleDriver</driver-class>
    <! -- Using the Oracle thin JDBC driver -- >
    <connection-url>
          jdbc:oracle:thin:@localhost:1521:orcl
    </connection-url>
    <user-name>scott</user-name>
    <password>tiger</password>
</login>
```

The web.xml Deployment Descriptor File

Your enterprise application is composed of a web application consisting of the `EmployeeServlet` servlet class with CMP and SB EJBs. Consequently, you need to provide a `web.xml` file for the servlet and EJB. Here is the `web.xml` file for the applications in this chapter. To learn more about the elements of this file, see Chapter 10 and Appendix A.

```
<?xml version = '1.0' encoding = 'windows-1252'?>
<!DOCTYPE web-app PUBLIC "-//Sun Microsystems,
 Inc.//DTD Web Application 2.3//EN"
 "http://java.sun.com/dtd/web-app_2_3.dtd">
<web-app>
  <description>
    Purchase web.xml file for Web Application
  </description>
  <servlet>
    <servlet-name>EmployeeServlet</servlet-name>
    <servlet-class>purchase.servlets.EmployeeServlet</servlet-class>
  </servlet>
  <servlet-mapping>
    <servlet-name>EmployeeServlet</servlet-name>
    <url-pattern>/EmployeeServlet</url-pattern>
  </servlet-mapping>
  <ejb-ref>
    <ejb-ref-name>ejb/PurchaseOrderManagement</ejb-ref-name>
    <ejb-ref-type>Session</ejb-ref-type>
    <home>purchase.ejb.sfsb.PurchaseOrderManagementHome</home>
    <remote>purchase.ejb.sfsb.PurchaseOrderManagement</remote>
    <ejb-link>PurchaseOrderManagement</ejb-link>
  </ejb-ref>
  <ejb-local-ref>
    <ejb-ref-name>ejb/local/LineItemLocal</ejb-ref-name>
    <ejb-ref-type>Entity</ejb-ref-type>
    <local-home>purchase.ejb.cmp.LineItemLocalHome</local-home>
    <local>purchase.ejb.cmp.LineItemLocal</local>
    <ejb-link>LineItemLocal</ejb-link>
```

```
  </ejb-local-ref>
  <ejb-local-ref>
    <ejb-ref-name>ejb/local/PurchaseOrderLocal</ejb-ref-name>
    <ejb-ref-type>Entity</ejb-ref-type>
    <local-home>purchase.ejb.cmp.PurchaseOrderLocalHome</local-home>
    <local>purchase.ejb.cmp.PurchaseOrderLocal</local>
    <ejb-link>PurchaseOrderLocal</ejb-link>
  </ejb-local-ref>
  <ejb-local-ref>
    <ejb-ref-name>ejb/local/ApprovalLocal</ejb-ref-name>
    <ejb-ref-type>Entity</ejb-ref-type>
    <local-home>purchase.ejb.cmp.ApprovalLocalHome</local-home>
    <local>purchase.ejb.cmp.ApprovalLocal</local>
    <ejb-link>ApprovalLocal</ejb-link>
  </ejb-local-ref>
</web-app>
```

Deploying and Packaging the Application

The first step in deploying an application is to package it. You can do this by creating WAR and EAR files. Let's start by creating the WAR file:

1. Open a command prompt, and position yourself in the web directory (for example, **c:\chapter11\web**).
2. Type the following:

   ```
   jar cvf chapter11-web.war *
   ```
3. Copy chapter11-web.war to the root directory, chapter11.
4. Position yourself in the classes directory.
5. Type the following:

   ```
   jar cvf chapter11-ejb.jar *
   ```
6. Copy chapter11-ejb.jar to the root directory, chapter11.
7. Position yourself in the root directory, chapter11.
8. Type the following:

   ```
   jar cvf chapter11.ear chapter11-web.war chapter11-ejb.jar
       META-INF\application.xml
   ```

You now have your chapter11.ear file and are ready to deploy.

Next, you will deploy the application. OC4J supports deployment of an EAR file conforming to the J2EE standard (as does our chapter11 directory structure).

Deploying an EAR File to OC4J

The steps to deploy an EAR file to OC4J are as follows:

1. Copy the `chapter11.ear` file to your OC4J installation's `applications` directory; if you installed OC4J under the `c:\OC4J` directory, then this will be `c:\OC4J\j2ee\home\applications`. The EAR file can be placed anywhere, but in this example, put it in the OC4J `applications` directory.

2. Edit the OC4J `server.xml` file, found under your `OC4J\j2ee\home\config` directory. Add the following entry:

```
<application name="chapter11" path="../applications/chapter11.ear"
auto-start="true" />
```

   The previous command tells OC4J the location of the `chapter11.ear` file.

3. Edit `http-web-site.xml` to bind your Web module to this J2EE application. Add the following entry:

```
<web-app application="chapter11" name="chapter11-web"
root="/chapter11" load-on-startup="true" />
```

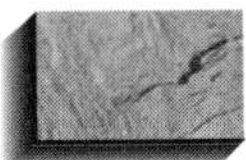

CAUTION

The name must correspond to whatever name you gave the WAR file; the root will be the virtual path where OC4J can reach your application.

Recall that OC4J supports hot deployment. Therefore, if OC4J is running, it will immediately pick up and deploy this application. If OC4J is not running, position yourself in the `OC4J/j2ee/home` directory and start OC4J by typing the following:

```
java -jar oc4j.jar -verbosity 10
```

Testing Your Application

To test your application, open a web browser and type the following URL:

```
http://localhost:port/chapter11/EmployeeServlet
```

where *localhost* is your machine, *port* is the port the web server is listening on, and chapter11 is the name that you defined in the <name> element of the `<application>` tag in the OC4J `server.xml` file.

Note that the default port for the stand-alone OC4J is 8888. The port can be found and changed in the OC4J `http-web-site.xml` file, located in the `OC4J_HOME/j2ee/home/config` directory.

In this chapter, you learned about JSP basic syntax, JSP architecture, and accessing the database using SQLJ, EJB, and TopLink from JSP pages. You also learned about the MVC pattern by developing a servlet controller. Finally, you learned how to deploy J2EE applications consisting of JSP files and other J2EE components to OC4J.

PART IV

Appendixes

APPENDIX A

OC4J XML Configuration Files

In the J2EE platform, XML is the preferred format for configuration files. The configuration files for applications and components are all XML-based. OC4J's configuration is also accomplished through the use of XML files. In this appendix, you will find brief definitions for OC4J server XML configuration files and then for J2EE and OC4J application deployment XML files.

Server Configuration Files

This section discusses the server OC4J server XML configuration files. These files, listed next, are the "heart" of the OC4J. These files tell the container things such as port numbers and security information.

- `server.xml`
- `data-sources.xml`
- `jms.xml`
- `rmi.xml`
- `http-web-site.xml`
- `principals.xml`
- `jazn.xml`
- `jazn-data.xml`

The server.xml File

The OC4J `server.xml` file contains the configuration information for the application server. This file is the root configuration file of the server and contains references to other configuration files. When you are ready to deploy your application to OC4J, one of the first steps in the deployment process is to update the `server.xml` file. The `server.xml` file is used in OC4J to deploy new applications or redeploy existing applications on to the server.

Use the `server.xml` file to specify the following:

- The library path, which is located in the application deployment descriptor
- The global application, the global web application, and the default web site served
- Maximum number of HTTP connections that the container allows

- Logging settings
- Java compiler settings
- Cluster ID
- Transaction timeout, in milliseconds
- SMTP host
- Location of the `data-sources.xml` configuration file
- Location of the configuration for JMS and RMI
- Location of the default and additional web sites. You specify these locations by adding entries that list the location of the web site configuration files. You can have multiple web sites. However, there is only one OC4J `default-web-site.xml` file and it defines a default web site. All other web sites are defined in `http-web-site.xml` configuration files.

Elements of the server.xml File

The `server.xml` file consists of the following elements:

`application-server` This is the top element of the `server.xml` file and contains the configuration information for OC4J. The attributes of the `<application-server>` element are as follows:

- **`application-auto-deploy-directory=".../applications/auto"`** Specifies the directory from which EAR files are automatically detected and deployed by the running OC4J server. It also performs the web application binding for the default application.
- **`auto-start-applications="true|false"`** When set to `true`, all applications defined in the `<applications>` elements are automatically started when the OC4J server is started. When set to `false`, the applications are not started unless their `auto-start` attribute is set to `true`. The default for `auto-start-applications` is `true`.
- **`application-directory=".../applications"`** Specifies a directory in which to store applications (EAR files). If no directory is specified, OC4J stores the information in the `j2ee/home/applications` directory. When you deploy an application with the `admin.jar` command-line tool, OC4J will store the information in its `applications` directory.
- **`deployment-directory=".../application-deployments"`** Specifies the master location where applications that are contained in EAR files

are deployed. The default for the master location is `j2ee/home/application-deployments/`.

- **`connector-directory=`** Specifies the location and filename of the `oc4j-connectors.xml` file. OC4J supports J2EE Connector Architecture for EIS applications that do not access relational databases. To learn about OC4J implementation of J2EE Connector Architecture, see the *Oracle9iAs Containers for J2EE, Release 2.0, Services Guide* technical manual.

- **`recovery-procedure="automatic|prompt|ignore">`** Specifies how the EJB container reacts for recovery of errors occurring in the middle of a global transaction using JTA. For example, if a CMP bean is in the middle of a global transaction, the EJB container saves the transactional state to a file. The next time OC4J is started, the server will use these attributes to recover the JTA transaction.

  - **`automatic`** When used, OC4J automatically attempts recovery. This is the default.

  - **`prompt`** When used, it prompts the user (system in/out).

  - **`ignore`** This indicates to ignore recovery. This attribute is useful in development environments or if you are never executing a CMP entity bean.

`<application>` An application is a entity with its own set of users, Web applications, and EJB JAR files.

- **`auto-start="true|false"`** Specifies whether the application should be automatically started when the OC4J server starts. The default is `true`.

- **`deployment-directory=".../application-deployments/chapter06"`** Specifies a directory in which to store your application deployment information. If no directory is specified (which is the default), OC4J looks in the global deployment-directory, and if none exists there, it stores the information inside the EAR file. The path can be relative or absolute. If relative, the path should be relative to the location of the `server.xml` file.

- **`name="anApplication"`** Specifies the name used to reference the application.

- **`parent="anotherApplication"`** Specifies the name of the optional parent application. The default is the global application. Children see the namespace of their parent application. This is used to share services such as Enterprise JavaBeans among multiple applications.

- **path=".../applications/chapter05.ear"** /> Specifies the path to the EAR file containing the application code. In this example, the EAR file is named `chapter05.ear`.

<compiler>

- **classpath="/myJDK/rt.jar"** Specifies an alternative/additional classpath when compiling. Some compilers need an additional classpath (such as Jikes, which needs the `rt.jar` file of the Java 2 VM to be included).
- **executable="jikes"** /> Specifies the name of the compiler executable to use, such as Jikes or JVC.

<cluster>

- **id="123" />** Specifies the unique cluster ID of the server.

<global-application> The default application for this server. This acts as a parent to other applications in terms of object visibility.

- **name="default"** Specifies the application.
- **path=".../application.xml"** /> Specifies the path to the OC4J global `application.xml` file, which contains the settings for the default application. The `application.xml` file provides global settings for all J2EE applications.

<global-web-app-config>

- **path=".../web-application.xml"** /> The path where the `web-application.xml` file is located.

<jms-config>

- **path=".../jms.xml"** Specifies the path to the `jms.xml` file.

<log>

<file>

- **path=".../log/server.log"** Specifies a relative or absolute path to a file where log events are stored.

<mail> Specifies an e-mail address where log events are forwarded. You must also specify a valid mail-session if you use this option.

- **address="my@mail.address"** Specifies the mail address.

<max-http-connections> Specifies the maximum number of concurrent connections any given web site can accept at a single point in time. If text exists inside the tag, it is used as a redirect-URL when the limit is reached.

- **max-connections-queue-timeout="10"** When the maximum number of connections are reached, this is the number of seconds that can pass before the connections are dropped and a message is returned to the client stating that the server is either busy or connections will be redirected. The default is 10 seconds.
- **socket-backlog** The number of connections to queue up before denying connections at the socket level. The default is 30.
- **value** The maximum number of connections.

<rmi-config> Use to configure RMI in OC4J. OC4J supports RMI over HTTP, a technique known as RMI tunneling. HTTP tunneling is one of the methods that allow Java programs to make outgoing calls through a local firewall. See Chapter 3 to learn how to configure RMI in OC4J.

- **path=".../rmi.xml"** Specifies the path to the OC4J `rmi.xml` file.

<transaction-config> Specifies transaction information for the server.

- **timeout="60000"** Specifies the maximum amount of time (in milliseconds) that a transaction can take to finish before it is rolled back due to a timeout. The default value is 60000.

<web-site> Specifies transaction information for the server.

- **path=".../my-web-site.xml"** /> The path to a `*web-site.xml` file that defines a web site. For each web site, you must specify a separate `*web-site.xml` file.

The data-sources.xml File

The `data-sources.xml` file contains configuration information for the data sources used. In addition, it contains information on how to establish connections to a data source. Refer to Chapter 2 to learn how to modify this file to create an application-specific OC4J data source. Use the `data-sources.xml` file to specify the following:

- JDBC driver

- JDBC URL
- JNDI paths to which to bind the data source
- User/password for the data source
- Database schema to use
- Inactivity timeout
- Maximum number of connections allowed to the database

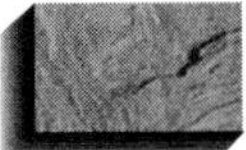

NOTE
Database schemas are used to make auto-generated SQL work with different database systems. OC4J contains an XML file format for specifying properties, such as type mappings and reserved words. OC4J comes with database schemas for MS SQL Server/MS Access, Oracle, and Sybase. You can edit these or make new schemas for your DBMS.

The jms.xml File

The `jms.xml` file contains the configuration for OC4J's in-memory JMS implementation. OC4J provides implementation classes for Oracle's Advanced Queuing and third-party messaging systems such as MQSeries, SonicMQ, and SwiftMQ. Refer to Chapter 7 to learn how to use Oracle Advanced Queuing to produce JMS messages that are handled by message-driven beans.

In the `jms.xml` file, specify the following:

- Hostname or IP address, and port number to which the JMS server binds
- Settings for queues and topics to be bound in the JNDI tree
- Log settings

The rmi.xml File

This file contains configuration for the Remote Method Invocation (RMI) system. It contains the setting for the RMI listener, which provides remote access for Enterprise JavaBeans. Refer to Chapter 3 to learn how to modify the OC4J `rmi.xml` file to accommodate your environment needs.

In the `rmi.xml` file, specify the following:

- Hostname or IP address, and port number to which the RMI server binds

- Remote servers to which to communicate
- Clustering settings
- Log settings

NOTE
If you do not modify the OC4J `rmi.xml` file, the default RMI port is 23791. You should modify the port number in the `rmi.xml` file if you will run multiple instances of OC4J on the same machine.

The http-web-site.xml File

This file contains the configuration information for a web site. Use the `http-web-site.xml` file to specify the following:

- Hostname or IP address, virtual host settings for this site, listener ports, and security using SSL
- Default web application for this site
- Additional web applications for this site
- Access-log format
- Settings for user web applications (for /~user/ sites)
- SSL configuration

This is the HTTP protocol listener. If you want to bypass OHS and go directly to OC4J, you use the port number defined in this file. However, you must be careful. The AJP port is chosen at random every time OC4J is started. If it chooses the same port number that is hard-coded in this XML file, there will be a conflict. The default HTTP port is 7777. The following shows the entry in the `http-web-site.xml` for an HTTP listener with a port number of 7777:

```
<web-site hostoc4j_host" port7777"
  protocolhttp" display-nameHTTP OC4J WebSit>
```

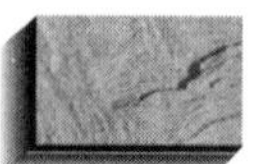

NOTE
In a UNIX environment, the port number should be greater than 1024, unless the process has administrative privileges.

OC4J is distributed with the following `http-web-site.xml` file:

```
<?xml version1.0" standalone='yes'?>
<!DOCTYPE web-site PUBLIC "Oracle9iAS XML
Web-sithttp://xmlns.oracle.com/ias/dtds/web-site.dt>

<!-- change the host name below to your own host name.
      Localhost will -->
<!-- not work with clustering -->
<!-- also add cluster-island attribute as below
<web-site hostlocalhost" port8888"
          display-nameOracle 9iAS Java HTTP WebSite"
                 cluster-island1" >
-->

<web-site port8888"
   display-nameOracle9iAS Containers for J2EE HTTP Web Sit>
        <!-- Uncomment the following line when using clustering -->
      <!-- <frontend hostyour_host_name" port80" /> -->
      <!-- The default web-app for this site, bound to the root -->
      <default-web-app applicationdefault" namedefaultWebApp" />
      <web-app applicationdefault" namedms0" root/dms0" />
      <web-app applicationdefault" namedms" root/dmsoc4j" />

        <!-- Uncomment the following to access these apps.
      <web-app applicationcallerInf
            namecallerInfo-web" root/jazn" />
      <web-app applicationnews" namenews-web" root/news" />
      <web-app applicationlogger" namemessagelogger-we
                  root/messagelogger" />
      <web-app applicationws_example" namews_exampl
                  root/webservices" />
        <web-app applicationojspdemos" nameojspdemos-we
               root/ojspdemos" />
        -->
      <!-- Access Log, where requests are logged to -->
      <access-log path="../log/http-web-access.log" />
</web-site>
```

The principals.xml File

This file contains security information for the OC4J server. Refer to Chapter 8 to learn how to modify this file. Use the `principals.xml` file to specify the following:

- Username and password for the client-admin console

- Name and description of users/groups, and real name and password for users
- Optional X.509 certificates for users

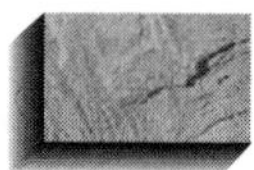

NOTE
OC4J is moving to JAZN security and moving away from `principals.xml`*. The configuration file for JAZN security is* `jazn-data.xml`*.*

The jazn.xml File

The `jazn.xml` file tells OC4J which data source to use for JAZN. By default, OC4J uses the `jazn-data.xml` file instead of the `jazn.xml` file. However, an LDAP directory can be specified to LDAP by modifying this file.

The jazn-data.xml File

The `jazn-data.xml` file contains the user roles, and group information. Refer to Chapter 8 to learn more about this file. The `jazn-data.xml` file is managed by the `jazn.jar` admin tool. Here are the `jazn.jar` admin tool usage and its options:

```
java -jar jazn.jar [-user <username> -password <password>]
[command]

-listusers [<realm> [-role <role>|-perm <permission>]] |

-listroles [<realm> [<user>|-role <role>]] |

-listrealms |

-listperms [<realm> { <user> |-role <role>}] |

-listperm <permission_name> |

-listprncpls |

-listprncpl <principal_name> |

-adduser <realm> <username> <password> |

-addrole <realm> <role> |

-addrealm <realm> <admin> {<adminpwd> <adminrole> | <adminrole>
  <userbase> <rolebase> <realmtype>}
```

```
-addperm <perm_name> <perm_class> <action> <target>
  [<description>] |

-addprncpl <prncpl_name> <prncpl_class> <params> [<description>] |

-remuser <realm> <user> |

-remrole <realm> <role> |

-remrealm <realm> |

-remperm <permission_name> |

-remprncpl <principal_name> |

-grantperm <realm> {user|-role <role>} <permission_class>
   <permission_params> |

-grantrole <role> <realm> {user|-role <to_role>} |

-revokeperm <realm> {user|-role <role>} <permission_class>
  <permission_params> |

-revokerole <role> <realm> {user|-role <from_role>} |

-setpasswd <realm> <user> <old_pwd> <new_pwd> |

-checkpasswd <realm> <user> [-pw <password>] |

-getconfig <default_realm> <admin> <password> |

-convert <filename> <realm> |

-shell

-help
```

J2EE and OC4J Deployment Files

The J2EE and OC4J-specific deployment XML files contain deployment information of an application. You can edit deployment XML files manually. These files are used by OC4J to map environment entries, resources references, and security roles to actual deployment-specific values. The OC4J-specific XML file begins with "orion." The OC4J-specific XML file will automatically be generated when you are using automatic deployment.

Here is a list of XML files that your application may need to deploy your J2EE application on OC4J:

- application.xml
- orion-application.xml
- ejb-jar.xml
- orion-ejb-jar.xml
- web.xml
- orion-web.xml
- application-client.xml
- orion-application-client.xml

Refer to Chapters 5 through 7 to learn how to write application.xml, ejb-jar.xml, and web.xml files. Remember that if you do not provide the orion-*xxx*.xml files, at deployment time, OC4J will automatically generate them for you.

The application.xml File

The application.xml file identifies the Web or EJB modules deployed to the global default application. This file has elements for EJB JAR, Web WAR, and client files.

The orion-application.xml File

The orion-application.xml file configures the OC4J-specific global application for the server. This file specifies the following:

- The default data source to use with CMP beans
- Security role mappings
- Specifying the user manager
- JNDI namespace-access rules (authorization)
- Whether to auto-create and auto-delete tables for CMP beans

The ejb-jar.xml File

The `ejb-jar.xml` file defines the deployment parameters for your Enterprise JavaBeans. Refer to Chapters 5 through 7 to learn how to define this file.

The orion-ejb-jar.xml File

This file is the OC4J-specific deployment descriptor for your EJB. The first time you deploy your application, OC4J generates this file using its default elements. However, if you provide the `orion-ejb-jar.xml` file with your application, OC4J will merge your file with the generated one. Refer to Chapters 5 through 7 to learn how to create this file or have OC4J generate it for you. In the `orion-ejb-jar.xml` file, you can specify the following:

- Timeout settings
- Transaction retry settings
- Session persistence settings
- Transaction isolation settings
- CMP mappings
- OR mappings
- Finder method specifications
- JNDI mappings

The web.xml File

This file contains deployment information about your web applications, such as information on servlets and JavaServer Pages (JSP). Refer to Chapters 10 and 11 for detailed information regarding the content of a `web.xml` file.

The orion-web.xml File

The `orion-web.xml` file is an OC4J-specific file to complement the `web.xml` file. This is the OC4J-specific deployment descriptor for mapping web settings. This XML file contains the following:

- Auto-reloading (including modification-check time-interval)

- Buffering
- Charsets
- Development mode
- Directory browsing
- Document root
- Locales
- Web timeouts
- Virtual directories
- Clustering
- Session tracking
- JNDI mappings

The application-client.xml File

The `application-client.xml` file contains JNDI information for accessing the server application from a client application.

The orion-application-client.xml File

The `orion-application-client.xml` file is an OC4J-specific file to complement the `application-client.xml` file. This deployment file is for client applications and contains JNDI mappings and entries for the client.

APPENDIX B

OC4J Security

his appendix provides the configuration instructions for the security mechanism of the application developed in Chapter 8 (based on the application developed in Chapter 5) and then presents the important packages in the Oracle9*i*AS JAAS API specification.

Configuring the Security Mechanism for the Chapter 8 Application

The following sections detail the prerequisites and configuration settings for running the application developed in Chapter 8.

Software Requirements

- OC4J Developer Preview installed
- Jakarta Ant, to build the application example
- Sun's JDK 1.3_01 or above

Notation

- **%OC4J_HOME%** The directory you installed OC4J to; for example, C:\
- **%J2EE_HOME%** The directory where the `oc4j.jar` file exists within OC4J. This typically is two directories under `%OC4J_HOME%`. For example, if you installed OC4J to `C:\`, then `%J2EE_HOME%` would be `C:\j2ee\home`.
- **%JAVA_HOME%** The directory where your JDK is installed.
- **JAZN** Oracle's JAAS provider.

Oracle9*i*AS JAAS 9.0.2.0.0 API Specification

The Oracle9*i*AS JAAS 9.0.2.0.0 API specification is the specification for JAZN (Java AuthoriZatioN), Oracle's authorization/policy provider for Java Authentication and Authorization Service (JAAS). This specification describes three packages, which are discussed in the following sections:

- `oracle.security.jazn`
- `oracle.security.jazn.policy`
- `oracle.security.jazn.realm`

Package oracle.security.jazn

The `oracle.security.jazn` package provides the classes and interfaces for Oracle's authorization/policy provider for JAAS. Besides providing a full implementation of `javax.security.auth.Policy`, JAZN enhances JAAS in the following ways:

- Defines a realm-based user and role management API
- Defines an administrative API for administering the following aspects of the authorization policy:
  - Permission-to-user assignment
  - Permission-to-role assignment
  - User-to-role assignment
- Provides Role-Based Access Control (RBAC) support via the Realm framework, with full support for role hierarchies

Interface Summary

The `oracle.security.jazn` package has one interface, `Persistable`, which is used for specifying settings and changes for persistence requirements.

Class Summary

The following table lists and describes the classes of the `oracle.security.jazn` package:

Class	Description
`JAZNConfig`	Specifies the JAZN configuration
`JAZNContext`	Provides a starting point for obtaining JAZN-related objects and a centralized place for managing JAZN properties
`JAZNPermission`	Used for authorization permissions

Exception Summary

The following table lists and describes the exceptions of the `oracle.security.jazn` package:

Exception	Description
`JAZNConfigException`	Represents an authorization exception
`JAZNException`	Represents an authorization exception
`JAZNInitException`	Thrown when an initialization error occurs
`JAZNNamingException`	Used to wrap a `javax.naming.NamingException`
`JAZNObjectExistsException`	Thrown when an attempt is made to create an object that already exists
`JAZNObjectNotFoundException`	Thrown when an attempt is made to access an object that does not already exist
`JAZNRuntimeException`	Represents an authorization exception

Package oracle.security.jazn.policy

The `oracle.security.jazn.policy` package provides the classes and interfaces for administering the authorization policy.

Interface Summary

The following table lists and describes the interfaces of the `oracle.security.jazn.policy` package:

Interface	Description
`GlobalPolicy`	Represents the "global" JAZN policy
`JAZNPolicy`	Represents the repository of authorization policies
`PermissionClassManager`*	Defines a manager for permission classes
`PolicyManager`*	Specifies policies for the JAZN
`PrincipalClassManager`*	Defines a manager for principal classes
`RealmPolicy`	Represents a realm-specific policy

* Interface is for Oracle internal use only and is subject to change without notice.

Class Summary

The following table lists and describes the classes of the `oracle.security.jazn.policy` package:

Class	Description
`AdminPermission`	Represents the right to administer a permission
`Grantee`	Represents a grantee in a policy entry
`PermissionClassDesc`	Defines the metadata for a permission type
`PrincipalClassDesc`	Defines the metadata for a principal type
`RoleAdminPermission`	Grants to the grantee the right to further grant/revoke the target role

Package oracle.security.jazn.realm

The `oracle.security.jazn.realm` package provides the classes and interfaces for the Realm framework.

Interface Summary

The following table lists and describes the interfaces of the `oracle.security.jazn.realm` package:

Interface	Description
`InitRealmInfo.RealmType`	Defines the different realm types supported by JAZN
`Realm`	Provides access to a store of roles and users
`Realm.LDAPProperty`	Defines the LDAP properties applicable for creating a realm (user manager and role manager) using LDAP directory as a backing store
`RealmPrincipal`	Extends from `java.security.Principal`
`RealmRole`	Defines a role associated with a realm
`RealmUser`	Defines a user associated with a realm
`RoleManager`	Defines the APIs for managing roles in a realm
`UserManager`	Defines the APIs for managing users in a realm

Class Summary

The following table lists and describes the classes of the `oracle.security.jazn.realm` package:

Class	Description
`InitRealmInfo`	Used as a placeholder for specifying realm properties when creating a new realm
`RealmLoginModule`	A realm-based login module
`RealmManager`	Manages realms
`RealmPermission`	Defined to represent permissions for a realm

For more information on JAAS, refer to the Oracle Technology Network at http://otn.oracle.com/docs/products/ias/doc_library/90200doc_otn/web.902/q20221/index.html.

APPENDIX C

Enterprise JavaBeans API Reference

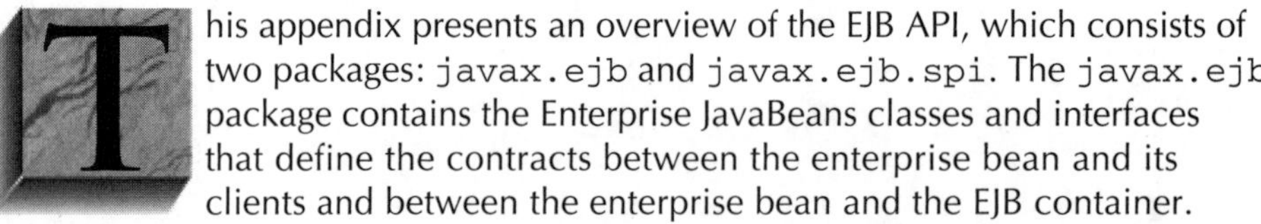

This appendix presents an overview of the EJB API, which consists of two packages: `javax.ejb` and `javax.ejb.spi`. The `javax.ejb` package contains the Enterprise JavaBeans classes and interfaces that define the contracts between the enterprise bean and its clients and between the enterprise bean and the EJB container. The `javax.ejb.spi` package defines a single interface that is implemented by the EJB container. The `javax.ejb.spi` interface is not used by application components. Vendors of EJB servers and containers must provide the implementation classes of the EJB interfaces. In this appendix, we also present the definition of the `javax.jms.MessageListener` interface.

Package javax.ejb

In this section, we present a summary of all the interfaces and exceptions of the `javax.ejb` package:

- **`EJBContext`** Provides access to the container-provided runtime context of a bean instance.
- **`EJBHome`** Must be extended by all enterprise beans' remote home interfaces.
- **`EJBLocalHome`** Must be extended by all enterprise beans' local home interfaces.
- **`EJBLocalObject`** Must be extended by all enterprise beans' local interfaces.
- **`EJBMetaData`** Provides access to EJB's metadata.
- **`EJBObject`** Must be extended by all EJB's remote interfaces.
- **`EnterpriseBean`** Must be implemented by every enterprise bean class.
- **`EntityBean`** Must be implemented by every entity enterprise bean class. See Chapter 6 to learn how to develop entity beans.
- **`EntityContext`** Extends the `EJBContext` and provides access to the container-provided runtime context of an entity bean instance.
- **`Handle`** Implemented by all EJB object handles.
- **`HomeHandle`** Implemented by all home object handles.
- **`MessageDrivenBean`** Implemented by every message-driven enterprise bean class. Additionally, all message-driven beans must implement the `javax.jms.MessageListener` interface. Note that a `MessageListener`

is used to receive asynchronously delivered messages. In the 1.3 release of the Java 2, Enterprise Edition (J2EE) platform, the JMS (Java Message Service) API has become an integral part of the J2EE platform. Application developers can use messaging with components using J2EE APIs. A detailed description of the `javax.jms.MessageListener` interface is presented in the "The javax.jms.MessageListener Interface" section of this appendix. To learn more about JMS and also develop message-driven beans, see Chapter 7.

- **`MessageDrivenContext`** Extends the `EJBContext` and provides access to the container-provided runtime context of a message-driven bean instance.
- **`SessionBean`** Implemented by every session enterprise bean class. See Chapter 6 to learn how to develop session beans.
- **`SessionContext`** Extends the `EJBContext` and provides access to the container-provided runtime context of a session bean instance.
- **`SessionSynchronization`** Used (optionally) by session beans to synchronize their state with transactions.

Exception Summary

Note that `XxxxLocalException` exceptions are thrown to local clients only.

- **`AccessLocalException`** Indicates that the caller does not have permission to call the method.
- **`CreateException`** Reports a failure to create an entity EJB object. This is a mandatory exception to be included in the **`throws`** clauses of all create methods defined in an enterprise bean's home interface.
- **`DuplicateKeyException`** Thrown if an entity EJB object cannot be created because an object with the same key already exists.
- **`EJBException`** Thrown by an enterprise bean instance, indicating that an invoked business method or callback method could not be completed.
- **`FinderException`** Reports a failure to find the requested EJB object(s). Must be included in the **`throws`** clause of every `findMETHOD(...)` method of an entity bean's home interface.
- **`NoSuchEntityException`** Thrown by an entity bean instance to its container to report that the invoked business method or callback method could not be completed because the entity bean does not exist in the permanent storage.

- **`NoSuchObjectLocalException`** Thrown when accessing an object that no longer exists.
- **`ObjectNotFoundException`** Thrown by a finder method when the specified object cannot be found.
- **`RemoveException`** Thrown when removing an EJB object when the enterprise bean or the container does not allow the EJB object to be removed. This exception is defined in the method signature to provide backward compatibility for enterprise beans written for the EJB 1.0 specification. Enterprise beans written for the EJB 1.1 specification and higher should throw `javax.ejb.EJBException` instead of this exception.
- **`TransactionRequiredLocalException`** Thrown when the target object did require a transaction.
- **`TransactionRolledbackLocalException`** Thrown when the transaction associated with processing of the request has been rolled back, or marked to roll back.

In the remaining sections of this appendix, we present a detailed definition of the interfaces of the EJB API.

The javax.ejb.EJBContext Interface

The `EJBContext` interface provides an instance access to the container runtime context. This interface is extended by the `SessionContext`, `EntityContext`, and `MessageDrivenContext` interfaces. Here is the definition of the `EJBContext` interface:

```
public interface EJBContext {
  java.security.Principal getCallerPrincipal(); // deprecated
  EJBHome getEJBHome();
  EJBLocalHome getEJBLocalHome();
  java.util.Properties getEnvironment();
  boolean getRollbackOnly();
  javax.transaction.UserTransaction
    getUserTransaction();
  boolean isCallerInRole
   (java.security.Identity role); // deprecated
  boolean isCallerInRole
    (java.lang.String roleName);
  void setRollbackOnly();
}  // End of EJBContext
```

The javax.ejb.EJBHome Interface

An EJB's remote home interface defines the methods that allow a remote client to create, find, and remove EJB objects. Additionally, the `EJBHome` interface defines home business methods that are not specific to a bean instance. The remote home interface is defined by the EJB provider and implemented by the EJB container. All EJB remote home interfaces must extend the `EJBHome` interface. Here is the definition of the `EJBHome` interface:

```
public interface EJBHome
     extends java.rmi.Remote {
  public void remove(Handle handle)
     throws java.rmi.RemoteException,
            RemoveException;
  public void remove(java.lang.Object primaryKey)
     throws java.rmi.RemoteException,
           RemoveException;
  public EJBMetaData getEJBMetaData()
    throws java.rmi.RemoteException;
  public HomeHandle getHomeHandle()
    throws java.rmi.RemoteException;
}  // End of EJBHome
```

The javax.ejb.EJBLocalHome Interface

An EJB's local home interface defines the methods that allow a local client to create, find, and remove EJB objects. Additionally, the `EJBLocalHome` interface defines home business methods that are not specific to a bean instance. The local home interface is defined by the EJB provider and implemented by the EJB container. All EJB local home interfaces must extend the `EJBLocalHome` interface. Here is the definition of the `EJBLocalHome` interface:

```
public interface EJBLocalHome {
  public void remove(java.lang.Object primaryKey)
     throws RemoveException, EJBException;
} // End of EJBLocalHome
```

The javax.ejb.EJBLocalObject Interface

An EJB's local interface provides the local client view of an EJB object. An EJB's local interface defines the business methods callable by local clients. The enterprise bean's local interface is defined by the EJB provider and implemented by the EJB container. All EJB local interfaces must extend the `EJBLocalObject` interface. Here is the definition of the `EJBLocalObject` interface:

```
public interface EJBLocalObject {
  public EJBLocalHome getEJBLocalHome()
```

```
      throws EJBException;
   public java.lang.Object getPrimaryKey()
      throws EJBException;
   public void remove()
      throws RemoveException,
             EJBException;
   public boolean isIdentical(EJBLocalObject obj)
      throws EJBException;
} // End of EJBLocalObject
```

The javax.ejb.EJBMetaData Interface

The metadata interface is not a remote interface. It is intended to be used by development tools. EJB client applications use the development tools to access enterprise beans. Here is the definition of the `EJBMetaData` interface:

```
public interface EJBMetaData{
   public EJBHome getEJBHome();
   public java.lang.Class getHomeInterfaceClass();
   public java.lang.Class getRemoteInterfaceClass();
   public java.lang.Class getPrimaryKeyClass();
   public boolean isSession();
   public boolean isStatelessSession();
}  // End of EJBMetaData
```

The javax.ejb.EJBObject Interface

An EJB's remote interface provides the remote client view of an EJB object. An EJB's remote interface defines the business methods callable by local clients. The enterprise bean's remote interface is defined by the EJB provider and implemented by the EJB container. All EJB remote interfaces must extend the `EJBObject` interface. Here is the definition of the `EJBObject` interface:

```
public interface EJBObject
     extends java.rmi.Remote {
   public EJBHome getEJBHome()
      throws java.rmi.RemoteException;
   public java.lang.Object getPrimaryKey()
      throws java.rmi.RemoteException;
   public void remove()
      throws java.rmi.RemoteException,
             RemoveException;
   public Handle getHandle()
      throws java.rmi.RemoteException;
   public boolean isIdentical(EJBObject obj)
      throws java.rmi.RemoteException;
} // End of EJBObject
```

The javax.ejb.EnterpriseBean Interface

This is the common super-interface for the SessionBean, EntityBean, and MessageDrivenBean interfaces. See Chapters 5, 6, and 7 to learn about entity, session, and message-driven beans. Here is the definition of the EnterpriseBean interface:

```
public interface EnterpriseBean
    extends java.io.Serializable {
}  // End of EnterpriseBean
```

The javax.ejb.EntityBean Interface

The container uses the EntityBean methods to notify the enterprise bean instances of the instance's life-cycle events. All entity bean classes must implement the EntityBean interface. Here is the definition of the EntityBean interface:

```
public interface EntityBean
    extends EnterpriseBean {
  public void setEntityContext(EntityContext ctx)
     throws EJBException,
            java.rmi.RemoteException;
  public void unsetEntityContext()
     throws EJBException,
            java.rmi.RemoteException;
  public void ejbRemove()
     throws EJBException,
           RemoveException;
  public void ejbActivate()
     throws EJBException,
            java.rmi.RemoteException;
  public void ejbPassivate()
     throws EJBException,
           java.rmi.RemoteException;
  public void ejbLoad()
     throws EJBException,
            java.rmi.RemoteException;
  public void ejbStore()
     throws EJBException,
            java.rmi.RemoteException;
}  // End of EntityBean
```

The javax.ejb.EntityContext Interface

The container passes the EntityContext interface to an entity bean's instance after the instance has been created. The EntityContext interface remains associated with the instance for the lifetime of the instance.

Here is the definition of the EntityContext interface:

```
public interface EntityContext
    extends EJBContext {
  public EJBLocalObject getEJBLocalObject()
     throws java.lang.IllegalStateException;
  public EJBObject getEJBObject()
     throws java.lang.IllegalStateException;
  public java.lang.Object getPrimaryKey()
     throws java.lang.IllegalStateException;
}  // End of EntityContext
```

The javax.ejb.Handle Interface

A Handle is an abstraction of a network reference to an EJB object. All EJB object handles implement the Handle interface. Here is the definition of the Handle interface:

```
public interface Handle
    extends java.io.Serializable {
  public EJBObject getEJBObject()
     throws java.rmi.RemoteException;
}  // End of Handle
```

The javax.ejb.HomeHandle Interface

All EJB home object handles must implement the HomeHandle interface. Here is the definition of the HomeHandle interface:

```
public interface HomeHandle
    extends java.io.Serializable {
  public EJBHome getEJBHome()
     throws java.rmi.RemoteException;
}  // End of HomeHandle
```

The javax.ejb.MessageDrivenBean Interface

All message-driven classes must implement the MessageDrivenBean interface. The container uses the MessageDrivenBean methods to notify the enterprise bean instances of the instance's life-cycle events. Here is the definition of the MessageDrivenBean interface:

```
public interface MessageDrivenBean
    extends EnterpriseBean {
  public void setMessageDrivenContext
          (MessageDrivenContext ctx)
```

```
      throws EJBException;
  public void ejbRemove()
      throws EJBException;
} // End of MessageDrivenBean
```

The javax.ejb.MessageDrivenContext Interface

Like the `EntityContext` interface, the `MessageDrivenContext` interface provides access to the runtime message-driven context provided by the container. The container passes the `MessageDrivenContext` interface to an instance after the instance has been created. The message-driven context remains associated with the instance for the lifetime of the instance. Here is the definition of the `MessageDrivenContext` interface:

```
public interface MessageDrivenContext
    extends EJBContext {
} // End of MessageDrivenContext
```

The javax.ejb.SessionBean Interface

All session bean classes must implement the `SessionBean` interface. The container uses the `SessionBean` methods to notify the enterprise bean instances of the instance's life-cycle events. Here is the definition of the `SessionBean` interface:

```
public interface SessionBean
    extends EnterpriseBean {
  public void setSessionContext
              (SessionContext ctx)
      throws EJBException,
             java.rmi.RemoteException;
  public void ejbRemove()
      throws EJBException,
             java.rmi.RemoteException;
  public void ejbActivate()
      throws EJBException,
             java.rmi.RemoteException;
  public void ejbPassivate()
      throws EJBException,
             java.rmi.RemoteException;
} // End of SessionBean
```

The javax.ejb.SessionContext Interface

Like the `EntityContext` and `MessageDrivenBeanContext` interfaces, the `SessionContext` interface provides access to the runtime session bean context provided by the container. The container passes the `SessionContext` interface to an instance after the instance has been created. The session context remains associated with the instance for the lifetime of the instance. Here is the definition of the `SessionContext` interface:

```
public interface SessionContext
    extends EJBContext {
  public EJBLocalObject getEJBLocalObject()
     throws java.lang.IllegalStateException;
  public EJBObject getEJBObject()
     throws java.lang.IllegalStateException;
}  // End of SessionContext
```

The javax.ejb.SessionSynchronization Interface

The `SessionSynchronization` interface allows a session bean instance to be notified by its container of transaction boundaries. A session bean class is not required to implement this interface. However, if you want the bean class to synchronize its state with the transactions, your session bean class should implement this interface. Here is the definition of the `SessionSynchronization` interface:

```
public interface SessionSynchronization {
  public void afterBegin()
     throws EJBException,
            java.rmi.RemoteException;
  public void beforeCompletion()
     throws EJBException,
            java.rmi.RemoteException;
  public void afterCompletion(boolean committed)
     throws EJBException,
            java.rmi.RemoteException;
}  // End of SessionSynchronization
```

Package javax.ejb.spi

This package consists of a single interface named `HandleDelegate`. The `HandleDelegate` interface is implemented by the EJB container. It is not used by EJB components or by client components. It is used by portable implementations of `javax.ejb.Handle` and `javax.ejb.HomeHandle`. It provides methods to serialize and deserialize `EJBObject` and `EJBHome` references to streams. The `HandleDelegate` object is obtained by JNDI lookup at the reserved name `java:comp/HandleDelegate`.

The HandleDelegate Interface

Here is the definition of the `HandleDelegate` interface:

```
public interface HandleDelegate {
  public void writeEJBObject
        (EJBObject ejbObject,
         java.io.ObjectOutputStream ostream)
     throws java.io.IOException;
  public EJBObject readEJBObject
        (java.io.ObjectInputStream istream)
     throws java.io.IOException,
            java.lang.ClassNotFoundException;
  public void writeEJBHome(EJBHome ejbHome,
              java.io.ObjectOutputStream ostream)
     throws java.io.IOException;
  public EJBHome readEJBHome
         (java.io.ObjectInputStream istream)
     throws java.io.IOException,
            java.lang.ClassNotFoundException;
}  // End of HandleDelegate
```

The javax.jms.MessageListener Interface

A `MessageListener` is used to receive asynchronously delivered messages. A message-driven bean is a special kind of `MessageListener`. See Chapter 7 to learn about message-driven beans. The following is the definition of the `javax.jms.MessageListener` interface:

```
public interface MessageListener {
  // This method passes
  // a message to the Listener
 public void onMessage(Message message);
} // End of MessageListener
```

To learn more about the EJB API and the JMS API, see http://java.sun.com/products/ejb/ and http://java.sun.com/products/jms/index.html, respectively. To learn how to use JMS, see Chapter 7.

APPENDIX D

OC4J J2EE-Specific DTD Reference

In this appendix, you will learn about the following: the structure of the OC4J deployment descriptor file, the elements of the `orion-ejb-jar.xml` DTD file, and the descriptions of the elements of the `orion-ejb-jar.xml` DTD file. In that section, you will also find element definitions for all EJB types.

The Structure of the OC4J Deployment Descriptor File

In this section, you will learn about the required ordering of the elements in the OC4J deployment descriptor XML file. Note that information regarding the OC4J-specific deployment descriptor file is covered in great detail in the *Oracle9iAS Containers For J2EE Enterprise JavaBeans Developer's Guide and Reference, Release 2.0* technical manual. You can find this manual at http://otn.oracle.com/tech/java/oc4j/pdf/oc4j_ent_jb_devguide_r2.pdf.

The OC4J-specific deployment descriptor file contains deployment information for all EJB types, such as session beans, entity beans, and message-driven beans, and security for these enterprise beans. The structure of the elements of the deployment descriptor is as follows:

```
<orion-ejb-jar deployment-time=...
         deployment-version=...>
 <enterprise-beans>
  <session-deployment ...></session-deployment>
  <entity-deployment ...></entity-deployment>
  <message-driven-deployment ...></message-driven-deployment>
  <jem-deployment ...></jem-deployment>
  <jem-server-extension ...></jem-server-extension>
 </enterprise-beans>
 <assembly-descriptor>
  <security-role-mapping ...></security-role-mapping>
  <default-method-access></default-method-access>
 </assembly-descriptor>
</orion-ejb-jar>
```

Two specific sections, the enterprise bean and the assembly descriptor sections, are listed under the `<orion-ejb-jar>` main tag.

The Enterprise JavaBeans Section

The enterprise beans section starts under the `<enterprise-beans>` tag. Here, you will find additional deployment information for all EJB types. Additionally, you will find deployment information for each specific enterprise bean. In this section, you will encounter the following information:

- Session bean
- Entity bean
- Message-driven bean
- Container-managed persistent (CMP) bean
- Method definitions

Session Bean

Under the `<session-bean>` tag, you find additional deployment information specific to session beans. The `<session-bean>` section contains the following structure:

```
<session-deployment call-timeout=...
      copy-by-value=... location=...
      max-tx-retries=... name=...
      persistence-filename=... timeout=...
      wrapper=...
 <env-entry-mapping name=...> </env-entry-mapping
 <ejb-ref-mapping location=... name=... />
 <resource-ref-mapping location=... name=... >
  <lookup-context location=...>
   <context-attribute name=... value=... />
  </lookup-context>
 </resource-ref-mapping>
</session-deployment>
```

Entity Bean

The `<entity-bean>` section consists of the following structure:

```
<entity-deployment call-timeout=...
       clustering-schema=... copy-by-value=...
       data-source=... exclusive-write-access=...
       isolation=... location=...
       max-tx-retries=... name=... table=...
       validity-timeout=... wrapper=...>
 <primkey-mapping>
```

```
  <cmp-field-mapping ejb-reference-home=...
       name=... persistence-name=...
       persistence-type=...></cmp-field-mapping>
 </primkey-mapping>
 <cmp-field-mapping ejb-reference-home=...
       name=... persistence-name=...
       persistence-type=...> </cmp-field-mapping>
 <finder-method partial=... query=... >
  <method></method>
 </finder-method>
 <env-entry-mapping name=...></env-entry-mapping>
 <ejb-ref-mapping location=... name=... />
 <resource-ref-mapping location=... name=... >
  <lookup-context location=...>
   <context-attribute name=... value=... />
  </lookup-context>
 </resource-ref-mapping>
</entity-deployment>
```

Message-Driven Bean

The <message-driven-bean> section consists of the following structure:

```
<message-driven-deployment
      connection-factory-location=...
      destination-location=... name=...>
 <env-entry-mapping name=...></env-entry-mapping>
 <ejb-ref-mapping location=... name=... />
 <resource-ref-mapping location=... name=... >
  <lookup-context location=...>
   <context-attribute name=... value=... />
  </lookup-context>
 </resource-ref-mapping>
</message-driven-deployment>
```

Next, you will learn the XML elements used for CMP persistent data field mapping within the `orion-ejb-jar.xml` file.

Container-Managed Persistent Field Mapping

The <cmp-field-mapping> element has the following structure:

```
<cmp-field-mapping ejb-reference-home=...
        name=... persistence-name=...
        persistence-type=...>
 <fields>
  <cmp-field-mapping ejb-reference-home=...
        name=... persistence-name=...
```

```
       persistence-type=...></cmp-field-mapping>
</fields>
<properties>
 <cmp-field-mapping ejb-reference-home=...
      name=... persistence-name=...
      persistence-type=...></cmp-field-mapping>
</properties>
<entity-ref home=...>
 <cmp-field-mapping ejb-reference-home=...
     name=... persistence-name=...
     persistence-type=...></cmp-field-mapping>
</entity-ref>
<list-mapping table=...>
 <primkey-mapping>
  <cmp-field-mapping ejb-reference-home=...
        name=... persistence-name=...
        persistence-type=...></cmp-field-mapping>
 </primkey-mapping>
 <value-mapping immutable="true|false" type=...>
  <cmp-field-mapping ejb-reference-home=...
        name=... persistence-name=...
        persistence-type=...></cmp-field-mapping>
 </value-mapping>
</list-mapping>
<collection-mapping table=...>
 <primkey-mapping>
  <cmp-field-mapping ejb-reference-home=...
       name=... persistence-name=...
       persistence-type=...></cmp-field-mapping>
 </primkey-mapping>
 <value-mapping immutable="true|false" type=...>
  <cmp-field-mapping ejb-reference-home=...
       name=... persistence-name=...
       persistence-type=...></cmp-field-mapping>
 </value-mapping>
</collection-mapping>
<set-mapping table=...>
 <primkey-mapping>
  <cmp-field-mapping ejb-reference-home=...
       name=... persistence-name=...
       persistence-type=...></cmp-field-mapping>
 </primkey-mapping>
 <value-mapping immutable="true|false" type=...>
  <cmp-field-mapping ejb-reference-home=...
       name=... persistence-name=...
       persistence-type=...></cmp-field-mapping>
 </value-mapping>
</set-mapping>
```

```
 <map-mapping table=...>
  <primkey-mapping>
   <cmp-field-mapping ejb-reference-home=...
        name=... persistence-name=...
        persistence-type=...></cmp-field-mapping>
  </primkey-mapping>
  <map-key-mapping type=...>
   <cmp-field-mapping ejb-reference-home=...
        name=... persistence-name=...
        persistence-type=...></cmp-field-mapping>
  </map-key-mapping>
  <value-mapping immutable="true|false" type=...>
   <cmp-field-mapping ejb-reference-home=...
        name=... persistence-name=...
        persistence-type=...></cmp-field-mapping>
  </value-mapping>
  </map-mapping>
</cmp-field-mapping>
```

Next, we present the structure that you need to use to specify the methods of the enterprise beans and possibly the parameters of these methods.

Method Definition

The <method> element consists of the following structure:

```
<method>
 <description></description>
 <ejb-name></ejb-name>
 <method-intf></method-intf>
 <method-name></method-name>
 <method-params>
  <method-param></method-param>
 </method-params>
</method>
```

When specifying methods in the deployment descriptor, you can use several styles to specify the methods of the EJB components.

Remote and Home Interface Methods

Use the following structure to specify all the methods of the remote and home interfaces of your EJB component:

```
<method>
  <ejb-name>EJBNAME</ejb-name>
  <method-name>*</method-name>
</method>
```

Overloaded Methods

Use the following structure to specify all overloaded methods of the same name method:

```
<method>
 <ejb-name>EJBNAME</ejb-name>
 <method-name>METHOD</method-name>
</method>
```

Single Method

Use the following structure to specify a single method within a set of overloaded methods. As shown, you can also specify each parameter within the method.

```
<method>
 <ejb-name>EJBNAME</ejb-name>
  <method-name>METHOD</method-name>
   <method-params>
     <method-param>PARAM-1</method-param>
     <method-param>PARAM-2</method-param>
     ...
     <method-param>PARAM-n</method-param>
   </method-params>
<method>
```

Next, you will learn about the assembly descriptor section of the OC4J deployment descriptor file.

Assembly Descriptor

Use the assembly descriptor section of the deployment descriptor file to specify the security-related information for the EJB beans that you want to deploy in OC4J. The `<assembly-descriptor>` consists of the following structure:

```
<assembly-descriptor>
 <security-role-mapping impliesAll=... name=...>
  <group name=... />
  <user name=... />
 </security-role-mapping>
 <default-method-access>
  <security-role-mapping impliesAll=... name=...>
   <group name=... />
   <user name=... />
  </security-role-mapping>
 </default-method-access>
</assembly-descriptor>
```

DTD Listing of orion-ejb-jar.xml

In this section, we present the elements of the `orion-ejb-jar.xml` file. The `orion-ejb-jar.xml` DTD file shows the ordering required for each element and its optional parameters. In the last section of this appendix, we present the definition of each element.

```
<!ELEMENT fields (cmp-field-mapping*)>
<!ELEMENT session-deployment
     (env-entry-mapping*, ejb-ref-mapping*,
     resource-ref-mapping*)>
<!ATTLIST session-deployment call-timeout
     CDATA #IMPLIED
     copy-by-value CDATA #IMPLIED
     location CDATA #IMPLIED
     max-tx-retries CDATA #IMPLIED
     name CDATA #IMPLIED
     persistence-filename CDATA #IMPLIED
     timeout CDATA #IMPLIED
     wrapper CDATA #IMPLIED
     replication CDATA #IMPLIED>
<!ELEMENT collection-mapping
    (primkey-mapping, value-mapping)>
<!ATTLIST collection-mapping table CDATA #IMPLIED>
<!ELEMENT resource-ref-mapping (lookup-context?)>
<!ATTLIST resource-ref-mapping
   location CDATA #IMPLIED
   name CDATA #REQUIRED>
<!ELEMENT method-intf (#PCDATA)>
<!ELEMENT entity-ref (cmp-field-mapping)>
<!ATTLIST entity-ref home CDATA #IMPLIED>
<!ELEMENT enterprise-beans
   ((session-deployment | entity-deployment |
   message-driven-deployment | jem-deployment)+,
   jem-server-extension?)>
<!ELEMENT ejb-ref-mapping (#PCDATA)>
<!ATTLIST ejb-ref-mapping location CDATA #IMPLIED
   name CDATA #REQUIRED>
<!ELEMENT primkey-mapping (cmp-field-mapping)>
<!ELEMENT description (#PCDATA)>
<!ELEMENT env-entry-mapping (#PCDATA)>
<!ATTLIST env-entry-mapping name CDATA #IMPLIED>
<!ELEMENT security-role-mapping (group*, user*)>
<!ATTLIST security-role-mapping impliesAll
     CDATA #IMPLIED
```

```
     name CDATA #IMPLIED>
<!ELEMENT method-params (method-param*)>
<!ELEMENT cmp-field-mapping
   (fields|properties|entity-ref|list-mapping|
   collection-mapping|set-mapping|
   map-mapping|field-persistence-manager)?>
<!ATTLIST cmp-field-mapping ejb-reference-home CDATA #IMPLIED
   name CDATA #IMPLIED
       persistence-name CDATA #IMPLIED
   persistence-type CDATA #IMPLIED>
<!ELEMENT list-mapping (primkey-mapping,
   value-mapping)>
<!ATTLIST list-mapping table CDATA #IMPLIED>
<!ELEMENT group (#PCDATA)>
<!ATTLIST group name CDATA #IMPLIED>
<!ELEMENT default-method-access
   (security-role-mapping)>
<!ELEMENT map-key-mapping (cmp-field-mapping)>
<!ATTLIST map-key-mapping type CDATA #IMPLIED>
<!ELEMENT map-mapping (primkey-mapping,
     map-key-mapping, value-mapping)>
<!ATTLIST map-mapping table CDATA #IMPLIED>
<!ELEMENT value-mapping (cmp-field-mapping)>
<!ATTLIST value-mapping immutable CDATA #IMPLIED
    type CDATA #IMPLIED>
<!ELEMENT method-param (#PCDATA)>
<!ELEMENT user (#PCDATA)>
<!ATTLIST user name CDATA #IMPLIED>
<!ELEMENT lookup-context (context-attribute+)>
<!ATTLIST lookup-context location CDATA #IMPLIED>
<!ELEMENT context-attribute (#PCDATA)>
<!ATTLIST context-attribute name CDATA #IMPLIED
    value CDATA #IMPLIED>
<!ELEMENT set-mapping (primkey-mapping, value-mapping)>
<!ATTLIST set-mapping table CDATA #IMPLIED>
<!ELEMENT message-driven-deployment
     (env-entry-mapping*, ejb-ref-mapping*,
       resource-ref-mapping*)>
<!ATTLIST message-driven-deployment cache-timeout CDATA #IMPLIED
      connection-factory-location CDATA #IMPLIED
      destination-location CDATA #IMPLIED
      max-instances CDATA #IMPLIED
      min-instances CDATA #IMPLIED
      name CDATA #IMPLIED>
<!ELEMENT jem-server-extension
     (description?, data-bus?)>
<!ATTLIST jem-server-extension
     data-source-location CDATA #REQUIRED
```

```
    scheduling-threads CDATA #IMPLIED>
<!ELEMENT data-bus EMPTY>
<!ATTLIST data-bus
    data-bus-name CDATA #REQUIRED
    url CDATA #IMPLIED>
<!ELEMENT jem-deployment
    (description?, data-bus?, called-by,
    security-identity)>
<!ATTLIST jem-deployment
    jem-name CDATA #REQUIRED
    ejb-name CDATA #REQUIRED>
<!ELEMENT called-by (caller+)>
<!ELEMENT caller EMPTY>
<!ATTLIST caller
    caller-identity CDATA #REQUIRED>
<!ELEMENT security-identity
    (description?,(use-caller-identity|
    run-as-specified-identity))>
<!ELEMENT use-caller-identity EMPTY>
<!ELEMENT run-as-specified-identity
    (description?, role-name)>
<!ELEMENT role-name (#PCDATA)>
<!ELEMENT ejb-name (#PCDATA)>
<!ELEMENT field-persistence-manager (property)>
<!ATTLIST field-persistence-manager
    class CDATA #IMPLIED>
<!ELEMENT property (#PCDATA)>
<!ATTLIST property name CDATA #IMPLIED
    value CDATA #IMPLIED>
<!ELEMENT finder-method (method)>
<!ATTLIST finder-method partial CDATA #IMPLIED
    query CDATA #IMPLIED>
<!ELEMENT method (description?, ejb-name,
    method-intf?, method-name,
    method-params?)>
<!ELEMENT entity-deployment (primkey-mapping?,
    cmp-field-mapping*,
    finder-method*, env-entry-mapping*,
    ejb-ref-mapping*, resource-ref-mapping*)>
<!ATTLIST entity-deployment call-timeout
    CDATA #IMPLIED
    clustering-schema CDATA #IMPLIED
    copy-by-value CDATA #IMPLIED
    data-source CDATA #IMPLIED
    exclusive-write-access CDATA #IMPLIED
    instance-cache-timeout CDATA #IMPLIED
    location CDATA #IMPLIED
    isolation (committed | serializable |
```

```
    uncommitted | repeatable_reads)
    CDATA #IMPLIED
    locking-mode (pessimistic | optimistic |
    read-only | old_pessimistic)
    max-instances CDATA #IMPLIED
    min-instances CDATA #IMPLIED
    max-instances-per-pk CDATA #IMPLIED
    min-instances-per-pk CDATA #IMPLIED
    max-tx-retries CDATA #IMPLIED
    update-changed-fields-only (true | false) "true"
    name CDATA #IMPLIED
    pool-cache-timeout CDATA #IMPLIED
    table CDATA #IMPLIED
    validity-timeout CDATA #IMPLIED
    wrapper CDATA #IMPLIED>
<!ELEMENT orion-ejb-jar (enterprise-beans,
    assembly-descriptor)>
<!ATTLIST orion-ejb-jar deployment-time
    CDATA #IMPLIED
```

Element Description

In this section, we present a description of each element of the `orion-ejb-jar.xml` file and its attributes, if any.

<assembly-descriptor>

This is the mapping of the assembly descriptor elements.

<cmp-field-mapping>

This is the description of container-managed persistence fields. Here, you can use subtags to define different behavior.

Attributes

- **ejb-reference-home** The JNDI-location of the field's remote **EJB-home** if the field is an entity **EJBObject** or an **EJBHome**.
- **name** The name of the field.
- **persistence-name** The name of the field in the database table.
- **persistence-type** The database type (which valid values varies from database to database) of the field.

<collection-mapping>

This tag specifies a relational mapping of a `Collection` type. The field containing the mapping must be of type `java.util.Collection`.

Attribute

- **`table`** The name of the table in the database.

<context-attribute>

This is an attribute sent to the context. The class name of the context factory implementation is `java.naming.factory.initial`, which is the only mandatory attribute in JNDI.

Attributes

- **`name`** The name of the attribute.
- **`value`** The value of the attribute.

<default-method-access>

Use as default access policy for methods that do not have a method-permission.

<description>

A short description.

<ejb-name>

Use the `ejb-name` element to specify an enterprise bean's name. The name must be unique among the names of the enterprise beans in the same `ejb-jar` file. The name must conform to the lexical rules for an NMTOKEN, a name composed of only name tokens as defined in XML. For example:

```
<ejb-name>EmployeeList</ejb-name>
```

<ejb-ref-mapping>

Use the `ejb-ref` tag to declare a reference of a bean to another enterprise bean's home.

Attributes

- **location** The JNDI location to look up the EJB home from.
- **name** The ejb-ref's name, which must match the name of an ejb-ref in ejb-jar.xml.

<enterprise-beans>

This section contains information regarding the beans in this ejb-jar file.

<entity-deployment>

Includes deployment information for an entity bean.

Attributes

- **call-timeout** The time (long milliseconds in decimal) to wait for an EJB if it is busy (before throwing a RemoteException). The default is 90 seconds.
- **clustering-schema** The name of the data source used if using container-managed persistence.
- **copy-by-value** Use this tag if your application does not assume copy-by-value semantics for these parameters. The default is true. Set to false.
- **data-source** The name of the data source used if using container-managed persistence.
- **disable-wrapper-cache** The default is false. If it is set to true, a pool of wrapper instances is not maintained.
- **exclusive-write-access** The default is false. Use this tag for entity beans that use a read_only locking mode. It enables better caching for common operations, thus improving performance.
- **instance-cache-timeout** The default is 60 seconds. It indicates the amount of time, in seconds, that entity wrapper instances are assigned to an identity. If you specify never, you retain the wrapper instances until they are garbage collected.
- **isolation** Specifies the isolation level for database actions. For Oracle databases, the valid values are serializable and committed. The

default is `committed`. Non-Oracle databases can be the following: `none`, `committed`, `serializable`, `uncommitted`, and `repeatable_read`.

- **`location`** Indicates to which JNDI name this bean will be bound.
- **`locking-mode`** Used for concurrency mode configuration—that is, the decision as to when to block to manage resource contention or when to execute in parallel. The concurrency modes are as follows:
    - **`PESSIMISTIC`** No parallel execution. Only one user at a time can execute the entity bean.
    - **`OPTIMISTIC`** Parallel is allowed. That is, multiple users can execute the bean in parallel. Note, however, that this tag does not monitor resource contention. Consequently, the burden of the data consistency is placed on the database isolation modes. This is the default.
    - **`READ-ONLY`** Multiple users can execute the entity bean in parallel. The container does not allow updating the bean's state.
- **`max-instances`** Used to indicate the maximum bean implementation instances that can be instantiated or pooled. The default is 10.
- **`min-instances`** Used to indicate the minimum bean implementation instances that can be instantiated or pooled. The default is 0.
- **`max-instances-per-pk`** Used to indicate the maximum wrapper instances that can be instantiated or pooled. The default is 50.
- **`min-instances-per-pk`** Used to indicate the minimum wrapper instances that can be instantiated or pooled. The default is 0.
- **`max-tx-retries`** Used to keep track of the number of times to retry a transaction that was rolled back due to system-level failures. The default is 3. Oracle recommends that you set this tag to 0 if you are using the `serializable` isolation level.
- **`name`** The name of the bean. Note that this name must match the name of a bean contained in the `ejb-jar.xml` assembly descriptor file.
- **`pool-cache-timeout`** Records the amount of time, in seconds, that the bean implementation instances can be kept in the "pooled" state. The default is 60. If you specify `never`, the instances are retained until they are garbage collected.
- **`table`** When using container-managed persistence, use this attribute to list the name of the database table.

- **validity-timeout** This attribute is only valid for entity beans with a locking mode of `read_only` and when `exclusive-write-access =true`. This attribute indicates the maximum amount of time (in milliseconds) that an entity is valid in the cache before being reloaded in memory.
- **update-changed-fields-only** Used to specify whether the container updates only modified fields or all fields to persistence storage for CMP entity beans when `ejbStore` is invoked. The default is `true`, which means to only update modified fields.
- **wrapper** Name of the OC4J wrapper class for this bean.

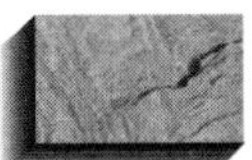

NOTE
Do not edit the `wrapper` attribute. This is an internal server attribute.

<entity-ref>

Use this tag to specify the configuration for persisting an entity reference via its primary key. The child tag of this tag is used to specify the configuration of how to persist the primary key.

Attribute

- **home** This is where the `lookup()` method locates the JNDI location of the `EJBHome` object.

<env-entry-mapping>

The value of this tag overrides the value of an `env-entry` in the assembly descriptor.

Attribute

- **name** The name of the context parameter.

<fields>

Specifies the configuration of a field-based mapping persistence for the Java class field.

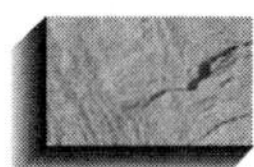

NOTE
The fields that you need to be persisted must be declared `public`*,* `non-static`*,* `non-final` *and the type of the containing object has to have an empty constructor.*

<finder-method>

Use this tag to specify the container-managed finder method. This defines the selection criteria in a `findByXXX()` method in the bean's home.

Attributes

- **`partial`** Used to specify that this is a partial query. A partial query is identified by a `WHERE` or an `ORDER` clause. Useful when doing advanced queries involving table joins and the like.
- **`query`** Used for the query part of the SQL statement. Use this section after the `WHERE` clause of the SQL statement. Special tokens are provided to identify a method argument number and a `cmp-field` name. The `$number` denotes a method argument number, whereas the `$name` denotes a `cmp-field` name. For example, in the `findByVendorZipcode(int zipcode)` query, the `cmp-field` named `zipcode` would be represented as follows:

```
$1 = $zipcode
```

<group>

This tag relates to the `<security-role-mapping>` role of the group. In this section, you will include all members of the group that are included in this role.

Attribute

- **`name`** The name of the specified group.

<message-driven-deployment>

Use this section to list deployment information for message-driven beans.

Attributes

- **connection-factory-location** JNDI location of the connection factory to use.
- **destination-location** JNDI location of the queue/topic destination to use.
- **max-instances** Used to indicate the maximum number of bean instances to instantiate. The default is `-1`, which indicates an infinite number.
- **min-instances** The minimum number of bean instances to instantiate.
- **name** The name of the bean; this matches the name of a bean in the assembly descriptor (`ejb-jar.xml`).

<method>

Used to specify the methods (and possibly parameters of those methods) of the bean.

<method-intf>

This tag allows a method element to differentiate between the methods with the same name and signature that are defined in both the remote and home interfaces. The `method-intf` element must be either `Home` or `Remote`.

<method-name>

Use this element to denote the name of a specific enterprise bean's method. If you want this element to denote all the methods of an enterprise bean's remote and home interfaces, then use the asterisk (`*`) character.

<method-param>

This element contains the fully qualified Java type name of a method parameter.

<method-params>

This element contains a list of the fully qualified Java type names of a method parameter.

<orion-ejb-jar>

The `orion-ejb-jar.xml` file contains the OC4J-specific deployment information for all types of EJBs.

NOTE

Importantly, at deployment time, OC4J automatically generates a new OC4J-specific XML file for you using its default elements. If you want to change these default elements and you do not want OC4J to generate a new file for you, Oracle recommends that you copy the `orion-ejb-jar.xml` file to wherever your original `ejb-jar.xml` file is located and change it in that location. The changes only stay constant when changed in the development directories. At deployment time, OC4J checks if an `orion-ejb-jar.xml` file exists in the specified deployed location. If the file exists, OC4J uses it, and thus does not overwrite your changes.

Attributes

- **`deployment-time`** The time, in long milliseconds, of the last deployment time. When you deploy a bean, OC4J uses an internal server value to check if that bean has already been deployed. If the last editing date of the JAR file does not match the OC4J's internal server value, then the bean gets redeployed.
- **`deployment-version`** Same scenario as `deployment-time`.

<primkey-mapping>

Specifies how the primary key is mapped.

<properties>

Used to show the mapping configuration of a bean's persistent field.

<resource-ref-mapping>

Use this element to specify external resources, such as a data source, JMS queue, or mail session. At deployment time, the `resource-ref-mapping` element ties the resource to a specific JNDI location.

Attributes

- **`location`** This element indicates the JNDI location in which to locate the resource.
- **`name`** The `resource-ref` name contained in the `ejb-jar.xml` file.

<security-role-mapping>

This element specifies the runtime mapping of a group and user role. It maps to a security role of the same name in the assembly descriptor.

Attributes

- **`impliesAll`** Indicates whether or not the mapping implies all users. The default is `false`.
- **`name`** The name of the role.

<session-deployment>

Deployment information specific to session beans.

Attributes

- **`cache-timeout`** Applicable only to session beans, this element indicates how long to keep stateless sessions cached in the pool. The default is 60. Legal values are positive integer values or `never`.
- **`call-timeout`** Wait time for an EJB if it is busy. When this time reaches a threshold, then a `RemoteException` is thrown treating it as a deadlock. The default value is 0, which means that OC4J waits forever.
- **`copy-value`** Specifies whether or not all incoming and outgoing parameters in EJB calls will be copied by value. The default is `true`. Set it to `false` if you do not want automatic copy creation of the EJB parameters.
- **`location`** This element indicates the JNDI location in which to locate the JNDI name of this bean.
- **`Max-tx-retries`** Indicates the number of times to retry a transaction that was rolled back due to system-level failures. The default is 3.
- **`name`** The name of the bean that you listed in the `ejb-jar.xml` file.

- **`Persistence-filename`** Path to the file where sessions are stored across restarts.
- **`timeout`** Inactivity timeout, in seconds. The default is 30 minutes. A 0 or negative value specifies that all timeouts are disabled.
- **`wrapper`** The name of the OC4J wrapper class for this bean.

<set-mapping>

Used to specify the relational mapping of the `Set` type. The field containing the mapping must be of type `java.util.Set`.

Attribute

- **`table`** The name of the table in the database.

<user>

A user that has the `security-role-mapping` role.

Attribute

- **`name`** The name of the user.

<value-mapping>

Indicates the mapping of the primary key part of a set of fields.

Attributes

- **`immutable`** Indicates whether or not the value can be trusted to be immutable once added to the Collection/Map. The default value is `true` for `set-mapping` and `map-mappings` and `false` for collection-mapping and list-mapping.
- **`type`** The fully qualified class name of the type of the value. For example, `purchase.ejb.cmp.PurchaseOrderPK` or `java.lang.String`.

In this appendix, you learned about the structure of the OC4J-specific deployment descriptor file and its major elements. To learn how to customize the OC4J-specific deployment descriptor file to deploy your EJB components, refer to Chapters 5 through 7.

Index

A

B

D

E

F

G

H

I

J

L

N

O

P

Q

R

S

T

U

V

W

X

Y

INTERNATIONAL CONTACT INFORMATION

AUSTRALIA
McGraw-Hill Book Company Australia Pty. Ltd.
TEL +61-2-9900-1800
FAX +61-2-9878-8881
http://www.mcgraw-hill.com.au
books-it_sydney@mcgraw-hill.com

CANADA
McGraw-Hill Ryerson Ltd.
TEL +905-430-5000
FAX +905-430-5020
http://www.mcgraw-hill.ca

GREECE, MIDDLE EAST, & AFRICA (Excluding South Africa)
McGraw-Hill Hellas
TEL +30-1-656-0990-3-4
FAX +30-1-654-5525

MEXICO (Also serving Latin America)
McGraw-Hill Interamericana Editores S.A. de C.V.
TEL +525-117-1583
FAX +525-117-1589
http://www.mcgraw-hill.com.mx
fernando_castellanos@mcgraw-hill.com

SINGAPORE (Serving Asia)
McGraw-Hill Book Company
TEL +65-863-1580
FAX +65-862-3354
http://www.mcgraw-hill.com.sg
mghasia@mcgraw-hill.com

SOUTH AFRICA
McGraw-Hill South Africa
TEL +27-11-622-7512
FAX +27-11-622-9045
robyn_swanepoel@mcgraw-hill.com

SPAIN
McGraw-Hill/Interamericana de España, S.A.U.
TEL +34-91-180-3000
FAX +34-91-372-8513
http://www.mcgraw-hill.es
professional@mcgraw-hill.es

UNITED KINGDOM, NORTHERN, EASTERN, & CENTRAL EUROPE
McGraw-Hill Education Europe
TEL +44-1-628-502500
FAX +44-1-628-770224
http://www.mcgraw-hill.co.uk
computing_neurope@mcgraw-hill.com

ALL OTHER INQUIRIES Contact:
Osborne/McGraw-Hill
TEL +1-510-549-6600
FAX +1-510-883-7600
http://www.osborne.com
omg_international@mcgraw-hill.com

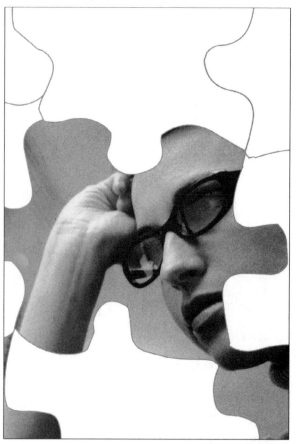

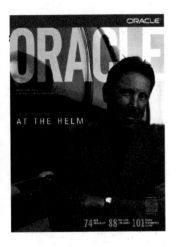